THE SPEAKERS OF THE HOUSE OF REPRESENTATIVES

The Johns Hopkins University
Studies in Historical and Political Science
103d Series (1985)

The Speakers of the U.S. House of Representatives:
A Bibliography, 1789–1984
Edited by Donald R. Kennon

THE SPEAKERS OF THE U.S. HOUSE OF REPRESENTATIVES

A Bibliography, 1789–1984

edited by

DONALD R. KENNON

UNITED STATES CAPITOL HISTORICAL SOCIETY

The Johns Hopkins University Press

BALTIMORE AND LONDON

© 1986 The Johns Hopkins University Press
All rights reserved
Printed in the United States of America

The Johns Hopkins University Press,
701 West 40th Street,
Baltimore, Maryland 21211
The Johns Hopkins Press Ltd, London

Library of Congress Cataloging in Publication Data

Kennon, Donald R., 1948–
    The speakers of the U.S. House of Representatives.

    Includes index.
    1. United States. Congress. House—Speaker—
Bibliography.   I. Title: The speakers of the United
States House of Representatives.
Z7165.U5K45   1985   016.32873′0762 85-45047
[JK1411]
ISBN 0-8018-2786-8

TABLE OF CONTENTS

JUL   1984

DETAILED TABLE OF CONTENTS

DETAILED TABLE OF CONTENTS

FOREWORD

The Speaker of the House of Representatives occupies the highest legislative position in the land. He serves as chief presiding officer of the House and is also the principal leader of his congressional party. In the event of the death, disability, or resignation of the president of the United States, only the vice-president ranks ahead of the Speaker in terms of succession. As Speaker Thomas B. Reed put it, the Speaker has "but one superior and no peer."

This bibliography on forty-six members of Congress who have served as Speaker of the U.S. House of Representatives is a remarkable piece of diligent research and scholarship that makes a major contribution to our understanding of the office of the Speaker.

The bibliography lists thousands of books, articles, and dissertations on the careers of the men who have held this office. It also contains an interesting biographical sketch of each Speaker and guides readers to the location of collections of the personal papers of former Speakers.

While there is a wealth of information here, I was surprised to find how little has been written about some of the former Speakers. There is a great deal more that we need to know about the history of the office and the lives of the men who have been Speaker.

The study of the Congress, especially by historians, has lagged behind the work that has been done on the executive branch of government. While all three branches of the federal government are complex institutions to study, the Congress is probably the most difficult; and within the Congress the House has been studied less than the Senate. Power is more diffuse in the House, with its 435 members and numerous committees and subcommittees, and this makes it difficult for students to chart the course of the decision-making process in the Congress. It is never easy to accurately describe the mix of local, national, and international concerns that affect legislation. Furthermore, the issues facing the Congress are not debated in a vacuum. The clash of personalities and political philosophies, while difficult to quantify, is an essential element in any attempt to describe the actions of the Congress. I believe it is impossible to understand how the Congress works without understanding the personalities of the men and women who serve there.

Under the Constitution, Congress is a coequal branch of government. Speaker Sam Rayburn underscored this status when he responded to a statement that he had served under eight presidents: "No, I haven't served under anybody. I have served *with* eight presidents." I would encourage students of American history and government not to neglect the study of the Congress simply because it is a difficult institution to research. It is important to have a balance in our studies of government just as it is important to have a balance of power between the branches themselves.

This bibliography will open the door to further research into the history of the Congress and contribute to a better understanding of the office of the Speaker and the Congress itself. I want to commend the United States Capitol Historical Society for the painstaking work that led to this volume. I hope that this publication will stimulate interest in congressional studies as we approach the two-hundredth anniversary of the Congress in 1989.

Thomas P. O'Neill, Jr.
Speaker, U.S. House of Representatives

PREFACE

"Why has not some publicist or statesman long since made the Speakership his study? Clearly to describe this office, and to show its tendencies, would be no easy task." Harvard professor of history and government Albert Bushnell Hart, in his introduction to Mary Parker Follett's classic *The Speaker of the House of Representatives* (1896), went on to conclude that one principal reason why the speakership had eluded scholarly study was "the volume and variety of the sources which have needed to be examined." Since the 1890s the volume and variety of sources has grown to such an extent that the scholar or student is at a loss without some basic reference guide. Though Follett's path-breaking work set high standards of scholarship for the history of the speakership, little has been written on the subject since the 1920s.[1] It is the purpose of this bibliography, and the hope of the United States Capitol Historical Society which sponsored it, to stimulate and facilitate research into the speakership and the forty-six men who have held the office.

The scholarly neglect of the office is in itself sufficient evidence of the need for a bibliography of the Speakers of the House. The significance of the office within the constitutional frame of government and the role that individual Speakers have played in American legislative history, moreover, justify and necessitate such a reference guide. Bibliographies are intended and designed to assist researchers at the outset of their research. In providing researchers with a guide to the basic sources, we hope that a deeper and more complete historical understanding of the office and the men who have occupied it will be developed. Mary Parker Follett may well have been correct when she concluded that "the whole history of the House of Representatives, from an institutional point of view, has been the history of the concentration of legislative power in the hands of the Speaker of the House." If this bibliography can generate the research to test, corroborate, or refute Follett's proposition, it will have fulfilled its purpose.

On a perhaps less exalted though no less compelling level, it is hoped that this bibliography will spur research into the careers of the forty-six Speakers, many of whom have been unjustly overlooked or wrongly dismissed on the basis of contemporary opinion. One brilliant Speaker, Thomas Brackett Reed, speaking with his characteristic lack of humility, may well have overstated the case when he claimed that "the Speaker has but one superior and no peer"; nevertheless, the significance of the office does demand a closer look at the men who have held it. Although the reputations and accomplishments of Speakers such as Henry Clay, Joseph Cannon, Champ Clark, and Sam Rayburn are well known, others have not received the study they deserve. Speakers such as Reed, Nathaniel Macon, John W. Taylor, Galusha Grow, Charles Crisp, and Nicholas Longworth all played a key legislative role in times of crisis, yet only Reed, largely owing to his intellect and caustic personality, has been the subject of much research. Moreover, several Speakers, including Joseph Varnum, John White, John W. Jones, John W. Davis, and William Pennington, still languish in relative obscurity, whether deserved or not.

This bibliography is the second major scholarly bibliographic project undertaken by the United States Capitol Historical Society. A private, nonprofit, educational organization chartered by Congress to promote the history of the Capitol and the Congress, the society earlier sponsored *The United States Capitol: An Annotated Bibliography*, edited by John R.

---

[1]Mary Parker Follett, *The Speaker of the House of Representatives* (New York: Longmans, Green, 1896), xi. For scholarship on the speakership see items 1-1 through 1-15.

Kerwood and published in 1973 by the University of Oklahoma Press in cooperation with the society.

At the inspiration of the president of the society, Fred Schwengel, research on this bibliography began in 1976 and was completed by the end of 1981. The research data accumulated by a team of researchers and interns were collected, reviewed, organized, and edited betweeen 1982 and 1984. An effort has been made to keep the bibliography up-to-date through the end of 1983. In the course of the research, hundreds of manuscript collections and thousands of books, articles, and dissertations were reviewed for inclusion in the bibliography. The criterion for published works included in the final manuscript was that they must contain (1) significant information on the speakership as an institution or (2) significant references to one or more Speakers. Works of only marginal value were weeded out in the editing process in order that the bibliography might be confined to a single, manageable volume while retaining references to those sources that can guide the reader in the direction of future research.

As the research on this bibliography proceeded, the project quickly outgrew its initial research design. *The Union Catalog of the Library of Congress, The Reader's Guide to Periodical Literature, America: History and Life,* and other indexes were searched for references to the speakership and each of the forty-six Speakers. When these references were reviewed, it became apparent that many more sources merited review. Each Speaker was then researched as an independent entity. Our researchers approached the task as if they were preparing a biography of the Speaker. Thus, footnotes and bibliographies in biographical sources were traced and reviewed. In addition, a thorough shelf search was conducted in the Library of Congress. The indexes of books in the American history section, the state and local history section, and the government and political science section were searched for references to the Speakers. In the course of research, scores of journals and periodicals, ranging from the *Journal of American History* and the *American Political Science Review* to *Time* and *Newsweek,* were searched. In some cases indexes were available; in others the journal or periodical had to be searched issue by issue. To facilitate the editing process, descriptive annotations were written for each reference reviewed.

The resulting bibliography is designed to guide the reader to the major published books and articles and unpublished doctoral dissertations on the institution of the speakership and the careers of the forty-six Speakers. While the bibliography is neither comprehensive nor encyclopedic, it does represent an exhaustive effort to identify both the volume and the variety of sources available for the study of the Speakers of the House. It includes all of the available published works (books, articles, letters, and speeches) written by each Speaker. Every published biography and all major biographical sketches of the Speaker's life, as well as all available genealogies and eulogies, are included. Every effort has been made to include all specific secondary studies devoted solely to some aspect of the Speaker's career. In addition, biographies and autobiographies of other political figures are included if they shed light on the Speaker's career. Other primary sources, such as articles in contemporary journals and periodicals, are included if the focus is on the speakership or the Speaker. Secondary studies in which the Speaker figures prominently but is not the central focus are also included. Only in the cases of Speakers Clay, Cannon, and Rayburn did the volume of available sources force the editor to exercise greater selectivity. There is no Political Associates category in the Clay bibliography, for example, since almost any work by or about a political figure of the first half of the nineteenth century makes at least some mention of Clay.

For the bibliography to fulfill its purpose it must be used. With that in mind, a word on the organization and methodology of this work is in order. The one guiding principle in compiling and organizing this bibliography was that it be useful to the reader. Thus the references contained herein are to books, articles, and dissertations that are, with but few exceptions, available at major research libraries, through interlibrary loan, or, in the case of dissertations, through University Microfilms.

The bibliography begins with a general section of works on the speakership as an institution and general works on Congress, congressional history, and guides to researching Congress. As this project neared completion, an excellent new bibliography on Congress appeared which all interested researchers should consult: Robert U. Goehlert and John R. Sayre, *The United States Congress: A Bibliography* (New York: Free Press, 1982).

The main body of this volume is divided into four chronological sections each of which is preceded by a brief list of works pertinent to the speakership and Speakers of that period. The works cited in these sections are not meant to be comprehensive. They include only works that have references to several Speakers of that period. The first section, 1789–1814, covers the development of the speakership from the first Speaker, Frederick A. C. Muhlenberg, through the consolidation of power in the hands of the seventh Speaker, Henry Clay. The second section, 1815–61, surveys the turbulent legislative period prior to the Civil War. The post–Civil War development of the speakership culminating in the revolt against Speaker Joseph Cannon is the subject of the third section, 1861–1911. The final section presents the Speakers of the modern era, 1911–84.

Beginning each of the chapters on the forty-six Speakers is a short biographical sketch, which is followed by a list of the available manuscript collections of the Speaker's papers. References to these collections were located through extensive correspondence with manuscript libraries. The two most helpful guides consulted are the National Union Catalog Manuscript Collections (NUCMC) and John J. McDonough, comp., *Members of Congress: A Checklist of Their Papers in the Manuscript Division, Library of Congress* (Washington, D.C.: Library of Congress, 1980). The former is an ongoing program of the Library of Congress cataloging the thousands of manuscript collections in American repositories. Each NUCMC citation is identified by a two-part number (i.e., 60-1271, Schuyler Colfax Papers in the Indiana State Library), the first part referring to the year in which the collection was cataloged by NUCMC. The latter is an excellent guide to the papers of the Speakers in the Library of Congress, identified herein by MC and the page number on which the particular collection is described (i.e., MC 92, Longworth Papers).

The bibliographic list of books, articles, and dissertations pertinent to each Speaker contains both primary and secondary published works. All items cited except those marked with an asterisk (*) were reviewed; items marked with an asterisk were unavailable for review. Early plans for a completely annotated bibliography were dropped when the volume of citations began to outweigh the advantages of annotation. Only works written by the Speakers, items of exceptional importance, or items that need explanation are annotated.

To offset the lack of annotation, the bibliography's 4,280 entries are divided into descriptive categories. The nature of the available sources determined the categories for each Speaker's bibliography. Although the categories vary from Speaker to Speaker, there are certain basic organizing principles. The first category in each Speaker's chapter is a comprehensive list of his published works. If the list is lengthy, the Speaker's works are subdivided according to type of work—books, articles, published letters, published speeches. The second category contains references to biographies, biographical sketches, genealogies, and eulogies. One category that is included in most, but not all, Speakers' chapters is entitled Political Associates. This category contains references to politicians and other public figures who either were closely associated with the Speaker or provided interesting and revealing insights into his public career. The Political Associates category provides a useful means of seeing the Speaker through the eyes of his political contemporaries. The other categories in each chapter are devoted to specific topics such as state and local history and politics and the Speaker's congressional career and speakership. These categories are arranged in a roughly chronological order, which makes it possible to follow the development of the Speaker's career.

Entries within each category are arranged alphabetically, with the exception of works authored by the Speaker, which are arranged chronologically by year of publication and alphabetically thereunder in order to give a chronological overview of the Speaker's output. Entries are numbered chapter by chapter and are identified and cross-referenced by a two-part numbering system, the first part referring to the chapter. Thus item number 7-15 refers to the fifteenth item in chapter 7.

The method of citation for books, journals, periodicals, and dissertations generally follows the University of Chicago Press *Manual of Style,* with the exceptions that total number of pages of books and month of publication for journals are cited to give the reader complete bibliographic information. Modern reprint editions are cited where available. Doctoral dissertations are identified by the University Microfilms order number.

We conclude with the question with which we began this project: Why has not some scholar made the speakership his or her study? With the interest in the speakership and the great Speakers of the past apparently on the rise, we may be closer than ever to an answer to that question.[2] This bibliography may be appearing at a most propitious time. If it can contribute to the study of the Speakers and the speakership, *The Speakers of the U.S. House of Representatives: A Bibliography, 1789–1984* will have repaid the trust and support given it by the United States Capitol Historical Society.

---

[2]Two recent books indicate the continuing interest in the speakership: Richard B. Cheney and Lynne V. Cheney, *Kings of the Hill: Power and Personality in the House of Representatives* (New York: Continuum Publishing, 1983); and Anthony Champagne, *Congressman Sam Rayburn* (New Brunswick, N.J.: Rutgers University Press, 1984).

NOWLEDGMENTS

ration of this one would not have been possible without
ple working toward a common goal. The success of this
tion, guidance, and devotion to historical scholarship of
ent of the United States Capitol Historical Society. As a
wa, Fred Schwengel learned the importance and power
nder Democratic Speaker Sam Rayburn, a man whom
and whose friendship and guidance he valued. Fred
his bibliography, and his patient and persistent support

e board of trustees of the society are to be commended
support this project. Past and present members of the
or M. Birely, Sen. David L. Boren, former Rep. Mar-
n, Rep. Barber Conable, Jr., Arthur M. Hanson, Carl
. Pickle, Sen. David Pryor, and Florian Thayn. Their
greatly benefited this project, as well as all of the

mmittee merits special acknowledgment. The late Dr.
nan of the history department of the University of
's chief academic advisor but the society's good friend
re especially valuable in the institution of many of the
bibliography. The society has also benefited from the
an of the University of Maryland. The editor would
fessor Hoffman for his wise counsel.
istorical bibliography and congressional history gra-
litor particularly benefited from the counsel of Arnold
sociation, Ruth Freitag and Edward McConomy of
or Thomas Helde of Georgetown University. Walter
Congressional Research Service shared their knowl-
provided advice and encouragement included: Jeff
Center for Congressional and Presidential Studies,
ongressional Research and Studies Center at the
Dulany of the Sam Rayburn Library.
ll of the librarians, archivists, and curators whose
f this project. The staff of the Library of Congress is
fulness. In particular, John J. McDonough and the
f Congress Manuscript Division, provided valuable
peakers' manuscript collections. Literally hundreds
ited States answered questions concerning publica-
metimes going beyond the call of duty. Nancy
lections at the University of Missouri, for example,
of the papers of Champ Clark and his son after we

homas P. O'Neill, Jr., for taking the time from his
busy schedule to write the foreword. Congress is beginning to realize the necessity for
studying its own history. Under the leadership of farsighted leaders such as Speaker

ACKNOWLEDGMENTS

O'Neill, both the House and the Senate have organized historical offices. The Senate Historical Office, led by Senate Historian Richard Baker, and the Office of the Bicentennial of the House of Representatives, directed by Historian Raymond W. Smock, are to be commended for their efforts to preserve, document, and promote congressional history.

The editor wishes to express a personal word of appreciation to the staff of the United States Capitol Historical Society for putting up with one who at times must have seemed to be a hopelessly befuddled and absent-minded bibliographer. Executive Secretary Cornelius Heine and staff members Joanne Hanson, Shirley Powell, Betty Davis, and Susan Malloy helped make this project a pleasant experience.

The editor's main debt of gratitude is to those whose labor made this bibliography possible. The early stages of research were directed by William M. Maury with the assistance of Maier B. Fox and, later, Anne M. Butler. Without Dr. Maury's skillful direction and the diligent support of Drs. Fox and Butler this bibliography could not have been completed. An able group of researchers including Michael Gaffney, Claudia Hodson, Joseph LaPiano, Frank J. Parisi, Elaine Rubin, and Richard Striner worked on the project at one point or another. Interns who either assisted with the research or double-checked bibliographic entries included Trudi Abel, Jennifer Brunet, Stacia Green, Tracy N. Gruis, Mary Lee Kerr, Stephen O'Brien, Stephen Oler, Neil Robinson, and Tim Touhey. Finally, a special word of appreciation is due to Peter Albert, who advised the editor on bibliographic matters and prepared the subject index, and to Ina Lintz, who expertly typed and retyped the manuscript through several drafts. The editor extends a personal word of appreciation to all of these dedicated individuals. Whatever merit this work may have is owing to their long hours of labor. The editor readily acknowledges that any remaining shortcomings or errors are his responsibility alone.

PART I

THE SPEAKERSHIP: AN OVERVIEW

1. General Bibliography

THE SPEAKERSHIP

The speakership has been the subject of little scholarly research. On the whole, the literature is dated and inadequate. During the controversial tenures of Speakers Reed and Cannon, at the turn of the twentieth century, the office was of great interest, which is reflected in Cockrell (1-3), Follett (1-4), Fuller (1-5), Greely (1-6), Hart (1-7), Hinds (1-8), and Taylor (1-15). Unfortunately, very little research has been done on the office recently.

A reading of Follett (1-4) and Fuller (1-5), together with Chiu (1-2), provides the best scholarly study of the speakership up to 1927. For the student of subsequent Speakers, the best introduction to the office can be found in chapters 4 and 5 of MacNeil (1-24). The introductory chapter to Mooney (1-12) is also an instructive starting point.

1-1. ALBERT, CARL B. *The Office and Duties of the Speaker of the House of Representatives*. Washington, D.C.: Government Printing Office, 1976. Unpaginated.

A short pamphlet outlining the speakership. *See also* Albert (50-3).

1-2. CHIU, CHANG-WEI. *The Speaker of the House of Representatives since 1896*. 1928. Reprint. New York: AMS Press, 1968. 347 p.

A scholarly analysis of the political and institutional changes in the speakership between 1896 and 1927.

1-3. COCKRELL, EWING. "The Place and the Man: The Speaker of the House of Representatives." *Arena* 22 (December 1899): 653–66.

1-4. FOLLETT, MARY P. *The Speaker of the House of Representatives*. New York: Longmans, Green, 1896. 378 p.

Both a history of the Speakers up to Crisp and an analysis of the development of the office.

1-5. FULLER, HUBERT BRUCE. *The Speaker of the House*. 1909. Reprint. New York: Arno Press, 1974. 311 p.

A history of the speakership from Muhlenberg to Cannon.

1-6. GREELY, A. W. "The Speaker and the Committees of the House of Representatives." *North American Review* 166 (January 1898): 24–31.

1-7. HART, ALBERT BUSHNELL. "The Speaker as Premier." In *Practical Essays on American Government*, pp. 1–19. 1893. Reprint. New York: Arno Press, 1974.

1-8. HINDS, ASHER C. "The Speaker of the House of Representatives." *American Political Science Review* 3 (May 1909): 155–66.

1-9. LEE, EUGENE C. *The Presiding Officer and Rules Committee in Legislatures of the United States*. Berkeley: University of California, Bureau of Public Administration, 1952. 49 p.

Contains only a brief institutional history of the speakership.

1-10. MACNEIL, NEIL. "The House Shall Chuse Their Speaker. . . ." *American Heritage* 28 (February 1977): 26–31.

A brief popular account. For his extended analysis of the speakership see MacNeil (1-24).

1-11. MAXEY, EDWIN. "The Powers of the Speaker." *Forum* 41 (April 1909): 344–50.

1-12. MOONEY, BOOTH. *Mr. Speaker: Four Men Who Shaped the United States House of Representatives*. Chicago: Follett Publishing, 1964. 226 p.

A brief overview of the office and sketches of Clay, Reed, Cannon, and Rayburn as Speaker.

1-13. MOSER, CHARLES A. *The Speaker and the House: Coalitions and Power in the United States House of Representatives*. Washington, D.C.: Free Congress Research and Education Foundation, 1979. 67 p.

An analysis of contested speakership elections that argues for a conservative coalition to control the House through election of the Speaker.

1-14. SMITH, WILLIAM H. *Speakers of the House of Representatives of the United States.* Baltimore: Simon J. Gaeng, 1928. 261 p.
Contains biographical sketches of Speakers Muhlenberg through Longworth.

1-15. TAYLOR, HANNIS. "The Speaker and His Powers." *North American Review* 188 (October 1908): 495–503.
A critique of the office and a comparison with the parliamentary model.

CONGRESS

An understanding of the speakership, the men who occupied the office, and the changes it has undergone requires a knowledge of Congress. The following sections list works on the history of Congress, rules and procedure, congressional leadership, the committee system, and the relationship between Congress and the executive branch.

Histories of Congress

1-16. ALEXANDER, DEALVA STANWOOD. *History and Procedure of the House of Representatives.* 1916. Reprint. New York: Burt Franklin, 1970. 435 p.

1-17. AMERICAN ASSEMBLY. *The Congress and America's Future.* Edited by David B. Truman. 2d ed. Englewood Cliffs, N.J.: Prentice-Hall, 1973. 220 p.

1-18. BATES, ERNEST S. *The Story of Congress, 1789–1935.* New York: Harper and Brothers, 1936. 468 p.

1-19. CONGRESSIONAL QUARTERLY. *Origins and Development of Congress.* Washington, D.C., 1976. 325 p.

1-20. FRIBOURG, MARJORIE C. *The U.S. Congress: Men Who Steered Its Course, 1787–1867.* Philadelphia: MacRea Smith, 1972. 280 p.

1-21. GALLOWAY, GEORGE B. *Congress at the Crossroads.* New York: Thomas Y. Crowell, 1946. 374 p.

1-22. ———. *History of the United States House of Representatives.* 2d ed., rev. Edited by Sidney Wise. New York: Thomas Y. Crowell, 1976. 408 p.

1-23. JOSEPHY, ALVIN T. *On the Hill: A History of the American Congress.* New York: Simon and Schuster, 1979. 414 p.

1-24. MACNEIL, NEIL. *Forge of Democracy: The House of Representatives.* New York: David McKay, 1963. 496 p.

Rules, Procedure, and the Legislative Process

1-25. CANNON, CLARENCE. *Cannon's Precedents of the House of Representatives of the United States.* 6 vols. Washington, D.C.: Government Printing Office, 1935–41.
Incorporates Hinds (1-33) into an updated three-volume index and supplements it with three volumes of precedents covering the period 1908–36.

1-26. DALZELL, JOHN. "The Rules of the House of Representatives." *Independent*, 12 March 1908, pp. 577–82.

1-27. DESCHLER, LEWIS. *Deschler's Precedents of the United States House of Representatives.* 6 vols. Washington, D.C.: Government Printing Office, 1977.
Covers the period 1936–76.

1-28. ———. *Deschler's Procedure: A Summary of the Modern Precedents and Practices of the U.S. House of Representatives, 86th–95th Congresses.* Washington, D.C.: Government Printing Office, 1979.
Updates Deschler's 1977 work (1-27).

1-29. FROMAN, LEWIS A., JR. *The Congressional Process: Strategies, Rules, and Procedures.* Boston: Little, Brown, 1967. 221 p.

1-30. GARDNER, AUGUSTUS P. "The Rules of the House of Representatives." *North American Review* 189 (February 1909): 233–41.

1-31. HARLOW, RALPH V. *The History of Legislative Methods in the Period before 1825.* New Haven: Yale University Press, 1917. 269 p.

1-32. HASBROUCK, PAUL D. *Party Government in the House of Representatives.* New York: Macmillan, 1927. 265 p.

1-33. HINDS, ASHER C. *Hinds' Precedents of the House of Representatives of the United States.* 8 vols. Washington, D.C.: Government Printing Office, 1907-8.

1-34. JONES, CHARLES O. "The Minority Party and Policy-Making in the House of Representatives." *American Political Science Review* 62 (June 1968): 481-93.

1-35. ———. *The Minority Party in Congress.* Boston: Little, Brown, 1970. 204 p.

1-36. LUCE, ROBERT. *Legislative Procedure: Parliamentary Practices and the Course of Business in the Framing of Statutes.* 1922. Reprint. New York: Da Capo Press, 1972. 628 p.

1-37. McCALL, SAMUEL W. *The Business of Congress.* New York: Columbia University Press, 1911. 215 p.

1-38. REMICK, HENRY C. *The Powers of Congress in Respect to Membership and Elections.* 2 vols. Princeton, N.J.: privately printed, 1929.

1-39. RIDDICK, FLOYD M. *The United States Congress: Organization and Procedure.* Manassas, Va.: National Capital Publishers, 1949. 459 p.

1-40. RIPLEY, RANDALL B. *Congress: Process and Policy.* New York: W. W. Norton, 1975. 316 p.

1-41. ROBINSON, JAMES A. *Congress and Foreign Policy Making: A Study in Legislative Influence and Initiative.* Homewood, Ill.: Dorsey Press, 1967. 254 p.

1-42. STEVENS, FREDERICK C. "The Rules of the House of Representatives: A Defense." *American Review of Reviews* 39 (April 1909): 470-74.

1-43. SWANSON, CLAUDE A. "The Rules of the House of Representatives: A Criticism." *American Review of Reviews* 39 (April 1909): 465-70.

1-44. TACHERON, DONALD G., AND UDALL, MORRIS K. *The Job of the Congressman: An Introduction to Service in the U.S. House of Representatives.* Indianapolis: Bobbs-Merrill, 1966. 446 p.

1-45. THURSTON, JOHN M. "The Rules of Congress." *Independent*, 24 April 1902, pp. 961-64.

Congressional Leadership

1-46. ABRAM, MICHAEL, AND COOPER, JOSEPH. "The Rise of Seniority in the House of Representatives." *Polity* 1 (Fall 1968): 52-85.

1-47. BOLLING, RICHARD. *House Out of Order.* New York: E. P. Dutton, 1965. 253 p.

1-48. ———. *Power in the House: A History of the Leadership of the House of Representatives.* New York: Capricorn Books, 1974. 284 p.

1-49. BROWN, GEORGE ROTHWELL. *The Leadership of Congress.* 1922. Reprint. New York: Arno Press, 1974. 311 p.

1-50. FROMAN, LEWIS A., JR., AND RIPLEY, RANDALL B. "Conditions for Party Leadership: The Case of the House Democrats." *American Political Science Review* 59 (March 1965): 52-63.

1-51. GALLOWAY, GEORGE B. "Leadership in the House of Representatives." *Western Political Quarterly* 12 (June 1959): 417-41.

1-52. McCLELLAN, GEORGE B. "Leadership in the House of Representatives." *Scribner's Magazine* 49 (May 1911): 594-99.

1-53. NELSON, GARRISON. "Partisan Patterns of House Leadership Change, 1789-1977." *American Political Science Review* 71 (September 1977): 918-39.

1-54. PEABODY, ROBERT L. *Leadership in Congress: Stability, Succession, and Change.* Boston: Little, Brown, 1976. 522 p.

1-55. ———. "Party Leadership Change in the United States House of Representatives." *American Political Science Review* 61 (September 1967): 675-93.

1-56. PEABODY, ROBERT L., AND POLSBY, NELSON W., EDS. *New Perspectives on the House of Representatives.* 3d ed. Chicago: Rand McNally, 1977. 420 p.

1-57. POLSBY, NELSON W. "The Institutionalization of the U.S. House of Representatives." *American Political Science Review* 62 (March 1968): 144-68.

1-58. POLSBY, NELSON W.; GALLAHER, MIRIAM; AND RUNDQUIST, BARRY SPENCER. "The Growth of the Seniority System in the U.S. House of Representatives." *American Political Science Review* 63 (September 1969): 787–807.

1-59. RIPLEY, RANDALL B. *Party Leaders in the House of Representatives*. Washington, D.C.: Brookings Institution, 1967. 221 p.

1-60. ⸺. "The Party Whip Organizations in the United States House of Representatives." *American Political Science Review* 58 (September 1964): 561–76.

Congressional Committees

1-61. McCONACHIE, LAUROS G. *Congressional Committees*. 1898. Reprint. New York: Burt Franklin, 1973. 441 p.

1-62. McCOWN, ADA C. *The Congressional Conference Committee*. 1927. Reprint. New York: AMS Press, 1967. 274 p.

1-63. MANLEY, JOHN F. *The Politics of Finance: The House Committee on Ways and Means*. Boston: Little, Brown, 1970. 395 p.

1-64. ROBINSON, JAMES A. "Decision Making in the Committee on Rules." Ph.D. dissertation, Northwestern University, 1957. 639 p. 00-24919.

1-65. ⸺. *The House Rules Committee*. Indianapolis: Bobbs-Merrill, 1963. 142 p.

1-66. SCHLESINGER, ARTHUR M., JR., AND BRUNS, ROGER, EDS. *Congress Investigates: A Documented History, 1792–1974*. 5 vols. New York: Chelsea House, 1975.

1-67. SHEPSLE, KENNETH A. *The Giant Jigsaw Puzzle: Democratic Committee Assignments in the Modern House*. Chicago: University of Chicago Press, 1978. 333 p.

1-68. VARDYS, V. STANLEY. "Select Committees of the House of Representatives." *Midwest Journal of Political Science* 6 (August 1962): 247–65.

Congress and the Executive

1-69. BINKLEY, WILFRED E. *The Powers of the President: Problems of American Democracy*. Garden City, N.Y.: Doubleday, 1937. 332 p.

1-70. HORN, STEPHEN. *The Cabinet and Congress*. New York: Columbia University Press, 1960. 310 p.

1-71. LEARNED, HENRY BARRETT. *The President's Cabinet: Studies in the Origin, Formation, and Structure of an American Institution*. 1912. Reprint. New York: Burt Franklin, 1972. 471 p.

POLITICS AND PARTIES

The following works on the American political system all make pertinent references to the speakership or to several Speakers.

1-72. AGAR, HERBERT. *The Price of Union*. Boston: Houghton Mifflin, 1950. 750 p.

1-73. BURNS, JAMES MACGREGOR. *The Deadlock of Democracy: Four-Party Politics in America*. Englewood Cliffs, N.J.: Prentice-Hall, 1963. 388 p.

1-74. GOLDMAN, RALPH M. *Search for Consensus: The Story of the Democratic Party*. Philadelphia: Temple University Press, 1979. 417 p.

1-75. HOLCOMBE, ARTHUR N. *Our More Perfect Union: From Eighteenth-Century Principles to Twentieth-Century Practice*. Cambridge, Mass.: Harvard University Press, 1950. 460 p.

1-76. HOYT, EDWIN P. *Jumbos and Jackasses: A Popular History of the Political Wars*. Garden City, N.Y.: Doubleday, 1960. 505 p.

1-77. JOHNSTON, ALEXANDER. *American Political History, 1763–1876*. Edited and supplemented by James Albert Woodburn. 2 vols. New York: G. P. Putnam's Sons, 1905.

1-78. KENT, FRANK R. *The Democratic Party: A History*. 1928. Reprint. New York: Johnson Reprint, 1968. 568 p.

1-79. LEWIS, STUART. *Party Principles and Practical Politics*. New York: Prentice-Hall, 1928. 523 p.

1-80. MAYER, GEORGE H. *The Republican Party, 1854–1966*. 2d ed. New York: Oxford University Press, 1967. 604 p.

1-81. MYERS, WILLIAM S. *The Republican Party: A History*. New York: Century, 1931. 517 p.

1-82. ROBINSON, EDGAR E. *The Evolution of American Political Parties: A Sketch of Party Development.* 1924. Reprint. New York: Johnson Reprint, 1970. 382 p.

1-83. SEILHAMER, GEORGE O. *History of the Republican Party.* 2 vols. New York: Judge Publishing, 1909.

1-84. SUNDQUIST, JAMES L. *Dynamics of the Party System: Alignment and Realignment of Political Parties in the United States.* Washington, D.C.: Brookings Institution, 1973. 388 p.

BIOGRAPHICAL DICTIONARIES

The following biographical compendia contain useful capsule biographies of most Speakers. The most reliable and scholarly sketches are in *The Dictionary of American Biography* (1-86), but the others may be useful on certain Speakers.

1-85. HERRINGSHAW, THOMAS WILLIAM. *Herringshaw's Encyclopedia of American Biography of the 19th Century.* Chicago: American Publisher's Association, 1904. 1,046 p.

Contains capsule biographies of most nineteenth-century Speakers.

1-86. JOHNSON, ALLEN, AND MALONE, DUMAS, EDS. *The Dictionary of American Biography.* 20 vols. Milford, Conn.: Charles Scribner's Sons, 1928–37.

The classic biographical dictionary for American history, it contains entries for thirty-eight of the forty-six Speakers.

1-87. *The National Cyclopedia of American Biography.* 75 vols. to date. New York: James T. White, 1898–.

Only four Speakers (Byrns, McCormack, Albert, and O'Neill) are omitted from this ongoing publication.

1-88. WILSON, JAMES GRANT, ED. *Appleton's Cyclopedia of American Biography.* 6 vols. New York: D. Appleton, 1886–1900.

Contains sketches on the first thirty-two Speakers (Muhlenberg to Henderson).

RESEARCHING CONGRESS

Researching the legislative process is a complex and sometimes confounding task. The variety and mass of governmental publications and their often confusing, unsystematic indexing create a severe handicap for the beginning researcher. Though it is beyond the scope of this bibliography to list all the necessary research tools, the following guides are useful. The works cited below are designed to guide researchers through the morass of documents and indices to the appropriate sources.

General Guides to the Legislative Process

The following works provide essential information on the legislative process. They give a valuable introduction to using the research guides cited in the following section. *See also* Ripley (1-40).

1-89. CONGRESSIONAL QUARTERLY. *Guide to Congress.* 3d ed. Washington, D.C., 1983. 721 p.

1-90. CUMMINGS, FRANK. *Capitol Hill Manual.* Washington, D.C.: Bureau of National Affairs, 1976. 331 p.

1-91. OLESZEK, WALTER. *Congressional Procedures and the Policy Process.* Washington, D.C.: Congressional Quarterly, 1976. 256 p.

1-92. ZINN, CHARLES. *How Our Laws Are Made.* Revised and updated by Joseph Fischer. Washington, D.C.: Government Printing Office, 1980. 73 p.

Legislative Research Guides

Researching legislation prior to the twentieth century presents special problems and the need for consulting the following guides. Folsom (1-95) is a clearly written handbook for beginners. Boyd (1-94) and Schmeckebier and Eastin (1-100) are especially valuable for researching congressional publications of the eighteenth and nineteenth centuries.

1-93. BITNER, HARRY, AND PRICE, MILES O. *Effective Legal Research.* 4th ed. Boston: Little, Brown, 1979. 643 p.

1-94. BOYD, ANNE MORRIS. *United States Government Publications*. 3d ed. Revised by Rae Elizabeth Rips. New York: Wilson, 1949. 627 p.

1-95. FOLSOM, GWENDOLYN B. *Legislative History: Research for the Interpretation of Laws*. Charlottesville: University Press of Virginia, 1972. 136 p.

1-96. GOEHLERT, ROBERT U. *Congress and Law Making: Researching the Legislative Process*. Santa Barbara, Calif.: Clio Books, 1979. 168 p.

1-97. MEYER, EVELYN S. "Reference Guides to Congressional Research." *RQ* 22 (Fall 1972): 30–36.

1-98. MOREHEAD, JOE. *Introduction to United States Public Documents*. Littleton, Colo.: Libraries Unlimited, 1975. 289 p.

1-99. NABORS, EUGENE. "Legislative History and Government Documents—Another Step in Legal Research." *Government Publications Review* 3 (Spring 1976): 15–41.

1-100. SCHMECKEBIER, LAURENCE F., AND EASTIN, ROY B. *Government Publications and Their Use*. 2d ed. Washington, D.C.: Brookings Institution, 1969. 502 p.

Records of Congressional Proceedings

Records of floor proceedings are particularly useful in following the Speaker's actions and rulings. The time periods covered are given in brackets.

1-101. *Annals of the Congress of the United States*. [1789–1824]. Washington, D.C.: Gales and Seaton, 1834–56.

1-102. *The Congressional Globe*. [1833–73]. Washington, D.C., 1835–73.

1-103. *Register of Debates in Congress*. [1824–37]. Washington, D.C.: Gales and Seaton, 1825–37.

1-104. U.S. CONGRESS. *The Congressional Record*. [1873–present]. Washington, D.C.: Government Printing Office, 1874–.

An indispensable source available in both daily editions and bound compilations, it includes the proceedings of both House and Senate, extensions of remarks, and a daily digest of congressional activities. It is not, however, a literal transcription. Remarks may be extended, altered, or deleted prior to printing and also prior to publication of bound volumes. The daily edition is therefore a more accurate account of what was said.

1-105. U.S. CONGRESS. HOUSE. *Journal of the House of Representatives of the United States of America*. [1789–present]. Washington, D.C.: Government Printing Office, 1789–.

The official minutes of the House of Representatives are published at the end of each session of Congress. The *House Journal* includes a "History of Bills and Resolutions," in which legislative actions are arranged by number, title, and action. The volumes also include a useful name, subject, and title index.

PART II

THE SPEAKERS, 1789–1814

2. General Bibliography, 1789–1814

The following general works are useful in researching the office and Speakers of the period 1789–1814.

GENERAL HISTORIES

2-1. ABERNETHY, THOMAS P. *The South in the New Nation, 1789–1819.* Baton Rouge: Louisiana State University Press, 1961. 529 p.

Attention is given to those Speakers who influenced the development of the South.

2-2. ADAMS, HENRY. *History of the United States during the Administrations of Jefferson and Madison.* 9 vols. New York: Charles Scribner's Sons, 1891–98.

A classic, richly detailed work.

PARTY POLITICS, 1789–1814

2-3. CHAMBERS, WILLIAM NISBET. *Political Parties in a New Nation: The American Experience, 1776–1809.* New York: Oxford University Press, 1963. 231 p.

2-4. GOLDMAN, PERRY M. " 'The Republic of Virtue' and Other Essays on the Politics of the Early National Period." Ph.D. dissertation, Columbia University, 1970. 310 p. 72-33421.

Discusses several early Speakers and changes in the office.

2-5. LYNCH, WILLIAM O. *Fifty Years of Party Warfare, 1789–1837.* 1931. Reprint. Gloucester, Mass.: Peter Smith, 1967. 506 p.

STUDIES OF CONGRESS, 1789–1814

2-6. BARLOW, WILLIAM RAY. "Congress during the War of 1812." Ph.D. dissertation, Ohio State University, 1961. 332 p. 62-02121.

2-7. BUTLER, JOHN P., ED. *Index: The Papers of the Continental Congress, 1774–1789.* 5 vols. Washington, D.C.: Government Printing Office, 1978.

A comprehensive guide to the papers of the Continental Congress held by the National Archives and Records Service. Useful for Speakers active in government or military service.

2-8. CHAMPAGNE, RAYMOND W., JR. "The House of Representatives and American Foreign Policy during the Washington Administration, 1789–1797." Ph.D. dissertation, Loyola University of Chicago, 1973. 328 p. 73-23138.

2-9. FRITZ, HARRY WILLIAM. "The Collapse of Party: President, Congress, and the Decline of Party Action, 1807–1817." Ph.D. dissertation, Washington University, 1971. 359 p. 71-19816.

2-10. FURLONG, PATRICK J. "The Evolution of Political Organization in the House of Representatives, 1789–1801." Ph.D. dissertation, Northwestern University, 1966. 380 p. 66-13982.

2-11. LIGHTFOOT, BILLY BOB. "The State Delegations in the Congress of the United States, 1789–1801." 2 vols. Ph.D. dissertation, University of Texas at Austin, 1958. 1,097 p. 58-3980.

THE WASHINGTON COMMUNITY, 1800–1814

2-12. WHARTON, ANNE H. *Social Life in the Early Republic.* Philadelphia: J. B. Lippincott, 1902. 346 p.

Contains anecdotal but illuminating insights into Washington society.

2-13. YOUNG, JAMES STERLING. *The Washington Community, 1800–1828.* New York: Columbia University Press, 1966. 307 p.

A scholarly study of the structure and interaction between the branches of the evolving federal government.

3. Frederick Augustus Conrad Muhlenberg
(1750–1801)
(Speaker, First and Third Congresses)

Frederick A. C. Muhlenberg, the first Speaker of the House of Representatives, was a member of an important Pennsylvania family and a politician with a clergyman's background. His father, eminent German Lutheran minister Henry Melchior Muhlenberg, was known as the Patriarch of the Lutheran Church in America. One of Frederick's brothers served as a brigadier general in the Continental army. Another brother was also a well-known minister.

Frederick Muhlenberg was born into this prominent family on January 1, 1750, at Trappe, Pennsylvania. He was sent with his two brothers to be educated in Germany, where he earned a degree in divinity from Halle University (1770). His fluency in German served him well among the German-speaking settlers in Pennsylvania, to which he returned in 1770. By 1775 Muhlenberg had become pastor of a congregation in New York, but his advocacy of independence forced him to return to Pennsylvania in 1776.

Muhlenberg resigned his ministerial office in 1779 to fill the unexpired term of a Pennsylvania representative to the Continental Congress. He subsequently served in the Pennsylvania General Assembly (1778–83), where he was elected speaker in 1780. From 1783 to 1784 he was president of the Council of Censors, a board that reviewed the state's laws and finances. Three years later he presided over the state convention that ratified the Federal Constitution (1787).

Muhlenberg's career in national politics began in 1789, when he was elected to the First Congress from Philadelphia, and ended with the closing of the Fourth Congress (1797). In 1789 he was elected Speaker as a Federalist, but sentiment favoring a rotation in the distribution of honors contributed to the election of Jonathan Trumbull as Speaker of the Second Congress (1791–93). Two years later Muhlenberg was elected Speaker of the Third Congress (1793–95) with the help of Republican votes. Between these terms, he joined congressmen James Monroe and Abraham Venable in investigating and clearing Secretary of the Treasury Alexander Hamilton of the charge of speculating with public funds. While chairman of the Committee of the Whole in 1795, Muhlenberg cast the deciding vote in favor of the bill appropriating funds to implement Jay's Treaty. In spite of criticism of his vote by Jeffersonian Republicans, Muhlenberg later became a member of Jefferson's party. After retiring from Congress in 1797, he was appointed collector general of the Pennsylvania Land Office in 1800. He died in Lancaster, Pennsylvania, on June 4, 1801.

The House of Representatives followed well-established colonial precedents in electing Muhlenberg as its first Speaker. Like the presiding officers of the British House of Commons and the colonial assemblies, Muhlenberg owed his election in large part to his experience and moderate views. Because he was a representative of the largest Middle Atlantic state at a time when the president was a Southerner and the vice-president was from New England, his selection helped to achieve sectional balance. In addition to ability, Muhlenberg brought to the Speaker's office a reputation for honesty, dignity, and impartiality. As Speaker he rarely took part in debates before the entire House. Although he was not a distinguished parliamentarian, he was able to establish workable procedures and precedents for the House.

MANUSCRIPT COLLECTIONS

Library of Congress, Manuscript Division, Washington, D.C.
  Muhlenberg Family Papers.
  15 items, 1773–1847.
  MC 110.
Muhlenberg College Library, Allentown, Pa.
  Muhlenberg Family Manuscript Collection.
  Journal, 24 items, 22 folders, 1775.
  NUCMC 61-2505.

In addition to the two major collections cited above, Frederick A. C. Muhlenberg manuscripts can be found in collections at the Historical Society of Pennsylvania and the Lutheran Theological Seminary Library, both located in Philadelphia, Pa.

BOOKS, ARTICLES, AND DISSERTATIONS

WORKS BY FREDERICK A. C. MUHLENBERG

The available published works of Frederick Muhlenberg center upon his Lutheran ministry (3-3, 3-4, and 3-5) and two speeches printed in German (3-1 and 3-2). The following items are listed chronologically by year of publication.

3-1. MUHLENBERG, FREDERICK AUGUSTUS CONRAD. *Rede bei der Feier des 20Ten Septembers* [Oration for the observance of the 20th of September]. Philadelphia, 1794.

3-2. ———. *Rede von der incorporirten Deutschen Gesellschaft in Philadelphia* [Speech about the Incorporated German Society in Philadelphia]. Philadelphia: Steiner and Kammerer, 1795.

3-3. ———. "Muhlenberg's Short Sketch of the Lutheran Congregation in Philadelphia, 1795." Edited by Julius F. Sachse. *Lutheran Church Review* 21 (January 1902): 81–87.

3-4. ———. "Diary of F. A. Muhlenberg from the Day of His Ordination, October 25, 1770, until June, 1774." Translated by J. W. Early. *Lutheran Church Review* 24 (January–October 1905): 127–37, 388–90, 562–71, 682–94; 25 (January–April 1906): 134–47, 345–58.

3-5. ———. "F. A. C. Muhlenberg's Report of His First Trip to Shamokin, Sent to His Father." *Lutheran Church Review* 25 (July 1906): 535–44.

BIOGRAPHICAL SKETCHES

The most complete, most detailed, and most scholarly biographical treatment of Muhlenberg is found in Wallace (3-9). Seidensticker (3-8), though less scholarly, is also useful and comprehensive.

3-6. MUHLENBERG, HENRY A. *The Life of Major-General Peter Muhlenberg of the Revolutionary War.* Philadelphia: Carey and Hart, 1849. 456 p.

3-7. RICHARDS, HENRY MELCHIOR MUHLENBERG. "Famous Pennsylvania-Germans: Frederick Augustus Conrad Muhlenberg." *Pennsylvania-German* 3 (April 1902): 51–60.

3-8. SEIDENSTICKER, OSWALD. "Frederick Augustus Conrad Muhlenberg: Speaker of the House of Representatives, in the First Congress, 1789." *Pennsylvania Magazine of History and Biography* 13 (July 1889): 184–206.
  Though dated, the article remains an indispensable sketch of Muhlenberg's career.

3-9. WALLACE, PAUL A. W. *The Muhlenbergs of Pennsylvania.* 1950. Reprint. Freeport, N.Y.: Books for Libraries Press, 1970. 358 p.
  Contains the best treatment of all phases of Muhlenberg's life.

EARLY LIFE AND LUTHERAN MINISTRY, 1750–1775

The published journal of Frederick Muhlenberg's father (3-17) offers the most complete and most detailed account of the future Speaker's childhood, adolescence, and early adult life. Kretschmann (3-16) and Schmucker (3-20) detail, respectively, Muhlenberg's religious life in Trappe and his pastorate in New York City.

3-10. DORPALEN, ANDREAS. "The German Element in Early Pennsylvania Politics, 1789–1800: A Study in Americanization." *Pennsylvania History* 9 (July 1942): 176–90.

3-11. EVANGELICAL LUTHERAN MINISTERIUM OF PENNSYLVANIA AND ADJACENT STATES. *Documentary History of the Evangelical Lutheran Ministerium of Pennsylvania and Adjacent States: Proceedings of the Annual Conventions, 1748–1821.* Philadelphia: General Council of the Evangelical Lutheran Church in North America, 1898. 619 p.

3-12. ──────. *Lutherans in Berks County: Two Centuries of Continuous Organized Church Life, 1723–1923.* Edited by H. S. Kidd. Reading, Pa.: William S. Rhode, 1923. 503 p.

3-13. HISTORICAL RECORDS SURVEY. New York (City). *Inventory of Church Archives in New York City: Lutheran.* New York, 1940. 152 p.

3-14. JACOBS, HENRY EYSTER. *A History of the Evangelical Lutheran Church in the United States.* New York: Christian Literature, 1893. 539 p.

3-15. KREIDER, HARRY JULIUS. *Lutheranism in Colonial New York.* 1942. Reprint. New York: Arno Press, 1972. 158 p.

3-16. KRETSCHMANN, ERNEST T., ED. *The Old Trappe Church, 1743–1893.* Philadelphia: Graig, Finley, 1893. 182 p.

3-17. MUHLENBERG, HENRY MELCHIOR. *The Journals of Henry Melchior Muhlenberg.* Translated by Theodore G. Tappert and John W. Doberstein. 3 vols. Philadelphia: Evangelical Lutheran Ministerium of Pennsylvania and the Muhlenberg Press, 1942–58.
  Volumes 2 and 3 are the most important documentary sources on Muhlenberg's early life, including his role in the church and in Pennsylvania politics.

3-18. PFATTEICHER, HELEN E. *The Ministerium of Pennsylvania: Oldest Lutheran Synod Founded in Colony Days.* Philadelphia: Ministerium Press, 1938. 176 p.

3-19. RICHARDS, HENRY MELCHIOR MUHLENBERG. *Descendents of Henry Melchior Muhlenberg.* Lancaster, Pa.: Pennsylvania-German Society, 1900. 89 p.

3-20. SCHMUCKER, REVEREND B. M. "The Lutheran Church in the City of New York." *Lutheran Church Review* 4 (April 1885): 127–51.
  A detailed account of Muhlenberg's activities as minister of Christ's Church, New York City.

3-21. WENTZ, ABDEL ROSS. *A Basic History of Lutheranism in America.* Rev. ed. Philadelphia: Fortress Press, 1964. 439 p.

THE REVOLUTION AND MUHLENBERG'S EARLY POLITICAL CAREER, 1776–1789

Wallace (3-34) provides a useful comparison of Muhlenberg's actions during the Revolution with those of his brother Peter. Hocker (3-23), a biography of Peter Muhlenberg, also contains ample references to Frederick. Brunhouse (3-22) analyzes Muhlenberg as a conservative German-American amid the political changes of the Revolutionary era.

3-22. BRUNHOUSE, ROBERT L. *The Counter-Revolution in Pennsylvania, 1776–1790.* 1942. Reprint. New York: Octagon Books, 1971. 368 p.

3-23. HOCKER, EDWARD W. *The Fighting Parson of the American Revolution: A Biography of General Peter Muhlenberg.* Philadelphia: privately printed, 1936. 191 p.

3-24. JENSEN, MERRILL, ED. *Ratification of the Constitution by the States: Pennsylvania.* The Documentary History of the Ratification of the Constitution, vol. 2. Madison: State Historical Society of Wisconsin, 1976. 779 p.

3-25. MEADER, LEWIS H. "The Council of Censors." *Pennsylvania Magazine of History and Biography* 22 (October 1898): 265–300.

3-26. NEVINS, ALLAN. *The American States during and after the Revolution, 1775–1789.* 1924. Reprint. New York: Augustus M. Kelley, 1969. 728 p.

3. FREDERICK AUGUSTUS CONRAD MUHLENBERG

3-27. PENNSYLVANIA. Council of Censors. 1783–84. *Journal of the Council of Censors, 1783–1784.* Philadelphia: Hall and Sellers, 1784. 179 p.

Muhlenberg served as president of the council in 1783 and 1784.

3-28. PENNSYLVANIA. General Assembly. *Minutes of the General Assembly of the Commonwealth of Pennsylvania, 1781–1782.* 8 vols. Philadelphia, 1781–90.

Muhlenberg was speaker of the Pennsylvania House from 1781 to 1783.

3-29. PENNSYLVANIA. Historical Society. *Pennsylvania and the Federal Constitution, 1787–1788.* Edited by John M. McMaster and Frederick D. Stone. 2 vols. 1880. Reprint. New York: Da Capo Press, 1970.

3-30. PENNSYLVANIA. Supreme Executive Council. *Minutes of the Supreme Council of Pennsylvania.* Vols. 12–16. Philadelphia, 1851–53.

3-31. RICHARDS, HENRY MELCHIOR MUHLENBERG. *The Pennsylvania-Germans in the Revolutionary War, 1775–1783.* Pennsylvania-German Society, Proceedings and Addresses, vol. 17. Lancaster, Pa.: Pennsylvania-German Society, 1908. 514 p.

3-32. TAPPERT, THEODORE G. "Henry Melchior Muhlenberg and the American Revolution." *Church History* 11 (December 1942): 284–301.

3-33. THOMAS, E. BRUCE. *Political Tendencies in Philadelphia, 1783–1794.* Philadelphia: Temple University Press, 1938. 231 p.

3-34. WALLACE, PAUL A. W. "The Muhlenbergs and the Revolutionary Underground." *Proceedings of the American Philosophical Society* 94 (1950): 119–26.

Examines Muhlenberg's behavior during the Revolution within the context of his family's actions.

3-35. ———. *Pennsylvania: Seedtime of a Nation.* New York: Harper and Row, 1962. 322 p.

MUHLENBERG AS CONGRESSMAN AND SPEAKER, 1789–1796

Muhlenberg's relationship with Alexander Hamilton is best described in Alberts (3-36),

Chidsey (3-40), Hamilton (3-47), and Miller (3-55). The Speaker's role in the debate over implementation of Jay's Treaty is discussed in Cobbett (3-42), Combs (3-43), McDonald (3-51), and Miller (3-56). *See also* Thomas (3-33).

3-36. ALBERTS, ROBERT C. *The Golden Voyage: The Life and Times of William Bingham, 1752–1804.* Boston: Houghton Mifflin, 1969. 570 p.

3-37. BOWERS, CLAUDE G. *Jefferson and Hamilton: The Struggle for Democracy in America.* Boston: Houghton Mifflin, 1925. 531 p.

3-38. BOWLING, KENNETH R. "Dinner at Jefferson's: A Note on Jacob E. Cooke's 'The Compromise of 1790.' " *William and Mary Quarterly,* 3d ser., 28 (October 1971): 629–48.

3-39. CARSON, HAMPTON L. "The First Congress of the United States." *Pennsylvania Magazine of History and Biography* 13 (July 1889): 129–52.

3-40. CHIDSEY, DONALD B. *Mr. Hamilton and Mr. Jefferson.* Nashville: Thomas Nelson, 1975. 207 p.

3-41. CLARK, BARBARA L. *E.B.: The Story of Elias Boudinot IV; His Family, His Friends, and His Country.* Philadelphia: Dorrance, 1977. 472 p.

3-42. COBBETT, WILLIAM. *Porcupine's Works.* Vols. 2, 3, 9. London: Cobbett and Morgan, 1783–1801.

3-43. COMBS, JERALD A. *The Jay Treaty: Political Battleground of the Founding Fathers.* Berkeley: University of California Press, 1970. 254 p.

3-44. CRESSON, WILLIAM P. *James Monroe.* 1946. Reprint. Hamden, Conn.: Archon, 1971. 577 p.

3-45. FREEMAN, DOUGLAS SOUTHALL. *George Washington.* 7 vols. New York: Charles Scribner's Sons, 1948–57.

3-46. GALLOWAY, GEORGE B. "Precedents Established in the First Congress." *Western Political Quarterly* 11 (September 1958): 454–68.

3-47. HAMILTON, ALEXANDER. *The Papers of Alexander Hamilton.* Edited by Harold C. Syrett. Vols. 10, 13–21, 25, 26. New York: Columbia University Press, 1961–79.

3-48. JENSEN, MERRILL, AND BECKER, ROBERT A., EDS. *Documentary History of the First Federal Elections, 1788–1790.* Vol. 1. Madison: University of Wisconsin Press, 1976. 896 p.

3-49. KURTZ, STEPHEN G. *The Presidency of John Adams: The Collapse of Federalism, 1795–1800.* Philadelphia: University of Pennsylvania Press, 1957. 448 p.

3-50. LUETSCHER, GEORGE D. *Early Political Machinery in the United States.* 1903. Reprint. New York: Da Capo Press, 1971. 160 p.

3-51. MCDONALD, FORREST. *The Presidency of George Washington.* Lawrence: University Press of Kansas, 1974. 210 p.

3-52. MACLAY, WILLIAM. *The Journal of William Maclay.* Edited with an introduction by Charles A. Beard. 1890. Reprint. New York: Frederick Unger, 1965. 429 p.

3-53. ———. *Sketches of Debates in the First Senate of the United States, 1789–1791.* Edited by George W. Harris. 1880. Reprint. New York: Burt Franklin, 1969. 357 p.

3-54. MARSH, PHILIP. "Hamilton and Monroe." *Mississippi Valley Historical Review* 34 (December 1947): 459–68.

3-55. MILLER, JOHN C. *Alexander Hamilton: Portrait in Paradox.* New York: Harper and Brothers, 1960. 659 p.

3-56. ———. *The Federalist Era, 1789–1801.* New York: Harper and Brothers, 1960. 304 p.

3-57. PERKINS, BRADFORD. *The First Rapprochement: England and the United States, 1795–1805.* Philadelphia: University of Pennsylvania Press, 1967. 257 p.

3-58. SACHSE, JULIUS F. *The Religious and Social Conditions of Philadelphia during the First Decade under the Federal Constitution, 1790–1800.* Philadelphia, 1901. 27 p.

3-59. STEWART, DONALD H. *The Opposition Press of the Federalist Period.* Albany: State University of New York Press, 1969. 957 p.

3-60. TINKCOM, HARRY MARLIN. *The Republicans and Federalists in Pennsylvania: A Study in National Stimulus and Local Response.* Harrisburg: Pennsylvania Historical and Museum Commission, 1950. 354 p.

3-61. WASHINGTON, GEORGE. *The Diaries of George Washington, 1748–1799.* Edited by Donald Jackson and Dorothy Twohig. 6 vols. Charlottesville: University Press of Virginia, 1976–79.

3-62. WILLIAMS, ROBERT P., ED. *The First Congress, March 4, 1789–March 3, 1791: A Compilation of Significant Debates.* New York: Exposition Press, 1970. 465 p.

3-63. WYNKOOP, HENRY. "The Letters of Judge Henry Wynkoop, Representative from Pennsylvania to the First Congress of the United States." Edited by Joseph M. Beatty. *Pennsylvania Magazine of History and Biography* 38 (January 1914): 39–64.

4. Jonathan Trumbull, Jr.
(1740–1809)
(Speaker, Second Congress)

Jonathan Trumbull, Jr., like his predecessor Frederick Muhlenberg, belonged to a distinguished American family and was chosen Speaker for his reputation as an honorable and talented statesman. Trumbull's mother, Faith Robinson, was a direct descendant of John and Priscilla Alden. His father, also named Jonathan, was governor of Connecticut and commissary general of the Continental army during the Revolution. Speaker Trumbull's younger brother, artist John Trumbull, gained fame from his heroic paintings of Revolutionary War scenes, including such works as *The Surrender of Lord Cornwallis at Yorktown* and *The Declaration of Independence.*

Jonathan Trumbull, Jr., was born in Lebanon, Connecticut, on March 26, 1740. He enrolled at Harvard College at the age of fifteen and graduated four years later as class valedictorian (1759). He entered local politics in Lebanon after over a decade as an active partner in the family trading business. Following his election to the Connecticut legislature in 1774, Trumbull offered his services to the Continental Congress and was appointed paymaster of the army in New York (1776). In June 1781 he succeeded Alexander Hamilton as George Washington's confidential secretary and aide.

Although he did not take an active role in either the formulation or the ratification of the new Constitution, Trumbull was elected to the First, Second, and Third Congresses (1789–95), where he aligned himself with the principles of Alexander Hamilton and the emerging Federalist party. Trumbull was unsuccessful in his bid to become the first Speaker of the House, but he was able to unseat Muhlenberg during the 1791–93 term. As an energetic, active first-term congressman, Trumbull had acquired a dominant influence among members from New England. As Speaker he used that influence to moderate and conciliate rising party spirits. The Connecticut legislature elected Trumbull to the U.S. Senate in 1794, after he had been defeated for the speakership of the Third Congress. He resigned from the Senate in 1796 to become deputy governor of Connecticut.

Trumbull succeeded to the governor's office after the death of Oliver Wolcott in December 1797. While he was Connecticut's chief executive (1797–1809) he continued to oppose Jefferson's influence over state and national politics. In 1799 he sought to curb the Jeffersonian Republicans by joining Hamilton and other Federalists in urging Washington to seek a third term. Trumbull's criticism of Republicanism climaxed in 1809, when he vigorously opposed the Embargo Acts and the request of the secretary of war to use the state militia to enforce the embargo. Trumbull died of heart failure on August 7, 1809, and was buried in Lebanon.

Trumbull's actions as Speaker did not depart significantly from those of his predecessor. He was certainly more sympathetic to Federalist policies and more closely aligned with Hamilton and Washington than Muhlenberg had been. Trumbull, in spite of his party allegiances, remained moderate and maintained an air of impartiality while Speaker. He was popular with his colleagues, who described him as cheerful and affable. A conscientious legislator, Trumbull was a dutiful and steadfast, if unspectacular, public servant.

MANUSCRIPT COLLECTIONS

Connecticut Historical Society, Hartford, Conn.
    Jonathan Trumbull, Jr., Papers.
    4 boxes, 6 vols., government letters, ca. 1,500 items, 1756–1809.
    NUCMC 61-2780.
Connecticut State Library, Hartford, Conn.
    Jonathan Trumbull, Jr., Papers.
    316 items, 1763–1903.
    NUCMC 60-1299.
Library of Congress, Manuscript Division, Washington, D.C.
    Jonathan Trumbull Checks and Letters.
    Ca. 175 items, 1792–94.
    MC 149.

Western Reserve Historical Society, Cleveland, Ohio.
    Jonathan Trumbull, Jr., Papers.
    Ca. 54 items relating to the Ohio Company, 1787–1811.
    NUCMC 75-1762.

The Connecticut Historical Society and the Connecticut State Library are the main repositories of Trumbull manuscripts. Both contain sizable Jonathan Trumbull, Sr., collections. There is a large collection of John Trumbull papers at the Yale University Library.

BOOKS, ARTICLES, AND DISSERTATIONS

WORKS BY JONATHAN TRUMBULL, JR.

4-1. TRUMBULL, JONATHAN, JR. *A Proclamation.* New Haven: Hudson and Goodwin, 1803. 1 p.
  The only published work by Trumbull, this one-page broadside promotes a missionary society.

BIOGRAPHIES, BIOGRAPHICAL SKETCHES, GENEALOGY, AND EULOGIES

The two works by Ifkovic (4-6 and 4-7) offer the most complete scholarly treatment of Trumbull's life. Also valuable is the biographical sketch included in Shipton (4-9). Representative eulogies include Dwight (4-4) and Ely (4-5). Lea (4-8) is a comprehensive and useful genealogy.

4-2. BARBER, JOHN WARNER. *Connecticut Historical Collections . . . Relating to the History and Antiquities of Every Town in Connecticut.* 1836. Reprint. New Haven: Durrie, Peck, and J. W. Barber, 1846. 576 p.

4-3. *Biographical Sketch of the Character of Governor Trumbull.* Hartford, Conn.: Hudson and Goodwin, 1809. 13 p.

4-4. DWIGHT, TIMOTHY. *A Discourse Occasioned by the Death of His Excellency Jonathan Trumbull, Esq., Governor.* New Haven: Oliver Steele, 1809. 28 p.

4-5. ELY, ZEBULON. *The Peaceful End to the Perfect Man: A Discourse Delivered in Lebanon at the Funeral of His Excellency Jonathan Trumbull.* Hartford, Conn.: Hudson and Goodwin, 1809. 27 p.

4-6. IFKOVIC, JOHN W. *Connecticut's Nationalist Revolutionary: Jonathan Trumbull, Junior.* Connecticut Bicentennial Series, no. 25. Hartford: American Revolutionary Bicentennial Commission of Connecticut, 1977. 103 p.
  A condensation of Ifkovic's dissertation (4-7), this work deals only with Trumbull's early career.

4-7. ———. "Jonathan Trumbull, Junior, 1740–1809: A Biography." Ph.D. dissertation, University of Virginia, 1974. 545 p. 74-12663.

Scholarly, comprehensive, and indispensable, this biography examines Trumbull's life and values within the context of his Puritan heritage.

4-8. LEA, JAMES HENRY. *A Genealogy of the Ancestors and Descendants of George Augustus and Louisa (Clap) Trumbull.* Fairhaven, Mass., 1886. 46 p.

4-9. SHIPTON, CLIFFORD K., ED. *Biographical Sketches of Those Who Attended Harvard College in the Classes 1756–1760.* Sibley's Harvard Graduates, vol. 14. Boston: Massachusetts Historical Society, 1968. 720 p.

4-10. SIZER, THEODORE. *The Works of Colonel John Trumbull: Artist of the American Revolution.* Rev. ed. New Haven: Yale University Press, 1967. 181 p.

4-11. TRUMBULL, JONATHAN. *Jonathan Trumbull: Governor of Connecticut, 1769–1784.* Boston: Little, Brown, 1919. 362 p.

4-12. WEAVER, GLEN. *Jonathan Trumbull: Connecticut's Merchant Magistrate, 1710–1785.* Hartford: Connecticut Historical Society, 1956. 182 p.

TRUMBULL AND THE REVOLUTION

Trumbull's service as Washington's aide can best be followed in Davis (4-17), Flexner (4-18), and Washington (4-24). *See also* Freeman (3-45) and Washington (3-61).

4-13. BURNETT, EDMUND CODY. *The Continental Congress.* 1941. Reprint. Westport, Conn.: Greenwood Press, 1975. 757 p.

4-14. ———, ED. *Letters of Members of the Continental Congress.* 8 vols. 1921–36. Reprint. Gloucester, Mass.: Peter Smith, 1963.

4-15. COLLIER, CHRISTOPHER. *Roger Sherman's Connecticut Yankee Politics and the American Revolution.* Middletown, Conn.: Wesleyan University Press, 1971. 409 p.

4-16. CONNECTICUT (COLONY). *The Public Records of the Colony of Connecticut.* Edited by J. H. Trumbull and Charles J. Hoadly. Vols. 13–15. 1850–90. Reprint. New York: AMS Press, 1968.

4-17. DAVIS, BURKE. *The Campaign That Won America: The Story of Yorktown.* New York: Dial Press, 1970. 319 p.

Trumbull's journal is used by the author as a perspective from which to describe Washington's actions.

4-18. FLEXNER, JAMES THOMAS. *George Washington.* 4 vols. Boston: Little, Brown, 1965–72.

4-19. HINE, REV. ORLO D. *Early Lebanon: An Historical Address Delivered . . . July 4, 1876.* Hartford, Conn.: Cage, Lockwood, and Brainard, 1880. 176 p.

4-20. RAKOVE, JACK N. *The Beginnings of National Politics: An Interpretive History of the Continental Congress.* New York: Alfred A. Knopf, 1979. 484 p.

4-21. *Record of Connecticut Men in the Military and Naval Service during the War of the Revolution, 1775–1783.* Edited by Henry P. Johnson. Hartford, Conn.: Cage, Lockwood, and Brainard, 1889. 779 p.

4-22. SPARKS, JARED, ED. *Correspondence of the American Revolution.* Vol. 3. 1853. Reprint. Freeport, N.Y.: Books for Libraries Press, 1970.

4-23. STARK, BRUCE P. "Lebanon, Connecticut: A Study of Society and Politics in the Eighteenth Century." Ph.D. dissertation, University of Connecticut, 1970. 524 p. 71-16043.

4-24. WASHINGTON, GEORGE. *The Writings of George Washington from the Original Manuscript Sources, 1745–1799.* Edited by John C. Fitzpatrick. Vols. 21–37. 1937–41. Reprint. Westport, Conn.: Greenwood Press, 1970.

These volumes provide documentary sources on Trumbull's association with Washington.

4-25. WEBB, SAMUEL BLACHLEY. *Correspondence and Journals of Samuel Blachley Webb.* Compiled and edited by Worthington C. Ford. 3 vols. 1893. Reprint. New York: Arno Press, 1969.

TRUMBULL AND THE POLITICS OF THE NEW NATION, 1789–1809

The Public Records of the State of Connecticut (4-27) are the most important source for Trumbull's career as a state official. His opposition to Jefferson and the Jeffersonian Republican party's ideology can be seen in Jennings (4-30), Purcell (4-32), and Robinson (4-33). *See also* Hamilton (3-47).

4-26. BURPEE, CHARLES W. *Burpee's "The Story of Connecticut."* 4 vols. New York: American Historical, 1939.

4-27. CONNECTICUT. General Assembly. *The Public Records of the State of Connecticut.* Edited by Charles J. Hoadly et al. 11 vols. Hartford: Connecticut State Library, 1894–1967.

4-28. FISHER, GEORGE P. *Life of Benjamin Silliman.* 2 vols. New York: Charles Scribner, 1866.

4-29. GIBBS, GEORGE. *Memoirs of the Administrations of Washington and John Adams.* Edited from the papers of Oliver Wolcott. 2 vols. 1846. Reprint. New York: Burt Franklin, 1971.

4-30. JENNINGS, WALTER W. *The American Embargo, 1807–1809.* Iowa City: University of Iowa Press, 1921. 242 p.

Discusses Trumbull's opposition to the embargo on the grounds of its unconstitutionality.

4-31. KENDALL, EDWARD AUGUSTUS. *Travels through the Northern Parts of the United States in the Years 1807 and 1808.* 3 vols. New York: I. Riley, 1809.

4-32. PURCELL, RICHARD J. *Connecticut in Transition, 1775–1818.* 1918. Reprint. Rev. ed., with a foreword by S. Hugh Brockunier. Middletown, Conn.: Wesleyan University Press, 1963. 305 p.

Trumbull is discussed within the context of the shift from Federalism to Republicanism in Connecticut.

4-33. ROBINSON, WILLIAM A. *Jeffersonian Democracy in New England.* 1916. Reprint. New York: AMS Press, 1969. 190 p.

4-34. SARGENT, WINTHROP, ED. *A Journal of the General Meeting of the Society of the Cincinnati in 1784.* Philadelphia: Historical Society of Pennsylvania, 1859. 59 p.

4-35. SAUNDERS, RICHARD F., JR. "The Origin and Early History of the Society of the Cincinnati: The Oldest Hereditary and Patriotic Association in the United States." Ph.D. dissertation, University of Georgia, 1970. 330 p. 71-03774.

4-36. THOMAS, EDMUND B., JR. "Politics in the Land of Steady Habits: Connecticut's First Political Party System, 1789–1820." Ph.D. dissertation, Clark University, 1972. 339 p. 72-27368.

4-37. TRUMBULL, HARRIET, AND TRUMBULL, MARIA. *A Season in New York, 1801: Letters of Har-*

riet and Maria Trumbull. Edited with an introduction by Helen M. Morgan. Pittsburgh: University of Pittsburgh Press, 1969. 189 p.
Letters from Trumbull's daughters to their parents.

4-38. WINGATE, CHARLES E. L. *Life and Letters of Paine Wingate.* 2 vols. Medford, Mass.: Mercury Printing, 1930.

5. Jonathan Dayton
(1760–1824)
(Speaker, Fourth and Fifth Congresses)

Jonathan Dayton served courageously in the Continental army and ably as third Speaker of the House of Representatives, yet his political career was marred by scandal and public disgrace. Dayton, who was born on October 16, 1760, in Elizabethtown, New Jersey, graduated from the College of New Jersey (now Princeton) in time to enlist in 1776 as paymaster of his father's regiment. He rose to the rank of captain and served not only under his father, General Elias Dayton, but also under the Marquis de Lafayette. He won high praise for gallantry in action before he was captured by the British. After the war, Dayton devoted himself to land speculation, law, and politics—the three interests that were to determine much of his future success and failure.

At twenty-seven, Dayton was the youngest delegate to the Constitutional Convention in 1787. He took part in the proceedings and signed the Constitution, even though he opposed some of its provisions. He was elected to the First Congress but declined to serve, preferring to remain in the New Jersey state legislature. He entered Congress in 1791 and served in the House until 1799.

As a loyal Federalist, Dayton was selected Speaker in the Fourth and Fifth Congresses (1795–99). His previous support of the Hamiltonian program ensured victory over Muhlen-

berg, whose Jeffersonian leanings were becoming apparent. Compared with his predecessors, Dayton was an active Speaker who used his position to influence other members. Among the measures that he favored and influenced were Jay's Treaty, Hamilton's fiscal program, and the suppression of the Whisky Rebellion. As Speaker at the outset of President John Adams's administration, Dayton found himself in the middle of Jeffersonian attacks on Hamilton's administration of the Treasury Department. The opposition party attacked Speaker Dayton's rulings with charges that he was biased by his friendship with the treasury secretary.

Dayton left the House at the close of the Fifth Congress to take a seat in the Senate, where he served but one term (1799–1805). He was an active debater, but he had less influence in the Senate than he had had in the House. He voted against repeal of the Judiciary Act of 1801 and the impeachment of Justice Chase, both on Federalist party lines, but he also supported the purchase of Louisiana after a trip to New Orleans in 1803.

The New Orleans trip was an indication of Dayton's interest in western lands. He speculated heavily in Ohio land with John Cleves Symmes, among others, and he was interested in a proposed canal around the Ohio Falls.

This interest may explain to some extent Dayton's involvement with Aaron Burr. Burr and Dayton had been childhood friends, had served together in the army, and in 1806 were working on a scheme involving the frontier. The degree of Dayton's participation in the Burr conspiracy remains as clouded as the details of Burr's intentions. Although Dayton was indicted for treason on June 25, 1807, he was not prosecuted because of the lack of conclusive evidence. The ill-health that prevented the former Speaker from accompanying Burr's expedition down the Ohio river probably saved him from conviction. Dayton was spared the humiliation of imprisonment, but he was not fully vindicated, and his national career was ended. He remained popular in New Jersey and held local offices while he continued to practice law. Dayton died on October 9, 1824, possibly from the stress and excitement of a visit from Lafayette.

Perhaps the estimate of one of Dayton's colleagues best sums up the man's character. "There is an impetuosity in his temper that is injurious to him," William Pierce wrote, "but there is an honest rectitude about him that makes him a valuable Member of Society."

MANUSCRIPT COLLECTIONS

New Jersey Historical Society, Newark, N.J.
Jonathan Dayton Papers.
67 items.
New-York Historical Society, New York, N.Y.
Jonathan Dayton Correspondence.
20 items, 1788–1824.
Princeton University, Princeton, N.J.
Jonathan Dayton Papers, 1734–1868.
45 items.
Rutgers University, New Brunswick, N.J.
Jonathan Dayton Papers, 1782–1820.
36 items.

University of Michigan Library, Ann Arbor, Mich.
Jonathan Dayton Papers.
2 ft.
Several other collections at the New Jersey Historical Society contain Dayton correspondence. The University of Virginia Library has a collection of Dayton-Burr items, and the Cincinnati Historical Society holds the papers of John Cleves Symmes, Dayton's associate in land speculation.

BOOKS, ARTICLES, AND DISSERTATIONS

WORKS BY JONATHAN DAYTON

5-1. DAYTON, JONATHAN. *Public Speculation Unfolded in Sixteen Letters.* New York: David Denniston, 1800. 18 p.
Dayton's only published writings consist of a collection of letters describing his involvement in land speculation. *See also* Symmes (5-58).

BIOGRAPHICAL SKETCHES

5-2. "Jonathan Dayton, 1760–1824: Patriot and Statesman and Founder of Dayton, Ohio." *New Jersey Genesis* 4 (October 1956): 113.

5-3. THAYER, THEODORE. *As We Were: The Story of Elizabethtown.* Collections of the New Jersey Historical Society, vol. 13. Elizabeth, N.J.: Grassman, 1964. 280 p.

DAYTON IN THE REVOLUTION AND CONSTITUTIONAL CONVENTION

Heitman (5-8) provides the best account of Dayton's military career. Though only a minor figure the Constitutional Convention in 1787, Dayton does receive treatment as a moderate nationalist in the works cited below. William Pierce's character sketch of Dayton included in *Constitutional Chaff* (5-16) is particularly noteworthy.

5-4. BEARD, CHARLES A. *An Economic Interpretation of the Constitution.* 1913. Reprint. New York: Free Press, 1965. 330 p.

5-5. *Documents Relating to the Revolutionary History of the State of New Jersey: Extracts from American Newspapers.* Edited by W. S. Stryker, F. B. Lee, W.

Nelson, and A. Scott. New Jersey Archives, 2d ser. 5 vols. 1901–17. Reprint. New York: AMS Press, 1977.

5-6. ELLIOT, JONATHAN, ED. *Debates in the Several State Conventions on the Adoption of the Federal Constitution.* 5 vols. 1827–30. Reprint. New York: Burt Franklin, 1968.

5-7. GOTTLIEB, THEODORE D. "New Jersey's Influence on the Constitutional Convention." *Proceedings of the New Jersey Historical Society,* 3d ser., 23 (April 1938): 140–48.

5-8. HEITMAN, FRANCIS B. *Historical Register of Officers of the Continental Army during the War of the Revolution, April 1775 to December 1783.* 1903. Reprint. Baltimore: Genealogical Press, 1967. 698 p.

A lengthy entry outlines Dayton's military career.

5-9. LEE, FRANCIS BAZLEY. *New Jersey as a Colony and as a State.* 5 vols. New York: Publishing Society of New Jersey, 1903.

5-10. McCORMICK, RICHARD P. *Experiment in Independence: New Jersey in the Critical Period, 1781–1789.* New Brunswick, N.J.: Rutgers University Press, 1950. 338 p.

5-11. McDONALD, FORREST. *We the People: The Economic Origins of the Constitution.* Chicago: University of Chicago Press, 1958. 436 p.

5-12. MURPHY, WILLIAM P. *The Triumph of Nationalism: State Sovereignty, the Founding Fathers, and the Making of the Constitution.* Chicago: Quadrangle Books, 1967. 434 p.

5-13. ROSSITER, CLINTON L. *1787: The Grand Convention.* New York: Macmillan, 1966. 443 p.

5-14. SCHACHNER, NATHAN. *The Founding Fathers.* 1954. Reprint. South Brunswick, N.J.: A. S. Barnes, 1970. 630 p.

5-15. TANSILL, CHARLES C., ED. *The Making of the American Republic: The Great Documents, 1774–1789.* 1927. Reprint. New Rochelle, N.Y.: Arlington House, 1972. 1,115 p.

5-16. UNITED STATES. Constitutional Convention, 1787. *Constitutional Chaff.* Compiled by Jane Butzner from the notes of James Madison, William Pierce, James McHenry, Rufus King, and Robert Yates. 1949. Reprint. Port Washington, N.Y.: Kennikat Press, 1970. 197 p.

5-17. ———. *The Records of the Federal Convention of 1787.* Edited by Max Farrand. 4 vols. 1911. Rev. ed. New Haven: Yale University Press, 1966.

The most detailed account of Dayton's actions at the Constitutional Convention.

DAYTON IN NEW JERSEY POLITICS

5-18. FEE, WALTER R. *The Transition from Aristocracy to Democracy in New Jersey, 1789–1829.* Somerville, N.J.: Somerset Press, 1933. 291 p.

5-19. McCORMICK, RICHARD P. "New Jersey's First Congressional Election, 1789: A Case Study in Political Skullduggery." *William and Mary Quarterly,* 3d ser., 6 (April 1949): 237–50.

A scholarly analysis of Dayton's candidacy in 1789, stressing the opposition from Republicans in West Jersey.

5-20. NELSON, WILLIAM. "The Election of Congressmen from New Jersey." *Proceedings of the New Jersey Historical Society,* 3d ser., 8 (July 1913): 80–83.

5-21. NEW JERSEY. Legislature. General Assembly. *Minutes of Votes and Proceedings of the . . . General Assembly of the State of New Jersey.* Trenton, N.J., 1786–90.

Dayton was a member from Essex County in the 11th, 12th, 14th, and 15th sessions.

5-22. PASLER, RUDOLPH J., AND PASLER, MARGARET C. *The New Jersey Federalists.* Rutherford, N.J.: Fairleigh Dickinson University Press, 1975. 266 p.

A full, scholarly account of Dayton's activities in New Jersey politics and on the national level.

5-23. PRINCE, CARL E. *New Jersey's Jeffersonian Republicans: The Genesis of an Early Party Machine, 1789–1817.* Chapel Hill: University of North Carolina Press, 1967. 266 p.

5-24. WOOD, GERTRUDE S. *William Paterson of New Jersey, 1745–1806.* Fairlawn, N.J.: Fairlawn Press, 1933. 217 p.

Dayton and Paterson were lifelong friends and political associates.

DAYTON AS SPEAKER AND SENATOR

See also Clark (3-41), Cobbett (3-42), Combs (3-43), Freeman (3-45), Hamilton (3-47), Kurtz (3-49), Stewart (3-59), and Gibbs (4-29).

5-25. BEVERIDGE, ALBERT J. *The Life of John Marshall.* 4 vols. Boston: Houghton Mifflin, 1916–19.

5-26. BOYD, GEORGE ADAMS. *Elias Boudinot: Patriot and Statesman, 1740–1821.* 1952. Reprint. Princeton: Princeton University Press, 1969. 321 p.
A biography of one of Dayton's colleagues that includes comprehensive coverage of Dayton's entire career.

5-27. BRANT, IRVING. *James Madison.* 6 vols. New York: Bobbs-Merrill, 1941–61.

5-28. BROWN, EVERETT S. *The Constitutional History of the Louisiana Purchase, 1803–1812.* 1920. Reprint. Clifton, N.J.: A. M. Kelley, 1972. 248 p.

5-29. CALLENDER, JAMES T. *The American Annual Register; or, Historical Memoirs of the United States, for the Year 1796.* Philadelphia: Biorem and Madan, 1797. 288 p.
Records the legislative activity of 1796.

5-30. ———. *The Political Register; or, Proceedings in the Session of Congress Commencing November 3, 1794, and Ending March 3, 1795.* 2 vols. Philadelphia: Thomas Dobson, 1795.
Dayton's legislative activity is described, and his speeches reprinted.

5-31. CHARLES, JOSEPH. *Origins of the American Party System.* Foreword by Frederick Merk. 1956. Reprint. New York: Harper and Row, 1961. 147 p.

5-32. CLANCY, HERBERT J. *The Democratic Party: Jefferson to Jackson.* New York: Fordham University Press, 1962. 240 p.

5-33. DAUER, MANNING J. *The Adams Federalists.* 1953. Reprint. Baltimore: Johns Hopkins Press, 1968. 292 p.

5-34. DESTLER, CHESTER MCARTHUR. *Joshua Coit: American Federalist, 1758–1798.* Middletown,

Conn.: Wesleyan University Press, 1962. 191 p.
Provides an account of Dayton's frequent disputes with Coit.

5-35. ERNST, ROBERT. *Rufus King: American Federalist.* Chapel Hill: University of North Carolina Press, 1968. 446 p.
King, a leading New York Federalist, clashed with Dayton over Jay's Treaty.

5-36. HAMILTON, JOHN C. *History of the Republic of the United States of America as Traced in the Writings of Alexander Hamilton and of His Contemporaries.* 7 vols. New York: D. Appleton, 1857–64.

5-37. HENDRICKSON, ROBERT A. *Hamilton.* 2 vols. New York: Mason, Charter, 1976.

5-38. MITCHELL, BROADUS. *Alexander Hamilton.* 2 vols. New York: Macmillan, 1957–62.

5-39. PLUMER, WILLIAM, JR. *William Plumer's Memorandum of Proceedings in the United States Senate, 1803–1807.* Edited by Everett S. Brown. 1923. Reprint. New York: Da Capo Press, 1969. 673 p.
A complete documentary record of Dayton's actions and opinions while a senator.

5-40. SMITH, JAMES MORTON. *Freedom's Fetters: The Alien and Sedition Laws and American Civil Liberties.* Ithaca, N.Y.: Cornell University Press, 1956. 464 p.
Examines Dayton's actions as Speaker, specifically his stand on the Alien and Sedition Acts.

5-41. SPARKS, JARED. *The Life of Gouverneur Morris, with Selections from His Correspondence and Miscellaneous Papers.* 3 vols. Boston: Gray and Bowen, 1832.
Includes letters to Dayton, 1803–6, concerning Federalist party intrigue.

5-42. STEVENS, JOHN A. *Albert Gallatin.* 1884. Reprint. New York: AMS Press, 1972. 423 p.

5-43. TURNER, KATHRYN. "The Appointment of Chief Justice Marshall." *William and Mary Quarterly,* 3d ser., 17 (April 1960): 143–63.

5-44. WALTERS, RAYMOND, JR. *Alexander James Dallas: Lawyer, Politician, Financier, 1759–1817.* 1943. Reprint. New York: Da Capo Press, 1969. 251 p.
Contains a brief reference to Dayton's friendship with Dallas.

5-45. Warfield, Ethelbert D. *The Kentucky Resolutions of 1798: An Historical Study*. 1894. Reprint. Freeport, N.Y.: Books for Libraries Press, 1969. 203 p.

5-46. Washington, George. *The Writings of George Washington from the Original Manuscript Sources, 1745–1799*. Edited by John C. Fitzpatrick. Vols. 18–37. 1937–41. Reprint. Westport, Conn.: Greenwood Press, 1970.

These volumes contain references and correspondence concerning Dayton from the time of his commission in the army until his appointment as an honorary general during the XYZ Affair.

5-47. Wood, John. *The Suppressed History of the Administration of John Adams, from 1797 to 1801*. Notes and appendix by John Henry Sherburne. 1846. Reprint. New York: Burt Franklin, 1968, 391 p.

DAYTON AND THE SOCIETY OF THE CINCINNATI

See also Sargent (4-34).

5-48. Society of the Cincinnati. New Jersey. *Bylaws and Rules of the New Jersey State Society of the Cincinnati*. Trenton, N.J.: James Oran, 1808. 128 p.

5-49. ———. *Excerpts of the Proceedings of the Society of the Cincinnati in the State of New Jersey from May 13, 1793 to July 4, 1906*. New Jersey: W. T. B. S. Imlay, 1908. 289 p.

5-50. ———. *The Society of the Cincinnati in the State of New Jersey*. 1898. Reprint. Bethlehem, Pa.: Times, 1960. 178 p.

LAND SPECULATION AND THE BURR CONSPIRACY

5-51. Abernethy, Thomas P. *The Burr Conspiracy*. 1954. Reprint. Gloucester, Mass.: Peter Smith, 1968. 301 p.

5-52. Alexander, Holmes M. *Aaron Burr: The Proud Pretender*. 3d ed. New York: Harper and Brothers, 1937. 390 p.

5-53. Blennerhassett, Harman. *The Blennerhassett Papers: Embodying the Private Journal of Harman Blennerhassett*. Edited by William H. Safford. 1864. Reprint. New York: Arno Press, 1971. 665 p.

5-54. Field, Mrs. Edward M. "The John Cleves Symmes Purchase." *Proceedings of the New Jersey Historical Society*, 3d ser., 14 (July 1929): 317–31.

5-55. Loth, David G. *Public Plunder: A History of Graft in America*. 1938. Reprint. Westport, Conn.: Greenwood Press, 1970. 436 p.

5-56. Parmet, Herbert S., and Hecht, Marie B. *Aaron Burr: Portrait of an Ambitious Man*. New York: Macmillan, 1967. 399 p.

5-57. Schachner, Nathan. *Aaron Burr: A Biography*. New York: Frederick A. Stokes, 1937. 563 p.

5-58. Symmes, John Cleves. *The Correspondence of John Cleves Symmes: Founder of the Miami Purchase*. Edited by Beverly W. Bond, Jr. New York: Macmillan, 1926. 312 p.

Includes twenty-nine letters from Dayton, as well as several addressed to him, relating to the purchase of Ohio land.

5-59. ———. *The Intimate Letters of John Cleves Symmes and His Family*. Edited by Beverly W. Bond, Jr. Cincinnati: Historical and Philosophical Society of Ohio, 1956. 174 p.

5-60. Vail, Philip [pseud.]. *The Great American Rascal: The Turbulent Life of Aaron Burr*. New York: Hawthorn Books, 1973. 243 p.

6. Theodore Sedgwick
(1746–1813)
(Speaker, Sixth Congress)

Theodore Sedgwick was the last in the line of Federalist Speakers elected by the House. He brought to the Sixth Congress (1799–1801) a reputation for honesty and integrity, as well as a strong partisanship bred of a New England background. Sedgwick, who was born in West Hartford, Connecticut, on May 9, 1746, entered Yale in 1761 with the intention of becoming a minister. He turned to the study of the law, however, and was admitted to the bar in 1766. He later developed a successful practice in Massachusetts.

The onset of the American Revolution found Sedgwick opposed to independence, but within two years he was actively involved in the rebellion. He took part in the ill-fated expedition to Canada in 1776 and later supplied provisions to the northern department of the Continental Congress. He also served as a representative to the provisional assembly of Massachusetts.

In the 1780s Sedgwick served in the state house of representatives (1780, 1782–83, 1787–88), the state senate (1784–85), and the Continental Congress (1785–88). During this time he became involved in cases concerning the legal rights of slaves in Massachusetts. In one 1783 case he won the freedom of Elizabeth Freeman, a runaway slave, who later became a servant in his household. Four years later Sedgwick organized local opposition to Shays' Rebellion (1787).

As a member of the Continental Congress, Sedgwick took particular interest in the Confederation's financial difficulties, which convinced him of the need for a stronger central government. Although he was not a delegate to the Constitutional Convention in 1787, Sedgwick was an advocate of the Federal Constitution at the ratification convention called in Massachusetts in 1788. He was elected to the First Congress and served in the House from 1789 to 1796; he resigned in 1796 to fill the Senate seat left vacant by the resignation of Caleb Strong. Sedgwick held a variety of key congressional committee posts, including that of chairman of the Finance Committee. He was also responsible for reporting the first fugitive slave law and parts of the Bill of Rights.

During his first terms in Congress, Sedgwick developed a reputation as a vigorous debater, an energetic legislator, and a dedicated proponent of Hamiltonian policies. He frequently engaged in verbal battles with Jeffersonians, especially his rival, Nathaniel Macon of North Carolina. He was hostile to France, though he was hardly an Anglophile, and he supported passage of Jay's Treaty for the sake of party unity. Sedgwick echoed these same concerns during partisan Senate debates over the undeclared naval war with France. He returned to the House upon the expiration of his Senate term in 1799, and he was elected Speaker in the wake of the Federalist victory of 1798. After a term marked by legislative frustration and waning party influence, Sedgwick retired from national politics. In 1802 he was appointed to the Massachusetts Supreme Court, where he served with dignity and distinction until his death on January 24, 1813.

As Speaker, Sedgwick displayed little tolerance for parliamentary maneuvering and dilatory tactics. To expedite the pace of congressional deliberations, he sought to make the speakership the focus of political power. Tradition and poor relations with the president prevented this innovation. Perhaps more than anything else, the partisanship that resulted from his strong Federalist principles set him apart from previous Speakers. Party bias had never been absent from the speakership, yet Sedgwick's attempt to bolster his party's waning political fortunes resulted in Congress's unprecedented refusal to vote him the customary resolution of thanks at the end of his term as Speaker.

MANUSCRIPT COLLECTIONS

Berkshire Athenaeum, Pittsfield, Mass.
  Sedgwick Family Papers.
Massachusetts Historical Society, Boston, Mass.
  Sedgwick Family Papers.
  5 vols., 108 boxes, 1698–1946.
  Includes Theodore Sedgwick papers: 38 letters, 1774–1807; manuscript diaries for 1785, 1787, 1790, 1791, and 1793; 101 letters, 1775–1813; and 204 letters, 1783–1811.

Stockbridge Public Library, Stockbridge, Mass.
  Sedgwick Family Papers.
  The following repositories contain small collections of miscellaneous Sedgwick letters: the Boston Athenaeum, Boston, Mass.; the Houghton Library, Harvard University, Cambridge, Mass.; and the Henry E. Huntington Library, San Marino, Calif.

BOOKS, ARTICLES, AND DISSERTATIONS

WORKS BY THEODORE SEDGWICK

6-1. SEDGWICK, THEODORE. "Letter of Theodore Sedgwick to Truman Wheeler." *Magazine of History* 11 (May 1910): 298.
  A single letter written during military duty in Canada is the only published work of Sedgwick.

BIOGRAPHY, BIOGRAPHICAL SKETCHES, AND GENEALOGY

Welch (6-8) is the only scholarly, book-length biography of Sedgwick. Other sources range from his daughter's reminiscences, Dewey (6-3), to a comprehensive biographical sketch included in Shipton (6-7).

6-2. BIRDSALL, RICHARD D. "Country Gentlemen of the Berkshires." *New-England Galaxy* 3 (Summer 1961): 16–25.

6-3. DEWEY, MARY E. *Life and Letters of Catharine M. Sedgwick.* New York: Harper and Brothers, 1871. 446 p.
  Sedgwick's daughter, a noted author, provides a loving personal account of her father.

6-4. FIELD, DAVID A. *A History of the County of Berkshire, Massachusetts.* Pittsfield, Mass.: Samuel W. Bush, 1829. 468 p.

6-5. GOODWIN, NATHANIEL. *Genealogical Notes; or, Contributions to the Family History of Some of the First Settlers of Connecticut and Massachusetts.* 1856. Reprint. Baltimore: Genealogical Press, 1969. 362 p.

6-6. SEDGWICK, H. D. "The Sedgwicks of Berkshire." *Collections of the Berkshire Historical and Scientific Society* 3 (1900): 91–106.

6-7. SHIPTON, CLIFFORD K., ED. *Biographical Sketches of Those Who Attended Harvard College in the Classes 1764–1767.* Sibley's Harvard Graduates, vol. 16. Boston: Massachusetts Historical Society, 1968. 598 p.

6-8. WELCH, RICHARD E., JR. *Theodore Sedgwick, Federalist: A Political Portrait.* Middletown, Conn.: Wesleyan University Press, 1965. 276 p.
  A scholarly biography depicting Sedgwick as a follower rather than a formulator of Federalist ideology.

SEDGWICK AND MASSACHUSETTS HISTORY AND POLITICS

The following local histories and studies place Sedgwick in the context of state history and political development. *See also* Birdsall (6-2) and Field (6-4).

6-9. BIRDSALL, RICHARD D. *Berkshire County: A Cultural History.* New Haven: Yale University Press, 1959. 401 p.

6-10. DAVIS, THOMAS L. "Aristocrats and Jacobins in Country Towns: Party Formation in Berkshire County, Massachusetts, 1775–1816." Ph.D. dissertation, Boston University, 1975. 469 p. 75-12245.
  Sedgwick's opinions and actions with respect to partisan politics are a central concern of this study.

6-11. JONES, ELECTA F. *Stockbridge, Past and Present; or, Records of an Old Mission Station.* Springfield, Mass.: Samuel Bowles, 1854. 275 p.

6-12. SEDGWICK, SARAH CABOT, AND MARQUAND, CHRISTINA SEDGWICK. *Stockbridge, 1739–1939: A Chronicle.* Foreword by Rachel Field. 1939. Reprint. Stockbridge, Mass.: Berkshire Traveller Press, 1974. 364 p.

SEDGWICK'S POLITICAL ASSOCIATES

As a prominent political leader, Sedgwick associated with many of the leading politicians of the period. The following biographies comment upon Sedgwick's role in national politics. *See also* Alberts (3-36), Hamilton (3-47), Gibbs (4-29), Destler (5-34), Ernst (5-35), Hendrickson (5-37), Mitchell (5-38), and Randall (6-45).

6-13. AMORY, THOMAS C. *Life of James Sullivan: With Selections from His Writings.* 2 vols. Boston: Phillips, Sampson, 1859.

6-14. BERNHARD, WINFRED E. A. *Fisher Ames: Federalist and Statesman, 1758–1808.* Chapel Hill: University of North Carolina Press, 1965. 372 p.

6-15. BORDEN, MORTON. *The Federalism of James A. Bayard.* 1954. Reprint. New York: AMS Press, 1968. 256 p.

6-16. BURR, AARON. *Memoirs of Aaron Burr.* Edited by Matthew Livingston Davis. 2 vols. 1836–37. Reprint. New York: Da Capo Press, 1971.

6-17. KING, RUFUS. *The Life and Correspondence of Rufus King.* Edited by Charles R. King. 6 vols. 1900. Reprint. New York: Da Capo Press, 1971.

6-18. LYCAN, GILBERT L. *Alexander Hamilton and American Foreign Policy: A Design for Greatness.* Norman: University of Oklahoma Press, 1970. 459 p.

6-19. RIVES, WILLIAM C. *History of the Life and Times of James Madison.* 3 vols. 1859–68. Reprint. Freeport, N.Y.: Books for Libraries Press, 1970.

6-20. SCHACHNER, NATHAN. *Alexander Hamilton.* 1946. Reprint. New York: Thomas Yoseloff, 1957. 488 p.

6-21. VAN SCHAACK, HENRY C. *The Life of Peter Van Schaack, LL.D.* New York: D. Appleton, 1842. 490 p.

SEDGWICK AND THE SLAVERY ISSUE IN MASSACHUSETTS

The following works describe Sedgwick's involvement in Massachusetts court cases concerning slavery in the 1780s.

6-22. MOORE, GEORGE H. *Notes on the History of Slavery in Massachusetts.* 1866. Reprint. New York: Negro Universities Press, 1968. 256 p.

6-23. WELCH, RICHARD E., JR. "Mumbet and Judge Sedgwick: A Footnote to the Early History of Massachusetts Justice." *Boston Bar Journal* 8 (January 1964): 12–19.

6-24. ZILVERSMIT, ARTHUR. "Quok Walker, Mumbet, and the Abolition of Slavery in Massachusetts." *William and Mary Quarterly,* 3d ser., 25 (October 1968): 614–24.

SEDGWICK, SHAYS' REBELLION, AND THE CONSTITUTION

See also Jensen and Becker (3-48).

6-25. HARDING, SAMUEL B. *The Contest over the Ratification of the Federal Constitution in the State of Massachusetts.* Harvard Historical Studies, vol. 2. 1896. Reprint. New York: Da Capo Press, 1970. 194 p.

6-26. MASSACHUSETTS. Constitutional Convention, 1789. *Debates and Proceedings in the Convention of the Commonwealth of Massachusetts.* Edited by Bradford K. Pierce and Charles Hale. 1789. Reprint. Boston: W. White, 1856. 442 p.

6-27. RILEY, STEPHEN T. "Dr. William Whiting and Shays' Rebellion." *Proceedings of the American Antiquarian Society* 66 (October 1956): 119–66.

6-28. STARKEY, MARION L. *A Little Rebellion.* New York: Alfred A. Knopf, 1955. 256 p.

6-29. TAYLOR, ROBERT J. *Western Massachusetts in the Revolution.* Brown University Studies, vol. 17. Providence, R.I.: Brown University Press, 1954. 227 p.

6-30. WILCOX, D. M. "An Episode of Shays' Rebellion." *Magazine of History* 22 (March 1916): 100–107.

Reprints three court documents filed by Sedgwick seeking the pardon of two men convicted for their part in the rebellion.

SEDGWICK, THE FEDERALIST PARTY, AND NATIONAL POLITICS, 1789–1815

Sedgwick and the Federalist Party in Massachusetts

6-31. BANNER, JAMES M., JR. *To the Hartford Convention: The Federalists and the Origins of Party Politics in Massachusetts, 1789–1815*. New York: Alfred A. Knopf, 1969. 378 p.

6-32. GOODMAN, PAUL. *The Democratic-Republicans of Massachusetts: Politics in a Young Republic*. Cambridge, Mass.: Harvard University Press, 1964. 281 p.

6-33. HALL, VAN BECK. *Politics without Parties: Massachusetts, 1780–1791*. Pittsburgh: University of Pittsburgh Press, 1972. 375 p.

Sedgwick in National Politics

See also Combs (3-43), Kurtz (3-49), Stewart (3-59), Rakove (4-20), Schachner (5-14), Callender (5-30), Dauer (5-33), and Hamilton (5-36).

6-34. AMES, WILLIAM E. *A History of the National Intelligencer*. Chapel Hill: University of North Carolina Press, 1972. 376 p.

Contains a good account of Speaker Sedgwick's opposition to press coverage of the House by the *National Intelligencer*.

6-35. BELL, RUDOLPH M. *Party and Faction in American Politics: The House of Representatives, 1789–1801*. Westport, Conn.: Greenwood Press, 1973. 311 p.

6-36. BOWERS, CLAUDE G. *Jefferson in Power: The Death Struggle of the Federalists*. Boston: Houghton Mifflin, 1936. 538 p.

6-37. BROWN, RALPH ADAMS. *The Presidency of John Adams*. Lawrence: University Press of Kansas, 1975. 248 p.

6-38. CALLENDER, JAMES T. *History of the United States for 1796: Including a Variety of Interesting Particulars Relative to the Federal Government Previous to That Period*. Philadelphia: Snowden and McCorkle, 1797. 312 p.

6-39. ———. *Sedgwick and Co.; or, Key to the Six Per-Cent Cabinet*. Philadelphia, 1798. 88 p.

Although the title bears his name, this pamphlet makes only scattered references to Sedgwick.

6-40. FERGUSON, E. JAMES. *The Power of the Purse: A History of American Public Finance, 1776–1790*. Chapel Hill: University of North Carolina Press, 1961. 358 p.

6-41. FISCHER, DAVID HACKETT. *The Revolution of American Conservatism: The Federalist Party in the Era of Jeffersonian Democracy*. New York: Harper and Row, 1969. 455 p.

6-42. FURLONG, PATRICK J. "John Rutledge, Jr., and the Election of a Speaker of the House in 1799." *William and Mary Quarterly*, 3d ser., 24 (July 1967): 432–35.

Furlong argues that Sedgwick's election as Speaker resulted from sectional differences among Federalists.

6-43. ———. "The Origins of the House Committee on Ways and Means." *William and Mary Quarterly*, 3d ser., 25 (October 1968): 587–604.

6-44. LIBBY, O. G. "Political Factions in Washington's Administrations." *Quarterly Journal of the University of North Dakota* 3 (July 1913): 293–318.

6-45. RANDALL, HENRY S. *The Life of Thomas Jefferson*. 3 vols. 1858. Reprint. New York: Da Capo Press, 1972.

SEDGWICK AND THE MASSACHUSETTS JUDICIARY, 1802–1813

6-46. BLISS, GEORGE. *An Address to the Members of the Bar of the Counties of Hampshire, Franklin and Hampden . . . September, 1826*. Springfield, Mass.: Tannatt, 1827. 85 p.

6-47. ELLIS, RICHARD E. *The Jeffersonian Crisis: Courts and Politics in the Young Republic*. New York: Oxford University Press, 1971. 377 p.

Considers Sedgwick's efforts for judicial reform in Massachusetts.

6-48. GRINNELL, FRANK W. "The Constitutional History of the Supreme Judicial Court of Massachusetts from the Revolution to 1813." *Massachusetts Law Quarterly* 2 (May 1917): 359–552.

Contains a description of Sedgwick's tenure on the court, including excerpts from four letters.

6-49. HANDLIN, OSCAR, AND HANDLIN, MARY F. *Commonwealth: A Study of the Role of Government in the American Economy; Massachusetts, 1774–1861.* Rev. ed. Cambridge, Mass.: Harvard University Press, 1969. 314 p.

6-50. MARSH, DANIEL L., AND CLARK, WILLIAM H., EDS. *The Story of Massachusetts.* Vol. 2. New York: American Historical Society, 1938. 486 p.

Includes an account of Sedgwick's career on the Massachusetts Supreme Court.

6-51. SULLIVAN, WILLIAM. *An Address to the Members of the Bar of Suffolk, Mass . . . 1824.* Boston: North American Review Office, 1825. 63 p.

6-52. WELCH, RICHARD E., JR. "The Parsons-Sedgwick Feud and the Reform of the Massachusetts Judiciary." *Essex Institute Historical Collections* 92 (April 1966): 171–87.

7. **Nathaniel Macon**
(1757–1837)
(Speaker, Seventh through Ninth Congresses)

Nathaniel Macon's political career was defined by opposition to the principles and policies of the Federalist party. As the first Jeffersonian Republican Speaker of the House, he was devoted to states' rights and slavery. Macon became Speaker in 1801, when Jefferson's election to the presidency marked the ascension of a new party in national politics.

Macon was born in North Carolina on December 17, 1757, of French Huguenot descent. After a childhood of private tutoring, he attended Princeton College for two years (1774–76). He joined the New Jersey militia in 1776, but he left the next year to study law in North Carolina and evidently took little interest in the Revolution during the following three years. He finally enlisted as a private in the militia when North Carolina was threatened with invasion in 1780. He was elected in 1781 to the state legislature, which he agreed to attend only at the insistence of his commanding officer, General Nathanael Greene.

Twice Macon was reelected to the North Carolina legislature (1782 and 1784), but he refused to serve when chosen to attend the Continental Congress in 1786. He opposed the Constitutional Convention of 1787 and urged the rejection of the Constitution. He was elected to the Second Congress in 1791 and subsequently served twelve consecutive terms (1791–1815). In 1815 he won election to the Senate, where he served until 1828. Macon died in retirement at his North Carolina estate on June 29, 1837.

Macon was an effective congressional spokesman for opponents of Federalist policy. He joined with Jefferson and Madison to oppose the Hamiltonian program of federal assumption of state war debts, the proposed national bank, and protective tariffs. In foreign policy he advocated closer ties with France and opposed Jay's Treaty, the Alien and Sedition Acts, the building of a navy, and the movement for war with France in 1798.

President Jefferson rewarded Macon by supporting his election to the speakership in 1801. Although Macon asserted that the Speaker was "the elect of the elect of all the people," historians have characterized him as a weak leader dominated by Jefferson. Macon supported the

Louisiana Purchase, repeal of the Judiciary Act of 1801, and Jefferson's foreign policy, but he later came under the influence of Jefferson's foe, John Randolph, and favored Monroe over Madison as the president's heir apparent. Jefferson retaliated by seeking Macon's defeat for the speakership in 1805. The attempt failed, but by such a narrow margin that Macon was convinced that he could not win the speakership of the Tenth Congress.

Macon returned to the rank and file of the House in 1807 and was appointed chairman of the Committee on Foreign Relations in 1809. In this capacity, he reported what became known as Macon's Bills No. 1 and 2, though he authored neither. The first bill was defeated, but Macon's Bill No. 2—to give the president the power to suspend trade with either France or Great Britain—which he did not support, was passed in May 1810. Macon abhorred war and only reluctantly lent his support to the War of 1812. He continued, however, to argue against higher taxes and conscription to meet the war effort.

As a Republican of the old school, Macon did not sympathize with younger leaders such as Henry Clay. He opposed internal improvements, a protective tariff, and the recharter of the Bank of the United States. In the Senate he fought against the Missouri Compromise and defended the rights of slaveholders. He was president *pro tempore* of the Senate from 1826 to 1828. After retirement in 1828 he remained an active correspondent and political advisor, and he presided over the North Carolina constitutional convention of 1835.

Compared with Theodore Sedgwick, Macon was a less partisan Speaker. He rarely interrupted debate unless the speaker went to extremes; he usually gave Federalists full representation on committees, and when possible he appointed men experienced or interested in a particular committee's work. Although some members of his party resented Macon's impartiality to the opposition and his favoritism toward John Randolph, he restored the regard for rules, procedures, and impartiality lost during Sedgwick's speakership.

MANUSCRIPT COLLECTIONS

Duke University Library, Durham, N.C.
  Nathaniel Macon Papers.
  37 items.
New-York Historical Society, New York, N.Y.
  Nathaniel Macon Correspondence.
  22 items, 1801–26, chiefly letters to Albert Gallatin.
North Carolina State Department of Archives and History, Raleigh, N.C.
  Nathaniel Macon Papers.
  117 items, 1773–1848.
  NUCMC 66-1868.

North Carolina State University Library, Raleigh, N.C.
  Nathaniel Macon Papers.
  1/4 cu. ft., 1804–37.
University of North Carolina Library, Southern Historical Collection, Chapel Hill, N.C.
  Nathaniel Macon Papers.
  50 items, 1794–1837.

BOOKS, ARTICLES, AND DISSERTATIONS

WORKS BY NATHANIEL MACON

Speech

7-1. MACON, NATHANIEL. *Speech of Mr. Nathaniel Macon on the Restriction of Slavery in Missouri*. N.p., 1820.

Other than the published letters cited below, Macon's Senate speech of January 20, 1820, opposing restrictions on slavery in the proposed Missouri Compromise, is his only published work.

Published Correspondence

7-2. BATTLE, KEMP P., ED. *Letters of Nathaniel Macon, John Steele, and William Barry Grove, with Sketches and Notes*. James Sprunt Historical Monographs, no. 3. Chapel Hill: University of North Carolina Press, 1902. 122 p.

Includes thirty letters to and from Macon dated 1794–1824.

7-3. JACKSON, ANDREW. *The Correspondence of Andrew Jackson*. Edited by John Spencer Bassett. Vols. 1, 5, 6. Washington, D.C.: Carnegie Institute of Washington, 1935.

Includes five Macon letters to Jackson.

7-4. "LETTERS BEARING ON THE WAR OF 1812." *John P. Branch Historical Papers* 1 (June 1902): 139–46.

Contains five letters from Macon to Joseph Nicholson dated 1812 and 1814.

7-5. MACON, NATHANIEL. "Letters from Nathaniel Macon to John Randolph of Roanoke." Edited by Elizabeth G. McPherson. *North Carolina Historical Review* 39 (April 1962): 195–211.

Comprises fourteen letters, dated 1810–30, from the Randolph Papers in the Library of Congress.

7-6. ———. "Macon Papers." Edited by William E. Dodd. *John P. Branch Historical Papers* 3 (June 1909): 27–93.

Contains sixty-two letters to leading political leaders dated 1798–1836.

7-7. ———. "Some Unpublished Letters of Nathaniel Macon." Edited by John Spencer Bassett. *Trinity College Historical Papers*, 6th ser., 1906, pp. 57–65.

Includes five letters from Macon to Andrew Jackson.

7-8. McPHERSON, ELIZABETH G., ED. "Unpublished Letters from North Carolinians to Jefferson." *North Carolina Historical Review* 12 (July–October 1935): 252–83, 354–80.

Includes eighteen Macon letters dated 1792–1826 from the Jefferson collection in the Library of Congress.

7-9. ———. "Unpublished Letters from North Carolinians to Van Buren." *North Carolina Historical Review* 15 (January 1938): 53–81.

Includes eight Macon letters dated 1823–37.

7-10. "NATHANIEL MACON AND BARTLETT YANCEY." *North Carolina University Magazine* 7 (October 1857): 89–100.

7-11. STEELE, JOHN. *The Papers of John Steele*. Edited by Henry M. Wagstaff. 2 vols. Raleigh: Edwards and Broughton, 1924.

Includes nine Macon letters dated 1794–1809.

7-12. WILSON, EDWIN MOOD. *The Congressional Career of Nathaniel Macon*. James Sprunt Historical Monographs, no. 2. Chapel Hill: University of North Carolina Press, 1900. 115 p.

Contains a brief outline of Macon's career and seventy-five pages of his letters to John R. Eaton and Bartlett Yancey.

BIOGRAPHIES AND BIOGRAPHICAL SKETCHES

Dodd's classic biography of Macon (7-15) is now dated. More recent scholarship is reflected in Helms (7-17), which deals with Macon's career through his three terms as Speaker.

7-13. COTTEN, EDWARD R. *Life of Hon. Nathaniel Macon, of North Carolina*. Baltimore: Lucas and Deaver, 1840. 272 p.

A eulogistic biography by an acquaintance.

7-14. DANIELS, JOSEPHUS. "Nathaniel Macon." In *Publications of the North Carolina Historical Commission*, 12:80–93. Raleigh: Edwards and Broughton, 1913.

7-15. DODD, WILLIAM E. *The Life of Nathaniel Macon*. 1903. Reprint. New York: Burt Franklin, 1970. 443 p.

7-16. ———. "The Place of Nathaniel Macon in Southern History." *American Historical Review* 7 (April 1902): 663–75.

7-17. HELMS, JAMES MARVIN, JR. "The Early Career of Nathaniel Macon: A Study in Pure Republicanism." Ph.D. dissertation, University of Virginia, 1962. 518 p. 62-05922.

7-18. PEELE, WILLIAM J., ED. *Lives of Distinguished North Carolinians*. Raleigh: North Carolina Publishing, 1898. 605 p.

7-19. PITTMAN, THOMAS M. *Nathaniel Macon*. Greensboro, N.C.: Guilford Battle Ground, 1902. 19 p.

7-20. POE, CLARENCE. "Nathaniel Macon: Cincinnatus of America." *South Atlantic Quarterly* 37 (January 1938): 12–21.

MACON'S POLITICAL ASSOCIATES

The following works comment upon Macon's political friendships and alliances, especially with John Randolph and Albert Gallatin. For Macon's relationship with Jefferson see items 7-47 to 7-56. *See also* King (6-17).

7-21. ADAMS, HENRY. *John Randolph*. 1898. Reprint. New York: AMS Press, 1972. 326 p.

7-22. ADAMS, JOHN QUINCY. *Memoirs of John Quincy Adams: Comprising Portions of His Diary from 1795 to 1848*. Edited by Charles Francis Adams. 12 vols. 1874–77. Reprint. Freeport, N.Y.: Books for Libraries Press, 1969.

7-23. BRUCE, WILLIAM CABELL. *John Randolph of Roanoke, 1773–1833*. 2 vols. New York: G. P. Putnam's Sons, 1922.

7-24. CASSELL, FRANK A. *Merchant Congressman in the Young Republic: Samuel Smith of Maryland, 1752–1839*. Madison: University of Wisconsin Press, 1971. 283 p.

7-25. CHAMBERS, WILLIAM NISBET. *Old Bullion Benton: Senator from the New West*. Boston: Little, Brown, 1956. 517 p.

7-26. CLARK, BENNETT CHAMP. *John Quincy Adams: Old Man Eloquent*. Boston: Little, Brown, 1932. 437 p.

7-27. GALLATIN, ALBERT. *The Writings of Albert Gallatin*. Edited by Henry Adams. Vol. 1. Philadelphia: J. B. Lippincott, 1879. 707 p.

7-28. GARLAND, HUGH A. *The Life of John Randolph of Roanoke*. 2 vols. 1859. Reprint. New York: Greenwood Press, 1969.

7-29. MEIGS, WILLIAM M. *The Life of Thomas Hart Benton*. 1904. Reprint. New York: Da Capo Press, 1970. 535 p.

7-30. MOONEY, CHASE C. *William H. Crawford*. Lexington: University of Kentucky Press, 1974. 364 p.

7-31. MUNROE, JOHN A. *Louis McLane: Federalist and Jacksonian*. New Brunswick, N.J.: Rutgers University Press, 1973. 763 p.

7-32. SMITH, ELBERT B. *Magnificent Missourian: The Life of Thomas Hart Benton*. Philadelphia: J. B. Lippincott, 1958. 351 p.

7-33. STOKES, WILLIAM E., JR. "Randolph of Roanoke: A Virginia Portrait. The Early Career of John Randolph of Roanoke, 1773–1805." Ph.D. dissertation, University of Virginia, 1955. 313 p. 00-13854.

MACON, STATES' RIGHTS, AND NORTH CAROLINA HISTORY AND POLITICS, 1781–1837

The following works reveal Macon's devotion to states' rights and his role in North Carolina politics.

7-34. BROWN, KATHERINE K. "The South's Reaction to the Tariffs and the Force Bill, 1828–1833." Ph.D. dissertation, Oklahoma State University, 1971. 308 p. 72-21839.

7-35. *Colonial and State Records of North Carolina*. Vols. 16–21. Charlotte: Observer Printing House, 1911.
These volumes include frequent references to Macon's activity in the state assembly.

7-36. COUNIHAN, HAROLD J. "The North Carolina Constitutional Convention of 1835: A Study in Jacksonian Democracy." *North Carolina Historical Review* 47 (October 1969): 335–64.

7-37. CUNNINGHAM, NOBLE E., JR. "Nathaniel Macon and the Southern Protest against Consolidation." *North Carolina Historical Review* 32 (July 1955): 376–84.

7-38. HOYT, WILLIAM H. *The Mecklenburg Declaration of Independence*. 1907. Reprint. New York: Da Capo Press, 1972. 284 p.

7-39. LEFLER, HUGH T., AND NEWSOME, ALBERT RAY. *North Carolina: The History of a Southern State*.

3d ed. Chapel Hill: University of North Carolina Press, 1973. 807 p.

7-40. McFarland, Daniel Miles. " 'Rip Van Winkle': Political Evolution in North Carolina, 1815–1835." Ph.D. dissertation, University of Pennsylvania, 1954. 504 p. 00-08566.

7-41. Montgomery, Lizzie Wilson. *Sketches of Old Warrenton, North Carolina: Traditions and Reminiscences of the Town and the People Who Made It.* Raleigh: Edwards and Broughton, 1924. 451 p.

7-42. Newsome, Albert Ray. *The Presidential Election of 1824 in North Carolina.* James Sprunt Studies in History and Political Science, vol. 23, no. 1. Chapel Hill: University of North Carolina Press, 1939. 202 p.

7-43. *Proceedings and Debates of the Convention of North Carolina, Called to Amend the Constitution of the State, 1835.* Raleigh: Joseph Gales and Son, 1836.

7-44. Sitterson, Joseph Carlyle. *The Secession Movement in North Carolina.* James Sprunt Studies in History and Political Science, vol. 23, no. 2. Chapel Hill: University of North Carolina Press, 1939. 285 p.

7-45. Wagstaff, Henry M. *State Rights and Political Parties in North Carolina, 1776–1861.* Johns Hopkins University Studies in Historical and Political Science, vol. 24, nos. 7–8. Baltimore: Johns Hopkins Press, 1906. 155 p.

7-46. Wheeler, John H. *Historical Sketch of North Carolina from 1584 to 1851.* 2 vols. Philadelphia: Lippincott, 1851.

MACON, THE JEFFERSONIAN REPUBLICAN PARTY, AND NATIONAL POLITICS

The two works by Cunningham (7-47 and 7-48) are excellent general studies that help place Macon in the context of the Jeffersonian Republican party. Macon's split with Jefferson is covered in Long (7-51) and MacPhee (7-52). *See also* Jennings (4-30), Plumer (5-39), Bell (6-35), Bowers (6-36), Furlong (6-43), and Randall (6-45).

7-47. Cunningham, Noble E., Jr. *The Jeffersonian Republicans in Power: Party Operations, 1801–1809.*

Chapel Hill: University of North Carolina Press, 1963. 318 p.

7-48. ———. *The Jeffersonian Republicans: The Formation of Party Organization, 1789–1801.* Chapel Hill: University of North Carolina Press, 1957. 279 p.

7-49. Jefferson, Thomas. *The Writings of Thomas Jefferson.* Edited by Andrew Lipscomb and Albert Bergh. Vols. 14 and 15. Washington, D.C.: Thomas Jefferson Memorial Association, 1903.

7-50. Jordan, Philip D. *The National Road.* 1948. Reprint. Gloucester, Mass.: Peter Smith, 1966. 442 p.

7-51. Long, Everett Lee. "Jefferson and Congress: A Study of the Jeffersonian Legislative System, 1801–1809." Ph.D. dissertation, University of Missouri, 1966. 494 p. 66-08998.

7-52. MacPhee, Donald A. "The Yazoo Controversy: The Beginning of the 'Quid Revolt.' " *Georgia Historical Quarterly* 49 (March 1965): 23–43.

7-53. Malone, Dumas. *Jefferson and His Time.* 6 vols. Boston: Little, Brown, 1948–81.

7-54. Miller, Zane L. "Senator Macon and the Public Domain, 1815–1828." *North Carolina Historical Review* 38 (October 1961): 482–99.

7-55. Remini, Robert V. *Andrew Jackson and the Course of American Empire, 1767–1821.* New York: Harper and Row, 1977. 502 p.

7-56. Risjord, Norman K. "The Old Republicans: Southern Conservatives in Congress, 1806–1824." Ph.D. dissertation, University of Virginia, 1960. 524 p. 60-04616.

MACON AND THE WAR OF 1812

See also Risjord (9-141) and Ingersoll (9-156).

7-57. Anderson, D. R. "The Insurgents of 1811." In *Annual Report of the American Historical Association,* 1:167–76. Washington, D.C.: Government Printing Office, 1912.

7-58. Fritz, Harry William. "The War Hawks of 1812: Party Leadership in the Twelfth Congress." *Capitol Studies* 5 (Spring 1977): 25–42.

7-59. LEMMON, SARAH McCULLOH. "Dissent in North America during the War of 1812." *North Carolina Historical Review* 49 (April 1972): 103–18.

7-60. ———. *Frustrated Patriots: North Carolina and the War of 1812.* Chapel Hill: University of North Carolina Press, 1973. 223 p.

MACON, SLAVERY, AND THE MISSOURI COMPROMISE

See also Cooper (10-28) and Moore (10-37).

7-61. BROWN, RICHARD H. "The Missouri Crisis, Slavery, and the Politics of Jacksonianism." *South Atlantic Quarterly* 65 (1966): 55–72.

7-62. DETWEILER, PHILIP F. "Congressional Debate on Slavery and the Declaration of Independence, 1819–1821." *American Historical Review* 63 (April 1958): 598–616.

7-63. JENKINS, WILLIAM SUMNER. *Pro-Slavery Thought in the Old South.* Chapel Hill: University of North Carolina Press, 1935. 381 p.

7-64. JOHNSON, GUION GRIFFIS. *Ante-Bellum North Carolina: A Social History.* Chapel Hill: University of North Carolina Press, 1937. 935 p.

7-65. PLUMER, WILLIAM, JR. *The Missouri Compromises and Presidential Politics, 1820–1825.* Edited by Everett S. Brown. 1926. Reprint. New York: Da Capo Press, 1970. 223 p.

8. Joseph Bradley Varnum
(1750–1821)
(Speaker, Tenth and Eleventh Congresses)

Joseph Bradley Varnum was the last Speaker of the House to have served in the American Revolution. A farmer, soldier, and statesman, he was a simple man of character. As an Antifederalist and Jeffersonian Republican in Federalist New England, he endured withering opposition while retaining the support of his home county.

Varnum was born to a farming family of limited means on January 29, 1750, in Dracut, Massachusetts. Unable to afford a formal education, he was largely self-taught. On his marriage in 1773, Varnum received a small farm from his father which remained his home for the rest of his life. Farming was Varnum's principal vocation, but he received more recognition for his military exploits.

The sight of British troops drilling in Boston in 1767 aroused Varnum's interest in military tactics, and by 1774 he had become an instructor of one of Dracut's militia companies. Varnum became captain of the Dracut Minutemen in 1776 and served in the 1777 campaign against Burgoyne. In 1778 he joined General Sullivan in Rhode Island. He remained in command of the militia through 1787 and participated in the suppression of Shays' Rebellion. Rising to the rank of major general, he was associated with the militia to the end of his life.

After serving in the lower house of the Massachusetts legislature (1780–85) and the state senate (1786–95), Varnum was elected to the Fourth Congress as a mild Antifederalist. He was reelected seven times, serving in the House from 1795 to 1811. Varnum's first election, won by a majority of eleven votes, was protested, but the subsequent investigation by the House confirmed his victory.

Varnum allied himself with the followers of Jefferson and became a leader among New England Jeffersonian Republicans. He opposed a standing army, the construction of a navy, and direct taxes and was an early critic of slavery and the slave trade. When Speaker Macon sided with John Randolph, Jefferson threw his support to Varnum, who was elected Speaker of the Tenth Congress (1807–9). Reelected Speaker of the Eleventh Congress (1809–11), Varnum supported the Embargo Act even though this action aroused severe criticism in New England. Although he was an unsuccessful candidate for lieutenant governor of Massachusetts in 1809, Varnum was elected by the Massachusetts legislature to succeed Timothy Pickering in the U.S. Senate in 1811.

Senator Varnum supported the War of 1812 in spite of bitter opposition in his home state and ran unsuccessfully for governor of Massachusetts on a prowar platform in 1814. He left the Senate at the end of his term in 1817, but he was elected to the state senate in the same year. Though he had been a soldier most of his life, Varnum became a pioneer member of the Massachusetts Peace Society. He also left the Congregational Church to become a Baptist. He died on September 11, 1821, and was buried in the Varnum Cemetery in Dracut.

Joseph Bradley Varnum was a humble, self-effacing man who wished to be remembered only for his contributions to farming and military service. His brief autobiography (8-2), written in the third person, concludes: "In fact, in regard to all the improvements which he has made in the arts and sciences, he was almost entirely self-taught; how far he has succeeded in those acquirements must be left for those who have been acquainted with him, and the world to judge."

MANUSCRIPT COLLECTIONS

Detroit Public Library, Detroit, Mich.
Varnum Family Papers.
1 box, 1788–1935.
Massachusetts Historical Society, Boston, Mass.
Varnum Family Papers.
8 letters, 1812–20.
University of Michigan, William L. Clements Library, Ann Arbor, Mich.
Jacob Butler Varnum Papers.

71 items, 1811–60 (includes Joseph Bradley Varnum correspondence).
NUCMC 66-858.

There are a few Varnum letters in scattered collections in the Library of Congress and the Massachusetts Historical Society, Boston. The Dracut Historical Society, Dracut, Mass., has a collection of old newspaper clippings and other documents concerning the Varnum family.

BOOKS, ARTICLES, AND DISSERTATIONS

WORKS BY JOSEPH B. VARNUM

The following items are listed chronologically by year of publication.

8-1. VARNUM, JOSEPH B. *An Address Delivered to the Third Division of Massachusetts Militia, at Review, on the Plains of Concord, 27th August, 1800.* Cambridge, Mass.: William Hilliard, 1800.

An address on the importance of discipline in the militia and in republican government.

8-2. ———. "Autobiography of General Joseph B. Varnum." *Magazine of American History* 20 (November 1888): 405–14.

Published Correspondence

8-3. BENTLEY, WILLIAM. "Selections from Dr. W. Bentley's Correspondence." *New England Historical and Genealogical Register* 27 (October 1873): 351–60.

Contains one Varnum letter.

8-4. MANNING, WILLIAM R., ED. *Diplomatic Correspondence of the United States: Canadian Relations, 1784–1860.* Vol. 1. 1940. Reprint. Millwood, N.Y.: Kraus Reprint, 1975. 947 p.

Includes Varnum's correspondence concerning the destruction of York, Canada, during the War of 1812.

8-5. VARNUM, JOSEPH B. "A New Englander Defends the War of 1812: Senator Varnum to Judge Thatcher." Edited by Lawrence S. Kaplan. *Mid-America* 46 (October 1964): 269–80.

BIOGRAPHICAL SKETCHES

There is no adequate biographical treatment of Varnum. In addition to Varnum's autobiography (8-2), the most valuable sketches are Coburn (8-6) and J. M. Varnum (8-9).

8-6. COBURN, FREDERICK W. *General Joseph Bradley Varnum: His Life and Times.* Lowell, Mass.: Press of the Courier-Citizen, 1933.

8-7. COBURN, GEORGE B. "A Sketch of the Life of General James M. Varnum." *Contributions of the Lowell Historical Society* 1 (November 1907): 69–78.
A sketch of Varnum's brother that also mentions Joseph Bradley Varnum.

8-8. GREEN, SAMUEL ABBOTT, ED. "Hon. Joseph B. Varnum." *Groton Historical Series* 3, no. 8 (1892): 374–76.

8-9. VARNUM, JOHN MARSHALL. *The Varnums of Dracutt.* Boston: David Clapp and Son, 1907. 308 p.
A genealogy of the Varnum family, it includes a lengthy sketch of Joseph Bradley Varnum's political career.

8-10. WOOD, FREDERICK A. "A New England Democrat of the Old School." *New England Magazine* 24 (July 1901): 474–86.

VARNUM AND MASSACHUSETTS HISTORY
AND POLITICS, 1780–1821

8-11. COBURN, SILAS R. *History of Dracutt, Massachusetts.* Lowell, Mass.: Press of the Courier-Citizen, 1922. 433 p.

8-12. HART, ALBERT BUSHNELL. *Commonwealth History of Massachusetts.* Vol. 3. 1929. Reprint. New York: Russell and Russell, 1966. 582 p.

8-13. HURD, D. HAMILTON. *History of Middlesex County, Massachusetts.* Vol. 2. Philadelphia: T. W. Lewis, 1890. 887 p.

8-14. RUSSELL, JAMES S. "How Pawtucket Bridge Was Built and Owned." *Contributions of the Old Residents' Historical Association, Lowell, Mass.* 4 (August 1888): 1–16.

8-15. SAWYER, ALFRED P. "Early Mining Operations Near Lowell." *Contributions of the Lowell Historical Society* 1 (July 1911): 316–42.

8-16. *Vital Records of Dracut, Massachusetts to the Year 1850.* Boston: New England Historic Genealogical Society, 1907. 301 p.

VARNUM'S POLITICAL CAREER, 1780–1820

See also Brown (5-28), Plumer (5-39), Bowers (6-36), Ellis (6-47), Helms (7-17), Bruce (7-23), Cunningham (7-47 and 7-48), Jefferson (7-49), Long (7-51), and Malone (7-53).

8-17. BURDICK, WILLIAM. *The Massachusetts Manual; or, Political and Historical Register, for the Political Year from June 1814 to June 1815.* Vol. 1. Boston: Charles Callendar, 1814. 219 p.

8-18. DEMPSEY, JOHN T. "Control of Congress over the Seating and Disciplining of Members." Ph.D. dissertation, University of Michigan, 1956. 386 p. 00-19691.

8-19. LACY, ALEXANDER B. "Jefferson and Congress: Congressional Method and Politics, 1801–1809." Ph.D. dissertation, University of Virginia, 1964. 330 p. 64-11269.

8-20. MORISON, SAMUEL ELIOT. *Harrison Gray Otis, 1765–1848: The Urbane Federalist.* Rev. ed. Boston: Houghton Mifflin, 1969. 561 p.

9. Henry Clay
(1777–1852)
(Speaker, Twelfth, Thirteenth [First Session], Fourteenth, Fifteenth, Sixteenth [First Session], and Eighteenth Congresses)

Henry Clay's election to the speakership in 1811 marked the end of an era and the beginning of a new role for the Speaker as the political leader of the House. Unlike the comparatively impartial parliamentary referees Muhlenberg and Trumbull or the highly partisan but ineffectual Sedgwick and Macon, Clay was the first to seize the possibilities the speakership offered to organize and lead the House. Clay's conception and exercise of the office demonstrated that in the hands of a master politician the Speaker could become the most dominant power in the House.

Clay was born in Hanover County, Virginia, on April 12, 1777. His father, a Baptist minister, died when Clay was four years old. His mother remarried, and though the family's financial condition improved, he did not receive a formal education. When the family moved to Kentucky in 1792, Clay remained in Virginia to study law under George Wythe, a signer of the Declaration of Independence and first professor of law in America. Clay was admitted to the bar in Richmond in 1797 and later that year moved to Lexington, Kentucky.

An ambitious young man, Henry Clay was supremely self-confident, independent, and public-spirited. A child of the Revolution, he quickly made himself a representative of the West. Clay, who possessed a keen insight into human nature, the versatility of an actor, and an astoundingly melifluous yet powerful voice that gave to his speeches an otherwise unwarranted popularity, became a successful frontier lawyer. Politics, however, was his destined calling. He was elected in 1803 to the Kentucky legislature, which selected him to fill unexpired terms in the U.S. Senate in 1806, when he was only twenty-nine, and again in 1810.

The Twelfth Congress, which assembled in Washington for a special session in November 1811, contained a number of new Western and Southern members who were collectively known as the war hawks. Two of the foremost war hawks were John C. Calhoun, twenty-nine, and the thirty-four-year-old Henry Clay. Clay had been chosen their leader prior to the opening of Congress, and on his first day in Congress he was elected Speaker of the House. He then pushed for war with Great Britain by appointing fellow war hawks to chair the Foreign Relations, Military Affairs, and Ways and Means committees. In 1814 he was appointed by President James Madison to the peace commission that negotiated the Treaty of Ghent.

In 1815 Clay returned to Congress and was again elected Speaker of the House. He served in that office for the following decade, with the exception of one term (1821–23) when financial necessity compelled him to return to his law practice in Kentucky. His major concern in this decade was his American System. The key provisions of Clay's balanced program were a protective tariff to assist American manufactures and create a home market for agricultural goods, a national bank to establish a sound currency, and internal improvements at federal expense to facilitate internal trade.

Opposition to Clay's nationalism was grounded in vested interests and sectional rivalries. The most important manifestations of sectionalism during Clay's speakership were the controversy over the admission of Missouri as a state in 1820 and the question of slavery in the Louisiana Territory. The passage of the Missouri Compromise through the House in 1821 was largely the result of Clay's efforts, which earned him the title the Great Compromiser.

Compromise was indeed Henry Clay's conception of politics. "All legislation," he once remarked, "all government, all society is founded upon the principle of mutual concession, politeness, comity, courtesy; upon these everything is based" (Mooney [1–12], p. 43). Although Clay's career after the speakership was marked by great accomplishments and equal disappointments, he remained a consummate politician. He was secretary of state under President John Quincy Adams (1825–29), senator from Kentucky (1831–42 and 1849–52), and an unsuccessful candidate for the presidency in 1824, 1832, and 1844. His final accomplishment, the Compromise of 1850, postponed but did not prevent the Civil War.

Clay was sentimental yet formal and dignified, democratic in principle yet aristocratic in bearing, fascinating to women yet faithful to his wife. He opposed slavery, but he feared the results of emancipation even more. He was unable to accept either the prospect of perpetual slavery or the coexistence of the races without slavery; his solution was the colonization of free blacks in Africa. He was the founder and president of the American Colonization Society, established in 1816. Clay did not free his slaves in his will but provided that all children of his women slaves would be liberated and sent to Africa.

By the very nature of his flawed but forceful personality, Clay made the speakership a political power. But even more than by his personal charm, eloquence, and self-confidence, he mastered the existing structure to take command of the House by using the power of appointment to select favorably inclined committee chairmen and by initiating the practice of the "previous question" to limit floor debate and force votes. Clay was the first to insist that the Speaker retained all of his rights as a member of the House to vote and to engage in debate. As Neil MacNeil has concluded, Clay's insistence on the concept of the Speaker as a political leader "made the United States Speaker in time the most powerful and influential political leader of any free legislature" ([1–24], p. 68).

MANUSCRIPT COLLECTIONS

Literally scores of collections possess Clay correspondence. *The Papers of Henry Clay* (9-11) are currently being edited and published by the University of Kentucky Press. Six volumes edited by James H. Hopkins and Mary W. M. Hargreaves have been published as of 1982. Robert Seager II assumed the editorship of volume 7 (1982), which includes a subject index for volumes 1–5, and volume 8 (1984). The project will be completed with publication of volume 10. Four manuscript collections account for the bulk of Clay papers included in the project: the Clay Papers in the Library of Congress Manuscript Division; the Clay Papers at the University of Kentucky, Lexington; the Clay Collection at Transylvania University, Lexington, Ky.; and various Department of State collections in the National Archives. Pending completion of the project, finding aids at these depositories will assist researchers.

BOOKS, ARTICLES, AND DISSERTATIONS

WORKS BY HENRY CLAY
Collected Works

The Papers of Henry Clay (9-11) will be the most complete collection of Clay letters and speeches. Also valuable is the seven-volume *Works of Henry Clay,* edited by Calvin Colton (9-10).

9-1. CARRIER, A. H. *Monument to the Memory of Henry Clay.* Philadelphia: Duane Rulison, 1859. 516 p.

Includes selected letters, speeches, and eulogies.

The following items are listed chronologically by year of publication and alphabetically thereunder.

9-2. CLAY, HENRY. *The Speeches of Henry Clay Delivered in the Congress of the United States.* Philadelphia: H. C. Carey and I. Lea, 1827. 381 p.

9-3. ———. *The Beauties of the Hon. Henry Clay, to Which Is Added a Biographical and Critical Essay.* New York: Edward Walker, 1839. 235 p.

9-4. ———. *Speeches of the Hon. Henry Clay of the Congress of the United States.* Edited by Richard Chambers. Cincinnati: Shepard and Stearns, 1842. 504 p.

9-5. ———. *The Life and Speeches of Henry Clay.* Edited by Horace Greeley. 2 vols. New York: Greeley and McElrath, 1843.

9-6. ———. *The Life and Speeches of the Hon. Henry Clay.* Compiled and edited by Daniel Mallory. 2 vols. 1843. Reprint. Hartford, Conn.: S. Andrus and Son, 1855.

9-7. ———. *The Ashland Text Book, Being a Compendium of Mr. Clay's Speeches on Various Public Measures, etc.* Boston: Redding, 1844. 72 p.

9-8. ———. *The Henry Clay Almanac . . . Containing Songs and Anecdotes and a Biographical Sketch of Henry Clay.* Philadelphia: Gregg and Elliot, 1844.

9-9. ———. *The Private Correspondence of Henry Clay.* Edited by Calvin Colton. 1855. Reprint. Freeport, N.Y.: Books for Libraries Press, 1971. 642 p.

9-10. ———. *The Works of Henry Clay.* Edited by Calvin Colton. 6 vols. 1855. Rev. ed., with an introduction by Thomas Brackett Reed. 7 vols. New York: G. P. Putnam's Sons, 1897.

9-11. ———. *The Papers of Henry Clay.* 8 vols. to date. Vols. 1–6 edited by James H. Hopkins and Mary W. M. Hargreaves. Vols. 7 and 8 edited by Robert Seager II. Lexington: University of Kentucky Press, 1959–.

Individually Published Speeches

The following Clay speeches are listed chronologically by year of publication and alphabetically thereunder.

*9-12. ———. *Speeches on the Line of Perdido.* N.p., 1810.

9-13. ———. *Speech Delivered by the Hon. Henry Clay . . . on the Bill for Raising an Additional Military Force of Twenty Thousand Men for One Year.* Washington, D.C.: National Intelligencer Office, 1813. 20 p.

*9-14. ———. *Speech of Henry Clay, Esq., Delivered in the House . . . on the Direct Tax, March, 1816.* New York: Sherman and Pudney, 1816. 23 p.

9-15. ———. *Speech of the Hon. Henry Clay . . . on the Seminole War.* [Washington, D.C.], 1819. 30 p.
Denounces Andrew Jackson's execution of two British agents.

*9-16. ———. *Speech of H. Clay on the Tariff Bill.* Pittsburgh, 1820. 126 p.

*9-17. ———. *Mr. Clay's Speech on Internal Improvements.* N.p., 1824. 24 p.

*9-18. ———. *Speech in Support of an American System for the Protection of American Industry.* Washington, D.C.: Columbian Office, 1824. 39 p.

9-19. ———. *To the People of the Congressional District Composed of the Counties of Fayette, Woodford and Clarke, in Kentucky.* Washington, D.C., 1825. 33 p.

9-20. ———. *An Address of Henry Clay . . . in Refutation of the Charges against Him Made by Gen. Andrew Jackson.* Washington, D.C.: Peter Force, 1827. 61 p.
A denial of the "corrupt bargain" charge that Clay threw his support to John Quincy Adams in the House vote to deny Andrew Jackson the presidency in 1824.

*9-21. ———. *The Address of Henry Clay to His Constituents and His Speech at the Dinner Given Him at Lewisburg, Va.* Louisville, Ky.: W. W. Worsley, 1827. 32 p.

9-22. ———. *Mr. Clay's Speech, at the Dinner at Noble's Inn, . . . July 12, 1827.* [Lexington, Ky., 1827]. 14 p.

9-23. ———. *Speech of the Hon. Henry Clay before the American Colonization Society . . . January 20, 1827.* Washington, D.C.: Columbian Office, 1827. 15 p.

9-24. ———. *A Supplement to the Address of Henry Clay to the Public . . . Touching the Last Presidential Election.* Washington, D.C.: Peter Force, 1828. 22 p.

*9-25. ———. *An Address, Delivered to the Colonization Society of Kentucky at Frankfort, December 17, 1829.* Lexington, Ky.: T. Smith, 1829. 26 p.

*9-26. ———. *Spanish America: Observations on the Instructions Given by the President of the United States of America, to the Representatives of That Republic, at the Congress held at Panama, in 1826.* London: E. Wilson, 1829. 68 p.

9-27. ———. *The Speech of Henry Clay, Delivered at the Public Dinner, at Fowler's Garden, . . . on the Sixteenth of May, 1829.* Richmond, Va.: Thomas W. White, 1829. 34 p.

A denunciation of Jackson and the spoils system.

9-28. ———. *Speech of the Hon. Henry Clay, Late Secretary of State, . . . on the 7th of March, 1829.* Xenia, Ohio: Richard C. Langdon, 1829.

9-29. ———. *Speech of Henry Clay Delivered at the Mechanics' Collation in the Apollonian Garden, in Cincinnati, on the 3d of August, 1830.* Baltimore: Patriot Office, 1830. 12 p.

Advocates rechartering the national bank.

*9-30. ———. *Mr. Clay's Speech: Debate in the United States Senate on the Return of the Bank Bill with Gen. Jackson's Veto.* Washington, D.C., 1832. 36 p.

*9-31. ———. *Speech of Henry Clay, in Defense of the American System against the British Colonial System.* Washington, D.C.: Gales and Seaton, 1832. 43 p.

9-32. ———. *Speech of Henry Clay . . . in Vindication of His Bill Entitled "An Act to Modify the Act of the 14th July 1832, and All Other Acts Imposing Duties on Imports."* N.p., 1833. 8 p.

House speech on the tariff of 1832.

*9-33. ———. *Report in the Senate of the United States by Mr. Clay . . . Regarding That Part of the President's Message as Relates to the State of Our Relations with France.* [Washington, D.C.], 1834. 23 p.

*9-34. ———. *A Speech Delivered by the Hon. H. Clay, on the Doctrines and on the Question of Recording the Protest of the President of the United States.* Washington, D.C.: Gales and Seaton, 1834. 20 p.

*9-35. ———. *Speech of the Hon. Henry Clay on the Subject of the Removal of the Deposits.* Washington, D.C.: Gales and Seaton, 1834. 48 p.

*9-36. ———. *Mr. Clay's Remarks . . . on the Message of President Jackson, Relating to Our Affairs with France.* N.p., 1836. 2 p.

9-37. ———. *Speech of Henry Clay, of Kentucky, on the Bill Imposing Additional Duties as Depositories, in Certain Cases, on Public Officers.* Boston: Benjamin H. Greene, 1837. 19 p.

*9-38. ———. *Speech of Mr. Clay, of Kentucky, on the Resolution to Expunge a Part of the Journal for the Session of 1833–1834.* Washington, D.C.: Moore, 1837. 41 p.

9-39. ———. *Speech of Mr. Clay, of Kentucky, Establishing a Deliberate Design, on the Part of the Late and Present Executive of the United States, to Break Down the Whole Banking System of the United States.* Washington, D.C.: Niles' National Register Office, 1838. 32 p.

*9-40. ———. *Speech of the Hon. Henry Clay, on the Sub-Treasury Scheme.* Troy, N.Y.: Tuttle, Belcher, and Burton, 1838. 48 p.

9-41. ———. *Free and Friendly Remarks and Speech . . . on the Subject of the Abolition of North American Slavery.* New York: Mahlon Day, 1839. 24 p.

9-42. ———. *Speech of Mr. Clay of Kentucky, on the Subject of Abolition Petitions.* Washington, D.C.: Gales and Seaton, 1839. 16 p.

*9-43. ———. *Speech on Introducing the Bill to Modify the Tariff.* [Charleston, S.C., 183?]. 8 p.

9-44. ———. *Speech of H. Clay, of Kentucky, on the Bill Commonly Called the Sub-Treasury Bill.* N.p., 1840. 16 p.

9-45. ———. *Speech of Mr. Clay of Kentucky, Delivered June 27, 1840, on the Occasion of a Public Dinner . . . at Taylorsville . . . Virginia.* N.p., 1840. 11 p.

9-46. ———. *Speeches Delivered by H. Clay of Ken-*

tucky . . . on the Message of President Tyler, Returning the Bank Bill, with His Veto. Washington, D.C., 1841. 16 p.

9-47. ———. Speech of Mr. Clay, of Kentucky, on the Amendment Proposed by Mr. Rives . . . to the Bill to "Incorporate the Subscribers to the Fiscal Bank of the United States." Washington, D.C., 1841. 4 p.

9-48. ———. Farewell Speech to the Senate of the United States by Henry Clay, the Friend and Advocate of Political and Civil Liberty and of Home Industry. Philadelphia: J. Crissy, 1842.

*9-49. ———. Speech Delivered at the Great Barbecue at Lexington (Ky.) June 1842. [New York: Sutherland, 1842]. 16 p.

*9-50. ———. Speech of Henry Clay, at Dayton, Ohio, September 29, 1842. Cincinnati, 1842. 24 p.

*9-51. ———. Speech of Mr. Clay, of Kentucky, upon His Resolutions concerning the Tariff, and Other Great Objects of Public Polity. Washington, D.C.: National Intelligencer Office, 1842. 23 p.

9-52. ———. Mr. Clay's Speech, Delivered in the City of Raleigh, April 13th, 1844. N.p., 1844. 17 p.

9-53. ———. Speech of Henry Clay at the Lexington Mass Meeting, 13th November, 1847. New York: George F. Nesbitt, 1847. 14 p.

A protest against the Mexican War.

*9-54. ———. Mr. Clay's Speech to the General Assembly of Kentucky, 1850. N.p., 1850. 13 p.

*9-55. ———. Speech in Reference to Diplomatic Relations with Austria. Washington, D.C.: Jonathan T. Towers, 1850. 8 p.

9-56. ———. Speech of Henry Clay, of Kentucky, on the Compromise Report. Washington, D.C.: Jonathan T. Towers, 1850. 16 p.

*9-57. ———. Speech of Henry Clay, of Kentucky, on the Report of the Committee of Thirteen. Washington, D.C.: Jonathan T. Towers, 1850. 16 p.

*9-58. ———. Speech of Mr. Clay, of Kentucky, in Support of His Propositions to Compromise on the Slavery Question. Washington, D.C.: Jonathan T. Towers, 1850. 32 p.

9-59. ———. Speech of Mr. Clay, of Kentucky, on the Measures of Compromise. Washington, D.C.: Jonathan T. Towers, 1850. 31 p.

*9-60. ———. Address before the American Colonization Society, Jan. 21, 1851. N.p., 1851.

*9-61. ———. The Rights of Maine Defended, Speech of Mr. Clay, in the Senate on the Boundary. [Washington, D.C.], n.d. 8 p.

*9-62. ROBERTSON, GEORGE. Addresses of George Robertson, President, and Henry Clay, Guest of the Day, at the Clay Festival at Lexington, Ky., Thursday, June 9th, 1842. Lexington, Ky.: W. R. Hervey, 1842. 28 p.

Other Published Correspondence

9-63. BOROME, JOSEPH A. "Henry Clay and James G. Birney: An Exchange of Views." Filson Club History Quarterly 35 (April 1961): 122–24.

Concerns Clay's views on gradual emancipation.

The following items are listed chronologically by year of publication and alphabetically thereunder.

*9-64. CLAY, HENRY. Letters of Messrs. Clay, Benton, and Barrow, on the Subject of the Annexation of Texas to the United States. Washington, D.C., 1844. 16 p.

*9-65. ———. Suppressed Letter Disavowing Anti-Slavery Sentiments. New York, 1844. 1 p.

*9-66. ———. Letter from Henry Clay on the Emancipation of Slavery in Kentucky. Cincinnati, 1849. 1 p.

*9-67. ———. Reply to Mr. Mendenhall, on the Occasion of the Presentation to Him, by Mr. M., of a Petition, Praying Him to Emancipate His Slaves in Kentucky. Philadelphia: Dyer and Webster, 1850. 8 p.

9-68. ———. "A Letter by Henry Clay." Quarterly Journal of Economics 2 (July 1888): 490–91.

A letter of March 1827 concerning the tariff issue.

9-69. ———. "Letter of Henry Clay: Written Thirty Years before the War, Giving His Views of Slavery." Register of the Kentucky State Historical Society 4 (May 1906): 71–72.

A letter of June 15, 1833, favoring gradual emancipation.

9-70. ———. "Letter of Henry Clay, July 1837." *Collector* 22 (May 1909): 75–76.

Discusses the failure to recharter the national bank.

9-71. ———. "Original Letters: Henry Clay to Thomas W. Gilmer (1836)." Edited by Lyon G. Tyler. *William and Mary Quarterly,* 1st ser., 20 (July 1911): 5–7.

Concerns distribution of proceeds from sales of public lands to the states.

9-72. ———. "Letters Relating to the Negotiations at Ghent, 1812–1814." *American Historical Review* 20 (October 1914): 108–29.

Includes three letters from Clay to William H. Crawford.

9-73. ———. "A Bit of New York History and an Unpublished Letter of Henry Clay." Edited by W. A. Titus. *Wisconsin Magazine of History* 7 (December 1923): 214–18.

Concerns Clay's strained relations with President Tyler.

*9-74. ———. *Henry Clay Asks Albert Gallatin to Represent the United States at the First Pan American Congress.* South Hadley Falls, Mass.: Hampshire Paper Co., 1928. 4 p.

9-75. ———. "Three Letters by Henry Clay: 1829, 1842, and 1851." *Filson Club History Quarterly* 9 (January 1935): 51–53.

9-76. ———. "Letters from Old Trunks: Two Letters from Henry Clay." *Virginia Magazine of History and Biography* 45 (April 1937): 147–48.

9-77. ———. "Letters of Henry Clay to John MacPherson Berrien." Edited by Lowry Axley. *Georgia Historical Quarterly* 29 (March 1945): 23–41.

Comprises nineteen letters dated 1841–46.

9-78. ———. "Henry Clay, Patron and Idol of White Sulphur Springs: His Letters to James Caldwell." Edited by Bernard Mayo. *Virginia Magazine of History and Biography* 55 (October 1947): 301–17.

Comprises seventeen letters dated 1826–42.

9-79. ———. "Henry Clay's Last Will." Edited by Clement Eaton. *University of Kentucky Libraries Bulletin* 1 (1949): 1–9.

9-80. ———. "Last Letters of Henry Clay." Edited by Sarah Agnes Wallace. *Register of the Kentucky Historical Society* 50 (October 1952): 307–18.

9-81. ———. "John G. Whittier Hears from Henry Clay." Edited by John C. Helper. *Register of the Kentucky Historical Society* 51 (April 1953): 171–72.

A Clay letter of July 22, 1837, expressing dissatisfaction with abolitionists.

9-82. COLEMAN, ANN MARY BUTLER. *The Life of John J. Crittenden: With Selections from His Correspondence and Speeches.* 2 vols. 1871. Reprint. New York: Da Capo Press, 1970.

Includes Clay letters and a eulogistic speech by Crittenden.

9-83. COLEMAN, CHRISTOPHER, ED. "Letters of Salmon P. Chase, Henry Clay, Henry George." *Indiana Quarterly Magazine of History* 7 (September 1911): 123–32.

A Clay letter of September 21, 1844, on his presidential campaign.

9-84. EDWARDS, NINIAN. *The Edwards Papers.* Edited by E. B. Washburne. Chicago Historical Society Collection, vol. 3. Chicago: Fergus Printing, 1884. 633 p.

Contains five Clay letters.

9-85. "Letters from Jackson, Clay, and Johnson." *American Historical Magazine* 5 (April 1900): 132–44.

9-86. LIEBMAN, WALTER H. "The Correspondence between Solomon Etting and Henry Clay." *Publications of the American Jewish Historical Society* 17 (1909): 81–88.

9-87. MANNING, WILLIAM R. *Diplomatic Correspondence of the United States: Canadian Relations, 1784–1860.* Vol. 2. 1942. Reprint. Millwood, N.Y.: Kraus Reprint, 1975. 1,016 p.

Includes Clay's correspondence as secretary of state concerning Canadian affairs.

9-88. NOBLE, NOAH. "Letters from Correspondence of Noah Noble." Edited by Esther Noble Carter. *Indiana Magazine of History* 22 (June 1926): 205–19.

Contains five Clay letters dated 1834–42.

9-89. PETERS, J. P. "Henry Clay and His Friends." *Nation* 63 (August 1896): 101–2.
Clay letter of October 2, 1849, on gradual emancipation.

9-90. "Sundry Old Letters." *Annals of Iowa* 5 (1901–3): 71–72.
Two letters dated 1806 and 1827 to General Joseph Street.

9-91. WEBSTER, DANIEL. *The Papers of Daniel Webster*. Edited by Charles M. Wiltse. Vols. 2 and 3. Hanover, N.H.: University Press of New England, 1976–77.
Includes twenty letters from Clay.

BIOGRAPHIES, GENEALOGY, AND EULOGIES

Biographies

The first biographies of Clay, by Prentice (9-97) and Sargent (9-98), were campaign biographies. Prior to 1937, the best and most thorough biography was Schurz's two-volume work (9-99). Both Mayo (9-95) and Van Deusen (9-100) were published in 1937; the first is colorful, the latter scholarly, and both are valuable. The most recent biography is Eaton's interpretive study (9-94). *See also* Winthrop (21-43).

9-92. CLAY, THOMAS HART. *Henry Clay*. Philadelphia: George W. Jacobs, 1910. 450 p.
An admiring, comprehensive biography by Clay's grandson.

9-93. COLTON, CALVIN. *The Life and Times of Henry Clay*. 2 vols. 1846–56. Reprint. New York: Garland, 1974.

9-94. EATON, CLEMENT. *Henry Clay and the Art of American Politics*. Boston: Little, Brown, 1957. 209 p.

9-95. MAYO, BERNARD. *Henry Clay: Spokesman of the New West*. Boston: Houghton, Mifflin, 1937. 570 p.
Colorful biography of Clay up to 1812.

9-96. POAGE, GEORGE R. *Henry Clay and the Whig Party*. 1936. Reprint. Gloucester, Mass.: Peter Smith, 1965. 295 p.

9-97. PRENTICE, GEORGE D. *Biography of Henry Clay*. Hartford, Conn.: Samuel Hammer, Jr., and John J. Phelps, 1831. 312 p.

9-98. SARGENT, EPES. *The Life and Public Services of Henry Clay down to 1848*. Edited and completed by Horace Greeley. Philadelphia: Porter and Coats, 1852. 423 p.

9-99. SCHURZ, CARL. *Life of Henry Clay*. 2 vols. 1887. Reprint. New York: Frederick Unger, 1968.

9-100. VAN DEUSEN, GLYNDON G. *The Life of Henry Clay*. Boston: Little, Brown, 1937. 448 p.

Genealogy

9-101. SMITH, ZACHARIAH F., AND CLAY, MRS. MARY ROGERS. *The Clay Family*. Louisville, Ky.: John P. Morton, 1899. 252 p.

Eulogies

9-102. ANDERSON, CHARLES. *A Funeral Oration on the Character, Life, and Public Services of Henry Clay*. Cincinnati: Ben Franklin Office, 1852. 38 p.

9-103. CHADBOURNE, JOHN S. *The Mortal and the Immortal: A Sermon Preached at St. James Church, Baton Rouge, in Improvement of the Character and Death of Henry Clay*. New Orleans: Office of the Picayune, 1852. 18 p.

9-104. COLEMAN, J. WINSTON, JR. *Last Days, Death, and Funeral of Henry Clay*. Lexington, Ky.: Winburn Press, 1951. 30 p.

9-105. FOSTER, THOMAS, ED. *Eulogies Delivered in the Senate and House of Representatives of the United States on the Life and Character of Hon. John C. Calhoun of South Carolina, Hon. Henry Clay of Kentucky, and Hon. Daniel Webster of Massachusetts*. Washington, D.C.: Foster and Cochran, 1853. 63, 103, 48 p.

9-106. M'CLUNG, ALEXANDER K. *Eulogy on the Life and Services of Henry Clay, Delivered in the Hall of the House of Representatives, October 11, 1852*. Jackson, Miss.: Palmer and Pickett, 1852. 23 p.

9-107. NEW YORK (CITY). Common Council. *Report of the Committee of Arrangements of the Common Council of New York of the Obsequies in Memory of the Hon. Henry Clay*. New York: Spedon and Baker, 1852. 362 p.

9-108. SMITH, SAMUEL L. *Eulogy upon the Life, Character and Services of Henry Clay*. Chicago: Daily Journal Office, 1852. 22 p.

CLAY AND THE AARON BURR TRIAL, 1806

In 1806 Clay successfully defended Aaron Burr against conspiracy charges in Kentucky. He dropped out of the case prior to the 1807 trial before Chief Justice John Marshall.

9-109. BURR, AARON. *The Trial of Col. Aaron Burr, on an Indictment for Treason, before the Circuit Court of the United States, Held in Richmond (Virginia) May Term, 1807*. 3 vols. Washington, D.C.: Wescott, 1807.

9-110. JILLSON, WILLARD ROUSE. "Aaron Burr's 'Trial' for Treason, at Frankfort, Kentucky, 1806." *Filson Club History Quarterly* 17 (October 1943): 202–29.

CLAY AND KENTUCKY POLITICS

9-111. BARTON, TOM K. "Henry Clay, Amos Kendall, and Gentlemen's Education: State-Supported Higher Education as a Political Issue in Kentucky, 1815–1825." *Rocky Mountain Social Science Journal* 3 (April 1966): 44–57.

9-112. ———. "Politics and Banking in Republican Kentucky, 1805–1824." Ph.D. dissertation, University of Wisconsin, 1968. 528 p. 68-15966.

9-113. BLAKELEY, GEORGE T. "Rendezvous with Republicanism: John Pope vs. Henry Clay in 1816." *Indiana Magazine of History* 62 (September 1966): 233–50.
Discusses Clay's 1816 campaign for Congress.

9-114. CHINN, GEORGE M. *Kentucky: Settlement and Statehood, 1750–1800*. Frankfort: Kentucky Historical Society, 1975. 616 p.

9-115. CLARK, T. D. "The Lexington and Ohio Railroad: A Pioneer Venture." *Register of the Kentucky State Historical Society* 31 (January 1933): 9–28.
Clay was a director of the railroad.

9-116. COLEMAN, J. WINSTON, JR. *Henry Clay's Last Criminal Case: An Interesting Episode of Lexington History in 1846*. Lexington, Ky.: Winburn Press, 1950. 23 p.

Clay served as chief counsel in the murder trial of Lafayette Shelby.

9-117. COLLINS, LEWIS. *Historical Sketches of Kentucky*. 1847. Reprint. New York: Arno Press, 1971. 560 p.

9-118. DUES, MICHAEL T. "Neither North nor South: The Rhetoric of Confrontation, Compromise, and Reaction in Kentucky, 1833–1868." Ph.D. dissertation, Indiana University, 1973. 177 p. 74-04668.

9-119. HAMMACK, JAMES W., JR. *Kentucky and the Second American Revolution: The War of 1812*. Lexington: University of Kentucky Press, 1976. 115 p.

9-120. JOHNSTON, J. STODDARD, ED. *Memorial History of Louisville from Its First Settlement to the Year 1896*. 2 vols. Chicago: American Biographical, 1897.

9-121. KENTUCKY. General Assembly. House of Representatives. *Journal of the House of Representatives of the Commonwealth of Kentucky*. Frankfort, 1803–9.

9-122. MATHIAS, FRANK F. "Henry Clay and His Kentucky Power Base." *Register of the Kentucky Historical Society* 78 (Spring 1980): 123–39.

9-123. ———. "The Turbulent Years of Kentucky Politics, 1820–1830." Ph.D. dissertation, University of Kentucky, 1966. 378 p. 69-19209.

9-124. SHALER, NATHANIEL S. *Kentucky: A Pioneer Commonwealth*. Boston: Houghton, Mifflin, 1855. 433 p.

9-125. STAPLES, CHARLES R. *The History of Pioneer Lexington, 1779–1806*. Lexington, Ky.: Transylvania Press, 1939. 361 p.

9-126. TURNER, WALLACE B. "Kentucky Politics in the Early 1850s." *Register of the Kentucky Historical Society* 56 (April 1958): 123–42.

CLAY AS SPEAKER OF THE HOUSE

9-127. FOLLETT, MARY PARKER. "Henry Clay as Speaker of the United States House of Representatives." In *Annual Report of the American Historical*

Association, 1891, 1:257–65. Washington, D.C.: Government Printing Office, 1892.

Argues that Clay was the first political Speaker.

9-128. HOAR, GEORGE F. "The Conduct of Business in Congress." *North American Review* 128 (February 1879): 113–34.

Reviews Clay's limitations on floor debate.

CLAY AND THE WAR OF 1812

See also Risjord (7-56) and Hammack (9-119).

9-129. BROWN, ROGER H. *The Republic in Peril, 1812.* New York: Columbia University Press, 1964. 238 p.

9-130. ———. "The War Hawks of 1812: An Historical Myth." *Indiana Magazine of History* 60 (June 1964): 137–58.

9-131. CAFFREY, KATE. *The Twilight's Last Gleaming: Britain vs. America, 1812–1815.* New York: Stein and Day, 1977. 340 p.

9-132. COLES, HARRY L. *The War of 1812.* Chicago: University of Chicago Press, 1965. 298 p.

9-133. HALL, ELLERY L. "Canadian Annexation Sentiment in Kentucky prior to the War of 1812." *Register of the Kentucky State Historical Society* 28 (October 1930): 372–80.

9-134. HAMMACK, JAMES W., JR. "Kentucky and Anglo-American Relations, 1803–1815." Ph.D. dissertation, University of Kentucky, 1974. 417 p. 74-21067.

9-135. HATZENBUEHLER, RONALD L. "The War Hawks and the Question of Congressional Leadership in 1812." *Pacific Historical Review* 45 (February 1976): 1–22.

9-136. HORSMAN, REGINALD. *The Causes of the War of 1812.* Philadelphia: University of Pennsylvania Press, 1962. 345 p.

9-137. ———. "Western War Aims, 1811–1812." *Indiana Magazine of History* 53 (March 1957): 1–18.

9-138. ———. "Who Were the War Hawks?" *Indiana Magazine of History* 60 (June 1964): 121–36.

9-139. MASON, PHILIP P., ED. *After Tippecanoe: Some Aspects of the War of 1812.* East Lansing: Michigan State University Press, 1963. 106 p.

9-140. PERKINS, BRADFORD. *Prologue to War: England and the United States, 1805–1812.* Berkeley: University of California Press, 1961. 457 p.

9-141. RISJORD, NORMAN K. "1812: Conservatives, War Hawks, and the Nation's Honor." *William and Mary Quarterly,* 3d ser., 18 (April 1961): 196–210.

9-142. ———. *The Old Republicans: Southern Conservatism in the Age of Jefferson.* New York: Columbia University Press, 1965. 340 p.

9-143. SMITH, THEODORE C. "War Guilt in 1812." *Proceedings of the Massachusetts Historical Society* 64 (June 1931): 319–45.

9-144. WILTSE, CHARLES M. "The Authorship of the War Report of 1812." *American Historical Review* 49 (January 1944): 253–59.

CLAY AND FOREIGN AFFAIRS

See also Manning (9-87).

Miscellaneous

9-145. BROOKS, PHILIP C. *Diplomacy and the Borderlands: The Adams-Onís Treaty of 1819.* Berkeley: University of California Press, 1939. 262 p.

9-146. BURTON, THEODORE E. "Henry Clay: Secretary of State, March 7, 1825, to March 3, 1829." In *The American Secretaries of State and Their Diplomacy,* edited by Samuel Flagg Bemis, 4: 115–58. 1928. Reprint. New York: Pageant Book, 1958.

9-147. CALLAHAN, JAMES MORTON. *American Foreign Policy in Canadian Relations.* 1937. Reprint. New York: Cooper Square Publishers, 1967. 576 p.

9-148. FULLER, HUBERT BRUCE. *The Purchase of Florida: Its History and Diplomacy.* Cleveland: Borrows Brothers, 1906. 399 p.

9-149. HOLT, WILLIAM STULL. *Treaties Defeated by the Senate: A Study of the Struggle between President and Senate over the Conduct of Foreign Relations.* Baltimore: Johns Hopkins Press, 1933. 328 p.

Analyzes Clay's opposition to the annexation of Texas.

9-150. SMITH, JUSTIN H. *The Annexation of Texas.* 1911. Reprint. New York: AMS Press, 1971. 496 p.

9-151. THOMAS, BENJAMIN P. *Russo-American Relations, 1815–1867.* 1930. Reprint. New York: Da Capo Press, 1970. 185 p.

Treaty of Ghent, 1815

9-152. BEMIS, SAMUEL FLAGG. *John Quincy Adams and the Foundations of American Foreign Policy.* New York: Alfred A. Knopf, 1949. 588 p.

9-153. BURT, ALFRED L. *The United States, Great Britain, and British North America: From the Revolution to the Establishment of Peace after the War of 1812.* New Haven: Yale University Press, 1940. 448 p.

9-154. ENGLEMAN, FRED L. *The Peace of Christmas Eve.* New York: Harcourt, Brace, and World, 1960. 333 p.

9-155. GALLATIN, JAMES. *The Diary of James Gallatin, Secretary to Albert Gallatin: A Great Peacemaker.* Edited by Count Gallatin. New York: Charles Scribner's Sons, 1915. 314 p.

9-156. INGERSOLL, CHARLES J. *Historical Sketch of the Second War between the United States of America and Great Britain.* 2 vols. Philadelphia: Lea and Blanchard, 1845–49.

9-157. UPDYKE, FRANK A. *The Diplomacy of the War of 1812.* Baltimore: Johns Hopkins Press, 1915. 494 p.

Latin America

9-158. BEMIS, SAMUEL FLAGG. *The Latin American Policy of the United States.* New York: Harcourt, Brace, 1943. 470 p.

9-159. CAMPBELL, RANDOLPH B. "Henry Clay and the Emerging Nations of South America." Ph.D. dissertation, University of Virginia, 1966. 395 p. 66-15164.

9-160. ————. "Henry Clay and the Poinsett Pledge Controversy of 1826." *Americas* 28 (April 1972): 429–40.

9-161. GRIFFIN, CHARLES C. *The United States and the Disruption of the Spanish Empire, 1810–1822: A Study of the Relations of the United States with Spain and with the Rebel Spanish Colonies.* New York: Columbia University Press, 1937. 317 p.

9-162. HACKETT, CHARLES WILSON. "The Development of John Quincy Adams' Policy with Respect to an American Confederation and the Panama Congress, 1822–1825." *Hispanic American Historical Review* 8 (November 1928): 496–526.

9-163. HOSKINS, HALFORD L. "The Hispanic American Policy of Henry Clay, 1816–1828." *Hispanic American Historical Review* 7 (August 1927): 460–78.

9-164. JOHNSON, GUION GRIFFIS. "The Monroe Doctrine and the Panama Congress." *James Sprunt Historical Studies* 19, no. 2 (1927): 53–73.

9-165. LATANÉ, JOHN H. *The Diplomatic Relations of the United States and Spanish America.* Baltimore: Johns Hopkins Press, 1900. 294 p.

9-166. LOGAN, JOHN A., JR. *No Transfer: An American Security Principle.* New Haven: Yale University Press, 1961. 430 p.

9-167. MANNING, WILLIAM R. "An Early Diplomatic Controversy between the United States and Brazil." *Hispanic American Historical Review* 1 (May 1918): 123–45.

9-168. ————. *Early Diplomatic Relations between the United States and Mexico.* Baltimore: Johns Hopkins Press, 1916. 406 p.

9-169. ————, ED. *Diplomatic Correspondence of the United States concerning the Independence of the Latin-American Nations.* 3 vols. New York: Oxford University Press, 1925.

9-170. MAY, ERNEST R. *The Making of the Monroe Doctrine.* Cambridge, Mass.: Harvard University Press, 1975. 306 p.

9-171. MOORE, JOHN BASSETT. "Henry Clay and Pan-Americanism." *Columbia University Quarterly* 17 (September 1915): 346–62.

9-172. PAXSON, FREDERICK L. *The Independence of the South American Republics: A Study in Recognition and Foreign Policy*. Philadelphia: Ferris and Leach, 1903. 264 p.

9-173. RIVES, GEORGE LOCKHART. *The United States and Mexico, 1821–1848*. 2 vols. New York: Charles Scribner's Sons, 1913.

9-174. ROBERTSON, WILLIAM SPENCE. "South America and the Monroe Doctrine." *Political Science Quarterly* 30 (March 1915): 82–105.

9-175. ROMERO, M[ATTIAS]. "The United States and the Liberation of the Spanish-American Colonies." *North American Review* 165 (July 1897): 70–86.

9-176. ———. "The United States and the Spanish American Colonies." *North American Review* 165 (November 1897): 553–71.

9-177. SHEPARD, WILLIAM R. "The Monroe Doctrine Reconsidered." *Political Science Quarterly* 39 (March 1924): 35–66.

9-178. STEWART, WATT. "The South American Commission, 1817–1818." *Hispanic American Historical Review* 9 (February 1929): 31–59.

9-179. TATUM, EDWARD H. *The United States and Europe, 1815–1823: A Study in the Background of the Monroe Doctrine*. New York: Russell and Russell, 1936. 315 p.

9-180. WHITAKER, ARTHUR P. *The United States and the Independence of Latin America, 1800–1830*. Baltimore: Johns Hopkins Press, 1941. 632 p.

CLAY AND EXPANSIONISM

9-181. JONES, THOMAS B. "Henry Clay and Continental Expansion, 1820–1844." *Register of the Kentucky Historical Society* 73 (July 1975): 241–62.

9-182. KLEIN, LARRY DEAN. "Henry Clay: Nationalist." Ph.D. dissertation, University of Kentucky, 1977. 267 p. 78-24404.

9-183. NEELY, MARK E., JR. "American Nationalism in the Image of Henry Clay: Abraham Lincoln's Eulogy on Henry Clay in Context." *Register of the Kentucky Historical Society* 73 (January 1975): 31–60.

CLAY, ECONOMIC ISSUES, AND THE AMERICAN SYSTEM

9-184. BENNS, F. LEE. *The American Struggle for the British West India Carrying Trade, 1815–1830*. 1923. Reprint. Clifton, N.J.: Augustus M. Kelley, 1972. 207 p.

9-185. BINKLEY, ROBERT W. "The American System: An Example of Nineteenth-Century Economic Thinking—Its Definition by Its Author, Henry Clay." Ph.D. dissertation, Columbia University, 1950. 361 p. 00-02524.

9-186. COULTER, E. MERTON. "The Genesis of Henry Clay's American System." *South Atlantic Quarterly* 25 (January 1926): 45–54.

9-187. EICHERT, MAGDALEN. "Henry Clay's Policy of Distribution of the Proceeds from Public Land Sales." *Register of the Kentucky Historical Society* 52 (January 1954): 25–32.

9-188. HARRISON, JOSEPH H. "The Internal Improvements Issue in the Politics of the Union, 1783–1825." Ph.D dissertation, University of Virginia, 1954. 711 p. 00-09646.

9-189. KRUEGER, DAVID W. "The Clay-Tyler Feud, 1841–1842." *Filson Club History Quarterly* 42 (April 1968): 162–75.

The feud centered on Clay's determination to reestablish a national bank.

9-190. LINDSEY, DAVID. *Henry Clay, Andrew Jackson: Democracy and Enterprise*. Cleveland: Howard Allen, 1962. 155 p.

9-191. McGRANE, REGINALD CHARLES. *The Panic of 1837: Some Financial Problems of the Jacksonian Era*. Chicago: University of Chicago Press, 1924. 260 p.

9-192. MILLER, RICHARD G. "The Tariff of 1832: The Issue That Failed." *Filson Club History Quarterly* 49 (July 1975): 221–30.

9-193. MORLEY, MARGARET RUTH. "The Edge of Empire: Henry Clay's American System and the Formulation of American Foreign Policy, 1810–1833." Ph.D. dissertation, University of Wisconsin, 1972. 218 p. 72-23064.

9-194. NAGEL, PAUL C. *This Sacred Trust: American Nationality, 1798–1898*. New York: Oxford University Press, 1971. 376 p.

9-195. NUSSBAUM, FREDERICK L. "The Compromise Tariff of 1833: A Study in Practical Politics." *South Atlantic Quarterly* 11 (October 1912): 337–49.

9-196. ROBBINS, ROY M. *Our Landed Heritage: The Public Domain, 1776–1936*. Princeton: Princeton University Press, 1942. 450 p.

9-197. SATO, SHOSUKE. *History of the Land Question in the United States*. Baltimore: Johns Hopkins Press, 1886. 398 p.

9-198. SETSER, VERNON G. *The Commercial Reciprocity Policy of the United States, 1774–1829*. Philadelphia: University of Pennsylvania Press, 1937. 305 p.

9-199. STEPHENSON, GEORGE M. *The Political History of the Public Lands from 1840 to 1862*. 1917. Reprint. New York: Russell and Russell, 1967. 296 p.

9-200. STEVENS, HARRY R. "Henry Clay, the Bank, and the West in 1824." *American Historical Review* 60 (July 1955): 843–48.

9-201. TAUSSIG, FRANK W. "The Early Protective Movement and the Tariff of 1828." *Political Science Quarterly* 3 (March 1888): 17–45.

9-202. WALTERS, RAYMOND, JR. "The Origins of the Second Bank of the United States." *Journal of Political Economy* 53 (June 1945): 115–31.

9-203. WELLINGTON, RAYNOR G. *The Political and Sectional Influence of the Public Lands, 1828–1842*. 1914. Reprint. New York: Burt Franklin, 1970. 131 p.

9-204. WELTER, RUSH. *The Mind of America, 1820–1860*. New York: Columbia University Press, 1975. 603 p.

9-205. ZAHLER, HELENE S. *Eastern Workingmen and National Land Policy, 1829–1862*. New York: Columbia University Press, 1941. 246 p.

CLAY, SLAVERY, AND THE AMERICAN
COLONIZATION SOCIETY

9-206. ALLEN, JEFFREY B. "The Debate over Slavery and Race in Antebellum Kentucky, 1792–1850." Ph.D. dissertation, Northwestern University, 1973. 327 p. 74-07699.

9-207. BENTON, THOMAS HART. *Historical and Legal Examination of That Part of the Decision of the Supreme Court of the United States in the Dred Scott Case*. 1857. Reprint. New York: Johnson Reprint, 1970. 193 p.

9-208. HILL, JOHN. *Opposing Principles of Henry Clay and Abraham Lincoln*. St. Louis: George Knapp, 1860. 14 p.
   Argues that Lincoln's views on slavery were directly opposite to those of Henry Clay.

9-209. KENWORTHY, LEONARD S. "Henry Clay at Richmond in 1842." *Indiana Magazine of History* 30 (December 1934): 353–59.
   Examines Clay's famous misstatements concerning slavery.

9-210. LIGHTFOOT, ALFRED. "Henry Clay and the Missouri Question." *Missouri Historical Review* 61 (January 1967): 143–65.

9-211. LINDLEY, HARLOW. "The Anti-Slavery Separation in Indiana and the 'Henry Clay Incident' in 1842." *Bulletin of Friends Historical Society* 6 (May 1915): 34–48.

9-212. LOGAN, RAYFORD W. "Some New Interpretations of the Colonization Movement." *Phylon* 4 (1943): 328–34.

9-213. MANESS, LONNIE EDWARD. "Henry Clay and the Problem of Slavery." Ph.D. dissertation, Memphis State University, 1980. 272 p. 81-09095.

9-214. OLIVER, ROBERT T. "Behind the Word: Studies in the Political and Social Views of the Slave-Struggle Orators." *Quarterly Journal of Speech* 23 (October 1937): 409–26.

9-215. VAN DEBURG, WILLIAM L. "Henry Clay: The Right of Petition, and Slavery in the Nation's Capital." *Register of the Kentucky Historical Society* 68 (April 1970): 132–46.

9-216. WICKSTROM, WERNER T. "The American Colonization Society and Liberia: An Historical Study in Religious Motivation and Achievement, 1817-1867." Ph.D. dissertation, Hartford Seminary Foundation, 1958. 388 p. 62-03064.

9-217. WINKLER, JAMES E. "Henry Clay: A Current Assessment." *Register of the Kentucky Historical Society* 70 (July 1972): 179-86.

CLAY AND THE WHIG PARTY

9-218. BROCK, WILLIAM R. *Parties and Political Conscience: American Dilemma, 1840-1850.* Millwood, N.Y.: KTO Press, 1979. 367 p.

9-219. BROWNLOW, WILLIAM G. *A Political Register, Setting Forth the Principles of the Whig and Locofoco Parties in the United States, with the Life and Public Services of Henry Clay.* Jonesborough, Tenn.: Jonesborough Whig Office, 1844. 349 p.

9-220. CARROLL, E. MALCOLM. *Origins of the Whig Party.* 1925. Reprint. New York: Da Capo Press, 1970. 260 p.

9-221. HOWE, DANIEL WALKER. *The Political Culture of the American Whigs.* Chicago: University of Chicago Press, 1979. 404 p.

9-222. MARSHALL, LYNN L. "The Strange Stillbirth of the Whig Party." *American Historical Review* 72 (January 1967): 445-68.

9-223. MILES, EDWIN A. "The Whig Party and the Menace of Caesar." *Tennessee Historical Quarterly* 27 (Winter 1968): 361-79.

9-224. PETERSON, MERRILL D. *The Jefferson Image in the American Mind.* New York: Oxford University Press, 1960. 548 p.

CLAY AND THE PRESIDENTIAL ELECTIONS
OF 1824-1844

General

9-225. BINKLEY, WILFRED E. *President and Congress.* New York: Random House, 1962. 312 p.

9-226. CHASE, JAMES S. *Emergence of the Presidential Nominating Convention, 1789-1832.* Urbana: University of Illinois Press, 1973. 332 p.

9-227. JOHNSON, GERALD W. *American Heroes and Hero-Worship.* New York: Harper and Brothers, 1943. 284 p.

9-228. ———. *America's Silver Age: The Statecraft of Clay, Webster, Calhoun.* New York: Harper and Brothers, 1939. 280 p.

9-229. PICKLESIMER, DORMAN, JR. "To Campaign or Not to Campaign: Henry Clay's Speaking Tour through the South." *Filson Club History Quarterly* 42 (July 1968): 235-42.

The Presidential Election of 1824

9-230. BROWN, EVERETT S. "The Presidential Election of 1824-1825." *Political Science Quarterly* 40 (September 1925): 384-403.

9-231. KREMER, GEORGE. *Kremer and Clay.* Washington, D.C., 1825. 23 p.

9-232. MORGAN, WILLIAM G. "Henry Clay's Biographers and the 'Corrupt Bargain' Charge." *Register of the Kentucky Historical Society* 66 (July 1968): 242-58.

9-233. NAGEL, PAUL C. "The Election of 1824: A Reconsideration Based on Newspaper Opinion." *Journal of Southern History* 26 (August 1960): 315-29.

The Presidential Election of 1828

9-234. REMINI, ROBERT V. *The Election of Andrew Jackson.* Philadelphia: J. B. Lippincott, 1963. 224 p.

9-235. WESTON, FLORENCE. *The Presidential Election of 1828.* Washington, D.C.: Ruddick Press. 1938. 217 p.

The Presidential Election of 1832

9-236. GAMMON, SAMUEL R. *The Presidential Campaign of 1832.* 1922. Reprint. Westport, Conn.: Greenwood Press, 1971. 180 p.

The Presidential Election of 1836

9-237. TEAGUE, WILLIAM J. "An Appeal to Reason: Daniel Webster, Henry Clay, and Whig Presidential Politics, 1836-1848." Ph.D. dissertation, North Texas State University, 1977. 384 p. 78-07847.

The Presidential Election of 1840

See also Teague (9-237).

9-238. GUNDERSON, ROBERT GRAY. *The Log-Cabin Campaign*. Lexington: University of Kentucky Press, 1957. 292 p.

9-239. ———. "The Magnanimous Mr. Clay." *Southern Speech Journal* 16 (December 1950): 133–40.

The Presidential Election of 1844

See also Teague (9-237).

9-240. FORD, WORTHINGTON C. *The Campaign of 1844*. Worcester, Mass.: Davis Press, 1909. 23 p.

9-241. LAMBERT, OSCAR D. *Presidential Politics in the United States, 1841–1844*. Durham, N.C.: Duke University Press, 1935. 220 p.

9-242. VAN DER LINDEN, FRANK. *Dark Horse*. San Antonio, Tex.: Naylor, 1944. 114 p.

THE CLAY-RANDOLPH DUEL

See also Adams (7-21), Bruce (7-23), and Garland (7-28).

9-243. CORTS, PAUL R. "Randolph vs. Clay: A Duel of Words and Bullets." *Filson Club History Quarterly* 43 (April 1969): 151–57.

9-244. SPAULDING, MYRA. "Dueling in the District of Columbia." *Records of the Columbia Historical Society* 29/30 (1928): 117–210.

CLAY AND THE COMPROMISE OF 1850

9-245. HAMILTON, HOLMAN. " 'The Cave of Winds' and the Compromise of 1850." *Journal of Southern History* 23 (August 1957): 331–53.

9-246. ———. "Democratic Senate Leadership and the Compromise of 1850." *Mississippi Valley Historical Review* 41 (December 1954): 403–18.

9-247. ———. *Prologue to Conflict: The Crisis and Compromise of 1850*. Lexington: University of Kentucky Press, 1964. 236 p.

9-248. HARMON, GEORGE D. "Douglas and the Compromise of 1850." *Journal of the Illinois State Historical Society* 21 (January 1929): 453–99.

9-249. HEARON, CLEO. "Mississippi and the Compromise of 1850." *Publications of the Mississippi Historical Society* 14 (1914): 7–229.

9-250. HODDER, FRANK H. "The Authorship of the Compromise of 1850." *Mississippi Valley Historical Review* 22 (March 1936): 525–36.

CONTEMPORARY ASSESSMENTS OF CLAY

9-251. BROWN, JAMES. "Letters of James Brown to Henry Clay, 1804–1835." Edited by James A. Padgett. *Louisiana Historical Quarterly* 24 (October 1941): 921–1177.
 Letters from Clay's brother-in-law concerning family matters.

9-252. ELLET, E[LIZABETH] F. *Court Circles of the Republic*. 1869. Reprint. New York: Arno Press, 1975. 586 p.

9-253. HAMILTON, THOMAS. *Men and Manners in America*. 1833. Reprint (2 vols. in 1). New York: Augustus M. Kelley, 1968.

9-254. MARRYAT, FREDERICK. *A Diary in America: With Remarks on Its Institutions*. 1839. Reprint. Edited by Sydney Jackson. New York: Alfred A. Knopf, 1962. 487 p.

9-255. MARTINEAU, HARRIET. *Retrospect of Western Travel*. Vol. 1. 1839. Reprint. New York: Greenwood Press, 1969. 318 p.

9-256. MAURY, SARAH MYTTON. *The Statesmen of America in 1846*. London: Longman, Brown, Green, and Longman, 1844. 261 p.

9-257. MURRAY, SIR CHARLES A. *Travels in North America during the Years 1834, 1835, and 1836*. Vol. 1. 1839. Reprint. New York: Da Capo Press, 1974. 473 p.

9-258. SEALSFIELD, CHARLES. *The United States of North America as They Are*. 1828. Reprint. New York: Johnson Reprint, 1970. 218 p.

9-259. SMITH, MARGARET [BAYARD]. *The First Forty Years of Washington Society: The Family Letters of Margaret Bayard Smith*. Edited by Gaillard Hunt. 1906. Reprint. New York: Frederick Unger, 1965. 424 p.

CLAY AS AN ORATOR

9-260. MATHEWS, WILLIAM. *Oratory and Orators*. Chicago: S. C. Griggs, 1878. 456 p.

9-261. [PARKER, E. A.]. "Henry Clay as an Orator." *Putnam's Monthly* 3 (May 1854): 493–502.

9-262. PECK, CHARLES H. "The Speeches of Henry Clay." *Magazine of History* 16 (July 1886): 58–67.

9-263. WRAGE, ERNEST J. "Henry Clay." In *A History and Criticism of American Public Addresses*, edited by William Norwood Brigance, 2:603–38. New York: McGraw-Hill, 1943.

CLAY'S ASHLAND ESTATE

9-264. CAPEN, OLIVER BRONSON. "Country Homes of Famous Americans, VII: Henry Clay." *Country Life in America* 6 (June 1904): 158–62.

9-265. ESTES, WORTH. "Henry Clay as a Livestock Breeder." *Filson Club History Quarterly* 32 (October 1958): 350–55.

9-266. HOPKINS, JAMES F., ED. "Henry Clay, Farmer and Stockman." *Journal of Southern History* 15 (February 1949): 89–96.

9-267. TROUTMAN, RICHARD LAVERNE. "Henry Clay and His 'Ashland' Estate." *Filson Club History Quarterly* 30 (April 1956): 159–74.

PART III

THE SPEAKERS, 1815–1861

10. General Bibliography, 1815–1861

GENERAL HISTORIES

10-1. BURGESS, JOHN W. *The Middle Period, 1817–1858*. New York: Charles Scribner's Sons, 1897. 544 p.

10-2. DANGERFIELD, GEORGE. *The Awakening of American Nationalism, 1815–1828*. New York: Harper and Row, 1965. 331 p.

10-3. ———. *The Era of Good Feelings*. New York: Harcourt, Brace, 1952. 525 p.
   Discusses the period 1811–29.

10-4. RHODES, JAMES FORD. *History of the United States from the Compromise of 1850 to the End of the Roosevelt Administration*. Vols. 1–3. 1900. Reprint. New York: Macmillan, 1966.

10-5. SCHLESINGER, ARTHUR M., JR. *The Age of Jackson*. Boston: Little, Brown, 1948. 577 p.

10-6. TURNER, FREDERICK JACKSON. *The United States, 1830–1850: The Nation and Its Sections*. 1935. Reprint. New York: W. W. Norton, 1965. 602 p.

10-7. VAN DEUSEN, GLYNDON G. *The Jacksonian Era, 1828–1848*. New York: Harper and Brothers, 1959. 291 p.

10-8. ———. *The Rise and Decline of Jacksonian Democracy*. New York: Van Nostrand Reinhold, 1970. 262 p.

10-9. WELLMAN, PAUL I. *The House Divides: The Age of Jackson and Lincoln, from the War of 1812 to the Civil War*. Garden City, N.Y.: Doubleday, 1966. 488 p.

10-10. WILSON, MAJOR L. *Space, Time, and Freedom: The Quest for Nationality and the Irrepressible Conflict, 1815–1861*. Westport, Conn.: Greenwood Press, 1974. 309 p.

10-11. WILTSE, CHARLES M. *The New Nation, 1800–1845*. New York: Hill and Wang, 1961. 237 p.

STUDIES OF CONGRESS, 1815–1861

10-12. BENTON, THOMAS HART. *Thirty Years' View; or, A History of the Working of the American Government for Thirty Years, from 1820 to 1850*. 2 vols. 1854–56. Reprint. Westport, Conn.: Greenwood Press, 1968.

10-13. BOYKIN, EDWARD C. *Congress and the Civil War*. New York: McBride, 1955. 325 p.

10-14. LIENTZ, GERALD R. "House Speaker Elections and Congressional Parties, 1789–1860." *Capitol Studies* 6 (Spring 1978): 63–89.

10-15. NIELSEN, GEORGE R. "The Indispensable Institution: The Congressional Party during the Era of Good Feelings." Ph.D. dissertation, University of Iowa, 1968. 356 p. 68-10681.

10-16. SILBEY, JOEL H. *The Shrine of Party: Congressional Voting Behavior, 1841–1852*. Pittsburgh: University of Pittsburgh Press, 1967. 292 p.

POLITICS AND PARTIES, 1815–1861

See also Brock (9-218).

10-17. COLE, ARTHUR C. *The Whig Party in the South*. Washington, D.C.: American Historical Association, 1913. 392 p.

10-18. CRANDALL, ANDREW W. *The Early History of the Republican Party, 1854–1856*. 1930. Reprint. Gloucester, Mass.: Peter Smith, 1960. 313 p.

10-19. DENT, LYNWOOD MILLER, JR. "The Virginia Democratic Party, 1824–1847." Ph.D. dissertation, Louisiana State University, 1974. 459 p. 75-01921.

10-20. FONER, ERIC. *Free Soil, Free Labor, Free Men: The Ideology of the Republican Party before the Civil War*. New York: Oxford University Press, 1970. 353 p.

10-21. LUTHIN, REINHARD H. *The First Lincoln Campaign.* Cambridge, Mass.: Harvard University Press, 1944. 328 p.

10-22. McCORMICK, RICHARD P. *The Second American Party System: Party Formation in the Jacksonian Era.* Chapel Hill: University of North Carolina Press, 1966. 389 p.

10-23. NAGEL, PAUL C. *One Nation Indivisible: The Union in American Thought, 1776–1861.* New York: Oxford University Press, 1964. 328 p.

10-24. NICHOLS, ROY FRANKLIN. *The Democratic Machine, 1850–1854.* 1923. Reprint. New York: AMS Press, 1967. 248 p.

10-25. PAUL, JAMES C. N. *Rift in Democracy.* Philadelphia: University of Pennsylvania Press, 1951. 200 p.
    Discusses the Democratic party in the 1840s.

10-26. POTTER, DAVID. *Lincoln and His Party in the Secession Crisis.* New Haven: Yale University Press, 1942. 408 p.

10-27. SIMMS, HENRY H. *The Rise of the Whigs in Virginia, 1824–1840.* Richmond: William Byrd Press, 1929. 204 p.

THE SLAVERY CONTROVERSY, 1820–1860

See also Plumer (7-65), Hamilton (9-247), and Hearon (9-249).

10-28. COOPER, WILLIAM J., JR. *The South and the Politics of Slavery, 1828–1856.* Baton Rouge: Louisiana State University Press, 1978. 401 p.

10-29. CRAVEN, AVERY O. *The Coming of the Civil War.* Chicago: University of Chicago Press, 1957. 491 p.

10-30. ———. *The Growth of Southern Nationalism, 1848–1861.* History of the South, vol. 6, edited by Wendell H. Stephenson. Baton Rouge: Louisiana State University Press, 1953. 433 p.

10-31. ———. *The Repressible Conflict, 1830–1861.* Baton Rouge: Louisiana State University Press, 1939. 97 p.

10-32. CRENSHAW, OLLINGER. *The Slave States in the Presidential Election of 1860.* 1945. Reprint. Gloucester, Mass.: Peter Smith, 1969. 332 p.

10-33. DIXON, SUSAN [BULLITT]. *History of the Missouri Compromise and Slavery in American Politics.* 1903. Reprint. New York: Johnson Reprint, 1970. 623 p.

10-34. EATON, CLEMENT. *The Growth of Southern Civilization, 1790–1860.* New York: Harper and Brothers, 1961. 357 p.

10-35. HOLT, MICHAEL F. *The Political Crisis of the 1850s.* New York: John Wiley and Sons, 1978. 330 p.

10-36. McCARDELL, JOHN. *The Idea of a Southern Nation: Southern Nationalists and Southern Nationalism, 1830–1860.* New York: W. W. Norton, 1979. 394 p.

10-37. MOORE, GLOVER. *The Missouri Controversy, 1819–1821.* 1953. Reprint. Gloucester, Mass.: Peter Smith, 1967. 383 p.

10-38. NEVINS, ALLAN. *The Emergence of Lincoln.* 2 vols. New York: Charles Scribner's Sons, 1950.

10-39. ———. *Ordeal of the Union.* 2 vols. New York: Charles Scribner's Sons, 1947.

10-40. POTTER, DAVID. *The Impending Crisis, 1848–1861.* Completed and edited by Don E. Fehrenbacher. New York: Harper and Row, 1976. 638 p.

10-41. ———. *The South and the Sectional Conflict.* Baton Rouge: Louisiana State University Press, 1968. 321 p.

10-42. RAWLEY, JAMES A. *Race and Politics: Bleeding Kansas and the Coming of the Civil War.* Philadelphia: J. B. Lippincott, 1969. 304 p.

10-43. RUSSEL, ROBERT R. *Economic Aspects of Southern Sectionalism, 1840–1861.* 1924. Reprint. New York: Arno Press, 1973. 325 p.

10-44. SIMMS, HENRY H. *A Decade of Sectional Controversy, 1851–1861.* Chapel Hill: University of North Carolina Press, 1942. 284 p.

10-45. STAMPP, KENNETH M. *And the War Came: The North and the Secession Crisis, 1860–1861.* 1950. Reprint. Baton Rouge: Louisiana State University Press, 1970. 331 p.

10-46. SYDNOR, CHARLES S. *The Development of Southern Sectionalism*. History of the South, vol. 5, edited by Wendell H. Stephenson and E. Merton Coulter. Baton Rouge: Louisiana State University Press, 1948. 400 p.

REMINISCENCES OF POLITICAL LIFE

10-47. HILLIARD, HENRY W. *Politics and Pen Pictures at Home and Abroad*. New York: G. P. Putnam's Sons, 1892. 445 p.

10-48. MCCLURE, ALEXANDER KELLY. *Colonel Alexander K. McClure's Recollections of Half a Century*. 1902. Reprint. New York: AMS Press, 1976. 502 p.

10-49. POORE, BENJAMIN PERLEY. *Perley's Reminiscences of Sixty Years in the National Metropolis*. 2 vols. 1886. Reprint. New York: AMS Press, 1971.

10-50. STANTON, HENRY B. *Random Recollections*. 3d ed. New York: Harper and Brothers, 1887. 298 p.

MISCELLANEOUS

10-51. STANWOOD, EDWARD. *American Tariff Controversies in the Nineteenth Century*. 2 vols. 1903. Reprint. New York: Garland Publishing, 1974.

10-52. WEINBERG, ALBERT K. *Manifest Destiny: A Study of Nationalist Expansionism in American History*. 1935. Reprint. New York: AMS Press, 1979. 559 p.

11. Langdon Cheves
(1776–1857)
⟨Speaker, Thirteenth Congress [Second Session]⟩

Langdon Cheves was born on September 17, 1776, amid the turmoil of the Revolutionary South Carolina back country. He grew up to serve his state and nation as a lawyer, politician, and banker. His childhood was inauspicious; his father had divided loyalties and eventually fled the country as a Loyalist. Left in the care of relatives, Cheves remained in the back country until his father returned in 1785 to open a shop in Charleston.

Cheves rose to prominence in Charleston through his own efforts as a merchant's clerk and as an aspiring law student who passed the bar examination in 1797 without completing the requisite preparations. Through his abilities as a lawyer, contacts as a member of a debating society, and public service as a trustee of an orphan asylum, Cheves gained popularity and political preference. He first served in the state house of representatives from 1802 to 1810 as a Jeffersonian Republican.

In 1810 Cheves was elected to Congress for the first time, as were John C. Calhoun and William Lowndes of South Carolina. Although he was elected to serve in the Twelfth Congress, Cheves was selected to fill the term of a congressman who had resigned before the end of the Eleventh Congress. Taking his seat in December 1810, Cheves served through the Fourteenth Congress (1810–15). He was considered a war hawk and resided at the same boardinghouse as Calhoun and Clay, with whom he helped plan the strategy that led to the War of 1812. Speaker Clay appointed Cheves chairman of the Select Committee on Naval Affairs, from which he called for major expansions in the size of the army and in the quality of maritime fortifications. He was a strong supporter of the war effort, but he broke with Clay on the imposition of trade restrictions, which Cheves argued harmed not only merchants but the entire economy. His bill for resumption of trade in 1813 was soundly defeated.

Henry Clay, nominated to the peace commission to negotiate an end to the war, left

Congress in January 1813. Cheves was elected Speaker of the second session of the Thirteenth Congress (1813–15) with the support of Federalists who shared his opposition to trade restrictions but lacked enough votes to elect one of their own. In contrast to Clay, with his easygoing, informal leadership style, Cheves was a strict Speaker who limited debate to pending matters and tolerated no personal attacks. During his tenure, trade restrictions were repealed (April 1814); and the British captured Washington and burned the Capitol (August 1814). In one notable debate, Cheves cast the deciding vote to defeat a bill proposing a national bank, although he was not opposed in principle to a national bank. Knowing that Clay would likely win the speakership when he returned to Congress, Cheves decided to retire rather than return to the rank and file. When Congress

adjourned in March 1815, the House adopted the customary resolution of appreciation to the retiring Speaker.

The highlight of Cheves's career came after he left Congress. In 1819 he was selected president of the Bank of the United States, after he had declined an offer of an appointment to the Supreme Court. During his three years as president (1819–22), Cheves rescued the bank from imminent collapse and restored it to fiscal responsibility. Later he served as chief commissioner of claims under the Treaty of Ghent (1823–28). His last years were devoted to rice cultivation on his plantation in South Carolina and to discussion of the states' rights issue. He was a delegate to the Nashville Convention (1850), where he called for united Southern resistance and secession. He died on June 26, 1857, at the age of eighty-one.

MANUSCRIPT COLLECTIONS

Duke University Library, Durham, N.C.
  Langdon Cheves Papers.
  6 items.
Georgia Historical Society, Savannah, Ga.
  Langdon Cheves Papers.
  NUCMC 79-779.
Historical Society of Pennsylvania, Philadelphia, Pa.
  Langdon Cheves Papers.
New-York Historical Society, New York, N.Y.
  Langdon Cheves Papers.
South Carolina Historical Society, Charleston, S.C.
  Cheves Family Papers.
  44 ft., 1777–1938.
  NUCMC 63-280.

University of North Carolina Library, Southern Historical Society, Chapel Hill, N.C.
  Langdon Cheves Papers.
  158 items, 1814–1919.
  NUCMC 64-57.
University of South Carolina Library, Columbia, S.C.
  Langdon Cheves Papers.
  Cheves manuscripts are numerous but scattered. The two major collections are those at the University of North Carolina Library, Chapel Hill, and the South Carolina Historical Society, Charleston.

BOOKS, ARTICLES, AND DISSERTATIONS

WORKS BY LANGDON CHEVES

See also Proceedings (11-49) and *Southern Rights Documents* (11-50).

11-1. BENNETT, SUSAN SMYTHE. "The Return of the Mace." *South Carolina Historical Magazine* 58 (October 1957): 243–45.

Contains Cheves's letters about the once-lost mace and his recommendation that it be saved for posterity.

The following items are listed chronologically by year of publication.

11-2. CHEVES, LANGDON. *Aristides; or, A Series of*

Papers on the Presidential Election. Charleston, S.C.: P. Freneau, 1808. 75 p.

Cheves favored the embargo and the election of James Madison in 1808.

11-3. ———. *An Oration Delivered in St. Philips Church.* Charleston, S.C.: E. S. Thomas, 1810. 18 p.

A patriotic Fourth of July speech.

11-4. ———. *Letter of the Hon. Langdon Cheves, to the Editors of the Charleston Mercury, Sept. 11, 1844.* Charleston, S.C.: Walker and Burke, 1844. 15 p.

Cheves's call for united Southern resistance to the tariff of 1842.

11-5. ———. *Speech of the Hon. Langdon Cheves in the Southern Convention at Nashville, Tennessee, November 14, 1850.* [Nashville]: Southern Rights Association, 1850. 30 p.

Cheves urged united Southern resistance and secession.

BIOGRAPHY AND BIOGRAPHICAL SKETCHES

Huff (11-11) is the only full-length, scholarly biography of Cheves. Of the other biographical sketches the most useful is Bennett (11-7).

11-6. ABBOT, ABIEL. "The Abiel Abbot Journals: A Yankee Preacher in Charleston Society, 1818–1827." Edited by John H. Moore. *South Carolina Historical Magazine* 68 (April–October 1967): 51–73, 115–39, 232–54.

11-7. BENNETT, SUSAN SMYTHE. "The Cheves Family of South Carolina." *South Carolina Historical and Genealogical Magazine* 35 (July–October 1934): 79–95, 130–52.

11-8. *Cyclopedia of Eminent and Representative Men of the Carolinas of the Nineteenth Century.* 2 vols. Madison, Wis.: Brant and Fuller, 1892.

11-9. DIFFENDERFER, F. R. "Langdon Cheves." *Historical Papers and Addresses of the Lancaster County Historical Society* 11 (January 1907): 45–58.

11-10. HENSEL, W. U. "A Reminiscence of Langdon Cheves." *Historical Papers and Addresses of the Lancaster County Historical Society* 15 (April 1911): 120–22.

11-11. HUFF, ARCHIE VERNON, JR. *Langdon Cheves of South Carolina.* Columbia: University of South Carolina Press, 1977. 276 p.

In this scholarly, comprehensive biography, Huff argues that Cheves consistently reflected the views of his South Carolina constituency.

11-12. O'NEALL, JOHN BELTON. *Biographical Sketches of the Bench and Bar of South Carolina.* 2 vols. 1859. Reprint. Spartanburg, S.C.: Reprint, 1975.

CHEVES'S POLITICAL ASSOCIATES

In his capacity as politician, Speaker, and president of the Bank of the United States, Cheves came into contact with many other political leaders. The following are the best sources on his political colleagues. *See also* Mooney (7-30), Munroe (7-31), Govan (11-33), and Jervey (11-46).

11-13. GOEBEL, DOROTHY B. *William Henry Harrison: A Political Biography.* 1926. Reprint. Philadelphia: Porcupine Press, 1974. 456 p.

11-14. PARKS, JOSEPH HOWARD. *Felix Grundy: Champion of Democracy.* Baton Rouge: Louisiana State University Press, 1940. 368 p.

11-15. ROBERTS, JONATHAN. "Memoirs of a Senator from Pennsylvania: Jonathan Roberts, 1771–1854." Edited by Philip S. Klein. *Pennsylvania Magazine of History and Biography* 61 (October 1937): 446–74; 62 (January–October 1938): 64–97, 213–48, 361–409, 502–51.

11-16. SIMMS, WILLIAM GILMORE. *The Letters of William Gilmore Simms.* Edited by Mary C. Simms Oliphant et al. 5 vols. Columbia: University of South Carolina Press, 1952–56.

11-17. THOMAS, EBENEZER S. *Reminiscences of the Last Sixty-Five Years.* 1840. Reprint (2 vols. in 1). New York: Arno Press, 1970.

11-18. VIPPERMAN, CARL J. "William Lowndes: South Carolina Nationalist, 1782–1822." Ph.D. dissertation, University of Virginia, 1966. 308 p. 67-03770.

CHEVES AND SOUTH CAROLINA HISTORY AND POLITICS

See items 11-44 to 11-50 for a discussion of his role in the nullification and states' rights issues.

11-19. BROUSSARD, JAMES H. "Party and Partisanship in American Legislatures: The South Atlantic States, 1800–1812." *Journal of Southern History* 43 (February 1977): 39–58.

11-20. KLOSKY, BETH ANN. *The Pendleton Legacy*. Columbia, S.C.: Sandlapper Press, 1971. 112 p.
    The story of Cheves's home district.

11-21. KOHN, AUGUST. *The Cotton Mills of South Carolina*. 1907. Reprint. Spartanburg, S.C.: Reprint, 1975. 228 p.

11-22. RATZLAFF, ROBERT KENT. "John Rutledge, Jr.: South Carolina Federalist, 1766–1819." Ph.D. dissertation, University of Kansas, 1975. 371 p. 76-16768.

11-23. STEPHENSON, NATHANIEL W. "Southern Nationalism in South Carolina in 1851." *American Historical Review* 36 (January 1931): 314–35.

11-24. WOLFE, JOHN HAROLD. *Jeffersonian Democracy in South Carolina*. James Sprunt Studies in History and Political Science, vol. 24, no. 1. Chapel Hill: University of North Carolina Press, 1940. 308 p.

CHEVES, THE WAR OF 1812, AND HIS CONGRESSIONAL CAREER

Cheves's advocacy of naval preparedness is discussed in Mahan (11-27) and Sprout and Sprout (11-28). The best treatments of Cheves as a war hawk are in Huff (11-25) and Latimer (11-26). *See also* Anderson (7-57), Fritz (7-58), Hatzenbuehler (9-135), Risjord (9-142), and Ingersoll (9-156).

11-25. HUFF, ARCHIE VERNON, JR. "Langdon Cheves and the War of 1812: Another Look at 'National Honor' in South Carolina." In *Proceedings of the South Carolina Historical Association* 17 (1970): 8–20.

11-26. LATIMER, MARGARET KINARD. "South Carolina: A Protagonist of the War of 1812." *American Historical Review* 61 (July 1956): 914–29.

11-27. MAHAN, ALFRED THAYER. *Sea Power in Its Relations to the War of 1812*. 2 vols. 1905. Reprint. New York: Haskell House, 1969.

11-28. SPROUT, HAROLD, AND SPROUT, MARGARET. *The Rise of American Naval Power, 1776–1918*. Princeton: Princeton University Press, 1939. 398 p.

CHEVES AND THE BANK OF THE UNITED STATES, 1819–1822

Cheves considered the presidency of the Bank of the United States his major accomplishment. The following works discuss his role in restoring the bank to financial responsibility. *See also* Walters (5-44 and 9-202).

11-29. CATTERALL, RALPH C. H. *The Second Bank of the United States*. Chicago: University of Chicago Press, 1903. 538 p.

11-30. CORRIGAN, M. SAINT PIERRE. "William Jones of the Second Bank of the United States: A Reappraisal." Ph.D. dissertation, St. Louis University, 1966. 139 p. 66-09104.
    Jones, who preceded Cheves as president of the bank, was a vocal critic of Cheves's administration.

11-31. DEWEY, DAVIS R. *Financial History of the United States*. 12th ed. 1934. Reprint. New York: A. M. Kelley, 1968. 600 p.

11-32. GOUGE, WILLIAM M. *A Short History of Paper Money and Banking in the United States*. 1833. Reprint (2 vols. in 1). New York: A. M. Kelley, 1968.

11-33. GOVAN, THOMAS P. *Nicholas Biddle: Nationalist and Public Banker, 1786–1844*. Chicago: University of Chicago Press, 1959. 428 p.
    Cheves reluctantly supported Biddle to succeed him as president of the bank.

11-34. HASKELL, LOUISA P. "Langdon Cheves and the United States Bank: A Study from Neglected Sources." In *Annual Report of the American Historical Association, 1896*, 1:361–71. Washington, D.C.: Government Printing Office, 1897.

11-35. KENT, FRANK R. *The Story of Alexander Brown and Sons*. Baltimore: Norman L. A. Munder, 1925. 215 p.

    Brown was influential in Cheves's selection as president of the bank.

11-36. KEYES, ROBERT W., III. "The Formation of the Second Bank of the United States, 1811–1817." Ph.D. dissertation, University of Delaware, 1975. 239 p. 75-22582.

11-37. KLEIN, PHILIP S. *Pennsylvania Politics, 1817–1832: A Game without Rules*. 1940. Reprint. Philadelphia: Porcupine Press, 1974. 430 p.

11-38. REDLICH, FRITZ. *The Molding of American Banking: Men and Ideas*. 1947–51. Reprint (2 vols. in 1). New York: Johnson Reprint, 1968.

11-39. SCHUR, LEON M. "The Second Bank of the United States and the Inflation after the War of 1812." *Journal of Political Economy* 68 (April 1960): 118–34.

11-40. SMITH, WALTER B. *Economic Aspects of the Second Bank of the United States*. 1953. Reprint. New York: Greenwood Press, 1969. 314 p.

11-41. WRIGHT, DAVID McCORD. *The Economic Library of the President of the Bank of the United States, 1819–1823*. Charlottesville: Bibliographic Society of the University of Virginia, 1950.

11-42. ———. "Langdon Cheves and Nicholas Biddle: New Data for a New Interpretation." *Journal of Economic History* 13 (Summer 1953): 305–19.

    Examines the Cheves-Biddle conflict over management of the bank.

THE TREATY OF GHENT CLAIMS COMMISSION, 1823–1828

11-43. MOORE, JOHN BASSETT. *History and Digest of the International Arbitrations to Which the United States Has Been a Party*. Vol. 1. Washington, D.C.: Government Printing Office, 1898. 989 p.

    Contains information on Cheves's service as a claims commissioner under the Treaty of Ghent.

CHEVES, NULLIFICATION, AND STATES' RIGHTS

11-44. FREEHLING, WILLIAM W. *Prelude to Civil War: The Nullification Controversy in South Carolina, 1816–1836*. New York: Harper and Row, 1965. 395.

11-45. HASSE, ADELAIDE R. "The Southern Convention of 1850." *Bulletin of the New York Public Library* 14 (April 1910): 239–40.

11-46. JERVEY, THEODORE D. *Robert Y. Hayne and His Times*. 1909. Reprint. New York: Da Capo Press, 1970. 555 p.

11-47. *Journal of the State Convention of South Carolina: Together with the Resolution and Ordinance*. Columbia, S.C.: Johnston and Cavis, 1852. 45 p.

    Cheves was a delegate to the convention.

11-48. *Journals of the Conventions of the People of South Carolina, Held in 1832, 1833, and 1852*. Columbia, S.C.: R. W. Gibbes, 1860. 173 p.

11-49. *Proceedings of the States' Rights Celebration at Charleston, S.C., July 1st, 1830*. Charleston: A. E. Miller, 1830. 56 p.

    Includes Cheves's speech against the tariff of 1828.

11-50. *Southern Rights Documents: Cooperation Meeting, Held in Charleston, S.C., July 29th, 1851*. Charleston, 1851. 23 p.

    Includes a letter of support from Cheves.

12. John W. Taylor
(1784–1854)
(Speaker, Sixteenth Congress [Second Session] and Nineteenth Congress)

John W. Taylor's career reflected the issues that agitated politics in the first half of the nineteenth century. The tariff, states' rights, and, above all, the issue of slavery propelled him to national prominence. For twenty years he was one of New York's leading congressmen. Taylor served as Speaker of the House on two different occasions and was defeated for reelection each time. In his opinion, both defeats were owing to his opposition to slavery.

Taylor was born March 26, 1784, at Charlton, New York. In 1803 he graduated from Union College in Schenectady. He was admitted to the New York bar in 1807 and established a law practice in Ballston Spa. Five years later he was elected to the state assembly for a single term (1812–13). In 1813 he won election to the Thirteenth Congress as a Republican. He served in the House of Representatives continuously from March 4, 1813, to March 3, 1833. Taylor was a nationalist who opposed states' rights while favoring a national bank and protective tariffs. In the 1830s he became a member of the Whig party to oppose the policies and tendencies of the Jacksonians.

It was not until the Missouri debates of the Sixteenth Congress that Taylor gained a national reputation for his outspoken opposition to the further extension of slavery. He supported James Talmadge's amendment to the Missouri bill, which would have forbidden the further introduction of slavery into the state and freed the children of slave parents at the age of twenty-five. Although the amendment failed, Taylor later introduced a similar amendment to the bill that organized the Arkansas territory. In support of his proposal to prohibit the introduction of slavery into territories north of the 36°30′ latitude, he argued that the power of Congress to admit states implied the power to refuse admission and hence the right to prescribe conditions. Clashing with Speaker Clay, Taylor attacked slavery as a moral evil that threatened the nation's economy and republican form of government.

When Henry Clay resigned the speakership prior to the second session of the Sixteenth Congress (1820–21), there developed a heated contest which Taylor finally won on the twenty-second ballot. Taylor presided with fairness, but the next Congress elected Philip P. Barbour of Virginia to the speakership.

Taylor, nominally a Republican, kept his seat in Congress from 1821 to 1825 while he continued an independent course. He supported John Quincy Adams's bid for the presidency in 1824; his vote gave the New York delegation to Adams when the election was decided in Congress. When the Nineteenth Congress (1825–27) convened, Taylor was chosen Speaker for the second time. Although he served with some distinction, he was again defeated for reelection to the speakership.

Anti-slavery sentiments hurt Taylor's career, but the most damaging opposition to him came from within New York. The anti-Clintonian faction in New York politics secured his defeat in 1821, and Van Buren Democrats manipulated the speakership election of 1827 by spreading malicious gossip about his private life. In 1832 Van Buren's followers prevented Taylor from being reelected to Congress. He returned to the practice of law in Ballston Spa, where he joined the Whig party in 1839. He was elected to the New York State senate in 1840, but a paralytic stroke forced him to retire in 1843. Taylor spent his last years with a daughter in Cleveland, Ohio, where he died on September 18, 1854.

MANUSCRIPT COLLECTIONS

New-York Historical Society, New York, N.Y.
John W. Taylor Correspondence.
Ca. 1,000 items touching on political issues, 1804–46.
NUCMC 60-2925.
New York Public Library, New York, N.Y.
John W. Taylor Papers.

New York State Library, New York, N.Y.
John W. Taylor Papers.
The only major collection of Taylor manuscripts is held by the New-York Historical Society, comprising some 1,000 items of correspondence.

BOOKS, ARTICLES, AND DISSERTATIONS

WORKS BY JOHN W. TAYLOR

The only published writings of John W. Taylor are a single letter addressed to Thomas Jefferson and two circular letters to his constituents.

12-1. CUNNINGHAM, NOBLE E., JR. *Circular Letters of Congressmen to Their Constituents, 1789–1829.* Vol. 3. Chapel Hill: University of North Carolina Press, 1978.

Contains Taylor's circular letters, including a controversial one of 1824.

12-2. IRWIN, RAY W., ED. "Documents on the Origin of the Phi Beta Kappa Society." *William and Mary Quarterly,* 2d ser., 19 (October 1939): 476–78.

BIOGRAPHY, BIOGRAPHICAL SKETCHES, AND GENEALOGY

Edward K. Spann's dissertation (12-6) is the only in-depth scholarly study of Taylor's career.

12-3. ALEXANDER, DEALVA STANWOOD. "John W. Taylor." *Quarterly Journal of the New York Historical Association* 1 (January 1920): 14–37.

A positive account of Taylor's career.

12-4. ———. "Only One Speaker from Empire State." *State Service* 6 (September–October 1922): 336–42.

12-5. GROSE, EDWARD F. *Centennial History of the Village of Ballston Spa.* Ballston Spa, N.Y.: Ballston Journal Office, 1907. 258 p.

Contains a sketch of Taylor and excerpts from his letters.

12-6. SPANN, EDWARD K. "John W. Taylor: The Reluctant Partisan, 1784–1854." Ph.D. dissertation, New York University, 1957. 498 p. 60-00522.

A scholarly and balanced biography placing Taylor in the context of his times.

12-7. TAYLOR, ELISHA. *Genealogy of Judge John Taylor and His Descendents.* Detroit: Richmond and Backus, 1886. 88 p.

A family genealogy including a short sketch of John W. Taylor.

TAYLOR'S POLITICAL ASSOCIATES

See also Munroe (7-31).

12-8. BEMIS, SAMUEL FLAGG. *John Quincy Adams and the Union.* New York: Alfred A. Knopf, 1956. 546 p.

12-9. IRWIN, RAY W. *Daniel D. Tompkins: Governor of New York and Vice-President of the United States.* New York: New-York Historical Society, 1968. 334 p.

12-10. LYNCH, DENIS TILDEN. *An Epoch and a Man: Martin Van Buren and His Times.* 1929. Reprint. Port Washington, N.Y.: Kennikat Press, 1971. 566 p.

12-11. REMINI, ROBERT V. "The Early Political Career of Martin Van Buren, 1782–1828." Ph.D. dissertation, Columbia University, 1951. 723 p. 00-02852.

12-12. ———. *Martin Van Buren and the Making of the Democratic Party.* New York: Columbia University Press, 1959. 271 p.

12-13. WILTSE, CHARLES M. *John C. Calhoun*. 3 vols. Indianapolis: Bobbs-Merrill, 1944–51.

TAYLOR AND NEW YORK POLITICS

Taylor's political career was largely shaped by the course of New York state politics. The following works place Taylor in the context of the state's political development.

12-14. ALEXANDER, DEALVA STANWOOD. *A Political History of the State of New York*. 4 vols. New York: Henry Holt, 1906–9.

12-15. HAMMOND, JABEZ D. *The History of Political Parties in the State of New York*. 2 vols. Albany: C. Van Benthuysen, 1842.

12-16. JENKINS, JOHN S. *History of Political Parties, in the State of New York*. 2d ed. Auburn, N.Y.: Alden and Parsons, 1849. 580 p.

12-17. KASS, ALVIN. *Politics in New York State, 1800–1830*. Syracuse: Syracuse University Press, 1965. 221 p.

Refers to Taylor's early political career, his position as a stockholder in Oneida Manufacturing, and his unsuccessful bid for reelection to the speakership.

12-18. MORRIS, JOHN DAVID. "The New York State Whigs, 1834–1842: A Study of Political Organization." Ph.D. dissertation, University of Rochester, 1970. 298 p. 70-17898.

12-19. NEW YORK. Legislature. Assembly. *Journal of the Assembly of the State of New York*. Albany, 1812–13.

Taylor served as a representative from Saratoga in the 35th and 36th sessions.

12-20. NEW YORK. Legislature. Senate. *Journal of the Senate of the State of New York*. Albany, 1841–42.

Taylor represented the Fourth District during the 64th session.

TAYLOR AND NATIONAL POLITICS

See also Carroll (9-220) and Remini (9-234).

12-21. LIVERMORE, SHAW, JR. *The Twilight of Federalism: The Disintegration of the Federalist Party,*

1815–1830. 1962. Reprint. New York: Gordian Press, 1972. 292 p.

12-22. MORGAN, WILLIAM G. "The Congressional Nominating Caucus of 1816: The Struggles against the Virginia Dynasty." *Virginia Magazine of History and Biography* 80 (October 1972): 461–75.

12-23. PESSEN, EDWARD. *Jacksonian America: Society, Personality, and Politics*. 1969. Reprint. Homewood, Ill.: Dorsey Press, 1978. 379 p.

TAYLOR, THE MISSOURI COMPROMISE, AND ANTI-SLAVERY

See also Detweiler (7-62) and Benton (9-207).

12-24. AMERICAN COLONIZATION SOCIETY. *Sixteenth Annual Report*. Washington, D.C.: James C. Dunn, 1833. 40 p.

12-25. JOHNSON, WILLIAM R. "Prelude to the Missouri Compromise: A New York Congressman's Efforts to Exclude Slavery from Arkansas Territory." *New-York Historical Society Quarterly Bulletin* 48 (January 1964): 31–50.

A detailed account of Taylor's role in the Missouri Compromise.

12-26. SIMPSON, ALBERT F. "The Political Significance of Slave Representation, 1787–1821." *Journal of Southern History* 7 (August 1941): 315–42.

12-27. TYLER, LYON G. "The Missouri Compromise." *Tyler's Historical and Genealogical Magazine* 13 (January 1932): 149–75.

12-28. WOODBURN, JAMES A. "The Historical Significance of the Missouri Compromise." In *Annual Report of the American Historical Association, 1893*, 1:249–97. Washington, D.C.: Government Printing Office, 1894.

TAYLOR AND THE SPEAKERSHIP ELECTIONS
OF 1821 AND 1827

12-29. RIVES, WILLIAM C. "Letters of William C. Rives." *Tyler's Historical and Genealogical Magazine* 7 (January 1926): 203–7.
Includes a letter on the political maneuvering during the 1827 speakership election.

12-30. SPANN, EDWARD K. "The Souring of Good Feelings: John W. Taylor and the Speakership Election of 1821." *New York History* 41 (October 1960): 379–99.
Details the political factionalism in New York that led to Taylor's defeat in 1821.

13. Philip Pendleton Barbour
(1783–1841)
(Speaker, Seventeenth Congress)

Philip P. Barbour, aristocratic slaveholder and states' rights advocate, contrasted sharply with his nationalistic and anti-slavery predecessor. As one of a new generation of Virginia leaders who looked upon the growing powers of the national government with alarm, he devoted most of his political life to the effort to restore Virginia to its former glory. His career as both a politician and a distinguished jurist illustrated the rising conflict between the forces of nationalism and those of the Southern states' rights movement.

The Barbour family was a prominent one in Virginia. Philip Barbour's father had been a leader in the House of Burgesses, and Philip's brother, James Barbour, was a senator, secretary of war under John Quincy Adams, and minister to England. Although the family was prominent, it was not prosperous during Philip's youth. As a result, he had few educational opportunities, even though he showed great aptitude in languages and classical studies. Following his legal studies, he traveled to Kentucky in 1800 to establish a practice. The following year, Barbour attended William and Mary College in Virginia for one session, after which he resumed the practice of law.

After he was elected to the Virginia House of Delegates in 1812, Barbour divided the rest of his life between the professions of law and politics. In 1814 he was elected to Congress, where he served fourteen years (1814–25 and 1827–30). From 1825 to 1827 he was a judge of the General Court for the Eastern District of Virginia, and for ten years he served in the federal judiciary (1830–41). In both careers Barbour championed states' rights and strict construction of the Constitution.

In Congress, Barbour consistently opposed all elements of the emerging nationalism represented in Clay's American System—tariffs and internal improvements—basing his position on the theory that a strict reading of the Constitution prohibited the national government from interfering with the internal commerce of the states. He also opposed the Missouri Compromise, on the grounds that the rights of citizens to take their property into any part of the nation could not be abridged. The extension of federal power through Marshall's doctrine of judicial review alarmed Barbour. In 1829 he introduced an unsuccessful bill to require the agreement of five of the seven justices on the Supreme Court in any decision that involved a constitutional question.

Barbour's election to the speakership in 1821 was owing to his well-known states' rights position and the general opposition in the House to Speaker John W. Taylor. Although his name was not presented on the first ballot, Barbour was elected Speaker by Taylor's opponents on the twelfth ballot. He served for only one term, returning to the rank and file when Clay resumed the speakership of the Twentieth Congress. Later Barbour served as president of the Virginia constitutional convention of 1829–30, where he opposed the demands of western counties for apportionment solely on the basis of white population. In 1832 there was a brief movement to substitute Barbour for Van Buren as Andrew Jackson's running mate. President Jackson appointed Barbour to the U.S. District

Court in Virginia in 1830 and named him to succeed Gabriel Duval on the Supreme Court in 1836. As a member of the Taney court, Barbour helped alter the emphasis of the court away from loose construction to a position closer to states' rights. Barbour delivered the court's opinion in the important Miln case (1837). An untimely death on February 25, 1841, at the age of fifty-seven, prevented him from exercising a greater impact upon the court.

MANUSCRIPT COLLECTIONS

University of Virginia Library, Charlottesville, Va.

Ambler and Barbour Family Papers.
9 ft., ca. 12,000 items, 1772–1800 (includes Philip Barbour Papers, 280 pieces, 1809–41). NUCMC 60-19.

Virginia Historical Society, Richmond, Va.
Barbour Family Papers.

1,353 items, 1741–1876.
NUCMC 78-587.

Other collections at the University of Virginia Library, Charlottesville, and the Virginia Historical Society, Richmond, also contain Barbour manuscripts and are worth consulting.

BOOKS, ARTICLES, AND DISSERTATIONS

WORKS BY PHILIP P. BARBOUR

The following Barbour speeches and letters are listed chronologically by year of publication.

13-1. BARBOUR, PHILIP P. *Speech Delivered in the House of Representatives of the United States, February 10, 1820.* Washington, D.C., 1820. 28 p.

Barbour's speech in opposition to Taylor's amendment authorizing Missouri to form a constitution prohibiting slavery.

13-2. ———. *Speech of Mr. P. P. Barbour, of Virginia, on the Tariff Bill, Delivered in the House of Representatives . . . March 26, 1824.* Washington, D.C.: Gales and Seaton, 1824. 38 p.

A speech opposing the 1824 protective tariff.

13-3. ———. *Speech of Mr. Philip P. Barbour, of Virginia, on the National Road Bill, Delivered in the House of Representatives, March, 1830.* Washington, D.C., 1830. 15 p.

A speech in opposition to construction of a road from Buffalo, N.Y., through Washington to New Orleans with federal funds.

13-4. ———. *Speech of Mr. Philip P. Barbour, of Virginia, on Internal Improvements, Delivered in the House of Representatives, January 15, 1824.* Washington, D.C., 1846.

A speech in opposition to federally funded internal improvements.

13-5. ———. "Letter from Philip P. Barbour to Andrew Glassell." *Virginia Magazine of History and Biography* 34 (July 1926): 277–78.

A letter dated December 16, 1822, containing legal advice.

13-6. VIRGINIA. *Calendar of Virginia State Papers and Other Manuscripts.* Edited by H. W. Flournoy. Vol. 10. Richmond: James E. Goode, 1892.

Includes references to Barbour's judicial actions and letters from Barbour on those actions.

13. PHILIP PENDLETON BARBOUR

BIOGRAPHICAL SKETCHES AND GENEALOGY

There is no book-length biography of Philip Barbour. Of the following biographical sketches the best is that by Gatell (13-7).

13-7. GATELL, FRANK OTTO. "Philip Pendleton Barbour." In *The Justices of the United States Supreme Court, 1789–1969,* compiled by Leon Friedman, 5:717–27. New York: R. R. Bowker, 1969.

13-8. GREEN, RALEIGH TRAVERS. *Genealogical and Historical Notes on Culpeper County, Virginia.* 1900. Reprint. Baltimore: Southern Book, 1958. 120, 160 p.

Includes a Barbour family genealogy.

13-9. LONG, W. S. "James Barbour." *John P. Branch Historical Papers of Randolph-Macon College* 4, no. 2 (June 1914): 34–64.

Discusses the confusion of James Barbour with Philip Barbour in some earlier works.

13-10. "Obituary: Mr. Justice Barbour." 15 *Peters* (1841): v–vii.

Comments on Barbour by Chief Justice Taney and Attorney General Gilpin.

13-11. SCOTT, W. W. *A History of Orange County, Virginia.* 1907. Reprint. Baltimore: Regional Publishing, 1974. 292 p.

Includes a brief biographical sketch of Barbour.

BARBOUR AND VIRGINIA POLITICS

See also Risjord (9-142) and Dent (10-19).

13-12. AMMON, HARRY. "The Republican Party in Virginia, 1789 to 1824." Ph.D. dissertation, University of Virginia, 1948. 107 p.

13-13. ———. "The Richmond Junto, 1800–1824." *Virginia Magazine of History and Biography* 61 (October 1953): 395–418.

Barbour was a leading member of the clique that dominated Virginia politics.

13-14. DAVIS, RICHARD B. *Intellectual Life in Jefferson's Virginia, 1790–1830.* Chapel Hill: University of North Carolina Press, 1964. 507 p.

13-15. VIRGINIA. General Assembly. House of Delegates. *Journal of the House of Delegates of the Commonwealth of Virginia.* Richmond, 1812–15.

Barbour was a delegate from Culpeper.

BARBOUR'S CONGRESSIONAL CAREER

Of the following, only Stenberg (13-17) gives any extended treatment of Barbour. For other references to Barbour's career and positions on key issues see Munroe (7-31), Brown (7-34), Brown (7-61), Harrison (9-188), Benton (9-207), Catterall (11-29), Rives (12-29), Spann (12-30), and Wayland (14-15).

13-16. ARNOLD, LINDA M. "Congressional Government of the District of Columbia, 1800–1846." Ph.D. dissertation, Georgetown University, 1974. 333 p. 74-16409.

13-17. STENBERG, RICHARD R. "The Jefferson Birthday Dinner." *Journal of Southern History* 4 (August 1938): 334–45.

BARBOUR AND THE VIRGINIA CONVENTION OF 1829–1830

Barbour's role as president of the convention is covered in the following sources.

13-18. ANDERSON, D. R. *William Branch Giles: A Study in the Politics of Virginia and the Nation from 1790 to 1830.* 1914. Reprint. Gloucester, Mass.: Peter Smith, 1965. 271 p.

13-19. CHRISTIAN, W. ASBURY. *Richmond: Her Past and Present.* 1912. Reprint. Spartanburg, S.C.: Reprint, 1973. 618 p.

13-20. GORDON, ARMISTEAD C. *William Fitzhugh Gordon: A Virginian of the Old School, His Life, Times, and Contemporaries, 1787–1858.* New York: Neale Publishing, 1909. 412 p.

13-21. GRIGSBY, HUGH B. *The Virginia Convention of 1829–30.* Richmond: Maclane and Ferguson, 1854. 104 p.

13-22. *Journal, Acts, and Proceedings of a General Convention of the Commonwealth of Virginia, 1829.* Richmond: Thomas Ritchie, 1829. 302, 187, 8 p.

13-23. PLEASANTS, HUGH R. "Sketches of the Virginia Convention of 1829–30." *Southern Literary Messenger* 17 (May 1851): 297–304.

13-24. SUTTON, ROBERT P. "The Virginia Constitutional Convention of 1829–30: A Profile Analysis of Late Jeffersonian Virginia." Ph.D. dissertation, University of Virginia, 1967. 329 p. 67-17625.

13-25. VIRGINIA. Constitutional Convention, 1829–30. *Proceedings and Debates of the Virginia State Convention of 1829–1830.* 2 vols. 1830. Reprint. New York: Da Capo Press, 1971.

BARBOUR'S VICE-PRESIDENTIAL BID, 1832

The following works refer to the unsuccessful attempt to gain the vice-presidential nomination for Barbour in 1832. *See also* Cooper (10-28) and Gordon (13-20).

13-26. BATTEN, J. M. "Governor John Floyd." *John P. Branch Historical Papers of Randolph-Macon College* 4, no. 1 (June 1913): 5–49.

13-27. FLOYD, JOHN. "Floyd's Letter to Gilmer." Edited by Lyon G. Tyler. *William and Mary Quarterly* 1st ser., 20 (January 1911): 191–95.

13-28. HOFFMAN, WILLIAM S. "John Branch and the Origins of the Whig Party in North Carolina." *North Carolina Historical Review* 35 (July 1958): 299–315.

13-29. "Letters from Jackson, Clay, and Johnson." *American Historical Magazine* 5 (April 1900): 132–44.
Includes a Jackson letter on Barbour's vice-presidential bid.

13-30. THORNTON, JONATHAN MILLS, III. "Politics and Power in a Slave Society: Alabama, 1806–1860." Ph.D. dissertation, Yale University, 1974. 658 p. 74-25778.

BARBOUR AND THE SUPREME COURT, 1836–1841

The following works cover Barbour's tenure on the Supreme Court. Most useful is Swisher (13-36). *See also* Gatell (13-7) and, for the Miln case, items 13-40 through 13-43.

13-31. ABRAHAM, HENRY J. *Justices and Presidents: A Political History of Appointments to the Supreme Court.* New York: Oxford University Press, 1974. 310 p.

13-32. CARSON, HAMPTON L. *The History of the Supreme Court of the United States.* 1902. Reprint. New York: Burt Franklin, 1971. 650 p.

13-33. KOHLMEIER, LOUIS M., JR. *God Save This Honorable Court!* New York: Charles Scribner's Sons, 1972. 309 p.

13-34. LEWIS, WALKER. *Without Fear or Favor: A Biography of Chief Justice Roger Brooke Taney.* Boston: Houghton Mifflin, 1965. 556 p.

13-35. LOTH, DAVID G. *Chief Justice John Marshall and the Growth of the Republic.* 1949. Reprint. New York: Greenwood Press, 1970. 395 p.

13-36. SWISHER, CARL BRENT. *Roger B. Taney.* New York: Macmillan, 1936. 608 p.

13-37. ————. *The Taney Period, 1836–64.* History of the Supreme Court of the United States, vol 5. New York: Macmillan, 1974. 1,041 p.

13-38. WARREN, CHARLES. *The Supreme Court in United States History.* 3 vols. Boston: Little, Brown, 1922.

13-39. WEISENBERGER, FRANCIS P. *The Life of John McLean: A Politician on the United States Supreme Court.* 1937. Reprint. New York: Da Capo Press, 1971. 244 p.

BARBOUR AND THE MILN CASE

13-40. DUNNE, GERALD T. *Justice Joseph Story and the Rise of the Supreme Court.* New York: Simon and Schuster, 1970. 458 p.

13-41. JACKSON, PERCIVAL E. *Dissent in the Supreme Court: A Chronology.* Norman: University of Oklahoma Press, 1969. 583 p.

13-42. MCCLELLAN, JAMES. *Joseph Story and the American Constitution: A Study in Political and Legal Thought.* Norman: University of Oklahoma Press, 1971. 413 p.

13-43. SMITH, CHARLES W., JR. *Roger B. Taney: Jacksonian Jurist.* 1936. Reprint. New York: Da Capo Press, 1973. 242 p.

14. Andrew Stevenson
(1784–1857)
(Speaker, Twentieth through Twenty-third Congresses)

Andrew Stevenson, a Jacksonian partisan, was Speaker of the House during the dramatic and turbulent years of the nullification crisis and the bank war. His unqualified support of Jackson's policies led to charges, since repeated, that he was merely the president's subservient tool. In spite of such charges, he presided over the House for nearly seven years, the longest consecutive service prior to Joseph Cannon's speakership. After he left Congress, Stevenson served as minister to Great Britain. In a career steeped in controversy, Stevenson reflected the heated partisan nature of the period.

Stevenson's early career followed the familiar pattern of political leadership. He was born the son of the rector of St. Mark's Parish in Culpeper County, Virginia, on January 21, 1784. He attended William and Mary College, studied law, and established a practice in Richmond before he entered politics. He was elected to the Virginia House of Delegates in 1809 and served there until 1821. In his speeches he espoused the political principles of Jeffersonian Republicanism, referring to the Constitution as a compact that divided sovereignty between the states and the Union. As a strict constructionist, he sought to preserve the rights of the states as the best means of maintaining the Union.

Stevenson lost two congressional elections to John Tyler (1814 and 1816) but was elected to Congress in 1821, when Tyler recommended him as his successor. Stevenson was a member of the Richmond Junto, the powerful controlling clique of Virginia politics. In Congress he became an early supporter of Martin Van Buren and joined the followers of Andrew Jackson. His election to the speakership of the Twentieth Congress in 1827 was reportedly owing to Van Buren's support. Because he was an eloquent orator and a gracious, courtly personality, Stevenson was considered an ideal choice to preside over the enactment of Jackson's policies.

As Speaker, Stevenson used the powers of his office to implement the Jacksonian party's program. He was not a legislative leader of the stature of Henry Clay, but he was also not the president's unprincipled mouthpiece as his enemies claimed. Speaker Stevenson used his influence to further Jacksonian measures because he shared the president's convictions. He appointed committees according to proportionate party strengths, which usually gave the Jacksonians a majority. Like other Speakers, he used the power of recognition to favor his party and to hinder the opposition. His long service testified to Stevenson's ability and success as a legislative manager.

When President Jackson nominated Stevenson to become minister to Great Britain in 1834, Whigs charged that the Speaker had solicited the appointment by improperly subordinating his office to the dictates of the president. This partisan accusation delayed Stevenson's confirmation until 1836. He served in London from July 1836 to October 1841, when the change in administrations brought the Whig party to power. Although untrained as a diplomat, Stevenson was, nonetheless, a popular ambassador. He succeeded in maintaining amicable relations with the British even through such potentially explosive issues as the *Caroline* and McLeod incidents, the northeastern boundary dispute, and Great Britain's attempt to suppress the international slave trade.

On his return to Virginia, Stevenson settled down to agricultural pursuits at Blenheim, his home in Albemarle County. He was elected president of the Virginia Society of Agriculture in 1845 and became a member of the board of visitors of the University of Virginia. Steven-son was chosen to be a rector of the university in 1856 but died soon thereafter, on January 25, 1857.

MANUSCRIPT COLLECTIONS

Library of Congress, Manuscript Division, Washington, D.C.
  Stevenson Family Papers.
  51 containers, ca. 12,000 items, 1756–1882.
  Register and index.
  NUCMC 76-174.
  Though this is the only Stevenson collection, his letters can also be found in scattered collections at the University of Virginia Library, Charlottesville, and the Virginia Historical Society, Richmond. Because of his diplomatic service, researchers would do well to consult the appropriate records in the Diplomatic Branch of the National Archives.

BOOKS, ARTICLES, AND DISSERTATIONS

WORKS BY ANDREW STEVENSON

14-1. "ANDREW STEVENSON." In *Historical Manuscripts in the Public Library of the City of Boston,* 5:210–12. Boston: published by the trustees, 1904.
  Includes two Stevenson letters, dated 1828 and 1840.

14-2. DONELSON, SAMUEL. "Selected Letters, 1846–1856, from the Donelson Papers." Edited by St. George L. Sioussat. *Tennessee Historical Magazine* 3 (December 1917): 257–91.
  Includes an 1851 Stevenson letter.

14-3. "MISSOURI COMPROMISE." *William and Mary Quarterly,* 1st ser., 10 (July 1901): 5–24.
  Includes a Stevenson letter pledging against any unconstitutional compromise.
  The following Stevenson speeches are listed chronologically by year of publication.

14-4. STEVENSON, ANDREW. *Speech on the Subject of Internal Improvements, Delivered in the House of Representatives of the United States, January 29, 1824.* Washington, D.C.: J. S. Meehan, 1824. 20 p.

14-5. ———. *Speech of Mr. Stevenson of Virginia on the Proposition to Amend the Constitution of the United States, Respecting the Election of President and Vice President.* Washington, D.C.: Gales and Seaton, 1826. 30 p.

14-6. ———. *Speech on the Powers of the General Government over Internal Improvements, Delivered in the House of Representatives, Feb. 2, 1829.* Washington, D.C.: Green, 1829. 32 p.

14-7. ———. *Address of Hon. Andrew Stevenson, Delivered before the Agricultural Society of Albemarle, at Its Annual Meeting, on the 29th of October, 1847.* Charlottesville, Va.: James Alexander, 1847. 28 p.

14-8. ———. *Address Delivered before the Penn'a State Agricultural Society, at Harrisburg, by the Hon. Andrew Stevenson.* Harrisburg, Pa.: M'Kinley and Lescure, 1851. 32 p.
  A speech delivered on October 31, 1851.

14-9. U.S. CONGRESS. HOUSE. COMMITTEE ON COMMERCE. *Report of Mr. Kennedy, of Maryland . . . on the Memorial of the Friends of African Colonization.* 1843. Reprint. Freeport, N.Y.: Books for Libraries Press, 1971. 1,088 p.
  Includes Minister Stevenson's official correspondence on the slave trade.

BIOGRAPHY AND BIOGRAPHICAL SKETCHES

The only scholarly, full-length biography of Stevenson is Wayland (14-15). For genealogical formation on the Stevenson family see Green (13-8).

14-10. CHALKLEY, LYMAN. *Chronicles of the Scotch-Irish Settlement in Virginia.* 3 vols. 1912. Reprint. Baltimore: Genealogical Publishing, 1965.

14-11. GARDNER, EUGENE NORFLEET. "Andrew Stevenson." *Richmond College Historical Papers* 1 (June 1915): 259–308.

14-12. JORDAN, DANIEL PORTER, JR. "Virginia Congressmen, 1801–1825." Ph.D. dissertation, University of Virginia, 1970. 479 p. 70-26630.
Includes a biographical sketch of Stevenson.

14-13. MEADE, WILLIAM. *Old Churches, Ministers, and Families of Virginia.* 2 vols. 1857. Reprint. Baltimore: Genealogical Publishing, 1966.

14-14. RUFFIN, EDMUND. "Extracts from the Diary of Edmund Ruffin." *William and Mary Quarterly,* 1st ser., 23 (April 1915): 240–58.

14-15. WAYLAND, FRANCIS FRY. *Andrew Stevenson: Democrat and Diplomat, 1785–1857.* Philadelphia: University of Pennsylvania Press, 1949. 290 p.
A thorough, scholarly study of Stevenson. Wayland defends Stevenson's reputation as a politician and diplomat.

STEVENSON AND VIRGINIA POLITICS

See also Dent (10-19), Ammon (13-12 and 13-13), and Davis (13-14).

14-16. AMBLER, CHARLES H. *Virginia and the Presidential Succession, 1840–1844.* N.p., 1911. 37 p.

14-17. ———. *Thomas Ritchie: A Study in Virginia Politics.* Richmond: Bell, Book, and Stationery, 1913. 303 p.

14-18. BRUCE, PHILIP ALEXANDER. *History of the University of Virginia, 1819–1919.* Vols. 1, 3, 4. New York: Macmillan, 1920–22.
Stevenson is discussed as a member of the board of visitors.

14-19. MOORE, JOHN HAMMOND. *Albemarle: Jefferson's County, 1727–1976.* Charlottesville: University of Virginia Press, 1976. 532 p.

14-20. VIRGINIA. GENERAL ASSEMBLY. HOUSE OF DELEGATES. *Journal of the House of Delegates of the Commonwealth of Virginia.* Richmond, 1810–21.

Contains a complete record of Stevenson's actions as a member and Speaker.

14-21. WOODS, EDGAR. *Albemarle County in Virginia.* 1901. Reprint. Bridewater, Va.: C. J. Carrier, 1932. 412 p.

STEVENSON'S CONGRESSIONAL CAREER, 1821–1834

See also Munroe (7-31) and Harrison (9-188).

14-22. ADAMS, CHARLES FRANCIS, JR. "John Quincy Adams and Speaker Andrew Stevenson of Virginia: An Episode of the Twenty-second Congress, (1832)." *Proceedings of the Massachusetts Historical Society,* 2d ser., 19 (December 1905): 504–53.
Adams and Stevenson clashed over the tariff.

14-23. FRASER, HUGH RUSSELL. *Democracy in the Making: The Jackson-Tyler Era.* Indianapolis: Bobbs-Merrill, 1938. 334 p.

14-24. HOYT, EDWIN P. *John Tyler: The Tenth President of the United States.* London: Abelard-Schuman, 1969. 159 p.

14-25. LAWRENCE, ALEXANDER A. *James Moore Wayne: Southern Unionist.* 1943. Reprint. Westport, Conn.: Greenwood Press, 1970. 250 p.

14-26. LOVE, JAMES. "Some Letters of James Love." Edited by Jimmie Hicks. *Register of the Kentucky Historical Society* 63 (April 1965): 121–39.
Comments upon the confusion in the House caused by Stevenson's nomination as minister to Great Britain.

14-27. MACOLL, JOHN DOUGLAS. "Congressman John Quincy Adams, 1831–1833." Ph.D. dissertation, University of Indiana, 1973. 252 p. 74-04685.

14-28. MOSER, HAROLD D. "Subtreasury Politics and the Virginia Conservative Democrats, 1835–1844." Ph.D. dissertation, University of Wisconsin, Madison, 1977. 527 p. 77-23722.

14-29. REMINI, ROBERT V. "Martin Van Buren and the Tariff of Abominations." *American Historical Review* 63 (July 1958): 903–17.

14-30. TYLER, LYON G. *The Letters and Times of the Tylers*. 3 vols. 1886. Reprint. New York: Da Capo Press, 1970.

STEVENSON'S MINISTRY TO GREAT BRITAIN, 1836–1841

See also Manning (8-4).

14-31. BLUFF, HARRY. "On the Right of Search." *Southern Literary Messenger* 8 (April 1842): 290–301.
Refers to Stevenson's position on the detention of American vessels by the British.

14-32. COREY, ALBERT B. *The Crisis of 1830–1842 in Canadian-American Relations*. New Haven: Yale University Press, 1941. 203 p.
A scholarly treatment of Stevenson's role in the McLeod case.

14-33. *The Court Journal: Gazette of the Fashionable World*. [London].
Volumes for the years 1836–41 contain many references to the Stevensons' social activities.

14-34. CURTIS, JAMES C. *The Fox at Bay: Martin Van Buren and the Presidency, 1837–1841*. Lexington: University of Kentucky Press, 1970. 233 p.

14-35. JONES, HOWARD. *To the Webster-Ashburton Treaty: A Study in Anglo-American Relations, 1783–1843*. Chapel Hill: University of North Carolina Press, 1977. 251 p.

14-36. JONES, WILBUR D. *The American Problem in British Diplomacy, 1841–1861*. London: Macmillan, 1974. 260 p.

14-37. REEVES, JESSE S. *American Diplomacy under Tyler and Polk*. 1906. Reprint. Gloucester, Mass.: Peter Smith, 1967. 335 p.

14-38. SOULSBY, HUGH G. *The Right of Search and the Slave Trade in Anglo-American Relations, 1814–1862*. Johns Hopkins University Studies in Historical and Political Science, 51st ser., no. 2. Baltimore: Johns Hopkins Press, 1933. 185 p.
Stevenson's role in the controversy is examined.

14-39. STEVENSON, SARAH COLES. "Mrs. Andrew Stevenson to Dr. Thomas Sewall, 1837, 1840." Edited by Grenville Howland Norcross. *Proceedings of the Massachusetts Historical Society* 44 (November 1910): 213–16.

14-40. ———. "Queen Victoria as Seen by an American: Being the Letters of Mrs. Sarah Coles Stevenson, Wife of the American Minister in London, 1836–1841." *Century* 87 (January–March 1909): 153–63, 508–18, 733–41.

14-41. WILLSON, BECKLES. *America's Ambassadors to England, 1785–1928*. 1928. Reprint. Freeport, N.Y.: Books for Libraries Press, 1969. 497 p.

THE STEVENSON-O'CONNELL AFFAIR

The following articles examine the controversy that arose when Daniel O'Connell, an Irish leader in the House of Commons, denounced Stevenson as a slavebreeder.

14-42. TEMPERLEY, HOWARD. "The O'Connell-Stevenson Contretemps: A Reflection of the Anglo-American Slavery Issue." *Journal of Negro History* 47 (October 1962): 217–33.

14-43. WAYLAND, FRANCIS FRY. "Slavebreeding in America: The Stevenson-O'Connell Imbroglio of 1838." *Virginia Magazine of History and Biography* 50 (January 1942): 47–54.

15. John Bell
(1797–1869)
(Speaker, Twenty-third Congress [Second Session])

The political career of John Bell was as stormy as the politics of the middle period of American history. Bell was an early Jacksonian Democrat and a founder of the Whig party. He was secretary of war under William Henry Harrison, but he resigned in protest when

Tyler became president. As a Border State politician, he attempted to prevent secession and civil war by running as the Constitutional Union party candidate for president in 1860. Lincoln's election and the Civil War that followed left Bell a broken figure, a sad emblem of the greater national tragedy.

Bell was born on February 15, 1797, in Tennessee. A precocious youth, he graduated from Cumberland College at the age of seventeen. He chose to pursue a legal career rather than his father's agricultural interests. Before his twenty-first birthday, Bell was admitted to the bar, established a practice in Franklin, Tennessee, and was elected to the state senate. These early accomplishments perhaps came too easily for Bell, who declined reelection to the senate and devoted the next ten years to the legal profession.

Bell entered national politics in 1826, when he defeated Felix Grundy for a seat in the Twentieth Congress. Grundy, one of Tennessee's political leaders since the War of 1812, was supported by Andrew Jackson, who had emerged as a national hero and a leading candidate for the presidency. Bell then aligned himself with Jackson and became a member of the Jacksonian party in Congress. Local rivalries and his own ambitions, however, forced him to break with Jackson. Bell refused to support Jackson's war on the national bank. The president responded by favoring Bell's personal enemy and leading rival in Tennessee, James K. Polk, in the speakership contest of 1834. Bell won the election with the support of anti-Jacksonian forces. The break with the president was completed when Bell supported Hugh Lawson White for the presidency in 1836 rather than Jackson's hand-picked successor, Martin Van Buren.

During Bell's one session as Speaker (1834–35), he was harassed by Jacksonians, which may have contributed to his defection to the Whig party. His popularity in Tennessee remained undiminished, and the Whig party became the dominant political force in Tennessee politics. He was defeated for the speakership of the Twenty-fourth Congress by Polk, who had the support of Van Buren and his Jacksonian followers.

Bell left Congress in 1841 to enter William Henry Harrison's cabinet as secretary of war March–September 1841), but he resigned when John Tyler succeeded to the presidency following Harrison's death. With the exception of Webster, the entire cabinet resigned rather than serve under Tyler, who had rejected Whig policies. Bell remained in retirement for six years before he was elected to the U.S. Senate in 1847.

Although he was a Border State slaveowner, Bell was not an uncompromising advocate of slavery. He supported the Compromise of 1850, even though he objected to some of its provisions. In spite of bitter criticism in the South, Bell refused to support the repeal of the Missouri Compromise, the doctrine of squatter sovereignty, or the Kansas-Nebraska Act of 1854. He briefly considered supporting the American party or joining with moderate Republicans and former Whigs, but with the ever-increasing threat of secession, Bell united with other moderates to form the Constitutional Union party in 1860. He was nominated as the party's candidate for president and campaigned on a platform pledged to preserving the Union. He won the electoral votes of only three states (Kentucky, Tennessee, and Virginia). Bell then argued against both secession and the use of force to maintain the Union. When the Civil War began and Tennessee was invaded, Bell's career came to an end. He died on September 10, 1869.

MANUSCRIPT COLLECTIONS

Library of Congress, Manuscript Division, Washington, D.C.
  John Bell Papers, 1815–61.
  1 container.
  NUCMC 62-4530.

MC 12.
Tennessee State Library and Archives, Nashville, Tenn.
  John Bell Papers.
  No significant collection of Bell manuscripts

is known to exist. The Bell Papers in the Library of Congress are not extensive. Bell's biographer, Joseph H. Parks, did find significant numbers of Bell letters in other collections.

Interested readers are directed to the critical essay on sources in Parks (15-27) for references.

BOOKS, ARTICLES, AND DISSERTATIONS

WORKS BY JOHN BELL

The following published speeches and letters constitute the available writings of John Bell, listed chronologically by year of publication and alphabetically thereunder.

15-1. BELL, JOHN. *Speech of the Hon. John Bell, Delivered at the Vauxhall Gardens, Nashville, on the 23rd of May, 1835*. Nashville: W. Hassell Hunt, 1835. 37 p.

Bell's speech endorsing Hugh Lawson White for the presidency, which signaled Bell's break with Jackson.

15-2. ———. *Speech of Mr. Bell, of Tennessee, on the Bill to Secure the Freedom of Elections*. N.p., [1837]. 16 p.

House speech of January 25, 1837.

15-3. ———. *Speech of Mr. Bell, of Tennessee, on the Message of the President of the United States*. Washington, D.C., 1838. 23 p.

15-4. ———. *Mr. Bell's Suppressed Report in Relation to Difficulties between the Eastern and Western Cherokees*. Washington, D.C., 1840. 23 p.

Report of the House Committee on Indian Affairs calling for reforms, sent by Bell to the *National Intelligencer*.

15-5. ———. *Speech of Mr. Bell of Tennessee on the Sub-Treasury Bill*. Washington, D.C.: Gales and Seaton, 1840. 43 p.

House speech of June 16–17, 1840.

15-6. ———. *An Address Delivered before the Alumni Society of the University of Nashville, October 3, 1843*. Nashville: W. F. Bang, 1844. 42 p.

15-7. ———. *Speech of John Bell, of Tennessee, on the Mexican War*. Washington, D.C.: Jonathan T. Towers, 1848. 32 p.

Senate speech of February 2–3, 1848, in opposition to the war.

15-8. ———. *Speech of John Bell, of Tennessee, on Slavery in the United States, and the Causes of the Present Dissensions between the North and the South*. Washington, D.C.: Gideon, 1850. 30 p.

15-9. ———. *Speech of Hon. John Bell, of Tennessee, . . . March 3, 1854*. Washington, D.C.: Congressional Globe Office, 1854. 16 p.

Senate speech opposing the Kansas Nebraska bill.

15-10. ———. *Speech of Hon. John Bell of Tennessee, on the Bill Reported from the Committee on Territories for the Admission of Kansas*. Washington, D.C.: Congressional Globe Office, 1856. 15 p.

Senate speech of July 2, 1856.

15-11. ———. *Speech of Hon. John Bell of Tennessee, on the Naval Retiring Board*. Washington, D.C.: Congressional Globe Office, 1856. 13 p.

Senate speech of April 28–29, 1856.

15-12. ———. *Speech of Hon. John Bell, of Tennessee, upon Our Relations with Great Britain*. Washington, D.C.: Congressional Globe Office, 1856. 15 p.

Senate speech of February 28, 1856.

15-13. ———. *Protection to American Industry*. Washington, D.C.: W. H. Moore, 1858. 8 p.

Excerpts from a Senate speech of May 26, 1858, indicating Bell's protectionism.

15-14. ———. *Speech of Hon. John Bell, on the Admission of Kansas under the Lecompton Constitution*. Washington, D.C.: Buell and Blanchard, 1858. 16 p.

Senate speech of March 18, 1858.

15-15. ———. "The Hon. John Bell on the Nebraska Bill." *Olympian* 1 (April 1903): 351–52.

A Bell letter of 1854 explaining his opposition to the Nebraska bill.

15-16. ———. "Interesting Letter of Hon. John Bell, of Tennessee, to the Hon. James R. Doolittle, of Wisconsin." Contributed by Duane Mowry. *American Historical Magazine* 9 (July 1904): 274–76.

A Bell letter of 1859 in response to Doolittle's internal colonization scheme.

15-17. ———. "Letters of John Bell to William B. Campbell, 1839–1857." Edited by St. George L. Sioussat. *Tennessee Historical Magazine* 3 (September 1917): 201–27.

Letters concerning major political issues and Bell's election campaigns.

15-18. ———. "John Bell: Seventh Congressional District." *Tennessee Historical Magazine* 9 (April 1925): 77–78.

An 1826 circular letter pledging support for Jackson.

15-19. *The Life, Speeches, and Public Services of John Bell*. New York: Rudd and Carleton, 1860. 118 p.

Campaign material containing excerpts from Bell's writings.

BIOGRAPHY AND BIOGRAPHICAL SKETCHES

The only full-length biography of Bell is Parks (15-27). The other sketches are of limited value.

15-20. BARTLETT, DAVID V. *Presidential Candidates: Containing Sketches, Biographical, Personal, and Political, of Prominent Candidates for the Presidency in 1860*. New York: A. B. Burdick, 1859. 360 p.

The chapter devoted to Bell stresses his positions on popular sovereignty and repeal of the Missouri Compromise.

15-21. CALDWELL, JOSHUA W. "John Bell of Tennessee: A Chapter of Political History." *American Historical Review* 4 (July 1899): 652–64.

15-22. ———. *Sketches of the Bench and Bar of Tennessee*. Knoxville: Ogden Brothers, 1898. 402 p.

Includes a concise, favorable summary of Bell's career.

15-23. "Death of Hon. John Bell." *DeBow's Review* 7 (October 1869): 888–89.

15-24. FOOTE, HENRY S. *The Bench and Bar of the South and South West*. St. Louis: Soule, Thomas, and Wentworth, 1876. 264 p.

15-25. McKELLAR, KENNETH D. *Tennessee Senators as Seen by One of Their Successors*. Kingsport, Tenn: Southern Publishers, 1942. 625 p.

15-26. ORDWAY, SALLIE FLEMING. "John Bell." *Gulf States Historical Magazine* 2 (July 1903): 35–44.

15-27. PARKS, JOSEPH HOWARD. *John Bell of Tennessee*. Baton Rouge: Louisiana State University Press, 1950. 435 p.

Scholarly biography that is particularly detailed on Bell's speakership.

15-28. PARKS, NORMAN L. "The Career of John Bell as Congressman from Tennessee, 1827–1841." *Tennessee Historical Quarterly* 1 (September 1942): 229–49.

Balanced account of Bell's congressional career, the speakership election of 1834, and Bell's interpretation of the Speaker's role.

15-29. SAVAGE, JOHN. *Our Living Representative Men*. Philadelphia: Childs and Peterson, 1860. 503 p.

15-30. TEMPLE, OLIVER P. *Notable Men of Tennessee from 1833 to 1875*. New York: Cosmopolitan Press, 1912. 467 p.

BELL AND TENNESSEE HISTORY AND POLITICS

General

15-31. ABERNETHY, THOMAS P. *From Frontier to Plantation in Tennessee: A Study in Frontier Democracy*. 1932. Reprint. University: University of Alabama Press, 1967. 392 p.

15-32. DOAK, H. M. "The Development of Education in Tennessee." *American Historical Magazine* 8 (January 1903): 64–90.

15-33. FOLMSBEE, STANLEY J., ET AL. *History of Tennessee*. 4 vols. New York: Lewis Historical Publishing, 1960.

15-34. FOLSOM, BURTON W., II. "The Politics of Elites: Prominence and Party in Davidson County, Tennessee, 1835–1861." *Journal of Southern History* 39 (August 1973): 359–78.

15-35. HAMER, PHILIP M. *Tennessee: A History, 1673–1932.* 4 vols. New York: American Historical Society, 1933.

15-36. HENRY, J. MILTON. "Summary of Tennessee Representation in Congress from 1845 to 1861." *Tennessee Historical Quarterly* 10 (June 1951): 140–48.

15-37. MOORE, JOHN TROTWOOD, AND FOSTER, AUSTIN P. *Tennessee: The Volunteer State, 1769–1923.* 4 vols. Chicago: S. J. Clarke, 1923.

15-38. PHELAN, JAMES. *History of Tennessee: The Making of A State.* Boston: Houghton Mifflin, 1888. 478 p.

15-39. TENNESSEE. GENERAL ASSEMBLY. HOUSE OF REPRESENTATIVES. *Journal of the House of Representatives . . . at the Twenty-seventh General Assembly.* Knoxville: James C. and Jonathan L. Moses, 1848.
   Bell served as a representative from Davidson county.

15-40. TENNESSEE. GENERAL ASSEMBLY. SENATE. *Journal of the Senate at the First Session of the Twelfth General Assembly.* Knoxville: George Wilson, 1817.
   Bell served as a senator from Davidson county.

State Politics: Jacksonian Democrats vs. Whigs, 1827–1841

See also Everett (16-56).

15-41. ABERNETHY, THOMAS P. "The Origin of the Whig Party in Tennessee." *Mississippi Valley Historical Review* 12 (March 1926): 504–22.
   Bell's break with Jackson was central to the creation of the Whig party in Tennessee.

15-42. BERGERON, PAUL H. "The Jacksonian Party on Trial: Presidential Politics in Tennessee, 1836–1856." Ph.D. dissertation, Vanderbilt University, 1965. 367 p. 65-10462.

15-43. ———. "Politics and Patronage in Tennessee during the Adams and Jackson Years." *Prologue* 2 (Spring 1970): 19–24.

15-44. GOHMANN, SISTER MARY DE LOURDES. *Political Nativism in Tennessee to 1860.* Washington, D.C.: Catholic University of America, 1938. 192 p.

15-45. KARSCH, ROBERT G. "Tennessee's Interest in the Texas Revolution, 1835-36." *Tennessee Historical Magazine,* 2d ser., 3 (January 1937): 206–39.

15-46. MURPHY, JAMES EDWARD. "Jackson and the Tennessee Opposition." *Tennessee Historical Quarterly* 30 (Spring 1971): 50–69.

15-47. OVERDYKE, W. DARRELL. *The Know-Nothing Party in the South.* 1950. Reprint. Gloucester, Mass.: Peter Smith, 1968. 322 p.

15-48. TRICAMO, JOHN EDGAR. "Tennessee Politics, 1845–1861." Ph.D. dissertation, Columbia University, 1965. 317 p. 65-14009.

15-49. WISE, HENRY A. *Seven Decades of the Union.* 1872. Reprint. Freeport, N.Y.: Books for Libraries Press, 1971. 320 p.
   Discusses Bell's role in the contest for the 1840 Whig presidential nomination.

State Politics: Secession and Civil War, 1850–1865

15-50. CAMPBELL, MARY EMILY ROBERTSON. *The Attitude of Tennesseans toward the Union, 1847–1861.* New York: Vantage Press, 1961. 308 p.

15-51. FERTIG, JAMES WALTER. *The Secession and Reconstruction of Tennessee.* 1898. Reprint. New York: AMS Press, 1972. 108 p.

15-52. HENRY, J. MILTON. "The Revolution in Tennessee: February, 1861, to June, 1861." *Tennessee Historical Quarterly* 18 (June 1959): 99–119.

15-53. LACY, ERIC RUSSELL. *Vanquished Volunteers: East Tennessee Sectionalism from Statehood to Secession.* Johnson City: East Tennessee State University Press, 1965. 242 p.

15-54. PARKS, JOSEPH HOWARD. "The Tennessee Whigs and the Kansas-Nebraska Bill." *Journal of Southern History* 10 (August 1944): 308–30.

15-55. Patton, James Welch. *Unionism and Reconstruction in Tennessee, 1860–1869.* 1934. Reprint. Gloucester, Mass.: Peter Smith, 1966. 267 p.

15-56. Sioussat, St. George L. "Tennessee and National Political Parties, 1850–1860." In *Annual Report of the American Historical Association, 1914,* 1:243–58. Washington, D.C.: Government Printing Office, 1916.

15-57. ———. "Tennessee, the Compromise of 1850, and the Nashville Convention." *Mississippi Valley Historical Review* 2 (December 1915): 313–47.

15-58. Temple, Oliver P. *East Tennessee and the Civil War.* 1889. Reprint. Freeport, N.Y.: Books for Libraries Press, 1971. 588 p.

BELL'S POLITICAL ASSOCIATES

The following works treat Bell in the context of his political alliances or feuds with other political figures of the period.

15-59. Alexander, Thomas B. *Thomas A. R. Nelson of East Tennessee.* Nashville: Tennessee Historical Commission, 1956. 186 p.

15-60. Barnes, Thurlow Weed. *Memoirs of Thurlow Weed.* 2 vols. Boston: Houghton Mifflin, 1884.

15-61. Brown, Norman D. *Edward Stanly: Whiggery's Tarheel Conqueror.* University: University of Alabama Press, 1974. 365 p.

15-62. Cassell, Robert. "Newton Cannon and State Politics, 1835–1839." *Tennessee Historical Quarterly* 15 (December 1956): 306–21.

15-63. Drake, James V. *Life of General Robert Hatton.* Nashville: Marshall and Bruce, 1867. 458 p.

15-64. Gresham, L. Paul. "The Public Career of Hugh Lawson White." *Tennessee Historical Quarterly* 3 (December 1944): 291–318.

15-65. Humphrey, Steve. *That D——d Brownlow.* Boone, N.C.: Appalachian Consortium Press, 1978. 412 p.
A biography of William G. Brownlow.

15-66. Kirwan, Albert D. *John J. Crittenden: The Struggle for the Union.* Lexington: University of Kentucky Press, 1962. 514 p.

15-67. McGavock, Randal W. *Pen and Sword: The Life and Journals of Randal W. McGavock.* Edited by Herschel Gower and Jack Allen. Nashville: Tennessee Historical Commission, 1959. 695 p.

15-68. Milton, George Fort. *The Eve of Conflict: Stephen A. Douglas and the Needless War.* Boston: Houghton Mifflin, 1934. 608 p.

15-69. Parks, Joseph Howard. *Felix Grundy: Champion of Democracy.* Baton Rouge: Louisiana State University Press, 1940. 368 p.

15-70. Randall, James G. *Lincoln the President.* 2 vols. New York: Dodd, Mead, 1945.

15-71. Scott, Nancy N. *A Memoir of Hugh Lawson White.* Philadelphia: J. B. Lippincott, 1856. 455 p.

15-72. Seward, Frederick W. *Seward at Washington as Senator and Secretary of State.* 2 vols. New York: Derby and Miller, 1891.

BELL, ANDREW JACKSON, AND THE WHIG PARTY

Bell's break with Jackson in the 1830s and his role in the formation of the Whig party are discussed in the following works. *See also* Abernethy (15-41) and Bergeron (15-43).

15-73. Goldman, Perry M. "Political Rhetoric in the Age of Jackson." *Tennessee Historical Quarterly* 29 (Winter 1970/71): 360–71.

15-74. Goodpasture, Albert V. "John Bell's Political Revolt and His Vauxhall Garden Speech." *Tennessee Historical Magazine* 2 (December 1916): 254–63.
A review of Bell's career up to his speech endorsing Hugh Lawson White, signaling his break with Jackson.

15-75. Moore, Powell. "The Political Background of the Revolt against Jackson in Tennessee." *East Tennessee Historical Society Publications* 4 (1932): 45–66.

15-76. ———. "The Revolt against Jackson in Tennessee, 1835–1836." *Journal of Southern History* 2 (August 1936): 335–59.

BELL AND THE HARRISON-TYLER CABINET, 1841

The following works describe Bell's short tenure as secretary of war and his resignation from Tyler's cabinet. *See also* Lambert (9-241).

15-77. EWING, THOMAS. "Diary of Thomas Ewing: August and September 1841." *American Historical Review* 18 (October 1912): 97–112.

A firsthand account by the secretary of the treasury, with several references to Bell.

15-78. KESILMAN, SYLVAN H. "John Tyler and the Presidency: Old School Republicanism, Partisan Realignment, and Support for His Administration." Ph.D. dissertation, Ohio State University, 1973. 289 p. 74-10985.

15-79. MORGAN, ROBERT J. *A Whig Embattled: The Presidency under John Tyler*. Lincoln: University of Nebraska Press, 1954. 199 p.

BELL AND INDIAN AFFAIRS

Although he was secretary of war for only a few months, Bell did take an interest in reforms in Indian policy. The following works devote some attention to Bell and Indian affairs.

15-80. FOREMAN, GRANT. *The Five Civilized Tribes*. 1934. Reprint. Muskogee, Okla.: C. T. Foreman, 1966. 455 p.

15-81. GRIMSLEY, THORNTON. "Letters of Colonel Thornton Grimsley to Secretary of War John Bell (1841)." Edited by T. C. Elliot. *Quarterly of the Oregon Historical Society* 24 (December 1923): 434–42.

15-82. LUMPKIN, WILSON. *The Removal of the Cherokee Indians from Georgia*. 1907. Reprint (2 vols. in 1). New York: Augustus M. Kelley, 1971.

15-83. PRUCHA, FRANCIS PAUL. *American Indian Policy in the Formative Years: The Indian Trade and Intercourse Acts, 1790–1834*. Cambridge, Mass.: Harvard University Press, 1962. 303 p.

Covers the proceedings of the House Indian Affairs Committee during the period when Bell was a member.

15-84. SATZ, RONALD N. *American Indian Policy in the Jacksonian Era*. Lincoln: University of Nebraska Press, 1975. 343 p.

Bell's favorable attitude toward Southern Indians while secretary of war is treated at length in this fine study.

BELL, ECONOMIC DEVELOPMENT, AND THE TRANSCONTINENTAL RAILROAD

15-85. BROOKS, ADDIE LOU. "The Building of the Trunk Line Railroads in West Tennessee, 1852–1861." *Tennessee Historical Quarterly* 1 (June 1942): 99–124.

15-86. *Journal of the Proceedings of the South-Western Convention, Began and Held at the City of Memphis, on the 12th November, 1845*. Memphis, 1845. 127 p.

15-87. ROBERSON, JERE W. "The Memphis Commercial Convention of 1853: Southern Dreams and 'Young America.' " *Tennessee Historical Quarterly* 33 (Fall 1974): 279–96.

15-88. RUSSEL, ROBERT R. *Improvement of Communication with the Pacific Coast as an Issue in American Politics: 1783–1864*. Cedar Rapids, Iowa: Torch Press, 1948. 332 p.

BELL, THE CONSTITUTIONAL UNION PARTY, AND THE ELECTION OF 1860

Campaign Literature

15-89. CONSTITUTIONAL UNION PARTY. NATIONAL COMMITTEE, 1860–64. *Address of the National Executive Committee of the Constitutional Union Party to the People of the United States*. Washington, D.C.: W. H. Moore, 1860. 8 p.

15-90. ———. *A Calm Appeal to the Friends of American Industry, Especially in the States of Pennsylvania and New Jersey*. Washington, D.C.: W. H. Moore, 1860. 8 p.

15-91. ———. *John Bell's Record . . . A Full Exposition of Mr Bell's Course on the Slavery Question from the Commencement of the Abolition-Petition Agitation in 1835 down to the Termination of his Congressional*

Career in 1859. Washington, D.C.: W. H. Moore, 1860. 31 p.

15-92. DEMOCRATIC PARTY. TENNESSEE. STATE CENTRAL COMMITTEE. *John Bell: His Past History Connected with the Public Service.* Nashville: Union and American Office, 1860. 40 p.

An anti-Bell propaganda sheet.

15-93. *The Public Record and Past History of John Bell and Edward Everett.* Washington, D.C.: National Democratic Executive Committee, 1860. 32 p.

General Works

See also Crenshaw (10-32).

15-94. CURL, DONALD WALTER. "The Baltimore Convention of the Constitutional Union Party." *Maryland Historical Magazine* 67 (Fall 1972): 254–77.

15-95. FITE, EMERSON DAVID. *The Presidential Campaign of 1860.* 1911. Reprint. Port Washington, N.Y.: Kennikat Press, 1967. 358 p.

15-96. HALSTEAD, MURAT. *Caucuses of 1860: A History of the National Political Conventions of the Current Presidential Campaign.* Columbus, Ohio: Follett, Foster, 1860. 232 p.

15-97. HAMER, MARGUERITE BARTLETT. "The Presidential Campaign of 1860 in Tennessee." *East Tennessee Historical Society Publication* 3 (1931): 3–22.

15-98. HODGSON, JOSEPH. *The Cradle of the Confederacy.* 1875. Reprint. Spartanburg, S.C.: Reprint, 1975. 528 p.

15-99. KELLEY, JACK. "John J. Crittenden and the Constitutional Union Party." *Filson Club History Quarterly* 49 (July 1974): 265–76.

15-100. MERING, JOHN V. "The Constitutional Union Campaign of 1860: An Example of the Paranoid Style." *Mid-America* 60 (April/July 1978): 95–106.

15-101. ———. "The Slave-State Constitutional Unionists and the Politics of Consensus." *Journal of Southern History* 43 (August 1977): 395–410.

15-102. NICHOLS, ROY FRANKLIN. *The Disruption of American Democracy.* New York: Macmillan, 1948. 612 p.

15-103. RICHARDSON, CHARLES F. "The Constitutional Union Party of 1860." *Yale Review* 3 (August 1894): 144–65.

15-104. STABLER, JOHN BURGESS. "A History of the Constitutional Union Party: A Tragic Failure." Ph.D. dissertation, Columbia University, 1954. 754 p. 00-10187.

BELL, SECESSION, AND CIVIL WAR

See also Potter (10-26).

15-105. ANDERSON, FRANK MALOY. *The Mystery of A Public Man.* Minneapolis: University of Minnesota Press, 1948. 256 p.

An anonymous diarist's account of the secession winter.

15-106. BARINGER, WILLIAM E. *A House Dividing: Lincoln as President-Elect.* Springfield, Ill.: Abraham Lincoln Association, 1945. 356 p.

15-107. BAUMGARDNER, JAMES L. "Abraham Lincoln, Andrew Johnson, and the Federal Patronage: An Attempt to Save Tennessee for the Union?" *East Tennessee Historical Society Publications* 45 (1973): 51–60.

15-108. BROWNLOW, WILLIAM G. *Sketches of the Rise, Progress, and Decline of Secession.* 1962. Reprint. New York: Da Capo Press, 1968. 458 p.

15-109. DEGLER, CARL N. *The Other South: Southern Dissenters in the Nineteenth Century.* New York: Harper and Row, 1974. 392 p.

15-110. DUMOND, DWIGHT L. *The Secession Movement, 1860–1861.* 1931. Reprint. New York: Negro Universities Press, 1968. 294 p.

15-111. FOOTE, HENRY S. *War of the Rebellion; or, Scylla and Charybdis.* New York: Harper and Brothers, 1866. 440 p.

Blames Bell for Tennessee's support of the Confederacy.

15-112. HALL, CLIFTON R. *Andrew Johnson: Military Governor of Tennessee.* Princeton: Princeton University Press, 1916. 234 p.

15-113. HALL, C. W. *Threescore Years and Ten*. Cincinnati: Elm Street Printing, 1884. 303 p.

    Blames Bell for Tennessee's support of the Confederacy.

15-114. HECK, FRANK H. "John C. Breckinridge in the Crisis of 1860–1861." *Journal of Southern History* 21 (August 1955): 316–46.

15-115. JOHNSON, ANDREW. *The Papers of Andrew Johnson*. 5 vols. to date. Edited by Leroy P. Graf and Ralph W. Haskins. Knoxville: University of Tennessee Press, 1967–.

15-116. PARKS, JOSEPH HOWARD. "John Bell and Secession." *East Tennessee Historical Society Publications* 16 (1944): 30–47.

15-117. WOOSTER, RALPH A. *The Secession Conventions of the South*. Princeton: Princeton University Press, 1962. 294 p.

15-118. WRIGHT, WILLIAM C. *The Secession Movement in the Middle Atlantic States*. Rutherford, N.J.: Fairleigh Dickinson University Press, 1973. 274 p.

16. James Knox Polk
(1795–1849)
(Speaker, Twenty-fourth and Twenty-fifth Congresses)

James K. Polk, the only Speaker ever elected president of the United States, was the eldest of ten children born to Samuel and Jane Knox Polk. In 1806, nearly eleven years after Polk's birth on November 2, 1795, the family moved from Mecklenburg County, North Carolina, to the valley of Duck River, Tennessee. Polk was a frail but intelligent youth. He attended the University of North Carolina, from which he graduated in 1818 with first honors in mathematics and the classics. He returned to Tennessee and quickly rose to prominence over the next seven years. He studied law with Felix Grundy, passed the bar in 1820, established his own law practice, and served two years in the state legislature (1823–25). During these years he formed a political alliance with Andrew Jackson, whose influence determined much of Polk's future career.

Polk began his congressional career in 1825, when he was elected to the Nineteenth Congress. In Congress he consistently opposed President John Quincy Adams and supported his political mentor, Andrew Jackson. After Jackson was elected president, Polk became Old Hickory's most trusted legislative lieutenant and was given the task of preventing the rechartering of the national bank. When John Bell deserted the Jacksonian camp, the president threw his support to Polk's candidacy for the speakership. Although he was defeated by Bell in 1834, Polk was elected Speaker of both the Twenty-fourth and Twenty-fifth Congresses (1835–39). Jackson's trust was well-founded. Polk proved to be an able Speaker, even though he had to deal with more verbal abuse than perhaps any of his predecessors. Virulent anti-Jacksonians saw Polk as an easy target; some even attempted to goad him into a duel. He maintained his composure and the dignity of the office by looking on such behavior with contempt.

In 1839 Polk reluctantly left Congress to return to Tennessee in an attempt to wrest political control of the state from the Whigs. He was elected governor in 1839 but was defeated in 1841 and 1843. In spite of these defeats, his public career was not at an end. Along with Richard M. Johnson, Polk was a prime candidate for the upcoming vice-presidential nomination on a ticket expected to be headed by Martin Van Buren. But when Van Buren took a stand against the annexation of Texas, which Polk favored, Jackson decisively threw his support to Polk. Polk was entered as a dark horse candidate at the Democratic convention in Baltimore, and he was nominated on the ninth ballot. He defeated Henry Clay in the election and took office in 1845 as the eleventh president of the United States.

The forty-nine-year-old Polk, who was known as Young Hickory, was younger than any previous president. He entered office with four main objectives, all of which he achieved in a single term. The four elements of Polk's program were: a reduction in the tariff, establishment of an independent treasury, settlement of the Oregon boundary dispute, and acquisition of California. Three goals were achieved in 1846: the Walker tariff placed import duties on a revenue-only basis; the independent-treasury bill reestablished the nation's financial system; and Great Britain agreed to the forty-ninth parallel as the boundary between Oregon and Canada.

His final objective, the acquisition of California, proved to be more difficult. After efforts to purchase the territory from Mexico failed, Polk asked for a declaration of war on the pretext that a Mexican attack along the contested Texas border constituted an invasion. Although the ensuing Mexican War revived the slavery controversy, Polk did obtain California and New Mexico by the Treaty of Guadalupe Hidalgo, which ended the war in 1848. Polk declined to seek a second term because of his frail health. He died on June 15, 1849, only three months after leaving office.

Polk's successes came through dedicated hard work. He possessed none of the personal charm, grace, or magnetism that distinguished politicians such as Clay, Calhoun, and Webster. Polk, who was reticent, even secretive, and had few close allies, seemed to court opposition. As a result, he was a controversial president in spite of his many accomplishments. He seemed reluctant to take an unequivocal stand on the slavery issue, which earned him the enmity of extremists on both sides. Contemporary critics have characterized Polk as either a willing tool of the slave power or a weak leader. He remains a controversial figure in the present scholarship on his life and career.

MANUSCRIPT COLLECTIONS

The *Correspondence of James K. Polk* (16-1) is presently being published by Vanderbilt University Press. The six volumes published to date contain correspondence from the years 1817–43. The chief sources of Polk's correspondence are the Polk Papers in the Library of Congress Manuscript Division and the Polk Papers in the Tennessee State Library, which also has custodial care of the Polk Papers in the Tennessee State Historical Society Archives.

BOOKS, ARTICLES, AND DISSERTATIONS

WORKS BY JAMES K. POLK

Collected Works

16-1. POLK, JAMES K. *Correspondence of James K. Polk.* 6 vols to date. Vols. 1–4 edited by Herbert Weaver and Paul H. Bergeron. Vols. 5–6 edited by Wayne Cutler. Nashville: Vanderbilt University Press, 1969–.

A comprehensive, scholarly edited collection of Polk correspondence.

16-2. ———. *The Diary of James K. Polk during His Presidency, 1845 to 1849.* Edited by Milo M. Quaife. 4 vols. Chicago: A. C. McClurg, 1910.

16-3. ———. *Polk: The Diary of a President, 1845–1849.* Edited by Allan Nevins. 1929. Reprint.

New York: Longmans, Green, 1952. 412 p.
A one-volume condensation of Polk's diary (16-2).

Published Correspondence

See also Cunningham (12-1) and Jackson (7-3 and 16-135).

16-4. BERGERON, PAUL H. "My Brother's Keeper: William H. Polk Goes to School." *North Carolina Historical Review* 44 (April 1967): 188–204.
Includes correspondence between Polk and his younger brother.

16-5. DAVIS, JEFFERSON. *The Papers of Jefferson Davis*. Edited by James T. McIntosh. Vol. 2. Baton Rouge: Louisiana State University Press, 1974. 806 p.

16-6. EWING, FRANCES. "The Senatorial Career of the Hon. Felix Grundy." *Tennessee Historical Magazine,* 2d ser., 2 (July 1932): 270–91.
Includes one Polk letter addressed to Martin Van Buren.

16-7. HOWE, M. A. DEWOLFE. "Bancroft Papers on the Mecklenberg Declaration, 1775, and on the Annexation of Texas, 1848." *Massachusetts Historical Society Proceedings* 43 (November 1909): 101–22.
Contains Polk letters to George Bancroft on the Mecklenberg Declaration and the annexation of Texas.

16-8. PARKS, JOSEPH HOWARD. "Letters from James K. Polk to Alfred O. P. Nicholson, 1835–49." *Tennessee Historical Quarterly* 3 (March 1944): 67–80.

16-9. ———. "Letters from James K. Polk to Samuel Laughlin, 1835–1844." *East Tennessee Historical Society Publications* 18 (1946): 147–67.

16-10. POLK, JAMES K. "James K. Polk to William C. Beach." *Boston Public Library Monthly Bulletin* 7 (July 1902): 316–17.

16-11. ———. "Mr. Polk Pleads a Case." Edited by Howard B. Gotlieb. *Yale University Library Gazette* 31 (January 1957): 134–36.

16-12. SIOUSSAT, ST. GEORGE L. "Letters of James K. Polk to Andrew J. Donelson, 1843–1848." *Tennessee Historical Magazine* 3 (March 1917): 51–73.

16-13. ———. "Letters of James K. Polk to Cave Johnson, 1833–1848." *Tennessee Historical Magazine* 1 (September 1915): 209–56.

16-14. TYLER, LYON G. "Some Letters of Tyler, Calhoun, Polk, Murphy, Houston and Donelson." *Tyler's Quarterly Historical and Genealogical Magazine* 6 (April 1925): 221–39; 7 (July 1925): 9–15.
Includes two Polk letters on Texas.

Executive Correspondence and Messages of the Governor of Tennessee

16-15. "Executive Correspondence of Governor James K. Polk." *American Historical Magazine and Tennessee Historical Society Quarterly* 8 (July–October 1908): 271–84, 371–76.

16-16. WHITE, ROBERT H., ed. *Messages of the Governors of Tennessee*. Vols. 3 and 4. Nashville: Tennessee Historical Commission, 1952–72.

Published Speeches

The following items are listed chronologically by year of publication and alphabetically thereunder.

16-17. POLK, JAMES K. *Speech of Mr. Polk, on the Proposition to Amend the Constitution of the United States, Respecting the Election of President and Vice-President*. [Washington, D.C., 1826]. 32 p.
House speech of March 13, 1826.

*16-18. ———. *Mr. Polk's Speech on the Maysville Veto, May 28, 1830*. [N.p., 1830]. 40 p.

16-19. ———. *Speech of Mr. James K. Polk, on the Bill to Construct a National Road from Buffalo to New Orleans*. Washington, D.C.: D. Green, 1830. 20 p.
House speech of March 29, 1830.

16-20. ———. *Speech of the Hon. James K. Polk of Tennessee, on His Motion to Re-commit . . . the Report of the Secretary of the Treasury on the Removal of the*

Deposits. Washington, D C.: Francis Preston Blair, 1834. 30 p.

House speech of December 30, 1833.

16-21. ———. *Speech of Hon. James K. Polk, Delivered at a Public Dinner at Mooresville, Maury County, Tennessee, on the 22nd Day of October, 1835*. [N.p., 1835]. 16 p.

A plea for Democratic unity in state politics.

16-22. ———. *Speech of Mr. Polk, of Tennessee, . . . on the Bill Regulating the Deposits of the Public Moneys in Certain Local Banks*. Washington, D.C.: Blair and Rives, 1835. 12 p.

House speech of February 10, 1835.

16-23. ———. *Answers of Ex-Gov. Polk to Two Series of Interrogatories Propounded to Him and Gov. Jones*. Memphis: Appeal Office, 1843. 32 p.

Campaign literature from Polk's 1843 gubernatorial contest.

16-24. ———. *Synopsis of Gov. Polk's Speech to the People of Madison and the Adjoining Counties*. [Jackson, Tenn.?, 1843?]. 30 p.

Presidential Messages and Papers

16-25. UNITED STATES. PRESIDENT. *A Compilation of the Messages and Papers of the Presidents*. Edited by James D. Richardson. Vols. 5 and 6. New York: Bureau of National Literature, 1897–1928.

Includes the official papers of President James K. Polk.

16-26. ———. *The State of the Union Messages of the Presidents, 1790–1966*. Edited by Fred L. Israel. 3 vols. New York: Chelsea House, 1966.

BIBLIOGRAPHICAL SOURCES

16-27. CRONIN, JOHN W., AND WISE, W. HARVEY, JR. *A Bibliography of William Henry Harrison, John Tyler, James Knox Polk*. Washington, D.C.: Riverford Publishing, 1935. 60 p.

A useful though dated bibliography with a brief biographical sketch and chronology.

16-28. FARRELL, JOHN J., ED. *James K. Polk, 1795–1849: Chronology, Documents, Bibliographical Aids*. Dobbs Ferry, N.Y.: Oceana Publications, 1970. 92 p.

Contains a brief chronology, selected public documents, and a bibliography of Polk's life.

16-29. HORN, JAMES J. "Trends in Historical Interpretation: James K. Polk." *North Carolina Historical Review* 42 (October 1965): 454–64.

A historiographical review of the literature on Polk published between 1880 and 1964.

BIOGRAPHIES, BIOGRAPHICAL SKETCHES, GENEALOGY, AND EULOGIES

Biographies

The most thorough and scholarly biography of Polk is Sellers (16-35). The contemporary biographies by Chase (16-31) and Jenkins (16-32) are both favorable accounts.

16-30. BRUCE, DAVID K. E. *Revolution to Reconstruction*. New York: Doubleday, 1939. 486 p.

A brief favorable biography of Polk.

16-31. CHASE, LUCIEN B. *History of the Polk Administration*. New York: George P. Putnam, 1850. 512 p.

16-32. JENKINS, JOHN S. *James Knox Polk and a History of His Administration*. Auburn, N.Y.: Derby, Miller, 1849. 395 p.

16-33. McCORMAC, EUGENE IRVING. *James K. Polk: A Political Biography*. 1922. Reprint. New York: Russell and Russell, 1965. 746 p.

16-34. McCOY, CHARLES A. *Polk and the Presidency*. Austin: University of Texas Press, 1960. 238 p.

16-35. SELLERS, CHARLES G., JR. *James K. Polk*. 2 vols. Princeton: Princeton University Press, 1957–66.

The two volumes cover the years 1795–1843 and 1843–46, respectively.

Biographical Sketches

See also Caldwell (15-22) and Temple (15-30).

16-36. BASSETT, JOHN SPENCER. "James Knox Polk, President." *South Atlantic Quarterly* 10 (January 1911): 70–78.

16-37. CHANDLER, WALTER. "Centenary of James K. Polk and His Administration." *West Tennessee Historical Society Papers* 3 (1949): 27–38.

16-38. GOODPASTURE, ALBERT V. "The Boyhood of President Polk." *Tennessee Historical Magazine* 7 (April 1921): 36–50.

16-39. PHILLIPS, MARGARET I. *The Governors of Tennessee.* Gretna, La.: Pelican Publishing, 1978. 193 p.

16-40. POLLARD, JAMES E. *The President and the Press.* 1947. Reprint. New York: Octagon Books, 1973. 866 p.
   Includes a chapter on Polk.

16-41. SELLERS, CHARLES G., JR. "James K. Polk's Political Apprenticeship." *East Tennessee Historical Society Publications* 25 (1953): 37–53.
   A study of Polk's single term in the Tennessee legislature.

16-42. ———. "Jim Polk Goes to Chapel Hill." *North Carolina Historical Review* 29 (April 1952): 189–203.
   A brief study of Polk's academic career.

16-43. STODDARD, WILLIAM O. *William Henry Harrison, John Tyler, and James Knox Polk.* New York: Frederick A. Stokes and Brother, 1888. 64, 96, 120 p.

16-44. TRICKEY, KATHARINE SHELBURNE. "Young Hickory and Sarah." *Tennessee Valley Historical Review* 1 (Spring 1972): 49–54.

16-45. WEST, EARL IRVIN. "Religion in the Life of James K. Polk." *Tennessee Historical Quarterly* 26 (Winter 1967): 357–71.

16-46. WILLIAMS, FRANK BROYLES. "Tennessee's Second President, Punctilious James." In *Tennessee's Presidents,* pp. 40–68. Knoxville: University of Tennessee Press, 1981.

16-47. WOLD, KARL C. *Mr. President: How Is Your Health?* St. Paul, Minn.: Bruce Publishing, 1948. 214 p.
   Includes a short discussion of Polk's recurring bouts with cholera and diarrhea.

Genealogy

16-48. ANGELLOTTI, MRS. FRANK. "The Polks of North Carolina and Tennessee." *New England Historical and Genealogical Register* 77 (April-

November 1923): 133–45, 213–27, 250–70; 78 (January-July 1924): 33–53, 159–77, 318–30.
   A detailed genealogical study.

Eulogies

16-49. BALLANTINE, E. *A Sermon Occasioned by the Death of Ex-President Polk.* Washington, D.C.: Robert A. Waters, 1849. 13 p.

16-50. FOOTE, HENRY S. *Eulogy upon the Life and Character of James K. Polk, Late President of the United States.* Washington, D.C.: Thomas Ritchie, 1849. 16 p.

16-51. GARRETT, SAMUEL B. *An Oration on the Life, Character, and Public Services of the Late President James K. Polk.* Lawrenceburg, Tenn.: Middle Tennessean Office, 1849. 39 p.

16-52. PORTER, JAMES M. *Eulogium upon James Knox Polk, Late President of the U.S.* Easton, Pa.: Easton Sentinel Office, 1849. 16 p.

16-53. WOODBURY, LEVI. *Eulogy on the Life, Character, and Public Services of the Late Ex-President Polk.* Boston: J. H. Eastburn, 1849. 31 p.

POLK AND TENNESSEE HISTORY AND POLITICS

See also Foote (15-24), Parks (15-27), Abernethy (15-31), Folmsbee et al. (15-33), Hamer (15-35), Moore and Foster (15-37), Phelan (15-38), Bergeron (15-42 and 15-43), and Sioussat (15-56 and 15-57).

16-54. BERGERON, PAUL H. "The Election of 1843: A Whig Triumph in Tennessee." *Tennessee Historical Quarterly* 22 (June 1963): 123–36.

16-55. ———. "James K. Polk and the Jacksonian Press in Tennessee." *Tennessee Historical Quarterly* 41 (Fall 1982): 257–77.

16-56. EVERETT, ROBERT B. "James K. Polk and the Election of 1844 in Tennessee." *West Tennessee Historical Society Papers* 16 (1962): 5–28.

16-57. FOLMSBEE, STANLEY J. *Sectionalism and Internal Improvements in Tennessee, 1796–1845.* Knoxville: East Tennessee Historical Society, 1939. 293 p.

16-58. HEISKELL, S. G. *Andrew Jackson and Early Tennessee History*. 3 vols. Nashville: Ambrose Printing, 1920.

16-59. HENRY, ROBERT SELPH. "Tennesseans and Territory." *Tennessee Historical Quarterly* 12 (September 1953): 195–203.
An assessment of the role of Andrew Jackson, Sam Houston, and James K. Polk in westward expansion.

16-60. MOONEY, CHASE C. *Slavery in Tennessee*. Bloomington: Indiana University Press, 1957. 250 p.

16-61. MOORE, POWELL. "James K. Polk and Tennessee Politics, 1839–1841." *East Tennessee Historical Society Publications* 9 (1937): 31–52.

16-62. ———. "James K. Polk and the 'Immortal Thirteen.'" *East Tennessee Historical Society Publications* 11 (1939): 20–33.

16-63. ———. "James K. Polk: Tennessee Politician." *Journal of Southern History* 17 (November 1951): 493–516.
Centers on the struggle between the Polk and White-Bell factions from 1834 to 1843.

16-64. PARKS, JOSEPH HOWARD. "Felix Grundy and the Depression of 1819 in Tennessee." *East Tennessee Historical Society Publications* 10 (1938): 19–43.

16-65. PUKL, JOSEPH M., JR. "James K. Polk's Congressional Campaigns, 1829–1833." *Tennessee Historical Quarterly* 40 (Winter 1981): 348–65.

16-66. ———. "James K. Polk's Congressional Campaigns of 1835 and 1837." *Tennessee Historical Quarterly* 41 (Summer 1982): 105–23.

16-67. ———. "James K. Polk's Early Congressional Campaigns of 1825 and 1827." *Tennessee Historical Quarterly* 39 (Winter 1980): 440–58.

16-68. SIOUSSAT, ST. GEORGE L. "Some Phases of Tennessee Politics in the Jackson Period." *American Historical Review* 14 (October 1908): 51–69.

16-69. WALTON, BRIAN G. "A Matter of Timing: Elections to the United States Senate in Tennessee before the Civil War." *Tennessee Historical Quarterly* 31 (Summer 1972): 129–48.

POLK'S POLITICAL ASSOCIATES

See also Adams (7-22), Chambers (7-25), Clark (7-26), Munroe (7-31), Smith (7-32), Van Deusen (9-100), Bemis (12-8), Swisher (13-36), Wise (15-49), Brown (15-61), Gresham (15-64), Kirwan (15-66), Milton (15-68), Parks (15-69), and Scott (15-71).

16-70. BAXTER, NATHANIEL. "Reminiscences." *American Historical Magazine* 8 (July 1903): 262–70.

16-71. BELOHLAVEK, JOHN M. *George Mifflin Dallas: Jacksonian Patrician*. University Park: Pennsylvania State University Press, 1977. 233 p.

16-72. BRADLEY, ERWIN STANLEY. *Simon Cameron: Lincoln's Secretary of War*. Philadelphia: University of Pennsylvania Press, 1966. 451 p.

16-73. COIT, MARGARET L. *John C. Calhoun: American Portrait*. Boston: Houghton Mifflin, 1961. 593 p.

16-74. CURTIS, GEORGE TICKNOR. *Life of James Buchanan, Fifteenth President of the United States*. 2 vols. New York: Harper and Brothers, 1883.

16-75. DONALD, DAVID H. *Charles Sumner and the Coming of the Civil War*. New York: Alfred A. Knopf, 1960. 392 p.

16-76. DYER, BRAINERD. *Zachary Taylor*. Baton Rouge: Louisiana State University Press, 1946. 455 p.

16-77. ELLIOT, CHARLES WINSLOW. *Winfield Scott: The Soldier and the Man*. New York: Macmillan, 1937. 817 p.

16-78. FALKNER, LEONARD. *The President Who Wouldn't Retire*. New York: Coward-McCann, 1967. 319 p.
An account of John Quincy Adams's congressional career.

16-79. FOLMSBEE, STANLEY J. "David Crockett and His Autobiography." *East Tennessee Historical Society Publications* 43 (1971): 3–18.

16-80. ———. "David Crockett and West Tennessee." *West Tennessee Historical Society Papers* 28 (1974): 5–24.

16-81. FOLMSBEE, STANLEY J., AND CATRON,

ANNA GRACE. "David Crockett: Congressman." *East Tennessee Historical Society Publications* 29 (1957): 40–78.

16-82. ———. "The Early Career of David Crockett." *East Tennessee Historical Society Publications* 28 (1956): 58–85.

16-83. FUESS, CLAUDE M. *Daniel Webster.* 2 vols. 1903. Reprint. Hamden, Conn.: Archon Books, 1963.

16-84. GARRATY, JOHN A. *Silas Wright.* New York: Columbia University Press, 1949. 426 p.

16-85. GILLET, RANSON H. *The Life and Times of Silas Wright.* 2 vols. Albany, N.Y.: Argus, 1874.

16-86. HAMILTON, HOLMAN. *Zachary Taylor.* 2 vols. Indianapolis: Bobbs-Merrill, 1941–51.

16-87. HOWE, M. A. DE WOLFE. *The Life and Letters of George Bancroft.* 2 vols. 1908. Reprint. New York: Da Capo Press, 1970.

16-88. JULIAN, GEORGE W. *The Life of Joshua R. Giddings.* Chicago: A. C. McClurg, 1892. 473 p.

16-89. MCKINLEY, SILAS B. *Old Rough and Ready: The Life and Times of Zachary Taylor.* New York: Vanguard Press, 1946. 329 p.

16-90. MCLANE, ROBERT M. *Reminiscences.* 1903. Reprint. Wilmington, Del.: Scholarly Resources, 1972. 165 p.

16-91. MEIGS, WILLIAM M. *The Life of John C. Calhoun.* 2 vols. New York: G. E. Stechert, 1917.

16-92. MEYER, LELAND W. *The Life and Times of Colonel Richard M. Johnson of Kentucky.* 1932. Reprint. New York: AMS Press, 1967. 508 p.

16-93. MITCHELL, ROBERT STEWART. *Horatio Seymour of New York.* 1938. Reprint. New York: Da Capo Press, 1970. 623 p.

16-94. NEVINS, ALLAN. *Frémont: The West's Greatest Adventurer.* 2 vols. New York: Harper and Brothers, 1928.

16-95. NYE, RUSSELL. *George Bancroft: Brahmin Rebel.* 1944. Reprint. New York: Octagon Books, 1972. 340 p.

16-96. PHILLIPS, CATHERINE C. *Jessie Benton Frémont: A Woman Who Made History.* San Francisco: Henry Nash, 1935. 361 p.

16-97. ROGERS, JOSEPH M. *Thomas Hart Benton.* Philadelphia: George W. Jacobs, 1905. 361 p.

16-98. ROOSEVELT, THEODORE. *Thomas Hart Benton.* 1891. Reprint. New York: AMS Press, 1972. 344 p.

16-99. SEAGER, ROBERT, II. *And Tyler Too: A Biography of John and Julia Gardiner Tyler.* New York: McGraw-Hill, 1963. 681 p.

16-100. SEWARD, WILLIAM HENRY. *Autobiography of William H. Seward from 1801 to 1834: With a Memoir of His Life and Selections from His Letters from 1831 to 1846.* Edited by Frederick W. Seward. New York: D. Appleton, 1877. 822 p.

16-101. SHACKFORD, JAMES ATKINS. *David Crockett: The Man and the Legend.* Edited by John B. Shackford. Chapel Hill: University of North Carolina Press, 1956. 388 p.

16-102. SHENTON, JAMES P. *Robert John Walker: A Politician from Jackson to Lincoln.* New York: Columbia University Press, 1961. 288 p.

16-103. SMITH, ARTHUR DOUGLAS HOWDEN. *Old Fuss and Feathers: The Life and Times of Lt.-General Winfield Scott.* New York: Greystone Press, 1937. 386 p.

16-104. SMITH, WILLIAM L. G. *Fifty Years of Public Life: The Life and Times of Lewis Cass.* New York: Derby and Jackson, 1856. 781 p.

16-105. WATSON, ELBERT L. "James Walker of Columbia: Polk's Critic and Compatriot." *Tennessee Historical Quarterly* 23 (March 1964): 24–37.

16-106. WOODFORD, FRANK B. *Lewis Cass: The Last Jeffersonian.* 1950. Reprint. New York: Octagon Books, 1973. 380 p.

POLK'S CONGRESSIONAL CAREER

See also Pukl (16-65, 16-66, and 16-67).

16-107. BASSETT, JOHN SPENCER. "James K. Polk and His Constituents: 1831–1832." *American Historical Review* 28 (October 1922): 68–77.

16-108. WISE, HENRY A. *Opinions of Hon. Henry A. Wise, upon the Conduct and Character of James K. Polk, as Speaker of the House of Representatives.* Washington, D.C., 1840.

POLK, JACKSON, AND VAN BUREN

See also Lynch (12-10) and Curtis (14-34).

16-109. ALEXANDER, HOLMES M. *The American Talleyrand: The Career and Contemporaries of Martin Van Buren, Eighth President.* New York: Harper and Brothers, 1935. 430 p.

16-110. EATON, CLEMENT. *A History of the Old South.* New York: Macmillan, 1949. 544 p.

16-111. JAMES, MARQUIS. *Andrew Jackson: Portrait of a President.* Indianapolis: Bobbs-Merrill, 1937. 627 p.

16-112. MACKENZIE, WILLIAM L. *The Life and Times of Martin Van Buren.* Boston: Cook, 1846. 308 p.

16-113. RAYBACK, JOSEPH G. "Martin Van Buren's Break with James K. Polk: The Record." *New York History* 36 (January 1955): 51–62.

16-114. SHEPARD, EDWARD M. *Martin Van Buren.* 1899. Reprint. New York: AMS Press, 1972. 499 p.

16-115. WHITEHURST, ALTO LEE. "Martin Van Buren and the Free Soil Movement." Ph.D. dissertation, University of Chicago, 1932. 219 p.

POLK AND THE PRESIDENTIAL ELECTION OF 1844

See also Ford (9-240), Lambert (9-241), and Van der Linden (9-242).

16-116. BURDETTE, FRANKLIN L. "First Dark Horse Candidate." *National Republic* 22 (October 1934): 5.

16-117. GRANT, C. L., ED. "The Politics behind a Presidential Nomination as Shown in Letters from Cave Johnson to James K. Polk." *Tennessee Historical Quarterly* 12 (June 1953): 152–81.

16-118. JULIAN, GEORGE W. "Some Ante-Bellum Politics." *North American Review* 163 (August 1896): 195–206.

16-119. LAMBERT, ROBERT S. "The Democratic Convention of 1844." *Tennessee Historical Quarterly* 14 (March 1955): 3–23.

16-120. *A Letter on the Subject of the Vice-Presidency in Favor of the Claims of Jas. K. Polk, of Tennessee, to the Nomination of the Democratic National Convention.* Washington, D.C.: Globe Office, 1844. 7 p.

16-121. STODDARD, HENRY L. *Presidential Sweepstakes: The Story of Political Conventions and Campaigns.* Edited by Francis W. Leary. New York: G. P. Putnam's Sons, 1948. 224 p.

16-122. THEISEN, LEE SCOTT. "James K. Polk: Not So Dark a Horse." *Tennessee Historical Quarterly* 30 (Winter 1971): 383–401.

16-123. TUGWELL, REXFORD G. *How They Became President: Thirty-Five Ways to the White House.* New York: Simon and Schuster, 1964. 587 p.

16-124. WASHBURN, CLARA BRACKEN. "Some Aspects of the 1844 Presidential Campaign in Tennessee." *Tennessee Historical Quarterly* 4 (March 1945): 58–74.

POLK'S PRESIDENCY

Expansion: General Works

16-125. BILLINGTON, RAY ALLEN. *Westward Expansion: A History of the American Frontier.* 4th ed. New York: Macmillan, 1974. 840 p.

16-126. BOURNE, EDWARD G. *Essays in Historical Criticism.* 1901. Reprint. Freeport, N.Y.: Books for Libraries Press, 1967. 304 p.

16-127. DEVOTO, BERNARD. *The Year of Decision: 1846.* 1943. Reprint. Boston: Houghton Mifflin, 1961. 538 p.

16-128. GRAEBNER, NORMAN A. *Empire on the Pacific: A Study in American Continental Expansion.* New York: Ronald Press, 1955. 278 p.

16-129. ———. "James K. Polk's Wartime Expansionist Policy." *East Tennessee Historical Society Publications* 23 (1951): 32–45.

16-130. MERK, FREDERICK. *Fruits of Propaganda in the Tyler Administration.* Cambridge, Mass.: Harvard University Press, 1971. 259 p.

16-131. ———. *Manifest Destiny and Mission in American History: A Reinterpretation.* New York: Alfred A. Knopf, 1963. 265 p.

16-132. ———. *The Monroe Doctrine and American Expansionism, 1843–1849.* New York: Alfred A. Knopf, 1966. 289 p.

16-133. VAN ALSTYNE, RICHARD W. *The Rising American Empire.* New York: W. W. Norton, 1974. 215 p.

16-134. ZWELLING, SHOMER S. *Expansion and Imperialism.* Chicago: Loyola University Press, 1970. 150 p.

The Annexation of Texas

See also Smith (9-150).

16-135. JACKSON, ANDREW. *Opinions of Gen. Andrew Jackson on the Annexation of Texas, February 12, 1844.* N.p., 1844. 8 p.
Includes a letter from Polk advocating the annexation of Texas.

16-136. MERK, FREDERICK. *Slavery and the Annexation of Texas.* New York: Alfred A. Knopf, 1972. 290 p.

16-137. PLETCHER, DAVID M. *The Diplomacy of Annexation: Texas, Oregon, and the Mexican War.* Columbia: University of Missouri Press, 1973. 656 p.

16-138. STENBERG, RICHARD R. "President Polk and the Annexation of Texas." *Southwestern Social Science Quarterly* 14 (March 1934): 333–56.

The Oregon Controversy

16-139. CUNNINGHAM, GERTRUDE. "The Significance of 1846 to the Pacific Coast." *Washington Historical Quarterly* 21 (January 1930): 31–54.

16-140. GRAEBNER, NORMAN A. "Maritime Factors in the Oregon Compromise." *Pacific Historical Review* 20 (November 1951): 331–45.

16-141. ———. "Polk, Politics, and Oregon." *East Tennessee Historical Society Publications* 24 (1952): 11–25.

16-142. JONES, WILBUR D., AND VINSON, J. CHAL. "British Preparedness and the Oregon Settlement." *Pacific Historical Review* 22 (November 1953): 353–64.

16-143. JUDSON, KATHARINE B. "Polk and Oregon: With a Pakenham Letter." *Oregon Historical Society Quarterly* 20 (September 1919): 301–2.

16-144. McCABE, JAMES O. "Arbitration and the Oregon Question." *Canadian Historical Review* 41 (December 1960): 308–27.

16-145. MERK, FREDERICK. *The Oregon Question: Essays in Anglo-American Diplomacy and Politics.* Cambridge, Mass.: Harvard University Press, 1967. 427 p.

16-146. PRATT, JULIUS W. "James K. Polk and John Bull." *Canadian Historical Review* 24 (December 1943): 341–49.

16-147. SCHUYLER, R. L. "Polk and the Oregon Compromise." *Political Science Quarterly* 26 (September 1911): 443–61.

16-148. SHIPPEE, LESTER BURRELL. "The Federal Relations of Oregon." *Oregon Historical Society Quarterly* 19 (March–December 1918): 89–133, 189–230, 283–311; 20 (March–December 1919): 35–93, 173–218, 261–95, 345–95.

16-149. SOWARD, F. W. "President Polk and the Canadian Frontier." In *Canadian Historical Association: Report of the Annual Meeting . . . 1930,* pp. 71–80. Ottawa: Department of Public Archives, 1930.

California

See also Bassett (16-36).

16-150. CLELAND, ROBERT GLASS. "Asiatic Trade and the American Occupation of the Pacific Coast." In *Annual Report of the American Historical Association, 1914,* 1:283–89. Washington, D.C.: Government Printing Office, 1916.

16-151. ———. "The Early Sentiment for the Annexation of California." *Southwestern Historical*

Quarterly 18 (July 1914–January 1915): 1–40, 121–61, 231–60.

16-152. COUGHLIN, SISTER MAGDALEN, C.S.J. "California Ports: A Key to Diplomacy for the West Coast, 1820–1845." *Journal of the West* 5 (April 1966): 153–72.

16-153. EGAN, FEROL. *Frémont: Explorer for a Restless Nation.* Garden City, N.Y.: Doubleday, 1977. 582 p.

16-154. STENBERG, RICHARD R. "Polk and Frémont, 1845–1846." *Pacific Historical Review* 7 (September 1938): 211–27.

16-155. ———. "President Polk and California: Additional Documents concerning the Slidell Mission." *Pacific Historical Review* 10 (June 1941): 217–19.

Foreign Diplomacy

See also Latané (9-165), Logan (9-166), and Reeves (14-37).

16-156. GOETZMANN, WILLIAM H. *When the Eagle Screamed: The Romantic Horizon in American Diplomacy, 1800–1860.* New York: John Wiley and Sons, 1966. 138 p.

16-157. MARRARO, HOWARD R. "William H. Polk's Mission to Naples, 1845–1847." *Tennessee Historical Quarterly* 4 (September 1945): 222–31.

16-158. PERKINS, DEXTER. *A History of the Monroe Doctrine.* Rev. ed. Boston: Little, Brown, 1963. 462 p.

16-159. ———. *The Monroe Doctrine, 1826–1867.* 1933. Reprint. Gloucester, Mass: Peter Smith, 1965. 580 p.

16-160. RAUCH, BASIL. *American Interest in Cuba, 1848–1855.* New York: Columbia University Press, 1948. 322 p.

16-161. REID, WHITELAW. *The Monroe Doctrine, the Polk Doctrine, and the Doctrine of Anarchism.* New York: De Vinne Press, 1903. 27 p.

16-162. RIPPY, J. FRED. *The United States and Mexico.* New York: F. S. Crofts, 1931. 423 p.

16-163. SOBEL, ROBERT. *Conquest and Conscience: The 1840s.* New York: Thomas Y. Crowell, 1971. 330 p.

Origins of the Mexican War

See also Rives (9-173).

16-164. BARKER, EUGENE C. "California as the Cause of the Mexican War." *Texas Review* 2 (1917): 213–21.

16-165. BERGE, DENNIS EUGENE. "Mexican Response to United States' Expansionism, 1841–1848."
Ph.D. dissertation, University of California, Berkeley, 1965. 341 p. 66-03545.

16-166. BINKLEY, WILLIAM C. *The Expansionist Movement in Texas, 1836–1850.* 1925. Reprint. New York: Da Capo Press, 1970. 235 p.

16-167. DODD, WILLIAM E. "The West and the War with Mexico." *Illinois State Historical Society Transactions* 17 (1912): 15–23.

16-168. FULLER, JOHN DOUGLAS P. *The Movement for the Acquisition of All Mexico, 1846–1848.* 1936. Reprint. New York: Da Capo Press, 1969. 174 p.

16-169. HARSTAD, PETER T., AND RESH, RICHARD W. "The Causes of the Mexican War: A Note on Changing Interpretations." *Arizona and the West* 6 (Winter 1964): 289–302.

16-170. HICKS, ROBERT S. "Diplomatic Relations with Mexico during the Administration of James K. Polk." *Historical Society of Southern California Publications* 12 (1922): 5–17.

16-171. JAY, WILLIAM. *A Review of the Causes and Consequences of the Mexican War.* 1849. Reprint. New York: Arno Press, 1969. 333 p.

16-172. KOHL, CLAYTON CHARLES. *Claims as a Cause of the Mexican War.* New York: New York University, 1914. 96 p.

16-173. LAMAR, QUINTON CURTIS. "The Role of Lucas Alaman in Mexican–United States Relations, 1824–1853." Ph.D. dissertation, Louisiana State University, 1971. 363 p. 71-20606.

16-174. LARGENT, ROBERT J. "Legal and Constitutional Aspects of President Polk's Mexican Policy." *Marshall Review* 1 (June 1937): 3–12.

16-175. LEONARD, GLEN MILTON. "Western Boundary-Making: Texas and the Mexican Cession, 1844–50." Ph.D. dissertation, University of Utah, 1970. 466 p. 70-23060.

6-176. MELTZER, MILTON. *Bound for the Rio Grande: The Mexican Struggle, 1845–1850*. New York: Alfred A. Knopf, 1974. 279 p.

16-177. MOODY, LORING. *Facts for the People: Showing the Relations of the United States Government to Slavery, Embracing a History of the Mexican War, its Origin and Objects*. 1847. Reprint. Freeport, N.Y.: Books for Libraries Press, 1971. 142 p.

16-178. PRICE, GLENN W. *Origins of the War with Mexico: The Polk-Stockton Intrigue*. Austin: University of Texas Press, 1967. 189 p.

16-179. SELBEY, JOHN. *The Eagle and the Serpent: The Spanish and American Invasions of Mexico, 1519 and 1846*. London: Hamish Hamilton, 1978. 163 p.

16-180. SMITH, JUSTIN H. "Polk and California." *Massachusetts Historical Society Proceedings* 50 (April 1917): 83–91.

16-181. STENBERG, RICHARD R. "Failure of Polk's Mexican War Intrigue of 1845." *Pacific Historical Review* 4 (March 1935): 39–68.

16-182. ULIBARRI, RICHARD ONOFRE. "American Interest in the Spanish-Mexican Southwest, 1803–1848." Ph.D. dissertation, University of Utah, 1963. 315 p. 64-03142.

The Mexican War

16-183. BAUER, K. JACK. *The Mexican War, 1846–1848*. New York: Macmillan, 1974. 454 p.

16-184. BILL, ALFRED HOYT. *Rehearsal for Conflict: The War with Mexico, 1846–1848*. 1947. Reprint. New York: Cooper Square, 1969. 342 p.

16-185. BISHOP, FARNHAM. *Our First War in Mexico*. New York: Charles Scribner's Sons, 1916. 225 p.

16-186. BOURNE, EDWARD G. "The Proposed Absorption of Mexico in 1847-48." In *Annual Report of the American Historical Association, 1899*, 1: 155–69. Washington, D.C.: Government Printing Office, 1900.

16-187. ———. "The United States and Mexico, 1847–1848." *American Historical Review* 5 (April 1906): 491–502.

16-188. BROOKS, N. C. *A Complete History of the Mexican War*. 1849. Reprint. Chicago: Rio Grande Press, 1965. 558 p.

16-189. CONNOR, SEYMOUR V., AND FAULK, ODIE B. *North America Divided: The Mexican War, 1846–1848*. New York: Oxford University Press, 1971. 300 p.

16-190. DEFOUR, CHARLES L. *The Mexican War: A Compact History, 1846–1848*. New York: Hawthorn Books, 1968. 304 p.

16-191. HENRY, ROBERT SELPH. *The Story of the Mexican War*. New York: Frederick Unger, 1950. 424 p.

16-192. JENKINS, JOHN S. *History of the War between the United States and Mexico from the Commencement of Hostilities to the Ratification of the Peace Treaty*. Auburn, N.Y.: Derby, Miller, 1849. 514 p.

16-193. MARTINEZ, ORLANDO. *The Great Landgrab: The Mexican-American War, 1846–1848*. London: Quartet Books, 1975. 166 p.
   A recent interpretation of the war from a Mexican viewpoint.

16-194. RIPLEY, ROSWELL SABINE. *The War with Mexico*. 2 vols. 1849. Reprint. New York: Burt Franklin, 1970.

16-195. SINGLETARY, OTIS A. *The Mexican War*. Chicago: University of Chicago Press, 1960. 181 p.

16-196. SMITH, JUSTIN H. *The War with Mexico*. 2 vols. New York: Macmillan, 1919.

16-197. WEEMS, JOHN EDWARD. *To Conquer a Peace: The War between the United States and Mexico*. Garden City, N.Y.: Doubleday, 1974. 500 p .

16-198. YOUNG, BOB, AND YOUNG, JAN. *Mr. Polk's War: The Conflict No One Wanted*. New York: Hawthorn Books, 1968. 176 p.

Domestic Opposition to the Mexican War

16-199. LOWELL, JAMES RUSSELL. *The Bigelow Papers.* 1848. Reprint. Edited by Thomas Wortham. DeKalb: Northern Illinois University Press, 1977. 316 p.

16-200. McENIRY, SISTER BLANCHE MARIE. "American Catholics in the War with Mexico." Ph.D. dissertation, Catholic University of America, 1937. 74 p.

16-201. MERK, FREDERICK. "Dissent in the Mexican War." In *Dissent in Three American Wars,* by Samuel Eliot Morison, Frederick Merk, and Frank Freidel, pp. 35–63. Cambridge, Mass.: Harvard University Press, 1970.

16-202. PARKER, THEODORE. *Sermons on War.* 1863. Reprint. Edited by Frances P. Cobbe. New York: Garland, 1973. 76 p.

16-203. SCHROEDER, JOHN H. *Mr. Polk's War: American Opposition and Dissent, 1846–1848.* Madison: University of Wisconsin Press, 1973. 184 p.

16-204. ———. "To Give 'Aid and Comfort': American Opposition to the Mexican War, 1846–1848." Ph.D. dissertation, University of Virginia, 1971. 297 p. 72-07210.

The Treaty of Guadalupe Hidalgo

16-205. BRENT, ROBERT A. "Nicholas P. Trist and the Treaty of Guadalupe Hidalgo." *Southwestern Historical Quarterly* 57 (April 1954): 454–74.

16-206. CHAMBERLAIN, EUGENE KEITH. "Nicholas Trist and Baja California." *Pacific Historical Review* 32 (February 1963): 49–63.

16-207. FARNHAM, THOMAS J. "Nicholas Trist and James Freaner and the Mission to Mexico." *Arizona and the West* 11 (Autumn 1969): 247–60.

16-208. GRAEBNER, NORMAN A. "Party Politics and the Trist Mission." *Journal of Southern History* 19 (May 1953): 137–56.

16-209. HAMMOND, GEORGE P., ED. *The Treaty of Guadalupe Hidalgo, February 2, 1848.* Berkeley, Calif.: Friends of the Bancroft Library, 1949. 79 p.

16-210. JOHNSON, KENNETH M. "Baja California and the Treaty of Guadalupe Hidalgo." *Journal of the West* 11 (April 1972): 328–47.

16-211. LOFGREN, CHARLES A. "Force and Diplomacy, 1846–1848: The View from Washington." *Military Affairs* 31 (Summer 1967): 57–64.

16-212. NELSON, ANNA KASTEN. "Mission to Mexico: Moses Y. Beach, Secret Agent." *New-York Historical Society Quarterly* 59 (July 1975): 226–45.

16-213. ———. "Secret Agents and Security Leaks: President Polk and the Mexican War." *Journalism Quarterly* 52 (Spring 1975): 9–14.

16-214. ———. "The Secret Diplomacy of James K. Polk during the Mexican War, 1846–1847." Ph.D. dissertation, George Washington University, 1972. 317 p. 73-04017.

16-215. NORTRUP, JACK. "Nicholas Trist's Mission to Mexico: A Reinterpretation." *Southwestern Historical Quarterly* 71 (January 1968): 321–46.

16-216. PITCHFORD, LOUIS CLEVELAND, JR. "The Diplomatic Representatives from the United States to Mexico from 1836 to 1848." Ph.D. dissertation, University of Colorado, 1965. 485 p. 66-03274.

16-217. REEVES, JESSE S. "The Treaty of Guadalupe Hidalgo." *American Historical Review* 10 (January 1905): 309–24.

16-218. SEARS, LOUIS MARTIN. "Nicholas P. Trist: A Diplomat with Ideals." *Mississippi Valley Historical Review* 11 (June 1924): 85–98.

Polk and the Slavery Issue

See also Harmon (9-248).

16-219. FONER, ERIC. "The Wilmot Proviso Revisited." *Journal of American History* 56 (September 1969): 262–79.

16-220. MORRISON, CHAPLAIN W. *Democratic Politics and Sectionalism: The Wilmot Proviso Controversy.* Chapel Hill: University of North Carolina Press, 1967. 244 p.

16-221. RAYBACK, JOSEPH G. *Free Soil: The Election of 1848.* Lexington: University Press of Kentucky, 1970. 326 p.

16-222. SMITH, ELBERT B. *The Death of Slavery: The United States, 1837–1865.* Chicago: University of Chicago Press, 1967. 225 p.

16-223. WALTON, BRIAN G. "James K. Polk and the Democratic Party in the Aftermath of the Wilmot Proviso." Ph.D. dissertation, Vanderbilt University, 1968. 406 p. 68-18001.

Evaluations of Polk's Presidency

See also Binkley (9-225) and McCoy (16-34).

16-224. BAILEY, THOMAS A. *Presidential Greatness: The Image and the Man from George Washington to the Present.* New York: Appleton-Century, 1966. 368 p.

16-225. BOWERS, CLAUDE G. *Making Democracy a Reality: Jefferson, Jackson, and Polk.* Memphis: Memphis State College Press, 1954. 170 p.

16-226. CHASE, LUCIEN B. "History of the Polk Administration." *Southern Quarterly Review* 19 (January 1851): 1–51.

16-227. FERSH, SEYMOUR H. "An Historical Analysis of the Changing Function of the Presidential 'State of the Union' Message from 1790 to 1955." Ph.D. dissertation, New York University, 1955. 405 p. 00-13606.

16-228. GRAEBNER, NORMAN A. "James K. Polk: A Study in Federal Patronage." *Mississippi Valley Historical Review* 38 (March 1952): 613–32.

16-229. ———. "James Polk." In *America's Eleven Greatest Presidents,* edited by Morton Borden, pp. 108–33. Chicago: Rand McNally, 1971.

16-230. LEARNED, HENRY BARRETT. "Cabinet Meetings under President Polk." In *Annual Report of the American Historical Society, 1914,* 1:231–42.

Washington, D.C.: Government Printing Office, 1916.

16-231. ———. "The Sequence of Appointments to Polk's Original Cabinet." *American Historical Review* 30 (October 1924): 77–83.

16-232. MITCHELL, ROBERT STEWART. "Four Legends about President Polk." *Proceedings of the American Antiquarian Society* 45 (October 1935): 267–87.

16-233. PLETCHER, DAVID M. "James K. Polk and the Rewards of Rashness." In *Makers of American Diplomacy: From Benjamin Franklin to Henry Kissinger,* edited by Frank J. Merli and Theodore A. Wilson, pp. 165–94. New York: Charles Scribner's Sons, 1974.

16-234. SCHLESINGER, ARTHUR M. *Paths to the Present.* 1949. Reprint. Boston: Houghton Mifflin, 1964. 293 p.

16-235. SCHOULER, JAMES. "President Polk's Administration." *Atlantic Monthly* 76 (September 1895): 371–87.

MISCELLANEOUS

See also Ellet (9-252).

16-236. ARMISTEAD, GEORGE H. "The Void Provision of a President's Will." *Tennessee Historical Quarterly* 15 (June 1956): 136–40.

Contains an analysis of Polk's will.

16-237. NELSON, ANSON, AND NELSON, FANNY. *Memorials of Sarah Childress Polk.* 1892. Reprint. Spartanburg, S.C.: Reprint, 1974. 284 p.

An account of Mrs. Polk's years as first lady.

16-238. POLK, SARAH C. "Letters of Mrs. James K. Polk to Her Husband." Edited by Sarah Agnes Wallace. *Tennessee Historical Quarterly* 11 (June–September 1952): 180–91, 282–88.

17. Robert Mercer Taliaferro Hunter
(1809–1887)
(Speaker, Twenty-sixth Congress)

Robert M. T. Hunter, who gained fame as a lawyer, planter, politician, and statesman, was born on April 21, 1809, in Essex County, Virginia. His father was a prominent planter, and his mother was from the locally influential Garnett family. Hunter was a serious, even grave, student particularly interested in politics and finance. He entered the University of Virginia's first class and graduated in July 1828. After studying law under Judge Henry St. George Tucker, Hunter was admitted to the bar in 1830.

In the political uncertainty of the 1830s, Hunter gradually moved into the camp of the states' rights Democrats. He was elected as an independent to the Virginia legislature and served there from 1834 to 1837. He was subsequently elected to Congress as a Whig in 1837, but he nevertheless supported most of Van Buren's Democratic proposals. Following his election to the speakership of the Twenty-sixth Congress (1839–41), Hunter embraced John C. Calhoun's states' rights philosophy and left the Whig party. Hunter's defection to the Democratic party ensured his defeat in the next election for the speakership.

After his failure to be reelected to Congress in 1843, Hunter worked to secure the Democratic presidential nomination for Calhoun in 1844. A campaign biography of the South Carolina senator appeared in 1843 and was attributed to Hunter; it was, however, most likely written by Calhoun himself. Although his efforts on Calhoun's behalf were futile, he did redirect the Virginia Democratic party along the lines of Calhoun's philosophy, an accomplishment that contributed to Hunter's election to Congress in 1845.

In 1847 Hunter was elected to the United States Senate. Because of his proslavery convictions, he advocated secession as early as 1850, but at other times he hoped for accommodation with the North. Hunter's conciliatory attitude made him a possible presidential candidate in 1860. Only after the Democratic party had irrevocably split into Northern and Southern wings did he throw his support to John Breckinridge, the Southern candidate. As one of the Senate committee of thirteen appointed to consider Southern grievances, Hunter urged conciliation and compromise following Lincoln's election. When compromise seemed hopeless, he withdrew from the Senate one month before Virginia seceded in 1861.

Hunter served the Confederacy as secretary of state from July 25, 1861, to February 18, 1862. He then sat in the Confederate Senate until the end of the war in 1865. As part of the Confederate delegation, he attended the Hampton Roads conference of February 3, 1865, in a futile attempt to negotiate a peace settlement short of unconditional surrender. Hunter surrendered after the fall of the Confederate government and was imprisoned for several months.

After the Civil War, Hunter devoted himself to rebuilding his personal finances and those of his home state. As treasurer of Virginia from 1874 to 1880, he argued that Virginia was honor-bound to pay its war debts without any assistance from West Virginia, which had been part of the state when the debts were contracted. In 1885 President Cleveland appointed Hunter collector of the port of Tappahannock, a position he held at his death on July 18, 1887.

MANUSCRIPT COLLECTIONS

Maine Historical Society Library, Portland, Me.

Robert M. T. Hunter Papers, 1834–71.
1 box.
NUCMC 76-1054.

University of Virginia Library, Charlottesville, Va.

Robert M. T. Hunter Papers, 1826–60.
Ca. 60 items.
NUCMC 67-2165.
Hunter-Garnett Family Papers, 1704–1940.
24 ft.
NUCMC 59-124.

Virginia Historical Society, Richmond, Va.

William Garnett Chisholm Collection, 1749–1955 (includes copies of Hunter letters).
NUCMC 61-2761.

Virginia State Library, Archives Division, Richmond, Va.

Robert M. T. Hunter Correspondence, 1820–76.
875 items.
NUCMC 62-886.

BOOKS, ARTICLES, AND DISSERTATIONS

WORKS BY ROBERT M. T. HUNTER

Manuscript Guide

17-1. Virginia. University. Library. *Guide to the Microfilm Edition of the Papers of R. M. T. Hunter, 1817–1887.* Edited by James L. Anderson and Mary F. Crouch. Charlottesville: University of Virginia Library, 1967. 44 p.

Published Correspondence

See also Johnson (15-115).

17-2. Boucher, Chauncey S., and Brooks, Robert P., eds. "Correspondence Addressed to John C. Calhoun, 1837–1849." In *Annual Report of the American Historical Association, 1929,* 1: 125–533. Washington, D.C.: Government Printing Office, 1930.
Includes two Hunter letters of 1843.

17-3. Calhoun, John C. "Correspondence of John C. Calhoun." Edited by J. Franklin Jameson. In *Annual Report of the American Historical Association, 1899,* 2:11–789. Washington, D.C.: Government Printing Office, 1900.

17-4. "The Failure of the Hampton Conference: With Unpublished Letters from Jefferson Davis and R. M. T. Hunter." *Century* 52 (July 1896): 476–78.

Includes a Hunter letter of 1870 discussing the Hampton Roads conference.
The following three Hunter items are listed chronologically by year of publication.

17-5. Hunter, Robert M. T. "Instructions to Hon. James M. Mason: Letter from Hon. R. M. T. Hunter, Secretary of State, C.S.A." *Southern Historical Society Papers* 7 (1879): 231–41.

17-6. ———. "Letter of Instructions to Hon. John Slidell." *Southern Historical Society Papers* 13 (1885): 455–66.

17-7. ———. *Correspondence of Robert M. T. Hunter, 1826–1876.* Edited by Charles H. Ambler. 1918. Reprint. New York: Da Capo Press, 1971. 383 p.
Consists primarily of letters addressed to Hunter.

17-8. Mason, Virginia. *The Public Life and Diplomatic Correspondence of James M. Mason.* Washington, D.C.: Neale Publishing, 1906. 603 p.

17-9. "Senator R. M. T. Hunter of Va." *United States Magazine and Democratic Review* 29 (July 1851): 77–81.
Comprises letters to and from Hunter.

17-10. Simms, Henry H. "Two Letters of 1865." *Tyler's Quarterly Historical and Genealogical Magazine* 24 (April 1943): 249–52.

Includes a Hunter letter to William Henry Seward on Reconstruction policy.

Published Speeches

The following speeches are listed chronologically by year of publication and alphabetically thereunder.

17-11. HUNTER, ROBERT M. T. *Remarks of Mr. Robert M. T. Hunter, of Virginia, on the Bill Imposing Additional Duties, as Repositories in Certain Cases, on Public Officers.* N.p., 1837. 8 p.

17-12. ————. *Speech of Mr. R. M. T. Hunter . . . on the Ten Regiment Bill.* Washington, D.C.: Towers, 1848. 15 p.
An 1848 Senate speech on the Mexican War.

17-13. ————. *Speech of R. M. T. Hunter . . . on the Resolution of Notice to Great Britain to Abrogate the Convention of Joint Occupancy to the Oregon Territory.* N.p., 1848. 8 p.
House speech recommending compromise of the Oregon question.

17-14. ————. *Speech of Hon. R. M. T. Hunter . . . on Suspending Our Diplomatic Relations with Austria.* Washington, D.C.: Congressional Globe Office, 1850. 7 p.

17-15. ————. *The Territorial Question.* Washington, D.C.: Congressional Globe Office, 1850. 15 p.
Senate speech on constitutional rights in the territories.

17-16. ————. *Speech of Hon. R. M. T. Hunter . . . against Increasing the Appropriation for the Collins Line of Steamers.* Washington, D.C.: Congressional Globe Office, 1852.

17-17. ————. *The Democratic Demonstration at Poughkeepsie: Speech of Hon. R. M. T. Hunter, of Virginia.* N.p., 1856. 14 p.
Speech on slavery and the territorial crisis.

17-18. ————. *Address Delivered before the Two Literary Societies of the Virginia Military Institute, July 3, 1857.* Richmond: MacFarlane and Fergusson, 1857. 59 p.

17-19. ————. *Hon. R. M. T. Hunter . . . on Invasion of States.* Washington, D.C.: Lemuel Towers, 1860. 16 p.
Senate speech defending slavery.

17-20. ————. *Speech of Hon. R. M. T. Hunter . . . on the Resolution Proposing to Retrocede the Forts, Dock-Yards, etc. to the States Applying for the Same.* Washington, D.C.: Lemuel Towers, 1861. 16 p.

Articles

The following articles are listed chronologically by year of publication and alphabetically thereunder.

17-21. HUNTER, ROBERT M. T. "Origin of the Late War." *Southern Historical Society Papers* 1 (1876): 2–13.
Hunter's explanation of the cause of the Civil War.

17-22. ————. "The Peace Commission of 1865." *Southern Historical Society Papers* 3 (1877): 168–76.
A personal account of the Hampton Roads conference of 1865.

17-23. ————. "The Peace Commission: Hon. R. M. T. Hunter's Reply to President Davis." *Southern Historical Society Papers* 4 (1877): 303–16.
Hunter's reply to Jefferson Davis's attack upon his article on the Hampton Roads conference (17-22).

17-24. ————. " 'The Republic of Republics.' " *Southern Historical Society Papers* 13 (1885): 342–55.
A review condemning the North, particularly Massachusetts.

BIOGRAPHIES, BIOGRAPHICAL SKETCHES, AND GENEALOGY

Biographies

17-25. FISHER, JOHN EUGENE. "Statesman of the Lost Cause: R. M. T. Hunter and the Sectional Controversy, 1847–1887." Ph.D. dissertation, University of Virginia, 1968. 297 p. 69-04026.
A scholarly study of Hunter's life and career with an emphasis on his post-speakership activities.

17-26. HUNTER, MARTHA T. *A Memoir of Robert M. T. Hunter.* Washington D.C.: Neale Publishing, 1903. 166 p.

A laudatory and uncritical account by Hunter's daughter.

17-27. SIMMS, HENRY H. *Life of Robert M. T. Hunter: A Study in Sectionalism and Secession.* Richmond, Va.: William Byrd Press, 1935. 234 p.

The standard biography of Hunter, with most attention accorded to his prewar activities.

Biographical Sketches and Genealogy

See also Bartlett (15-20) and Savage (15-29).

17-28. ANDERSON, JAMES L. "Robert Mercer Taliaferro Hunter." *Virginia Cavalcade* 18 (Autumn 1968): 9–13.

An informative, popularly written sketch.

17-29. CHISHOLM, WILLIAM GARNETT. "The Garnetts of Essex County and Their Homes." *Virginia Magazine of History and Biography* 42 (January–October 1934): 72–85, 166–80, 256–67, 358–66.

Includes genealogical information on Hunter's family.

17-30. GARNETT, T. S. "Address of Hon. T. S. Garnett upon Presenting the Portrait of Hon. R. M. T. Hunter, to the Circuit Court of Essex County, at Tappahanock, Va., June 20, 1898." *Southern Historical Society Papers* 27 (1899): 151–55.

17-31. HENRY, WILLIAM WIRT, AND SPOFFARD, AINSWORTH R. *Eminent and Representative Men of Virginia and the District of Columbia of the Nineteenth Century.* Madison, Wis.: Brant and Fuller, 1893. 600 p.

17-32. JONES, CHARLES C., JR. *Hon. R. M. T. Hunter: Post-Bellum Mortality among Confederates: Address before the Confederate Survivors Association.* Atlanta: Chronicle Publishing, 1887. 9 p.

17-33. TYLER, LYON G., ED. *Encyclopedia of Virginia Biography.* Vol. 3. New York: Lewis Historical Publishing, 1915.

17-34. WASHINGTON, COL. L. Q. "Hon. R. M. T. Hunter." *Southern Historical Society Papers* 25 (1897): 193–205.

HUNTER AND THE UNIVERSITY OF VIRGINIA

17-35. BRUCE, PHILIP ALEXANDER. *History of the University of Virginia, 1819–1919.* Vols. 1, 3, 4, 5. New York: Macmillan, 1920–22.

HUNTER'S CONGRESSIONAL CAREER

17-36. FISHER, JOHN E. "The Dilemma of a States' Rights Whig: The Congressional Career of R. M. T. Hunter, 1837–1841." *Virginia Magazine of History and Biography* 81 (October 1973): 387–404.

17-37. SHIELDS, JOHANNA N. "The Making of American Congressional Mavericks: A Contrasting of the Cultural Attitudes of Mavericks and Conformists in the United States House of Representatives, 1836–1860." Ph.D. dissertation, University of Alabama, 1973. 344 p. 73-19560.

17-38. SILBEY, JOEL H. "The Southern National Democrats, 1845–1861." *Mid-America* 47 (July 1965): 176–90.

HUNTER'S POLITICAL ASSOCIATES

The following works on notable political figures of the ante-bellum and Civil War periods help explain Hunter's career. *See also* Adams (7-22), Tyler (14-30), Kirwan (15-66), Milton (15-68), and Curtis (16-74).

17-39. BANCROFT, FREDERIC. *The Life of William H. Seward.* 2 vols. 1900. Reprint. Gloucester, Mass.: Peter Smith, 1967.

17-40. BEVERIDGE, ALBERT J. *Abraham Lincoln, 1809–1858.* 2 vols. Boston: Houghton Mifflin, 1928.

17-41. BONEY, F. N. *John Letcher of Virginia: The Story of Virginia's Civil War Governor.* University: University of Alabama Press, 1966. 319 p.

17-42. CRAVEN, AVERY O. *Edmund Ruffin, Southerner: A Study in Secession.* New York: D. Appleton, 1932. 283 p.

17-43. DAVIS, WILLIAM C. *Breckenridge: Statesman, Soldier, Symbol.* Baton Rouge: Louisiana State University Press, 1974. 687 p.

17-44. DODD, WILLIAM E. *Jefferson Davis*. 1907. Reprint. New York: Russell and Russell, 1966. 396 p.

17-45. ECKENRODE, HAMILTON J. *Jefferson Davis: President of the South*. 1923. Reprint. Freeport, N.Y.: Books for Libraries Press, 1971. 371 p.

17-46. FLOWER, FRANK A. *Edwin McMasters Stanton: The Autocrat of Rebellion, Emancipation, and Reconstruction*. 1905. Reprint. New York: AMS Press, 1973. 425 p.

17-47. FREEMAN, DOUGLAS SOUTHALL. *R. E. Lee: A Biography*. 4 vols. New York: Charles Scribner's Sons, 1935.

17-48. GOODE, JOHN. *Recollections of a Lifetime*. New York: Neale Publishing, 1906. 266 p.

17-49. HENDRICK, BURTON J. *Statesmen of the Lost Cause: Jefferson Davis and His Cabinet*. Boston: Little, Brown, 1939. 452 p.

17-50. HUNT, GAILLARD. *John C. Calhoun*. Philadelphia: George W. Jacobs, 1907. 335 p.

17-51. McELROY, ROBERT M. *Jefferson Davis: The Unreal and the Real*. 2 vols. New York: Harper and Brothers, 1937.

17-52. MEAD, ROBERT D. *Judah P. Benjamin: Confederate Statesman*. New York: Oxford University Press, 1943. 432 p.

17-53. PARRISH, WILLIAM E. *David Rice Atchison of Missouri: Border Politician*. Columbia: University of Missouri Press, 1961. 271 p.

17-54. PATRICK, REMBERT W. *Jefferson Davis and His Cabinet*. Baton Rouge: Louisiana State University Press, 1944. 401 p.

17-55. PIERCE, EDWARD L. *Memoir and Letters of Charles Sumner*. 4 vols. 1877. Reprint. New York: Arno Press, 1969.

17-56. RUFFIN, EDMUND. *The Diary of Edmund Ruffin*. Edited by William K. Scarborough. 2 vols. Baton Rouge: Louisiana State University Press, 1972.

17-57. SIMPSON, CRAIG MICHAEL. "Henry A. Wise in Antebellum Politics, 1850–1861." Ph.D. dissertation, Stanford University, 1973. 344 p. 73-14981.

17-58. STEPHENS, ALEXANDER H. *Recollections of Alexander H. Stephens*. Edited by Myrta Lockett Avery. 1910. Reprint. New York: Da Capo Press, 1971. 572 p.

17-59. STRODE, HUDSON. *Jefferson Davis: Confederate President*. 3 vols. New York: Harcourt, Brace, 1955–64.

HUNTER AND THE 1843 CALHOUN BIOGRAPHY

Hunter's authorship of the 1843 *Life of John C. Calhoun* (17-62) has been called into question. The works cited below attribute authorship to Calhoun himself. *See also* Hunt (17-50).

17-60. ANDERSON, JAMES L., AND HEMPHILL, W. EDWIN. "The 1843 Biography of John C. Calhoun: Was R. M. T. Hunter Its Author?" *Journal of Southern History* 38 (August 1972): 469–73.

17-61. CAPERS, GERALD M. *John C. Calhoun, Opportunist: A Reappraisal*. Gainesville: University of Florida Press, 1960. 275 p.

17-62. *Life of John C. Calhoun: Presenting a Condensed History of Political Events from 1811 to 1843*. New York: Harper and Brothers, 1843. 544 p.

17-63. RHETT, ROBERT BARNWELL. "Robert Barnwell Rhett on the Biography of Calhoun, 1854." Edited by Gaillard Hunt. *American Historical Review* 13 (January 1908): 310–12.

A Rhett letter credits Hunter with only a very brief contribution to the Calhoun biography.

HUNTER AND THE SECESSION CRISIS

17-64. AMBLER, CHARLES H. "The Cleavage between Eastern and Western Virginia." *American Historical Review* 15 (July 1910): 762–80.

17-65. ———. *Sectionalism in Virginia from 1776 to 1861*. 1910. Reprint. New York: Russell and Russell, 1964. 366 p.

17-66. ARNOLD, CARROLL C. "The Senate Committee of Thirteen, December 6–31, 1861." In

Anti-Slavery and Disunion, 1858–1861, edited by Jeffrey J. Auer, pp. 300–310. 1963. Reprint. Gloucester, Mass.: Peter Smith, 1968.

17-67. AUCHAMPAUGH, PHILIP GERALD. *James Buchanan and His Cabinet on the Eve of Secession.* Lancaster, Pa.: Lancaster Press, 1921. 42 p.

17-68. CROW, JEFFREY J. "R. M. T. Hunter and the Secession Crisis, 1860–1861: A Southern Plan for Reconstruction." *West Virginia History* 34 (April 1973): 374–90.

17-69. MONTEIRO, MARGARET KEAN. "The Presidential Election of 1860 in Virginia." *Richmond College Historical Papers* 1 (June 1916): 222–58.

17-70. SHANKS, HENRY T. *The Secession Movement in Virginia, 1847–1861.* 1934. Reprint. New York: AMS Press, 1971. 296 p.

HUNTER AND THE CONFEDERACY

The following works cover Hunter's service to the Confederacy first as secretary of state and then as senator.

17-71. CALLAHAN, JAMES MORTON. *The Diplomatic History of the Southern Confederacy.* 1901. Reprint. New York: Greenwood Press, 1968. 304 p.

The essential work for study of Hunter's service as secretary of state for the Confederacy.

17-72. CHESTNUT, MARY BOYKIN. *A Diary from Dixie.* Edited by Ben Ames Williams. Boston: Houghton Mifflin, 1949. 572 p.

17-73. CONFEDERATE STATES OF AMERICA. CONGRESS. *Journal of the Provisional Congress of the Confederate States of America.* 7 vols. Washington, D.C.: Government Printing Office, 1904.

17-74. CONFEDERATE STATES OF AMERICA. PRESIDENT. *The Messages and Papers of Jefferson Davis and the Confederacy.* Edited by James D. Richardson. 2 vols. 1905. Reprint. New York: Chelsea House, 1966.

17-75. FREEMAN, DOUGLAS SOUTHALL, AND VANDIVER, FRANK E., EDS. *Proceedings of the First Confederate Congress: Sessions One to Four.* Southern Historical Society Papers, vols. 44–50. Richmond: Virginia Historical Society, 1923–53.

17-76. JONES, J. B. *A Rebel War Clerk's Diary at the Confederate States Capital.* 2 vols. Philadelphia: J. B. Lippincott, 1866.

17-77. KEAN, ROBERT GARLICK HILL. *Inside the Confederate Government: The Diary of Robert Garlick Hill Kean.* Edited by Edward Younger. New York: Oxford University Press, 1957. 241 p.

17-78. OWSLEY, FRANK LAWRENCE. *King Cotton Diplomacy: Foreign Relations of the Confederate States of America.* 2d ed., rev. Edited by Harriet Chappell Owsley. Chicago: University of Chicago Press, 1959. 614 p.

The standard work on Confederate diplomacy.

17-79. *The Rebellion Record: A Diary of American Events, with Documents, Narratives, Illustrative Incidents, Poetry, etc.* Edited by Frank Moore. 11 vols. 1864. Reprinted. New York: Arno Press, 1977.

17-80. REID, WILLIAM G. "Confederate Opponents of Arming the Slaves, 1861–1865." *Journal of Mississippi History* 22 (October 1960): 249–72.

17-81. THOMAS, EMORY M. *The Confederate Nation, 1861–1865.* New York: Harper and Row, 1979. 384 p.

17-82. YEARNS, WILFRED B. "The Peace Movement in the Confederate Congress." *Georgia Historical Quarterly* 41 (March 1957): 1–18.

HUNTER AND THE HAMPTON ROADS CONFERENCE

See also Hunter (17-22 and 17-23).

17-83. CAMPBELL, JOHN A. "The Hampton Roads Conference." *Transactions of the Southern Historical Society* 1 (January/December 1874): 187–94.

17-84. CONNOR, HENRY G. *John Archibald Campbell: Associate Justice of the United States Supreme Court, 1853–1861.* Boston: Houghton Mifflin, 1920. 310 p.

17-85. KIRKLAND, EDWARD C. *The Peacemakers of 1864.* 1927. Reprint. New York: AMS Press, 1969. 279 p.

HUNTER AND RECONSTRUCTION

17-86. MADDEX, JACK P., JR. *The Virginia Conservatives, 1867–1879*. Chapel Hill: University of North Carolina Press, 1970. 328 p.

17-87. PERMAN, MICHAEL. *Reunion without Compromise: The South and Reconstruction, 1865–1868.*

Cambridge, Mass.: Harvard University Press, 1973. 376 p.

17-88. SQUIRES, WILLIAM H. T. *Unleashed at Long Last: Reconstruction in Virginia, April 9, 1865–January 26, 1870*. 1939. Reprint. New York: Negro Universities Press, 1970. 486 p.

18. John White
(1805–1845)
(Speaker, Twenty-seventh Congress)

John White has remained an obscure figure in American history in spite of his accomplishments as a prominent lawyer, Whig politician, five-term congressman, and Speaker of the House in the Twenty-seventh Congress. He was well equipped by background and training for political success. The White family, into which he was born on February 14, 1805, was one of the leading families in Kentucky and Tennessee. His father was a wealthy and influential entrepreneur, and one of his kinsmen was Hugh Lawson White, a Tennessee senator and independent presidential candidate in 1840. White was educated at Greenville College in Tennessee. He later studied law under Governor William Owsley and was admitted to the bar in Richmond, Kentucky, in 1823.

By all accounts, White was a forceful and persuasive lawyer. He came under the influence of Henry Clay, entered the Whig party, and won election to Congress in 1835. He was a capable but unremarkable congressman during the Twenty-fourth through the Twenty-eighth Congresses (1835–45). John Quincy Adams noted that though White was an "able debater, . . . his manner is so vehement and his articulation so rapid that it becomes altogether indistinct." He was chosen Speaker in 1841, however, because of his reputation as a skilled parliamentarian. His speakership was marred by President Tyler's desertion of the Whig party and the agitation over slavery and the annexation of Texas, but it was notable for two significant rules changes. One change was the 1841 adoption of the one-hour rule limiting floor debate. The other innovation was the Speaker's ruling that only a simple majority vote of the House was needed to approve a special resolution from the Rules Committee, a precedent that was seized in the 1880s to facilitate legislation and limit debate even further.

In 1845 White left Congress to accept an appointment to the bench in Kentucky. His death on September 22, 1845, was an apparent suicide; it followed the revelation that one of his final House speeches had been a plagiarized version of a speech given years earlier by Aaron Burr. The ignominy of White's death has seemingly ensured his relative anonymity.

MANUSCRIPT COLLECTIONS

There is no known collection of John White's manuscripts. A thorough survey of NUCMC and finding aids for major manuscript repositories has located only three White letters. Two are in the James K. Polk Papers in the Library of Congress Manuscript Division, and one is in the Leverett Saltonstall Papers in the Massachusetts Historical Society in Boston. Though White was a Kentuckian, the Kentucky Historical Society does not report any White documents or correspondence in its collections.

BOOKS

WORKS BY JOHN WHITE

The following items are listed chronologically by year of publication.

18-1. WHITE, JOHN. *Speech of Mr. White, of Kentucky, Delivered in Committee of the Whole on the State of the Union, in Opposition to the Sub-Treasury Bill.* Washington, D.C.: Gideon's Office, 1840. 48 p.

House speech of June 5, 1840.

18-2. ———. *Speech of Hon. John White, of Kentucky, in Defense of Mr. Clay, upon the Charge of "Bargain and Sale."* Washington, D.C.: Gideon's Office, 1844. 8 p.

House speech of April 23, 1844.

BIOGRAPHICAL SOURCES

John White has been the subject of little research. The few references to him are slender and unrevealing. The best biographical sketch is found in Levin (18-8). *See also* Adams (7-22), Poage (9-96), Bemis (12-8), Wiltse (12-13), Barnes (15-60), and Falkner (16-78).

18-3. *Biographical Encyclopedia of Kentucky of the Dead and Living Men of the Nineteenth Century.* Cincinnati: J. M. Armstrong, 1878. 792 p.

Includes a brief statement on the life and accomplishments of John White.

18-4. CLIFT, GARRETT GLENN. *Kentucky Obituaries, 1787–1854.* Baltimore: Genealogical Publishing, 1977. 254 p.

Contains newspaper notices of White's suicide.

18-5. COLEMAN, J. WINSTON, JR., ED. *A Bibliography of Kentucky History.* Lexington: University of Kentucky Press, 1949. 516 p.

18-6. DORRIS, JONATHAN T., AND DORRIS, MAUD W. *Glimpses of Historic Madison County, Kentucky.* Nashville: Williams Printing, 1955. 334 p.

Features a short description of White's career and accomplishments, including the speakership.

18-7. KENTUCKY. General Assembly. House of Representatives. *Journal of the House of Representatives of the Commonwealth of Kentucky.* Frankfort: Albert G. Hodges, 1832.

White was a representative from Madison County in 1832.

18-8. LEVIN, H., ED. *The Lawyers and Lawmakers of Kentucky.* Chicago: Lewis Publishing, 1897. 777 p.

Contains a brief biographical sketch of White's life and career.

18-9. ROBERTSON, GEORGE. *Scrap Book on Law and Politics, Men and Times.* Lexington, Ky.: A. E. Elder, 1855. 404 p.

18-10. WILLIS, GEORGE LEE. *Kentucky Democracy: A History of the Party and Its Representatives Past and Present.* 3 vols. Louisville: Democratic Historical Society, 1935.

19. John Winston Jones
(1791–1848)
(Speaker, Twenty-eighth Congress)

The historical record reveals little about John W. Jones other than the barest outlines of his political career. He was born in Amelia County, Virginia, on November 22, 1791, the eldest son of Alexander and Mary Ann Jones. Following his father's death in 1802, he was tutored by an uncle. Jones later taught school for several years in Amelia and Lynchburg. He graduated from the law department of William and Mary College in 1813 and began practice that year in Chesterfield County, Virginia.

Jones advanced quickly in the legal profession. In 1818 he was appointed prosecuting attorney for the Fifth Judicial Circuit of Virginia, a position that he held for fifteen years. In 1829 he was chosen to attend the state constitutional convention. Although he had not sought election, he served faithfully if modestly. Jones was elected as a Democrat to the House of Representatives in 1834 and served in the Twenty-fourth through Twenty-eighth Congresses (1835–45). He was chairman of the Ways and Means Committee (1841–43) and Speaker of the House in the Twenty-eighth Congress (1843–45).

Since Jones's election to Congress was under contest in 1843, he scrupulously asked to be relieved of the responsibility for naming the committee on elections that would examine his own election. A Speaker *pro tempore* was chosen to appoint the committee, an action that established a precedent for choosing committees in which the Speaker might have a personal stake. Little has been written on Jones's speakership, although John Quincy Adams found it too partisan.

In 1844 Jones declined reelection to the House and returned to his law practice and agricultural pursuits. In a famous 1846 case, he won acquital on the grounds of self-defense for Thomas Ritchie, Jr., who had been charged with the murder of John Hampden Pleasants in a duel. Jones was a member of the Virginia House of Delegates from 1846 until an illness compelled him to resign in December 1847. He died soon thereafter, on January 29, 1848, at the age of fifty-six.

MANUSCRIPT COLLECTIONS

Virginia Historical Society, Richmond, Va.
John Winston Jones Account Book, 1815–23. 324 p.
There are two letters from Jones in the Nash Family Papers in the Virginia Historical Society in Richmond and two letters in the Martin Van Buren Papers in the Library of Congress Manuscript Division in Washington, D.C.

BOOKS AND ARTICLES

WORKS BY JOHN W. JONES

The following works are listed chronologically by year of publication.

*19-1. JONES, JOHN WINSTON. *Speech of Mr. Jones, of Virginia, on the Bill to Postpone the Fourth Installment of Deposite with the States.* Washington, D.C.: Blair and Rives, 1837. 15 p.
House speech of September 20, 1837.

*19-2. ———. *Speech of Mr. Jones, of Virginia, . . . on the Bill to Authorize the Issuing of Treasury Notes to Meet the Current Expenses of the Government.* N.p., 1838. 16 p.
House speech of May 16, 1838.

*19-3. ———. *Speech of Mr. Jones, of Virginia, on the Bill Making Appropriations for the Civil and Diplomatic Expenses of the Government for the Year 1840.* Washington, D.C.: Blair and Rives, 1840. 23 p.
House speech of April 11, 1840.

19-4. ———. *Speech of Mr. Jones, of Virginia, on the Loan Bill.* Washington, D.C.: Blair and Rives, 1841. 16 p.
House speech of July 12, 1841, in opposition to the measure.

BIOGRAPHICAL SOURCES

The following list suggests the paucity of information on John W. Jones. The best of the short biographical sketches is included in the *Dictionary of American Biography* (1-86). *See also* Jackson (7-3), Adams (7-22), Lambert (9-241), Grigsby (13-21), Wayland (14-15), Curtis (14-34), Falkner (16-78), Grant (16-117), Calhoun (17-3), Hunter (17-7), and Mason (17-8).

19-5. "A List of the Portraits and Pieces of Statuary in the Virginia State Library." *Bulletin of the Virginia State Library* 13 (January/April 1920): 1–29.

Contains a brief sketch of Jones.

19-6. DODSON, E. GRIFFITH. *Speakers and Clerks of the Virginia House of Delegates, 1776–1955*. Richmond, 1956. 152 p.

19-7. FOTHERGILL, AUGUSTA B. *Peter Jones and Richard Jones Genealogies*. Richmond, Va.: Old Dominion Press, 1924. 363 p.

Contains genealogical information on Jones's family.

19-8. HUGHES, THOMAS P., JR., AND STANDEFER, JEWEL B., EDS. *Petersburg, Virginia, Hustings Court: Marriage Bonds, Marriage Register, and Ministers' Returns, 1784-1854*. Memphis: Thomas P. Hughes, Jr., 1971. 178 p.

19-9. KENNEDY, MARY SELDEN. *Seldens of Virginia and Allied Families*. 2 vols. New York: Frank Allaben Genealogical, 1911.

Contains some genealogical information on Jones's family.

19-10. LUTZ, FRANCIS EARLE. *Chesterfield: An Old Virginia County*. Richmond: William Byrd Press, 1954. 385 p.

19-11. PULLIAM, DAVID L. *The Constitutional Conventions of Virginia*. Richmond: John T. West, 1901. 180 p.

19-12. VALENTINE, EDWARD PLEASANTS. *The Edward Pleasants Valentine Papers*. Edited by Clayton Torrence. Vol. 4. Baltimore: Genealogical Publishing, 1979.

Includes some information on deed exchanges involving Jones.

19-13. VIRGINIA. General Assembly. House of Delegates. *Journal of the House of Delegates of Virginia*. Richmond: Samuel Shepard, 1846–48.

19-14. WATSON, WALTER A. *Notes of Southside Virginia*. Edited by Mrs. Walter A. Watson. Baltimore: Genealogical Publishing, 1977. 346 p.

20. John Wesley Davis
(1799–1859)
(Speaker, Twenty-ninth Congress)

John W. Davis once wrote that his disposition was "changeful," an observation confirmed by his versatile career as a physician, Indian commissioner, judge, politician, diplomat, and territorial governor. His versatility was an expression not of genius but of a kind of comfortable mediocrity.

Davis was born on April 16, 1799, in New Holland, Pennsylvania, and grew up on a farm near Shippensburg. He was apprenticed first to a clockmaker and then to a storekeeper, but ill-health prevented him from pursuing either occupation. He then attended a Latin school in Shippensburg and studied medicine with a local physician. After studying at the University of Maryland in Baltimore (1819–21), Davis unsuccessfully attempted to establish a medical practice in Pennsylvania. His career fared better in Allegany County, Maryland, where he practiced medicine before moving on to Carlisle, Indiana, in 1823.

Although he was attracted to politics, Davis lost his first attempt at public office in 1828, when he ran for the Indiana state senate. He was elected probate judge of Sullivan County the following year and served on the bench for two uneventful years (1829–31). In 1831 he won election to the state house of representatives. In all, Davis was a member of the state legislature six times (1831–33, 1841–43, 1851–52, and 1857). After he was defeated for election to Congress in 1833, he accepted a presidential appointment to an Indian peace-treaty commission, but he succeeded only in impressing the Indian representatives as a pompous fool.

Davis was elected to the Twenty-fourth Congress (1835–37) as a Democrat. He also served in the Twenty-sixth, Twenty-eighth, and Twenty-ninth Congresses (1839–41, 1843–45, and 1845–47) and was elected Speaker of the Twenty-ninth Congress. Davis was an ardent Democrat who supported the Southern wing of the party in its defense of slavery. As Speaker, he supported President Polk's expansionist policy and the war with Mexico.

When Davis declined to run for reelection in 1847, Polk appointed him commissioner to China, a post he held from 1848 to 1850. He later presided over the 1852 Democratic national convention, which nominated Franklin Pierce. After Pierce's election, Davis was appointed governor of the Oregon Territory, a position he first declined but later accepted. His tenure in Oregon (1853–54) was difficult and unhappy. He returned to Indiana to serve two final terms in the state legislature. He died on August 22, 1859.

MANUSCRIPT COLLECTIONS

Oregon Historical Society, Portland, Ore.
  John W. Davis Collection.
  The only manuscript collection that bears Davis's name consists entirely of letters written to him while governor of the Oregon Territory.

There are also a few Davis letters in scattered collections at the Indiana State Library, the Indiana Historical Society, and the Oregon Historical Society.

BOOKS, ARTICLES, AND DISSERTATIONS

WORKS BY JOHN W. DAVIS

20-1. DAVIS, JOHN W. *Speech . . . June 27, 1840 on the Independent Treasury Bill*. New York: New Era, 1840. 7 p.

*20-2. ———. *Speech of Mr. Davis of Indiana, on an Appropriation for the Cumberland Road*. Washington, D.C., 1840. 7 p.

*20-3. ROBERTSON, NELLIE A., AND RIKER, DOROTHY, EDS. *The John Tipton Papers*. Indiana Historical Collections, vol. 25. Indianapolis: Indiana Historical Bureau, 1942. 184 p.
  Contains several Davis letters on Indiana politics.

BIOGRAPHICAL SKETCHES

20-4. BEDFORD, HOPE. "John Wesley Davis." M.A. thesis, Butler University, 1930. 45 p.

Though merely adequate, this is still the only substantial biographical treatment of Davis.

20-5. MONKS, LEANDER J. *Courts and Lawyers of Indiana*. 3 vols. Indianapolis: Federal Publications, 1916.

20-6. "Some Self-Made Indianans." *Indiana Magazine of History* 1 (1905): 153–55.

20-7. WOOLLEN, WILLIAM WESLEY. *Biographical and Historical Sketches of Early Indiana*. Indianapolis: Hammond, 1883. 568 p.

DAVIS AND INDIANA HISTORY AND POLITICS

20-8. BEELER, DALE. "The Election of 1852 in Indiana." *Indiana Magazine of History* 11 (December 1915): 301–23; 12 (March 1916): 34–52.

20-9. ELLIOTT, JOSEPH PETER. *A History of Evansville and Vanderburgh County, Indiana*. Evansville: Keller, 1897. 499 p.

20-10. ESAREY, LOGAN. *A History of Indiana from Its Exploration to 1850*. 2 vols. Indianapolis: B. F. Bowen, 1918.

20-11. *History of Greene and Sullivan Counties, Indiana*. 1884. Reprint. Evansville: Unigraphic, 1975. 881 p.

20-12. INDIANA. General Assembly. House of Representatives. *Journal of the House of Representatives of the State of Indiana*. Indianapolis: N. Bolton et al., 1831–57.

20-13. JENNINGS, JONATHAN. "Unedited Letters of Jonathan Jennings." With notes by Dorothy Riker. *Indiana Historical Society Publications* 10 (1932): 148–278.

20-14. KEMPER, GEN. W. H. *A Medical History of the State of Indiana*. Chicago: American Medical Association Press, 1911. 393 p.

20-15. LEONARD, ADAM. "Personal Politics in Indiana, 1816–1840; State Politics, 1828 to 1840." *Indiana Magazine of History* 19 (September 1923): 241–81.

20-16. MYERS, BURTON DORR. *Trustees and Officers of Indiana University, 1820–1850*. Bloomington: Indiana University Press, 1951. 537 p.

20-17. ROLL, CHARLES. *Indiana: One Hundred and Fifty Years of American Development*. 5 vols. Chicago: Lewis Publishing, 1931.

20-18. SMITH, OLIVER H. *Early Indiana Trials and Sketches*. Cincinnati: Moore, Wilstach, Keys, 1858. 646 p.

20-19. STUART, BENJAMIN F. "The Deportation of Menominee and His Tribe of the Pottawattomie Indians." *Indiana Magazine of History* 18 (September 1922): 255–65.

20-20. VAN BOLT, ROGER H. "Indiana in Political Transition, 1851–1853." *Indiana Magazine of History* 49 (June 1953): 131–60.

20-21. WOLFE, THOMAS J., ED. *A History of Sullivan County, Indiana*. 2 vols. New York: Lewis Publishing, 1909.

DAVIS'S POLITICAL CAREER

See also Falkner (16-78).

20-22. DEMOCRATIC PARTY. National Convention. Baltimore, 1852. *Proceedings of the Democratic National Convention Held at Baltimore, June 1852*. Washington, D.C.: Buell and Blanchard, 1852. 44 p.

20-23. GOING, CHARLES BUXTON. *David Wilmot, Free Soiler: A Biography of the Great Advocate of the Wilmot Proviso*. New York: D. Appleton, 1924. 787 p.

20-24. HODDER, FRANK H. "Genesis of the Kansas-Nebraska Act." *Wisconsin State Historical Society Proceedings*, October 1912, pp. 69–86.

20-25. TURPIE, DAVID H. *Sketches of My Own Times*. 1903. Reprint. New York: AMS Press, 1975. 387 p.

DAVIS AND CHINA

20-26. DAVIDS, JULES, ED. *American Diplomatic and Public Papers: The United States and China*. Ser. 1. 21 vols. Wilmington, Del.: Scholarly Resources, 1973.

Volumes 19–21 contain information on Davis.

20-27. DENNETT, TYLER. *Americans in Eastern Asia: A Critical Study of the Policy of the United States with Reference to China, Japan, and Korea in the 19th Century*. 1922. Reprint. New York: Barnes and Noble, 1941. 725 p.

Features a good account of Davis's activities in China.

20-28. FOSTER, JOHN W. *American Diplomacy in the Orient*. Boston: Houghton Mifflin, 1903. 498 p.

20-29. HARRINGTON, GORDON K. "The Relations between the United States and China, 1840–1860." Ph.D. dissertation, University of Chicago, 1960. 151 p.

20-30. SWISHER, EARL. *China's Management of the American Barbarians: A Study of Sino-American Relations, 1841–1861, with Documents*. New York: Octagon Books, 1972. 844 p.

20-31. TONG, TE-KONG. *United States Diplomacy in China, 1844–60*. Seattle: University of Washington Press, 1964. 332 p.

DAVIS AND THE OREGON TERRITORY

20-32. Bancroft, Hubert Howe. *The Works of Hubert Howe Bancroft.* Vols. 29 and 30. 1883–90. Reprint. New York: Arno Press and McGraw-Hill, 1960.

Volumes 29 and 30, Bancroft's *History of Oregon*, include a detailed account of Davis's tenure as territorial governor.

20-33. Carey, Charles, H. *A General History of Oregon prior to 1861.* 2 vols. Portland: Metropolitan Press, 1936.

20-34. Hendrickson, James E. *Joe Lane of Oregon: Machine Politics and the Sectional Crisis, 1849–1861.* New Haven: Yale University Press, 1967. 274 p.

20-35. Johansen, Dorothy O., and Gates, Charles M. *Empire of the Columbia: A History of the Pacific Northwest.* 2d ed. New York: Harper and Row, 1967. 654 p.

20-36. Lyman, Horace S. *History of Oregon: The Growth of an American State.* 4 vols. New York: North Pacific Publishing Society, 1903.

20-37. North Pacific History Company. *History of the Pacific Northwest: Oregon and Washington.* 2 vols. Portland, 1889.

20-38. Williams, George H. "Political History of Oregon, 1853–1865." *Quarterly of the Oregon Historical Society* 2 (March 1901): 1–35.

20-39. Woodward, Walter C. *The Rise and Early History of Political Parties in Oregon, 1843–1868.* Portland: J. K. Gill, 1913. 276 p.

21. Robert Charles Winthrop
(1809–1894)
(Speaker, Thirtieth Congress)

Robert C. Winthrop was born into one of Massachusetts' most distinguished families on May 12, 1809. He was a sixth-generation descendant of the first governor of Massachusetts, John Winthrop. His father was Lieutenant Governor Lindall Winthrop, a prominent Boston merchant and politician. Robert C. Winthrop was educated at private schools and attended Harvard University, where he excelled not only in academics but also in extracurricular social activities. At commencement in 1828 Winthrop delivered his first oration, "Public Station."

The Winthrops were a wealthy family with a long tradition of public service. It came as no surprise, therefore, that Robert C. Winthrop entered law and politics. He studied law in Daniel Webster's office and was admitted to the bar in 1831. The legal profession did not monopolize Winthrop's life; he found time to indulge in a full social life and to pursue his military interests as captain in the Boston light infantry, lieutenant of the ancient and honorable artillery, and aide-de-camp to three state governors.

In politics Winthrop was a Whig who followed the leadership of Henry Clay. He served from 1834 to 1840 in the Massachusetts legislature, where he demonstrated great oratorical powers in opposing Andrew Jackson's policies. In one speech he characterized the president's removal of the deposits as a "tyrannous design to set up his arbitrary and despotic will as the sole standard of government." Winthrop was elected to the Twenty-sixth Congress to fill a vacancy in 1840; he served until 1842, when he resigned to be with his dying wife. He was reelected in 1842 and served in the House until 1850.

Winthrop's speeches in Congress enhanced

his reputation as an orator and parliamentarian. In some of his more noted speeches he supported the right of petition over the gag rule, which automatically tabled all anti-slavery petitions; opposed the annexation of Texas and the Mexican War; and favored settlement of the Oregon crisis through negotiation. When the Thirtieth Congress convened in 1848, the Whigs had a small majority and selected Winthrop as Speaker of the House. His single term as Speaker was not an easy one; other Whigs accused him of being too mild in his opposition to slavery. Winthrop did oppose the extension of slavery, but he believed that the Constitution prevented any tampering with slavery where it existed. His stand on the issue contributed to his defeat for the speakership in 1849, when he lost to Howell Cobb on the sixty-third ballot.

Winthrop was appointed to fill the Senate seat vacated when Daniel Webster became President Fillmore's secretary of state in 1850. He served only a few months and was defeated for election to a full term by Charles Sumner. Winthrop was also an unsuccessful candidate for governor of Massachusetts on the Whig ticket in 1850. Thereafter, he devoted himself to literary and philanthropic endeavors.

In the following years Winthrop became a familiar sight at historic celebrations. He prepared and delivered eloquent speeches for the laying of the Washington monument cornerstone in 1848, the monument's completion in 1885, the 250th anniversary of the landing of the Pilgrims in 1870, and the centennials of the Boston Tea Party in 1873 and the Battle of Yorktown in 1881. For thirty years (1855–84) he was president of the Massachusetts Historical Society. He served as president of the Boston Provident Association and as chairman of the Poor of Boston. His most noteworthy philanthropic contribution came as president of the board of trustees of the Peabody Education Fund. Winthrop, who had suffered a severe attack of pneumonia several years earlier, died on November 16, 1894, after a long illness.

As a brilliant orator, a cultivated scholar, and a wealthy philanthropist, Winthrop approached politics with a sense of social obligation and corresponding expectations of success. Unfortunately, politics had changed; leadership and deference were no longer accorded merely on the basis of status or even in recognition of demonstrated virtue. Winthrop never adjusted to the new realities of politics, since he believed that personal recriminations and the lowered tone of politics were "unnatural and revolting." Although he was never a policy maker, he did strive to conserve the values of his ancestors through oratory and philanthropy.

MANUSCRIPT COLLECTIONS

American Antiquarian Society, Worcester, Mass.

Winthrop Letters, 1843–85.

1 folder, 17 items.

Massachusetts Historical Society, Boston, Mass.

Winthrop Family Papers, 1544–1963.

28 ft.

NUCMC 65-189.

Several collections at the Massachusetts Historical Society and the Library of Congress Manuscript Division contain numerous Winthrop letters. Most notable are the Edward Everett Papers in the Massachusetts Historical Society, which include over three hundred letters from Winthrop.

BOOKS, ARTICLES, AND DISSERTATIONS

WORKS BY ROBERT C. WINTHROP

Books

The following books are listed chronologically by year of publication.

21-1. WINTHROP, ROBERT C. *Addresses and Speeches on Various Occasions.* 4 vols. Boston: Little, Brown, 1852–86.

A compendium of Winthrop's public speeches.

21-2. ———. *Memoir of the Hon. Nathan Appleton, LL.D.* 1861. Reprint. New York: Greenwood Press, 1969. 79 p.

Includes laudatory remarks and a bibliography of Appleton's writings.

21-3. ———. *Life and Letters of John Winthrop: Governor of the Massachusetts-Bay Company at Their Emigration to New England, 1630.* 2 vols. Boston: Ticknor and Fields, 1864–67.

A detailed biography of Winthrop's ancestor, the first governor of the Massachusetts Bay colony.

21-4. ———. *Washington, Bowdoin, and Franklin: As Portrayed in Occasional Addresses.* Boston: Little, Brown, 1876. 186 p.

21-5. ———. *Some Account of the Early Generations of the Winthrop Family in Ireland.* Cambridge, Mass.: John Wilson and Son, 1883. 24 p.

An account of the Winthrop ancestry.

21-6. ———. *To George Washington.* (Boston): privately printed, (1889). 2 p.

An epic poem in praise of George Washington.

21-7. ———. *Reminiscences of Foreign Travel: A Fragment of Autobiography.* (Boston): privately printed, 1894. 104 p.

Articles

The following articles are listed chronologically by year of publication. *See also Proceedings of the Massachusetts Historical Society* (21-122).

21-8. WINTHROP, ROBERT C. "Personal Recollections of Baron Visconti." *Proceedings of the American Antiquarian Society* 1 (October 1880): 52–57.

Winthrop recounts his friendship with the Italian archaeologist who introduced him to Rome's antiquities.

21-9. ———. "Historic Moments: The Death of John Quincy Adams in the Capitol." *Scribner's Magazine* 13 (March 1893): 389–92.

Winthrop was Speaker when John Quincy Adams was fatally stricken in the Capitol.

21-10. ———. "Webster's Reply to Hayne, and His General Methods of Preparation." *Scribner's Magazine* 15 (January 1894): 118–28.

As a clerk in Webster's law office in 1830, Winthrop knew his mentor's informal approach to speech writing.

Published Letters

See also Coleman (9-82) and Phillips (22-14).

21-11. BUCHANAN, JAMES. *The Works of James Buchanan.* Compiled and edited by John Bassett Moore. 12 vols. Philadelphia: J. B. Lippincott, 1911.

21-12. EMERSON, RALPH WALDO. *The Letters of Ralph Waldo Emerson.* Edited by Ralph L. Rusk. 6 vols. New York: Columbia University Press, 1939.

21-13. FORD, WORTHINGTON C. "Sumner's Oration on the 'True Grandeur of Nations,' July 4, 1845." *Proceedings of the Massachusetts Historical Society* 50 (March 1917): 249–307.

A series of Sumner letters, including one from Winthrop dated July 9, 1845.

21-14. PRESCOTT, WILLIAM H. *The Correspondence of William Hickling Prescott, 1833–1847.* Edited by Roger Wolcott. 1925. Reprint. New York: Da Capo Press, 1970. 691 p.

Includes two 1847 letters from Winthrop to the historian Prescott.

21-15. STEINER, BERNARD C., ED. "Some Letters from Correspondence of James Alfred Pearce." *Maryland Historical Magazine* 16 (June 1921): 150–78.

Includes a Winthrop letter of 1855.

21-16. WINTHROP, ROBERT C. "Two Letters of Robert Charles Winthrop." Edited by Joseph A. Borome. *Mississippi Valley Historical Review* 38 (September 1951): 289–96.

Published Speeches

The following list, arranged chronologically by year of publication and alphabetically thereunder, provides a good representative sample of Winthrop's extensive oratory.

21-17. WINTHROP, ROBERT C. *An Address Delivered before the New England Society, in the City of New York,*

December 23, 1839. New York: Gould, Newman, and Saxton, 1840. 60 p.

A speech on the Pilgrim fathers.

21-18. ———. *Remarks of Mr. Winthrop . . . on the Distribution Bill*. Washington, D.C., 1841. 9 p.

House speech of July 2, 1841, on public lands.

21-19. ———. *Speech . . . the Exchequer Plan Ought Not to Be Adopted*. Washington, D.C., 1842. 8 p.

House speech of January 25, 1842.

21-20. ———. *Speech of Mr. Winthrop . . . on the Annexation of Texas*. Washington, D.C.: J. and G. S. Gideon, 1845. 16 p.

House speech of January 6, 1845, favoring the annexation of Texas.

21-21. ———. *An Address Delivered before the Boston Mercantile Library Association, on . . . October 15, 1845*. Boston: T. R. Marvin, 1845. 38 p.

A plea for morality in business.

21-22. ———. *Speech of Mr. Winthrop . . . on the Oregon Question*. Washington, D.C.: J. and G. S. Gideon, 1846. 14 p.

House speech of January 3, 1846, calling for arbitration of the Oregon dispute between the United States and Great Britain.

21-23. ———. *Speech of Mr. Winthrop . . . on the River and Harbor Bill*. Washington, D.C.: J. and G. S. Gideon, 1846. 16 p.

House speech of March 12, 1846.

21-24. ———. *Speech of Mr. Winthrop . . . on the Tariff*. Washington, D.C.: J. and G. S. Gideon, 1846. 20 p.

House speech of June 25, 1846.

21-25. ———. *Speech of Mr. Winthrop . . . on the Mexican War*. Washington, D.C.: J. and G. S. Gideon, 1847. 16 p.

House speech of January 8, 1847, opposing Polk's prosecution of the war.

21-26. ———. *An Address Delivered before the Maine Historical Society, at Bowdoin College*. Boston: Ticknor, Reed, and Fields, 1849. 68 p.

Speech of September 5, 1849, on the life and times of James Bowdoin.

21-27. ———. *Admission of California: Speech of Mr. Winthrop on the President's Message, Transmitting the Constitution of California*. Washington, D.C.: Gideon, 1850. 28 p.

House speech of May 8, 1850, in opposition to the Compromise of 1850.

21-28. ———. *Transactions of the Society of Middlesex Husbandmen and Manufactures, for the Year 1851: Including the Speeches of the Hon. Edward Everett and Hon. Robert C. Winthrop*. N.p., 1852. 57 p.

Winthrop's speech expresses praise for the society and the American farmer.

21-29. ———. *An Address Delivered before the Association of the Alumni of Harvard College, July 22, 1852*. Cambridge, Mass.: J. Bartlett, 1852. 59 p.

21-30. ———. *American Agriculture: An Address Delivered before the Bristol County Agricultural Society, on . . . Oct. 15, 1852*. Boston: John Wilson and Son, 1853. 31 p.

A speech in praise of American agriculture.

21-31. ———. *Archimedes and Franklin: A Lecture Introductory to a Course on the Application of Science to Art, Delivered before the Massachusetts Charitable Mechanic Association, November 29, 1853*. Boston: T. R. Marvin, 1853. 47 p.

21-32. ———. *Algernon Sidney: A Lecture Delivered before the Boston Mercantile Library Association, December 21, 1853*. Boston: S. K. Whipple, 1854. 43 p.

A laudatory speech on Sidney's life.

21-33. ———. *Oration at the Inauguration of the Statue of Benjamin Franklin . . . September 17, 1856*. Boston: T. R. Marvin, 1856. 28 p.

21-34. ———. *An Address Delivered at the Music Hall, Boston, . . . on the Evening of May 13, 1859*. Boston: Little, Brown, 1859. 60 p.

Speech in praise of Washington and the fine arts.

21-35. ———. *Addresses by His Excellency Governor John A. Andrew, Hon. Edward Everett, Hon. B. F. Thomas, and Hon. Robert C. Winthrop, Delivered at the Mass Meeting . . . on Wednesday, August 27, 1862*. Boston: J. E. Farwell, 1862. 16 p.

Includes Winthrop's call to arms for recruits to fight the Civil War.

21-36. ———. *Speech of Hon. Robert C. Winthrop at the Great Ratification Meeting in Union Square, New York, September 17, 1864.* [New York, 1864]. 8 p.

1864 Democratic campaign literature.

21-37. ———. *Introductory Lecture to the Course on the Early History of Massachusetts.* Boston: John Wilson and Son, 1869. 27 p.

Lecture given at the Lowell Institute in Boston on January 5, 1869.

21-38. ———. *Eulogy Pronounced at the Funeral of George Peabody . . . February 8, 1870.* Boston: John Wilson and Son, 1870. 25 p.

Eulogy in honor of educational reformer Peabody.

21-39. ———. *Oration on the Two Hundred and Fiftieth Anniversary of the Landing of the Pilgrim Fathers at Plymouth, December 21, 1870.* Boston: John Wilson and Son, 1871. 93 p.

21-40. ———. *Address at the Dedication of the New Town Hall of Brookline.* Cambridge, Mass.: John Wilson and Son, 1873. 42 p.

Speech of February 22, 1873.

21-41. ———. *Oration on the Centennial Anniversary of the Declaration of Independence Delivered in the Music Hall, . . . Boston, July 4, 1876.* Boston: John Wilson and Son, 1876. 55 p.

21-42. ———. *Address at the Unveiling of the Statue of Daniel Webster in Central Park, New York, November 25, 1876.* Boston: John Wilson and Son, 1876. 14 p.

21-43. ———. *Memoir of Henry Clay.* Cambridge, Mass.: John Wilson and Son, 1880. 39 p.

21-44. ———. *Address at the Unveiling of the Statue of Colonel William Prescott on Bunker Hill, June 17, 1881.* Cambridge, Mass: John Wilson and Son, 1881. 33 p.

21-45. ———. *Oration on the Hundredth Anniversary of the Surrender of Lord Cornwallis . . . Delivered at Yorktown, October 19, 1881.* Boston: Little, Brown, 1881. 73 p.

Speech celebrating the American victory at Yorktown.

21-46. ———. *The Portraits of John Hampden, in the Executive Mansion in Washington, and of Lafayette, in the Hall of the House of Representatives of the United States.* Cambridge, Mass.: John Wilson and Son, 1881. 17 p.

Winthrop discusses the importance of each portrait and how they came to hang in their respective locations.

21-47. ———. *Bunker Hill Monument Association . . . Mr. Winthrop's Address at the Annual Meeting, June 18, 1883.* [Boston, 1883]. 16 p.

21-48. ———. *The Character of Washington: From the Oration of Hon. Robert C. Winthrop at the Laying of the Corner-stone of the National Monument to Washington, July 4, 1848.* Boston, 1885. 7 p.

Excerpts from Winthrop's speech at the cornerstone ceremonies for the Washington monument in 1848.

21-49. ———. *Oration on the Completion of the National Monument to Washington . . . February 21, 1885.* Boston: Little, Brown, 1885. 39 p.

21-50. ———. *Tribute to Eben Sperry Stearns, D.D., LL.D., Chancellor of the University and President of the Normal College at Nashville, Tennessee, at the Annual Meeting . . . of the Peabody Education Fund, New York, October 5, 1887.* Cambridge, Mass.: John Wilson and Son, 1887. 6 p.

21-51. ———. *Tribute to William Aiken, Ex-Governor of South Carolina, at the Annual Meeting of . . . the Peabody Education Fund, New York, October 5, 1887.* Cambridge, Mass.: John Wilson and Son, 1887. 7 p.

Winthrop's tribute to Aiken's activities on behalf of the fund.

21-52. ———. *Notice of Jeremiah Morrow and Samuel F. Vinton, of Ohio.* [Boston, 1890]. 6 p.

An attempt to redeem the reputation of two Ohioans.

21-53. ———. *Introductory Remarks of Hon. Robert C. Winthrop at the Annual Meeting of the Peabody Trustees, October 12, 1892.* [Boston, 1892]. 5 p.

An address on the merits and goals of the fund.

21-54. ———. *Introductory Remarks of the Hon. Robert C. Winthrop at the Annual Meeting of the Pea-*

body Trustees of Southern Education, in New York, October 6, 1893. [Boston, 1893]. 9 p.

Similar to the address of the previous year (21-53).

21-55. ———. *Music in New England: An Address at the Opening of the First Musical Festival in Boston, May, 21, 1857.* [Boston: Directors of the Old South Work, 1908]. 20 p.

Speech on the origins and qualities of New England's music.

BIOGRAPHICAL SKETCHES AND EULOGIES

The most useful source is the memoir written by Winthrop's son, Robert C. Winthrop, Jr. (21-72), which draws heavily on his father's letters and speeches. *See also* Maury (9-256) and Reed (35-30).

21-56. BANCROFT, FREDERIC. "The Late Robert C. Winthrop." *Harper's Weekly,* 1 December 1894, p. 1135.

21-57. BOLTON, ETHEL STANWOOD. "Two Notable Wax Portraits." *Old Time New England* 13 (July 1922): 3–13.

Includes a brief biographical sketch of Winthrop.

21-58. CRAWFORD, MARY CAROLINE. *Famous Families of Massachusetts.* 2 vols. Boston: Little, Brown, 1930.

21-59. EVERETT, WILLIAM. "Robert Charles Winthrop." *Harvard Graduates' Magazine* 3 (March 1895): 294–301.

An affectionate sketch by a lifelong friend.

21-60. FORBES, ABNER, AND GREENE, J. W. *The Rich Men of Massachusetts.* Boston: Fetridge, 1851. 208 p.

Includes a brief sketch of Winthrop, who had an estimated worth of two hundred thousand dollars.

21-61. FREIBERG, MALCOLM. "The Winthrops and Their Papers." *Proceedings of the Massachusetts Historical Society* 80 (1968): 55–70.

An account of how the Winthrop papers were deposited in the Massachusetts Historical Society.

21-62. GOODWIN, DANIEL. *In Memory of Robert C. Winthrop.* Chicago: R. R. Donnelley and Sons, 1894. 64 p.

21-63. LEE, HENRY. *Memoir of Colonel Henry Lee.* Edited by John T. Morse, Jr. Boston: Little, Brown, 1905. 441 p.

Includes a tribute to Winthrop.

21-64. "Life and Public Service of the Honorable Robert Charles Winthrop, Speaker of the House of Representatives." *American Review* 29 (March 1848): 275–79.

21-65. LORING, JAMES SPEAR. *The Hundred Boston Orators from 1770 to 1852.* 4th ed. Boston: John P. Jewett, 1855. 730 p.

Includes a sketch of Winthrop's career to 1852.

21-66. MASSACHUSETTS HISTORICAL SOCIETY. *Tributes to the Memory of Robert C. Winthrop, December 13, 1894.* Boston: Massachusetts Historical Society, 1894. 40 p.

A collection of eulogies on Winthrop's death.

21-67. MAYO, LAWRENCE SHAW. *The Winthrop Family in America.* Boston: Massachusetts Historical Society, 1948. 507 p.

Includes a very full and sympathetic essay on Winthrop's career.

21-68. PEABODY EDUCATION FUND. *Tribute to the Memory of the Hon. Robert C. Winthrop.* N.p., 1895.

21-69. ROBERTS, OLIVER A. *History of the Military Company of Massachusetts.* 4 vols. Boston: Alfred Mudge and Son, 1895–1901.

Includes a brief description of Winthrop's military career and a biographical sketch.

21-70. ROBINSON, MRS. WILLIAM S. [HARRIET J.], ED. *Warrington Pen-Portraits: A Collection of Personal and Political Reminiscences, from 1848 to 1876, from the Writings of William S. Robinson.* Boston: Lee and Shepard, 1877. 587 p.

21-71. WILSON, JAMES GRANT. "Tributes to Hon. Hamilton Fish, Hon. John Jay, Hon. Robert C. Winthrop, and Others." In *Annual Report of the American Historical Association, 1894,* pp. 55–61. Washington, D.C.: Government Printing Office, 1895.

Includes a eulogy on Winthrop's death in 1894.

21-72. WINTHROP, ROBERT C., JR. *A Memoir of Robert C. Winthrop.* Boston: Little, Brown, 1897. 358 p.

A glowing tribute, focusing on Winthrop's political career.

WINTHROP AND MASSACHUSETTS HISTORY AND POLITICS

21-73. ANDERSON, GODFREY T. *The Slavery Issue as a Factor in Massachusetts Politics from the Compromise of 1850 to the Outbreak of the Civil War.* Chicago: University of Chicago Press, 1944. 359 p.

21-74. BRUNET, MICHEL. "The Secret Ballot Issue in Massachusetts Politics from 1851 to 1853." *New England Quarterly* 25 (September 1952): 354–62.

Analyzes the causes for Winthrop's defeat in the 1851 gubernatorial election.

21-75. DARLING, ARTHUR B. *Political Changes in Massachusetts, 1824–1848: A Study of Liberal Movements in Politics.* 1925. Reprint. Cos Cob, Conn.: J. E. Edwards, 1968. 392 p.

21-76. TRUSTY, NORMAN LANCE. "Massachusetts Public Opinion and the Annexation of Texas: 1835–1845." Ph.D. dissertation, Boston University, 1964. 195 p. 64-11615.

WINTHROP AND THE WHIG PARTY

See also Brock (9-218).

21-77. APPLETON, WILLIAM S. "The Whigs of Massachusetts." *Proceedings of the Massachusetts Historical Society,* 2d ser., 11 (March 1897): 278–82.

Examines the break between the Winthrop and Sumner factions. Also printed as a pamphlet in 1897.

21-78. BRAUER, KINLEY J. *Cotton versus Conscience: Massachusetts Whig Politics and Southwestern Expansion, 1843–1848.* Lexington: University Press of Kentucky, 1967. 272 p.

A fine scholarly study of the schism between Cotton and Conscience Whigs over the issues of Texas and Mexico in the late 1840s.

21-79. DAVIS, STUART JOHN. "Liberty before Union: Massachusetts and the Coming of the Civil War." Ph.D. dissertation, University of Massachusetts, 1975. 300 p. 76-05328.

Treats Winthrop as a leading Cotton Whig.

21-80. HAUN, CHERYL. "The Whig Abolitionists' Attitude toward the Mexican War." *Journal of the West* 11 (April 1972): 260–72.

21-81. HAWS, ROBERT J. "Massachusetts Whigs, 1833–1854." Ph.D. dissertation, University of Nebraska, 1973. 298 p. 74-12986.

Winthrop is identified as an important Cotton Whig in Massachusetts politics.

21-82. MATTHEWS, J. V. " 'Whig History': The New England Whigs and a Usable Past." *New England Quarterly* 51 (June 1978): 193–208.

A discussion of the social philosophies of New England Whigs.

21-83. MAYFIELD, JOHN RUSSELL. "Free Soil: Politics and Beliefs." Ph.D. dissertation, Johns Hopkins University, 1973. 397 p. 76-11222.

Includes a comprehensive account of the 1848 Cotton versus Conscience dispute in the Whig party in Massachusetts.

21-84. MEADE, SISTER MARY CATHERINE. "Daniel Webster and the Decline of the Whig Party in Massachusetts, 1848–1852." Ph.D. dissertation, Boston College, 1972. 451 p. 72-19773.

21-85. O'CONNOR, THOMAS H. "Cotton Whigs and Union: The Textile Manufacturers of Massachusetts and the Coming of the Civil War." Ph.D. dissertation, Boston University, 1958. 259 p. 58-03114.

21-86. ————. *Lords of the Loom: The Cotton Whigs and the Coming of the Civil War.* New York: Charles Scribner's Sons, 1968. 214 p.

21-87. RICH, ROBERT. " 'A Wilderness of Whigs': The Wealthy Men of Boston." *Journal of Social History* 4 (Spring 1971): 263–76.

A quantitative analysis of Boston's Whig elite that includes Winthrop.

21-88. ——. "Politics and Pedigrees: The Wealthy Men of Boston, 1798–1852." Ph.D. dissertation, University of California, Los Angeles, 1975. 313 p. 75-25185.

21-89. SWEENY, KEVIN. "Rum, Romanism, Representation, and Reform: Coalition Politics in Massachusetts, 1847–1853." *Civil War History* 72 (June 1976): 116–37.

21-90. WHIG PARTY. *Proceedings of the Whig State Convention Held at Worcester, October 2, 1855.* Boston: Boston Courier Office, 1855. 16 p.

Includes Winthrop's warning against the organization of a sectional party.

WINTHROP'S POLITICAL ASSOCIATES

See also Adams (7-22), Brown (15-61), Kirwan (15-66), Falkner (16-78), Fuess (16-83), Hamilton (16-86), Julian (16-88), and Going (20-23).

21-91. ABBOTT, RICHARD H. *Cobbler in Congress: The Life of Henry Wilson, 1812–1875.* Lexington: University Press of Kentucky, 1972. 289 p.

21-92. ADAMS, CHARLES FRANCIS, JR. *Charles Francis Adams.* 1900. Reprint. New York: AMS Press, 1972. 426 p.

21-93. BOHNER, CHARLES H. *John Pendleton Kennedy: Gentleman from Baltimore.* Baltimore: Johns Hopkins Press, 1961. 266 p.

21-94. CORNING, CHARLES R. *Amos Tuck.* Exeter, N.H.: News-Letter Press, 1902. 99 p.

21-95. DALZELL, ROBERT F. *Daniel Webster and the Trial of American Nationalism, 1843–1852.* Boston: Houghton Mifflin, 1972. 363 p.

21-96. DANA, RICHARD HENRY. *The Journal of Richard Henry Dana.* 3 vols. Edited by Robert F. Lucid. Cambridge, Mass.: Harvard University Press, 1968.

21-97. DONALD, DAVID H. *Charles Sumner and the Rights of Man.* New York: Alfred A. Knopf, 1970. 595 p.

Winthrop is mentioned throughout both volumes of Donald's acclaimed biography of Sumner. *See also* Donald (16-75).

21-98. DUBERMAN, MARTIN B. *Charles Francis Adams, 1807–1886.* 1961. Reprint. Stanford: Stanford University Press, 1968. 525 p.

21-99. FROTHINGHAM, PAUL REVERE. *Edward Everett: Orator and Statesman.* 1925. Reprint. Port Washington, N.Y.: Kennikat Press, 1971. 495 p.

21-100. FUESS, CLAUDE M. *The Life of Caleb Cushing.* 2 vols. 1923. Reprint. Hamden, Conn.: Archon Books, 1965.

21-101. GARRISON, WENDELL PHILLIPS, AND GARRISON, FRANCIS JACKSON. *William Lloyd Garrison, 1805–1879: The Story of His Life Told by His Children.* 4 vols. 1889. Reprint. New York: Arno Press, 1969.

21-102. GATELL, FRANK OTTO. *John Gorham Palfrey and the New England Conscience.* Cambridge, Mass.: Harvard University Press, 1963. 337 p.

21-103. McKAY, ERNEST A. *Henry Wilson, Practical Radical: A Portrait of a Politician.* Port Washington, N.Y.: Kennikat Press, 1971. 262 p.

21-104. MERRIAM, GEORGE S. *The Life and Times of Samuel Bowles.* Vol. 1. 1885. Reprint. St. Clair Shores, Mich.: Scholarly Press, 1970. 419 p.

21-105. NATHANS, SYDNEY. "Daniel Webster: Massachusetts Man." *New England Quarterly* 39 (June 1966): 161–81.

21-106. NEVINS, ALLAN. *Hamilton Fish: The Inner History of the Grant Administration.* Rev. ed. New York: Frederick Unger, 1957. 932 p.

21-107. PEARSON, HENRY GREENLEAF. *The Life of John A. Andrew: Governor of Massachusetts, 1861–1865.* 2 vols. Boston: Houghton Mifflin, 1904.

21-108. RICE, JESSIE PEARL. *J. L. M. Curry: Southerner, Statesman, and Educator.* New York: King's Crown Press, 1949. 242 p.

21-109. RIDDLE, DONALD W. *Congressman Abraham Lincoln.* 1957. Reprint. Westport, Conn.: Greenwood Press, 1979. 280 p.

21-110. STEWART, JAMES BREWER. *Joshua R. Giddings and the Tactics of Radical Politics.* Cleveland: Press of Case Western Reserve University, 1970. 318 p.

21-111. STOREY, MOORFIELD, AND EMERSON, EDWARD W. *Ebenezer Rockwood Hoar: A Memoir.* Boston: Houghton Mifflin, 1911. 355 p.

21-112. SUMNER, CHARLES. *Complete Works.* Vol. 1. 1883. Reprint. New York: Negro Universities Press, 1969. 382 p.

21-113. TYACK, DAVID B. *George Ticknor and the Boston Brahmins.* Cambridge, Mass.: Harvard University Press, 1967. 289 p.

21-114. WELLES, GIDEON. *Diary of Gideon Welles.* Vol. 2. 1911. Reprint. Edited by Howard K. Beale. New York: W. W. Norton, 1960. 653 p.

WINTHROP'S CONGRESSIONAL CAREER
AND SPEAKERSHIP

See also Hamilton (9-247), Merk (16-201), Corning (21-94), and Gatell (21-102).

21-115. GATELL, FRANK OTTO. "Palfrey's Vote: The Conscience Whigs, and the Election of Speaker Winthrop." *New England Quarterly* 31 (June 1958): 218-31.

21-116. GIDDINGS, JOSHUA R. *History of the Rebellion.* New York: Follett, Foster, 1864. 498 p.
Contains a detailed account of Winthrop's election to the speakership in 1847.

21-117. ———. *Speeches in Congress.* 1853. Reprint. New York: Negro Universities Press, 1968. 511 p.
Includes a speech on the Winthrop-Cobb speakership election of 1849.

21-118. PALFREY, JOHN GORHAM. *A Letter to a Friend.* Cambridge, Mass.: Metcalf, 1850.
Palfrey explains his refusal to support Winthrop for the speakership.

21-119. WHEELER, HENRY G. *History of Congress.* Vol. 1. New York: Harper and Brothers, 1848. 568 p.

WINTHROP AND RECONSTRUCTION

21-120. BUCK, PAUL H. *The Road to Reunion, 1865-1900.* Boston: Little, Brown, 1937. 320 p.
Describes Winthrop's efforts to reconcile North and South.

21-121. WARE, EDITH ELLEN. *Political Opinion in Massachusetts during Civil War and Reconstruction.* 1917. Reprint. New York: AMS Press, 1968. 219 p.

WINTHROP AND THE MASSACHUSETTS
HISTORICAL SOCIETY

21-122. *Proceedings of the Massachusetts Historical Society.* Vols. 2-20 (1855-84).
Winthrop served as president of the society from 1855 to 1884. His contributions to the *Proceedings* are too numerous to list individually. There is a complete index to volumes 1-20 which will direct interested readers to references concerning Winthrop.

WINTHROP AND THE PEABODY EDUCATION
FUND

21-123. PEABODY EDUCATION FUND. *Proceedings of the Trustees of the Peabody Education Fund.* Vols. 1-6. Cambridge, Mass., 1869-1914.
Volumes 1-6 contain the minutes of Winthrop's activities.

22. Howell Cobb
(1815–1868)
(Speaker, Thirty-first Congress)

Howell Cobb was one of the South's leading ante-bellum politicians. He believed that the continued existence of slavery was necessary for the South's prosperity, but he was not a fire-eating demagogue. Throughout his congressional career he endeavored to keep the Union intact and strong. After Lincoln was elected in 1860, Cobb nonetheless called for secession and joined the Confederacy, which he later served as a general in the army.

Howell Cobb was born into a wealthy and prominent Georgia family with a long tradition of public service on September 7, 1815. Cobb attended school in Athens, Georgia, and graduated in 1834 from Franklin College (then a part of the University of Georgia). He was married the same year to Mary Ann Lamar, daughter of another prominent Georgia family. He studied law and passed the bar exam in 1836. In 1837 he was elected solicitor general of the state's western circuit, an area of small farms, few slaves, and strong Unionist sentiment. Cobb was elected to Congress in 1842; he served from 1843 to 1851 and again from 1855 to 1857.

Cobb's congressional career coincided with territorial expansion and the sectional crisis over the extension of slavery. Cobb, a Southern Democrat, supported the annexation of Texas and the war with Mexico. He also proposed that the slavery question be settled by extending the Missouri Compromise line to the Pacific. When John C. Calhoun suggested that members of Congress from the South withdraw from their national parties and form a Southern bloc, Cobb refused, arguing that a unified Democratic party was the best protection for Southern interests.

His moderate, pro-Union stance helped Cobb become the Democratic congressional leader. He was elected Speaker in 1849 when he defeated the Whig incumbent, Robert C. Winthrop, on the sixty-third ballot. As Speaker of the Thirty-first Congress (1849–51), he presided over the debates that culminated in the Compromise of 1850.

Leaving Congress in 1851, Cobb returned to Georgia, where he ran for governor. With the state Democratic party divided into Southern Rights and Union factions, Cobb, leader of the Union wing, was elected governor by a large majority. After a single term in the governor's office, he returned to Congress in 1855. He was a close friend of James Buchanan, whom he helped nominate for the presidency in 1856. After Buchanan's election, Cobb was rewarded with the post of secretary of the treasury. His handling of the financial crisis of 1857 earned praise, but he was forced out when Buchanan reorganized the cabinet in late 1860.

After Lincoln's election in 1860, Cobb called for immediate secession. He was selected chairman of the Montgomery convention to organize the Confederacy. He was briefly considered for the Confederacy's presidency, in spite of his lack of military training and his former Union sympathy. He organized a regiment of Georgia troops and ultimately rose to the rank of major general. The war nearly destroyed Cobb's wealth. After the war, he returned to the practice of law in Athens, where he strongly opposed Radical Reconstruction. He died while visiting New York on October 9, 1868.

MANUSCRIPT COLLECTIONS

Emory University Library, Atlanta, Ga.
  Howell Cobb Papers.
  18 items.
Georgia Department of Archives and History, Atlanta, Ga.
  Miscellaneous Manuscripts Collection, file 2.
  1 folder of Howell Cobb items.
Library of Congress, Manuscript Division, Washington, D.C.
  Howell Cobb Letters.

  3 items.
  MC 34.
University of Georgia Library, Athens, Ga.
  Howell Cobb Collection.
  200 boxes of Cobb family correspondence.
  Some of Howell Cobb's correspondence of the 1840s and 1850s has been published in Brooks (22-1) and Phillips (22-14). Most of the published material was taken from the large collection now held at the University of Georgia Library.

BOOKS, ARTICLES, AND DISSERTATIONS

WORKS BY HOWELL COBB

See also Hunter (17-7).

22-1. BROOKS, ROBERT P., ED. "Howell Cobb Papers." *Georgia Historical Quarterly* 5, nos. 1–4 (March–December 1921): 50–61, 29–52, 35–55, 43–64.

A collection of 150 Cobb letters dating from 1840 to 1867.

22-2. CANDLER, ALLEN D. *The Confederate Records of the State of Georgia.* Vol. 3. New York: AMS Press, 1972. 746 p.

Includes the official correspondence between Cobb and Governor Joseph E. Brown.

The following works by Cobb are listed chronologically by year of publication.

22-3. COBB, HOWELL. *Speech of Mr. Cobb . . . on the Oregon Question.* Washington, D.C.: Union Office, 1846. 8 p.

House speech of January 8, 1846.

22-4. ———. *Necessity for Party Organization.* Washington, D.C.: Congressional Globe Office, 1848. 8 p.

House speech of July 1, 1848.

22-5. ———. *Remarks of Mr. Cobb . . . on the Organization of the House.* Washington, D.C.: Congressional Globe Office, 1855. 8 p.

House speech of December 21, 1855, denying that the Democrats were to blame for the failure to elect a Speaker.

22-6. ———. *A Scriptural Examination of the Institution of Slavery in the United States.* 1856. Reprint. Freeport, N.Y.: Books for Libraries Press, 1972. 173 p.

A defense of slavery on scriptural grounds.

22-7. ———. "The Cabinet—Report of Secretary Cobb." *United States Magazine and Democratic Review* 41 (January 1858): 34–45.

Cobb's annual report for 1858 as secretary of the treasury.

22-8. ———. *Communication from Hon. Howell Cobb Enclosing the Report of Major John C. Whitner.* Richmond, 1865. 4 p.

Cobb expresses his concern for the preparation of the journals of the Provisional Congress of the Confederacy.

22-9. ———. *Great Speech of General Howell Cobb, Delivered in Atlanta, Ga., July 23, 1868.* Augusta, Ga.: Chronicle and Sentinel Office, [1868]. 8 p.

A Democratic campaign speech.

22-10. ———. "Editorial Notes." *Magazine of Western History* 7 (November 1887): 100.

Includes a Cobb letter of 1857 on the civil service question.

22-11. ———. *Speech of Hon. Howell Cobb . . . Delivered in Concord, N.H., at a Mass Meeting of the Democratic Party of Merrimac County.* N.p., n.d. 12 p.

A campaign speech on behalf of Buchanan urging Democrats to unite on the principles of the Kansas-Nebraska Act.

22-12. FLEMING, WALTER LYNWOOD. *Documentary History of Reconstruction.* 2 vols. 1906. Reprint. New York: McGraw-Hill, 1966.

Contains a Cobb letter of 1865 with suggestions on Reconstruction.

22-13. FRANKLIN, JOHN HOPE. "Georgia and the Confederacy." *American Historical Review* 1 (October 1895): 97–102.

Includes two letters from Cobb in 1865 advising against the arming of slaves.

22-14. PHILLIPS, ULRICH BONNELL, ED. *The Correspondence of Robert Toombs, Alexander H. Stephens, and Howell Cobb.* 1913. Reprint. New York: Da Capo Press, 1970. 759 p.

Cobb's letters, dated 1844–68, concern his activities while Speaker, secretary of the treasury, and general in the Confederate army.

22-15. U. S. CONGRESS. HOUSE. SELECT COMMITTEE ON ASSAULT UPON SENATOR SUMNER. *Alleged Assault upon Senator Sumner . . . Report . . . of the Select Committee.* Washington, D.C., 1856. 142 p.

Includes a minority report submitted by Cobb.

BIOGRAPHIES AND BIOGRAPHICAL SKETCHES

The only recent full-length biography, Simpson (22-25), depicts Cobb unfavorably. Boykin (22-16) treats Cobb in a favorable but uncritical light. *See also* Savage (15-29).

22-16. BOYKIN, SAMUEL, ED. *A Memorial Volume of the Hon. Howell Cobb of Georgia.* Philadelphia: J. B. Lippincott, 1870. 280 p.
Includes a comprehensive sketch of Cobb with details of his death, funeral, and the eulogies delivered.

22-17. "Hon. Howell Cobb." *United States Magazine and Democratic Review* 41 (February 1858): 131–40.
A sketch of Cobb's career up to 1858.

22-18. JOHNSON, ZACHARY TAYLOR. *The Political Policies of Howell Cobb.* Nashville: George Peabody College for Teachers, 1929. 187 p.
An account of Cobb's political career from 1842 to 1861.

22-19. KNIGHT, LUCIAN L. *Reminiscences of Famous Georgians.* Vol. 1. Atlanta: Franklin-Turner, 1908. 763 p.
Contains a brief, favorable biographical sketch.

22-20. MAYS, ELIZABETH. "Mrs. Howell Cobb." *Georgia Historical Quarterly* 24 (March–June 1940): 1–21, 101–23.
Biographical account of Mary Ann Lamar Cobb.

22-21. NORTHERN, WILLIAM T., ED. *Men of Mark in Georgia.* Vol. 3. Atlanta: A. B. Caldwell, 1910. 581 p.

22-22. "Popular Portraits with Pen and Pencil: Howell Cobb, of Georgia." *United States Magazine and Democratic Review* 25 (September 1849): 266–76.

22-23. RAMAGE, C. J. "Howell Cobb." *Virginia Law Register* 28 (November 1922): 486–91.

22-24. RAND, CLAYTON. *Sons of the South.* New York: Holt, Rinehart, and Winston, 1961. 212 p.

22-25. SIMPSON, JOHN EDDINS. *Howell Cobb: The Politics of Ambition.* Chicago: Adams Press, 1973. 198 p.

COBB AND GEORGIA HISTORY AND POLITICS

See also Beck (22-66), Craven (22-68), Doherty (22-69), Johnson (22-70), Montgomery (22-71), Bass (22-73), Bryan (22-76), Christian (22-77), Coleman (22-80), Conway (22-92), and Thompson (22-93).

22-26. AVERY, I. W. *The History of the State of Georgia from 1850 to 1881.* 1881. Reprint. New York: AMS Press, 1972. 754 p.

22-27. BUTLER, JOHN C. *Historical Record of Macon and Central Georgia.* 1879. Reprint. Macon, Ga.: J. W. Burke, 1958. 351 p.

22-28. COULTER, E. MERTON. *College Life in the Old South.* 1928. Reprint. Athens: University of Georgia Press, 1951. 320 p.

22-29. ———. "A Georgia Educational Movement during the Eighteen Hundred Fifties." *Georgia Historical Quarterly* 9 (March 1925): 1–33.

22-30. GREENE, HELEN IONE. "Politics in Georgia, 1853–54: The Ordeal of Howell Cobb." *Georgia Historical Quarterly* 30 (September 1946): 185–211.
Details Cobb's advocacy of the Democratic states' rights program.

22-31. GRICE, WARREN. *The Georgia Bench and Bar.* Vol. 1. Macon, Ga.: J. W. Burke, 1931.

22-32. HULL, AUGUSTUS LONGSTREET. *Annals of Athens, Georgia, 1801–1901.* 1906. Reprint. Danielsville, Ga.: Heritage Papers, 1978. 568 p.

22-33. JOHNSON, ZACHARY TAYLOR. "Geographic Factors in Georgia Politics in 1850." *Georgia Historical Quarterly* 17 (March 1933): 26–36.

22-34. MONTGOMERY, HORACE. *Cracker Politics.* Baton Rouge: Louisiana State University Press, 1950. 278 p.

22-35. ———. "The Crisis of 1850 and Its Effect on Political Parties in Georgia." *Georgia Historical Quarterly* 24 (December 1940): 293–322.

22-36. ———. "The Two Howell Cobbs: A Case of Mistaken Identity." *Journal of Southern History* 28 (August 1962): 348–55.

An effort to clear the confusion between Speaker Howell Cobb and author Howell Cobb of Houston County.

22-37. MORRIS, SYLVANUS. *Strolls about Athens during the Early Seventies*. 1912. Reprint. Athens, Ga.: Athens Historical Society, 1969. 62 p.

22-38. PHILLIPS, ULRICH BONNELL. *Georgia and State Rights*. 1902. Reprint. Yellow Springs, Ohio: Antioch Press, 1968. 224 p.

22-39. SHRYOCK, RICHARD HARRISON. *Georgia and the Union in 1850*. 1926. Reprint. New York: AMS Press, 1968. 406 p.

COBB'S POLITICAL ASSOCIATES

See also Milton (15-68), Hamilton (16-86), Shenton (16-102), Hendrick (17-49), McElroy (17-51), and Going (20-23).

22-40. CAPERS, GERALD M. *Stephen A. Douglas: Defender of the Union*. Boston: Little, Brown, 1959. 239 p.

22-41. COULTER, E. MERTON. *Lost Generation: The Life and Death of James Barrow, C.S.A.* Tuscaloosa, Ala.: Confederate Publishing, 1956. 118 p.

Barrow was Cobb's staff adjutant during the Civil War.

22-42. FIELDER, HERBERT. *A Sketch of the Life and Times and Speeches of Joseph E. Brown*. Springfield, Mass.: Press of Springfield, 1883. 785 p.

22-43. FLIPPIN, PERCY SCOTT. *Herschel V. Johnson of Georgia: States' Rights Unionist*. Richmond, Va.: Dietz, 1931. 336 p.

22-44. HILL, LOUISE BILES. *Joseph E. Brown and the Confederacy*. 1939. Reprint. Westport, Conn.: Greenwood Press, 1972. 360 p.

22-45. JOHNSTON, RICHARD MALCOM, AND BROWNE, WILLIAM HAND. *Life of Alexander H. Stephens*. 1878. Reprint. Freeport, N.Y.: Books for Libraries Press, 1971. 619 p.

22-46. MCCASH, WILLIAM B. *Thomas R. R. Cobb: The Making of a Southern Nationalist*. Macon, Ga.: Mercer University Press, 1983. 356 p.

22-47. MURPHY, JAMES B. *L. Q. C. Lamar: Pragmatic Patriot*. Baton Rouge: Louisiana State University Press, 1973. 294 p.

22-48. PEARCE, HAYWOOD J. *Benjamin H. Hill: Secession and Reconstruction*. 1928. Reprint. New York: Negro Universities Press, 1969. 330 p.

22-49. PHILLIPS, ULRICH BONNELL. *The Life of Robert Toombs*. 1913. Reprint. New York: B. Franklin, 1968. 281 p.

22-50. STOVALL, PLEASANT A. *Robert Toombs: Statesman, Speaker, Soldier, Sage*. New York: Alexander Cassell, 1892. 396 p.

22-51. THOMPSON, WILLIAM Y. *Robert Toombs of Georgia*. Baton Rouge: Louisiana State University Press, 1966. 281 p.

22-52. VON ABELE, RUDOLPH R. *Alexander H. Stephens: A Biography*. 1946. Reprint. Westport, Conn.: Negro Universities Press, 1971. 337 p.

COBB'S CONGRESSIONAL CAREER

See also Brock (9-218), Hamilton (9-245 and 9–247), Shields (17-37), and Giddings (21-117).

22-53. BROOKS, ROBERT P. "Howell Cobb and the Crisis of 1850." In *Georgia Studies: Selected Writings of Robert Preston Brooks*, edited by Gregor Sebba. 1952. Reprint. Freeport, N.Y.: Books for Libraries Press, 1969. 309 p.

22-54. FRANKLIN, JOHN HOPE. "The Southern Expansionists of 1846." *Journal of Southern History* 25 (August 1959): 323–38.

22-55. HUBBELL, JOHN T. "Three Georgia Unionists and the Compromise of 1850." *Georgia Historical Quarterly* 51 (September 1967): 307–23.

An account of the efforts of Cobb, Stephens, and Toombs to secure passage of the compromise measures of 1850.

22-56. SIMPSON, JOHN EDDINS. "Prelude to Compromise: Howell Cobb and the House Speakership Election of 1849." *Georgia Historical Quarterly* 58 (Winter 1974): 389–99.

COBB AND THE BUCHANAN CABINET

See also Nichols (15-102) and Auchampaugh (17-67).

22-57. BRIGANCE, WILLIAM NORWOOD. *Jeremiah Sullivan Black*. 1934. Reprint. New York: Da Capo Press, 1971. 303 p.

Includes references to Cobb as secretary of the treasury in Buchanan's cabinet.

22-58. KLEIN, PHILIP S. *President James Buchanan: A Biography*. University Park: Pennsylvania State University Press, 1962. 506 p.

22-59. MONTGOMERY, HORACE. "Georgia's Howell Cobb Stumps for James Buchanan in 1856." *Pennsylvania History* 29 (January 1962): 40–52.

Details Cobb's campaign efforts on behalf of Buchanan which were rewarded with the treasury post.

22-60. SMITH, ELBERT B. *The Presidency of James Buchanan*. Lawrence: University Press of Kansas, 1975. 225 p.

22-61. STENBERG, RICHARD R. "An Unnoted Factor in the Buchanan-Douglas Feud." *Journal of the Illinois State Historical Society* 25 (January 1933): 271–84.

Notes the emergence of a rivalry between Cobb and Buchanan shortly before Cobb resigned from the cabinet.

22-62. "Three Letters of William Henry Trescott to Howell Cobb, 1861." *South Carolina Historical Magazine* 68 (January 1967): 22–30.

These letters, written in January and February 1861, were written to keep Cobb informed of events after his resignation as secretary of the treasury.

22-63. TRESCOTT, WILLIAM H. "Narrative and Letter of William H. Trescott concerning the Negotiations between South Carolina and President Buchanan in December, 1860." Edited by Gaillard Hunt. *American Historical Review* 13 (April 1908): 531–56.

Informative on the circumstances surrounding Cobb's resignation from the Buchanan cabinet.

22-64. VAN VLECK, GEORGE W. *The Panic of 1857: An Analytical Study*. 1943. Reprint. New York: AMS Press, 1967. 126 p.

Discusses measures taken by Secretary of the Treasury Cobb to meet the financial crisis.

COBB AND THE PRESIDENTIAL ELECTION OF 1860

See also Bartlett (15-20) and Savage (15-29).

22-65. SIMPSON, JOHN EDDINS. "Howell Cobb's Bid for the Presidency." *Georgia Historical Quarterly* 55 (Spring 1971): 102–13.

COBB AND THE SECESSION MOVEMENT

See also Degler (15-109) and Silbey (17-38).

22-66. BECK, N. B. "The Secession Debate in Georgia: November, 1860–January, 1861." In *Anti-Slavery and Disunion, 1858–1861,* edited by Jeffrey J. Auer, pp. 331–59. 1963. Reprint. Gloucester, Mass.: Peter Smith, 1968.

22-67. COLE, ARTHUR C. "The South and the Right of Secession in the Early Fifties." *Mississippi Valley Historical Review* 1 (December 1914): 376–99.

22-68. CRAVEN, AVERY O. "Georgia and the South." *Georgia Historical Quarterly* 23 (September 1939): 219–35.

22-69. DOHERTY, HERBERT J., JR. "Union Nationalism in Georgia." *Georgia Historical Quarterly* 37 (March 1953): 18–38.

22-70. JOHNSON, MICHAEL P. *Toward a Patriarchal Republic: The Secession of Georgia*. Baton Rouge: Louisiana State University Press, 1977. 244 p.

22-71. MONTGOMERY, HORACE. "Howell Cobb and the Secession Movement in Georgia." *Papers of the Athens Historical Society* 1 (1963): 35–39.

22-72. ———. "The Solid South Movement of 1855." *Georgia Historical Quarterly* 26 (June 1942): 101–28.

COBB AND THE CONFEDERACY

See also Confederate States of America (17-73), Jones (17-76), and *Rebellion Record* (17-79).

22-73. BASS, JAMES HORACE. "The Attack upon the Confederate Administration in Georgia in the Spring of 1864." *Georgia Historical Quarterly* 18 (September 1934): 228–47.

22-74. BERINGER, RICHARD E. "The Unconscious 'Spirit of Party' in the Confederate Congress." *Civil War History* 18 (December 1972): 312–33.

22-75. BRUMGARDT, JOHN RAYMOND. "Alexander H. Stephens and the Peace Issue in the Confederacy, 1863–1865." Ph.D. dissertation, University of California, 1974. 476 p. 76-28355.

22-76. BRYAN, T. CONN. *Confederate Georgia*. Athens: University of Georgia Press, 1953. 299 p.

22-77. CHRISTIAN, REBECCA. "Georgia and the Confederate Policy of Impressing Supplies." *Georgia Historical Quarterly* 28 (March 1944): 1–33.

22-78. COBB, THOMAS R. R. "The Correspondence of Thomas Reade Rootes Cobb, 1860–1862." Edited by Augustus Longstreet Hull. *Publications of the Southern History Association* 11 (May–November 1907): 147–81, 233–60, 312–28.
His brother's letters include many references to Howell Cobb's actions.

22-79. ———. "The Making of the Confederate Constitution." Edited by Augustus Longstreet Hull. *Publications of the Southern History Association* 9 (September 1905): 272–92.
Includes many references to Howell Cobb.

22-80. COLEMAN, KENNETH. *Confederate Athens*. Athens: University of Georgia Press, 1967. 214 p.

22-81. COULTER, E. MERTON. *The Confederate States of America, 1861–1865*. A History of the South, vol. 7. Baton Rouge: Louisiana State University Press, 1950. 644 p.

22-82. CURRY, J. L. M. *Civil History of the Government of the Confederate States with Some Personal Reminiscences*. Richmond, Va.: B. F. Johnson, 1901. 318 p.

22-83. DAVIS, RUBY SELLERS. "Howell Cobb: President of the Provisional Congress of the Confederacy." *Georgia Historical Quarterly* 46 (March 1962): 20–33.

22-84. FREEMAN, DOUGLAS SOUTHALL. *Lee's Lieutenants: A Study in Command*. 3 vols. New York: Charles Scribner's Sons, 1942–44.

22-85. HAY, THOMAS ROBSON. "The South and the Arming of the Slaves." *Mississippi Valley Historical Review* 6 (June 1919): 34–73.
Cobb argued against arming the slaves even as a last resort.

22-86. HESSELTINE, WILLIAM B. *Civil War Prisons: A Study in War Psychology*. 1930. Reprint. Kent, Ohio: Kent State University Press, 1972. 123 p.

22-87. JOHNSON, ROBERT V., AND BUEL, C. C., EDS. *Battles and Leaders of the Civil War*. 4 vols. New York: Century, 1887.

22-88. LEE, CHARLES ROBERT, JR. *The Confederate Constitutions*. 1963. Reprint. Westport, Conn.: Greenwood Press, 1974. 225 p.

22-89. MONTGOMERY, HORACE. *Howell Cobb's Confederate Career*. Tuscaloosa, Ala.: Confederate Publishing, 1959. 144 p.
A well-written account of Cobb's military career in the Confederate army.

22-90. MOORE, ALBERT BURTON. *Conscription and Conflict in the Confederacy*. New York: Macmillan, 1924. 367 p.

22-91. YEARNS, WILFRED B. *The Confederate Congress*. Athens: University of Georgia Press, 1960. 293 p.

COBB AND RECONSTRUCTION

22-92. CONWAY, ALAN. *The Reconstruction of Georgia*. Minneapolis: University of Minnesota Press, 1966. 248 p.

22-93. THOMPSON, C. MILDRED. *Reconstruction in Georgia: Economic, Social, Political, 1865–1872*. 1915. Reprint. Savannah, Ga.: Beehive Press, 1972. 397 p.

23. Linn Boyd
(1800–1859)
(Speaker, Thirty-second and Thirty-third Congresses)

Born in Nashville, Tennessee, on November 22, 1800, Linn Boyd grew up in an atmosphere politically dominated by Andrew Jackson. Boyd's father had fought in the American Revolution and then migrated to Nashville with Jackson. The Boyds remained close to Jackson even after the family moved to Kentucky in 1803. When Linn Boyd was nineteen, he was appointed to assist the commissioners who negotiated the Jackson Purchase of land from the Chickasaw Indians. He had little education, but he was vigorous, handsome, popular, and ambitious. Boyd moved to a farm in Calloway County in 1826. The following year he was elected to the Kentucky legislature, where he served from 1827 to 1832.

In 1834 Boyd was elected to Congress as a Jacksonian Democrat. He so steadfastly defended the president's opposition to the Bank of the United States that he angered his constituents and lost the 1836 election. President Jackson rewarded Boyd's loyalty, however, by lending his influence to further the career of the son of his old friend. Boyd was reelected in 1839 and served until 1855. Throughout his congressional career he was a vigorous and influential leader of the Democratic party.

Boyd favored the annexation of Texas and is credited with divising the plan whereby annexation was adopted by resolution. As chairman of the Committee on Military Affairs and later the Committee on Territories, he supported the war with Mexico and favored a compromise resolution of the problems caused by the acquisition of territory from Mexico. He led the House passage of the Compromise of 1850 and was Speaker of the House during his last four years in Congress (1851–55).

Boyd's popularity and his ambition led to aspirations to higher office. After he returned to Kentucky in 1855, he became the state's favorite-son candidate for the vice-presidency in 1856. Boyd had intended to run for the Senate, but first he was nominated for lieutenant governor of Kentucky in 1859. When he was elected, he was too ill to hold office. He died on December 17, 1859, in Paducah, Kentucky.

MANUSCRIPT COLLECTIONS

University of Kentucky Libraries, Lexington, Ky.
  Boyd Family Papers, 1830–1915.

1,071 pieces (includes 93 letters, 1850–58, from Linn Boyd to his wife).

BOOKS, ARTICLES, AND DISSERTATIONS

WORKS BY LINN BOYD

The following works by Boyd are listed chronologically by year of publication.

23-1. BOYD, LINN. *To the Citizens of the First Congressional District in the State of Kentucky.* Washington, D.C., 1843. 8 p.
  An attack upon the Whig party.

23-2. ———. *Speech of Mr. Linn Boyd . . . in Reply to the Hon. John White, Relative to the Charge of Bargain between Messrs. Adams and Clay, in the Presidential Election of 1824–25.* Washington, D.C., 1844. 23 p.

23-3. ———. *Speech of Hon. Linn Boyd . . . on Granting Bounty Lands to the Army.* Washington,

D.C.: Congressional Globe Office, 1847. 7 p.

A speech of January 26, 1847, in favor of extending the grant to include soldiers who fought in the Mexican War.

BIOGRAPHICAL SOURCES

For a political leader who served two terms as Speaker of the House, surprisingly little has been written about Linn Boyd. The best account of his political career can be found in Hamilton (23-7), an analysis of Boyd's role in the Compromise of 1850. Short biographical sketches are included in *Biographical Encyclopedia of Kentucky* (18-3), Levin (18-8), Clift (23-5), and Thompson (23-17). *See also* Colton (9-93), Poage (9-96), Hamilton (9-245 and 9-247), Hodder (9-250), Nichols (15-102), Davis (17-43), Willis (18-10), Corning (21-94), Brooks (22-1), and Phillips (22-14).

23-4. CHASE, SALMON P. *Diary and Correspondence of Salmon P. Chase.* Edited by Edward G. Bourne. 1902. Reprint. New York: Da Capo Press, 1971. 527 p.

23-5. CLIFT, GARRETT GLENN. *Governors of Kentucky, 1792–1942.* Kentucky Sesquicentennial Edition. Cynthiana, Ky.: Hobson Press, 1942. 361 p.

23-6. DICK, EVERETT N. *The Dixie Frontier: A Social History of the Southern Frontier from the First Transmontane Beginnings to the Civil War.* 1948. Reprint. New York: Octagon Books, 1974. 374 p.

23-7. HAMILTON, HOLMAN. "Kentucky's Linn Boyd and the Dramatic Days of 1850." *Register of the Kentucky Historical Society* 55 (July 1957): 185–95.

A scholarly analysis of Boyd's role in the Compromise of 1850.

23-8. HECK, FRANK H. *Proud Kentuckian: John C. Breckinridge, 1821–1875.* Lexington: University Press of Kentucky, 1976. 171 p.

23-9. KENTUCKY. GENERAL ASSEMBLY. *Speeches and Proceedings upon the Announcement of the Death of the Hon. Linn Boyd . . . December 20, 1859.* Frankfort, Ky.: Yeoman Office, 1860. 52 p.

Contains an announcement of Boyd'd death, brief eulogies, and a biographical sketch.

23-10. KENTUCKY. GENERAL ASSEMBLY. HOUSE OF REPRESENTATIVES. *Journal of the House of Representatives of the Commonwealth of Kentucky.* Frankfort: Jacob H. Holeman, 1827–30.

Boyd represented the counties of Hickman, Graves, Calloway, and McCracken.

23-11. LITTLE, LUCIUS P. *Ben Hardin: His Times and Contemporaries.* Louisville, Ky., 1887. 640 p.

23-12. McELROY, ROBERT M. *Kentucky in the Nation's History.* New York: Moffat, Yard, 1909. 590 p.

23-13. NEUMAN, FRED G. *Paducahans in History.* Paducah, Ky.: Young, 1922.

Includes a short biographical sketch.

23-14. PIERCE, FRANKLIN. "Some Papers of Franklin Pierce, 1852–1862." Edited by P. O. Ray. *American Historical Review* 10 (October 1904–January 1905): 110–27, 350–70.

Includes an 1852 letter referring to Boyd as a possible presidential contender.

23-15. PIERSON, HAMILTON W. *In the Brush: An Old-Time Social, Political, and Religious Life in the Southwest.* New York: D. Appleton, 1881. 321 p.

Includes an interesting account of Boyd's background, campaign style, and political accomplishments.

23-16. SADLER, RICHARD W. "The Impact of the Slavery Question on the Whig Party in Congress, 1843–1854." Ph.D. dissertation, University of Utah, 1969. 407 p. 69-19001.

23-17. THOMPSON, GEORGE W. *Biographical Sketch of Hon. Linn Boyd, of Kentucky, the Present Speaker of the House of Representatives of the United States.* Washington, D.C.: Congressional Globe Office, 1855. 15 p.

24. Nathaniel Prentice Banks
(1816–1894)
(Speaker, Thirty-fourth Congress)

The life of Nathaniel P. Banks suggests the myth of the self-made man. His career as a poor mill-town boy who made good as a congressman, governor of Massachusetts, and Union general had all the apparent elements of the American rags-to-riches success story. Yet his willingness to subordinate principle for personal gain and his overweening ambition also suggest the tragic flaw in the drive for upward mobility.

The urge to get ahead was deeply instilled in Banks during his early years. He was born the eldest of seven children on January 30, 1816, in Waltham, Massachusetts. Although his father was a foreman for the Boston Manufacturing Company, young Banks was forced to leave school at age eleven to work in the mill. His job was replacing empty bobbins, which later earned him the nickname the Bobbin Boy of Massachusetts. Banks found a means to escape mill life through politics. He developed talents easily transferred to politics by studying Latin and Spanish, joining a debating club, lecturing on temperance, and even organizing a theatrical society. He later studied law, was admitted to the bar, and started a local weekly newspaper—all with little success. Finally he found his calling in politics by linking his fortunes with the Democratic party and by soliciting a patron, Robert Rantoul, Jr. In 1843 Banks was given a post in the Boston customs house by Rantoul, who was then collector of the port of Boston.

Banks ran for the Massachusetts legislature seven times before he won a seat in 1849. Politics became his vocation; for him, political office and financial success were identical. To win office he followed the prevailing political currents. His career charted the ebb and flow of politics in Massachusetts; during his tenure in ten Congresses (1853–57, 1865–73, 1875–79, and 1889–91) he represented four different party alignments. After successfully presiding over the state constitutional convention of 1853, Banks entered Congress as a Democrat. Although he was elected to the following Congress as a candidate of the American, or Know-Nothing, party, Banks embraced the position of the Free Soil party and was elected Speaker of the House on the 133d ballot. He filled the office well, and many considered him the ablest Speaker since Henry Clay. In 1859 Banks forsook both the American party and Congress to accept the Republican nomination for governor of Massachusetts. He was elected by a large majority and held office from 1858 to 1860.

Banks had just assumed the financially rewarding presidency of the Illinois Central Railroad when the Civil War began. He immediately offered his services to President Lincoln and was commissioned a major general. Although he lacked any military training and subsequently displayed little military aptitude, Banks was given command first in Annapolis, then in the Shenandoah Valley, then in Washington, D.C., and finally in New Orleans, where he succeeded the controversial Benjamin F. Butler. The task at New Orleans was a challenging one of balancing military operations with the administration of a difficult if not perverse civilian population. His greatest military success came in July 1863, when Port Hudson fell after a protracted seige. The Red River campaign of 1864 into northwest Louisiana, however, was a disastrous failure. Banks's administration of Louisiana also proved to be controversial for his attempt to reform the labor system and to reconstruct the state government.

Mustered out of the army in August 1865, Banks returned to Massachusetts and was elected to the Thirty-ninth Congress to fill a vacancy. He was defeated for reelection when he refused to support Grant in 1872, but he was elected to the Forty-fourth Congress two years later. He served as U.S. marshal for Massachusetts (1879–88) before one final term in Congress (1889–91). Banks died at home in Waltham on September 1, 1894.

MANUSCRIPT COLLECTIONS

American Antiquarian Society, Manuscript Collections, Worcester, Mass.
Nathaniel P. Banks Correspondence, ca. 1852–85.
1 box, 261 items.
NUCMC 75-1891.
Duke University Library, Durham, N.C.
Nathaniel P. Banks Papers, 1850–80.
107 items.
NUCMC 69-1468.
Illinois State Historical Society, Springfield, Ill.
Nathaniel P. Banks Papers, 1840–94.
2,300 pieces.

Library of Congress, Manuscript Division, Washington, D.C.
Nathaniel Prentice Banks Papers, 1840–1911.
205 containers.
Register and index.
MC 8.
Louisiana State University, Department of Archives and Manuscripts, Baton Rouge, La.
Nathaniel P. Banks Letterbook, 1863–64.
1 vol.
NUCMC 70-202.

BOOKS, ARTICLES, AND DISSERTATIONS

WORKS BY NATHANIEL P. BANKS

The following items by Banks are listed chronologically by year of publication and alphabetically thereunder.

24-1. BANKS, NATHANIEL P. *Speech of N. P. Banks . . . on the Employment of Army Officers in the National Armories.* Washington, D.C., 1854. 16 p.
House speech of July 17, 1854.

24-2. ———. *Address of . . . Nathaniel P. Banks, to the Two Branches of the Legislature of Massachusetts.* Boston: William White, 1858.
Governor Banks's annual address delivered on January 7, 1858.

24-3. ———. *Valedictory Address of . . . Nathaniel P. Banks, to the Two Branches of the Legislature of Massachusetts.* Boston: William White, 1861. 38 p.
Banks's final annual message, delivered on January 3, 1861.

24-4. ———. *Emancipated Labor in Louisiana: Address Delivered before the Young Men's Christian Commission, Boston, October 30, 1864, and Charlestown, Mass., November 1, 1864.* [New York, 1864]. 45 p.
A speech on the condition of black labor in Louisiana.

24-5. ———. *An Address Delivered . . . at the Customhouse, New Orleans, on the Fourth of July, 1865.* New Orleans, 1865. 15 p.
Banks called for the enfranchisement of blacks.

24-6. ———. *The Reconstruction of the States: Letter of Major-General Banks to Senator Lane.* New York: Harper and Brothers, 1865. 23 p.
A letter justifying the new Louisiana state constitution.

24-7. ———. *Speech of Hon. N. P. Banks . . . upon the Representation of the United States at the Exhibition of the World's Industry, Paris, 1867.* Washington, D.C.: Mansfield and Martin, 1866. 24 p.
House speech of March 14, 1866, in favor of American participation in the exhibition.

24-8. ———. *Remarks of Hon. N. P. Banks . . . on the Death of Senator Foot.* Washington, D.C.: Congressional Globe Office, [1866].
Eulogy delivered on April 12, 1866.

24-9. ———. *Speech of Hon. Nathaniel P. Banks, . . . on Revision of the Tariff.* Washington, D.C., 1878. 36 p.
House speech of May 7, 1878, opposing higher tariffs.

24-10. HARRINGTON, FRED HARVEY, ED. "A Peace

Mission of 1863." *American Historical Review* 46 (October 1940): 76–86.

A series of letters between Banks and Lincoln's emissary, Dr. Issachar Zacharie.

24-11. HARVARD UNIVERSITY. *Addresses at the Inauguration of Cornelius Felton, LL.D., as President of Harvard College . . . July 19, 1860.* Cambridge, Mass.: Seves and Francis, 1860. 149 p.

Includes a speech by Governor Banks on education and Harvard.

24-12. "The Story of the Illinois Central Lines during the Civil Conflict, 1861–5: General Banks." *Illinois Central Magazine* 2 (July/August 1913): 13–22.

Includes letters that Banks wrote as president of the railroad.

BIOGRAPHY AND BIOGRAPHICAL SKETCHES

The only biography of Banks, Harrington (24-13), is an excellent scholarly study emphasizing the political aspects of Banks's military service. *See also* Robinson (21-70).

24-13. HARRINGTON, FRED HARVEY. *Fighting Politician: Major General N. P. Banks.* 1948. Reprint. Westport, Conn.: Greenwood Press, 1970. 301 p.

24-14. MASSACHUSETTS. EXECUTIVE DEPARTMENT. *A Record of the Dedication of the Statue of Major General Nathaniel Prentiss Banks, September 16, 1908.* Boston: Wright and Potter, 1909. 58 p.

Comprises addresses praising Banks.

24-15. "Obituary." *Outlook,* 8 September 1894, p. 374.

A brief review of Banks's career.

24-16. WALTHAM, MASS. *Celebration of the Centennial of the Birth of General Nathaniel Prentiss Banks.* Waltham, 1916. 31 p.

BANKS'S CONGRESSIONAL CAREER AND SPEAKERSHIP

24-17. BIGELOW, JOHN. *Retrospections of an Active Life.* Vols. 1, 2, 4. Garden City, N.Y.: Doubleday, Page, 1909-13.

24-18. GREELEY, HORACE. *Recollections of a Busy Life.* 1868. Reprint. Miami, Fla.: Mnemosyne, 1969. 624 p.

24-19. HARRINGTON, FRED HARVEY, ED. "A Note on the Ray Explanation of the Origin of the Kansas-Nebraska Act." *Mississippi Valley Historical Review* 25 (June 1938): 79–81.

Concerns Banks's 1855 speech opposing popular sovereignty.

24-20. HENRY, MILTON LYMAN, JR. "Henry Winter Davis: Border State Radical." Ph.D. dissertation, Louisiana State University, 1974. 427 p. 75-01929.

Includes a discussion of the speakership contest of 1855–56.

24-21. MORGAN, EDWIN B. "A Congressman's Letters on the Speaker Election in the Thirty-fourth Congress." Edited by Temple B. Hollcroft. *Mississippi Valley Historical Review* 43 (December 1956): 444–58.

These letters stress slavery as the divisive factor in Banks's speakership contest.

24-22. NIVEN, JOHN. *Gideon Welles: Lincoln's Secretary of the Navy.* New York: Oxford University Press, 1973. 676 p.

Discusses the meeting at which Banks was selected as a candidate for the speakership.

24-23. VAN HORNE, WILLIAM E. "Lewis D. Campbell and the Know-Nothing Party in Ohio." *Ohio History* 76 (Autumn 1966): 202–21.

Contains an account of the 1855 speakership race in which Campbell ran against Banks.

BANKS, ANTI-SLAVERY POLITICS, AND THE REPUBLICAN PARTY

See also Baringer (15-106).

24-24. BARINGER, WILLIAM E. *Lincoln's Rise to Power.* 1937. Reprint. St. Clair Shores, Mich.: Scholarly Press, 1971. 373 p.

24-25. BARTLETT, RUHL JACOB. *John C. Frémont and the Republican Party.* 1930. Reprint. New York: Da Capo Press, 1970. 146 p.

24-26. HARRINGTON, FRED HARVEY. "Frémont and the North Americans." *American Historical*

Review 44 (July 1939): 842–48.

Discusses Banks's role in the 1856 presidential campaign.

24-27. ———. "Nathaniel Prentiss Banks: A Study in Anti-Slavery Politics." *New England Quarterly* 9 (December 1936): 626–54.

Harrington contends that Banks's opposition to slavery was mild and politically motivated.

24-28. ———. "The Reception of the Frémont-Robinson Letter (A Note on the 1856 Campaign)." *New England Quarterly* 12 (September 1939): 545–48.

24-29. KEHOE, MARY CORLEEN. "Massachusetts Takes a Stand: The Growth of Republican Ideology and Politics, 1850–1856." Ph.D. dissertation, University of Maryland, 1975. 320 p. 76–17811.

24-30. KLEEBERG, GORDEN S. P. *The Formation of the Republican Party as a National Political Organization.* 1911. Reprint. New York: B. Franklin, 1970. 245 p.

24-31. MCKAY, ERNEST A. "Henry Wilson and the Coalition of 1851." *New England Quarterly* 36 (September 1963): 338–57.

24-32. MALIN, JAMES C. "Speaker Banks Courts the Free Soilers: The Frémont-Robinson Letter of 1856." *New England Quarterly* 12 (March 1939): 103–12.

Banks is suggested as the architect of the first Republican presidential campaign.

24-33. SEWELL, RICHARD H. *Ballots for Freedom: Antislavery Politics in the United States.* New York: Oxford University Press, 1976. 379 p.

24-34. STONE, EBEN F. "Sketch of John Albion Andrew." *Historical Collections of the Essex Institute* 27 (January/March 1890): 1–30.

Discusses Banks in the context of Massachusetts anti-slavery politics.

BANKS AND THE MASSACHUSETTS CONSTITUTIONAL CONVENTION OF 1853

24-35. SCHOULER, JAMES. "The Massachusetts Convention of 1853." *Proceedings of the Massachu-*

setts Historical Society, 2d ser., 38 (November 1903): 30–48.

24-36. SHAPIRO, SAMUEL. "The Conservative Dilemma: The Massachusetts Constitutional Convention of 1853." *New England Quarterly* 33 (June 1960): 207–24.

BANKS AS GOVERNOR OF MASSACHUSETTS, 1858–1860

See also Davis (21-79).

24-37. HARRINGTON, FRED HARVEY. "A Royal Tour of 1860." *South Atlantic Quarterly* 38 (July 1939): 332–41.

24-38. ROE, ALFRED S. "The Governors of Massachusetts: Clifford to Crane." *New England Magazine* 31 (February 1902): 651–72.

Includes a brief review of Banks's career.

BANKS AND THE CIVIL WAR

Military Operations

The following works include information on Banks's military career, including his three major campaigns in the Shenandoah, at Port Hudson, and in the Red River Valley. *See also* Johnson and Buel (22-87).

24-39. BERRY, MARY F. "Negro Troops in Blue and Gray: The Louisiana Native Guards, 1861–1863." *Louisiana History* 8 (Spring 1967): 165–90.

Refers to Banks's attitude toward black officers and his strategy in the seige of Port Hudson.

24-40. BROWN, GEORGE WILLIAM. *Baltimore and the Nineteenth of April, 1861: A Study of the War.* Baltimore: N. Murray, 1887. 176 p.

Includes a section on Banks as commander of the Department of Annapolis.

24-41. DENISON, GEORGE S. "Some Letters of George Stanton Denison, 1854–1866: Observations of a Yankee on Conditions in Louisiana and Texas." Edited by James A. Padgett. *Louisiana Historical Quarterly* 23 (September 1940): 1132–1249.

Includes observations on Banks as a military commander.

24-42. Farragut, Loyall. *The Life of David Glasgow Farragut, First Admiral of the United States Navy, Embodying His Journal and Letters.* New York: D. Appleton, 1879. 586 p.

24-43. Flinn, Frank M. *Campaigning with Banks in Louisiana, '63 and '64, and with Sheridan in the Shenandoah Valley in '64 and '65.* Lynn, Mass.: Thomas P. Nichols, 1887. 239 p.

24-44. Gordon, George H. *Brook Farm to Cedar Mountain in the War of the Great Rebellion, 1861–62.* Boston: James R. Osgood, 1883. 376 p.

The final chapter focuses exclusively on Banks.

24-45. ———. *History of the Campaign of the Army of Virginia.* Boston: Houghton, Osgood, 1880. 498 p.

24-46. ———. *History of the Second Massachusetts Regiment of Infantry, Third Paper.* Boston: Alfred Mudge and Son, 1875. 231 p.

24-47. Grant, Ulysses S. *The Papers of Ulysses S. Grant.* Edited by John Y. Simon. Vols. 7 and 8. Carbondale: Southern Illinois University Press, 1979.

24-48. ———. *Personal Memoirs.* 2 vols. New York: C. L. Webster, 1885.

24-49. Greene, Francis Vinton. *The Mississippi.* The Army in the Civil War, vol. 8. New York: Charles Scribner's Sons, 1882. 276 p.

24-50. Johnson, Ludwell H. *Red River Campaign: Politics and Cotton in the Civil War.* Baltimore: Johns Hopkins Press, 1958. 317 p.

An account of the Red River campaign centering on its political and economic aspects.

24-51. Kassel, Charles. "Opening the Mississippi: A Civil War Drama." *Open Court* 40 (March 1926): 145–54.

Defends Banks's actions in the Port Hudson campaign.

24-52. Landers, Col. H. L. "Wet Sand and Cotton: Banks's Red River Campaign." *Louisiana Historical Quarterly* 19 (January 1936): 150–95.

24-53. Longacre, Edward G. "The Port Hudson Campaign." *Civil War Times Illustrated* 10 (February 1972): 20–34.

24-54. McClellan, George B. *McClellan's Own Story.* New York: Charles L. Webster, 1887. 678 p.

24-55. McDowell, John E. "Nathaniel P. Banks: Fighting Politico." *Civil War Times Illustrated* 9 (January 1973): 4.

24-56. Morse, John T., Jr. *Memoir of Colonel Henry Lee with Selections from His Writings and Speeches.* Boston: Little, Brown, 1905. 441 p.

24-57. Quint, Alonzo H. *The Potomac and the Rapidan: Army Notes, from the Failure at Winchester to the Reinforcement of Rosecrans, 1861–63.* Boston: Crosby and Nichols, 1864. 407 p.

24-58. Sherman, William T. *The Sherman Letters: Correspondence between General and Senator Sherman from 1837 to 1891.* Edited by Rachel Sherman Thorndike. 1894. Reprint. New York: AMS Press, 1971. 398 p.

24-59. ———. *Some Letters of General Sherman.* Edited by Mark A. DeWolfe Howe. New York: Charles Scribner's Sons, 1909. 412 p.

24-60. Smith, George Winston. "The Banks Expedition of 1862." *Louisiana Historical Quarterly* 26 (April 1943): 341–60.

24-61. Strother, P. D. "Personal Recollections of the War." *Harper's* 33 (September–October 1866): 409–28, 545–66; 34 (January–May 1867): 172–91, 423–49, 713–34.

24-62. Thomas, Benjamin P., and Hyman, Harold M. *Stanton: The Life and Times of Lincoln's Secretary of War.* New York: Alfred A. Knopf, 1962. 642 p.

Discusses Banks's military failures and shortcomings as commander of the Department of the Gulf.

24-63. Welles, Gideon. *Diary of Gideon Welles.* 3 vols. 1911. Reprint. Edited by Howard K. Beale. New York: W. W. Norton, 1960.

24-64. West, Richard S., Jr. *The Second Admiral: A Life of David Dixon Porter, 1813–1891.* New York: Coward-McCann, 1937. 376 p.

24-65. Williams, Richard Hobson. "General Banks's Red River Campaign." *Louisiana Historical Quarterly* 32 (January 1939): 103–44.

24-66. WINTERS, JOHN D. *The Civil War in Louisiana*. Baton Rouge: Louisiana State University Press, 1963. 534 p.

Banks and the Department of the Gulf

The following works provide insight into Banks's civil administration of New Orleans.

24-67. BRAGG, JEFFERSON DAVIS. *Louisiana in the Confederacy*. Baton Rouge: Louisiana State University Press, 1941. 341 p.

24-68. BUTLER, BENJAMIN F. *Autobiography and Personal Reminiscences of Major-General Benjamin F. Butler: Ben Butler's Book*. Boston: A. M. Thayer, 1892. 1,154 p.

24-69. ———. *Private and Official Correspondence of Gen. Benjamin F. Butler during the Period of the Civil War*. Compiled by Jessie Ames Marshall. 5 vols. Norwood, Mass.: Plimpton Press, 1917.

24-70. BYRNE, FRANK L. " 'A Terrible Machine': General Neal Dow's Military Government on the Gulf Coast." *Civil War History* 12 (March 1966): 5–22.

24-71. CAPERS, GERALD M. "Confederates and Yankees in Occupied New Orleans, 1862–1865." *Journal of Southern History* 30 (November 1964): 405–26.

24-72. ———. *Occupied City: New Orleans under the Federals, 1862–1865*. Lexington: University of Kentucky Press, 1965. 248 p.

24-73. CASKEY, WILLIE MALVIN. *Secession and Restoration of Louisiana*. 1938. Reprint. New York: Da Capo Press, 1970. 318 p.

24-74. DOYLE, ELISABETH JOAN. "Greenbacks, Car Tickets, and the Pot of Gold: The Effects of Wartime Occupation on the Business Life of New Orleans, 1861–1865." *Civil War History* 5 (December 1959): 347–62.

24-75. ———. "Nurseries of Treason: Schools in Occupied New Orleans." *Journal of Southern History* 26 (May 1960): 161–79.

24-76. FREIDEL, FRANK. "General Orders 100 and Military Government." *Mississippi Valley Historical Review* 33 (March 1946): 541–56.

24-77. HAY, JOHN. *Lincoln and the Civil War in the Diaries and Letters of John Hay*. Edited by Tyler Dennett. 1939. Reprint. Westport, Conn.: Negro Universities Press, 1972. 348 p.

Includes frequent references to Banks.

24-78. HEPWORTH, GEORGE H. *The Whip, Hoe, and Sword; or, The Gulf Department in '63*. 1864. Reprint. Edited by Joe Gray Taylor. Baton Rouge: Louisiana State University Press, 1979. 304 p.

24-79. REED, EMILY HAZEN. *Life of A. P. Dostie; or, The Conflict in New Orleans*. New York: William P. Tomlinson, 1868. 374 p.

24-80. SOUTHWARD, MARION. *Beauty and Booty: The Watchword of New Orleans*. New York: privately printed, 1867. 303 p.

24-81. STROTHER, DAVID HUNTER. *A Virginia Yankee in the Civil War: The Diaries of David Hunter Strother*. Edited by Cecil D. Eby, Jr. Chapel Hill: University of North Carolina Press, 1961. 294 p.

24-82. UNITED STATES ARMY. DEPARTMENT OF THE GULF. *Historical Sketch of Major Gen. N. P. Banks' Civil and Military Administration in Louisiana*. New York, 1864. 12 p.

24-83. ———. *To the People of Louisiana*. New Orleans, 1862. 3 p.

Banks's proclamation of December 24, 1862, explaining the Emancipation Proclamation.

24-84. WAITZ, JULIA ELLEN [LE GRAND]. *The Journal of Julia Le Grand: New Orleans, 1862–1863*. Edited by Kate Mason Rowland and Agnes E. Croxall. Richmond, Va.: Everett Waddey, 1911. 318 p.

24-85. WILLIAMS, T. HARRY. "General Banks and the Radical Republicans in the Civil War." *New England Quarterly* 12 (June 1939): 268–80.

Discusses Radical Republican criticism of Banks's administration.

24-86. ———. *Lincoln and the Radicals*. Madison: University of Wisconsin Press, 1941. 413 p.

Banks, Freedmen, and the Labor System in Louisiana

The following works describe Banks's efforts to assist freedmen and to reform Louisiana's labor system.

24-87. Cornish, Dudley Taylor. *The Sable Arm: Negro Troops in the Union Army, 1861–1865.* New York: W. W. Norton, 1966. 337 p.

24-88. Cox, LaWanda. "The Promise of Land for Freedmen." *Mississippi Valley Historical Review* 45 (December 1958): 413–40.

24-89. Gerteis, Louis S. *From Contraband to Freedman: Federal Policy toward Southern Blacks, 1861–1865.* Westport, Conn.: Greenwood Press, 1973. 255 p.

24-90. Grosz, Agnes Smith. "The Political Career of Pickney Benton Stewart Pinchback." *Louisiana Historical Quarterly* 27 (April 1944): 527–612.

24-91. Kassel, Charles. "Educating the Slave: A Forgotten Chapter of Civil War History." *Open Court* 41 (April 1927): 239–56.

24-92. ———. "The Labor System of General Banks: A Lost Episode of Civil War History." *Open Court* 42 (January 1928): 38–50.

24-93. McPherson, James M. *The Negro's Civil War: How American Negroes Felt and Acted during the War for the Union.* 1965. Reprint. Urbana: University of Illinois Press, 1982. 364 p.

24-94. ———. *The Struggle for Equality: Abolitionists and the Negro in the Civil War and Reconstruction.* Princeton: Princeton University Press, 1964. 474 p.

24-95. May, J. Thomas. "Continuity and Change in the Labor Program of the Union Army and the Freedmen's Bureau." *Civil War History* 17 (September 1971): 245–54.

24-96. Messner, William F. "Black Education in Louisiana, 1863–1865." *Civil War History* 22 (March 1976): 41–59.

24-97. U.S. War Department. *The Mastership and Its Fruits: The Emancipated Slave Face to Face with His Old Master.* New York: Loyal Publication Society, 1864. 38 p.

24-98. White, Howard Ashley. *The Freedmen's Bureau in Louisiana.* Baton Rouge: Louisiana State University Press, 1970. 227 p.

24-99. Wiley, Bell I. *Southern Negroes, 1861–1865.* 1938. Reprint. Baton Rouge: Louisiana State University Press, 1974. 366 p.

Banks and the Louisiana Cotton and Sugar Industries

24-100. Prichard, Walter. "The Effects of the Civil War on the Louisiana Sugar Industry." *Journal of Southern History* 5 (August 1939): 315–32.

24-101. Roberts, A. Sellew. "The Federal Government and Confederate Cotton." *American Historical Review* 32 (January 1927): 262–75.

24-102. Roland, Charles P. "Difficulties of Civil War Sugar Planting in Louisiana." *Louisiana Historical Quarterly* 38 (October 1955): 40–62.

24-103. ———. *Louisiana Sugar Plantations during the Civil War.* Leiden: E. J. Brill, 1957. 150 p.

Banks and Reconstruction

24-104. Belz, Herman. *A New Birth of Freedom: The Republican Party and Freedmen's Rights, 1861–1866.* Westport, Conn.: Greenwood Press, 1976. 199 p.

24-105. ———. *Reconstructing the Union: Theory and Policy during the Civil War.* 1969. Reprint. Westport, Conn.: Greenwood Press, 1979. 336 p.

24-106. Dawson, Joseph Green. "The Long Ordeal: Army Generals and Reconstruction in Louisiana, 1862–1877." Ph.D. dissertation, Louisiana State University Press, 1978. 568 p. 78-15617.

24-107. Ficklen, John Rose. *History of Reconstruction in Louisiana.* 1910. Reprint. Freeport, N.Y.: Books for Libraries Press, 1971. 234 p.

24-108. Hesseltine, William B. *Lincoln's Plan of Reconstruction.* 1960. Reprint. Chicago: Quadrangle Books, 1967. 154 p.

24-109. Lowrey, Walter McGehee. "The Political Career of James Madison Wells." *Louisiana Historical Quarterly* 31 (October 1948): 995–1123.

24-110. McCarthy, Charles Hallan. *Lincoln's Plan of Reconstruction*. New York: McClure, Phillips, 1901. 531 p.

24-111. McCrary, Peyton. *Abraham Lincoln and Reconstruction: The Louisiana Experiment*. Princeton: Princeton University Press, 1978. 423 p.

24-112. Randall, James G. *Constitutional Problems under Lincoln*. Rev. ed. Urbana: University of Illinois Press, 1951. 596 p.

24-113. Scott, Eben Greenough. *Reconstruction during the Civil War in the United States of America*. 1895. Reprint. New York: Negro Universities Press, 1969. 432 p.

24-114. Taylor, Joe Gray. *Louisiana Reconstructed, 1863–1877*. Baton Rouge: Louisiana State University Press, 1974. 552 p.

24-115. ———. "New Orleans and Reconstruction." *Louisiana History* 9 (Summer 1968): 189–208.

BANKS AND LABOR

24-116. Bruce, Robert V. *1877: The Year of Violence*. Indianapolis: Bobbs-Merrill, 1959. 389 p.
Refers to Banks's view on the labor problem.

24-117. Montgomery, David. *Beyond Equality: Labor and the Radical Republicans*. 1967. Reprint. Urbana: University of Illinois Press, 1981. 535 p.
Contains several references to Banks's strong support for labor.

BANKS AND THE FENIAN MOVEMENT

The following works refer to Banks's support of the Fenian movement.

24-118. D'Arcy, William. *The Fenian Movement in the United States, 1858–1886*. 1947. Reprint. New York: Russell and Russell, 1971. 453 p.

24-119. Jenkins, Brian. *Fenians and Anglo-American Relations during Reconstruction*. Ithaca, N.Y.: Cornell University Press, 1969. 346 p.

BANKS AND FOREIGN AFFAIRS

See also Logan (9-166).

24-120. Bemis, George. *American Neutrality: Its Honorable Past, Its Expedient Future*. Boston: Little, Brown, 1866. 211 p.

24-121. Dozer, Donald Marquand. "Anti-Expansionism during the Johnson Administration." *Pacific Historical Review* 12 (September 1943): 253–75.

24-122. Dunning, William A. "Paying for Alaska." *Political Science Quarterly* 27 (September 1912): 385–98.

24-123. Holbo, Paul S. *Tarnished Expansion: The Alaska Scandal, the Press, and Congress, 1867–1871*. Knoxville: University of Tennessee Press, 1983. 145 p.

24-124. Reid, Virginia Hancock. *The Purchase of Alaska: Contemporary Opinion*. Long Beach, Calif.: Press-Telegram Printers, 1939. 134 p.

24-125. Smith, Joe Patterson. *The Republican Expansionists of the Early Reconstruction Era*. Chicago, 1933. 129 p.

24-126. Smith, Theodore C. "Expansion after the Civil War, 1865–71." *Political Science Quarterly* 16 (September 1901): 412–36.

24-127. Warner, Donald F. *The Idea of Continental Union: Agitation for the Annexation of Canada to the United States, 1849–1893*. Lexington: University of Kentucky Press, 1960. 276 p.

25. James Lawrence Orr
(1822–1873)
(Speaker, Thirty-fifth Congress)

James L. Orr was a political realist, a Southern Unionist who led South Carolina's secession, and a Confederate senator who championed Reconstruction. His early background and education provided a strong foundation for a successful political career. The Orr family emigrated from Ireland to Pennsylvania in the 1730s and later moved to the Carolinas. Orr was born in Anderson County, South Carolina, on May 12, 1822. He attended the local schools, clerked in his father's store, and entered the University of Virginia in 1839 to study mathematics, law, and political economy. After graduation in 1842 he returned to South Carolina to practice law. Following a brief venture into journalism he concentrated on law and politics.

At the age of twenty-two, Orr was elected as a Democrat to the South Carolina legislature, where he gained attention as an advocate of public-school reform. An admirer of John C. Calhoun, he nonetheless opposed nullification, and in one of his earliest speeches he defended the Union. Orr, who was a powerful speaker and a popular campaigner, was elected to Congress in 1848 and served there until 1859. During part of his service in Congress, Orr was chairman of the Committee on Indian Affairs. He used this position to champion the cause of justice for Indians. Orr continued to express Unionist sentiments, but he opposed all attempts to limit the existence of slavery, including the Compromise of 1850. As head of the South Carolina delegation to the National Democratic Convention of 1856, he worked to undermine growing secessionist impulses by supporting the candidacy of Stephen A. Douglas. He also opposed the nativist, anti-Catholic prejudices of the Know-Nothing party.

In 1857 Orr was elected Speaker of the Thirty-fifth Congress (1857–59). Although he clearly supported slavery, he presided with fairness over heated debates concerning the application of the concept of popular sovereignty to Kansas. But public sentiment in South Carolina was changing, and Orr was defeated in a bid for the Senate in 1858. He abruptly reversed his position and embraced secession. He called for South Carolina to leave the Union in 1860, and as a member of the secession convention, he signed the ordinance of secession. Orr, who hoped for a peaceful dissolution of the Union, was one of three commissioners sent to Washington to negotiate the surrender of the Charleston forts. When war broke out, he organized and briefly led Orr's Regiment of Rifles. He was elected to the Confederate Senate in 1861 and served until the end of the war. With defeat seemingly inevitable, Orr advocated a negotiated peace, a position that did nothing to increase his popularity with Southern leaders, who already questioned his earlier Unionist sympathies.

Orr played a prominent role in the reconstruction of South Carolina by supporting President Johnson's policies. After he was elected governor of the state as a Republican in 1866, he favored compromise and cooperation as the state's best response to Reconstruction. Orr's affiliation with the Republican party and his acceptance of Radical Reconstruction only increased the contempt in which he was held by the South's former leaders. He remained steadfast, though, and supported Grant's candidacy at the Republican National Convention in 1872. President Grant rewarded Orr by appointing him minister to Russia. He was physically and emotionally drained from years of controversy, and his health broke under the severe Russian climate. He died from pneumonia in St. Petersburg on May 5, 1873.

MANUSCRIPT COLLECTIONS

Duke University Library, Durham, N.C.
James L. Orr Papers.
Evansville Museum of Arts and Sciences, Evansville, Ind.
James L. Orr Papers.
South Carolina Department of Archives, Columbia, S.C.

James L. Orr Gubernatorial Papers.
8 cu. ft., 1865–68.
University of North Carolina Library, Southern Historical Collection, Chapel Hill, N.C.
Orr-Patterson Papers, 1799–1905 (includes James L. Orr Papers, 350 items, 2 vols.).

BOOKS, ARTICLES, AND DISSERTATIONS

WORKS BY JAMES L. ORR

The following Orr items are listed chronologically by year of publication and alphabetically thereunder.

*25-1. ORR, JAMES L. *Address Delivered before the Literary Society of Erskine College, . . . September 16, 1846.* Greenville, S.C.: O. H. Wells, 1846.

25-2. ———. *Speech of the Hon. James L. Orr . . . on the Slavery Question.* Washington, D.C.: Jonathan T. Towers, 1850. 7 p.
House speech of May 8, 1850.

25-3. ———. *Speech of Hon. James L. Orr . . . on the Bill to Indemnify the Public Printer.* Washington, D.C.: Congressional Globe Office, 1851. 16 p.
House speech of February 21, 1851.

25-4. ———. *Speech of Hon. J. L. Orr . . . on the Bill Granting Public Lands to Missouri to Aid in Constructing Railroads.* Washington, D.C.: Congressional Globe Office, 1852. 7 p.
House speech of February 24, 1852.

*25-5. ———. *Speech of Hon. James L. Orr, of South Carolina, on the Presidency.* N.p., 1852.
House speech of June 9, 1852.

25-6. ———. *Report on the Bill Defining the Terms on Which Treaties Shall Hereafter Be Made with Certain Tribes of Indians.* Washington, D.C., 1854. 7 p.

25-7. ———. *An Address Delivered before the Philosophian and Adelphian Societies of the Furman University.* Greenville, S.C.: G. E. Elford, 1855. 27 p.
A discourse on the value of education.

25-8. ———. *The Cincinnati Convention.* Washington, D.C.: H. Polkinhorn's Steam Book and Job Printing Office, 1855. 7 p.
A speech on South Carolina's representation at the Democratic National Convention in Cincinnati.

*25-9. ———. *Speech . . . on the French Spoliation Bill.* N.p., 1855. 7 p.

25-10. ———. *National Politics: Speech of Hon. James L. Orr, of South Carolina, on the Assault on Mr. Sumner.* Washington, D.C., 1856. 8 p.
House speech of July 14, 1856.

*25-11. ———. *Address of the Hon. James L. Orr, Governor Elect, Delivered before the Legislature of South Carolina, November 29, 1865.* Columbia, S.C.: Julian A. Selby, 1865. 7 p.

*25-12. ———. *Message of Gov. Orr to Gentlemen of the Senate and House of Representatives, December 5, 1865.* Columbia, S.C.: Columbia Phoenix, 1865. 4 p.

*25-13. ———. *Letter from Governor James L. Orr, of South Carolina, to His Excellency the President of the United States, in Reference to the Sea Island Lands.* Washington, D.C.: Gibson Brothers, 1866. 8 p.

*25-14. ———. *Message No. 1 of His Excellency Gov. J. L. Orr, with Accompanying Documents.* Columbia, S.C.: Julian A. Selby, 1866. 34 p.

*25-15. ———. *Message No. 1 (to the General Assembly Convened in Extra-Ordinary Session) September 4, 1866.* N.p., 1866. 8 p.

*25-16. ———. *Message (No. 3) of His Excellency the Governor, on the Subject of the Institution of the Deaf and Dumb and the Blind, at Cedar Springs, S.C.* Columbia, S.C.: F. G. De Fontaine, 1866. 19 p.

*25-17. ———. *Message No. 1 of His Excellency Gov. J. L. Orr, with Accompanying Documents, Prepared for the Called Session of the Legislature, July 1868.* Columbia, S.C.: Phoenix Book and Job Power Press, 1868. 198 p.

25-18. ———. *Southern Politics: Ex-Governor Orr's Reasons for Joining the Republican Party in South Carolina.* Washington, D.C.: Union Republican Congressional Executive Committee, 1870. 4 p.

25-19. ———. "Statement of ex-Governor Orr, of South Carolina, as to 'Preserving the Status' of the Forts at Charleston." *Southern Historical Society Papers* 12 (January/February 1884): 60–63.

Orr's account of the discussions between the South Carolina commissioners and President Buchanan concerning Forts Sumter and Moultrie.

25-20. ———. "James L. Orr on Congressional Reconstruction." Edited by Martin Abbott. *South Carolina Historical Magazine* 54 (July 1953): 141–42.

25-21. ———. "A Letter of James L. Orr, Minister to Russia, 1873." Edited by Joseph O. Bayless. *South Carolina Historical Magazine* 61 (October 1960): 225–31.

25-22. *Political Correspondence between J. L. Orr and A. Kendall.* Washington, D.C.: National Intelligencer Office, 1860. 10 p.

A dialogue concerning the "impending storm" of secession.

25-23. SCHOOLCRAFT, HENRY R. *Historical and Statistical Information Respecting the History, Condition, and Prospects of the Indian Tribes of the United States.* Vol. 5. 1855. Reprint. New York: Paladian Press, 1969. 712 p.

Contains an eight-page speech by Orr calling for more perceptive and humane policies.

BIOGRAPHY AND BIOGRAPHICAL SKETCHES

The only scholarly biography of Orr is Leemhuis (25-25). *See also Cyclopedia of Eminent*

and *Representative Men of the Carolinas* (11-8), Klosky (11-20), Bartlett (15-20), and Savage (15-29).

25-24. HESSELTINE, WILLIAM B. *Confederate Leaders in the New South.* 1950. Reprint. Westport, Conn.: Greenwood Press, 1970. 146 p.

25-25. LEEMHUIS, ROGER P. *James L. Orr and the Sectional Conflict.* Washington, D.C.: University Press of America, 1979. 218 p.

A sympathetic scholarly biography.

25-26. ———. "James L. Orr: The Civil War and Reconstruction Years." Ph.D. dissertation, University of Wisconsin, 1970. 327 p. 70-13924.

25-27. LIVINGSTON, JOHN. *Portraits of Eminent Americans Now Living: Including President Pierce and His Cabinet.* New York: R. Craighead, 1854. 542 p.

25-28. TOPPING, W. H. "Hon. James L. Orr, of South Carolina." *National Democratic Quarterly Review* 1 (April 1856): 328–42.

An admiring sketch of Orr's career up to 1856.

ORR'S POLITICAL ASSOCIATES

See also Simms (11-16).

25-29. BROADUS, JOHN A. *Memoir of James Petigru Boyce, D.D., LL.D.* New York: A. C. Armstrong and Son, 1893. 371 p.

25-30. COX, WILLIAM VAN ZANDT, AND NORTHRUP, MILTON HARLOW. *Life of Samuel Sullivan Cox.* Syracuse: M. H. Northrup, 1899. 280 p.

25-31. EDMUNDS, JOHN B., JR. "Francis W. Pickens: A Political Biography." Ph.D. dissertation, University of South Carolina, 1967. 268 p. 68-03929.

25-32. KIBLER, LILLIAN ADELE. *Benjamin F. Perry: South Carolina Unionist.* Durham, N.C.: Duke University Press, 1946. 562 p.

25-33. SWANBERG, W. A. *Sickles the Incredible.* New York: Charles Scribner's Sons, 1956. 433 p.

25-34. TRESCOTT, WILLIAM H. *Memorial of the Life of J. Johnston Pettigrew.* Charleston, S.C.: John Russel, 1870. 65 p.

25-35. WELLMAN, MANLY W. *Giant in Gray: A Biography of Wade Hampton of South Carolina*. New York: Charles Scribner's Sons, 1949. 387 p.

ORR'S CONGRESSIONAL CAREER AND SPEAKERSHIP

See also Nichols (15-102).

25-36. FEHRENBACHER, DON E. *Prelude to Greatness: Lincoln in the 1850s*. Stanford: Stanford University Press, 1962. 205 p.

ORR AND THE SLAVERY ISSUE

25-37. FORAN, WILLIAM A., ED. "The Attempted Conversion of James L. Orr." *Journal of Negro History* 39 (January 1954): 137.
Comprises a letter from one of Orr's slaves.

25-38. TAKAKI, RONALD. "The Movement to Reopen the African Slave Trade in South Carolina." *South Carolina Historical Magazine* 66 (January 1965): 38–54.
Orr was one of the most vigorous opponents of reopening the slave trade.

ORR, UNIONISM, AND SECESSION IN SOUTH CAROLINA

See also Potter (10-26), Halstead (15-96), and Anderson (15-105).

25-39. BOUCHER, CHAUNCEY S. "South Carolina on the Eve of Secession, 1852 to 1860." *Washington University Studies* 6 (April 1919): 79–144.

25-40. BREESE, DONALD H. "James L. Orr, Calhoun, and the Cooperationist Tradition in South Carolina." *South Carolina History Magazine* 80 (October 1979): 273–85.

25-41. CAUTHEN, CHARLES EDWARD. "South Carolina's Decision to Lead the Secession Movement." *North Carolina Historical Review* 18 (October 1941): 360–72.

25-42. *The Diary of a Public Man: An Intimate View of the National Administration, December 28, 1860 to March 15, 1861*. Prefatory notes by F. Lauriston Bullard. Foreword by Carl Sandburg. Chicago, 1945. 117 p.

An anonymous account of Orr's mission to negotiate the surrender of the Charleston forts.

25-43. HAMER, PHILIP M. *The Secession Movement in South Carolina, 1847–1852*. 1918. Reprint. New York: Da Capo Press, 1971. 152 p.

25-44. KIBLER, LILLIAN ADELE. "Unionist Sentiment in South Carolina in 1860." *Journal of Southern History* 4 (August 1938): 346–66.

25-45. MAY, JOHN A., AND FAUNT, JOAN R., EDS. *South Carolina Secedes*. Columbia: University of South Carolina Press, 1960. 231 p.

25-46. SCHULTZ, HAROLD S. *Nationalism and Sectionalism in South Carolina, 1852–1860*. 1950. Reprint. New York: Da Capo Press, 1969. 259 p.

25-47. SOUTH CAROLINA. CONVENTION JOURNAL, 1860–62. *Journal of the Convention of the People of South Carolina, Held in 1860, 1861 and 1862, Together with the Ordinances, Reports, Resolutions, Etc*. Columbia, S.C.: R. W. Gibbs, 1862. 873 p.
The complete transcript of the convention at which Orr played an important role.

25-48. WHITE, LAURA A. "The National Democrats in South Carolina, 1852 to 1860." *South Atlantic Quarterly* 28 (October 1929): 370–89.

ORR AND THE CONFEDERACY

See also Chestnut (17-72), Confederate States of America (17-73), Freeman and Vandiver (17-75), and Yearns (22-91).

25-49. CALDWELL, J. F. J. *The History of a Brigade of South Carolinians*. Philadelphia: King and Bard, 1866. 247 p.
Includes an account of Orr's Rifles.

25-50. CAUTHEN, CHARLES EDWARD. *South Carolina Goes to War, 1860–1865*. James Sprunt Studies in History and Political Science, vol. 32. Chapel Hill: University of North Carolina Press, 1950. 256 p.

25-51. CONFEDERATE STATES OF AMERICA. CONGRESS. SENATE. COMMITTEE ON FOREIGN RELATIONS. *Report of the Committee on Foreign Relations, on the Resolution of the Senate Asking for the Facts in Relation to the Lawless Seizure and Capture of the Confeder-*

ate Steamer Florida *in the Bay of Bahia, Brazil.* N.p., 1864. 8 p.

The report was submitted by Orr.

25-52. CONFEDERATE STATES OF AMERICA. CONGRESS. SENATE. SELECT COMMITTEE TO WHOM WAS REFERRED THAT PORTION OF THE MESSAGE OF THE PRESIDENT OF THE CONFEDERATE STATES, OF THE 13TH INSTANT, RELATING TO THE ACTION OF CONGRESS DURING THE PRESENT SESSION. *Report* . . . . N.p., 1865. 8 p.

Orr chaired this select committee which responded to President Jefferson Davis's plan to use slaves as soldiers.

ORR AND RECONSTRUCTION IN

SOUTH CAROLINA

See also Perman (17-87).

25-53. BALL, WILLIAM W. *The State That Forgot: South Carolina's Surrender to Democracy.* Indianapolis: Bobbs-Merrill, 1932. 307 p.

25-54. BROOKS, U. R. *South Carolina Bench and Bar.* Columbia, S.C.: State, 1909. 381 p.

25-55. HENRY, ROBERT SELPH. *The Story of Reconstruction.* Indianapolis: Bobbs-Merrill, 1938. 633 p.

25-56. HOLLIS, DANIEL W. *The University of South Carolina.* 2 vols. Columbia: University of South Carolina Press, 1956.

Contains an examination of Orr's efforts as governor to transform South Carolina College into the University of South Carolina.

25-57. HOLLIS, JOHN P. *The Early Period of Reconstruction in South Carolina.* Johns Hopkins University Studies in Historical and Political Science, 23d ser. Baltimore: Johns Hopkins Press, 1905. 129 p.

25-58. KINCAID, LARRY G. "The Legislative Origins of the Military Reconstruction Act, 1865–1867." Ph.D. dissertation, Johns Hopkins University, 1968. 377 p. 68-16437.

25-59. KNIGHT, EDGAR W. "Reconstruction and Education in South Carolina." *South Atlantic Quarterly* 18 (October 1919): 350–64.

25-60. LELAND, JOHN A. *A Voice from South Carolina.* 1879. Reprint. Freeport, N.Y.: Books for Libraries Press, 1971. 231 p.

Severely criticizes Orr for the changes that Reconstruction brought to the state.

25-61. MOORE, W. G. "Notes of Colonel W. G. Moore: Private Secretary to President Johnson, 1866–1868." *American Historical Review* 19 (October 1913): 98–132.

25-62. PERMAN, MICHAEL. "The South and Congress's Reconstruction Policy, 1866–67." *Journal of American Studies* 4 (February 1971): 181–200.

25-63. RANDEL, WILLIAM P. *The Ku Klux Klan: A Century of Infamy.* Philadelphia: Chilton, 1965. 300 p.

25-64. REYNOLDS, JOHN S. *Reconstruction in South Carolina, 1865–1877.* 1905. Reprint. New York: Negro Universities Press, 1969. 522 p.

25-65. SIMKINS, FRANCIS BUTLER, AND WOODY, ROBERT HILLIARD. *South Carolina during Reconstruction.* 1932. Reprint. Gloucester, Mass.: Peter Smith, 1966. 590 p.

25-66. SNOWDEN, YATES. *History of South Carolina.* 5 vols. Chicago: Lewis, 1920.

25-67. TAYLOR, ALRUTHEUS A. *The Negro in South Carolina during Reconstruction.* 1925. Reprint. New York: AMS Press, 1971. 341 p.

25-68. THOMPSON, HENRY T. *Ousting the Carpetbagger from South Carolina.* 1926. Reprint. New York: Negro Universities Press, 1969. 182 p.

25-69. TROWBRIDGE, JOHN T. *A Picture of the Desolated States and the Work of Restoration, 1865–1868.* Hartford, Conn.: L. Stebbins, 1868. 690 p.

25-70. ———. *The South: A Tour of Its Battlefields and Ruined Cities, a Journey through the Desolated States.* Hartford, Conn.: L. Stebbins, 1866. 590 p.

25-71. WALLACE, DAVID DUNCAN. *The History of South Carolina.* 4 vols. New York: American Historical Society, 1934.

25-72. WILLIAMSON, JOEL. *After Slavery: The Negro in South Carolina during Reconstruction, 1861–1877.* 1965. New York: W. W. Norton, 1975. 442 p.

ORR AS AMBASSADOR TO RUSSIA

25-73. U.S. DEPARTMENT OF STATE. *Papers Relating to the Foreign Relations of the United States, Transmitted to Congress, with the Annual Message of the President, December 1, 1873.* 2 vols. Washington, D.C.: Government Printing Office, 1873.
   Includes the three communiqués that Orr sent to Secretary of State Hamilton Fish.

26. William Pennington
(1796–1862)
(Speaker, Thirty-sixth Congress)

William Pennington was an undistinguished politician. He was chosen Speaker of the House in 1859 as the least objectionable compromise candidate. Born in Newark, New Jersey, on May 4, 1796, he was the son of New Jersey Governor William Sandford Pennington. He attended local schools and graduated from Princeton in 1813. Pennington studied law with Theodore Frelinghuysen and was licensed as an attorney in 1817. He served as clerk of the district and circuit courts in Newark from 1817 to 1826, while his father was district judge. He joined the Whig party after being elected to the state assembly as a Democrat in 1828.

When the Whigs gained control of the state legislature in 1837, Pennington was elected governor and chancellor of New Jersey. Although he was reelected five times, the only notable event of his tenure (1837–43) was the "broad seal war" of 1838–39. In the 1838 congressional elections, five Democratic candidates contested the election returns of their Whig opponents. Governor Pennington, exercising his legal prerogative, certified the election of the five Whigs by issuing their commissions under the state seal. The rejected Democrats took their case to Congress and contested the seating of the New Jersey delegation. Ten days of heated debate culminated with the seating of the five Democrats and the selection of Robert M. T. Hunter as Speaker of the House. Pennington was severely criticized for not ordering an investigation into the contested election returns, even though he had no legal recourse but to accept the returns as reported.

After he was defeated for reelection in 1843, Pennington returned to his legal practice. He had ambitions to become chancellor, an appointive office under the new constitution, or minister to a European country. He declined offers to become governor of the Minnesota Territory or a claims judge under the Treaty of Guadalupe Hidalgo.

In 1858, at the age of sixty-two, Pennington was elected to Congress as a Republican. When the House convened in 1859, no political faction had a clear majority. Democrats were split over President Buchanan's Kansas policy, and Republicans lacked enough votes to elect their candidate, John Sherman of Ohio, as Speaker. The House debated and balloted for eight weeks before it finally settled on the relatively unknown and untried Pennington as a compromise candidate. He proved to be a less than adequate Speaker, so ignorant of parliamentary law that he reportedly had to ask the advice of a page. After he was defeated for reelection in 1860, Pennington returned to Newark, where he died on February 16, 1862, from an overdose of morphine evidently administered by mistake.

MANUSCRIPT COLLECTIONS

New Jersey Historical Society, Newark, N.J.
  William Pennington Papers, ca. 1820–62.
  Ca. 400 items.
  NUCMC 60-982.

BOOKS, ARTICLES, AND DISSERTATIONS

WORKS BY WILLIAM PENNINGTON

*26-1. PENNINGTON, WILLIAM. *Opinion of Governor Pennington, of New Jersey, . . . in Relation to the Powers and Duty of the Governor and Privy Council, in Canvassing the Votes for Representatives in Congress.* Washington, D.C.: Niles' National Register, [1839?]. 12 p.

*26-2. ———. *Special Message of Governor of New Jersey, January 14, 1840.* Trenton, N.J., 1840.

BIOGRAPHICAL SKETCHES

There is no biography of Pennington. The following biographical sketches are inadequate; the sketch in *A History of Newark* (26-7), by Pennington's grandson, is more detailed than the others.

26-3. ATKINSON, JOSEPH. *The History of Newark, New Jersey.* Newark: William B. Guild, 1878. 334 p.

26-4. *The Biographical Encyclopaedia of New Jersey of the Nineteenth Century.* Philadelphia: Galaxy, 1877. 574 p.

26-5. EGBERT, DONALD DREW. *Princeton Portraits.* Princeton: Princeton University Press, 1947. 360 p.

26-6. ELMER, LUCIUS Q. C. *The Constitution and Government of the Province and State of New Jersey, with Biographical Sketches of the Governors from 1776 to 1845 and Reminiscences of the Bench and Bar during More than Half a Century.* Newark: Martin R. Dennis, 1872. 495 p.

26-7. *A History of Newark, New Jersey: Embracing Practically Two and a Half Centuries, 1666–1913.* Vol. 2. New York: Lewis, 1913. 1,125 p.

PENNINGTON AND PRINCETON, 1813

See also Egbert (26-5).

26-8. GIFFORD, ARTHUR N. "Reminiscences of the War of 1812." *Proceedings of the New Jersey Historical Society* 2 (October 1917): 218.
A letter from a Princeton classmate comments upon Pennington's alleged personality change after 1813.

PENNINGTON AND NEW JERSEY HISTORY AND POLITICS

See also Lee (5-9).

26-9. CHUTE, WILLIAM J. "The New Jersey Whig Campaign of 1840." *Proceedings of the New Jersey Historical Society* 77 (October 1959): 223–39.
Pennington is treated within the context of the broad seal war.

26-10. ERSHKOWITZ, HERBERT. "New Jersey Politics during the Era of Andrew Jackson, 1820–1837." Ph.D. dissertation, New York University, 1965. 314 p. 66-05657.

26-11. ———. "Samuel L. Southard: A Case Study of Whig Leadership in the Age of Jackson." *Proceedings of the New Jersey Historical Society* 88 (Spring 1970): 5–24.

26-12. FALLAW, WALTER R., JR. "The Rise of the Whig Party in New Jersey." Ph.D. dissertation, Princeton University, 1967. 466 p. 67-09599.
A useful analysis of Whig factionalism and the impact of the broad seal war.

26-13. HERRMANN, FREDERICK M. "Stress and Structure: Political Change in Antebellum New

Jersey." Ph.D. dissertation, Rutgers University, 1976. 378 p. 76-27007.

Analyzes the important changes in the structure of state government that occurred during Pennington's term as governor.

26-14. KNAPP, CHARLES M. *New Jersey Politics during the Period of Civil War and Reconstruction.* Geneva, N.Y.: W. F. Humphrey, 1924. 212 p.

26-15. KULL, IRVING S., ED. *New Jersey: A History.* 6 vols. New York: American Historical Society, 1930.

26-16. LOCKARD, DUANE. *The New Jersey Governor: A Study in Political Power.* New Jersey Historical Series, vol. 14. Princeton: D. Van Nostrand, 1964. 153 p.

26-17. LUTZKER, MICHAEL A. "Abolition of Imprisonment for Debt in New Jersey." *Proceedings of the New Jersey Historical Society* 84 (October 1966): 1–29.

26-18. MYERS, WILLIAM S. "New Jersey Politics from the Revolution to the Civil War." *Americana* 37 (July 1943): 395–449.

A full, favorable examination of Pennington's actions as governor during the broad seal war.

26-19. NEW JERSEY. LEGISLATURE. GENERAL ASSEMBLY. *Minutes of Votes and Proceedings of the Sixty-Third General Assembly of the State of New Jersey.* 1838. Newark: M. S. Harrison, 1839.

A complete record of Pennington's legislative actions while governor.

26-20. ———. *Votes and Proceedings of the Fifty-third General Assembly of the State of New Jersey.* Woodbury, N.J.: P. J. Gray, 1829.

Pennington served as a representative of Essex County.

26-21. SHAW, WILLIAM H. *History of Essex and Hudson Counties, New Jersey.* Vol. 1. Philadelphia: Everts and Peck, 1884. 678 p.

PENNINGTON'S POLITICAL ASSOCIATES

See also Drake (15-63), Davis (26-27), and Henig (26-29).

26-22. CHAMBERS, TALBOT W. *Memoir of the Life and Character of the Late Hon. Theo. Frelinghuysen,*

LL.D. New York: Harper and Brothers, 1863. 289 p.

26-23. SMITH, CHARLES PERRIN. *New Jersey Political Reminiscences, 1828–1882.* Edited by Herman K. Platt. New Brunswick, N.J.: Rutgers University Press, 1965. 278 p.

26-24. SMITH, WILLIAM E. *The Francis Preston Blair Family in Politics.* 2 vols. 1933. Reprint. New York: Da Capo Press, 1969.

26-25. STEINER, BERNARD C. *Life of Henry Winter Davis.* Baltimore: John Murphy, 1916. 416 p.

PENNINGTON AND THE SPEAKERSHIP

See also Drake (15-63), Mering (15-101), Nichols (15-102), Adams (21-92), Giddings (21-116), and Henry (24-20).

26-26. ADAMS, CHARLES FRANCIS, JR. *An Autobiography, 1835–1915: With a Memorial Address Delivered November 17, 1915 by Henry Cabot Lodge.* 1916. Reprint. Westport, Conn.: Greenwood Press, 1973. 224 p.

Adams recalls Pennington's incompetence as Speaker in several sharp anecdotes.

26-27. DAVIS, REUBEN. *Recollections of Mississippi and Mississippians.* Rev. ed. with an introduction by William D. McCain. Hattiesburg: University Press of Mississippi, 1972. 456 p.

Includes an account of Pennington's election and first actions as Speaker.

26-28. HENIG, GERALD S. "Henry Winter Davis and the Speakership Contest of 1859–60." *Maryland Historical Magazine* 68 (Spring 1973): 1–19.

Analyzes Davis's motives for casting the deciding ballot for Pennington.

26-29. ———. *Henry Winter Davis: Antebellum and Civil War Congressman from Maryland.* New York: Twayne, 1973. 332 p.

Davis played a major role in the speakership election, casting the deciding ballot for Pennington.

26-30. HICKEN, VICTOR. "John A. McClernand and the House Speakership Struggle of 1859." *Journal of the Illinois State Historical Society* 53 (Summer 1960): 163–78.

26-31. NICKLASON, FRED. "The Secession Winter and the Committee of Five." *Pennsylvania History* 38 (October 1971): 372–88.

26-32. NIXON, JOHN T. "Election of William Pennington, of New Jersey, as Speaker of the Thirty-sixth Congress." *Proceedings of the New Jersey Historical Society,* 2d ser., 2 (1872): 205–20.

Nixon, a member of the Thirty-sixth Congress, suggests that his demand for Sherman's withdrawal secured the nomination for Pennington.

26-33. SUTHERLAND, KEITH ALAN. "Congress and Crisis: A Study in the Legislative Process, 1860." Ph.D. dissertation, Cornell University, 1966. 359 p. 67-01417.

Contains a chapter on the 1859–60 speakership contest.

26-34. TULSA, FRANK J. "Congressional Politics in the Secession Crisis, 1859–61." Ph.D. dissertation, Pennsylvania State University, 1975. 261 p. 75-22716.

Features the most comprehensive study of Pennington's actions as Speaker.

27. Galusha Aaron Grow
(1823–1907)
(Speaker, Thirty-seventh Congress)

The volatile political climate preceding the Civil War centered on the issue of slavery, but for many Northerners the question of the disposition of western lands was an equally pressing concern. Galusha A. Grow's political career illustrates how these two issues converged in the late 1850s.

Grow was born in Connecticut on August 31, 1823. He grew up on small farms in Connecticut and in Pennsylvania, where the family moved after his father's death. He developed an interest in politics and an opposition to slavery while attending Amherst College. After graduation in 1844, he studied law and eventually formed a partnership in Towanda, Pennsylvania, with David Wilmot, author of the famous Wilmot Proviso. Grow, a Democrat, was not as vocally anti-slavery as his partner, who joined the Free Soil party in 1848. In the congressional elections of 1850, Wilmot withdrew from the race so that Grow, as a fusion candidate acceptable to both Free Soil and Democratic parties, might defeat the Whig candidate.

As he entered national politics, Grow at first tried to avoid the extremism on both sides of the slavery issue. He was elected to the Thirty-second Congress (1851–54), which he entered as its youngest member. Throughout his congressional career he pursued an interest in the disposition of public lands. His first speech in Congress, "Man's Right to the Soil," expressed his proposal to give free homesteads to settlers who would live on the land and cultivate it for a given number of years. Grow's proposal encountered hostile opposition from Southern members, who viewed such a system as tantamount to an attack upon slavery. "Free soil" and "free labor" were becoming inextricably linked slogans in the political vocabulary of the 1850s. Grow, by siding with the concept of free soil, had moved squarely into the anti-slavery camp.

With the increasingly aggressive posture of Southern defenders of slavery, Grow acted upon the implications of his principles by joining the Republican party in 1857. He had served three terms as a Democrat (1851–57), and he served three more as a Republican (1857–63). Although he suffered from chronic indigestion, Grow, who stood six feet two inches, was sturdily built. When he was physically challenged on the House floor by Congressman Laurence Keitt of South Carolina, the same man who had stood guard while Preston Brooks had savagely caned Charles Sumner in the Senate chamber, Grow defended himself and floored Keitt with a single blow.

Grow was elected Speaker when President Lincoln called Congress into special session following the firing on Fort Sumter. Although he served only one term as Speaker, Grow was able to take advantage of the absence of Southern opposition to push through the Homestead Act in 1862. Pennsylvania changed the boundaries of Grow's district, making it a Demo-cratic stronghold, which resulted in his defeat for reelection. For the next thirty years Grow devoted himself to business. From 1871 to 1875 he was president of the International and Great Northern Railroad Company in Houston, Texas. He returned to Pennsylvania and engaged in lumbering, land surveying, and coal mining. In 1894 he was elected to the Fifty-third Congress to complete an unexpired term. He was subsequently reelected to the Fifty-fourth through Fifty-seventh Congresses (1895–1903). Grow retired in 1903 and was rewarded for his service with a pension from Andrew Carnegie. He died in 1907.

MANUSCRIPT COLLECTIONS

Susquehanna County Historical Society, Montrose, Pa.

Galusha Grow Papers.

Grow manuscripts are quite rare, since most of his private papers were destroyed in a house fire. There are about a dozen letters in scattered collections at the Pennsylvania Historical Society and nine letters in the Lincoln, Garfield, Harrison, and McKinley collections in the Library of Congress Manuscript Division.

BOOKS, ARTICLES, AND DISSERTATIONS

WORKS BY GALUSHA A. GROW

The following items are listed chronologically by year of publication and alphabetically thereunder. *See also* Egle (27-34).

27-1. GROW, GALUSHA A. *Man's Right to the Soil: A Speech of Hon. G. A. Grow of Pennsylvania . . . on the Homestead Bill.* Washington, D.C.: Congressional Globe, 1852.
House speech of March 30, 1852, advocating homestead legislation.

*27-2. ———. *Remarks of Hon. G. A. Grow, of Pennsylvania, on the Finality of the Compromise.* Washington, D.C.: Congressional Globe, 1852. 6 p.
House speech of May 27, 1852.

27-3. ———. *A Homestead Bill: A Speech of Hon. G. A. Grow.* Washington, D.C.: Congressional Globe, 1854.
House speech of February 21, 1854.

27-4. ———. *Nebraska and Kansas: A Speech of Hon. G. A. Grow.* N.p., 1854. 8 p.
House speech of May 10, 1854, in opposition to the Kansas-Nebraska Act.

27-5. ———. *Affairs in Kansas: A Speech of Hon. Galusha A. Grow.* Washington, D.C.: Buell and Blanchard, 1856. 8 p.
House speech of March 5, 1856, defending the rights of citizens in the Kansas Territory.

27-6. ———. *Admission of Kansas: A Speech of Hon. G. A. Grow . . . on Closing the Debate on the Bill Reported from the Committee on Territories for the Admission of Kansas into the Union as a State.* Washington, D.C.: Buell and Blanchard, 1856. 8 p.
An argument for the admission of Kansas delivered in the House on June 30, 1856.

*27-7. ———. *Delegate from Kansas: Remarks of Hon. G. A. Grow, of Pennsylvania, . . . on the Question of Administering the Oath of Office to John W. Whitfield, as the Delegate from Kansas Territory.* Washington, D.C.: Buell and Blanchard, 1856. 7 p.
House speech of December 1, 1856.

27-8. ———. *Remarks of Messrs. Grow, Quitman, and T. L. Harris, on the Missouri Compromise, and the Responsibility for the Organization of the House.* Washington, D.C.: Congressional Globe, 1856. 8 p.

A spirited debate held in the House on January 18 and 19, 1856.

27-9. ———. *Kansas: The Lecompton Constitution, Speech of Hon. G. A. Grow.* Washington, D.C.: Buell and Blanchard, 1858. 8 p.

House speech of March 25, 1858, in opposition to the admission of Kansas on the basis of the Lecompton Constitution.

27-10. ———. *Responsibility for Organizing the House and for the Defeat of the Post Office Appropriations Bill: Remarks of Hon. Galusha A. Grow.* N.p., 1859. 8 p.

House speech of December 22, 1859, criticizing Speaker Cobb.

27-11. ———. *Free Homes for Free Men (Land for the Landless): Speech of Hon. G. A. Grow.* N.p., 1860. 8 p.

House speech of February 29, 1860, in favor of homestead legislation.

27-12. ———. *Speeches of Hon. Galusha A. Grow . . . on Homestead, Tariff, and Election of Speaker for Thirty-seventh Congress.* Washington, D.C.: Scammell, 1862. 16 p.

Includes Grow's February 29, 1860, speech (27-11), his May 1860 speech on the tariff, and his speech upon election to the speakership.

*27-13. ———. *Speech of Hon. G. A. Grow on the Currency and Resumption of Specie Payments, Made at a Mass Meeting in Philadelphia, September 25, 1875.* N.p., 1875. 7 p.

27-14. ———. *Money and Its Uses; Hard Times, Their Cause and Cure: Speech of Hon. Galusha A. Grow, Delivered at Oil City, Pa., August 10, 1878.* N.p., 1878. 24 p.

*27-15. ———. *Let Well Enough Alone: Speech.* Pittsburgh, 1880.

27-16. ———. *Hawaiian Policy of the Administration: A Speech of Hon. Galusha A. Grow.* Washington, D.C., 1894.

House speech of April 18, 1894, criticizing Cleveland's Hawaiian policy.

27-17. ———. *Home Labor to Supply Home Markets: A Speech.* Washington, D.C., 1894.

House speech of June 7, 1894, in favor of increased domestic production.

27-18. ———. *National Banks instead of State Banks: Speech of Hon. Galusha A. Grow.* N.p., 1894.

House speech of May 26, 1894, advocating the creation of more national banks than state-controlled banks.

27-19. ———. *The President's Message, Free Coinage of Silver, Protective Tariff Best for Revenue: Speeches of Hon. Galusha A. Grow.* Washington, D.C., 1896. 20 p.

House speeches of December 12, 1895, and February 13 and March 17, 1896, critical of Cleveland's policies.

27-20. ———. *Protective Duties on Imported Articles Do Not Necessarily Enhance the Price of Such Articles to the Consumer: Remarks of Hon. Galusha A. Grow.* N.p., 1897.

House speech of March 25, 1897, critical of a protective tariff.

27-21. ———. *Annexation of the Hawaiian Islands: A Speech of Hon. Galusha A. Grow.* Washington, D.C., 1898. 8 p.

House speech of June 14, 1898, in favor of annexation.

27-22. ———. *The Civil Service: A Speech.* Washington, D.C., 1898.

House speech of January 5, 1898, arguing for an independent, efficient civil service.

27-23. ———. *Free Homes for Pioneer Settlers: A Speech.* Washington, D.C., 1898.

House speech of March 10, 1898, reviewing the impact of homestead legislation.

27-24. ———. *The Government's Plighted Faith in the Payment of Its Debts: Speech of Hon. Galusha A. Grow.* Washington, D.C., 1898. 16 p.

House speech of May 26, 1898, arguing for the payment of debts in specie rather than paper currency.

27-25. ———. *Independence of Cuba: Remarks of Hon. Galusha A. Grow.* Washington, D.C.: Government Printing Office, 1898. 4 p.

House speech of March 31, 1898, in support of Cuban independence.

27-26. ———. *Justice to the Pioneer Settler: Speech of Hon. Galusha A. Grow.* Washington, D.C.: Government Printing Office, 1900. 15 p.

House speech of May 3, 1900, urging an extension of existing homestead legislation.

BIOGRAPHY AND BIOGRAPHICAL SKETCHES

The only biography of Grow, Dubois and Mathews (27-28), is dated but adequate.

27-27. Brockett, Linus P. *Men of Our Day: Biographical Sketches of Patriots, Orators, Statesmen, Generals, Reformers, Financiers, and Merchants.* Philadelphia: Zeigler, McCurdy, 1868. 696 p.

27-28. Dubois, James T., and Mathews, Gertrude S. *Galusha Grow: Father of the Homestead Law.* Boston: Houghton Mifflin, 1917. 305 p.

27-29. Watrous, A. E. "Galusha A. Grow." *Harper's Weekly,* 24 February 1894, p. 211.

Discusses Grow's return to the House after thirty years and includes a short sketch of his life.

GROW AND PENNSYLVANIA HISTORY
AND POLITICS

27-30. Blackman, Emily C. *History of Susquehanna County, Pennsylvania.* 1873. Reprint. Baltimore: Regional, 1970. 685 p.

27-31. Bradley, Erwin Stanley. *The Triumph of Militant Republicanism: A Study of Pennsylvania and Presidential Politics, 1860–1872.* Philadelphia: University of Pennsylvania Press, 1964. 467 p.

27-32. Davis, Stanton Ling. *Pennsylvania Politics, 1860–1863.* Cleveland: Case Western Reserve University Press, 1935. 334 p.

27-33. Stocker, Rhamanthus M. *Centennial History of Susquehanna County, Pennsylvania.* 1887. Reprint. Baltimore: Regional, 1974. 927 p.

GROW'S POLITICAL ASSOCIATES

See also Bradley (16-72), Going (20-23), and Steiner (26-25).

27-34. Egle, William Henry, ed. *Andrew Gregg Curtin: His Life and Services.* Philadelphia: Avil Printing, 1895. 521 p.

In the chapter entitled "Curtin and Pennsylvania at the Beginning of the War" Grow writes much about Governor Curtin's actions as well as his own.

27-35. Magdol, Edward. *Owen Lovejoy: Abolitionist in Congress.* New Brunswick, N.J.: Rutgers University Press, 1967. 493 p.

27-36. Mayes, Edward. *Lucius Q. C. Lamar: His Life, Times, and Speeches, 1825–1893.* 1896. Reprint. New York: AMS Press, 1974. 820 p.

27-37. Schurz, Carl. *Intimate Letters of Carl Schurz, 1841–1869.* Translated and edited by Joseph Schafer. 1928. Reprint. New York: Da Capo Press, 1970. 491 p.

GROW'S CONGRESSIONAL CAREER AND
SPEAKERSHIP

See also Fite (15-95), Nichols (15-102), Nicklason (26-31), Sutherland (26-33), and Tulsa (26-34).

27-38. Brichford, Maynard J. "Congress at the Outbreak of the War." *Civil War History* 3 (June 1957): 153–62.

27-39. Gobright, Lawrence A. *Recollections of Men and Things at Washington during the Third of a Century.* Philadelphia: Claxton, Remsen, and Hoffelfinger, 1869. 420 p.

27-40. Hart, Charles Desmond. "The Natural Limits of Slavery Expansion: Kansas-Nebraska, 1854." *Kansas Historical Quarterly* 34 (Spring 1968): 32–50.

27-41. Hutchins, John. "Opening Scenes in the Thirty-sixth Congress: By an Eyewitness." *Magazine of Western History* 10 (May 1889): 102–10.

27-42. Martin, Edward Winslow [James D. McCabe]. *Behind the Scenes in Washington.* 1873. Reprint. New York: Arno Press, 1974. 518 p.

27-43. Simms, Henry H. "The Controversy over the Admission of the State of Oregon." *Missis-*

sippi Valley Historical Review 32 (December 1945): 355–74.

27-44. U. S. CONGRESS. HOUSE. COMMITTEE ON THE TERRITORIES. *Reports and Documents relating to the Constitution adopted by the People of Kansas. . . .* Washington, D.C.: Government Printing Office, 1860. 55 p.

> Grow was one of the principal authors of the majority report in favor of the constitution adopted by the people of Kansas on October 4, 1859.

GROW AND THE HOMESTEAD ACT

See also Robbins (9-196), Stephenson (9-199), and Zahler (9-205).

27-45. COMMONS, JOHN R. "Horace Greeley and the Working Class Origins of the Republican Party." *Political Science Quarterly* 24 (September 1909): 468–88.

27-46. DONALDSON, THOMAS. *The Public Domain: Its History, with Statistics.* 1881. Reprint. New York: Johnson Reprint, 1970. 1,343 p.

> Details Grow's part in the formulation and enactment of the Homestead Act.

27-47. GREELEY, HORACE, AND CLEVELAND, JOHN F. *A Political Textbook for 1860.* 1860. Reprint. New York: Negro Universities Press, 1969. 248 p.

> Includes a chapter on the public lands, featur-

ing reprints of Grow's position on homestead legislation.

27-48. ILISERICH, ROBERT D. "Galusha Grow: Pennsylvania's Champion of the Homestead Act." *Western Pennsylvania Historical Magazine* 40 (Fall 1957): 205–16.

> Argues that Grow played an even greater role in the success of homestead legislation than is usually acknowledged.

27-49. MAXEY, EDWIN. "Galusha A. Grow: Father of the Homestead Bill." *Overland Monthly* 52 (July 1908): 74–77.

27-50. MIDDLETON, THOMAS J. "Andrew Johnson and the Homestead Law." *Sewanee Review* 15 (July 1907): 316–20.

27-51. ROBBINS, ROY M. "Horace Greeley: Land Reform and Unemployment, 1837–1862." *Agricultural History* 7 (January 1933): 18–41.

27-52. WILSON, MAJOR L. "The Controversy over Slavery Expansion and the Concept of the Safety Valve: Ideological Confusion in the 1850s." *Mississippi Quarterly* 24 (Spring 1971): 135–53.

> Argues that Grow sought to use land to balance the evils of an advancing civilization.

27-53. WILSON, RUFUS R. "The Maker of Four Million Homes." *World's Work* 1 (March 1901): 475–76.

PART IV

THE SPEAKERS, 1861–1911

28. General Bibliography, 1861–1911

GENERAL HISTORIES

28-1. Dewey, Davis R. *National Problems, 1885–1897.* 1907. Reprint. New York: Greenwood Press, 1968. 360 p.

28-2. Faulkner, Harold U. *Politics, Reform, and Expansion, 1890–1900.* New York: Harper and Brothers, 1959. 312 p.

28-3. Ford, Henry Jones. *The Cleveland Era: A Chronicle of the New Order in Politics.* 1919. Reprint. New York: United States Publishers Association, 1972. 232 p.

28-4. Haworth, Paul L. *The United States in Our Own Times, 1865–1920.* New York: Charles Scribner's Sons, 1935. 626 p.

28-5. Morgan, H. Wayne. *From Hayes to McKinley: National Party Politics, 1877–1896.* Syracuse: Syracuse University Press, 1969. 618 p.

28-6. Oberholtzer, Ellis P. *A History of the United States since the Civil War.* 5 vols. 1928. Reprint. New York: Negro Universities Press, 1969.

28-7. Randall, James G., and Donald, David H. *The Civil War and Reconstruction.* 2d ed. Lexington, Ky.: D. C. Heath, 1969. 866 p.

28-8. Rhodes, James Ford. *History of the United States from the Compromise of 1850 to the End of the Roosevelt Administration.* Vol. 8. 1936. Reprint. New York: Macmillan, 1966. 620 p.

NATIONAL POLITICS

28-9. Benedict, Michael Les. *A Compromise of Principle: Congressional Republicans and Reconstruction, 1863–1869.* New York: W. W. Norton, 1974. 493 p.

28-10. Coleman, Charles H. *The Election of 1868.* 1933. Reprint. New York: Octagon Books, 1971. 407 p.

28-11. Curtis, Francis. *The Republican Party: A History of Its Fifty Years' Experience.* 2 vols. 1904. Reprint. New York: AMS Press, 1978.

28-12. Eaton, Herbert. *Presidential Timber: A History of Nominating Conventions, 1868–1960.* New York: Free Press, 1964. 528 p.

28-13. Hoogenboom, Ari. *Outlawing the Spoils: A History of the Civil Service Reform Movement, 1861–1883.* 1961. Reprint. Westport, Conn.: Greenwood Press, 1982. 306 p.

28-14. Jones, Stanley L. *The Presidential Election of 1896.* Madison: University of Wisconsin Press, 1964. 436 p.

28-15. Knoles, George Harmon. *The Presidential Campaign and Election of 1892.* 1942. Reprint. New York: AMS Press, 1971. 268 p.

28-16. Merrill, Horace Samuel, and Merrill, Marion Galbraith. *The Republican Command, 1897–1913.* Lexington: University of Kentucky Press, 1971. 360 p.

28-17. Milton, George Fort. *The Age of Hate: Andrew Johnson and the Radicals.* 1930. Reprint. Hamden, Conn.: Archon Books, 1965. 788 p.

28-18. Morgan, H. Wayne, ed. *The Gilded Age: A Reappraisal.* Syracuse: Syracuse University Press, 1963. 329 p.

28-19. Tarbell, Ida M. *The Tariff in Our Times.* New York: Macmillan, 1911. 375 p.

28-20. Trefousse, Hans L. *The Radical Republicans: Lincoln's Vanguard for Racial Justice.* 1968. Reprint. Baton Rouge: Louisiana State University Press, 1975. 492 p.

28-21. Tweedy, John. *A History of the Republican National Conventions from 1856–1908.* Danbury, Conn.: J. Tweedy, 1910. 408 p.

28-22. Williams, R. Hal. *Years of Decision: American Politics in the 1890s.* New York: John Wiley and Sons, 1978. 219 p.

POLITICAL MEMOIRS

28-23. Barry, David S. *Forty Years in Washington.* 1924. Reprint. New York: Beckman, 1974. 349 p.

28-24. Cole, Cyrenus. *I Remember, I Remember: A Book of Reminiscences.* Iowa City: State Historical Society of Iowa, 1936. 543 p.

28-25. Cox, James M. *Journey through My Years.* New York: Simon and Schuster, 1946. 463 p.

28-26. Cox, Samuel S. *Union—Disunion—Reunion: Three Decades of Federal Legislation, 1855 to 1885.* 1885. Reprint. Freeport, N.Y.: Books for Libraries Press, 1970. 726 p.

28-27. Cullom, Shelby M. *Fifty Years of Public Service.* 1911. Reprint. New York: Da Capo Press, 1969. 467 p.

28-28. Dunn, Arthur Wallace. *From Harrison to Harding: A Personal Narrative Covering a Third of a Century, 1888–1921.* 2 vols. 1922. Reprint. Port Washington, N.Y.: Kennikat Press, 1971.

28-29. Foraker, Joseph Benson. *Notes of a Busy Life.* 2 vols. Cincinnati: Stewart and Kidd, 1917.

28-30. Gompers, Samuel P. *Seventy Years of Life and Labor: An Autobiography.* 2 vols. 1925. Reprint. New York: Augustus M. Kelley, 1967.

28-31. Heaton, John L. *The Story of a Page.* 1913. Reprint. New York: Arno Press, 1970. 364 p.

28-32. Hoar, George F. *Autobiography of Seventy Years.* 2 vols. New York: Charles Scribner's Sons, 1906.

28-33. McCulloch, Hugh. *Men and Measures of Half a Century.* 1888. Reprint. New York: Da Capo Press, 1970. 542 p.

28-34. Peck, Harry Thurston. *Twenty Years of the Republic, 1885–1905.* New York: Dodd, Mead, 1913. 811 p.

28-35. Powers, Samuel Leland. *Portraits of a Half Century.* Boston: Little, Brown, 1925. 285 p.

28-36. Riddle, Albert Gallatin. *Recollections of War Times: Reminiscences of Men and Events in Washington, 1860–1865.* New York: G. P. Putnam's Sons, 1895. 380 p.

28-37. Robinson, John B. *Midshipman to Congress.* Media, Pa.: privately printed, 1916. 323 p.

28-38. Roper, Daniel C., and Lovette, Frank H. *Fifty Years of Public Life.* 1941. Reprint. New York: Greenwood Press, 1968. 422 p.

28-39. Schurz, Carl. *The Reminiscences of Carl Schurz.* 3 vols. New York: McClure, 1907–8.

28-40. Sherman, John. *Recollections of Forty Years in the House, Senate, and Cabinet: An Autobiography.* 2 vols. 1895. Reprint. New York: Greenwood Press, 1968.

28-41. Stealey, Orlando O. *Twenty Years in the Press Gallery.* New York: Publishers Printing, 1906. 497 p.

28-42. Watson, James E. *As I Knew Them.* Indianapolis: Bobbs-Merrill, 1936. 330 p.

BIOGRAPHICAL COLLECTIONS

28-43. Buttolph, C. E. *Our Great Men.* Atlanta: Crescent Publishing, 1887. 704 p.

28-44. Gates, Merrill E. *Men of Mark in America.* 2 vols. Washington D.C.: Men of Mark Publishing, 1906.

28-45. Headley, P. C. *Public Men of To-Day.* Hartford, Conn.: S. S. Scranton, 1882. 799 p.

28-46. *Our Statesmen: Who They Are, How They Look.* New York: Brentano's, 1888. 64 p.

28-47. Waterloo, Stanley, and Hanson, John Wesley, Jr., eds. *Eminent Sons and Daughters of Columbia.* Chicago: International Publishing, 1896. 518 p.

THE SPEAKERSHIP

See also Cockrell (1-3), Follett (1-4), Fuller (1-5), Greely (1-6), Hart (1-7), Hinds (1-8), and Taylor (1-15).

28-48. ATKINSON, C. R., AND BEARD, CHARLES A. "The Syndication of the Speakership." *Political Science Quarterly* 26 (September 1911): 381–414.

28-49. BRADY, DAVID W., AND ALTHOFF, PHILLIP. "Party Voting in the House of Representatives, 1890–1910: Elements of a Responsible Party System." *Journal of Politics* 36 (August 1974): 753–75.

28-50. BROOKS, SYDNEY. "Congress and Parliament: A Contrast." *North American Review* 170 (January 1900): 78–86.

28-51. COCKRELL, EWING. "Congress or Parliament?" *Arena* 23 (June 1900): 593–605.

28-52. LEWIS, ALFRED H. "An Amiable Tyrant: The Speaker and His Rule of Gag." *Saturday Evening Post,* 16 April 1904, pp. 8–9.

28-53. SMITH, HENRY H. "Parliamentary Reform in the National House of Representatives." *Chautauquan* 30 (December 1899): 239–45.

29. Schuyler Colfax
(1823–1885)
(Speaker, Thirty-eighth through Fortieth Congresses)

Although he was uncharitably described by his opponents as a demagogue, Schuyler Colfax was a popular, successful leader in a time of political crisis. He was the first Speaker to subsequently win election to the vice-presidency; the taint of scandal, however, prevented him from seeking an even higher office.

Colfax was born in New York City on March 23, 1823, four months after his father's death. He was forced to leave school at the age of ten to help support his mother. After she remarried, the family moved to New Carlisle, Indiana, where Colfax studied law. He was appointed deputy county auditor by his stepfather in 1841. His interests turned to journalism in 1845, and he established a newspaper, the *St. Joseph Valley Register,* at South Bend.

Colfax's earliest political sympathies, like those of many other ambitious young men who idolized Henry Clay, were with the Whigs. He made campaign speeches for Clay in 1844 and supported his candidacy at the 1848 Whig national convention. After an unsuccessful bid for election to Congress as a Whig in 1851, Colfax took an active role in the formation of the Republican party in Indiana. He won election to the Thirty-fourth Congress (1855–57) as a Republican and was reelected for six consecutive terms (1857–69).

In his first congressional term, Colfax earned a reputation as a brilliant orator. His first major speech, delivered in June 1856, championed the freedom of speech in the heated Kansas debates. His oratory won him a measure of public favor in the North. As chairman of the Committee on Post Offices and Post Roads, Colfax oversaw the extension of mail service to California and advocated the construction of a transcontinental railroad.

Following the 1860 presidential election, Colfax was recommended for the office of postmaster general in Lincoln's administration. The president declined to appoint him, since he believed that Colfax would be of greater influence in the House. The culmination of Colfax's legislative career was his election to the speakership of the Thirty-eighth Congress. He was a popular leader throughout his tenure as Speaker (1863–69). The real power in the House, however, was Thaddeus Stevens of Pennsylvania, chairman of the Appropriations Committee and Republican floor leader. It was Stevens, not Colfax, who managed the House's impeachment of Andrew Johnson.

Elected vice-president in 1868 as Grant's running mate, Colfax was not renominated in 1872, primarily because regular party leaders had learned that he was under consideration as a presidential candidate by the Liberal Republicans. He left public office in 1873 under a cloud of scandal. Implicated in the Crédit Mobilier scandal, Colfax was alleged to have accepted stock and dividends to influence legislation while Speaker of the House. He denied any wrongdoing, and an investigating commit-

tee declined to censure him on the grounds that any alleged wrongdoing would have occurred before he became vice-president. Although he claimed complete exoneration, Colfax's political career was at an end.

In retirement the last decade of his life, Colfax continued to be a popular figure on the lecture circuit. His life ended suddenly on January 13, 1885, when he stepped onto the train platform at Mankato, Minnesota, and dropped dead.

MANUSCRIPT COLLECTIONS

Chicago Historical Society, Chicago, Ill.
Schuyler Colfax Papers.
45 items, 1845–85.

Illinois State Historical Library, Springfield, Ill.
Schuyler Colfax Papers.
3 letters and 1 manuscript speech.

Indiana Historical Society Library, Indianapolis, Ind.
Schuyler Colfax Papers.
100 items, 1843–81.
NUCMC 75-1981.

Indiana State Library, Indianapolis, Ind.
Schuyler Colfax Papers.
300 items, 1778–1926.
NUCMC 60-1271.

Indiana University Library, Bloomington, Ind.
Schuyler Colfax Papers.

Library of Congress, Manuscript Division, Washington, D.C.
Schuyler Colfax Papers.

152 items, 1837–82.
NUCMC 64-1559.
MC 34.

New York Public Library, New York, N.Y.
Schuyler Colfax Papers.
2 folders, ca. 1860–80.
NUCMC 68-1099.

Northern Indiana Historical Museum, South Bend, Ind.
Schuyler Colfax Papers.
Letters and a journal, 1863–73.

Rutherford B. Hayes Memorial Library, Fremont, Ohio.
Schuyler Colfax Papers.
34 items, 1855–76.

University of Rochester Library, Rochester, N.Y.
Schuyler Colfax Papers.
59 items, 1841–85.
NUCMC 61-1252.

BOOKS, ARTICLES, AND DISSERTATIONS

WORKS BY SCHUYLER COLFAX

The following Colfax speeches are arranged chronologically by year of publication and alphabetically thereunder. *See also* Barnes (29-56).

29-1. COLFAX, SCHUYLER. *The Laws of Kansas: A Speech of the Hon. Schuyler Colfax.* New York: Greeley and McElrath, 1856. 15 p.
Colfax's House speech of June 22, 1856, which established his reputation as an orator.

29-2. ———. *Kansas: The Lecompton Constitution, a Speech of Hon. Schuyler Colfax.* Washington, D.C.: Buell and Blanchard, 1858. 14 p.
House speech of March 20, 1858.

29-3. ———. *Frémont's Hundred Days in Missouri: Speech . . . in Reply to Mr. Blair, of Missouri.* Washington, D.C.: Scammell, 1862. 15 p.
House speech of March 7, 1862.

29-4. ———. *Speech of Schuyler Colfax . . . on Confiscation.* Washington, D.C.: Scammell, 1862. 4 p.

House speech of April 23, 1862, in support of a bill to confiscate the property and slaves of the leaders of the Confederacy.

29-5. ———. *Speech of Schuyler Colfax . . . on His Resolution Declaring Mr. Long, of Ohio, an Unworthy Member of the House.* N.p., [1864]. 8 p.
House speech in which Speaker Colfax argued for the expulsion of Alexander Long of Ohio.

29-6. ———. *Life and Principles of Abraham Lincoln.* Philadelphia: James B. Rodgers, 1865. 29 p.
Colfax's popular lecture on Lincoln.

29-7. ———. *The Mormon Question: Being a Speech of Vice-President Schuyler Colfax at Salt Lake City.* Salt Lake City: Deseret News Office, 1870. 25 p.
A lively debate on polygamy, Colfax speaking against it.

29-8. ———. *Example and Effort: An Address, Delivered before the Congressional Temperance Society, at Washington, D.C.* New York: National Temperance Society and Publication House, 1872. 16 p.
An argument on the need for abstention.

29-9. PHILLIPS, CATHERINE C. *Cornelius Cole: California Pioneer and United States Senator.* San Francisco: Henry Nash, 1929. 379 p.
Includes Colfax correspondence.

BIOGRAPHIES AND BIOGRAPHICAL SKETCHES

From the standpoint of scholarship, the best biography of Colfax is Smith (29-15). *See also* Monks (20-5), Turpie (20-25), Brockett (27-27), Smith (29-26, 29-27, 29-54, and 29-71), and the section on campaign literature (items 29-74 through 29-85) for campaign biographies and biographical sketches of Colfax.

29-10. BANTA, RICHARD E. *Indiana Authors and Their Books.* Crawfordsville, Ind.: Wabash College, 1949. 352 p.

29-11. CROFFUT, WILLIAM A. *An American Procession, 1855–1914: A Personal Chronicle of Famous Men.* 1931. Reprint. Freeport, N.Y.: Books for Libraries Press, 1968. 321 p.

29-12. FURLONG, PATRICK J., AND HARTDAGEN, GERALD E. "Schuyler Colfax: A Reputation Tar-

nished." In *Gentlemen from Indiana: National Party Candidates, 1836–1940,* edited by Ralph D. Gray, pp. 55–82. Indianapolis: Indiana Historical Bureau, 1977.
A reinterpretation of Colfax's life and career that argues that he was neither corrupt nor great but rather a product of his social and political milieu.

29-13. GRINNELL, JOSIAH BUSHNELL. *Men and Events of Forty Years: Autobiographical Reminiscences of an Active Career.* Boston: D. Lothrup, 1891. 426 p.
Includes a comprehensive and favorable sketch of Colfax.

29-14. HOLLISTER, O. V. *Life of Schuyler Colfax.* New York: Funk and Wagnalls, 1886. 535 p.
An adulatory biography important for its documentation and insights into Colfax's character.

29-15. SMITH, WILLARD H. *Schuyler Colfax: The Changing Fortunes of a Political Idol.* Indiana Historical Collections, vol. 33. Indianapolis: Indiana Historical Bureau, 1952. 475 p.
A scholarly, well-researched biography that treats Colfax in a favorable light.

29-16. SUTHERLAND, JAMES. *Biographical Sketches of the Members of the Forty-first General Assembly of the State of Indiana.* Indianapolis: Indianapolis Journal, 1861. 210 p.

COLFAX AND INDIANA HISTORY AND POLITICS

See also Roll (20-17), Smith (20-18), and Van Bolt (20-20).

29-17. BARTHOLOMEW, PAUL C. *The Indiana Third Congressional District: A Political History.* South Bend, Ind.: University of Notre Dame Press, 1970. 238 p.
Features a detailed analysis of the issues and the election returns from each of Colfax's seven congressional elections.

29-18. HARBISON, WINFRED A. "Indiana Republicans and the Re-election of President Lincoln." *Indiana Magazine of History* 34 (March 1938): 42–64.

29-19. HOWARD, TIMOTHY E. *A History of St. Joseph County, Indiana.* 2 vols. Chicago: Lewis, 1907.

29-20. INDIANA. CONSTITUTIONAL CONVENTION, 1850. *Journal of the Convention.* Indianapolis: Austin H. Brown, 1851. 1,085 p.

The official record of Colfax's actions as a delegate, including his resolutions on banking and a proposed referendum on black suffrage.

29-21. LONDON, LENA. "Homestead Exemption in the Indiana Constitution of 1851." *Indiana Magazine of History* 44 (September 1948): 267–80.

Characterizes Colfax as an influential leader who favored homestead legislation.

29-22. MILLER, JOHN WILLIAM. "The Pioneer Newspapers of Indiana, 1804–1850." Ph.D. dissertation, Purdue University, 1975. 371 p. 76-00562.

29-23. NOLAN, VAL, JR. "Unicameralism and the Indiana Constitutional Convention of 1850." *Indiana Law Journal* 26 (Spring 1951): 349–59.

Discusses in detail Colfax's proposal for a unicameral state legislature.

29-24. ROLL, CHARLES. "Indiana's Part in the Nomination of Abraham Lincoln for President in 1860." *Indiana Magazine of History* 25 (March 1929): 1–13.

29-25. SHARP, WALTER R. "Henry S. Lane and the Formation of the Republican Party in Indiana." *Mississippi Valley Historical Review* 7 (September 1920): 93–112.

29-26. SMITH, WILLARD H. "Schuyler Colfax and the Political Upheaval of 1854–1855." *Mississippi Valley Historical Review* 28 (December 1941): 383–98.

An examination of Colfax's rise to prominence in Indiana politics.

29-27. ———. "Schuyler Colfax: Whig Editor, 1845–1855." *Indiana Magazine of History* 34 (September 1938): 262–82.

29-28. STAMPP, KENNETH M. *Indiana Politics during the Civil War.* Rev. ed. Bloomington: Indiana University Press, 1970. 300 p.

29-29. THORNBROUGH, EMMA LOU. *Indiana in the Civil War Era, 1850–1880.* History of Indiana, vol. 3. Indianapolis: Indiana Historical Bureau and Indiana Historical Society, 1965. 758 p.

29-30. TOMLINSON, KENNETH L. "Indiana Republicans and the Negro Suffrage Issue." Ph.D. dissertation, Ball State University, 1971. 253 p. 72-07520.

29-31. VAN BOLT, ROGER H. "Fusion out of Confusion, 1854." *Indiana Magazine of History* 49 (December 1953): 353–90.

Examines the rise of the Know-Nothing party and Colfax's position in Indiana.

29-32. ———. "The Hoosiers and the Eternal Agitation, 1848–1850." *Indiana Magazine of History* 48 (December 1952): 331–68.

Discusses Colfax's opinions on the state of the Whig party from 1848 to 1850.

29-33. ———. "The Rise of the Republican Party in Indiana, 1855–1856." *Indiana Magazine of History* 51 (September 1955): 185–220.

Colfax is characterized as a skillful politician able to formulate a viable alternative to the Democratic party.

29-34. ZIMMERMAN, CHARLES. "The Origin and Rise of the Republican Party in Indiana from 1854 to 1860." *Indiana Magazine of History* 13 (September–December 1917): 211–69, 349–412.

COLFAX AND THE REPUBLICAN PARTY

See also Sharp (29-25), Tomlinson (29-30), Van Bolt (29-33), and Zimmerman (29-34).

29-35. FLOWER, FRANK A. *History of the Republican Party: Embracing Its Origin, Growth, and Mission.* Grand Rapids, Mich.: Union Book, 1884. 623 p.

29-36. LIVINGSTONE, WILLIAM. *Livingstone's History of the Republican Party.* 2 vols. Detroit: William Livingstone, 1900.

29-37. REPUBLICAN PARTY. NATIONAL CONVENTIONS. *Proceedings of the First Three Republican National Conventions of 1856, 1860, and 1864.* Minneapolis: Charles W. Johnson, 1893. 264 p.

29-38. ———. *National Conventions of 1868, 1872, 1876, and 1880.* Minneapolis: Charles W. Johnson, 1903. 682 p.

29-39. Ross, Earle D. *The Liberal Republican Movement.* 1919. Reprint. Seattle: University of Washington Press, 1970. 267 p.

COLFAX'S POLITICAL ASSOCIATES

See also Flower (17-46), Abbot (21-91), McKay (21-103), and Russell (30-30).

29-40. Caldwell, Robert G. *James A. Garfield: Party Chieftain.* New York: Dodd, Mead, 1931. 383 p.

29-41. Hesseltine, William B. *Ulysses S. Grant: Politician.* 1935. Reprint. New York: Frederick Unger, 1957. 480 p.

29-42. Isely, Jeter Allen. *Horace Greeley and the Republican Party, 1853–1861: A Study of the New York Tribune.* 1946. Reprint. New York: Octagon Books, 1965. 368 p.

The close relationship between Colfax and Greeley is documented with selections from their correspondence.

29-43. Logan, Mary Simmerson. *Reminiscences of a Soldier's Wife: An Autobiography.* New York: Charles Scribner's Sons, 1913. 470 p.

29-44. McKee, Irving. *Ben-Hur Wallace: The Life of General Lew Wallace.* Berkeley: University of California Press, 1947. 301 p.

29-45. Oberholtzer, Ellis P. *Jay Cooke: Financier of the Civil War.* 2 vols. 1907. Reprint. New York: Burt Franklin, 1970.

29-46. Orth, Godlove S. "The Letters of Godlove S. Orth." Edited by J. Herman Schavinger. *Indiana Magazine of History* 39 (December 1943): 365–400; 40 (March–June 1944): 51–66, 158–78.

29-47. Riddleberger, Patrick W. *George Washington Julian, Radical Republican: A Study in Nineteenth-Century Politics and Reform.* Indianapolis: Indiana Historical Bureau, 1966. 344 p.

29-48. Sievers, Harry J. *Benjamin Harrison: Hoosier Statesman.* New York: University Publishers, 1959. 502 p.

29-49. Van Deusen, Glyndon G. *Horace Greeley: Nineteenth-Century Crusader.* 1953. Reprint. New York: Hill and Wang, 1964. 444 p.

29-50. Wallace, Lew. *An Autobiography.* 2 vols. New York: Harper and Brothers, 1906.

COLFAX'S CONGRESSIONAL CAREER, 1855–1863

See also Shields (17-37) and Brichford (27-38).

29-51. Carman, Harry J., and Luthin, Reinhard H. *Lincoln and the Patronage.* 1943. Reprint. Gloucester, Mass.: Peter Smith, 1964. 375 p.

Colfax is discussed with regard to the controversy over cabinet appointments.

29-52. Hendrick, Burton J. *Lincoln's War Cabinet.* Boston: Little, Brown, 1946. 482 p.

29-53. Linden, Glenn M. "'Radicals' and Economic Policies: The House of Representatives, 1861–1873." *Civil War History* 13 (March 1967): 51–65.

29-54. Smith, Willard H. "The Colfax-Turpie Congressional Campaigns, 1862–1866." *Indiana Magazine of History* 38 (June 1942): 123–42.

COLFAX, THE SPEAKERSHIP, AND RECONSTRUCTION, 1863–1869

29-55. Barnes, William H. *The Fortieth Congress of the United States.* 2 vols. New York: George E. Perine, 1869.

A comprehensive account of the session with a favorable sketch of Speaker Colfax.

29-56. ———. *History of the Thirty-ninth Congress of the United States.* 1867. Reprint. New York: Negro Universities Press, 1969. 636 p.

Speaker Colfax, who wrote the preface to this work, figured prominently in this Congress.

29-57. BEALE, HOWARD K. *The Critical Year: A Study of Andrew Johnson and Reconstruction*. New York: Frederick Unger, 1958. 454 p.

29-58. BROCK, WILLIAM R. *An American Crisis: Congress and Reconstruction, 1865–1867*. New York: St. Martin's Press, 1963. 312 p.

29-59. BURGESS, JOHN W. *Reconstruction and the Constitution, 1866–1876*. 1902. Reprint. New York: AMS Press, 1972. 342 p.

29-60. CLEMENCEAU, GEORGES. *American Reconstruction, 1865–1870, and the Impeachment of President Johnson*. Edited with an introduction by Fernand Baldensperger. 1928. Reprint. New York: Da Capo Press, 1969. 300 p.

29-61. CRAVEN, AVERY O. *Reconstruction: The Ending of the Civil War*. New York: Holt, Rinehart, and Winston, 1969. 330 p.

29-62. DONALD, DAVID H. *The Politics of Reconstruction, 1863–1867*. 1965. Reprint. Westport, Conn.: Greenwood Press, 1982. 105 p.

29-63. DUNNING, WILLIAM A. *Reconstruction: Political and Economic*. New York: Harper and Brothers, 1907. 378 p.

29-64. FLACK, HORACE E. *The Adoption of the Fourteenth Amendment*. 1908. Reprint. Gloucester, Mass.: Peter Smith, 1965. 285 p.

29-65. JAMES, JOSEPH B. *The Framing of the Fourteenth Amendment*. Urbana: University of Illinois Press, 1956. 220 p.

29-66. ———. "The Immediate Purpose of the Fourteenth Amendment." *Indiana Magazine of History* 39 (December 1943): 345–61.

29-67. McKITRICK, ERIC L. *Andrew Johnson and Reconstruction*. Chicago: University of Chicago Press, 1960. 533 p.

29-68. McPHERSON, EDWARD. *The Political History of the United States of America during the Period of Reconstruction*. 1871. Reprint. New York: Da Capo Press, 1972. 653 p.

29-69. NICOLAY, JOHN G., AND HAY, JOHN. *Abraham Lincoln: A History*. Volumes 2, 3, 7, 8. New York: Century, 1886–90.

29-70. NIEMAN, DONALD G. "Andrew Johnson, the Freedmen's Bureau, and the Problem of Equal Rights, 1865–1866." *Journal of Southern History* 44 (August 1978): 399–420.

29-71. SMITH, WILLARD H. "Schuyler Colfax and Reconstruction Policy." *Indiana Magazine of History* 39 (December 1943): 323–44.

29-72. TREFOUSSE, HANS L. "The Acquittal of Andrew Johnson and the Decline of the Radicals." *Civil War History* 14 (June 1968): 148–61.

29-73. VOEGELI, V. JACQUE. *Free But Not Equal: The Mid-West and the Negro during the Civil War*. Chicago: University of Chicago Press, 1967. 215 p.
A fine study that details Colfax's position on Lincoln's peace plan and emancipation.

CAMPAIGN LITERATURE, 1868

Colfax figures prominently in the following representative pieces of campaign literature from the presidential and vice-presidential campaigns of 1868. *See also* Brockett (27-27).

29-74. BRISBIN, JAMES S. *The Lives of Ulysses S. Grant and Schuyler Colfax*. Cincinnati: C. F. Vent, 1869. 411 p.

29-75. COPPEE, HENRY. *Life and Services of Gen. U. S. Grant*. Chicago: Western News, 1868. 566 p.
Includes a short, favorable biography of Colfax.

29-76. *The Life and Times of Hon. Schuyler Colfax, Speaker of the United States House of Representatives and Republican Candidate for the Vice-Presidency*. New York: E. B. Treat, 1868. 50 p.

29-77. *The Lives and Public Services of General U. S. Grant, U.S.A., and of Hon. Schuyler Colfax, Speaker of the House of Representatives*. Philadelphia, 1868. 24 p.

29-78. *Lives of Ulysses S. Grant and Schuyler Colfax . . . Containing, also, a Correct Genealogical Summary of the Grant Family*. Cincinnati: Padrick, 1868. 104 p.

29-79. MANSFIELD, EDWARD D. *Popular and Authentic Lives of Ulysses S. Grant and Schuyler Colfax*. Cincinnati: R. W. Carroll, 1868. 425 p.

29-80. MARTIN, EDWARD WINSLOW [JAMES D. McCABE]. *The Life and Public Services of Schuyler Colfax: Together with His Most Important Speeches.* New York: United States, 1868. 512 p.

29-81. MOORE, AMBROSE Y. *The Life of Schuyler Colfax.* Philadelphia: T. B. Peterson and Brothers, 1868. 394 p.

29-82. *The People's Edition of the Lives of the Candidates for President and Vice-President of the United States.* Albany, N.Y.: R. Duncan, 1868. 46 p.

29-83. PHELPS, CHARLES A. *Life and Public Services of General Ulysses S. Grant: From His Boyhood to the Present Time and a Biographical Sketch of Hon. Schuyler Colfax.* Boston: Lee and Shepard, 1868. 344 p.

29-84. RICHARDSON, ALBERT D. *A Personal History of Ulysses S. Grant . . . with a Portrait and Sketch of Schuyler Colfax.* Hartford, Conn.: American Publishing, 1868. 560 p.

29-85. *Sketches of the Lives and Services of Ulysses S. Grant and Schuyler Colfax, National Republican Candidates for President and Vice-President of the United States.* Washington, D.C.: Chronicle Printer, 1868. 8 p.

COLFAX AND THE VICE-PRESIDENCY

29-86. BARZMAN, SOL. *Madmen and Geniuses: The Vice-Presidents of the United States.* Chicago: Follett, 1974. 335 p.

29-87. CURTIS, RICHARD, AND WELLS, MAGGIE. *Not Exactly a Crime: Our Vice-Presidents from Adams to Agnew.* New York: Dial Press, 1972. 202 p.

29-88. HARWOOD, MICHAEL. *In the Shadow of Presidents: The American Vice-Presidency and Succession System.* Philadelphia: J. B. Lippincott, 1966. 239 p.

29-89. HILL, ADAMS SHERMAN. "The Chicago Convention." *North American Review* 107 (July 1868): 167–86.
Examines the selection of Colfax as Grant's running mate.

29-90. YOUNG, KLYDE H., AND MIDDLETON, LAMAR. *Heirs Apparent: The Vice-Presidents of the United States.* 1948. Reprint. Freeport, N.Y.: Books for Libraries Press, 1969. 314 p.

COLFAX AND THE CRÉDIT MOBILIER SCANDAL

See also Loth (5-55) and Brigance (22-57).

29-91. CRAWFORD, JAY B. *The Crédit Mobilier of America: Its Origins and History.* 1880. Reprint. New York: AMS Press, 1971. 229 p.
A detailed study of the scandal generated by the financial institution that underwrote the Union Pacific Railroad.

29-92. SEITZ, DON C. *The Dreadful Decade, 1869–1879.* 1926. Reprint. New York: AMS Press, 1970. 311 p.

29-93. U.S. CONGRESS. HOUSE. *Report of the Select Committee to Investigate the Alleged Crédit Mobilier Bribery . . . February 18, 1873.* 42d Cong., 3d sess., 1873. Washington, D.C.: Government Printing Office, 1873. 523 p.
A complete record of the charges relating to the Crédit Mobilier in which Colfax is quoted often and at length.

MISCELLANEOUS

See also Martin (27-42).

29-94. AMES, MARY CLEMMER. *Ten Years in Washington: Life and Scenes in the National Capital as a Woman Sees Them.* Hartford, Conn.: Worthington, 1873. 587 p.
A journalist's account of Washington politics and society.

29-95. BOWLES, SAMUEL. *Across the Continent: A Summer's Journey to the Rocky Mountains, the Mormons, and the Pacific States, with Speaker Colfax.* 1865. Reprint. Ann Arbor: University Microfilms, 1966. 452 p.
A colorful account of Colfax's trip to the West in 1865.

29-96. ———. *Our New West: Record of Travel between the Mississippi River and the Pacific Ocean.* 1869. Reprint. New York: Arno Press, 1973. 524 p.

29-97. BROOKS, NOAH. *Washington in Lincoln's Time.* 1895. Reprint. New York: Rinehart, 1958. 309 p.
A journalist's account of the capital during the Civil War.

29-98. DONALDSON, PASHAL. *The Odd-Fellow's Text-Book and Manual*. Rev. ed. Philadelphia: Moss, 1869. 406 p.

Includes an account of Speaker Colfax's activities as a member.

29-99. HARPER, JOSEPH HENRY. *The House of Harper: A Century of Publishing in Franklin Square*. New York: Harper and Brothers, 1912. 689 p.

Includes anecdotes about Colfax by the noted publisher and by cartoonist Thomas Nast.

29-100. LEECH, MARGARET. *Reveille in Washington, 1860–1865*. 1941. Reprint. Westport, Conn.: Greenwood Press, 1971. 483 p.

Colfax is mentioned in the context of the social and political history of Washington during the Civil War.

29-101. RICHARDSON, ALBERT D. *Beyond the Mississippi: From the Great River to the Great Ocean*. Hartford, Conn.: American, 1867. 572 p.

A firsthand account of a trip to the West with Speaker Colfax.

30. James Gillespie Blaine
(1830–1893)
(Speaker, Forty-first through Forty-third Congresses)

James G. Blaine, like his early role model, Henry Clay, never attained the office he so deeply desired. Though he never gained the presidency, Blaine, like Clay, did serve with distinction as Speaker of the House, senator, and secretary of state. With a commanding physical presence, magnetic eyes, and striking powers of oratory, he was a leading politician in a period of American history marked by corruption and mediocrity.

Blaine was born on January 31, 1830, at West Brownsville, Pennsylvania. After private tutoring, he entered Washington College at the age of thirteen and studied the classics, English, and mathematics. Teaching was Blaine's first profession. From 1848 to 1852 he taught at the Western Military Institute at Georgetown, Kentucky, and from 1852 to 1854 he was on the staff of the Pennsylvania Institute for the Blind in Philadelphia.

While in Kentucky, Blaine secretly married Harriet Stanwood in 1850. To remove any doubts as to the legality of their marriage, the couple remarried in Pennsylvania in 1851. Three years later they moved to Augusta, Maine, where Harriet Blaine's brothers arranged for Blaine to become editor of the *Kennebec Journal*. Blaine was a great admirer of Henry Clay, and he was equally opposed to slavery. He adopted the Republican party's cause in 1854 and was a delegate to the first Republican national convention in 1856. Two years later he was elected to the Maine state legislature (1858–62), and he served the last two years of his term as speaker of the state house of representatives.

Blaine was elected to Congress in 1862. He served in the House from 1863 to 1876 and in the Senate from 1876 to 1881. During the Civil War and Reconstruction he was a moderate who supported Lincoln's approach to preserving and reuniting the Union. He clashed with Thaddeus Stevens on several matters, most notably Radical Reconstruction. After Stevens died, Blaine, William Boyd Allison of Iowa, and James A. Garfield of Ohio became the power brokers in the House. He also made one lifelong enemy and rival, Roscoe Conkling of New York.

In 1869 Blaine was elected to the speakership of the Forty-first Congress. He served as Speaker until the end of the Forty-third Congress in 1875. During those years he used his position as a platform to prepare for a presidential bid in 1876. The Republican party was split. One faction, the Stalwarts, included Conkling and supported President Grant and his policies; the other faction, the Half-Breeds, opposed Grant. Blaine, a leading Half-Breed, might have won the Republican presidential nomination had not two incidents intervened. The first was the implication that he had been involved in railroad graft while serving as Speaker. Blaine denied those charges and in the famous Mulligan letters incident produced letters that purported to clear him of any wrongdoing. Then, just days before the convention, he was incapacitated by a sunstroke, which some people thought might prove fatal. As a result, his support waned, and the nomination went to Rutherford B. Hayes.

Although Blaine was denied the Republican nomination again in 1880, President Garfield appointed Blaine secretary of state in 1881. After Garfield was assassinated, Blaine's influence in the administration declined, and he left office in December 1881. He remained in Washington, wrote the first volume of his memoirs, *Twenty Years of Congress,* and maintained an active involvement in party politics.

Blaine won the Republican nomination in 1884, but he lost the election to Grover Cleveland. The loss has been attributed largely to an unfortunate statement by one of his supporters characterizing the Democratic party as the party of "rum, Romanism, and rebellion." Following the election, Blaine wrote the second volume of his memoirs, published a collection of speeches, and traveled in Europe. He declined to be a serious candidate in 1888, but he was instrumental in the selection of Benjamin Harrison as the Republican party's nominee. After Harrison was elected, Blaine was again appointed secretary of state, an office he held from March 1889 to June 1892. Although he was somewhat ignorant of diplomacy and international law, he championed American interests, chiefly through advocacy of trade reciprocity and the concept of Pan-Americanism. Blaine, who was chronically plagued by poor health, died on January 27, 1893, at the age of sixty-two.

MANUSCRIPT COLLECTIONS

Iowa State Department of History and Archives, Des Moines, Iowa.
James G. Blaine Papers.
1 box.
NUCMC 62-2606.
Library of Congress, Manuscript Division, Washington, D.C.
James G. Blaine Family Papers, 1777–1945.
40 containers.
Register.
Includes 550 items of James G. Blaine correspondence, 1850–92.
NUCMC 63-326.
MC 16.
Maine State Archives, Augusta, Me.

Records of the Adjutant General of Maine, Civil War Correspondence (includes approximately 200 Blaine letters, 1861–65, concerning the war and the Washington political scene).

In addition to the three collections listed above, several hundred Blaine letters are contained in the James A. Garfield and the Benjamin Harrison collections in the Library of Congress Manuscript Division. Blaine correspondence can be found in many of the manuscript collections of other politicians of the period. Researchers should also consult the National Archives for materials relating to Blaine's service as secretary of state.

BOOKS, ARTICLES, AND DISSERTATIONS

WORKS BY JAMES G. BLAINE

The following Blaine items are arranged chronologically by year of publication and alphabetically thereunder. *See also* Hollister (29-14).

30-1. Blaine, James G. *Memoir of Luther Severance.* Augusta, Me.: Office of the Kennebec Journal, 1856. 33 p.

30-2. ———. *Municipal Debt in the United States.* Augusta, Me.: Sprague, Owen, and Nash, 1874. 25 p.

Text of a speech delivered October 1, 1874, in Oshkosh, Wisconsin.

30-3. ———. *Speaker Blaine's Letter of Acceptance.* Augusta, Me., 1874. 4 p.

30-4. ———. *Address of Hon. James G. Blaine, at the Minneapolis Fair, Minnesota, Tuesday, Sept. 3, 1878.* Augusta, Me.: Office of the Kennebec Journal, 1878. 10 p.

30-5. ———. *Chinese Immigration: Speech of Hon. James G. Blaine . . . Delivered in the United States Senate, February 14, 1879.* Washington, D.C.: R. O. Polkinhorn, 1879. 16 p.

30-6. ———. "Ought the Negro to Be Disfranchised? Ought He to Have Been Enfranchised?" *North American Review* 128 (March 1879): 225–83.

30-7. ———. *Twenty Years of Congress.* 2 vols. Norwich, Conn.: Henry Bill Publishing, 1884.

Blaine's political memoirs, written in the third person.

30-8. ———. *Words on the Issues of the Day.* Edited by Walter S. Vail. Boston: D. L. Guernsey, 1884. 303 p.

Comprises excerpts from Blaine's speeches on a variety of issues and a brief review of his career.

30-9. ———. *Political Discussions: Legislative, Diplomatic, and Popular, 1856–1886.* Norwich, Conn.: Henry Bill Publishing, 1887. 525 p.

A compilation of Blaine's speeches and writings over his thirty-year career.

30-10. ———. *Welcome Home and Campaign Speeches of James G. Blaine.* New York: J. S. Ogilvie, 1888. 92, 65 p.

30-11. ———. "Some Personal Traits of General Sherman." In *Memoirs of W. T. Sherman,* by William Tecumseh Sherman, pp. 485–93. New York: Charles L. Webster, 1891.

30-12. ———. "The Presidential Election of 1892." *North American Review* 155 (November 1892): 513–25.

30-13. ———. "The Progress and Development of the Western World." In *Columbus and Columbia: A Pictorial History of the Man and the Nation,* by James G. Blaine et al., pp. 33–62. Philadelphia: Historical Publishing, 1892.

30-14. ———. *Condensed History of American Tariff Acts and Their Effects upon Industries.* Boston: Home Market Club, 1902. 8 p.

A Blaine speech of September 29, 1888, in pamphlet form.

30-15. ———. *Memorial Address on the Life and Character of James A. Garfield.* Washington, D.C.: Government Printing Office, 1903. 18 p.

Blaine's eulogy of Garfield, delivered before a joint session of Congress on February 27, 1882.

30-16. ———. "North American Relations with South America." In *We Hold These Truths,* edited by Stuart Gray Brown, pp. 267–69. New York: Harper and Brothers, 1948.

A Blaine letter to the U.S. minister to Chile outlining his Latin American policy.

30-17. Detroit Post and Tribune. *Zachariah Chandler: An Outline and Sketch of His Life and Public Services.* Detroit, 1880. 396 p.

Includes a brief eulogistic letter from Blaine.

30-18. Gotlieb, Howard B. "A Revealing Letter from James G. Blaine." *Colby Library Quarterly,* 4th ser., August 1958, pp. 274–77.

30-19. Hunt, Gaillard. *Israel, Elihu, and Cadwallader Washburn: A Chapter in American Biography.* 1925. Reprint. Freeport, N.Y.: Books for Libraries Press, 1971. 397 p.

Includes several letters from Blaine to Israel Washburn dated 1856 to 1869.

30-20. McCLURE, J. B. *Life and Great Speeches of James G. Blaine.* Chicago: Rhodes and McClure, 1890. 287 p.
Comprises a seventy-page biography and two hundred pages of Blaine speeches.

30-21. VOLWILER, ALBERT T., ED. *The Correspondence between Benjamin Harrison and James G. Blaine, 1882–1893.* Philadelphia: American Philosophical Society, 1940. 314 p.

BIOGRAPHIES, BIOGRAPHICAL SKETCHES, GENEALOGIES, AND EULOGIES

Biographies

Of the several biographies of Blaine, the most scholarly to date is that of Muzzey (30-27). In addition to the nineteenth-century biographies cited below, see the campaign biographies listed in the section on the presidential election of 1884 (30-140 through 30-158).

30-22. BOYD, JAMES P. *Life and Public Services of Hon. James G. Blaine, the Illustrious American Orator, Diplomat, and Statesman.* Philadelphia: Publisher's Union, 1893. 704 p.

30-23. CRAWFORD, THERON C. *James G. Blaine: A Study of His Life and Career.* Philadelphia: Edgewood Publishing, 1893. 644 p.

30-24. DODGE, MARY ABIGAIL [GAIL HAMILTON]. *Biography of James G. Blaine.* Norwich, Conn.: Henry Bill Publishing, 1895. 722 p.

30-25. JOHNSON, WILLIS F. *An American Statesman: The Works and Words of James G. Blaine.* Philadelphia: A. R. Keller, 1892. 578 p.
A second edition was published in 1893 under the title *Life of James G. Blaine: The Plumed Knight.*

30-26. MANN, EDWARD C. *Hon. James G. Blaine's Place in American History.* Albany, N.Y.: Matthew Bender, 1893. 34 p.

30-27. MUZZEY, DAVID S. *James G. Blaine: A Political Idol of Other Days.* 1934. Reprint. Port Washington, N.Y.: Kennikat Press, 1963. 514 p.

The most scholarly and accurate Blaine biography.

30-28. PIERCE, JAMES W. *Life of the Hon. James G. Blaine.* Baltimore: R. N. Woodward, 1893. 565 p.

30-29. RIDPATH, JOHN C., ET AL. *Life and Work of James G. Blaine.* Philadelphia: Historical Publishing, 1893. 505 p.

30-30. RUSSELL, CHARLES EDWARD. *Blaine of Maine: His Life and Times.* New York: Cosmopolitan Book, 1931. 446 p.

30-31. SHERMAN, THOMAS H. *Twenty Years with James G. Blaine: Reminiscences by His Private Secretary.* New York: Grafton Press, 1928. 194 p.

30-32. STANWOOD, EDWARD. *James Gillespie Blaine.* 1905. New York: AMS Press, 1972. 377 p.

Biographical Sketches

30-33. BEALE, HARRIET S. BLAINE. "James G. Blaine." In *Just Maine Folks,* pp. 26–38. Lewiston, Me.: Journal Printshop, 1924.
The reminiscences of Blaine's daughter.

30-34. BRADFORD, GAMALIEL. "James Gillespie Blaine." *Atlantic Monthly* 126 (October 1920): 509–19.

30-35. ———. "James Gillespie Blaine." In *American Portraits, 1875–1900,* pp. 113–41. 1922. Reprint. Port Washington, N.Y.: Kennikat Press, 1969.

30-36. BRIGHAM, JOHNSON. *Blaine, Conkling, and Garfield: A Reminiscence and a Character Study.* Des Moines, 1915. 36 p.

30-37. BROOKS, NOAH. "James G. Blaine." In *Statesmen,* pp. 280–312. New York: Charles Scribner's Sons, 1893.

30-38. CHASE, HENRY, ED. *Representative Men of Maine.* Portland, Me.: Lakeside Press, 1893. 250 p.

30-39. HOYER, EVA H. "James Gillespie Blaine: The Father of the Pan American Union, 1830–1898." In *Sixteen Exceptional Americans,* pp. 129–50. New York: Vantage Press, 1959.

30-40. HOYT, EDWIN P. "James G. Blaine." In *Lost Statesmen,* pp. 129-46. Chicago: Reilly and Lee, 1961.

30-41. JUDSON, HARRY P. "American Politics: A Study of Four Careers." *American Review of Reviews* 7 (March 1893): 159-72.
Reviews Blaine's career and compares it with that of Henry Clay.

30-42. MACARTNEY, CLARENCE E. N. "James G. Blaine." In *Men Who Missed It,* pp. 87-95. Philadelphia: Dorrance, 1940.

30-43. MORRIS, CHARLES. "James G. Blaine, the Plumed Knight of Republicanism." In *Heroes of Progress in America,* edited by Charles Morris, pp. 278-86. Philadelphia: J. B. Lippincott, 1906.

30-44. ROBERTS, HENRY G. "James G. Blaine." In *A History and Criticism of American Public Address,* edited by William Norwood Brigance, 2:878-90. 1943. Reprint. New York: Russell and Russell, 1960.

30-45. SEITZ, DON C. "James G. Blaine." In *The Also Rans: Great Men Who Missed Making the Presidential Goal,* pp. 282-97. 1928. Reprint. Freeport, N.Y.: Books for Libraries Press, 1968.

30-46. SPENCER, WILBUR D. *Maine Immortals: Including Many Unique Characters in Early Maine History.* Augusta, Me.: Northeastern Press, 1932. 316 p.

30-47. STONE, IRVING. "Main Chance Politicos." In *They Also Ran,* pp. 231-50. Garden City, N.Y.: Doubleday, 1966.

30-48. WATTS, FREDERICK. "James Gillespie Blaine, A Brief Biographical Sketch." In *The American Government,* edited by William H. Barnes, 2: 7-12. Washington, D.C.: W. H. Barnes, 1875.

Genealogies

30-49. BLAINE, JOHN EWING, ED. *The Blaine Family: James Blaine, Emigrant, and His Children.* Cincinnati: Ebbert and Richardson, 1920. 99 p.

30-50. LITTLE, GEORGE T. *Genealogical and Family History of the State of Maine.* Vol. 2. New York: Lewis Historical Publishing, 1909.

Eulogies

30-51. EDWARDS, E. JAY. "Reminiscences of James G. Blaine." *Chautauquan* 17 (April 1893): 44-48.

30-52. "James G. Blaine." *Harper's Weekly,* 4 February 1893, pp. 98-103.

30-53. LONG, JOHN D. "James G. Blaine." *Education* 8 (April 1893): 455-61.

30-54. MICHIGAN. LEGISLATURE. *Memorial of James G. Blaine.* Lansing: Robert Smith, 1893. 36 p.

30-55. *Proceedings of the Senate and Assembly of the State of New York on the Life and Character of James Gillespie Blaine.* Albany: James B. Lyon, 1893. 58 p.

BLAINE AND MAINE HISTORY AND POLITICS

30-56. HATCH, LOUIS C. *Maine: A History.* Vols. 2 and 3. 1919. Reprint. Somersworth: New Hampshire Publishing, 1974.

30-57. KINGSBURY, HENRY D., AND DEYO, SIMEON L., EDS. *Illustrated History of Kennebec County.* 2 vols. New York: H. W. Blake, 1892.

30-58. WHALON, MICHAEL WINTERS. "Maine Republicans, 1854-1866: A Study in Growth and Political Power." Ph.D. dissertation, University of Nebraska, 1968. 381 p. 69-09659.

BLAINE'S CONGRESSIONAL CAREER AND SPEAKERSHIP

General

See also Ross (29-39) and Barnes (29-55).

30-59. COULTER, E. MERTON. "Amnesty for All Except Jefferson Davis: The Hill-Blaine Debate of 1876." *Georgia Historical Quarterly* 56 (Winter 1972): 453-94.

30-60. DESANTIS, VINCENT P. *Republicans Face the Southern Question: The New Departure Years, 1877-1897.* Johns Hopkins University Studies in Historical and Social Science, 77th ser., no. 1. Baltimore: Johns Hopkins Press, 1959. 275 p.

30-61. DOBSON, JOHN M. *Politics in the Gilded Age: A New Perspective on Reform.* New York: Praeger, 1972. 200 p.

30-62. GARFIELD, JAMES A. *Garfield-Hinsdale Letters: Correspondence between James Abram Garfield and Burke Aaron Hinsdale.* Ann Arbor: University of Michigan Press, 1949. 556 p.

Includes observations on Blaine's actions as Speaker and his presidential ambitions.

30-63. HAM, EDWARD B. "Amnesty and Blaine of Maine." *New England Quarterly* 28 (June 1955): 255–58.

30-64. HOUSE, ALBERT V., JR. "The Speakership Contest of 1875: Democratic Response to Power." *Journal of American History* 50 (September 1965): 252–74.

A detailed analysis of the election in which Blaine lost to Michael Crawford Kerr.

30-65. HOWARD, VINCENT. "The Two Congresses: A Study of the Changing Roles and Relationships of the National Legislature and Washington Reporters as Revealed Particularly in the Press Accounts of Legislative Activity, 1860–1913." Ph.D. dissertation, University of Chicago, 1976.

30-66. KITSON, JAMES TALCOTT. "The Congressional Career of James G. Blaine." Ph.D. dissertation, Case Western Reserve University, 1971. 354 p. 72-00061.

A well-researched survey that portrays Blaine as ambitious, aggressive, and sometimes shady in his political behavior.

30-67. KLINKHAMER, SISTER MARIE CAROLYN. "The Blaine Amendment of 1875: Private Motives for Political Action." *Catholic Historical Review* 42 (April 1956): 15–49.

Examines Blaine's reasons for opposing public funding for religious schools.

30-68. MEYER, ALFRED W. "The Blaine Amendment and the Bill of Rights." *Harvard Law Review* 64 (April 1951): 939–45.

30-69. "Mrs. Logan's Recollections of Mr. Blaine as Speaker." *American Review of Reviews* 5 (June 1892): 590–91.

30-70. SHARKEY, ROBERT P. *Money, Class, and Party: An Economic Study of Civil War and Reconstruction.* Johns Hopkins University Studies in Historical and Social Science, 77th ser., no. 2. Baltimore: Johns Hopkins Press, 1959. 346 p.

30-71. THOMPSON, MARGARET S. "The 'Spider Web': Congress and Lobbying in the Age of Grant." Ph.D. dissertation, University of Wisconsin, 1979. 570 p. 80-11405.

30-72. TOWNSEND, GEORGE A. *Washington, Outside and Inside.* Cincinnati: James Betts, 1873. 751 p.

Blaine's election to the speakership in 1869 is given particular attention.

30-73. UNGER, IRWIN. *The Greenback Era: A Social and Political History of American Finance, 1865–1879.* Princeton: Princeton University Press, 1964. 467 p.

The Blaine-Conkling Feud

30-74. BOUTWELL, GEORGE S. "Blaine and Conkling and the Republican Convention of 1880." *McClure's* 14 (January 1900): 281–86.

30-75. CHIDSEY, DONALD B. *The Gentleman from New York: A Life of Roscoe Conkling.* New Haven: Yale University Press, 1935. 438 p.

30-76. DECASSERES, BENJAMIN. "Plumed Knight and Turkey Gobbler." *American Mercury* 18 (October 1929): 215–21.

A light, irreverent article. The title refers to Blaine's and Conkling's respective nicknames.

30-77. FRY, JAMES B. *The Conkling and Blaine-Fry Controversy in 1866.* New York: A. G. Sherwood, 1893. 341 p.

30-78. INGALLS, JOHN J. *The Writings of John James Ingalls.* Kansas City, Mo.: Hudson Kimberly Publishing, 1902. 536 p.

30-79. POWERS, G. C. "A Feud That Made History." *National Republic* 8 (December 1933): 16; 9 (January 1934): 18.

The Mulligan Letters Controversy

See also the House *Report* of the Crédit Mobilier investigating committee (29-93) and Cannon (38-21).

30-80. *Mr. Blaine and the Mulligan Letters: The Whole Story.* Boston: J. S. Cushing, 1884. 54 p.

A verbatim reprint of Blaine's story as told in the House on June 5, 1876.

30-81. STOREY, MOORFIELD. *Mr. Blaine's Record: The Investigation of 1876 and the Mulligan Letters.* Boston: Committee of One Hundred, [1884?]. 68 p.

30-82. TROTTMAN, NELSON S. *History of the Union Pacific: A Financial and Economic Survey.* 1923. Reprint. New York: Augustus M. Kelley, 1966. 412 p.

BLAINE'S POLITICAL ASSOCIATES

The diaries, autobiographies, reminiscences, and biographies of almost all politicians of the period contain references to Blaine. The items in the following list have been found useful.

Diaries, Autobiographies, and Reminiscences

See also McClure (10-48), Barry (28-23), Peck (28-34), and Schurz (28-39).

30-83. BELMONT, PERRY. *An American Democrat: The Recollections of Perry Belmont.* New York: Columbia University Press, 1940. 729 p.

30-84. CARNEGIE, ANDREW. *Autobiography of Andrew Carnegie.* Boston: Houghton Mifflin, 1920. 385 p.

30-85. COOLIDGE, T. JEFFERSON. *Autobiography of T. Jefferson Coolidge.* Boston: Houghton Mifflin, 1923. 311 p.

30-86. DEPEW, CHAUNCEY M. *My Memories of Eighty Years.* New York: Charles Scribner's Sons, 1922. 417 p.

30-87. GARFIELD, JAMES A. *The Diary of James A. Garfield.* Edited by Harry James Brown and Frederick D. Williams. Vols. 2 and 3. East Lansing: Michigan State University Press, 1967.

30-88. HAYES, RUTHERFORD B. *Diary and Letters of Rutherford Birchard Hayes.* Edited by Charles R. Williams. Vols. 3–5. Columbus: Ohio State Archaeological and Historical Society, 1922–26.

30-89. HUDSON, WILLIAM C. *Random Recollections of an Old Political Reporter.* New York: Cupples and Leon, 1911. 271 p.

30-90. MCDOUGAL, HENRY C. *Recollections, 1844–1909.* Kansas City, Mo.: Franklin Hudson Publishing, 1910. 466 p.

30-91. PLATT, THOMAS C. *The Autobiography of Thomas Collier Platt.* Edited by Louis J. Lang. 1910. Reprint. New York: Arno Press, 1974. 556 p.

30-92. SMITH, THEODORE C. *The Life and Letters of James Abram Garfield.* 2 vols. 1925. Reprint. Hamden, Conn.: Archon Books, 1968.

30-93. STODDARD, HENRY L. *As I Knew Them: Presidents and Politics from Grant to Coolidge.* 1927. Reprint. Port Washington, N.Y.: Kennikat Press, 1971. 571 p.

30-94. WATTERSON, HENRY. *Marse Henry.* 2 vols. 1919. Reprint. New York: Beekman Press, 1971.

Biographies

See also Nevins (21-106), Storey and Emerson (21-111), Pearce (22-48), Caldwell (29-40), Hesseltine 9-41), Oberholtzer (29-45), Sievers (29-48), McCall (35-47), and Robinson (35-49).

30-95. BARNARD, HARRY. *Rutherford B. Hayes and His America.* Indianapolis: Bobbs-Merrill, 1954. 606 p.

30-96. COOLING, BENJAMIN. *Benjamin Franklin Tracy.* Hamden, Conn.: Archon Books, 1973. 211 p.

30-97. CORTISSOZ, ROYAL. *The Life of Whitelaw Reid.* 2 vols. New York: Charles Scribner's Sons, 1921.

30-98. CRAMER, CLARENCE H. *Royal Bob: The Life of Robert G. Ingersoll.* Indianapolis: Bobbs-Merrill, 1952. 314 p.

30-99. CROLY, HERBERT. *Marcus Alonzo Hanna: His Life and Work.* 1912. Reprint. Hamden, Conn.: Archon Books, 1965. 495 p.

30-100. DINGLEY, EDWARD NELSON. *The Life and Times of Nelson Dingley, Jr.* Kalamazoo, Mich.: Ibling Brothers and Everard, 1902. 497 p.

30-101. DUNCAN, BINGHAM. *Whitelaw Reid: Journalist, Politician, Diplomat.* Athens: University of Georgia Press, 1975. 305 p.

30-102. FESSENDEN, FRANCIS. *Life and Public Services of William Pitt Fessenden.* 2 vols. 1907. Reprint. New York: Da Capo Press, 1970.

30-103. Fuess, Claude M. *Carl Schurz: Reformer.* 1932. Reprint. Port Washington, N.Y.: Kennikat Press, 1963. 421 p.

30-104. Garraty, John A. *Henry Cabot Lodge: A Biography.* New York: Alfred A. Knopf, 1953. 433 p.

30-105. Gosnell, Harold F. *Boss Platt and His New York Machine: A Study of the Political Leadership of Thomas C. Platt, Theodore Roosevelt, and Others.* 1924. Reprint. New York: Russell and Russell, 1969. 370 p.

30-106. Gresham, Matilda. *Life of Walter Quintin Gresham, 1832–1895.* 2 vols. 1919. Reprint. Freeport, N.Y.: Books for Libraries Press, 1970.

30-107. Hendrick, Burton J. *The Life of Andrew Carnegie.* Vol. 1. New York: Harper and Row, 1969. 434 p.

30-108. Howe, George F. *Chester A. Arthur: A Quarter Century of Machine Politics.* 1934. Reprint. New York: Frederick Unger, 1957. 307 p.

30-109. Hunt, H. Draper. *Hannibal Hamlin of Maine: Lincoln's First Vice-President.* Syracuse: Syracuse University Press, 1969. 292 p.

30-110. Lambert, Oscar D. *Stephen Benton Elkins.* Pittsburgh: University of Pittsburgh Press, 1955. 336 p.

30-111. Larson, Henrietta M. *Jay Cooke: Private Banker.* 1936. Reprint. New York: Greenwood Press, 1968. 512 p.

30-112. Leech, Margaret, and Brown, Harry J. *The Garfield Orbit.* New York: Harper and Row, 1978. 369 p.

30-113. Lynch, Denis Tilden. *Grover Cleveland: A Man Four Square.* New York: Horace Liveright, 1932. 581 p.

30-114. Morris, Edmund. *The Rise of Theodore Roosevelt.* New York: Coward, McCann, and Geoghegan, 1979. 886 p.

30-115. Nevins, Allan. *Abram S. Hewitt: With Some Account of Peter Cooper.* 1935. Reprint. New York: Octagon Books, 1967. 623 p.

30-116. ———. *Grover Cleveland: A Study in Courage.* New York: Dodd, Mead, 1934. 832 p.

30-117. Parker, William B. *The Life and Public Services of Justin Smith Morrill.* 1924. Reprint. New York: Da Capo Press, 1971. 378 p.

30-118. Pepper, Charles M. *The Life and Times of Henry Gassaway Davis, 1823–1916.* New York: Century, 1920. 318 p.

30-119. Peskin, Allan. *Garfield.* Kent, Ohio: Kent State University Press, 1978. 716 p.

30-120. Reeves, Thomas C. *Gentleman Boss: The Life of Chester Alan Arthur.* New York: Alfred A. Knopf, 1975. 500 p.

30-121. Richardson, Leon B. *William E. Chandler, Republican.* New York: Dodd, Mead, 1940. 758 p.

30-122. Rogers, Cameron. *Colonel Bob Ingersoll: A Biographical Narrative of the Great American Orator and Agnostic.* Garden City, N.Y.: Doubleday, 1927. 293 p.

30-123. Sage, Leland L. *William Boyd Allison: A Study in Practical Politics.* Iowa City: State Historical Society of Iowa, 1956. 401 p.

30-124. Sievers, Harry J. *Benjamin Harrison: Hoosier President, the White House and After.* Indianapolis: Bobbs-Merrill, 1968. 319 p.

30-125. Taylor, John M. *Garfield of Ohio: The Available Man.* New York: W. W. Norton, 1970. 336 p.

30-126. Trefousse, Hans L. *Ben Butler: The South Called Him Beast!* 1957. Reprint. New York: Octagon Books, 1974.

30-127. Wallace, Willard M. *Soul of the Lion: A Biography of General Joshua L. Chamberlain.* New York: Thomas Nelson and Sons, 1960. 357 p.

30-128. Welch, Richard E., Jr. *George Frisbie Hoar and the Half-Breed Republicans.* Cambridge, Mass.: Harvard University Press, 1971. 364 p.

30-129. Williams, Charles R. *The Life of Rutherford Birchard Hayes, Nineteenth President of the United States.* 2 vols. 1914. Reprint. New York: Da Capo Press, 1971.

30-130. YOUNGER, EDWARD. *John A. Kasson.* Iowa City: State Historical Society of Iowa, 1955. 450 p.

BLAINE AND PRESIDENTIAL POLITICS, 1876–1892

General

See also Stoddard (16-121) and Morgan (28-5).

30-131. GARRATY, JOHN A. *The New Commonwealth, 1877–1890.* New York: Harper and Row, 1968. 364 p.

30-132. GINGER, RAY. *Age of Excess: The United States from 1877 to 1914.* New York: Macmillan, 1975. 419 p.

30-133. HARRISON, ROBERT. "Blaine and the Camerons: A Study in the Limits of Machine Power." *Pennsylvania History* 49 (July 1982): 157–75.

30-134. HOAR, GEORGE F. "Four National Conventions." *Scribner's* 25 (February 1899): 152–74.

30-135. JOSEPHSON, MATTHEW P. *The Politicos, 1865–1896.* New York: Harcourt, Brace, and World, 1938. 760 p.

30-136. MARCUS, ROBERT D. *Grand Old Party: Political Structure in the Gilded Age, 1880–1896.* New York: Oxford University Press, 1971. 323 p.

The Presidential Election of 1876

30-137. POLAKOFF, KEITH I. *The Politics of Inertia: The Election of 1876 and the End of Reconstruction.* Baton Rouge: Louisiana State University Press, 1973. 343 p.

30-138. REPUBLICAN PARTY. NATIONAL CONVENTION. CINCINNATI, 1876. *Proceedings of the Republican National Convention, Held at Cincinnati, Ohio, . . . 1876.* Concord, N.H.: Republican Press Association, 1876. 120 p.

The Presidential Election of 1880

30-139. CLANCY, HERBERT J. *The Presidential Election of 1880.* Chicago: Loyola University Press, 1958. 294 p.

The Presidential Election of 1884

30-140. BALCH, WILLIAM R. *An American Career and Its Triumph: The Life and Public Services of James G. Blaine, with the Facts in the Career of John A. Logan.* Philadelphia: Thayer, Merriam, 1884. 546 p.

30-141. BALESTIER, CHARLES W. *James G. Blaine: A Sketch of His Life, with a Brief Record of the Life of John A. Logan.* New York: John W. Lovell, 1884. 296 p.

30-142. BARKER, WHARTON. "Blaine's Nomination and Defeat." *Pearson's Magazine* 35 (June 1916): 506–12.

30-143. *Biographies of Blaine and Logan, with the Proceedings of the National Convention and an Account of the Issues of the Campaign of '84.* N.p., 1884. 96 p.

30-144. BOYD, THOMAS B. *The Blaine and Logan Campaign of 1884.* Chicago: J. L. Reagan, 1884. 234 p.

30-145. BUEL, JAMES W. *The Standard Bearers: The Authorized Pictorial Lives of James Gillespie Blaine and John Alexander Logan.* New York: N. D. Thompson, 1884. 502 p.

30-146. CONWELL, RUSSELL H. *The Life and Public Services of James G. Blaine.* Springfield, Mass.: Enterprise Publishing, 1884. 504 p.

30-147. COOK, SHERWIN L. *Torchlight Parade: Our Presidential Pageant.* 1929. Reprint. Freeport, N.Y.: Books for Libraries Press, 1970. 307 p.

30-148. COOPER, THOMAS V. *Campaign of '84.* Chicago: Baird and Dillon, 1884. 313 p.

30-149. CRAIG, HUGH. *The Biography and Public Services of Hon. James G. Blaine, Giving a Full Account of Twenty Years in the National Capitol.* New York: N. S. Goodspeed, 1884. 712 p.

30-150. CRESSEY, E. K. *Pine to Potomac: Life of James G. Blaine.* Boston: James H. Earle, 1884. 421 p.

30-151. DOBSON, JOHN M. "The Mugwump Protest in the Election of 1884." Ph.D. dissertation, University of Wisconsin, 1966. 451 p. 66-13407.

30-152. FARRELLY, DAVID G. " 'Rum, Romanism, and Rebellion' Resurrected." *Western Political Quarterly* 8 (June 1955): 262–70.

30-153. KNOX, THOMAS W. *The Lives of James G. Blaine and John A. Logan, Republican Candidates of 1884*. Hartford, Conn.: Hartford Publishing, 1884. 502 p.

30-154. LANDIS, JOHN H., AND CLARE, ISRAEL S. *The Life of James Gillespie Blaine*. Lancaster, Pa.: New Era Printing, 1884. 220 p.

30-155. *Official Proceedings of the Republican National Conventions, 1884, 1888*. Minneapolis, Minn.: Charles W. Johnson, 1903.

30-156. RAMSDELL, H. J. *Life and Public Services of James G. Blaine*. Philadelphia: Hubbard Brothers, 1884. 678 p.

30-157. THOMAS, HARRISON C. *The Return of the Democratic Party to Power in 1884*. 1919. Reprint. New York: AMS Press, 1969. 261 p.

30-158. WILLIAMS, C. R. *Lives of Blaine and Logan*. Philadelphia: E. T. Haines, 1884. 64 p.

The Presidential Election of 1892

See Knoles (28-15).

BLAINE AND FOREIGN AFFAIRS

General

See also Van Alstyne (16-133).

30-159. "American Policy as Conceived by Mr. Blaine." *American Review of Reviews* 7 (March 1893): 133–34.

30-160. BASSETT, JOHN SPENCER. *Expansion and Reform, 1889–1926*. 1926. Reprint. Port Washington, N.Y.: Kennikat Press, 1971. 355 p.

30-161. CAMPBELL, CHARLES S., JR. *The Transformation of American Foreign Relations, 1865–1900*. New York: Harper and Row, 1976. 393 p.

30-162. COXE, JOHN E. "The New Orleans Mafia Incident." *Louisiana Historical Quarterly* 20 (October 1937): 1067–1110.

30-163. FISH, CARL RUSSELL. *The Path of Empire: A Chronicle of the United States as a World Power*. 1919. New York: U.S. Publishing, 1978. 305 p.

30-164. FOSTER, JOHN W. *Diplomatic Memoirs*. 2 vols. Boston: Houghton Mifflin, 1909.

30-165. GRENVILLE, JOHN A. S., AND YOUNG, GEORGE BERKELEY. *Politics, Strategy, and American Diplomacy: Studies in Foreign Policy, 1873–1917*. New Haven: Yale University Press, 1966. 352 p.

30-166. HENDERSON, JOHN B. *American Diplomatic Questions*. New York: Macmillan, 1901. 529 p.

30-167. LaFEBER, WALTER. *The New Empire: An Interpretation of American Expansion, 1860–1898*. Ithaca, N.Y.: Cornell University Press, 1963. 444 p.

30-168. LANGLEY, LESTER D. "James Gillespie Blaine: The Ideologue as Diplomatist." In *Makers of American Diplomacy: From Benjamin Franklin to Henry Kissinger*, edited by Frank J. Merli and Theodore A. Wilson, pp. 253–78. New York: Charles Scribner's Sons, 1974.

30-169. LOCKEY, JOSEPH B. "James Gillespie Blaine." In *The American Secretaries of State and Their Diplomacy*, edited by Samuel Flagg Bemis, 7:263–97; 8:109–84. 1928. Reprint. New York: Pageant Book, 1958.

30-170. MOORE, JOHN BASSETT. *History and Digest of the International Arbitrations to Which the United States Has Been a Party*. Vols. 1–3. Washington, D.C.: Government Printing Office, 1898.

30-171. MORGAN, JAMES M. *America's Egypt: Mr. Blaine's Foreign Policy*. New York: H. Bartsch, 1884. 15 p.

30-172. PLETCHER, DAVID M. *The Awkward Years: American Foreign Relations under Garfield and Arthur*. Columbia: University of Missouri Press, 1962. 381 p.

30-173. "Private Letters from the British Embassy in Washington to the Foreign Secretary Lord Granville." Edited by Paul Knaplund and Carolyn M. Clewes. In *Annual Report of the American Historical Association, 1941*, 1: 73–189. Washington, D.C.: Government Printing Office, 1942.

30-174. SMITH, THEODORE C. "The Garfield-Blaine Tradition." *Massachusetts Historical Society Proceedings* 57 (March 1924): 291–307.

30-175. SPETTER, ALLAN B. "Harrison and Blaine: Foreign Policy, 1889–93." Ph.D. dissertation, Rutgers University, 1967. 397 p. 67-09267.

A condensed version of this dissertation was published under the same title in *Indiana Magazine of History* 65 (September 1969): 215–27.

30-176. SPRING-RICE, SIR CECIL ARTHUR. *The Letters and Friendships of Sir Cecil Arthur Spring-Rice.* Edited by Stephen Gwynn. Vol. 1. 1929. Reprint. Freeport, N.Y.: Books for Libraries Press, 1972. 504 p.

30-177. STROBEL, EDWARD H. *Mr. Blaine and His Foreign Policy: An Examination of His Most Important Dispatches while Secretary of State.* Boston: H. W. Hall, 1884. 69 p.

30-178. TANSILL, CHARLES C. *The Foreign Policy of Thomas F. Bayard, 1885–1897.* New York: Fordham University Press, 1940. 800 p.

30-179. TYLER, ALICE FELT. *The Foreign Policy of James G. Blaine.* 1927. Reprint. Hamden, Conn.: Archon Books, 1965. 411 p.

30-180. U.S. DEPARTMENT OF STATE. *Papers Relating to the Foreign Relations of the United States, 1881.* Washington, D.C.: Government Printing Office, 1882.
See also the volumes for the years 1889–93.

30-181. VOLWILER, ALBERT T. "Harrison, Blaine, and American Foreign Policy, 1889–1893." *Proceedings of the American Philosophical Society* 79 (November 1938): 637–48.

30-182. WILLIAMS, WILLIAM APPLEMAN. *The Roots of the Modern American Empire.* New York: Random House, 1969. 547 p.

30-183. WINCHESTER, RICHARD C. "James G. Blaine and the Ideology of American Expansionism." Ph.D. dissertation, University of Rochester, 1966. 277 p. 69-10831.

The Bering Sea Controversy, 1889–1892

30-184. CAMPBELL, CHARLES S., JR. "The Anglo-American Crisis in the Bering Sea, 1890–1891." *Mississippi Valley Historical Review* 48 (December 1961): 393–414.

30-185. ———. "The Bering Sea Settlements of 1892." *Pacific Historical Review* 32 (August 1963): 347–67.

30-186. GAY, JAMES T. "Harrison, Blaine, and Cronyism . . . Some Facets of the Bering Sea Controversy of the Late Nineteenth Century." *Alaska Journal* 3 (Winter 1973): 12–19.

30-187. ROSEN, BARON ROMAN ROMANOVICH. *Forty Years of Diplomacy.* Vol. 1. New York: Alfred A. Knopf, 1922.

Canada

See also Callahan (9-147) and Warner (24-127).

30-188. KEENLEYSIDE, HUGH L. *Canada and the United States: Some Aspects of the History of the Republic and the Dominion.* 1929. Reprint. Port Washington, N.Y.: Kennikat Press, 1971. 396 p.

30-189. SPETTER, ALLAN B. "Harrison and Blaine: No Reciprocity for Canada." *Canadian Review of American Studies* 12 (Fall 1981): 143–56.

Hawaii and the Pacific

30-190. BAKER, GEORGE W., JR. "Benjamin Harrison and Hawaiian Annexation: A Reinterpretation." *Pacific Historical Review* 33 (August 1964): 295–309.

30-191. RYDEN, GEORGE H. *The Foreign Policy of the United States in Relation to Samoa.* 1933. Reprint. New York: Octagon Books, 1975. 634 p.

30-192. STEVENS, SYLVESTER K. *American Expansion in Hawaii, 1842–1898.* 1945. New York: Russell and Russell, 1968. 320 p.

Latin America and Pan-Americanism

See also Bemis (9-158) and Latane (9-165).

30-193. BASTERT, RUSSELL H. "A New Approach to the Origins of Blaine's Pan American Policy." *Hispanic American Historical Review* 39 (August 1959): 375–412.

30-194. CALLAHAN, JAMES MORTON. *American Foreign Policy in Mexican Relations.* 1932. Reprint. New York: Cooper Square, 1967. 644 p.

30-195. FLINT, CHARLES R. *Memories of an Active Life: Men, and Ships, and Sealing Wax.* New York: G. P. Putnam's Sons, 1923. 349 p.

30-196. FORD, GUY STANTON. "A Yankee Pan-American." In *On and Off Campus*, pp. 474–76. Minneapolis: University of Minnesota Press, 1938. 511 p.

30-197. *International American Conference*. Vol. 1. Washington, D.C.: Government Printing Office, 1890. 905 p.

Contains Blaine's opening remarks to the conference, as well as the committee reports and discussions.

30-198. LOCKEY, JOSEPH B. "The Pan Americanism of Blaine." In *Essays in Pan Americanism*, pp. 51–69. 1939. Reprint. Port Washington, N.Y.: Kennikat Press, 1967.

30-199. LOGAN, RAYFORD W. *The Diplomatic Relations of the United States with Haiti, 1776–1891*. Chapel Hill: University of North Carolina Press, 1941. 516 p.

30-200. MILLINGTON, HERBERT. *American Diplomacy and the War of the Pacific*. 1948. Reprint. New York: Octagon Books, 1975. 172 p.

30-201. MONTAGUE, LUDWELL L. *Haiti and the United States, 1714–1938*. 1940. Reprint. New York: Russell and Russell, 1966. 308 p.

30-202. PIKE, FREDERICK B. *Chile and the United States, 1880–1962*. South Bend, Ind.: University of Notre Dame Press, 1963. 466 p.

30-203. ROBERTSON, WILLIAM SPENCE. *Hispanic-American Relations with the United States*. New York: Oxford University Press, 1923. 470 p.

30-204. ROMERO, M[ATTIAS]. "Mr. Blaine and the Boundary Question between Mexico and Guatemala." *Bulletin of the American Geographical Society* 39, no. 3 (1897): 281–330.

The Mexican minister to Washington's version of Blaine's role in the 1881 dispute.

30-205. ———. "The Pan American Conference." *North American Review* 151 (September/October 1890): 407–21.

30-206. "Secretary Blaine and the Panama Canal." *Commercial and Financial Chronicle* 33 (October 1881): 456–57.

30-207. SMITH, JOSEPH. *Illusions of Conflict: Anglo-American Diplomacy, 1865–1896*. Pittsburgh: University of Pittsburgh Press, 1979. 276 p.

30-208. WILGUS, A. CURTIS. "James G. Blaine and the Pan American Movement." *Hispanic American Historical Review* 5 (November 1922): 622–708.

30-209. WILLIAMS, MARY WILHELMINE. *Anglo-American Isthmian Diplomacy, 1815–1915*. Gloucester, Mass.: Peter Smith, 1965. 356 p.

Trade Reciprocity and Commercial Policy

30-210. CRAPOL, EDWARD P. *America for Americans: Economic Nationalism and Anglophobia in the Late Nineteenth Century*. Westport, Conn.: Greenwood Press, 1973. 248 p.

30-211. "A Glance at Mr. Blaine's Commercial Policy." *Review of Reviews* 5 (June 1892): 546–50.

30-212. LAUGHLIN, J. LAURENCE, AND WILLIS, H. PARKER. *Reciprocity*. New York: Baker and Taylor, 1903. 583 p.

30-213. MILLS, ROGER Q. "The Gladstone-Blaine Controversy." *North American Review* 150 (February 1890): 145–76.

30-214. MORRILL, JUSTIN S. "Free Trade or Protection: A Continuation of the Gladstone-Blaine Controversy." *North American Review* 150 (March 1890): 281–300.

30-215. "Mr. Blaine and Free Trade." *Spectator* 59 (October 1886): 1409–10.

30-216. "Mr. Blaine on Our Navigation Laws." *Commercial and Financial Chronicle* 28 (May 1879): 487–88.

30-217. TARBELL, IDA M. "The Tariff in Our Times." *American Magazine* 63 (March 1907): 473–88.

30-218. TERRILL, TOM E. *The Tariff, Politics, and American Foreign Policy, 1874–1901*. Westport, Conn.: Greenwood Press, 1973. 306 p.

DOMESTIC LIFE

30-219. BALDWIN, ELBERT F. "Intimate Glimpses of a Statesman's Home Life." *Outlook* 91 (February 1909): 316–18.

30-220. BLAINE, HARRIET BAILEY [STANWOOD]. *Letters of Mrs. James G. Blaine.* Edited by Harriet S. Blaine Beale. 2 vols. New York: Duffield, 1898.

30-221. "Blaine Centennial." *Maine Library Association Bulletin* 15 (January 1930): 78–83.
  Includes material on books about Blaine, his home, and the memorial to be erected in his memory.

30-222. BRADFORD, GAMALIEL. *Wives.* 1925. Reprint. New York: Arno Press, 1972. 298 p.

30-223. DAMROSCH, WALTER. *My Musical Life.* 1930. Reprint. Westport, Conn.: Greenwood Press, 1972. 376 p.

30-224. HUNT, H. DRAPER. *The Blaine House.* Portland: Maine Historical Society, 1974. 136 p.

30-225. MOORE, KATRINA. "Blaine House." *Down East* 5 (May 1959): 24–39.

31. Michael Crawford Kerr
(1827–1876)
(Speaker, Forty-fourth Congress)

From his deathbed Michael C. Kerr reportedly told his only child, "I have nothing to leave you, my son, except my good name." Kerr died as he had lived—a poor but honest and principled man. Little is known about Kerr other than the bare outlines of his career. Kerr was born into a family of modest means on March 15, 1827, near Titusville, Pennsylvania. After graduation from Erie Academy in 1845, he married and moved to Bloomfield, Kentucky, where he accepted a teaching position and studied law and political economy in his spare time. He later enrolled in Louisville University and earned a Bachelor of Laws degree in 1851. Kerr then moved his family to New Albany, Indiana, to establish a law practice with one of his classmates.

After being elected city attorney of New Albany in 1854 and prosecuting attorney of Floyd County in 1855, Kerr rose to prominence in the state Democratic party organization. He was elected to a single term in the Indiana legislature in 1856. When Benjamin Harrison left his post as reporter of the state supreme court in 1862 to serve in the Civil War, Kerr was selected to fill the post, perhaps the most lucrative position in the state government at that time. He edited five volumes of *Reports of the Cases Decided in the Supreme Court of Indiana* while serving as state supreme court reporter from 1862 to 1865.

During the Civil War, Kerr was associated with the Peace Democrats, who favored a Union restored by negotiation rather than one restored by war. He was a member of the controversial Knights of the Golden Circle, also known as the Sons of Liberty, but the degree of his participation in their schemes remains uncertain. In 1864 he was largely responsible for exposing the society's plot to oust Indiana's Republican governor, Oliver P. Morton.

Following his election to the Thirty-ninth Congress in 1864, Kerr supported the Democratic party's call for the immediate restoration of the Southern states, which he argued had never left the Union. As a member of the Land Claims and Elections committees, Kerr advocated a liberal policy in the payment of Southern war claims and leniency toward unreconstructed Southerners involved in contested elections. He favored abolition of the test oath and opposed the readmission of Georgia and Alabama under constitutions framed by the Republican party. He denied the constitutionality of black suffrage, opposed the Freedmen's Bureau, and defended the Ku Klux Klan.

During the Forty-second Congress, Kerr served as Democratic floor leader. Although he was defeated for reelection to the Forty-third Congress, he was mentioned as a possible candidate for the speakership upon his election to the Forty-fourth Congress. Humorless, distant, and often uncompromising, he was not a popular man. A long bout with tuberculosis made many doubt that he could control the predictably turbulent House of Representatives.

Because of his limitations, especially his failing health, Kerr did not initially seek the speakership. His prominent friends Manton Marble and August Belmont believed that Kerr's reputation for honesty and integrity would benefit the party's image in the upcoming 1876 presidential campaign. With his candidacy for the speakership championed by Marble's *New York World*, Kerr narrowly defeated Samuel J. Randall for the caucus nomination.

Kerr's speakership proved to be a disappointment to his party. His committee assignments alienated some important party leaders, and illness compelled him to be absent on many occasions. By the middle of February 1876, Kerr was so ill that Samuel S. Cox was named Speaker *pro tempore*. In June, Kerr entered a sanatorium in Rockbridge Alum Springs, Virginia, where he died on August 19, 1876.

MANUSCRIPT COLLECTIONS

Kerr's papers were scattered following the death of his only child, Samuel Kerr. Although no Kerr manuscript collection is known to exist, he is listed as a principal correspondent in the Manton Marble Papers in the Library of Congress Manuscript Division.

BOOKS, ARTICLES, AND DISSERTATIONS

WORKS BY MICHAEL C. KERR

31-1. HALSELL, WILLIE D., ED. "Advice from Michael C. Kerr to a Reconstructed Rebel Congressman." *Indiana Magazine of History* 33 (September 1941): 257–61.

A long letter to Lucius Q. C. Lamar containing advice on how to aid the cause of sectional reconciliation.

The following Kerr items are listed chronologically by year of publication and alphabetically thereunder.

*31-2. KERR, MICHAEL C. *Reconstruction: Speech in the House of Representatives, January 16, 1868*. Washington, D.C., 1868.

*31-3. ———. *Rights of American Citizens: Speech . . . in the House of Representatives, January 11, 1868*. Washington, D.C.: Congressional Globe Office, 1868.

*31-4. ———. *Speech against the Bill for the Ratification of the Constitution of Alabama, Delivered in the House of Representatives, March 28, 1868*. Washington, D.C., 1868.

*31-5. ———. *Power of Congress over Railroads and to Regulate Their Traffic and Commerce . . . Speech Delivered in the House of Representatives, February 4 and 9, 1869*. Washington, D.C., 1869. 8 p.

*31-6. ———. *Power of Congress to Regulate Suffrage in the States: Speech Delivered in the House of Representatives, January 27, 1869*. Washington, D.C., 1869.

31-7. ———. *United States Courts in Indiana*. Washington, D.C.: Congressional Globe Office, 1869. 4 p.

House speech of December 22, 1869, discussing unsatisfactory court facilities in Indiana.

31-8. ———. *The Finances: Needful Reforms*. Washington, D.C.: F. and J. Rives and George A. Bailey, 1870. 14 p.

House speech of January 22, 1870, indicting Republican economic policy.

*31-9. ———. *Tariff: Speech . . . Delivered in the*

House of Representatives, March 21, 1870. Washington, D.C., 1870. 15 p.

*31-10. ———. *Against the Employment of the Bayonet at the Ballot Box: Speeches of C. A. Eldridge, S. S. Cox, M. C. Kerr, and D. W. Voorhees, Delivered in the House of Representatives, February 15, 1871.* Washington, D.C.: Judd and Detweiler, 1871.

31-11. ———. *The Claim of William McGarrahan, alias the Panoche Grande Quicksilver Mining Company of New York, vs. the United States.* Washington, D.C.: Gibson Brothers, 1871. 15 p.
House speech of February 18, 1871.

31-12. ———. *Contested Election Cases. . . .* Washington, D.C.: H. Polkinhorn, 1871. 8 p.

31-13. ———. *Election Contest: Sheafe vs. Tillman.* Washington, D.C.: Congressional Globe Office, 1871. 8 p.

31-14. ———. *Enforcement of Fourteenth Amendment: Speech Delivered in the House of Representatives, March 28, 1871.* Washington, D.C., 1871. 14 p.

*31-15. ———. *National Education: Speech Delivered in the House of Representatives, February 18, 1871.* Washington, D.C., 1871.

31-16. ———. *Negotiation of Loan: Speeches of Hon. M. C. Kerr, of Indiana, and Hon. J. B. Beck, of Kentucky.* Washington, D.C.: Congressional Globe Office, 1872. 15 p.
House speech of January 31, 1872.

31-17. ———. *What Is a Tariff for Revenue? Speech of Hon. Michael C. Kerr, of Indiana, Delivered in the House of Representatives, March 16, 1872.* Washington, D.C.: F. and J. Rives and George A. Bailey, 1872. 15 p.
A speech in opposition to protective tariffs.

*31-18. ———. *French Spoliation Claims: Speech in the House of Representatives, February 26, 1873.* Washington, D.C., 1873.

*31-19. ———. *The James River and Kanawha Canal: Speeches of Hon. Job E. Stevenson of Ohio, Hon. Michael C. Kerr, of Indiana, in the House of Representatives, February 13, 1873.* Washington, D.C., 1873.

*31-20. ———. *Refunding of Cotton Tax: Speech in

the House of Representatives, February 18, 1873. Washington, D.C., 1873.

*31-21. ———. *Restoration of the Union: Speech . . . Delivered in the House of Representatives, January 21, 1876.* Washington, D.C.: Government Printing Office, 1876.

*31-22. U.S. Congress. House. Committee on the Judiciary. *Two Percent Claims of Ohio, Indiana, and Illinois . . . with Remarks on the Same Subject by J. M. Wilson, M. C. Kerr, J. B. Hawley, and J. A. Bingham, in the House of Representatives, December, 1872.* Washington, D.C., 1872. 23 p.

BIOGRAPHICAL SKETCHES AND EULOGIES

There is no full-length biography of Kerr. For the most adequate biographical sketch see Woollen (20-7). *See also* Monks (20-5).

31-23. *A Biographical Directory of the Indiana General Assembly.* Edited by Rebecca A. Shepard et al. Indianapolis: Select Committee on the Centennial History of the Indiana General Assembly, 1980–.

31-24. *A Biographical History of Eminent and Self-made Men of the State of Indiana.* Vol. 1. Cincinnati: Western Biographical Publishing, 1880.

31-25. Cotton, C. W. *1889 Biographical and Historical Souvenir, Floyd County, Indiana.* 1889. Reprint. Knightstown, Ind.: Bookmark, 1977. 152 p.

31-26. Cox, Samuel S. *Memorial Eulogies Delivered in the House of Representatives of the United States.* Washington, D.C.: Government Printing Office, 1883. 86 p.

31-27. Goodrich, DeWitt C., and Tuttle, Charles R. *An Illustrated History of the State of Indiana.* Edited and revised by W. S. Haymond. Indianapolis: S. L. Marrow, 1879. 736 p.

31-28. Gresham, Otto. *Memorial Address Delivered at the Unveiling of the Monument to Michael C. Kerr, May 30, 1928.* N.p., n.d.

31-29. Reed, George Irving, ed. *Encyclopedia of Biography of Indiana.* Vol. 1. Chicago: Century, 1895. 412 p.

31-30. U.S. CONGRESS. HOUSE. *Memorial Addresses on the Life and Character of Michael Crawford Kerr.* 44th Cong., 2d sess. Washington, D.C.: Government Printing Office, 1877. 88 p.

A collection of twenty eulogies delivered by Kerr's colleagues.

KERR AND INDIANA HISTORY AND POLITICS

General

31-31. DUNN, JACOB P. *Indiana and Indianans.* Vols. 1–3. Chicago: American Historical Society, 1919.

31-32. NEW ALBANY, INDIANA. CENTENNIAL COMMITTEE, 1813-1913. *Souvenir History: New Albany Centennial Celebration, October 12–16, 1913.* New Albany, Ind.: G. L. Russell, 1913.

31-33. ROBBINS, D. P. *The Advantages and Surroundings of New Albany, Indiana.* New Albany, Ind.: Ledger, 1892. 98 p.

31-34. SMITH, WILLIAM H. *The History of the State of Indiana from the Earliest Explorations by the French to the Present Time.* 2 vols. Indianapolis: Western Publishing, 1903.

Kerr as Reporter of the State Supreme Court

31-35. INDIANA. SUPREME COURT. *Reports of the Cases Decided in the Supreme Court of Indiana.* Vols. 18–22. Indianapolis: Hall and Hutchinson, 1863–64.

The five volumes edited by Kerr.

31-36. MOLL, THEOPHILUS J. "Indiana Contributors to Legal Literature." *Indiana State Bar Association,* 1922, pp. 54–103.

Includes a brief sketch of Kerr as court reporter.

Indiana and the Civil War

See also Stampp (29-28) and Thornbrough (29-29).

31-37. FESLER, MAYO. "Secret Political Societies in the North during the War." *Indiana Magazine of History* 14 (September 1918): 183–286.

Discusses Kerr's membership in the Knights of the Golden Circle.

31-38. PITMAN, BEN, ED. *The Trials for Treason at Indianapolis.* Cincinnati: Moore, Wilstach, and Baldwin, 1865. 340 p.

A transcript of the trial of the Knights of the Golden Circle that contains testimony on Kerr's involvement in the order and his discovery of the plot to oust Governor Morton.

31-39. STAMPP, KENNETH M. "The Milligan Case and the Election of 1864 in Indiana." *Mississippi Valley Historical Review* 31 (June 1944): 41–58.

A scholarly analysis of the Knights of the Golden Circle conspiracy.

31-40. STIDGER, FELIX G. *Treason History of the Order of Sons of Liberty.* Chicago, 1903. 246 p.

31-41. TREDWAY, GILBERT RILEY. *Democratic Opposition to the Lincoln Administration in Indiana.* Indiana Historical Collections, vol. 48. Indianapolis: Indiana Historical Bureau, 1973. 433 p.

The published version of Tredway's dissertation (31-42).

31-42. ———. "Indiana against the Administration, 1861–1865." Ph.D. dissertation, Indiana University, 1962. 434 p. 63-05086.

KERR'S POLITICAL ASSOCIATES

See also Cox and Northrup (25-30), Mayes (27-36), Belmont (30-83), Smith (30-92), and Gresham (30-106).

31-43. CALHOUN, CHARLES W. "The Ragged Edge of Anxiety: A Political Biography of Walter Q. Gresham." Ph.D. dissertation, Columbia University, 1977. 613 p. 79-24857.

31-44. FOULKE, WILLIAM D. *Life of Oliver P. Morton.* Vol. 1. 1899. Reprint. New York: AMS Press, 1974. 488 p.

31-45. McJIMSEY, GEORGE T. *Genteel Partisan: Manton Marble, 1834–1917.* Ames: Iowa State University Press, 1971. 333 p.

31-46. SYLVESTER, LORNA LUTES. "Oliver P. Morton and Hoosier Politics during the Civil War." Ph.D. dissertation, Indiana University, 1968. 329 p. 68-15468.

KERR'S CONGRESSIONAL CAREER AND SPEAKERSHIP

The most scholarly account of Kerr's election to the speakership is House (30-64). *See also* Barnes (29-55 and 29-56), Flack (29-64), Thompson (30-71), Unger (30-73), and Terrill (30-218).

31-47. "The Democratic Speaker and the House Committees." *Republic* 6 (February 1876): 98–104.

> Assesses the domination of Southern Democrats in Kerr's committee assignments.

31-48. GILLETTE, WILLIAM. *Retreat from Reconstruction, 1869–1879*. Baton Rouge: Louisiana State University Press, 1979. 463 p.

31-49. GROSSMAN, LAWRENCE. "The Democratic Party and the Negro: A Study in Northern and National Politics, 1868–1892." Ph.D. dissertation, City University of New York, 1973. 504 p. 73-21051.

31-50. HOUSE, ALBERT V., JR. "Northern Congressional Democrats as Defenders of the South during Reconstruction." *Journal of Southern History* 6 (February 1940): 46–71.

31-51. HYMAN, HAROLD M. *Era of the Oath: Northern Loyalty Tests during the Civil War and Reconstruction*. 1954. Reprint. New York: Octagon Books, 1978. 229 p.

31-52. ———. *A More Perfect Union: The Impact of the Civil War and Reconstruction on the Constitution*. 1973. Reprint. Boston: Houghton Mifflin, 1975. 562 p.

31-53. "Record of the Democratic Speaker." *Republic* 6 (February 1876): 104–17.

> An outline of the issues in the first months of Kerr's speakership.

31-54. "The Speakership." *Nation*, 9 December 1875, pp. 3–66.

> An analysis of Kerr's victory over Randall for the speakership.

32. Samuel Jackson Randall
(1828–1890)
(Speaker, Forty-fourth through Forty-sixth Congresses)

Samuel J. Randall, who was elected Speaker after Michael C. Kerr's death in 1876, was the son of a prominent Philadelphia lawyer, Whig politician, and protective-tariff advocate. Randall was born on October 10, 1828, in Philadelphia. He attended University Academy and later established his own iron and coal company. He shared his father's political views and consistently supported high tariffs to protect American industries from foreign competition.

Randall became a Democrat following the disintegration of the Whig party in the early 1850s. He sat on the city council from 1852 to 1856 and was elected to the state senate in 1858. He served in the Union army during the Civil War and was elected to Congress in 1862.

Although he was a Democrat representing an overwhelmingly Republican city, Randall was able to win election to every Congress from the Thirty-eighth through the Fifty-first (1863–90). His success at the polls came primarily because his sincere support for high tariffs coincided with the views of his constituency; such views, however, made him suspect at the national party level.

In other respects Randall's views were quite in keeping with those of the majority within his own party. During Reconstruction he was a friend to the South. He not only sponsored amnesty legislation but also filibustered against the civil rights and force bills in 1875. Randall earned a reputation during the Grant administration as a "retrenchment" or "economy in-government" man by supporting cuts in government spending and calling for investigations of the Crédit Mobilier and other scandals. By the end of 1875 he had gained effective control of the Democratic organization in Pennsylvania and had emerged as a national party leader.

Although he was defeated by Kerr for the speakership in December 1875, Randall was appointed chairman of the powerful Committee on Appropriations. After Kerr died in August 1876, Randall was elected to the speakership in December. One of his first duties involved the disputed Hayes-Tilden presidential ballot count. He was instrumental in resolving the electoral crisis once the Hayes "bargain" with the South was negotiated.

As Speaker of the Forty-fifth and Forty-sixth Congresses, Randall proved to be highly partisan. He thwarted any attempt at tariff reform and crippled or killed most attempts to secure government subsidies. His rulings did much to augment the power of the Rules Committee, and he presided over the condensation of the House rules into forty-five compact rules.

In 1881 the Republicans regained control of the House and elected J. Warren Keifer to the speakership. When the Democrats prevailed at the next election, they bypassed Randall to choose John G. Carlisle for the speakership. Randall retained substantial power, however, as chairman of the Committee on Appropriations.

Because of his impact on the nomination and election of Grover Cleveland, Randall's influence within the Democratic party remained strong through the mid-1880s. His political fortunes declined after he refused to support President Cleveland's call for tariff reform in 1887. Control over the Pennsylvania patronage was taken from him by the party leadership, and former congressional allies deserted him. Even though Randall's physical energy was diminished by cancer, he worked on to the end. He died in Washington, D.C., on April 13, 1890.

MANUSCRIPT COLLECTIONS

Henry E. Huntington Library, San Marino, Calif.
  Samuel J. Randall Correspondence, 1856–61.
  81 items.
  NUCMC 61-1765.
Pennsylvania Historical and Museum Commission, Philadelphia, Pa.
  Samuel J. Randall Correspondence, 1879–89.
  81 items.
  NUCMC 60-2878.
University of Pennsylvania Library, Philadelphia, Pa.

  Samuel J. Randall Papers, 1844–90.
  270 boxes.
  NUCMC 68-460.
Wyoming (County) Historical and Geological Society, Wilkes-Barre, Pa.
  Samuel J. Randall Papers, 1871–89.
  Ca. 100 items.
  NUCMC 71-2003.
  There are approximately thirty-five additional letters in various collections in the Pennsylvania Historical Society, Philadelphia, and over one hundred letters in the Grover Cleveland Papers in the Library of Congress Manuscript Division.

BOOKS, ARTICLES, AND DISSERTATIONS

WORKS BY SAMUEL J. RANDALL

The following works are listed chronologically by year of publication.

32-1. RANDALL, SAMUEL J. *The Lehigh University: Exercises at the Celebration of the Founder's Day, Thursday, October 13, 1881, with the Memorial Address by the Hon. Samuel J. Randall, of Pennsylvania.* Reading, Pa.: B. F. Owen, 1881. 23 p.

32-2. ———. *An Address Delivered before the Literary Societies of Dickinson College, Carlisle, Penna., Ninety-eighth Commencement, by the Hon. Samuel J. Randall.* Carlisle, Pa.: George H. McCully, 1882. 20 p.

32-3. ———. *Speech of Hon. Samuel J. Randall, of Pennsylvania, in the House of Representatives, Friday, May 5, 1882.* Washington, D.C.: Government Printing Office, 1883. 13 p.

A speech on tariff and tax policy.

32-4. ———. *The Tariff: Speech of Hon. Samuel J. Randall, of Pennsylvania, in the House of Representatives, Tuesday, May 6, 1884.* N.p., n.d. 16 p.

A speech on tariff protectionism.

BIOGRAPHY, BIOGRAPHICAL SKETCHES, AND EULOGIES

The only extended biographical treatment of Randall is Albert V. House's 1934 dissertation (32-11). The other biographical sketches are inadequate.

32-5. ADAMS, THOMAS R. "The Samuel J. Randall Papers." *Pennsylvania History* 21 (January 1954): 45–54.

Comprises a biographical sketch and a description of the Randall papers at the University of Pennsylvania Library.

32-6. *The Biographical Annual.* New York: L. Klopsch, 1884. 160 p.

32-7. *The Biographical Encyclopedia of Pennsylvania.* Philadelphia: Galaxy Publishing, 1874. 672 p.

32-8. CHAMBERLAIN, EUGENE T. *Early Life and Public Services of Hon. Grover Cleveland and Hon. Thomas A. Hendricks.* Chicago: Caxton Publishing, 1884. 510 p.

Includes a capsule biography of Randall.

32-9. *Contemporary American Biography.* 3 vols. New York: Atlantic Publishing, 1895.

32-10. DEACON, CHARLES RIDGWAY. *A Biographical Album of Prominent Pennsylvanians.* 3 vols. Philadelphia: American Biographical Publishing, 1888–90.

32-11. HOUSE, ALBERT V., JR. "The Political Career of Samuel Jackson Randall." Ph.D. dissertation, University of Wisconsin, Madison, 1934. 290 p.

A positive evaluation of Randall's congressional career.

32-12. SHENK, HIRAM H., ED. *Encyclopedia of Pennsylvania.* Harrisburg, Pa.: National Historical Association, 1932. 593 p.

32-13. SHIMMELL, L. S. *A History of Pennsylvania.* Harrisburg, Pa.: R. L. Myers, 1900. 348 p.

Includes a biographical sketch of Randall.

32-14. U.S. CONGRESS. *Memorial Addresses on the Life and Character of Samuel J. Randall.* 51st. Cong., 1st sess., 1889–90. Washington, D.C.: Government Printing Office, 1891. 157 p.

Contains thirty-five eulogies delivered by Randall's colleagues in the House and Senate.

RANDALL AND PENNSYLVANIA HISTORY AND POLITICS

32-15. BARNES, JAMES A. "Protection, Politics, and Pennsylvania." *Pennsylvania History* 31 (January 1964): 1–21.

An extended discussion of Randall's protectionism in the context of Pennsylvania politics.

32-16. BEERS, PAUL B. *The Pennsylvania Sampler.* Harrisburg, Pa.: Stackpole, 1970. 256 p.

32-17. COLLINS, HERMAN LEROY, AND JORDAN, WILFRED. *Philadelphia: A Story of Progress.* 4 vols. New York: Lewis Historical Publishing, 1941.

32-18. DUNAWAY, WAYLAND FULLER. *A History of Pennsylvania.* 2d ed. New York: Prentice-Hall, 1948. 724 p.

32-19. EVANS, FRANKLIN B. *Pennsylvania Politics, 1872–1877: A Study in Political Leadership.* Harrisburg, Pa.: Pennsylvania Historical and Museum Commission, 1966. 360 p.

A very useful study of Pennsylvania politics with numerous references to Randall's political career up to 1877.

32-20. HOUSE, ALBERT V., JR. "Men, Morals, and Manipulation of the Pennsylvania Democracy of 1875." *Pennsylvania History* 23 (April 1956): 248–66.

A scholarly study of Randall's attempt to expose a ring of corruption and promote his own political fortunes.

32-21. KLEIN, PHILIP S., AND HOOGENBOOM, ARI. *A History of Pennsylvania*. New York: McGraw-Hill, 1973. 559 p.

32-22. STEVENS, SYLVESTER K. *Pennsylvania: The Heritage of a Commonwealth*. 4 vols. West Palm Beach, Fla.: American Historical, 1968.

RANDALL'S POLITICAL ASSOCIATES

See also Caldwell (29-40), Oberholtzer (29-45), Belmont (30-83), Garfield (30-87), Smith (30-92), Barnard (30-95), Dingley (30-100), Leech and Brown (30-112), Lynch (30-113), Nevins (30-115 and 30–116), Pepper (30-118), Peskin (30-119), Taylor (30-125), Williams (30-129), and Barnes (34-12).

32-23. CLEVELAND, GROVER. *Letters of Grover Cleveland, 1850–1908*. Edited by Allan Nevins. 1933. Reprint. New York: Da Capo Press, 1970. 640 p.

32-24. ECKENRODE, HAMILTON J. *Rutherford B. Hayes: Statesman of Reunion*. 1930. Reprint. Port Washington, N.Y.: Kennikat Press, 1963. 363 p.

32-25. FLICK, ALEXANDER CLARENCE. *Samuel Jones Tilden: A Study in Political Sagacity*. 1939. Reprint. Westport, Conn.: Greenwood Press, 1973. 597 p.

32-26. HAYNES, FRED EMORY. *James Baird Weaver*. 1919. New York: Arno Press, 1975. 494 p.

32-27. HAZELTINE, RALPH. "Victor E. Piollet: Portrait of a Country Politician." *Pennsylvania History* 40 (January 1973): 1–18.

32-28. HIRSCH, MARK D. *William C. Whitney: Modern Warwick*. 1948. Reprint. Hamden, Conn.: Archon Books, 1969. 622 p.

32-29. KATZ, IRVING. *August Belmont: A Political Biography*. New York: Columbia University Press, 1968. 296 p.

32-30. NEWBERRY, FARRAR. *James K. Jones: The Plumed Knight of Arkansas*. Arkadelphia, Ark.: Siftings-Herald Printing, 1913. 338 p.

32-31. NIXON, RAYMOND B. *Henry W. Grady: Spokesman of the New South*. 1943. Reprint. New York: Russell and Russell, 1969. 360 p.

32-32. OLSON, JAMES C. *J. Sterling Morton*. 1942. Reprint. Lincoln: Nebraska State Historical Society, 1972. 451 p.

32-33. SANBORN, ALVAN F. *Reminiscences of Richard Lathers*. New York: Grafton Press, 1907. 425 p.

32-34. STEPHENSON, ISAAC. *Recollections of a Long Life*. Chicago: R. R. Donnelly and Sons, 1915. 264 p.

32-35. TANSILL, CHARLES C. *The Congressional Career of Thomas Francis Bayard*. Washington, D.C.: Georgetown University Press, 1946. 362 p.

RANDALL'S CONGRESSIONAL CAREER AND SPEAKERSHIP

General

See also Barnes (29-55 and 29–56), Josephson (30-135), Clancy (30-139), Thomas (30-157), and Pletcher (30-172).

32-36. HOUSE, ALBERT V., JR. "Internal Conflict in Key States in the Democratic Convention of 1880." *Pennsylvania History* 27 (April 1960): 188–216.

32-37. KELLER, MORTON. *Affairs of State: Public Life in Late Nineteenth-Century America*. Cambridge, Mass.: Harvard University Press, 1977. 631 p.

32-38. SHANNON, FRED A. *The Centennial Years*. Garden City, N.Y.: Doubleday, 1967. 362 p.

32-39. "The Week." *Nation,* 27 December 1883, p. 519; 24 December 1885, pp. 519–20; 17 June 1886, p. 497; 22 March 1888, p. 228; 17 April 1890, p. 305.

Brief notes on Randall's legislative activity.

The Speakership

See also House (30-64) and "The Speakership" (31-54).

32-40. HOUSE, ALBERT V., JR. "The Contributions of Samuel J. Randall to the Rules of the National House of Representatives." *American Political Science Review* 29 (October 1935): 837–41.

House interprets Randall's speakership as a foreshadowing of the powerful leadership of Reed and Cannon.

32-41. "The Week." *Nation,* 9 December 1875, p. 363; 18 October 1877, p. 233; 20 March 1879, p. 191.

Brief notes on Randall's speakership.

Reconstruction and the Hayes-Tilden Disputed Election

See also Bruce (24-116), McPherson (29-68), Polakoff (30-137), and House (31-50).

32-42. BERGAMINI, JOHN D. *The Hundredth Year.* New York: G. P. Putnam's Sons, 1976. 402 p.

32-43. HAWORTH, PAUL L. *The Hayes-Tilden Disputed Election of 1876.* 1906. Reprint. New York: AMS Press, 1979. 365 p.

32-44. PATRICK, REMBERT W. *The Reconstruction of the Nation.* New York: Oxford University Press, 1967. 324 p.

32-45. PESKIN, ALLAN. "Was There a Compromise of 1877?" *Journal of American History* 60 (June 1973): 63–75.

32-46. ROBINSON, LLOYD. *The Stolen Election: Hayes versus Tilden, 1876.* Garden City, N.Y.: Doubleday, 1968. 240 p.

32-47. VAUGHAN, HAROLD CECIL. *The Hayes-Tilden Election of 1876: A Disputed Presidential Election in the Gilded Age.* New York: Franklin Watts, 1972. 89 p.

32-48. WOODWARD, C. VANN. *Reunion and Reaction: The Compromise of 1877 and the End of Reconstruction.* Boston: Little, Brown, 1966. 263 p.

32-49. ———. "Yes, There Was a Compromise of 1877." *Journal of American History* 60 (June 1973): 215–23.

Randall and the Tariff Issue

See also Sharkey (30-70), Unger (30-73), and Barnes (32-15).

32-50. HENDRICK, BURTON J. "Shall We Have Responsible Government?" *World's Work* 31 (December 1915): 189–202.

32-51. "Mr. Randall on the Tariff Question." *Nation,* 17 September 1885, p. 232.

32-52. TERRILL, TOM E. "David A. Wells, the Democracy, and Tariff Reduction, 1877–1894." *Journal of American History* 56 (December 1969): 540–55.

32-53. WEINSTEIN, ALLEN. *Prelude to Populism: Origins of the Silver Issue, 1867–1878.* New Haven: Yale University Press, 1970. 433 p.

33. Joseph Warren Keifer
(1836–1932)
(Speaker, Forty-seventh Congress)

J. Warren Keifer, a soldier and a politician, served with distinction in both fields during his long career. He rose to the brevet rank of major general in the Civil War, and he commanded the American forces that occupied Havana during the Spanish-American War. He was elected to the House of Representatives seven times and served as Speaker of the Forty-seventh Congress. Keifer's accomplishments, however, never quite attained the magnitude or brilliance necessary to make him one of the leading figures of the period.

The youngest of fourteen children, Keifer was born in Clark County, Ohio, on January 30, 1836. He turned to the study of the law in a local office after his father's death forced him to leave Antioch College. In 1858 he established a law practice in Springfield, Ohio, and became active in local Republican party affairs.

At the outset of the Civil War, Keifer volunteered for military duty and was commissioned a major of the Third Ohio Volunteers. He won several battlefield promotions, including the brevet rank of major general, awarded on April 9, 1865, shortly after his twenty-ninth birthday. Although he suffered four wounds, he served until the end of the war and took part in the grand review in Washington, D.C.

A good military record enhanced Keifer's political image. He was elected to the Ohio Senate in 1867 and served during the 1868–69 session. He was elected to the House of Representatives in 1876 and served from 1877 to 1885 and from 1905 to 1911. Keifer worked diligently on the Committee on Claims in the Forty-fifth Congress and the Committee on Elections in the Forty-sixth Congress to preserve black voting rights. He even went as far as to call for the stationing of troops at the polls. With a reputation for persistent, even combative, behavior and with little experience in parliamentary procedure, Keifer seemed ill-prepared to assume the speakership of the Forty-seventh Congress (1881–83). The Republican majority in the House was badly divided between Stalwarts, Half-Breeds, and Independents. As the Stalwart candidate, Keifer prevailed. His own rugged personality, compounded with the problems of party factionalism, made his speakership a troubled and stormy one, however. His committee appointments and personnel decisions aroused charges of favoritism and partisanship from members of both parties.

With the Democrats back in control of the Forty-eighth Congress, Keifer returned to the rank and file. He retired at the end of that Congress and devoted himself to the practice of law and to writing about his military exploits. He offered his services to President McKinley when war with Spain was declared in 1898. Appointed major general of volunteers, he commanded the American troops that occupied Havana in 1899. He returned to Congress in 1905 and served three more terms. During this tenure he tried unsuccessfully to protect the voting rights of blacks from such discriminatory practices as literacy tests and poll taxes. He returned to private life in 1911 and died on April 22, 1932, at the age of ninety-six.

MANUSCRIPT COLLECTIONS

Clark County Historical Society, Springfield, Ohio.
   Joseph Warren Keifer Papers.
   Ca. 1 ft.
   NUCMC 76-1822.
Library of Congress, Manuscript Division, Washington, D.C.
   Joseph Warren Keifer Papers, 1861–65.

   6 containers.
   NUCMC 62-893.
   MC 80.
Syracuse University Library, Syracuse, N.Y.
   Joseph Warren Keifer Papers.
   269 items.
   NUCMC 66-213.

BOOKS, ARTICLES, AND DISSERTATIONS

WORKS BY J. WARREN KEIFER

33-1. JACOBY, J. WILBUR. "Marion Centennial Celebration." *Ohio Archaeological and Historical Quarterly* 31 (October 1922): 380–413.

The following works by Keifer are listed chronologically by year of publication and alphabetically thereunder.

33-2. KEIFER, J. WARREN. *Official Reports of J.*

Warren Keifer, Brevet Major General of Volunteers, U.S.A., while Serving in the Armies of the Potomac and Shenandoah. Springfield, Ohio: Daily Republic, 1866. 50 p.

33-3. ———. *The Ohio Democratic Platform Reviewed*. Springfield, Ohio, 1877. 12 p.
A speech delivered in Springfield on September 10, 1877.

33-4. ———. *Ohio's Contribution, Sacrifice, and Service in the War*. Springfield, Ohio: Republic Printing, 1878. 15 p.
A speech delivered on July 22, 1878.

33-5. ———. *Memorial Day Oration of Gen'l J. Warren Keifer of Ohio at Arlington National Cemetery, May 30, 1879*. Washington, D.C.: Gibson Brothers, 1879. 10 p.

33-6. ———. *Deputy Marshalls: Shall Election Laws Be Enforced by the Executive Power?* Washington, D.C., 1880.
House speech of June 11, 1880.

33-7. ———. *Decoration Day Oration of Gen. J. Warren Keifer at Bellefontaine, Ohio, May 30, 1881*. Springfield, Ohio: Republic Printing, 1881. 10 p.

33-8. ———. *Campaign of '82*. Springfield, Ohio: Republic Printing, 1882.
Campaign speech delivered on September 4, 1882, in Springfield.

33-9. ———. *Campaign 1883: The Parties, Wool Tariff, State Issues*. N.p., n.d. 10 p.
Speech delivered at Carey, Ohio, on September 10, 1883.

33-10. ———. *Speeches and Decisions as Speaker of Hon. J. Warren Keifer of Ohio*. Washington, D.C.: Government Printing Office, 1883.
A valuable collection of Keifer's major speeches in the Forty-fifth and Forty-sixth Congresses and his parliamentary rulings as Speaker of the Forty-seventh Congress.

33-11. ———. *Charges against Boynton and Shaw: Remarks of Hon. J. Warren Keifer, in the House of Representatives, Tuesday, January 29, 1884*. [Washington, D.C., 1884]. 8 p.

33-12. ———. *Fitz-John Porter: Speech of Hon. J. Warren Keifer of Ohio in the House of Representatives,* Friday, January 25, 1884. Washington, D.C., 1884. 20 p.

33-13. ———. *Oration of J. Warren Keifer, at the Unveiling of the Statue of James Abram Garfield*. Springfield, Ohio: Globe, 1887. 37 p.

33-14. ———. *Historical Address by Major General J. Warren Keifer, . . . Columbus, Ohio, September 12, 1888*. Zanesville, Ohio: George Lilienthal, 1888.
A review of Keifer's brigade's service in the war.

33-15. ———. "The Battle of Sailor's Creek." In *Sketches of War History, 1861–1865*, edited by Robert Hunter, 3:1–20. Cincinnati: Robert Clarke, 1890.

33-16. ———. *Slavery and Four Years of War: A Political History of Slavery in the United States, Together with a Narrative of the Campaigns and Battles of the Civil War in Which the Author Took Part, 1861–1865*. 2 vols. 1900. Reprint. Miami, Fla.: Mnemosyne Publishing, 1969.
Keifer's major work, it contains much autobiographical material, including his own evaluation of his speakership.

33-17. ———. "Military History." In *The Centenniel Celebration of Springfield, Ohio*, edited by Benjamin F. Prince, pp. 185–202. Springfield, Ohio: Springfield Publishing, 1901.
An article concerning the military history of Clark County, Ohio.

33-18. ———. *The Military History of Ohio from the War of 1812*. Columbus, Ohio: F. J. Heer, 1903.
Speech delivered at the Ohio centennial celebration at Chillicothe on May 20, 1903.

33-19. ———. "Did William Shakesper [sic] Write Shakespeare?" *Open Court* 18 (January 1904): 15–36.
Keifer concludes that the Bard of Avon did not write the Shakespeare plays.

33-20. ———. "O.K." *Ohio Archaeological and Historical Quarterly* 8 (July 1904): 350–54.
An article on the origin of the expression "o.k."

33-21. ———. "The Shakesper [sic] Controversy." *Open Court* 8 (June 1904): 377–82.

A rebuttal to criticisms of his earlier article (33-19).

33-22. ———. "Equality of Representation in Congress and the Electoral College." *Independent,* 21 June 1906, pp. 1479–82.

Keifer argues that those states that deny a class of citizens the right to vote should have their representation reduced.

33-23. ———. *Federal Quarantine: Yellow Fever, How Transmitted, and How Prevented.* Washington, D.C., 1906.

House speech of April 3, 1906.

33-24. ———. "Power of Congress to Reduce Representation in Congress and in the Electoral College: A Reply." *North American Review* 187 (February 1906): 228–38.

Keifer argues for the reduction in representation for those states denying voting rights to blacks.

33-25. ———. *The Battle of Rich Mountain and Some Incidents.* Cincinnati, 1911. 24 p.

A paper read before the Ohio assembly of the Loyal Legion on December 6, 1911.

33-26. ———. "A Century of Peace: Neutralization of the Great American Lakes." In *Official Souvenir Program of the Perry's Victory Centennial,* pp. 21–33. Akron, Ohio: New Werner, 1913.

33-27. ———. "Address of General J. Warren Keifer." *Ohio Archaeological and Historical Quarterly* 22 (July 1913): 435–54.

An address dedicating the Fort Recovery monument.

33-28. ———. "The Story of a Flag." *Ohio Archaeological and Historical Quarterly* 31 (October 1922): 414–21.

33-29. INTER-PARLIAMENTARY UNION. *Union Inter-parlementaire: Compte Rendu de la XVIe Conference Tenue a Bruxelles du 30 Aout au 1er Septembre 1910* (Interparliamentary Union: Report of the Sixteenth Conference held at Brussels from August 30 to September 1, 1910). Brussels: Misch and Thron, 1910. 141 p.

Includes an address by Keifer in which he proposes opening the Panama Canal to all nations upon its completion.

BIOGRAPHICAL SKETCHES AND EULOGIES

There is no adequate biography or biographical sketch of Keifer. Those cited below are typically straightforward and uncritical accounts.

33-30. BRENNAN, J. FLETCHER. *A Biographical Cyclopaedia and Portrait Gallery of Distinguished Men, with an Historical Sketch of the State of Ohio.* Cincinnati: John C. Yorston, 1879. 504 p.

33-31. FESS, SIMEON D. *Ohio: A Four Volume Reference Library on the History of a Great State.* Vol. 3. Chicago: Lewis Publishing, 1937. 463 p.

33-32. GALBREATH, CHARLES B. "General Keifer Honored." *Ohio Archaeological and Historical Quarterly* 35 (April 1926): 418–26.

33-33. ———. *History of Ohio.* Vol. 5. Chicago: American Historical Society, 1925. 563 p.

33-34. "General J. Warren Keifer." *Ohio Archaeological and Historical Quarterly* 41 (July 1932): 572–75.

A eulogy.

33-35. "General J. Warren Keifer: Tribute of Clark County Bar Association." *Ohio Archaeological and Historical Quarterly* 41 (July 1932): 575–82.

A eulogy.

33-36. *The History of Clark County, Ohio.* 1881. Reprint. Evansville, Ind.: Unigraphic, 1979. 92 p.

33-37. MARSHALL, CARRINGTON T., ED. *A History of the Courts and Lawyers of Ohio.* Vol. 4. New York: American Historical Society, 1934. 404 p.

33-38. PRINCE, BENJAMIN F. *A Standard History of Springfield and Clark County, Ohio.* 2 vols. Chicago: American Historical Society, 1922.

33-39. REED, GEORGE IRVING; RANDALL, EMILIUS OVIATT; AND GREVE, CHARLES THEODORE. *Bench and Bar of Ohio.* Vol. 1. Chicago: Century Publishing, 1897. 470 p.

33-40. RUST, ORTON G. *History of West Central Ohio.* Vol. 2. Indianapolis: Historical Publishing, 1934.

33-41. TAYLOR, WILLIAM A. *Ohio in Congress from 1803 to 1901.* Columbus, Ohio: Century Publishing, 1900. 318 p.

KEIFER AND THE CIVIL WAR

The best sources on Keifer's service in the Civil War are his own writings. *See* Keifer (33-2, 33-15, and 33-16).

33-42. BEATH, ROBERT B. *History of the Grand Army of the Republic.* New York: Bryan Taylor, 1889. 702 p.

33-43. BEATTY, JOHN. *The Citizen-Soldier; or, Memoirs of a Volunteer.* Cincinnati: Wilstach, Baldwin, 1879.

33-44. REID, WHITELAW. *Ohio in the War.* 2 vols. New York: Moore, Wilstach, and Baldwin, 1868.

KEIFER'S CONGRESSIONAL CAREER AND SPEAKERSHIP

See also Howard (30-65), Smith (30-92), Dingley (30-100), Younger (30-130), McCall (35-47), and Robinson (35-49).

33-45. BARTHOLDT, RICHARD. *From Steerage to Congress: Reminiscences and Reflections.* Philadelphia: Dorrance, 1930. 447 p.

33-46. BEATTY, JOHN. "The Diary of John Beatty." *Ohio Archaeological and Historical Quarterly* 58 (April–October 1949): 119–51, 390–427; 59 (January–April 1950): 58–91, 165–95.

33-47. "Speakership Contests." *Nation,* 1 December 1881, pp. 428–29.
A summary of the candidates for the speakership with comments on Keifer.

33-48. "The Speakership of the House of Representatives." *Nation,* 8 December 1881, p. 447.
A discussion of the speakership and Keifer's qualifications.

33-49. SWIFT, DONALD CHARLES. "The Ohio Republicans, 1866–1880." Ph.D. dissertation, University of Delaware, 1967. 219 p. 68-09611.

33-50. WALTERS, EVERETT. *Joseph Benson Foraker: An Uncompromising Republican.* Columbus: Ohio History Press, 1948. 315 p.

33-51. "The Week." *Nation,* 12 January 1882–20 April 1882, pp. 21, 46, 242, 262, 284–85, 326; 27 December 1883, p. 519.
Brief notes on Keifer's actions as Speaker.

34. John Griffin Carlisle
(1835–1910)
(Speaker, Forty-eighth through Fiftieth Congresses)

John G. Carlisle was born amid humble surroundings on September 5, 1835, in Campbell (now Kenton) County, Kentucky. The hardships of farm life in rural Kentucky served only to intensify Carlisle's ambition. After he had acquired all the formal education he could, he moved to Covington, studied law, and was admitted to the bar in 1858. He was elected as a Democrat to the state legislature in 1859. Like many Border State politicians, Carlisle was ambivalent concerning the issues of the Civil War. He served on the committee that drafted Kentucky's neutrality resolutions in

May 1861, and he refused to support either side in the war. After the war, he served in the state senate (1866–71) and was elected lieutenant governor (1871–75).

Carlisle was elected to the Forty-fifth Congress and served in the House of Representatives from 1877 to 1890. He quickly became the acknowledged House Democratic leader. In 1883 he was elected Speaker of the Forty-eighth Congress. Carlisle was an effective Speaker who helped set the stage for the powerful speakerships of Reed and Cannon. His knowledge of parliamentary law and House rules commanded bipartisan support; moreover, his fairness and impartiality permitted the exercise of considerable power without provoking the objections that attended Reed's and Cannon's speakerships.

As a member of the House and as Speaker, Carlisle advocated tariff reform, in sharp contrast to the aggressive protectionism of his Democratic colleague Samuel J. Randall. He resigned his House seat in 1890 to fill the Senate vacancy caused by the death of James B. Beck. In 1893 he left the Senate to become secretary of the treasury in Grover Cleveland's second administration (1893–97).

Soon after Carlisle assumed his duties a major financial panic created a serious drain on the gold reserve. Carlisle and President Cleveland upheld the gold standard, in spite of the hostility that their stand aroused within those elements of the Democratic party that favored the free and unlimited coinage of silver. Initially Carlisle had been a cautious supporter of bimetallism, but he became a strong supporter of the gold standard by the mid-1890s.

Carlisle's position made him attractive as a prospective presidential candidate among sound money Democrats in 1896. President Cleveland's delay in ruling out his own candidacy for reelection robbed Carlisle of much-needed support and prevented him from winning the nomination. Carlisle continued to speak out for the gold standard even after William Jennings Bryan was nominated. The hostility to his speeches was so great that he was nearly mobbed in Covington, his hometown. Carlisle refused to return to Kentucky after 1896 because of these animosities. He established a legal practice in New York City and retired from politics except for serving as a vice-president of the Anti-Imperialist League. He died in New York City on July 31, 1910.

MANUSCRIPT COLLECTIONS

Library of Congress, Manuscript Division, Washington, D.C.

John G. Carlisle Papers, 1881, 1883.

2 items.

Western Kentucky University, Kentucky Library and Museum, Bowling Green, Ky.

John G. Carlisle Papers, 1883–96.

5 items.

Although no sizable Carlisle manuscript collection is known to exist, some Carlisle correspondence can be found in the collections of his contemporaries. The Grover Cleveland Papers in the Library of Congress Manuscript Division, for example, contain over seventy Carlisle items. Moreover, Carlisle's long career produced a wealth of public papers that can be found in the gubernatorial papers of Kentucky and among the documents of the State and Treasury Departments.

BOOKS, ARTICLES, AND DISSERTATIONS

WORKS BY JOHN G. CARLISLE

The following works are listed chronologically by year of publication and alphabetically thereunder.

34-1. CARLISLE, JOHN G. *Remonetization of Silver.* Washington, D.C., 1878. 13 p.

House speech of February 21, 1878.

34-2. ———. "The Limitations of the Speakership." *North American Review* 150 (March 1890): 382–99.

Carlisle and Thomas Brackett Reed debate the merits of Reed's method of obtaining quorum calls.

34-3. ———. "The Recent Election." *North American Review* 151 (December 1890): 641–49.

A broad attack upon Republican "abuse of power."

34-4. ———. "Republican Promises and Performances." *Forum* 9 (May 1890): 243–54.

34-5. ———. "The Tariff and the Farmer." *Forum* 8 (January 1890): 475–88.
Carlisle explains his opposition to high tariffs.

34-6. ———. "The Vanishing Surplus." *Forum* 10 (February 1891): 597–606.
Carlisle blames government deficits on Republican policies.

34-7. ———. *Increased Cost of Living and Reduced Wages.* Washington, D.C.: Government Printing Office, 1892. 16 p.
Senate speech of July 29, 1892, on the McKinley tariff.

34-8. ———. *The Free Coinage of Silver.* N.p., 1895. 59 p.
Four speeches of May and June 1895.

34-9. ———. "Dangerous Defects of Our Electoral System, I." *Forum* 24 (November 1897): 257–66.
A critique of the electoral college system as undemocratic.

34-10. ———. "Dangerous Defects of Our Electoral System, A Remedy." *Forum* 24 (February 1898): 651–59.
Suggestions for the reform of the electoral college system.

34-11. ———. "Our Future Policy." *Harper's* 97 (October 1898): 720–28.
Carlisle argues that American foreign policy should avoid colonialism.

BIOGRAPHY, BIOGRAPHICAL SKETCHES, AND EULOGIES

See also Chamberlain (32-8).

34-12. BARNES. JAMES A. *John G. Carlisle: Financial Statesman.* 1931. Reprint. Gloucester, Mass.: Peter Smith, 1967. 552 p.
The only full-length biography of Carlisle.

34-13. BOYD, JAMES P. *Parties, Problems, and Leaders of 1896.* Philadelphia: Publisher's Union, 1896. 615 p.
Includes a capsule biography of Carlisle.

34-14. "John Griffin Carlisle." *Outlook,* 13 August 1910, p. 808.
A biographical sketch on Carlisle's death.

34-15. KERR, CHARLES. *Some Great Lawyers of Kentucky.* N.p., 1931. 40 p.
An address before the Kentucky bar association in 1931 praising Carlisle's political and public career.

34-16. LEE, IVY. "The Modern Lawyer." *World's Work* 8 (June 1904): 4878.
A portrait of Carlisle as a successful corporation lawyer.

34-17. MCAFEE, JOHN J. *Kentucky Politicians: Sketches of Representative Corn-Crackers and Other Miscellany.* Louisville, Ky.: Courier-Journal Job Printing, 1886. 259 p.
Includes a short biographical sketch.

34-18. "Mr. Carlisle." *Nation,* 4 August 1910, pp. 93–94.
A respectful eulogy.

CARLISLE AND KENTUCKY HISTORY AND POLITICS

34-19. CHANNIN, STEVEN A. *Kentucky: A Bicentennial History.* New York: W. W. Norton, 1977. 222 p.

34-20. COULTER, E. MERTON. *The Civil War and Readjustment in Kentucky.* 1926. Reprint. Gloucester, Mass.: Peter Smith, 1966. 468 p.

34-21. TAPP, HAMBLETON, AND KLOTTER, JAMES C. *Kentucky: Decades of Discord, 1865–1900.* Frankfort, Ky.: Kentucky Historical Society, 1977. 553 p.

CARLISLE'S POLITICAL ASSOCIATES

See also Belmont (30-83), McDougal (30-90), Lynch (30-113), Nevins (30-116), McJimsey (31-45), Cleveland (32-23), Haynes (32-26), Hirsch (32-28), Newberry (32-30), and Olson (32-32).

34-22. BASS, HERBERT J. *I Am a Democrat: The Political Career of David Bennett Hill.* Syracuse: Syracuse University Press, 1961. 315 p.

34-23. BIGELOW, JOHN. *The Life of Samuel J. Tilden.* 2 vols. New York: Harper and Brothers, 1895.

34-24. HOVEY, CARL. *The Life Story of J. Pierpont Morgan.* 1911. Reprint. New York: Books for Libraries Press, 1971. 352 p.

34-25. JAMES, HENRY. *Richard Olney and His Public Service.* 1923. Reprint. New York: Da Capo Press, 1971. 335 p.

34-26. JONES, BURR W. "Reminiscences of Nine Decades." *Wisconsin Magazine of History* 20 (September 1936–June 1937): 10–33, 143–64, 270–90, 404–36.

34-27. KLOTTER, JAMES C. *William Goebel: The Politics of Wrath.* Lexington: University Press of Kentucky, 1977. 137 p.

34-28. LA FOLLETTE, ROBERT M. "La Follette's Autobiography." *American Magazine* 73 (November 1911): 3–15.

34-29. O'FERRALL, CHARLES T. *Forty Years of Active Service.* New York: Neale Publishing, 1904. 367 p.

34-30. SCOTT, JAMES BROWN. *Robert Bacon: Life and Letters.* 1923. Reprint. New York: Arno Press, 1975. 459 p.

34-31. STICKES, ARNDT M. *Simon Bolivar Buckner: Borderland Knight.* Chapel Hill: University of North Carolina Press, 1940. 446 p.

34-32. WHITTLE, JAMES LOWRY. *Grover Cleveland.* London: Bliss, Sands, 1896. 240 p.

34-33. WILLIAMSON, HAROLD F. *Edward Atkinson: The Biography of an American Liberal.* 1934. Reprint. New York: Arno Press, 1972. 304 p.

CARLISLE'S CONGRESSIONAL CAREER
AND SPEAKERSHIP

See also Josephson (30-135), Pletcher (30-172), Keller (32-37), Shannon (32-38), and Terrill (32-52).

34-34. "Mr. Carlisle's Election." *Nation,* 6 December 1883, p. 462.
Interprets Carlisle's election to the speakership as a reaction against the existing tariff.

34-35. TARBELL, IDA M. "The Tariff in Our Times." *American Magazine* 64 (June 1907): 169–83.

34-36. U.S. CONGRESS. HOUSE. *Thobe vs. Carlisle: Notice of Contested Election in the Sixth Congressional District of Kentucky.* 50th Cong., 1st sess., 1887–89. Washington, D.C.: Government Printing Office, 1888.
Comprises documents regarding the contested election involving Carlisle.

34-37. "The Week." *Nation,* 31 December 1885, p. 543.
Comments on Carlisle's appointment of Richard P. Bland to chair the Coinage Committee.

CARLISLE AS SECRETARY OF THE TREASURY,
1893–1897

See also LaFeber (30-167).

34-38. BARNES, JAMES A. "The Gold-Standard Democrats and the Party Conflict." *Mississippi Valley Historical Review* 17 (December 1930): 422–50.

34-39. CLEVELAND, GROVER. " 'The Cleveland Bond Issue': A Detailed History of the Crime Charged against an Administration That Issued Bonds of the Government in Time of Peace." *Saturday Evening Post,* 7 May 1904, p. 1.

34-40. ———. *Presidential Problems.* 1904. Reprint. New York: Books for Libraries Press, 1971. 281 p.

34-41. DAWES, CHARLES G. *A Journal of the McKinley Years.* Chicago: Lakeside Press, 1950. 458 p.

34-42. HEPBURN, A. BARTON. *A History of Currency in the United States.* Rev. ed. New York: A. M. Kelley, 1967. 573 p.

34-43. HOLLINGSWORTH, J. ROGERS. *The Whirligig of Politics: The Democracy of Cleveland and Bryan.*

Chicago: University of Chicago Press, 1963. 263 p.

34-44. LAUCK, WILLIAM JETT. *The Causes of the Panic of 1893*. Boston: Houghton Mifflin, 1907. 122 p.

34-45. "Mr. Carlisle's Speech." *Nation,* 30 November 1893, pp. 405–6.
An approving report of a gold-standard speech by Carlisle.

34-46. "Mr. Carlisle's Statement." *Nation,* 22 June 1893, p. 448.
Praises Carlisle's statement concerning the financial crisis of 1893.

34-47. NOYES, ALEXANDER. *Forty Years of American Finance*. 1909. Reprint. New York: Arno Press, 1980. 418 p.

34-48. "Secretary Carlisle. . . ." *Nation,* 28 December 1893, p. 480; 25 July–19 December 1895, pp. 58–59, 380–81, 440; 6 August 1896, p. 98.

Favorable reviews of Carlisle's actions as secretary of the treasury.

34-49. UNDERWOOD, OSCAR W. *Drifting Sands of Party Politics*. New York: Century, 1928. 422 p.

34-50. "The Week." *Nation,* 20 December 1894, p. 453; 17 January 1895, p. 39.

34-51. WILSON, WOODROW. "Mr. Cleveland's Cabinet." *Review of Reviews* 7 (April 1893): 286–97.

CARLISLE AND ANTI-IMPERIALISM

34-52. CARLETON, WILLIAM G. "Isolationism and the Middle West." *Mississippi Valley Historical Review* 33 (December 1946): 377–90.

34-53. WELCH, RICHARD E., JR. *Response to Imperialism*. Chapel Hill: University of North Carolina Press, 1979. 215 p.

35. **Thomas Brackett Reed**
(1839–1902)
(Speaker, Fifty-first, Fifty-fourth, and Fifty-fifth Congresses)

Thomas Brackett Reed possessed a penetrating intellect and a pungent wit which permitted him, more than any previous Speaker since Henry Clay, to transform the speakership into a position from which to control the House of Representatives. Reed, a complicated man of apparent paradoxes, was over six feet three inches tall and weighed nearly 300 pounds, yet he displayed a soft, bland countenance that has been described as almost cherubic. He was a cultured, droll, and affable companion in private life, but in his public career he was a sarcastic and inflexible debater and a nearly autocratic ruler of the House.

Reed was born into a family of modest means on October 18, 1839, in Portland, Maine. He demonstrated a reflective temperament and attended Bowdoin College with the intention of entering the ministry. By the time he graduated in 1860 he had become a confirmed freethinker and had turned his attention to law. He moved to California in late 1861 and was admitted to the bar at San Jose in 1863. He returned to Portland soon thereafter and served as a navy paymaster for eighteen months in 1864–65.

Admitted to the Maine bar in 1865, Reed won election to the state legislature two years later. He then served as attorney general of Maine for three years (1870–73). During this time he earned a reputation as an energetic and fearless prosecutor. During the following three years, which he devoted to his private law practice, Reed was active in Republican party affairs. He was elected to Congress in 1876 and served in the House of Representatives from 1877 to 1899.

Reed's rise to prominence in Congress was rapid. His wit and intellect quickly gained him a reputation as a formidable foe. As a member of the select committee investigating charges of corruption in the 1876 election, he demonstrated great skill in uncovering evidence and conducting cross-examinations. Moreover, he championed Republican causes such as voting rights for blacks, protective tariffs, and sound money.

As a member of the Rules Committee and the Ways and Means Committee in the 1880s, Reed unsuccessfully campaigned for reform of the House rules to make it possible for the majority in Congress to govern. By the mid–1880s he had emerged as the acknowledged House Republican leader. After the Republicans gained control of the Fifty-first Congress in 1888, Reed was elected Speaker of the House, in December 1889. Immediately he set about reforming the House rules. In order to combat such dilatory tactics as the "disappearing quorum," he counted as present all members in the chamber, not simply those who answered the roll call. The famous Reed Rules, adopted over the Democratic minority's vehement objections, made it possible for the Republican majority to enact the most extensive legislative program of the post–Civil War era.

The Democrats won control of the Fifty-second and Fifty-third Congresses and rescinded Reed's Rules. Reed returned to the rank and file, where he was able to use obstructionist tactics to such effect that the Democrats were forced to readopt the very rules that they had so bitterly opposed. He resumed the speakership in the Fifty-fourth and Fifty-fifth Congresses. Once again he ruled the House by the sheer force of his personality, which earned him the nickname "Czar" Reed. Although he was considered a strong candidate for the presidential nomination in 1896, he refused to court favor or to make the deals that might have given him the Republican nomination. Reed's opposition to McKinley's imperialism turned to bitter frustration with the annexation of Hawaii, the intervention in Cuba, and the acquisition of the Philippines. He resigned from the House in disgust on September 4, 1899, and established a law practice in New York City. Reed died on December 7, 1902, while visiting Washington, D.C.

MANUSCRIPT COLLECTIONS

Bowdoin College Library, Brunswick, Me.
  Thomas Brackett Reed Papers, 1870–1944.
  1 ft., ca. 200 items.
  NUCMC 71-38.

BOOKS, ARTICLES, AND DISSERTATIONS

WORKS BY THOMAS BRACKETT REED

See also Clay (9-10) and Carlisle (34-2).

The following works by Reed are listed chronologically by year of publication and alphabetically thereunder.

35-1. REED, THOMAS BRACKETT. *Address of Hon. Thomas B. Reed, at Grand Army Reunion, Old Orchard, August 1, 1884.* Portland, Me.: Stephen Berry, 1884. 3 p.

A tribute to Civil War veterans.

35-2. ———. *Centennial Oration, Delivered at Portland, July 6, 1886, by Hon. Thomas B. Reed.* Portland, Me., 1886.

An address on the centenary of the incorporation of Portland, Maine.

35-3. ———. "Democracy at St. Louis." *North American Review* 147 (July 1888): 37–44.

An analysis of the Democratic National Convention.

35-4. ———. "An Outlying Province." *North American Review* 146 (January 1888): 86–95.

An article on the climate, geography, and living conditions of Alaska.

35-5. ———. "The President's Letter." *North American Review* 147 (October 1888): 385–93.

Comments upon Cleveland's acceptance of the Democratic nomination for president.

35-6. ———. *Speeches of Hon. Thomas B. Reed, of Maine, on Protection,* . . . New York: M. J. Ivers, 1888. 45 p.

35-7. ———. "Obstructions in the National House." *North American Review* 149 (October 1889): 421–28.

Reed explains his opposition to dilatory parliamentary tactics.

35-8. ———. "Rules of the House of Representatives." *Century Magazine* 37 (March 1889): 792–95.

A proposal to reform House rules to allow the majority to govern.

35-9. ———. "Contested Elections." *North American Review* 151 (July 1890): 112–20.

Reed suggests reforms in the method of resolving contested elections.

35-10. ———. "The Federal Control of Elections." *North American Review* 150 (June 1890): 671–80.

A call for federal supervision of Southern elections.

35-11. ———. "Reforms Needed in the House." *North American Review* 150 (May 1890): 537–46.

A defense of his rules from critics such as former Speaker Carlisle. *See* Carlisle (34-2).

35-12. ———. "A Reply to X.M.C." *North American Review* 151 (August 1890): 228–36.

A reply to criticisms of his reforms. *See* X.M.C. (35-154).

35-13. ———. "A Deliberative Body." *North American Review* 152 (February 1891): 148–56.

Another defense of Reed's reforms.

35-14. ———. "Mr. Speaker." *North American Review* 154 (January 1892): 9–16.

A further comment on the efficiency of government by the majority.

35-15. ———. "Spending Public Money." *North American Review* 154 (March 1892): 319–28.

Reed charges the House Democrats with parsimony in appropriations.

35-16. ———. "Two Congresses Contrasted." *North American Review* 155 (August 1892): 227–36.

Reed contrasts the virtues of his Fifty-first Congress with the vices of the Democratic Fifty-second Congress.

35-17. ———. "The Political Situation." *North American Review* 157 (September 1893): 257–67.

Comments on several related economic and political issues.

35-18. ———. "Issues of the Coming Election." *North American Review* 159 (October 1894): 394–403.

A partisan analysis of the upcoming election.

35-19. ———. "The Present Administration of National Affairs." *North American Review* 159 (July 1894): 1–10.

A biting criticism of Cleveland's administration.

35-20. ———. "Silver and the Tariff at Washington." *Fortnightly Review* 61 (June 1894): 837–38.

An interview with Reed on economic issues.

35-21. ———. "Tariff and Business." *North American Review* 158 (January 1894): 110–18.

35-22. ———. "Historic Political Upheavals." *North American Review* 160 (January 1895): 109–16.

Another criticism of the Cleveland administration.

35-23. ———. "A Last Tribute." *North American Review* 160 (April 1895): 385–95.

A sarcastic criticism of the conduct of the Democratic party during the preceding Congress.

35-24. ———. "As Maine Goes, So Goes the Union." *Forum* 22 (November 1896): 257–62.

A commentary on the silver issue and Maine's reputation as a national political barometer.

35-25. ———. "The Safe Pathway of Experience." *North American Review* 163 (October 1896): 385–94.

The adoption of free silver by the Democrats is seen as an unnecessarily risky venture.

35-26. ———. "Concerning Hard Times." *Illustrated American*, 28 August 1897, pp. 264–65.

An examination of the historical cycles of feast and famine.

35-27. ———. "Concerning Who Goes First." *Illustrated American*, 3 July 1897, pp. 8–10.

Reed discusses protocol.

35-28. ———. "Critics and Leaders." *Illustrated American*, 23 October 1897, pp. 525–26.

A criticism of modern critics.

35-29. ———. "Empire Can Wait." *Illustrated American*, 4 December 1897, pp. 713–14.

An argument against imperialism.

35-30. ———. "A Great Yankee Leader of the Past Generation." *Illustrated American*, 9 October 1897, pp. 456–57.

A tribute to former Speaker Robert C. Winthrop.

35-31. ———. "A Half-Forgotten Leader." *Illustrated American*, 17 July 1897, pp. 70–71.

35-32. ———. "How Congress Gets Reported." *Illustrated American*, 6 November 1897, pp. 590–91.

A contrast between the British and American ways of reporting legislative proceedings.

35-33. ———. "How the House Does Business." *North American Review* 164 (June 1897): 641–50.

A description of House procedure under Reed's rules.

35-34. ———. "How Klondike May Look in History." *Illustrated American*, 20 November 1897, pp. 648–49.

An attempt to put the Alaska gold rush in historical perspective.

35-35. ———. "The New Navy." *Illustrated American*, 25 September 1897, pp. 392–93.

A comment on the constant need to upgrade and equip the navy.

35-36. ———. "The Newspaper's Intrusion upon Privacy." *Illustrated American*, 18 December 1897, pp. 776–77.

Reed argues that the press, in spite of its abuses, is necessary for a free republic.

35-37. ———. "The Passage of the Tariff Bill." *Illustrated American*, 14 August 1897, pp. 198–99.

35-38. ———. "Should the Cabinet Officers Have Seats in Congress?" *Illustrated American*, 31 July 1897, pp. 137–38.

35-39. ———. "Wealth and One of Its Results." *Illustrated American*, 11 September 1897, pp. 329–30.

Reed praises wealth for making available leisure time in which to pursue intellectual matters.

35-40. ———. "The Nicaragua Canal." *North American Review* 168 (May 1899): 552–62.

Reed supports construction of a transisthmian canal in Nicaragua.

35-41. ———. "Orators and Oratory of Today." *Saturday Evening Post*, 9 February 1901, pp. 1–2.

35-42. ———. "Mr. Reed's Last Speech." *Harper's Weekly*, 20 December 1902, pp. 1981–82.

35-43. ———. "What Shall We Do with the Tariff." *North American Review* 175 (December 1902): 746–55.

Reed's last published article calls for the maintenance of the protective tariff.

35-44. ———. "The Life of a Congressman." In *The Ship of State: By Those at the Helm*, pp. 43–66. Boston: Ginn, 1903.

An essay for young audiences.

35-45. ———. *Orations and Addresses Delivered by Thomas Brackett Reed*. Portland, Me., 1911. 170 p.

Contains six of Reed's speeches.

35-46. ———, ED. *Modern Eloquence*. 10 vols. Philadelphia: John D. Morris, 1900–1903.

Reed served as the general series editor and authored a piece entitled "Oratory, Past and Present" in volume 4.

BIOGRAPHIES, BIOGRAPHICAL SKETCHES, AND EULOGIES

Biographies

35-47. McCall, Samuel W. *The Life of Thomas Brackett Reed.* 1914. Reprint. New York: AMS Press, 1972. 303 p.

35-48. Offenberg, Richard Stanley. "The Political Career of Thomas Brackett Reed." Ph.D. dissertation, New York University, 1963. 198 p. 63-07227.

A scholarly account that is critical of many of Reed's actions but admiring of his character.

35-49. Robinson, William A. *Thomas B. Reed: Parliamentarian.* New York: Dodd, Mead, 1930. 423 p.

The most comprehensive and useful biography of Reed

Biographical Sketches

See also Powers (28-35), Headley (28-45), and Chase (30-38).

35-50. Brownson, W. H. "Thomas B. Reed." *New England Magazine* 8 (April 1890): 188–93.

35-51. DeCasseres, Benjamin. "Tom Reed." *American Mercury* 19 (February 1930): 221–28.

35-52. Lodge, Henry Cabot. "The Hon. Thomas B. Reed." *Harper's Weekly,* 17 March 1894, pp. 257–58.

35-53. ———. "Thomas Brackett Reed: The Statesman, the Wit, and the Man." *Century Magazine* 81 (February 1911): 613–21.

35-54. McCall, Samuel W. *Address by Hon. Samuel W. McCall upon the Unveiling of the Monument of Hon. Thomas Brackett Reed at Portland, Maine, August 31, 1910.* Washington, D.C.: Government Printing Office, 1911. 18 p.

35-55. McIntyre, Philip W., and Blanding, William F., eds. *Biographical Sketches and Portraits of Leaders in Business and Professional Life in and of the State of Maine.* Boston: New England Magazine, 1897. 626 p.

35-56. Munsey, Frank A. "Thomas Brackett Reed." *Munsey's Magazine* 9 (April 1893): 85–88.

35-57. Neale, Walter, ed. *Autobiographies and Portraits.* 2 vols. Washington, D.C.: Neale, 1899.

35-58. Newman, Eugene William [Savoyard]. *Essays on Men, Things, and Events.* New York: Neale, 1904. 287 p.

35-59. Porter, Robert P. "Thomas B. Reed of Maine: The Man and His Home." *McClure's* 1 (October 1893): 374–89.

35-60. Ruoff, Henry W. *Leaders of Men.* Springfield, Mass.: King-Richardson, 1903. 695 p.

35-61. Smalley, George W. *Anglo-American Memories.* London: Duckworth, 1911. 391 p.

35-62. Stewart, John C. "Biographical Sketches of Natives of Maine Who Have Served in the Congress of the United States." *Sprague's Journal of Maine History* 11 (April/June 1923): 69.

35-63. Tuchman, Barbara W. *The Proud Tower: A Portrait of the World before the War, 1890–1914.* New York: Macmillan, 1966. 528 p.

Includes an excellent chapter on Reed.

Eulogies

35-64. Clark, Francis E. "Thomas B. Reed as a Neighbor." *Independent,* 8 January 1903, pp. 82–84.

35-65. Clemens, Samuel Langhorne [pseud. Mark Twain]. *The Complete Essays of Mark Twain.* Edited by Charles Neider. Garden City, N.Y.: Doubleday, 1963. 705 p.

Includes a two-page eulogy of Reed by his friend Samuel Clemens.

35-66. Clemens, Samuel Langhorne [pseud. Mark Twain], et al. "Thomas Brackett Reed." *Harper's Weekly,* 20 December 1902, pp. 1979–81.

35-67. "The Contributors' Club—Thomas Brackett Reed." *Atlantic Monthly* 91 (February 1903): 281–83.

35-68. DAY, HOLMAN F. "Tom Reed among His Neighbors." *Saturday Evening Post,* 3 January 1903, pp. 1–2.

35-69. "Death of Thomas Brackett Reed." *Gunton's Magazine* 24 (January 1903): 1–6.

35-70. HUBBARD, THOMAS H. "Memorial of Thomas Brackett Reed." *Annual Report of the Association of the Bar of the City of New York,* 1904, pp. 137–44.

35-71. KNIGHT, ENOCH. "Thomas B. Reed: An Appreciation." *New England Magazine* 30 (April 1904): 215–24.

35-72. LEUPP, FRANCIS E. "Personal Recollections of Thomas B. Reed." *Outlook,* 3 September 1910, pp. 36–40.

35-73. MCFARLAND, HENRY B. F. "Thomas Brackett Reed." *Review of Reviews* 27 (January 1903): 36–38.

35-74. MAINE. LEGISLATURE. *Memorial Addresses on the Life and Character of Thomas Brackett Reed Delivered in Joint Assembly of the Two Branches of the Legislature.* Augusta, Me.: Kennebec Journal, 1903. 40 p.

35-75. "Speaker Reed." *Nation,* 11 December 1902, p. 456.

35-76. THOMAS BRACKETT REED MEMORIAL ASSOCIATION. *Exercises at the Unveiling of the Statue of Thomas Brackett Reed, at Portland, Maine, August 31, 1910.* Portland, Me.: Stephen Berry, 1911. 84 p.

35-77. "Thomas B. Reed." *Outlook,* 13 December 1902, pp. 864–66.

35-78. "Tributes to Thomas B. Reed." *Gunton's Magazine* 24 (January 1903): 55–60.

35-79. WEBB, RICHARD. "Public Career of Thomas B. Reed." *Collections of the Maine Historical Society,* 3d ser., 1 (1904): 369–89.

REED AND MAINE HISTORY

General

See also Hatch (30-56).

35-80. COE, HARRIET B., ED. *Maine: Resources,*

Attractions, and Its People, A History. 4 vols. New York: Lewis Historical, 1928.

Reed's Legal Practice

35-81. *Anson Atwood, complt., vs. Portland Co. . . .* Portland, Me.: Stephen Berry, 1879.

The record of a case in which Reed served as attorney for the complainant.

35-82. TOWNSHEND, EDWARD W. "Some Anecdotes of Thomas B. Reed." *Harper's Weekly,* 30 January 1904, p. 180.

REED'S POLITICAL ASSOCIATES

See also Barry (28-23), Dunn (28-28), Hoar (28-32), Peck (28-34), Stealey (28-41), Watson (28-42), Blaine (30-7), McDougal (30-90), Smith (30-92), Stoddard (30-93), Cortissoz (30-97), Croly (30-99), Dingley (30-100), Garraty (30-104), Morris (30-114), Nevins (30-115), Sage (30-123), Welch (30-128), Stephenson (32-34), Bartholdt (33-45), Walters (33-50), Barnes (34-12), Jones (34-26), O'Ferrall (34-29), Bolles (38-33), Busbey (38-34), Gwinn (38-35), Clark (40-38), Webb (40-52), and Gillett (41-7).

35-83. ADAMS, HENRY. *Letters of Henry Adams.* 3 vols. Edited by Worthington C. Ford. 1938. Reprint. Cambridge, Mass.: Harvard University Press, 1983.

35-84. BEER, THOMAS. *Hanna.* 1929. Reprint. New York: Octagon Books, 1973. 325 p.

35-85. COOLIDGE, LOUIS A. *An Old-fashioned Senator: Orville H. Platt.* 1910. Reprint. Port Washington, N.Y.: Kennikat Press, 1971. 655 p.

35-86. COWLES, ANNA ROOSEVELT. *Letters from Theodore Roosevelt to Anna Roosevelt Cowles, 1870–1918.* New York: Charles Scribner's Sons, 1924. 323 p.

35-87. CRISSEY, FORREST. *Theodore E. Burton: American Statesman.* Cleveland: World Publishing, 1956. 352 p.

35-88. DREISER, THEODORE. *A Book about Myself.* New York: Boni and Liveright, 1922. 502 p.

PART IV. THE SPEAKERS, 1861–1911

35-89. ELLIS, ELMER. *Henry Moore Teller: Defender of the West*. Caldwell, Idaho: Caxton Printers, 1941. 409 p.

35-90. EVANS, LAWRENCE B. *Samuel W. McCall: Governor of Massachusetts*. Boston: Houghton Mifflin, 1916. 241 p.

35-91. GODKIN, E. L. *Life and Letters of Edwin Lawrence Godkin*. Edited by Rollo Ogden. 2 vols. 1907. Reprint. Westport, Conn.: Greenwood Press, 1972.

35-92. GRIFFIN, SOLOMON BULKLEY. *People and Politics Observed by a Massachusetts Editor*. Boston: Little, Brown, 1923. 510 p.

35-93. ———. *W. Murray Crane: A Man and a Brother*. Boston: Little, Brown, 1926. 202 p.

35-94. HALSTEAD, MURAT. *Life and Distinguished Services of William McKinley*. Chicago: Memorial Association, 1901. 540 p.

35-95. JOHNSON, ROBERT UNDERWOOD. *Remembered Yesterdays*. Boston: Little, Brown, 1923. 624 p.

35-96. KENNEDY, AMBROSE. *American Orator: Bourke Cockran, His Life and Politics*. Boston: Bruce Humphries, 1948. 225 p.

35-97. KERR, WINFIELD S. *John Sherman: His Life and Public Services*. 2 vols. Boston: Sherman, French, 1908.

35-98. KOENIG, LOUIS W. *Bryan: A Political Biography of William Jennings Bryan*. New York: G. P. Putnam's Sons, 1971. 736 p.

35-99. LA FOLLETTE, BELLE CASE, AND LA FOLLETTE, FOLA. *Robert M. La Follette*. 2 vols. 1953. Reprint. New York: Hafner, 1971.

35-100. LA FOLLETTE, ROBERT M. *La Follette's Autobiography: A Personal Narrative of Political Experiences*. 1913. Reprint. Madison: University of Wisconsin Press, 1960. 349 p.

35-101. LODGE, HENRY CABOT. *Selections from the Correspondence of Theodore Roosevelt and Henry Cabot Lodge*. 2 vols. 1925. Reprint. New York: Da Capo Press, 1971.

35-102. LONG, JOHN D. *The Papers of John Davis Long*. Edited by Gardner Weld Allen. Boston: Massachusetts Historical Society, 1939. 464 p.

35-103. McELROY, ROBERT M. *Levi Parsons Morton: Banker, Diplomat, and Statesman*. 1930. Reprint. New York: Arno Press, 1975. 340 p.

35-104. MORGAN H. WAYNE. *William McKinley and His America*. Syracuse: Syracuse University Press, 1963. 595 p.

35-105. MYERS, ELISABETH P. *Benjamin Harrison*. Chicago: Reilly and Lee, 1969. 165 p.

35-106. ORCUTT, WILLIAM DANA. *Burrows of Michigan and the Republican Party: A Biography and a History*. 2 vols. New York: Longmans, Green, 1917.

35-107. OSBORN, GEORGE C. *John Sharp Williams: Planter-Statesman of the Deep South*. 1943. Reprint. Gloucester, Mass.: Peter Smith, 1964. 501 p.

35-108. PAINE, ALBERT BIGELOW. *Mark Twain: A Biography*. 3 vols. 1912. Reprint. New York: Chelsea House, 1980.

35-109. PRINGLE, HENRY F. *Theodore Roosevelt: A Biography*. New York: Harcourt, Brace, 1931. 435 p.

35-110. ROOSEVELT, THEODORE. *The Letters of Theodore Roosevelt*. 2 vols. Edited by Elting E. Morison. Cambridge, Mass.: Harvard University Press, 1951–54.

35-111. ROSS, THOMAS RICHARD. *Jonathan Prentiss Dolliver: A Study in Political Integrity and Independence*. Iowa City: State Historical Society of Iowa, 1958. 366 p.

35-112. STEPHENSON, NATHANIEL W. *Nelson W. Aldrich: A Leader in American Politics*. 1930. Reprint. Port Washington, N.Y.: Kennikat Press, 1971. 496 p.

35-113. STEVENSON, ADLAI E. *Something of Men I Have Known*. Chicago: A. C. McClurg, 1909. 442 p.

35-114. STONE, WILLIAM A. *The Tale of a Plain Man*. Philadelphia: John C. Winston, 1918. 318 p.

35-115. WHITE, ANDREW DICKSON. *Autobiography of Andrew Dickson White.* 2 vols. New York: Century, 1905.

35-116. WHITE, WILLIAM ALLEN. *The Autobiography of William Allen White.* New York: Macmillan, 1946. 669 p.

35-117. WILSON, WOODROW. *The Papers of Woodrow Wilson.* Edited by Arthur S. Link. Vols. 6, 7, 10. Princeton: Princeton University Press, 1968–71.

35-118. WOODWARD, C. VANN. *Tom Watson: Agrarian Rebel.* New York: Macmillan, 1938. 430 p.

REED AS SPEAKER OF THE HOUSE

See also Hinds (1-8), Alexander (1-16), Swanson (1-43), Stanwood (10-51), Merrill and Merrill (28-16), Tarbell (28-19), Williams (28-22), Brady and Althoff (28-49), Lewis (28-52), DeSantis (30-60), Howard (30-65), Ginger (30-132), Josephson (30-135), Marcus (30-136), Keller (32-37), Shannon (32-38), and Cannon (38-23).

35-119. BRADY, DAVID W. *Congressional Voting in a Partisan Era.* Lawrence: University Press of Kansas, 1973. 273 p.

35-120. LEECH, MARGARET. *In the Days of McKinley.* 1959. Reprint. Westport, Conn.: Greenwood Press, 1975. 686 p.

35-121. MONTGOMERY, KIRT EARL. "Thomas B. Reed's Theory and Practice of Congressional Debating." *Speech Monographs* 17 (March 1950): 65–74.

35-122. "Mr. Reed to Leave Congress." *Review of Reviews* 19 (May 1899): 528–29.

35-123. RHODES, JAMES FORD. *The McKinley and Roosevelt Administrations.* 1922. Reprint. Port Washington, N.Y.: Kennikat Press, 1965. 418 p.

35-124. ROOSEVELT, THEODORE. *The Works of Theodore Roosevelt.* Vol. 14. Edited by Hermann Hagedorn. New York: Charles Scribner's Sons, 1926. 403 p.

35-125. "Speaker Reed's Assumption of a Protectorate." *Review of Reviews* 17 (March 1898): 268–69.

35-126. "Speaker Reed's Retirement." *Gunton's Magazine* 16 (May 1899): 320–28.

35-127. STERN, CLARENCE A. *Golden Republicanism: The Crusade for Hard Money.* Oshkosh, Wis., 1970. 118 p.

35-128. ———. *Protectionist Republicanism: Republican Tariff Policy in the McKinley Period.* Oshkosh, Wis., 1971. 138 p.

35-129. ———. *Republican Heyday.* Oshkosh, Wis., 1962. 97 p.

35-130. STRUNSKY, SIMEON. " 'Czar' Reed: Speaker of the House." *Current History* 34 (April 1931): 58–62.

35-131. TUCHMAN, BARBARA W. "Czar of the House." *American Heritage* 14 (December 1962): 33–35.

35-132. "The Week." *Nation,* 6 February–6 June 1890, pp. 101, 143, 459, 479, 499; 10 July–23 October 1890, pp. 21, 201, 219, 237, 313; 5 February–26 February 1891, pp. 103–4, 128, 170–71; 7 September 1893, p. 164; 14 June 1894, p. 237; 12 July 1894, p. 21; 26 December 1895, p. 457; 13 February 1896, p. 130; 18 March 1897, p. 193; 9 March 1899, p. 173.
Brief notices concerning Reed's congressional and parliamentary actions.

35-133. WELLBORN, FRED. "The Influence of the Silver-Republican Senators, 1889–1891." *Mississippi Valley Historical Review* 14 (March 1928): 462–80.

Contemporary Assessments of Reed's Speakership

See also Smith (28-53) and Carlisle (34-2).

35-134. BRYCE, JAMES. "A Word as to the Speakership." *North American Review* 151 (October 1890): 385–98.

35-135. CHAMBERLAIN, DANIEL H. " 'Counting a Quorum': Or Speaker Reed's Change of Rules."

New Englander and Yale Review 53 (December 1890): 510–25.

35-136. HAZELTINE, MAYO W. "Speaker Reed and the House of Representatives." *North American Review* 165 (August 1897): 232–39.

35-137. "The House Rules." *Nation,* 11 February 1892, p. 102.

35-138. "How 'One-Man Power' Works." *Nation,* 13 February 1890, pp. 124–25.

35-139. "How the Speakership Looks Now." *Nation,* 30 June 1898, pp. 493–94.

35-140. "The Issue in the House." *Nation,* 25 September 1890, p. 240.

35-141. JUDEX [PSEUD.]. "The Speaker and His Critics." *North American Review* 151 (August 1890): 237–50.

35-142. LEE, MARY URQUHART. *Parliamentary Lessons.* Chicago: Rand McNally, 1899. 59 p.

35-143. "Mr. Reed's Speech." *Nation,* 6 August 1896, p. 98.

35-144. "Notes." *Nation,* 15 March 1894, pp. 199–200.

A testy review of Reed's rules.

35-145. "The Official Explanation at Last." *Nation,* 20 November 1890, pp. 393–94.

35-146. "Our Ruler the Speaker." *Nation,* 21 January 1897, pp. 43–44.

35-147. PALGRAVE, REGINALD F. D. "The Recent Crisis in Congress." *North American Review* 151 (September 1890): 367–75.

35-148. ROOSEVELT, THEODORE. "Thomas Brackett Reed and the Fifty-first Congress." *Forum* 20 (December 1895): 410–18.

35-149. "Speaker Reed in 1890." *Nation,* 5 December 1895, p. 402.

35-150. "Speaker Reed's Error." *Nation,* 17 July 1890, pp. 44–45.

35-151. "Speaker Reed's Reply." *Nation,* 7 August 1890, pp. 104–5.

35-152. "The Speaker's Rights." *Nation,* 17 December 1891, p. 461.

35-153. "The Struggle in the House." *Nation,* 6 February 1890, pp. 104–5.

35-154. X.M.C. "Speaker Reed's Error." *North American Review* 151 (July 1890): 90–111.

REED AND THE PRESIDENTIAL ELECTION OF 1896

See also Jones (28-14).

35-155. FALLOWS, SAMUEL, ED. *Life of William McKinley: Our Martyred President.* Chicago: Regan Printing, 1901. 453 p.

35-156. GLAD, PAUL W. *McKinley, Bryan, and the People.* Philadelphia: J. B. Lippincott, 1964. 222 p.

35-157. JOSEPHSON, MATTHEW P. *The President Makers.* 1940. Reprint. New York: G. P. Putnam, 1979. 584 p.

35-158. LEUPP, FRANCIS E. "The Presidency and Mr. Reed." *Atlantic Monthly* 77 (February 1896): 250–56.

35-159. "Speaker and Candidate." *Nation,* 12 December 1895, pp. 422–23.

35-160. WARREN, SIDNEY. *The Battle for the Presidency.* Philadelphia: J. B. Lippincott, 1968. 426 p.

REED'S ANTI-IMPERIALISM

See also Campbell (30-161), LaFeber (30-167), and Welch (34-53).

35-161. BEISNER, ROBERT L. *Twelve against Empire.* New York: McGraw-Hill, 1968. 310 p.

35-162. BUTLER, NICHOLAS MURRAY. "Things Seen and Heard in Politics—Speaker Reed on the American Idea of War." *Scribner's* 100 (September 1936): 154–61.

35-163. COLETTA, PAOLO E., ED. *Threshold to American Internationalism.* New York: Exposition Press, 1970. 334 p.

35-164. DULLES, FOSTER RHEA. *Prelude to World Power.* New York: Macmillan, 1965. 238 p.

35-165. HARRINGTON, FRED HARVEY. "The Anti-Imperialist Movement in the United States, 1898–1900." *Mississippi Valley Historical Review* 22 (September 1935): 211–30.

35-166. HEALY, DAVID F. *U.S. Expansionism: The Imperialist Urge in the 1890s.* Madison: University of Wisconsin Press, 1970. 315 p.

35-167. MAY, ERNEST R. *Imperial Democracy.* New York: Harcourt, Brace, and World, 1961. 318 p.

35-168. MILLIS, WALTER. *The Martial Spirit.* 1931. Reprint. New York: Arno Press, 1979. 427 p.

35-169. MORGAN, H. WAYNE. *America's Road to Empire.* New York: John Wiley and Sons, 1965. 124 p.

35-170. TOMPKINS, E. BERKELEY. *Anti-Imperialism in the United States: The Great Debate, 1890–1920.* Philadelphia: University of Pennsylvania Press, 1970. 344 p.

35-171. WELCH, RICHARD E., JR. "Motive and Policy Objectives of Anti-Imperialists, 1898." *Mid-America* 51 (April 1969): 119–29.

35-172. WOLFF, LEON. *Little Brown Brother.* 1961. Reprint. New York: Kraus Reprint, 1970. 383 p.

36. Charles Frederick Crisp
(1845–1896)
(Speaker, Fifty-second and Fifty-third Congresses)

Charles F. Crisp, the son of an English theatrical couple, was born in Sheffield, England, on January 29, 1845. His parents, who were naturalized American citizens, returned to the United States soon after their son's birth and settled in Georgia. Though they owned a number of theaters in the South, the family was not wealthy; consequently, Crisp's education was limited to the public schools of Macon and Savannah. He enlisted in the Confederate army at the age of sixteen, served three years, and rose to the rank of lieutenant. He spent the last year of the war as a Union prisoner.

After the war, Crisp settled in Americus, Georgia, where he was admitted to the bar. In 1872 he was appointed solicitor general of the superior court in the southwestern circuit. From 1877 to 1882 he served as a judge of the superior court. In 1882 he was elected as a Democrat to Congress, where he served from 1883 until his death in 1896. Throughout his congressional career Crisp was an effective and skilled parliamentarian. His instrumental role in the passage of the Interstate Commerce Act of 1887 helped him become House Democratic

leader after John G. Carlisle went into the Senate in 1890. When the Democrats gained control of the House in 1891, Crisp was elected Speaker, and he held office through the Fifty-second and Fifty-third Congresses (1891–95).

Crisp's speakership was characterized by a running feud with his predecessor, Thomas Brackett Reed. Crisp had been one of Reed's principal detractors; now he found Reed using the same dilatory tactics to harass him. Eventually Crisp and his Democratic colleagues were forced to adopt the Reed Rules in order to govern effectively.

In the 1890s Crisp's main concern was currency reform. He supported the Sherman Silver Purchase Act of 1890. In 1892 he argued that farmers should be granted economic relief through tariff reduction or compensatory assistance. As a candidate for the Senate on a silver platform in 1896, he held a series of four debates in prominent Georgia towns with Hoke Smith, then secretary of the interior in Cleveland's cabinet. Although he was an ardent "silverite," Crisp was not on good terms with the Farmers' Alliance or populist leaders, especially fellow Georgian Tom Watson. Georgia elected a decidedly prosilver legislature in 1896, which made Crisp's election to the Senate a virtual certainty. He died suddenly, however, of a heart attack in Atlanta on October 23, 1896. At the beginning of the following Congress, his old foe, Thomas Brackett Reed, resumed the speakership.

MANUSCRIPT COLLECTIONS

There is no known major collection of Charles F. Crisp papers. The Georgia Department of Archives and History, in Atlanta, has a folder containing three letters, a speech, and a newspaper clipping. There are also a few Crisp letters in the Grover Cleveland Papers and the Benjamin Harrison Papers in the Library of Congress Manuscript Division.

BOOKS, ARTICLES, AND DISSERTATIONS

WORKS BY CHARLES F. CRISP

The following items are listed chronologically by year of publication and alphabetically thereunder.

36-1. CRISP, CHARLES F. "Contested Election Case: Chalmers vs. Manning; Speech of Hon. Charles F. Crisp." In *Forty-eighth Congress Speeches*, vol. 2, no. 22. Washington, D.C.: Government Printing Office, 1884.

Crisp's House speech of February 13, 1884, on a contested election in Mississippi's Second District.

36-2. ———. "Post-Office Appropriation Bill: Speech of Hon. Charles F. Crisp, of Georgia, in the House of Representatives, Tuesday, March 18, 1884." In *Forty-eighth Congress Speeches*, vol. 2, no. 23. Washington, D.C.: Government Printing Office, 1884.

Crisp's speech in favor of rural mail delivery.

36-3. ———. "Protection: A Help to Few, a Hindrance to Many." *American Journal of Politics* 1 (August 1892): 160–71.

An attack upon protectionism and a plea for a more equitable tax system.

36-4. ———. *Coin Redemption Fund: Speech of Charles F. Crisp, of Georgia, in the House of Representatives, Friday, February 14, 1896*. Washington, D.C., 1896. 18 p.

A plea for the coining of gold and silver on the pre–1873 basis.

36-5. ———. "How Congress Votes Money: A Rejoinder." *North American Review* 162 (January 1896): 14–20.

A response to criticisms of the congressional appropriations procedure.

36-6. ———. *Remarks of Hon. Charles F. Crisp, of Georgia, in the House of Representatives of the United States, on Election Contests, Tariff Bill, and Bond Bill, December 17, 26, and 28, 1895*. Washington, D.C.: Government Printing Office, 1896. 24 p.

A speech on Southern elections, tariffs, and monetary policy.

BIOGRAPHICAL SKETCHES AND EULOGIES

There is no biography of Crisp. The best biographical sketch is Martin (36-11).

36-7. CANDLER, ALLEN D., AND EVANS, CLEMENT A., EDS. *Georgia: Comprising Sketches of Counties, Towns, Events, Institutions and Persons*. 4 vols. 1906. Reprint. Spartanburg, S.C.: Reprint, 1972.

36-8. EVANS, LAWTON B. *A History of Georgia*. 1898. Reprint. Spartanburg, S.C.: Reprint, 1972. 360 p.

36-9. HAM, HENRY WILKES JONES. *Representative Georgians*. Savannah: Morning News, 1887. 233 p.

36-10. KNIGHT, LUCIAN L. *Reminiscences of Famous Georgians*. Vol. 2. Atlanta: Franklin-Turner, 1908. 723 p.

36-11. Martin, Sidney Walter. "Charles F. Crisp, Speaker of the House." *Georgia Review* 8 (Summer 1954): 167–77.

36-12. U.S. Congress. *Memorial Addresses on the Life and Character of Charles Frederick Crisp.* 54th Cong., 2d sess., 1896–97. Washington, D.C.: Government Printing Office, 1897. 196 p.

Thirty-eight eulogies delivered by Crisp's colleagues in Congress.

CRISP AND GEORGIA HISTORY AND POLITICS

See also Avery (22-26).

36-13. Arnett, Alex M. *The Populist Movement in Georgia.* 1922. Reprint. New York: AMS Press, 1967. 239 p.

36-14. Bonner, James C. *The Georgia Story.* Oklahoma City: Harlow Publishing, 1961. 499 p.

36-15. Coleman, Kenneth, ed. *A History of Georgia.* Athens: University of Georgia Press, 1977. 445 p.

36-16. Coulter, E. Merton. *A Short History of Georgia.* Chapel Hill: University of North Carolina Press, 1933. 457 p.

36-17. Frech, Mary L., ed. *Chronology and Documentary Handbook of the State of Georgia.* Dobbs Ferry, N.Y.: Oceana Publications, 1973. 119 p.

36-18. Johnson, Amanda. *Georgia as Colony and State.* Atlanta: Walter W. Brown Publishing, 1938. 1,064 p.

36-19. Knight, Lucian Lamar. *A Standard History of Georgia and Georgians.* 6 vols. Chicago: Lewis Publishing, 1917.

36-20. Williford, William Bailey. *Americus through the Years.* Atlanta: Cherokee Publishing, 1975. 544 p.

CRISP'S POLITICAL ASSOCIATES

See also Dunn (28-28), Dingley (30-100), Bass (34-22), O'Ferrall (34-29), McCall (35-47), Robinson (35-49), Koenig (35-98), Stone (35-114), Woodward (35-118), and Clark (40-38).

36-21. Grantham, Dewey W., Jr. *Hoke Smith and the Politics of the New South.* Baton Rouge: Louisiana State University Press, 1958. 396 p.

36-22. Lambert, John R. *Arthur Pue Gorman.* Baton Rouge: Louisiana State University Press, 1953. 397 p.

CRISP'S CONGRESSIONAL CAREER AND SPEAKERSHIP

See also Lewis (28-52) and Smith (28-53).

36-23. "The House Rules." *Nation,* 11 February 1892, p. 102.

Notes that Crisp would not be given the powers exercised by Reed in the previous Congress.

36-24. "The New Speaker of the House." *Harper's Weekly,* 19 December 1891, p. 1020.

36-25. "An Object Lesson." *Nation,* 22 August 1895, pp. 128–29.

Criticizes Crisp for being too partisan.

36-26. "The Progress of the World: Speaker Crisp Stands Fast." *Review of Reviews* 9 (May 1894): 520.

Reports Crisp's rejection of an appointment to a vacated Senate seat.

36-27. "The Quorum Trouble." *Nation,* 26 April 1894, pp. 306–7.

Comments upon the readoption of Reed's quorum-counting methods.

36-28. "The Week." *Nation,* 10 December 1891, p. 437; 7 September 1893, p. 164; 19 November 1896, p. 376.

Brief notes concerning Crisp's election to the speakership, his debate with Reed over rules, and his death.

37. David Bremner Henderson
(1840–1906)
(Speaker, Fifty-sixth and Fifty-seventh Congresses)

Six years after he was born in Old Deer, Scotland, on March 14, 1840, David B. Henderson immigrated to the United States with his parents. The family settled first in Illinois; then in 1849 they moved to Iowa, where Henderson attended school and helped run the family farm. He attended Upper Iowa University but left before graduation to join the Union army in 1861. He enlisted as a private in the Twelfth Iowa Infantry, but his comrades elected him a first lieutenant. Henderson was wounded in the neck at Fort Donelson and was more severely wounded in the leg at Corinth; the later wound caused the amputation of part of his left leg. The leg never healed properly, which made further degrees of amputation necessary in the 1890s, at the very height of his congressional career.

After the war, Henderson opened a legal practice in Dubuque, Iowa, where he was appointed to several minor federal offices. In 1882 he was elected to represent Iowa's Third District as a moderate, standpat Republican. He was an avowed protectionist and a prominent supporter of pensions and veterans' benefits. He also backed a number of specific reform issues, most notably railroad safety legislation and rural mail delivery. He supported the temperance movement, even though he personally opposed prohibition. In Iowa politics he was so frequently aligned with Senator William Boyd Allison and Congressman Jonathan P. Dolliver that he was considered the powerful Allison's protégé in the House. By the late 1890s Henderson had become such a pow-

erful fixture in the Iowa Republican leadership that he was a target of the reform faction led by Albert Baird Cummins.

Henderson served in the House from 1883 to 1903 and was elected Speaker of the Fifty-sixth and Fifty-seventh Congresses (1899–1903). In contrast to his predecessor, the brilliant and often imperious Thomas Brackett Reed, Henderson became known as a popular, though not brilliant, Speaker. Where Reed had ruled the House like a czar, Henderson managed affairs in a straightforward, businesslike manner. Even though he had scheduled beforehand which members would be recognized, Reed had maintained the ritual display of having members clamor around the Speaker's desk to seek recognition. Henderson, on the other hand, insisted that members remain decorously seated as he recognized them according to the prearranged schedule.

Henderson stunned Washington in 1903 with the sudden announcement of his retirement. The ostensible reason for this decision was the marked upsurge of anti-protectionist sentiment in his home district, which supposedly jeopardized his political effectiveness and diminished his enthusiasm for politics. Henderson's deteriorating health may have been the real reason for his retirement. A painful series of leg operations had impaired his mental capacity, and shortly before his death he suffered a complete mental breakdown. Except for a brief visit to California, he spent his last years at home in Iowa, where he died on February 25, 1906.

MANUSCRIPT COLLECTIONS

Dubuque County Historical Society, Dubuque, Iowa.
> David Bremner Henderson Papers.
> 73 items.

University of Iowa Libraries, Special Collec-

tions Department, Iowa City, Iowa.
> David Bremner Henderson Papers, 1884–1951.
> 53 items.

BOOKS, ARTICLES, AND DISSERTATIONS

WORKS BY DAVID B. HENDERSON

37-1. HALSELL, WILLIE D., ED. "Republican Factionalism in Mississippi, 1882–1884." *Journal of Southern History* 7 (February 1941): 92–95.

Includes a letter from Henderson to William Chandler dated July 4, 1882, discussing Mississippi factions and racial politics.

The following works by Henderson are arranged chronologically by year of publication and alphabetically thereunder.

37-2. HENDERSON, DAVID B. "Annual Oration by General D. B. Henderson." In *Report of the Proceedings of the Society of the Army of the Tennessee, at the Twenty-fifth Meeting, Held at Chicago, Illinois, Sept. 12th, and 13th, 1893,* pp. 67–75, 99–100. Cincinnati: F. W. Freeman, 1893.

A powerful anti-war address and condemnation of violence by labor unions.

37-3. ———. "First Toast: Lincoln and Grant." In *Report of the Proceedings of the Society of the Army of the Tennessee, at the Twenty-fourth Meeting, Held at St. Louis, Mo., Nov. 16th and 17th, 1892,* pp. 101–4. Cincinnati: F. W. Freeman, 1893.

A tribute to Lincoln and Grant.

37-4. ———. "Address, Col. Henderson." In *Report of the Proceedings of the Society of the Army of the Tennessee, at the Twenty-sixth Meeting, Held at Council Bluffs, Iowa, Oct. 3d and 4th, 1894,* pp. 127–28. Cincinnati: F. W. Freeman, 1895.

A speech on the progress of legislation creating the Shiloh National Battlefield Park.

37-5. ———. "Ninth Toast: Col. Henderson." In *Report of the Proceedings of the Society of the Army of the Tennessee, at the Twenty-seventh Meeting, Held at Cincinnati, Ohio, and Chattanooga, Tenn., Sept. 16–21, 1895,* pp. 135–36. Cincinnati: F. W. Freeman, 1896.

A toast in commemoration of the army's final campaigns in the Civil War.

37-6. ———. "Telegram from Col. Henderson." In *Report of the Proceedings of the Society of the Army of the Tennessee, at the Twenty-ninth Meeting, Held at Milwaukee, Wisconsin, Oct. 27–28, 1897,* p. 80. Cincinnati: F. W. Freeman, 1897.

Henderson telegraphs his regrets at not being able to attend owing to another leg operation.

37-7. ———. "Address, Col. Henderson." In *Report of the Proceedings of the Society of the Army of the Tennessee, at the Thirty-second Meeting, Held at Detroit, Mich., Nov. 14–15, 1900,* pp. 92–94. Cincinnati: F. W. Freeman, 1901.

An informal series of remarks.

37-8. ———. "Fourth Toast, Gen. D. B. Henderson." In *Report of the Proceedings of the Society of the Army of the Tennessee at the Thirty-third Meeting, Held at Indianapolis, Indiana, Nov. 13–14, 1901,* pp. 159–61. Cincinnati: F. W. Freeman, 1902.

Henderson toasts war as the most abominable of last resorts.

37-9. ———. "Oration, Col. David B. Henderson." In *Report of the Proceedings of the Society of the Army of the Tennessee at the Thirty-fourth Meeting, Held at Washington, D.C., Oct. 15–16, 1903,* pp. 85–94. Cincinnati: F. W. Freeman, 1906.

A patriotic address that has been attributed to David B. Henderson but may have been delivered by Thomas J. Henderson.

BIOGRAPHICAL SKETCHES AND EULOGIES

See also Neale (35-57).

37-10. FITZPATRICK, T. J. "Notes and Comment." *Iowa Journal of History* 4 (1906): 332.
Obituary notice.

37-11. GUE, BENJAMIN F. *History of Iowa.* Vol. 4. New York: Century History, 1903. 325 p.

37-12. HARLAN, EDGAR RUBEY. *A Narrative History of the People of Iowa.* Vol. 2. Chicago: American Historical Society, 1931. 473 p.

37-13. HOING, WILLARD L. "David B. Henderson, Speaker of the House." *Iowa Journal of History* 55 (1957): 1–34.

A biographical sketch with a balanced assessment of Henderson's speakership.

37-14. "Letter from Mrs. D. B. Henderson." In *Report of the Proceedings of the Society of the Army of the Tennessee at the Thirty-fifth Meeting, Held at Cincin-*

nati, Ohio, Oct. 5–6, 1905, pp. 147–48. Cincinnati: F. W. Freeman, 1906.

A melancholy letter detailing Henderson's final illness.

37-15. *Memorial Exercises in Honor of David B. Henderson in the Hall of the House of Representatives in Des Moines, Iowa, Thursday, March 9, 1906.* N.p., n.d. 28 p.

A program of tribute and eulogies by Iowa leaders.

37-16. MILLS, GEORGE S. *Rogues and Heroes from Iowa's Amazing Past.* Ames: Iowa State University Press, 1972. 252 p.

37-17. "Notable Deaths: Colonel Henderson." *Annals of Iowa* 7 (April 1906): 394–95.

37-18. PERKINS, GEORGE DOUGLAS. *David B. Henderson: Eulogy at Funeral.* Dubuque, Iowa, 1906. 7 p.

37-19. RICHARDS, JULIAN W. "The Passing of Speaker Henderson." *Independent,* 19 March 1903, pp. 651–55.

A positive evaluation of Henderson's record as Speaker, with an account of his relationship with Theodore Roosevelt.

37-20. SAGE, LELAND L. *A History of Iowa.* Ames: Iowa State University Press, 1974. 376 p.

37-21. STILES, EDWARD H. *Recollections and Sketches of Notable Lawyers and Public Men of Early Iowa.* Des Moines, Iowa: Homestead Publishing, 1916. 988 p.

HENDERSON AND IOWA HISTORY

See also Gue (37-11), Harlan (37-12), Mills (37-16), Sage (37-20), and Stiles (37-21).

37-22. COLE, CYRENUS. *A History of the People of Iowa.* Cedar Rapids, Iowa: Torch Press, 1921. 572 p.

37-23. ———. *Iowa through the Years.* Iowa City: State Historical Society of Iowa, 1940. 547 p.

37-24. FULLER, WAYNE E. "Rural Free Delivery in Hardin County." *Annals of Iowa* 41 (Fall 1972): 1049–72.

37-25. JENSEN, RICHARD. *The Winning of the Midwest: Social and Political Conflict, 1888–1896.* Chicago: University of Chicago Press, 1971. 357 p.

37-26. MOTT, DAVID C. "The Pivotal Convention of 1883." *Annals of Iowa* 26 (April 1945): 254–60.

HENDERSON AND THE CIVIL WAR

Henderson's own writings provide the best account of his military career and his thoughts on war.

37-27. PARKER, L. F. "Fort Donelson: The Second Iowa Infantry." *Iowa Historical Record* 2 (July 1886): 344–50.

HENDERSON'S POLITICAL ASSOCIATES

See also Cole (28-24), Dunn (28-28), Sage (30-123), Ross (35-111), Stephenson (35-112), and Clark (40-38).

37-28. BRIGGS, JOHN ELY. *William Peters Hepburn.* Iowa City: State Historical Society of Iowa, 1919. 469 p.

37-29. HARRINGTON, ELBERT W. "A Survey of the Political Ideas of Albert Baird Cummins." *Iowa Journal of History* 39 (October 1941): 339–86.

37-30. SAYRE, RALPH MILLS. "Albert Baird Cummins and the Progressive Movement in Iowa." Ph.D. dissertation, Columbia University, 1958. 575 p. 58-02602.

HENDERSON'S CONGRESSIONAL CAREER AND SPEAKERSHIP

See also Cockrell (1-3), Merrill and Merrill 28-16), Lewis (28-52), and Smith (28-53).

37-31. CHAPPLE, JOE MITCHELL. "The Personal Side of Speaker Henderson." *National Magazine* 11 (October 1899): 3–8.

37-32. "Colonel Henderson, the New Speaker." *Review of Reviews* 20 (October 1899): 479–80.

37-33. "Contemporary Celebrities—David B. Henderson." *Current Literature* 29 (July 1900): 24.

37-34. "Contemporary Celebrities—The New Speaker." *Current Literature* 27 (February 1900): 114–15.

37-35. "Czar Reed's Successor Presumptive." *Review of Reviews* 20 (July 1899): 19.

37-36. A FRIEND OF GEN. HENDERSON. "A Word to the Next Speaker." *Forum* 28 (September 1899): 57–65.

37-37. "Mr. Henderson in the Speaker's Chair." *American Monthly Review of Reviews* 21 (January 1900): 11.

37-38. NELSON, HENRY LOOMIS. "The Next Speaker and the Next Session." *Harper's Weekly,* 11 November 1899, p. 1138.

37-39. "Our Washington Letter: Speaker Henderson and Mr. Roberts." *Independent,* 14 December 1899, pp. 3356–58.

37-40. RICHARDS, JULIAN W. "Henderson and His Critics." *Independent,* 20 March 1902, pp. 677–79.

37-41. "Speaker Henderson's Retirement." *Review of Reviews* 26 (October 1902): 387–89.

37-42. "Speaker Henderson's Surrender." *Nation,* 25 September 1902, pp. 238–39.
Speculates on Henderson's motives for retiring from Congress.

37-43. TOWNSHEND, EDWARD W. "The Opening of Congress." *Harper's Weekly,* 9 December 1899, p. 1227.

37-44. "The Week." *Nation,* 4 March 1886, p. 180; 19 June 1890, p. 479; 7 December 1899, p. 417.
Brief notes on Henderson in reference to pension legislation and his election to the speakership.

38. Joseph Gurney Cannon
(1836–1926)
(Speaker, Fifty-eighth through Sixty-first Congresses)

No Speaker exerted more control over the House of Representatives than Joseph G. Cannon. A hard-shell, conservative Republican instinctively opposed to change, he ruled the House with a force that lacked any of the subtlety or wit exercised by Reed and Clay. Cannon, who was uncouth and essentially vulgar, cultivated and relished his image as "foul-mouthed Joe," "the Hayseed Member from Illinois." He was popular with colleagues for his gregarious homespun nature, which earned him the nickname "Uncle Joe." Yet his heavy-handed exercise of power ultimately provoked a reaction against the speakership that led to the imposition of restraints on the Speaker's prerogatives.

Cannon was born into a Quaker family on May 7, 1836, in New Garden, North Carolina.

A few years later the family moved to a new Quaker settlement in Indiana. When he was fourteen years old, his father died, forcing Cannon to take a job in a country store. Later he studied law for six months at the Cincinnati Law School and began his own practice at Shelbyville, Illinois, in 1858. He later moved to Tuscola, Illinois, and he finally established a permanent residence in Danville, Illinois, in 1876.

Cannon embarked on his political career in 1861, when he became district attorney of Coles County, a post he occupied until 1868. He ran for Congress as a Republican in 1870 but was defeated. He was elected to the Forty-third Congress and held office from 1873 to 1891, from 1893 to 1913, and from 1915 to 1923, for a total of forty-six years. He was an energetic and demonstrative orator, constantly in motion. Champ Clark once referred to him as "the dancing dervish of Illinois." His speeches were direct and to the point, though his language was coarse, even racy at times. He worked hard on the committees to which he was assigned and rigidly adhered to the Republican party line. Yet, in all his forty-six years in Congress he originated no important piece of constructive legislation; his forte was expediting party measures and blocking any reform legislation.

In 1889 Cannon first seriously tried for the speakership but lost to Thomas Brackett Reed, who nonetheless made Cannon his parliamentary lieutenant. Cannon was defeated for reelection in 1891, but he returned to Congress in 1893 and served as chairman of the Committee on Appropriations from 1897 to 1903. Finally, after thirty years in Congress, he was elected Speaker of the Fifty-eighth Congress in 1903.

As a conservative, Cannon opposed the rising demands for changes, such as tariff reform, woman's suffrage, conservation, and labor unionism. Relying on a private leadership style, he ruled the House in an arbitrary and partisan manner. The Reed Rules, the binding party caucus, and the Speaker's power to appoint committee chairmen gave Uncle Joe the tools to control the House. Opponents—both Democrats and Progressive Republicans—came to resent what they termed "Cannonism."

Cannon's control of the House and his intransigent opposition to reform obstructed the administrations of both Theodore Roosevelt and William Howard Taft. Roosevelt courted Cannon with a White House dinner and private consultations, but Uncle Joe refused to alter his opposition to reform legislation. In 1908 Cannon challenged Taft for the Republican presidential nomination, but he received only the support of his home state of Illinois.

The increasing opposition to Cannon in the House included the Democrats under the leadership of Champ Clark, as well as a growing number of "insurgent" Republicans led by George W. Norris of Nebraska and Victor Murdock of Kansas. Attempts to curb Cannon's exercise of power began as early as 1907, but not until 1910 was the opposition able to seriously impair his power by removing control of the all-important Rules Committee from the Speaker. Cannon remained in office until 1913, but he was not elected to the following Congress.

When Cannon rejoined the rank and file in 1915, he again became a popular character who regaled his listeners with salty stories of forty years in politics. His colleagues commemorated Cannon's eightieth birthday in 1916 to prove that they held no grudges. He retired to Danville in 1923 and died there on November 12, 1926, at the age of ninety.

MANUSCRIPT COLLECTIONS

Illinois State Historical Library, Springfield, Ill.
> Joseph G. Cannon Correspondence, 1883–1926.
> 62 items.
> NUCMC 65-157.
> The only collection of Cannon's papers is rather meager for a politician of his stature and longevity. Many other Cannon letters can be found in the papers of his contemporaries, including some twenty-eight items in the Theodore Roosevelt Papers and thirty-eight items in the William Howard Taft Papers, both in the Library of Congress Manuscript Division.

BOOKS, ARTICLES, AND DISSERTATIONS

WORKS BY JOSEPH G. CANNON

38-1. AVBERE, JEWELL H. "A Reminiscence of Abraham Lincoln: A Conversation with Speaker Cannon." *World's Work* 13 (February 1907): 8528–30.

38-2. BUSBEY, L. WHITE. *Made in Germany: The*

Hon. Joseph G. Cannon's Definition of International Socialism. Washington, D.C.: Government Printing Office, 1919. 34 p.

Comprises Cannon's thoughts on the origins of socialism in the United States.

The following works by Cannon are listed chronologically by year of publication and alphabetically thereunder.

38-3. CANNON, JOSEPH G. *Security of Elections: Speech of Hon. Joseph G. Cannon, of Illinois.* Washington, D.C.: Government Printing Office, 1875. 22 p.

House speech of February 27, 1875, supporting federal supervision of Southern elections.

38-4. ———. *Repeal of the Resumption Act.* Washington, D.C.: National Republican Printing House, 1877. 8 p.

House speech against repeal of the resumption of specie payments for currency.

*38-5. ———. *The Reduction of the Surplus, the Protective System, Free Sugar: Speech . . .* N.p., 1888. 16 p.

House speech of May 10, 1888.

38-6. ———. *Extracts from Debates in the House of Representatives and Votes on Important Measures: Remarks of Hon. J. G. Cannon, of Illinois.* Washington, D.C.: George R. Ray, 1890.

Includes Cannon's remarks on a variety of issues from pensions to irrigation.

*38-7. ———. *Appropriations Fifty-first Congress: Speech of Hon. Joseph G. Cannon, of Ill.* Washington, D.C., 1891. 5 p.

House speech of March 4, 1891.

38-8. ———. *Amending Interstate-Commerce Act by Legalizing Pooling.* Washington, D.C.: Government Printing Office, 1895.

House speech of December 11, 1894, in support of pooling arrangements between railroad companies.

*38-9. ———. *$1,050,000 in the Pockets of the American Tobacco Trust: Speech of Hon. Joseph G. Cannon of Illinois.* N.p., 1900. 16 p.

House speech of February 27, 1900.

38-10. ———. *Revenue for Puerto Rico: Speech of Hon. Joseph G. Cannon, of Illinois.* Washington, D.C., 1900. 16 p.

House speech of February 27, 1900, in opposition to receiving revenue from Puerto Rico.

*38-11. ———. *Speech of Hon. Joseph G. Cannon: The House . . . Having under Consideration the Bill (H.R. 8245) to Regulate the Trade of Puerto Rico.* Washington, D.C., 1900. 14 p.

38-12. ———. "The Power of the Speaker: Is He an Autocrat or a Servant?" *Century Magazine* 78 (June 1909): 306–12.

Speaker Cannon defends his exercise of power as being consistent with the principle of majority rule.

38-13. ———. *Speech of Hon. J. G. Cannon Delivered at Kansas City, Mo., Friday Night, November 26, 1909.* Washington, D.C.: Government Printing Office, 1909. 16 p.

A speech in praise of the West and a rebuttal to the charges by the insurgents.

38-14. ———. *Abraham Lincoln: Speech before the Chamber of Commerce, Pittsburgh, Pa.* Washington, D.C.: Government Printing Office, 1910. 15 p.

A speech praising Lincoln and the Republican party.

38-15. ———. *Ulysses S. Grant, the Modest, Courageous Man, the Normal American.* Washington, D.C., 1910. 15 p.

A speech praising Grant and "regular" Republicans.

*38-16. ———. *Reciprocity with Canada.* Washington, D.C.: Government Printing Office, 1911. 32 p.

House speech of April 19, 1911.

38-17. ———. "Followers after Strange Gods." *Saturday Evening Post,* 3 May 1913, p. 3.

Cannon attacks political reformers and the Democratic administration.

38-18. ———. *Speeches at the Dinner in Honor of Honorable Joseph G. Cannon of Illinois.* Washington, D.C.: Government Printing Office, 1913. 29 p.

A bipartisan tribute to Cannon that includes a Cannon speech on loyalty and unity.

38-19. ———. "The Native American." *Outlook,* 5 April 1916, pp. 787–97.

An excerpt from a House speech denouncing immigration restrictions.

38-20. ———. "We Are at War with Mexico." *Independent,* 10 July 1916, p. 55.

A call for military intervention in Mexico.

38-21. ———. "Dramatic Scenes from My Career in Congress, I: Blaine and the Mulligan Letters." *Harper's Magazine* 140 (December 1919): 39–48.

Cannon's recollections of the Mulligan letters scandal. *See also* items 30-80 through 30-82.

38-22. ———. "The National Budget." *Harper's Magazine* 139 (October 1919): 617–28.

A plea for an end to executive interference in the budget process.

38-23. ———. "Dramatic Scenes from My Career in Congress, II: When Reed Counted a Quorum." *Harper's Magazine* 140 (March 1920): 433–41.

Cannon's interpretation of Reed's quorum count as a parliamentary revolution.

38-24. ———. "Women in Politics? Ever since Eve." *Delineator* 97 (September 1920): 5.

Though he opposed woman's suffrage, Cannon acknowledged the contributions of women to politics.

38-25. ———. "Party Discipline." *Saturday Evening Post,* 27 September 1924, p. 3.

Personal and political memoirs.

38-26. ———. *I Knew Abraham Lincoln.* N.p., 1934. 8 p.

A speech at the dedication of a Lincoln marker in Danville, Illinois, on October 20, 1922.

38-27. ———. "Uncle Joe and Abe Lincoln." *National Republic* 22 (January 1935): 19–20.

An adaptation of Cannon's speech on Lincoln (38-26).

*38-28. ———. *Pension Appropriations Reduced $20,099,504.85.* N.p., n.d. 4 p.

38-29. Davis, James J. *The Iron Puddler.* Indianapolis: Bobbs-Merrill, 1922. 275 p.

Features an introduction by Cannon.

38-30. Moore, Charles, ed. *The Promise of American Architecture.* Washington, D.C.: American Institute of Architects, 1905. 80 p.

Includes an address by Cannon on architecture and appropriations in which he explains his opposition to government funding.

38-31. "A Suppressed Interview." *Colliers,* 1 January 1910, p. 18.

An edited transcript of an interview with Cannon.

38-32. Wolf, Simon. *The Presidents I Have Known from 1860–1918.* Washington, D.C.: Byron S. Adams, 1918. 459 p.

Includes a speech made by Cannon before the B'nai B'rith in 1912.

BIOGRAPHIES, BIOGRAPHICAL SKETCHES, AND EULOGIES

Biographies

38-33. Bolles, Blair. *Tyrant from Illinois: Uncle Joe Cannon's Experiment with Personal Power.* 1951. Reprint. Westport, Conn.: Greenwood Press, 1974. 248 p.

Focuses upon Cannon's fight with the insurgents.

38-34. Busbey, L. White. *Uncle Joe Cannon: The Story of a Pioneer American.* 1927. Reprint. St. Clair Shores, Mich.: Scholarly Press, 1970. 362 p.

A rambling reminiscence by Cannon's personal secretary.

38-35. Gwinn, William Rea. *Uncle Joe Cannon: Archfoe of Insurgency.* New York: Bookman Associates, 1957. 314 p.

Not a full biography, the book focuses upon the rise and fall of Cannonism.

Biographical Sketches and Eulogies

38-36. Davenport, Walter. "Uncle Joe Got Tired." *Collier's,* 13 November 1926, p. 28.

Eulogistic anecdotes about Cannon's career.

38-37. "Forty Years of Uncle Joe." *Literary Digest,* 20 May 1916, pp. 1492–98.

Excerpts from speeches at Cannon's eightieth birthday celebration.

38-38. "Joseph Cannon." *Nation,* 24 November 1926, p. 521.

An obituary notice.

38-39. "Long Service in Congress." *Nation,* 1 December 1926, p. 550.

An assessment of Cannon's contributions to American democracy.

38-40. "Political Notes: Cannonism." *Time,* 22 November 1926, p. 11.

An obituary notice of Cannon's death with remarks on the highlights of his career.

38-41. *Proceedings in the House of Representatives on the Eightieth Anniversary of His Birth.* Washington, D.C.: Government Printing Office, 1916. 53 p.

Includes bipartisan testimonials to Cannon's long career.

38-42. "Taps for 'Uncle Joe,' Old-fashioned American." *Literary Digest,* 4 December 1926, pp. 36–42.

38-43. THOMPSON, CHARLES WILLIS. *Party Leaders of the Time: Character Studies of Public Men at Washington.* New York: G. W. Dillingham, 1906. 422 p.

38-44. " 'Uncle Joe' Cannon." *Outlook,* 24 November 1926, p. 393.

An obituary.

38-45. " 'Uncle Joe' Cannon—Age 75." *Illinois Statesman,* 13 May 1911, p. 6.

An anecdotal profile.

CANNON AND ILLINOIS STATE AND LOCAL HISTORY

38-46. BURFORD, CARY CLIVE. *The History and Romance of Danville Junction.* Danville, Ill.: Interstate Printers and Publishers, 1942. 304 p.

38-47. ———. "Vermilion County in Illinois History." *Journal of the Illinois State Historical Society* 34 (December 1941): 472–81.

38-48. CHURCH, CHARLES A. *History of the Republican Party in Illinois, 1854–1912.* Rockford, Ill.: Wilson Brothers, 1912. 248 p.

38-49. DRURY, JOHN. *Old Illinois Houses.* 1948. Reprint. Chicago: University of Chicago Press, 1977. 220 p.

38-50. FULLINWIDER, JAMES W. "The Governor and the Senator: Executive Power and the Struc-

ture of the Illinois Republican Party, 1880–1917." Ph.D. dissertation, Washington University, 1974. 347 p. 75-14897.

38-51. JONES, LOTTIE E. *History of Vermilion County, Illinois.* 2 vols. Chicago: Pioneer Publishing, 1911.

38-52. *Past and Present of Vermilion County, Illinois.* Chicago: S. J. Clarke Publishing, 1903. 1,158 p.

38-53. STRAETZ, RALPH A. "The Progressive Movement in Illinois, 1910–1916." Ph.D. dissertation, University of Illinois, 1951.

38-54. TARR, JOEL A. "President Theodore Roosevelt and Illinois Politics, 1901–1904." *Journal of the Illinois State Historical Society* 58 (Autumn 1965): 245–64.

CANNON'S POLITICAL ASSOCIATES

See also Merrill and Merrill (28-16), Cox (28-25), Cullom (28-27), Dunn (28-28), Gompers (28-30), Watson (28-42), Platt (30-91), Stoddard (30-93), Garraty (30-104), Lambert (30-110), Bartholdt (33-45), Walters (33-50), McCall (35-47), Robinson (35-49), Evans (35-90), Koenig (35-98), La Follette (35-99), La Follette (35-100), Morgan (35-104), Osborn (35-107), Ross (35-111), Stephenson (35-112), White (35-116), Briggs (37-28), Sayre (37-30), Clark (40-38), Morrison (40-47), Webb (40-52), Fisher (43-15), James (43-16), and Waller (44-22).

38-55. BELLAMY, JOHN D. *Memoirs of an Octogenarian.* Charlotte, N.C.: Observer Printing House, 1942. 201 p.

38-56. BOWERS, CLAUDE G. *Beveridge and the Progressive Era.* Boston: Houghton Mifflin, 1932. 610 p.

38-57. BRAEMAN, JOHN. *Albert J. Beveridge: American Nationalist.* Chicago: University of Chicago Press, 1971. 370 p.

38-58. BULLARD, THOMAS R. "From Businessman to Congressman: The Careers of Martin B. Madden." Ph.D. dissertation, University of Illinois at Chicago Circle, 1973. 344 p. 73-22624.

38-59. Childs, Marquis W. *I Write from Washington.* New York: Harper and Brothers, 1942. 331 p.

38-60. Collier, J. W. "Quarter Century in Congress." *National Republic* 21 (May/June 1933): 3–13.

38-61. Dickson, Harris. *An Old-fashioned Senator: A Story-Biography of John Sharp Williams.* New York: Frederick A. Stokes, 1925. 204 p.

38-62. Fausold, Martin L. *James W. Wadsworth, Jr.: The Gentleman from New York.* Syracuse: Syracuse University Press, 1975. 457 p.

38-63. Frear, James A. *Forty Years of Progressive Public Service: Reasonably Filled with Thorns and Flowers.* Washington, D.C.: Associated Writers, 1937. 315 p.

38-64. Greenbaum, Fred. *Robert Marion La Follette.* Boston: Twayne, 1975. 275 p.

38-65. Harvey, Rowland Hill. *Samuel Gompers: Champion of the Toiling Masses.* 1935. Reprint. New York: Octagon Books, 1975. 376 p.

38-66. Haynes, George H. *The Life of Charles G. Washburn.* Boston: Houghton Mifflin, 1931. 302 p.

38-67. Hull, Cordell. *The Memoirs of Cordell Hull.* 2 vols. New York: Macmillan, 1948.

38-68. Hutchinson, William T. *Lowden of Illinois: The Life of Frank O. Lowden.* 2 vols. Chicago: University of Chicago Press, 1957.

38-69. Johnson, Evans C. *Oscar W. Underwood: A Political Biography.* Baton Rouge: Louisiana State University Press, 1980. 480 p.

38-70. La Guardia, Fiorello H. *The Making of an Insurgent: An Autobiography.* 1948. Reprint. New York: Capricorn Books, 1961. 222 p.

38-71. Lief, Alfred. *Democracy's Norris: The Biography of a Lonely Crusade.* 1939. Reprint. New York: Octagon Books, 1977. 546 p.

38-72. Longworth, Alice Roosevelt. *Crowded Hours: Reminiscences of Alice Roosevelt Longworth.* 1933. Reprint. New York: Arno Press, 1980. 355 p.

38-73. Lowitt, Richard. *George W. Norris: The Making of a Progressive.* 1963. Reprint. Westport, Conn.: Greenwood Press, 1980. 341 p.

38-74. Margulies, Herbert F. *Senator Lenroot of Wisconsin: A Political Biography, 1900–1929.* Columbia: University of Missouri Press, 1977. 432 p.

38-75. Neilson, James W. *Shelby M. Cullom: Prairie State Republican.* Urbana: University of Illinois Press, 1962. 328 p.

38-76. Neuberger, Richard L., and Kahn, Stephen B. *Integrity: The Life of George W. Norris.* New York: Vanguard Press, 1937. 401 p.

38-77. Norris, George W. *Fighting Liberal: The Autobiography of George W. Norris.* New York: Collier Books, 1961. 414 p.

38-78. Osborn, George C. "Joseph G. Cannon and John Sharp Williams." *Indiana Magazine of History* 35 (September 1939): 283–84.

38-79. Pennypacker, Samuel Whitaker. *The Autobiography of a Pennsylvanian.* Philadelphia: John C. Winston, 1918. 564 p.

38-80. Petterchak, Janice A. "Conflict of Ideals: Samuel Gompers vs. 'Uncle Joe' Cannon." *Journal of the Illinois State Historical Society* 74 (Spring 1981): 31–40.

38-81. Pinchot, Gifford. *Breaking New Ground.* 1947. Reprint. Seattle: University of Washington Press, 1972. 522 p.

38-82. Russell, Francis. *The Shadow of Blooming Grove: Warren G. Harding in His Times.* New York: McGraw-Hill, 1968. 691 p.

38-83. Sageser, Adelbert Bower. *Joseph L. Bristow: Kansas Progressive.* Lawrence: University of Kansas Press, 1968. 197 p.

38-84. Tarr, Joel A. *A Study in Boss Politics: William Lorimer of Kansas.* Urbana: University of Illinois Press, 1971. 376 p.

38-85. Washburn, Charles G. *The Life of John W. Weeks.* Boston: Houghton Mifflin, 1928. 349 p.

38-86. Wilson, Woodrow. *The Papers of Woodrow Wilson.* Edited by Arthur S. Link. Vols. 16, 19–25. Princeton: Princeton University Press, 1973–78.

38-87. Yates, Richard. *Serving the Republic: Richard Yates, Illinois Governor and Congressman, Son of Richard Yates, Civil War Governor, an Autobiography.* Edited by John H. Krenkel. Danville, Ill.: Interstate Printers and Publishers, 1968. 268 p.

CANNON'S SPEAKERSHIP

Profiles of Cannon as Speaker

See also Abram and Cooper (1-46) and Lewis (28-52).

38-88. ABBOT, WILLIS J. *Watching the World Go By.* 1933. Reprint. New York: Beekman Publishers, 1974. 358 p.

38-89. ALBERT, ALLEN D., JR. "Speaker Cannon." *Munsey's Magazine* 35 (July 1906): 420–24.

38-90. ALEXANDER, DEALVA STANWOOD. "The Speaker, the Committees, and the House." *Outlook,* 16 May 1908, pp. 129–30.

38-91. "The American Speaker." *Harper's Weekly,* 30 April 1910, p. 4.

38-92. "As to Speaker Cannon." *American Review of Reviews* 41 (February 1910): 140–42.

38-93. "Cannon." *Collier's,* 5 September 1908, p. 7.

38-94. CARMICHAEL, OTTO. " 'Uncle Joe' Cannon as Speaker." *World's Work* 7 (December 1903): 4195–99.

38-95. CLUBB, JEROME M. "Congressional Opponents of Reform, 1901–1913." Ph.D. dissertation, University of Washington, 1963. 359 p. 64-00405.

38-96. FITCH, GEORGE. "A Survey and Diagnosis of Uncle Joe Cannon." *American Magazine* 65 (December 1907): 185–92.

38-97. GOODWIN, GEORGE, JR. *The Little Legislatures: Committees of Congress.* Amherst: University of Massachusetts Press, 1970. 284 p.

38-98. GROSS, BERTRAM M. *The Legislative Struggle: A Study in Social Combat.* 1953. Reprint. Westport, Conn.: Greenwood Press, 1978. 472 p.

38-99. HARD, WILLIAM. " 'Uncle Joe' Cannon: Unmasking the 'Czar' in the House." In *The Muckrakers,* edited by Arthur M. Weinberg and

Lila Weinberg, pp. 87–98. New York: Simon and Schuster, 1961.

38-100. HINDS, ASHER C. "The Speaker and the House." *McClure's* 35 (June 1910): 195–202.

38-101. "How Uncle Joe Works." *Collier's,* 2 July 1910, p. 21.

38-102. JONES, CHARLES O. "Joseph G. Cannon and Howard W. Smith: An Essay on the Limits of Leadership in the House of Representatives." *Journal of Politics* 30 (August 1968): 617–46.

38-103. LEUPP, FRANCIS E. "The New Speaker." *Outlook,* 21 November 1903, pp. 684–88.

38-104. LOW, A. MAURICE. " 'Uncle Joe' Cannon: The New Speaker." *Harper's Weekly,* 14 November 1903, pp. 1824–25.

38-105. LUCAS, WILLIAM DENNIS. "A Study of the Speaking and Debating of Joseph Gurney Cannon." Ph.D. dissertation, Northwestern University, 1948.

38-106. MENTOR. "Speaker Cannon: A Character Sketch." *American Monthly Review of Reviews* 28 (December 1903): 673–76.

38-107. MESSENGER, NORTH OVERTON. "The Speaker Prospective of the Next House." *Independent,* 5 February 1903, pp. 306–11.

38-108. "The Most Striking and Positive Character in the House of Representatives." *Current Literature* 40 (June 1906): 599–600.

38-109. "The Next Speaker of the House of Representatives." *Harper's Weekly,* 10 January 1903, p. 70.

38-110. PARSHALL, GERALD. "Czar Cannon." *American History Illustrated* 11 (June 1976): 34–41.

38-111. PATTERSON, CALEB PERRY. *Presidential Government in the United States: The Unwritten Constitution.* Chapel Hill: University of North Carolina Press, 1947. 301 p.

38-112. PAYNE, WILL. "A Plutocrat in Homespun." *Saturday Evening Post,* 28 July 1906, pp. 10–12.

38-113. "The Retirement of a Veteran." *American Review of Reviews* 67 (April 1923): 350.

38-114. "The Speaker." *Outlook,* 9 April 1910, pp. 789–92.

38-115. "The Speaker and His Power." *Independent,* 3 March 1910, pp. 653–54.

38-116. "Speaker Cannon and the Lunatic." *Harper's Weekly,* 23 February 1907, p. 283.

38-117. STRONG, DENNIS FULTON. "Conservative Social Thought in the Progressive Era." Ph.D. dissertation, University of Washington, 1959. 402 p. 59-05476.

38-118. SULLIVAN, MARK. *The Education of an American.* 1938. Reprint. New York: Johnson Reprint, 1970. 320 p.

38-119. ———. *Our Times, 1900–1925.* 4 vols. 1932. Reprint. New York: Charles Scribner's Sons, 1972.

38-120. "Uncle Joe." *Current Opinion* 72 (May 1922): 597–98.

38-121. "Uncle Joe." *Harper's Weekly,* 26 March 1910, p. 5.

38-122. "Uncle Joe Cannon." *Current Literature* 29 (August 1900): 162.

38-123. " 'Uncle Joe' Cannon." *Outlook,* 12 January 1921, p. 44.

38-124. " 'Uncle Joe' Quits with Optimism and a Smile." *Literary Digest,* 17 March 1923, pp. 47–48.

38-125. "The Week." *Nation,* 4 September 1890, p. 180.

38-126. WILSON, WOODROW. *The New Freedom.* 1913. Reprint. Englewood Cliffs, N.J.: Prentice-Hall, 1961. 173 p.

Cannon and Pure Food and Drug Legislation

38-127. "Speaker Cannon's Contentment with Present Foods." *Literary Digest,* 16 June 1906, pp. 894–95.

38-128. "Speaker Cannon's Reply to His Critics." *Literary Digest,* 30 June 1906, p. 960.

Cannon, Theodore Roosevelt, and William Howard Taft

See also Pringle (35-109) and Roosevelt (35-110).

38-129. ANDERSON, DONALD F. *William Howard Taft: A Conservative's Conception of the Presidency.* Ithaca, N.Y.: Cornell University Press, 1973. 355 p.

38-130. ANDERSON, JUDITH I. "A Mountain of Misery: An Intimate History of William Howard Taft." Ph.D. dissertation, University of California, Los Angeles, 1973. 414 p. 73-28666.

38-131. BLUM, JOHN MORTON. *The Republican Roosevelt.* 2d ed. Cambridge, Mass.: Harvard University Press, 1977. 170 p.

38-132. COLETTA, PAOLO E. *The Presidency of William Howard Taft.* Lawrence: University Press of Kansas, 1973. 306 p.

38-133. DAVIS, OSCAR KING. *Released for Publication: Some Inside Political History of Theodore Roosevelt and His Times, 1898–1918.* Boston: Houghton Mifflin, 1925. 468 p.

38-134. DUFFY, HERBERT S. *William Howard Taft.* New York: Minton, Balch, 1930. 345 p.

38-135. GATEWOOD, WILLARD B., JR. *Theodore Roosevelt and the Art of Controversy: Episodes of the White House Years.* Baton Rouge: Louisiana State University Press, 1970. 294 p.

38-136. HARBAUGH, WILLIAM HENRY. *The Life and Times of Theodore Roosevelt.* Rev. ed. New York: Collier Books, 1963. 542 p.

38-137. HATCH, CARL E. *The Big Stick and the Congressional Gavel: A Study of Theodore Roosevelt's Relations with His Last Congress.* New York: Pageant Press, 1967. 99 p.

38-138. McHALE, FRANCIS. *President and Chief Justice: The Life and Public Services of William Howard Taft.* Philadelphia: Dorrance, 1931. 321 p.

38-139. MANNERS, WILLIAM. *TR and Will: A Friendship That Split the Republican Party.* New York: Harcourt, Brace, and World, 1969. 335 p.

38-140. MAYHILL, GEORGE ROGER. "Speaker Cannon under the Roosevelt Administration,

1903–1907." Ph.D. dissertation, University of Illinois, 1942. 230 p.

38-141. MOORE, J. HAMPTON. *Roosevelt and the Old Guard.* Philadelphia: Macrae Smith, 1925. 300 p.

38-142. MOWRY, GEORGE E. *The Era of Theodore Roosevelt, 1900–1912.* New York: Harper and Brothers, 1958. 330 p.

38-143. ————. *Theodore Roosevelt and the Progressive Movement.* Madison: University of Wisconsin Press, 1946. 405 p.

38-144. "The President and the People." *World's Work* 19 (March 1910): 12648–51.

38-145. "The President and the Speaker." *Harper's Weekly,* 21 September 1907, p. 1369.

38-146. PRINGLE, HENRY F. *The Life and Times of William Howard Taft: A Biography.* 2 vols. 1939. Reprint. Hamden, Conn.: Archon Books, 1964.

38-147. ROOSEVELT, THEODORE, AND LODGE, HENRY CABOT. *Selections from the Correspondence of Theodore Roosevelt and Henry Cabot Lodge, 1884–1918.* 2 vols. 1925. Reprint. New York: Da Capo Press, 1971.

38-148. SOLVICK, STANLEY D. "William Howard Taft and the Progressive Movement: A Study in Conservative Thought and Politics." Ph.D. dissertation, University of Michigan, 1962. 339 p. 63-06955.

38-149. ————. "William Howard Taft and Cannonism." *Wisconsin Magazine of History* 48 (Autumn 1964): 48–58.

38-150. TAFT, HORACE DUTTON. *Memories and Opinions.* New York: Macmillan, 1942. 336 p.

38-151. THAYER, WILLIAM ROSCOE. *Theodore Roosevelt: An Intimate Biography.* Boston: Houghton Mifflin, 1919. 474 p.

Cannon and the Presidential Election of 1908

38-152. BARRY, DAVID S. "Men and Affairs at Washington." *New England Magazine* 43 (November 1907): 345–59.

38-153. BOUTELL, HENRY S. "The Claims of the Candidates: Joseph Gurney Cannon." *North American Review* 187 (May 1908): 641–47.

38-154. ————. "Speaker Cannon and the Presidency." *Independent,* 23 April 1908, pp. 894–99.

38-155. "Cannon in the Race." *Collier's,* 11 April 1908, p. 26.

38-156. "Cannon's Strength." *Harper's Weekly,* 29 February 1908, p. 5.

38-157. "Presidential Possibilities." *Living Age,* 6 June 1908, pp. 585–86.

38-158. ROSEWATER, VICTOR. *Back Stage in 1912: The Inside Story of the Split Republican Convention.* Philadelphia: Dorrance, 1932. 227 p.

38-159. "Speaker Cannon's Key-Note Speech." *Harper's Weekly,* 1 September 1906, pp. 1232–33.

38-160. "Uncle Joe and the Hoosier Paragon." *Saturday Evening Post,* 14 March 1908, p. 14.

Cannon and the Tariff

38-161. BAKER, RICHARD CLEVELAND. *The Tariff under Roosevelt and Taft.* Hastings, Nebr.: Democratic Printing, 1941. 218 p.

38-162. BARFIELD, CLAUDE E. " 'Our Share of the Booty': The Democratic Party, Cannonism, and the Payne-Aldrich Tariff." *Journal of American History* 57 (September 1970): 308–23.

38-163. "Cannon and Ridder Dispute." *La Follette's Weekly,* 20 November 1909, pp. 12–13.

38-164. DETZER, DAVID W. "The Politics of the Payne-Aldrich Tariff of 1909." Ph.D. dissertation, University of Connecticut, 1970. 267 p. 71-15975.

38-165. "Mr. Cannon in the Role of the Worm That Turns." *Arena* 40 (November 1908): 508–9.

38-166. "Progressives Score against House Machine." *La Follette's Weekly,* 17 April 1909, pp. 5–6.

38-167. "Prospects of an Honest Bill." *American Review of Reviews* 39 (January 1909): 6–7.

38-168. SULLIVAN, MARK. "The Lower House and Standard Oil." *Collier's,* 24 April 1909, p. 11.

38-169. "Uncle Joe as a Tariff Reformer." *Saturday Evening Post,* 25 April 1908, p. 16.

38-170. "Uncle Joe Explained." *Saturday Evening Post,* 30 May 1908, p. 16.

38-171. "The Week." *Nation,* 27 April 1911, p. 411.

38-172. WILLIS, H. PARKER. "The Impending Tariff Struggle." *Journal of Political Economy* 17 (January 1909): 1–18.

38-173. ———. "The Tariff of 1909." *Journal of Political Economy* 17 (November 1909): 589–619; 18 (January–March 1910): 1–33, 173–96.

Cannon and the Insurgency: Primary Sources

See also Maxey (1-11), Gardner (1-30), and Morrison (40-93).

38-174. ABBOT, E. H. "The Liberation of the House." *Outlook,* 2 April 1910, pp. 750–54.

38-175. "The Attack on Cannonism." *Outlook,* 2 April 1910, pp. 635–40.

38-176. "The Autocratic House of Representatives." *Outlook,* 10 April 1909, pp. 807–9.

38-177. "The Battle in the House." *Harper's Bazaar* 44 (May 1910): 335.

38-178. "A Body Blow for Cannonism." *La Follette's Weekly,* 15 January 1910, pp. 5–6.

38-179. "Cannon Denies Parson's Charge." *La Follette's Weekly,* 16 October 1909, p. 12.

38-180. "Cannon's Revenge." *La Follette's Weekly,* 14 August 1909, p. 4.

38-181. "Cannon Standing by His Guns." *Literary Digest,* 30 July 1910, pp. 153–55.

38-182. "Cannon Viewed by His Own Party." *Literary Digest,* 29 January 1910, pp. 169–70.

38-183. "Cannon Volleyed and Thundered." *Collier's,* 6 November 1909, p. 12.

38-184. "The Degradation of the House of Representatives." *Arena* 39 (May 1908): 615–18.

38-185. "The Demotion of Fowler." *La Follette's Weekly,* 28 August 1909, pp. 3–4.

38-186. "Effect of the Revolt in the House." *Independent,* 31 March 1910, pp. 667–68.

38-187. "The Fight against Cannon." *Nation,* 17 September 1908, pp. 251–52.

38-188. "Fighting for New Rules." *American Review of Reviews* 39 (April 1909): 395–97.

38-189. "Fowler Exposes Cannon." *La Follette's Weekly,* 4 September 1909, pp. 12–13.

38-190. "Government by Oligarchy." *Outlook,* 2 May 1908, pp. 12–14.

38-191. " 'Government of the People, by'—the Speaker." *La Follette's Weekly,* 13 February 1909, p. 5.

38-192. HALE, WILLIAM BAYARD. "The Speaker or the People?" *World's Work* 19 (April 1910): 12805–12.

38-193. "The House Insurgents." *Outlook,* 20 March 1909, p. 626.

38-194. "Insurgency Rampant." *American Review of Reviews* 41 (April 1910): 396–99.

38-195. "The Insurgents' First Taste of Blood." *Current Literature* 48 (February 1910): 127–31.

38-196. "A Lesson in Cannonism." *La Follette's Weekly,* 14 August 1909, pp. 4–5.

38-197. LEWIS, ALFRED H. "What Is 'Joe' Cannon?" *Cosmopolitan* 48 (April 1910): 567–75.

38-198. LOWRY, EDWARD G. "The Downfall of Cannon." *Harper's Weekly,* 26 March 1910, p. 8.

38-199. ———. "In the 'Insurgent' Camp." *Harper's Weekly,* 2 April 1910, p. 8.

38-200. MACADAMS, HASTINGS. "The Insurgent." *Everybody's Magazine* 27 (July 1912): 770–81.

38-201. McCALL, SAMUEL W. "Cannonism— How the Speaker Looks to the Regulars." *Saturday Evening Post,* 15 January 1910, p. 3.

38-202. "The March of Events." *World's Work* 37 (April 1919): 613–14.

38-203. "The Meaning of Cannonism." *La Follette's Weekly,* 5 February 1910, pp. 3–4.

38-204. MURDOCK, VICTOR. "After Cannonism—What?" *Independent,* 22 September 1910, pp. 622–25.

38-205. ———. "The Insurgent Movement in Congress." *North American Review* 191 (April 1910): 510–16.

38-206. ———. "Usurping Rights of Congressmen." *La Follette's Weekly,* 20 March 1909, p. 7.

38-207. NEEDHAM, HENRY B. "The Insurgents vs. Aldrich, Cannon, et al." *Everybody's Magazine* 22 (January 1910): 102–9.

38-208. NORRIS, GEORGE W. "The Secret of His Power: A History of the Insurgent Movement in the House of Representatives." *La Follette's Weekly,* 8 January 1910, pp. 7–9.

38-209. "Opposition to Speaker Cannon." *Independent,* 25 August 1910, pp. 384–85.

38-210. "Our House of Petitioners." *La Follette's Weekly,* 6 February 1909, p. 6.

38-211. A PARLIAMENTARIAN. "Cannon: The Servant in the House." *Harper's Weekly,* 9 April 1910, p. 8.

38-212. "Party Machines Uphold Cannonism." *La Follette's Weekly,* 20 March 1909, p. 6.

38-213. "The Progress of the World." *American Review of Reviews* 41 (April 1910): 387–417.

38-214. "The Real Issue." *La Follette's Weekly,* 11 December 1909, p. 3.

38-215. "Reform of the House Rules." *La Follette's Weekly,* 20 February 1909, p. 6.

38-216. "Republican Disaffection." *Literary Digest,* 2 April 1910, pp. 627–30.

38-217. "Republican Press on the Party Split." *Literary Digest,* 22 January 1910, pp. 125–27.

38-218. "Republicans Repudiate Cannon." *La Follette's Weekly,* 26 February 1910, p. 3.

38-219. "Repudiating Cannon." *La Follette's Weekly,* 22 January 1910, p. 4.

38-220. "Revolt against Speaker Cannon." *Independent,* 24 March 1910, pp. 599–600.

38-221. "The Revolution in the House." *Harper's Weekly,* 26 March 1910, p. 4.

38-222. "Shaking the Throne of the Czar." *La Follette's Weekly,* 26 March 1910, pp. 4–6.

38-223. "Silly Cannon Threats." *La Follette's Weekly,* 12 March 1910, p. 6.

38-224. "The Skirmish in the House." *La Follette's Weekly,* 26 March 1910, p. 3.

38-225. "The Speaker and the Rules." *Nation,* 18 March 1909, p. 268.

38-226. "Speaker Cannon and His Foes." *Current Literature* 47 (January 1910): 9–12.

38-227. "Speaker Cannon and the Complete Destruction of Popular Rule in the House of Representatives." *Arena* 40 (July 1908): 89–91.

38-228. "Speaker Cannon as the Friend of Privileged Interests and the Money-Controlled Machines." *Arena* 36 (September 1906): 307–8.

38-229. "The Speakership Struggle." *Nation,* 24 March 1910, p. 280.

38-230. "Spiking Cannon." *Collier's,* 2 April 1910, p. 11.

38-231. SULLIVAN, MARK. "Comment on Congress." *Collier's,* 1 January 1910, p. 9.

38-232. ———. "Comment on Congress." *Collier's,* 2 April 1910, p. 15.

38-233. ———. "Fight against Cannonism." *Collier's,* 27 March 1909, p. 11.

38-234. ———. "The People's One Hour in Two Years." *Collier's,* 13 March 1909, pp. 10–11.

38-235. ———. "Shall We Have an Insurgent Congress?" *Collier's,* 12 March 1910, p. 9.

38-236. "Taking the Patronage Club to the Insurgents." *Literary Digest,* 15 January 1910, pp. 86–87.

38-237. "Tammany and Cannon." *Nation,* 7 October 1909, pp. 319–20.

38-238. "Trying to Drop Cannon." *Literary Digest,* 3 September 1910, p. 330.

38-239. "Uncle Joe on Regularity." *Saturday Evening Post,* 11 June 1910, p. 20.

38-240. "Uncle Joe's Graveyard." *Collier's,* 18 April 1908, p. 10.

38-241. "Uncle Joe's Pet." *Saturday Evening Post,* 7 May 1910, p. 27.

38-242. "The Uprising against Cannon." *Literary Digest,* 26 March 1910, pp. 573–74.

38-243. "The Vindication of the Speaker." *Saturday Evening Post,* 29 January 1910, p. 18.

38-244. WELLIVER, J. C. "The End of Cannonism." *Success* 13 (January 1910): 7.

38-245. "We Shall See, Mr. Cannon." *La Follette's Weekly,* 30 October 1909, p. 3.

38-246. "Will Uncle Joe Retire?" *Harper's Weekly,* 14 August 1909, p. 4.

Cannon and the Insurgency: Secondary Sources

See also Straetz (38-53).

38-247. BAKER, JOHN D. "The Character of the Congressional Revolution of 1910." *Journal of American History* 60 (December 1973): 679–91.

38-248. BARFIELD, CLAUDE E. "The Democratic Party in Congress, 1909–1913." Ph.D. dissertation, Northwestern University, 1965. 488 p. 65-12047.

38-249. BOWDEN, ROBERT D. *The Evolution of the Politician: A Short Study of the Corruption of Politics.* Boston: Stratford, 1924. 248 p.

38-250. BRADEN, WALDO W. "The Cummins-Cannon Controversy of 1909." *Iowa Journal of History* 49 (July 1951): 211–20.

38-251. DEWITT, BENJAMIN P. *The Progressive Movement.* New York: Macmillan, 1915. 376 p.

38-252. FILLER, LOUIS. *Crusaders for American Liberalism.* Yellow Springs, Ohio: Antioch Press, 1961. 428 p.

38-253. FLEMING, JAMES S. "Re-establishing Leadership in the House of Representatives: The Case of Oscar W. Underwood." *Mid-America* 54 (October 1972): 234–50.

38-254. HECHLER, KENNETH WILLIAM. *Insurgency: Personalities and Politics in the Taft Era.* 1940. Reprint. New York: AMS Press, 1970. 252 p.

38-255. HOLT, LAURENCE JAMES. *Congressional Insurgents and the Party System, 1909–1916.* Cambridge, Mass.: Harvard University Press, 1967. 188 p.

38-256. LOWITT, RICHARD. "The Making of an Insurgent." *Mid-America* 42 (April 1960): 105–15.

38-257. REGIER, CORNELIUS C. *The Era of the Muckrakers.* Chapel Hill: University of North Carolina Press, 1932. 254 p.

PART V

THE SPEAKERS, 1911–1984

39. General Bibliography, 1911–1984

NATIONAL POLITICS

39-1. BLAKEY, ROY G., AND BLAKEY, GLADYS C. *The Federal Income Tax.* London: Longmans, Green, 1940. 640 p.

39-2. GOLDMAN, ERIC F. *Rendezvous with Destiny.* New York: Alfred A. Knopf, 1952. 503 p.

39-3. KING, JUDSON. *The Conservation Fight: From Theodore Rossevelt to the Tennessee Valley Authority.* Washington, D.C.: Public Affairs Press, 1959. 316 p.

39-4. MANCHESTER, WILLIAM R. *The Glory and the Dream: A Narrative History of America, 1932–1972.* Boston: Little, Brown, 1974. 1,397 p.

39-5. MARTIN, RALPH G. *Ballots and Bandwagons.* Chicago: Rand McNally, 1964. 480 p.

39-6. SCHLESINGER, ARTHUR M., JR. *The Age of Roosevelt.* 3 vols. Boston: Houghton Mifflin, 1957–60.

39-7. SUNDQUIST, JAMES L. *Politics and Policy: The Eisenhower, Kennedy, and Johnson Years.* Washington, D.C.: Brookings Institution, 1968. 560 p.

39-8. WARREN, HARRIS GAYLORD. *Herbert Hoover and the Great Depression.* 1959. Reprint. Westport, Conn.: Greenwood Press, 1980. 372 p.

STUDIES OF CONGRESS

39-9. COOPER, JOSEPH, AND BRADY, DAVID W. "Institutional Context and Personal Leadership Style: The House from Cannon to Rayburn." *American Political Science Review* 75 (June 1981): 411–25.

39-10. DAVIDSON, ROGER H.; KOVENACK, DAVID M.; AND O'LEARY, MICHAEL K. *Congress in Crisis: Politics and Congressional Reform.* Belmont, Calif.: Wadsworth Publishing, 1966. 208 p.

39-11. KEFAUVER, ESTES B., AND LEVIN, JACK. *A Twentieth-Century Congress.* 1947. Reprint. New York: Greenwood Press, 1959. 236 p.

39-12. PATTERSON, JAMES T. *Congressional Conservatism and the New Deal: The Growth of the Conservative Coalition in Congress, 1933–1939.* 1967. Reprint. Westport, Conn.: Greenwood Press, 1981. 369 p.

39-13. PORTER, DAVID L. *The Seventy-sixth Congress and World War II, 1939–1940.* Columbia: University of Missouri Press, 1979. 236 p.

39-14. SCHWARZ, JORDAN A. *The Interregnum of Despair: Hoover, Congress, and the Depression.* Urbana: University of Illinois Press, 1970. 281 p.

39-15. SINCLAIR, BARBARA. "The Speaker's Task Force in the Post-Reform House of Representatives." *American Political Science Review* 75 (June 1981): 397–410.

39-16. WALDMAN, SIDNEY. "Majority Leadership in the House of Representatives." *Political Science Quarterly* 95 (Fall 1980): 373–93.

MEMOIRS AND REMINISCENCES

39-17. ABELL, GEORGE, AND GORDON, EVELYN. *Let Them Eat Caviar.* New York: Dodge Publishing, 1937. 304 p.

39-18. BLOOM, VERA. *There's No Place Like Washington.* New York: G. P. Putnam's Sons, 1944. 296 p.

39-19. MOLEY, RAYMOND. *The First New Deal.* New York: Harcourt, Brace, and World, 1966. 577 p.

39-20. ———. *27 Masters of Politics: In a Personal Perspective.* 1949. Reprint. Westport, Conn.: Greenwood Press, 1972. 276 p.

39-21. WEARIN, OTHA D. *Country Roads to Washington.* Des Moines, Iowa: Wallace Homestead, 1976. 181 p.

40. James Beauchamp ("Champ") Clark
(1850–1921)
(Speaker, Sixty-second through Sixty-fifth Congresses)

James Beauchamp Clark, who was born on a farm near Lawrenceburg, Kentucky, on March 7, 1850, early adopted Champ as the name by which he would be known. His father, a carriage and buggy maker, hired Champ out at the age of eight to a local farmer. While he worked on the farm for several years, Clark managed to acquire enough learning on his own to become a teacher by the age of fifteen. He attended Kentucky University at Lexington for three years but was expelled for fighting. He graduated from Bethany College three years later, in 1873.

Following graduation Clark accepted the presidency of Marshall College, in West Virginia, for a year, after which he entered the Cincinnati Law School. He went to Kansas in 1875 with the intention of establishing a practice at Wichita, but he moved to the town of Louisiana, Missouri, in 1876 and to Bowling Green, Missouri, in 1880. He first entered Democratic party politics in 1880 as a presidential elector. He was also city attorney for Bowling Green, assistant county attorney for four years, and county attorney for four years. In 1888 he won election to the Missouri legislature. Although he served only from 1889 to 1891, Clark authored the Missouri anti-trust law and the law that introduced the secret-ballot system to the state.

Following his election to the Fifty-third Congress (1893–95), Clark remained in the House, with the exception of the Fifty-fourth Congress, until his death in 1921. He quickly rose to prominence in the House by serving on the Foreign Affairs and the Ways and Means committees. For several years he was also Democratic minority leader John Sharp Williams's chief assistant. Clark strongly supported the Spanish-American War, but he opposed the annexation of Hawaii. In all other matters he strictly followed the Democratic party platform.

After Clark became Democratic minority leader of the Sixtieth Congress (1907–9), he led the fight against Speaker Joseph Cannon, partly in opposition to Cannon's arbitrary exercise of power and partly out of partisan considerations. By cultivating the insurgents, Clark skillfully exploited the opposition to Cannon within the Republican party. When the combined forces of Republican insurgents and Democrats were able to overthrow Cannonism in 1911, the results were doubly beneficial to Clark. First, the coup consolidated his leadership and standing among Democrats, and second, it divided the Republican party and made a Democratic triumph in the 1912 congressional election a virtual certainty.

Clark's first tangible benefit from the overthrow of Cannon was his election in 1911 to the speakership, an office he held until 1919. Clark had aspirations to even higher office. In the 1912 Democratic convention at Baltimore he was the leading contender for the presidential nomination. He received 440.5 votes on the first ballot, compared with 324 for his closest challenger, Woodrow Wilson. Clark continued to lead through the fourteenth ballot, but then William Jennings Bryan switched his support to Wilson, possibly in the hope that the convention would deadlock and allow Bryan to win the nomination. In any event, Wilson won the nomination, and Clark held Bryan responsible for his defeat.

Clark nonetheless supported Wilson in the campaign, although he later opposed the president on both intervention in World War I and the Selective Service Act of 1917. He was minority leader of the Sixty-sixth Congress, but he was defeated for reelection in 1920. He died on March 2, 1921.

MANUSCRIPT COLLECTIONS

Bethany College Library, Bethany, W. Va.
  Champ Clark Correspondence, 1905-15.
  1 ft.
  NUCMC 78-75.
  Other than the small collection of Clark correspondence at Bethany College, no major collection of Clark manuscripts is known to exist.

As this bibliography neared completion, the Western Historical Manuscript Collection at the University of Missouri Columbia accessioned a major collection of the papers of Champ Clark and his son, Senator Bennett Champ Clark.

BOOKS, ARTICLES, AND DISSERTATIONS

WORKS BY JAMES B. CLARK

The following works are listed chronologically by year of publication and alphabetically thereunder.

*40-1. CLARK, JAMES B. *The Necessity of Political Morality: An Address Delivered before the Missouri Press Association at Jefferson City, Mo., May 12th 1881.* N.p., 1881. 16 p.

40-2. ———. *Silver: Speech of Hon. Champ Clark, of Missouri, August 19, 1893.* Washington, D.C.: Government Printing Office, 1893. 18 p.
  House speech in favor of free silver.

40-3. ———. *Improvement of the Missouri River: Remarks of Hon. Champ Clark, of Missouri, in the House of Representatives, Monday, March 19, 1894.* N.p., 1894.

40-4. ———. *Oklahoma: Remarks of Hon. Champ Clark, of Missouri, in the House of Representatives, Friday, December 15, 1893.* N.p., 1894.
  An argument in favor of the admission of New Mexico and Oklahoma into the Union.

40-5. ———. *Tariff: Remarks of Hon. Champ Clark, of Missouri, in the House of Representatives, Jan. 15, 16, 19, and 24, 1894.* N.p., 1894. 21 p.
  A speech in favor of the Wilson tariff bill.

40-6. ———. *Remarks . . . on the Bill to Establish a Public Library in the City of Washington.* Washington, D.C., 1895.
  Clark opposed using federal funds to establish a public library in Washington.

40-7. ———. *Cuba: The Monroe Doctrine as Interpreted by a Missouri Democrat.* Washington, D.C., 1898. 8 p.
  A House speech of January 20, 1898, requesting the recognition of Cuba's independence.

40-8. ———. *Hawaii: Speech of the Hon. Champ Clark, of Missouri, . . . in the House of Representatives, Saturday, June 11, 1898.* Washington, D.C., 1898. 24 p.
  A lengthy anti-imperialist speech arguing against the annexation of Hawaii.

40-9. ———. *The Spanish War, Silver, Greenbacks, Income Tax, and Patriotism: Remarks of Champ Clark, of Missouri.* Washington, D.C., 1898. 16 p.
  House speech of May 3, 1898, discoursing on all the issues mentioned in the title.

40-10. ———. *The Financial Bill: Remarks of Champ Clark, of Missouri, in the House of Representatives, December 16, 1899.* Washington, D.C., 1899.
  Another speech arguing for free silver.

40-11. ———. *The Philippine Problem: Speech of Hon. Champ Clark, of Missouri, in the House of Representatives, Monday, February 5, 1900.* Washington, D.C., 1900. 15 p.
  A speech opposing annexation of the Philippines.

40-12. ———. *Remarks of Champ Clark, of Missouri, Delivered in the House of Representatives, on Richard Park Bland, the Hepburn-Gabe Letter, the Postal Bill, the Hawaiian Government Bill, the Chinese-*

Japanese Commission, and the Lieutenant-Generalcy. Washington, D.C., 1900.

40-13. ———. "Spellbinders and Spellbinding." *Saturday Evening Post,* 15 September 1900, pp. 2–3.
   A discussion of oratorical technique.

40-14. ———. "Stumping in Old Missouri." *Saturday Evening Post,* 29 September 1900, p. 10.
   A humorous account of campaigning Missouri-style.

40-15. ———. "The Use of Wit, Humor, and Anecdote in Public Speech." *Saturday Evening Post,* 1 June 1901, p. 4.
   An entertaining survey of wit in political and social life.

40-16. ———. *Chinese Exclusion: Speech of Hon. Champ Clark, of Missouri, in the House of Representatives, Friday, April 4, 1902.* N.p., 1902. 16 p.
   An argument for more stringent restrictions on Chinese immigration.

40-17. ———. *Reply to General Grosvenor: Remarks of Champ Clark, of Missouri, in the House of Representatives, January 13, 1903.* Washington, D.C., 1903.

40-18. ———. "As to the Vice-Presidency— What the Office Really Amounts To." *Saturday Evening Post,* 2 April 1904, pp. 8–9.
   An examination of the office and its importance to the American system of government.

40-19. ———. "The Lure of Department Life— A Riddle of Public Life That Has But a Sad Reading." *Saturday Evening Post,* 28 May 1904, p. 3.
   Examines the benefits and abuses of the Washington bureaucracy.

*40-20. ———. *The President's Message.* N.p., 1908. 16 p.
   House speech of February 13, 1908.

40-21. ———. "A Defense of Missouri." *Independent,* 4 March 1909, pp. 482–83.
   Clark defends Missouri election laws against charges of discrimination.

40-22. ———. "Where Champ Clark Lives." *Current Literature* 46 (March 1909): 265.
   Clark's rhapsodic tribute to his home district.

40-23. ———. "Is Congressional Oratory a Lost Art?" *Century Magazine* 81 (December 1910): 307–10.
   Clark observes a decline in speaking ability in Congress.

40-24. ———. "The Political Situation in the United States." *Forum* 43 (June 1910): 634–36.
   Clark's analysis of the resurgence of the Democratic party.

40-25. ———. *The President and the Tariff: Remarks of Champ Clark, of Missouri, Delivered in the House of Representatives on Saturday, May 21, 1910.* Washington, D.C., 1910. 29 p.
   A partisan speech against the tariff.

40-26. ———. "The Work of the Democratic House." *North American Review* 194 (September 1911): 337–43.
   A review of the accomplishments of Clark's party during the previous session.

40-27. ———. "The Duty of the Democrats." *Independent,* 25 January 1912, pp. 176–79.
   A discussion of the Democratic program, stressing tariff reform and governmental efficiency.

40-28. ———. "The Vacation Period." *Independent,* 6 June 1912, pp. 1247–50.
   A defense of the Chautauqua movement.

40-29. ———. "A Perennial National Problem." *North American Review* 200 (July 1914): 25–34.
   A plea to improve the harbors and tributaries of the Mississippi River.

40-30. ———. "Cloture." *North American Review* 201 (April 1915): 516–20.
   A review of the history and usage of cloture.

40-31. ———. "How Much Preparedness?" *Independent,* 24 April 1916, p. 133.
   Clark argues that the public mood justifies preparedness and a tax on war munitions.

40-32. ———. "What We Are Trying to Do." *Independent,* 4 December 1916, p. 392.
   A justification of the actions of the Democratic majority in Congress.

40-33. ———. *Address by Speaker Champ Clark, of Missouri, in Presenting the Washington Memorial Arch at Valley Forge to the State of Pennsylvania on Tuesday, June 19, 1917.* Washington D.C.: Government Printing Office, 1917. 8 p.

40-34. ———. "Democracy is Safe." *Forum* 58 (November 1917): 517–25.

A call for unity in the face of war, with the assurance that democracy is strong enough to survive.

*40-35. ———. *Volunteers vs. Conscripts: Speech of Champ Clark, of Missouri.* Washington, D.C., 1917. 15 p.

40-36. ———. "The Bible and Public Life." *World Outlook* 4 (March 1918): 3–4.

Clark analyzes how and why the Bible is so often quoted in American politics.

40-37. ———. "Why We Need a Democratic Congress." *Outlook,* 23 October 1918, pp. 289–90.

An argument for a Democratic Congress based on past performances.

40-38. ———. *My Quarter Century of American Politics.* 2 vols. New York: Harper and Brothers, 1920.

Clark's memoirs.

40-39. ———. "Missourians and the Nation during the Last Century." *Missouri Historical Review* 15 (April 1921): 433–48.

A breezy reminiscence of Missouri political leaders.

40-40. ———. "The Country Lawyer Vindicated." *United States Law Review* 73 (October/November 1939): 520–24.

Reprint of an 1891 letter in which Clark defends the image of the country lawyer.

40-41. WILSON, WOODROW, AND CLARK, CHAMP. *Celebration of the Rededication of Congress Hall.* Washington, D.C., 1913. 10 p.

Includes a stirring patriotic address given by Clark at the ceremonies held on October 25, 1913.

BIOGRAPHIES, BIOGRAPHICAL SKETCHES, AND EULOGIES

See also Neale (35-57).

40-42. BAKER, RAY STANNARD. "What About the Democratic Party?" *American Magazine* 70 (June 1910): 147–60.

A short, contemporary biographical sketch.

40-43. *The Bench and Bar of St. Louis, Kansas City, Jefferson City, and Other Missouri Cities.* St. Louis: American Biographical Publishing, 1884. 504 p.

Includes a short biographical sketch that highlights Clark's early legal career.

40-44. "Champ Clark, 'Almost President.' " *Literary Digest,* 26 March 1921, pp. 51–53.

An obituary notice that recalls and applauds Clark's accomplishments.

40-45. HOLLISTER, WILFRED R. *Five Famous Missourians.* Kansas City, Mo.: Hudson-Kimberly Publishing, 1900. 386 p.

Includes a favorable biographical sketch of Clark.

40-46. LEWIS, ALFRED H. "The Honorable Champ." *Cosmopolitan* 51 (November 1911): 760–65.

An admiring biographical sketch.

40-47. MORRISON, GEOFFREY F. "A Political Biography of Champ Clark." Ph.D. dissertation, St. Louis University, 1972. 337 p. 72-23979.

The most recent and well-researched biographical treatment of Clark.

40-48. "The New Leader of the Democrats in Congress." *Current Literature* 46 (January 1909): 39–41.

A favorable biographical sketch.

40-49. SHOEMAKER, FLOYD CALVIN. *Missouri's Hall of Fame: Lives of Eminent Missourians.* Columbia, Mo.: Missouri Book, 1918. 269 p.

Includes a short biographical sketch.

40-50. U.S. CONGRESS. HOUSE. *Champ Clark (Late Representative from Missouri): Memorial Addresses Delivered in the House of Representatives of the United States.* 66th Cong., 3d sess., 1920–21. Washington, D.C.: Government Printing Office, 1922. 99 p.

Contains thirty-one eulogies by Clark's colleagues in Congress.

40-51. WEBB, MARY G., AND WEBB, EDNA L., EDS. *Famous Living Americans.* Greencastle, Ind.: Charles Webb, 1915. 594 p.

Includes a biographical sketch of Clark by Wallace D. Bassford.

40-52. WEBB, WILLIAM LARKIN. *Champ Clark.* New York: Neale Publishing, 1912. 256 p.

A campaign biography including excerpts from several speeches.

40-53. WHITE, HOLLIS L. "Champ Clark, the 'Leather-Bound Orator.'" *Missouri Historical Review* 56 (October 1961): 25–39.

40-54. ———. "A Rhetorical Criticism of the Speeches of Speaker Champ Clark of Missouri." Ph.D. dissertation, University of Missouri, 1950.

A comprehensive study of the content and delivery of Clark's speeches.

CLARK AND MISSOURI HISTORY AND POLITICS

40-55. CRIGHTON, JOHN CLARK. *Missouri and the World War, 1914–1917.* Columbia: University of Missouri Press, 1947. 199 p.

40-56. CULMER, FREDERIC ARTHUR. *A New History of Missouri.* Mexico, Mo.: McIntyre Publishing, 1938. 592 p.

40-57. GRANT, PHILIP A., JR. "Missourians in Congress, 1916–1920." *Missouri Historical Society Bulletin* 34 (April 1978): 151–56.

40-58. *The History of Pike County, Missouri: An Encyclopedia of Useful Information, and a Compendium of Actual Facts.* Des Moines, Iowa: Mills, 1883. 1,038 p.

40-59. JACKSON, WILLIAM RUFUS. *Missouri Democracy: A History of the Party and Its Representative Members Past and Present.* Vol. 1. Chicago: S. J. Clarke Publishing, 1935. 841 p.

40-60. MITCHELL, FRANKLIN D. *Embattled Democracy: Missouri Democratic Politics, 1919–1932.* Columbia: University of Missouri Press, 1966. 219 p.

40-61. MURASKIN, JACK DAVID. "Missouri Politics during the Progressive Era." Ph.D. dissertation, University of California, Berkeley, 1969. 413 p. 70-06174.

40-62. NEILSON, JAMES W. "Congressional Opinion in Missouri on the Spanish-American War." *Missouri Historical Review* 51 (April 1957): 245–56.

40-63. SHOEMAKER, FLOYD CALVIN. *Missouri and Missourians: Land of Contrasts and People of Achievements.* 5 vols. Chicago: Lewis Publishing, 1943.

40-64. STEVENS, WALTER B. *Centennial History of Missouri: One Hundred Years in the Union.* 4 vols. St. Louis: S. J. Clarke Publishing, 1921.

CLARK'S POLITICAL ASSOCIATES

See also Cox (28-25), Dunn (28-28), Gompers (28-30), Roper and Lovette (28-38), Watson (28-42), Belmont (30-83), Bartholdt (33-45), Koenig (35-98), Bolles (38-33), Gwinn (38-35), Frear (38-63), Johnson (38-69), La Guardia (38-70), Lief (38-71), Lowitt (38-73), Margulies (38-74), Abbot (38-88), Coletta (38-132), Brown (43-14), Fisher (43-15), James (43-16), and Waller (44-22).

40-65. ACHESON, SAM HANNA. *Joe Bailey: The Last Democrat.* 1932. Reprint. Freeport, N.Y.: Books for Libraries Press, 1970. 420 p.

40-66. BAKER, RAY STANNARD. *Woodrow Wilson: Life and Letters.* 6 vols. Garden City, N.Y.: Doubleday, Doran, 1927–37.

40-67. BILLINGTON, MONROE. *Thomas P. Gore: The Blind Senator from Oklahoma.* Lawrence: University of Kansas Press, 1967. 229 p.

40-68. BLUM, JOHN MORTON. *Joe Tumulty and the Wilson Era.* 1951. Reprint. Hamden, Conn.: Archon Books, 1969. 337 p.

40-69. BRYAN, WILLIAM JENNINGS. *The Memoirs of William Jennings Bryan.* 1925. Reprint. New York: Haskell House, 1971. 560 p.

40-70. BUTT, ARCHIBALD W. *Taft and Roosevelt: The Intimate Letters of Archie Butt, Military Aide.* 2 vols. 1930. Reprint. Port Washington, N.Y.: Kennikat Press, 1971.

40-71. COBEN, STANLEY. *A. Mitchell Palmer: Politician.* 1963. Reprint. New York: Da Capo Press, 1972. 351 p.

40-72. COLETTA, PAOLO E. *William Jennings Bryan.* 3 vols. Lincoln: University of Nebraska Press, 1964–69.

40-73. CRAMER, CLARENCE H. *Newton D. Baker: A Biography.* 1961. Reprint. New York: Garland Publishing, 1979. 310 p.

40-74. GEIGER, LOUIS G. *Joseph W. Folk of Missouri.* Columbia: University of Missouri Press, 1953. 206 p.

40-75. GLAD, PAUL W. *The Trumpet Soundeth: William Jennings Bryan and His Democracy, 1896–1912.* Lincoln: University of Nebraska Press, 1960. 242 p.

40-76. HAINES, LYNN, AND HAINES, DORA B. *The Lindberghs.* New York: Vanguard Press, 1931. 307 p.

40-77. HARRISON, CARTER H. *Stormy Years: The Autobiography of Carter H. Harrison, Five Times Mayor of Chicago.* New York: Bobbs-Merrill, 1935. 361 p.

40-78. HIBBEN, PAXTON. *The Peerless Leader: William Jennings Bryan.* 1929. Reprint. New York: Russell and Russell, 1967. 446 p.

40-79. INGLE, HOMER L. "Pilgrimage to Reform: A Life of Claude Kitchin." Ph.D. dissertation, University of Wisconsin, 1967. 278 p. 67-06801.

40-80. JONES, MARVIN. *Marvin Jones' Memoirs, 1917–1973: Fifty-six Years of Continuing Service in All Three Branches of the Federal Government.* Edited by Joseph M. Ray. El Paso: Texas Western Press, University of Texas, 1973. 183 p.

40-81. LONG, JOHN CUTHBERT. *Bryan: The Great Commoner.* New York: D. Appleton, 1928. 421 p.

40-82. MILNER, COOPER. "The Public Life of Cordell Hull: 1907–1924." Ph.D. dissertation, Vanderbilt University, 1960. 486 p. 60-02731.

40-83. MOON, ANNA MARY, AND PHILLIPS, JOE. *John A. Moon: Father of the Parcel Post.* Chattanooga, Tenn.: Chattanooga Publishing, 1941. 229 p.

40-84. MULLEN, ARTHUR F. *Western Democrat.* New York: Wilfred Funk, 1940. 360 p.

40-85. ROSSER, CHARLES McDANIEL. *The Crusading Commoner: A Close-up of William Jennings Bryan and His Times.* Dallas, Tex.: Mathis, Van Nort, 1937. 355 p.

40-86. SLAYDEN, ELLEN MAURY. *Washington Wife: Journal of Ellen Maury Slayden from 1897–1919.* New York: Harper and Row, 1963. 385 p.

40-87. THURMAN, A. L. "Joseph Wingate Folk: The Politician as Speaker and Public Servant." *Missouri Historical Review* 59 (January 1965): 173–91.

40-88. VILLARD, OSWALD G. *Fighting Years: Memoirs of a Liberal Editor.* New York: Harcourt, Brace, 1939. 543 p.

CLARK AND IMPERIALISM IN THE 1890S

See also Hollingsworth (34-43).

40-89. PRATT, JULIUS W. *Expansionists of 1898: The Acquisition of Hawaii and the Spanish Islands.* 1936. Reprint. New York: Peter Smith, 1951. 393 p.

40-90. RUSS, WILLIAM ADAM, JR. *The Hawaiian Republic, 1894–98, and Its Struggle to Win Annexation.* Selingsgrove, Pa.: Susquehanna University Press, 1961. 398 p.

CLARK AND THE REVOLT AGAINST CANNONISM

See also Barfield (38-162), McCall (38-201), and Barfield (38-248).

40-91. "A Committee on Committees." *Outlook,* 31 December 1910, pp. 987–88.

40-92. "The House and Its Methods." *American Review of Reviews* 39 (April 1909): 395–97.

40-93. MORRISON, GEOFFREY F. "Champ Clark and the Rules Revolution of 1910." *Capitol Studies* 2 (Winter 1974): 43–56.

40-94. SARASOHN, DAVID. "The Democratic Surge, 1905–1912: Forging a Progressive Majority." Ph.D. dissertation, University of California at Los Angeles, 1976. 332 p. 77-09353.

CLARK AND THE SPEAKERSHIP

See also Fleming (38-253).

40-95. "Democratic Opportunities." *Literary Digest,* 15 April 1911, pp. 715–17.

40-96. Gastit, Horace D. "As to Champ." *Harper's Weekly,* 14 January 1911, p. 6.

40-97. Lowry, Edward G. "The New Deal in Congress." *Harper's Weekly,* 17 December 1910, p. 24.

40-98. ———. "Opening the New Congress." *Harper's Weekly,* 15 April 1911, p. 7.

40-99. ———. "What Profit Hath a Man?" *New Republic,* 12 January 1921, pp. 197–99.

40-100. "The Next Speaker." *Outlook,* 24 December 1910, pp. 914–16.

40-101. "A Self-Ruling House." *Harper's Weekly,* 24 December 1910, p. 4.

40-102. "The Senator's Secretary." *Saturday Evening Post,* 10 December 1910, pp. 25–27.

40-103. "The Sequel of Cannonism." *La Follette's Weekly,* 13 June 1914, p. 4.

40-104. Smith, T. Berry. "When Champ's in the Chair." *Harper's Weekly,* 25 February 1911, p. 6.

40-105. Vieillard [pseud.]. "Mr. Speaker." *Nation,* 24 June 1915, pp. 707–8.

CLARK AND THE TARIFF

40-106. "Anti-Tariff Thunders." *Literary Digest,* 4 June 1910, pp. 1105–7.

40-107. "Clark Makes Answer." *La Follette's Weekly,* 9 September 1911, p. 9.

40-108. "Democracy Facing the Tariff." *Literary Digest,* 28 January 1911, pp. 137–38.

40-109. "Democrats and Tariff Revision." *Harper's Weekly* 28 January 1910, p. 27.

40-110. "Rushing Tariff Revision." *Current Literature* 46 (May 1909): 465–69.

40-111. U.S. Congress. House. Committee on Ways and Means. *Tariff Hearings.* . . . 60th Cong.

9 vols. Washington, D.C.: Government Printing Office, 1909.

40-112. ———. *To Provide Revenue, Equalize Duties, Encourage the Industries of the United States, and for Other Purposes: Views of the Minority.* Washington, D.C.: Government Printing Office, 1909.

CLARK AND THE 1912 PRESIDENTIAL NOMINATION

See also Kent (1-78), Eaton (28-12), Josephson (35-157), and Manners (38-139).

40-113. Baker, Ray Stannard. "Our Next President and Some Others." *American Magazine* 74 (June 1912): 131–43.

40-114. Bennett, Ira E. "The Race to the White House." *North American Review* 192 (September 1910): 326–40.

40-115. Broesamle, John J. *William Gibbs McAdoo: A Passion for Change, 1863–1917.* Port Washington, N.Y.: Kennikat Press, 1973. 304 p.

40-116. Coletta, Paolo E. "Bryan at Baltimore, 1912: Wilson's Warwick?" *Nebraska History* 57 (Summer 1976): 200–225.

40-117. Graves, John Temple. "Champ Clark." *Independent,* 2 November 1911, pp. 959–63.

40-118. Harvey, George. "Two Democratic Candidates." *North American Review* 195 (June 1912): 721–39.

40-119. "Is Clark a 'Stalking Horse'?" *La Follette's Weekly,* 16 March 1912, p. 13.

40-120. Kelly, Frank K. *The Fight for the White House: The Story of 1912.* New York: Thomas Y. Crowell, 1961. 308 p.

40-121. Kerney, James. *The Political Education of Woodrow Wilson.* New York: Century, 1926. 503 p.

40-122. Lathrop, John E. "The Views of Champ Clark." *Outlook,* 11 May 1912, pp. 65–73.

40-123. Link, Arthur S. *Woodrow Wilson and the Progressive Era, 1910–1917.* New York: Harper and Brothers, 1954. 331 p.

40-124. LORD, WALTER. *The Good Years: From 1900 to the First World War.* New York: Harper and Brothers, 1960. 369 p.

40-125. LYONS, MAURICE F. *William F. McCombs: The President Maker.* Cincinnati: Bancroft, 1922. 147 p.

40-126. MCADOO, WILLIAM GIBBS. *Crowded Years: The Reminiscences of William Gibbs McAdoo.* 1931. Reprint. Port Washington, N.Y.: Kennikat Press, 1971. 542 p.

40-127. MCCOMBS, WILLIAM F. *Making Woodrow Wilson President.* Edited by Louis J. Lang. New York: Fairview Publishing, 1921. 309 p.

40-128. MORGENTHAU, HENRY. *All in a Lifetime.* Garden City, N.Y.: Doubleday, Page, 1922. 454 p.

40-129. RIDGWAY, ERMAN J. "Weighing the Candidates." *Everybody's Magazine* 26 (May 1912): 579–92.

40-130. WALWORTH, ARTHUR C. *Woodrow Wilson.* 1965. Reprint. New York: W. W. Norton, 1978. 438 p.

40-131. "Why Bryan Abandoned Clark." *La Follette's Weekly,* 6 July 1912, p. 12.

40-132. WILSON, WOODROW. *The Papers of Woodrow Wilson.* Edited by Arthur S. Link. Vols. 20–30. Princeton: Princeton University Press, 1975–79.

40-133. WISEMAN, JOHN B. "Dilemmas of a Party Out of Power: The Democracy, 1904–1912."
Ph.D. dissertation, University of Maryland, 1967. 260 p. 68-03396.

CLARK AND WORLD WAR I

See also Crighton (40-55).

40-134. ARNETT, ALEX M. *Claude Kitchin and the Wilson War Policies.* 1937. Reprint. New York: Russell and Russell, 1971. 341 p.

40-135. BARNES, HARRY ELMER. *The Genesis of the World War: An Introduction to the Problem of War Guilt.* 1926. Reprint. Grosse Pointe, Mich.: Scholarly Press, 1968. 754 p.

40-136. BILLINGTON, MONROE L. "The Sunrise Conference: Myth or Fact?" *Southwestern Social Science Quarterly* 37 (March 1957): 330–40.

40-137. HORNER, RICHARD KENNETH. "The House at War: The House of Representatives during World War I, 1917–1919." Ph.D. dissertation, Louisiana State University, 1977. 467 p. 77-25383.

40-138. LIVERMORE, SEWARD W. *Politics Is Adjourned: Woodrow Wilson and the War Congress, 1916–1918.* Middletown, Conn.: Wesleyan University Press, 1966. 324 p.

40-139. VIERECK, GEORGE S. *The Strangest Friendship in History: Woodrow Wilson and Colonel House.* 1932. Reprint. Westport, Conn.: Greenwood Press, 1976. 375 p.

41. Frederick Huntington Gillett
(1851–1935)
(Speaker, Sixty-sixth through Sixty-eighth Congresses)

The reserved and scholarly Frederick H. Gillett served for thirty-two years in the House of Representatives, including six years as Speaker, and for six years in the Senate. Gillett was born in Westfield, Massachusetts, on October 16, 1851, the son of one of the leading lawyers of western Massachusetts. He attended school at Westfield and then traveled abroad for a year with a private tutor. At Amherst College he won several prizes for English composition.

After he graduated from Harvard Law School in 1877, he began a law practice in Springfield, Massachusetts.

From 1879 to 1882 Gillett served as assistant attorney general of Massachusetts. In 1890 he was elected to the state house of representatives, where he served two terms and was chairman of the judiciary committee. He was elected as a Republican to the Fifty-third Congress (1893–95) and to the fifteen succeeding Congresses (1895–1925). During his lengthy tenure, he served on the Appropriations, Judiciary, Foreign Affairs, Military Affairs, Civil Service Reform, and Merchant Marine and Fisheries committees. As chairman of the Committee on Civil Service Reform for twelve years, he became known as the stepfather of the merit system.

Gillett was elected Speaker of the House in 1919, after being Republican minority leader of the House during World War I. He served as Speaker for three Congresses before he ran for the Senate in 1924. He was persuaded to become the party's nominee for the Senate from Massachusetts after the original candidate had been chosen Coolidge's campaign manager.

During his years in the Senate (1925–31) Gillett supported the World Court, even though he opposed the League of Nations. He also endorsed a department of education and public welfare, prohibition, the Eighteenth Amendment, and the Volstead Act. He was both a close friend of Calvin Coolidge and one of the president's closest advisors. Gillett retired from public life in 1931 and authored a biography of George Frisbie Hoar published in 1934. He died in Springfield, Massachusetts, on July 31, 1935.

MANUSCRIPT COLLECTIONS

Harvard University, Houghton Library, Cambridge, Mass.
  Frederick H. Gillett Papers.
  8 items.
Massachusetts Historical Society, Boston, Mass.

Frederick H. Gillett Papers, 1896–1935.
6 letters.

Gillett burned virtually all his papers. The Ohio Historical Society in Columbus, Ohio, however, does have over forty-five Gillett letters in the Warren G. Harding Papers.

BOOKS, ARTICLES, AND DISSERTATIONS

WORKS BY FREDERICK H. GILLETT

See also U.S. Congress, House (40-50). The following works by Gillett are listed chronologically by year of publication and alphabetically thereunder.

*41-1. GILLETT, FREDERICK H. *Civil Service in the Census Bureau.* Washington, D.C., 1902. 4 p. House speech of January 10, 1902.

41-2. ———. "Develop Navigation and Power on the Connecticut River." *Western New England* 2 (November 1912): 317-23.
  Gillett encourages commercial development of the river.

*41-3. ———. *The Democratic Administration and the Merit System.* Washington, D.C., 1913. 13 p. House speech of December 16, 1913.

41-4. ———. "Does U. S. Navy Need Fifteen Cruisers?" *Congressional Digest* 8 (January 1929): 16-17.
  An argument in favor of appropriations for sixteen new cruisers.

41-5. ———. "Herbert Putnam." In *Essays Offered to Herbert Putnam by His Colleagues and Friends on His Thirtieth Anniversary as Librarian of Congress,* edited by William Warner Bishop and Andrew Keogh, p. 4. New Haven: Yale University Press, 1929.

Gillett's brief remarks congratulate Putnam for making the Library of Congress a national institution.

41-6. ———. *The United States and the World Court*. New York: American Foundation, 1930. 18 p.

An argument in favor of the World Court.

41-7. ———. *George Frisbie Hoar*. Boston: Houghton Mifflin, 1934. 311 p.

A well-written biography of a nineteenth-century congressman and senator from Massachusetts.

41-8. REPUBLICAN PARTY. NATIONAL CONVENTION. CHICAGO, 1920. *Official Report of the Proceedings of the Seventeenth Republican National Convention*. New York: Tenny Press, 1920. 292 p.

Includes Gillett's address nominating Coolidge for president.

BIOGRAPHICAL SKETCHES AND EULOGIES

41-9. "The Classes: 1874." *Amherst Graduates' Quarterly* 25 (November 1935): 44–45.

Includes a brief but informative sketch of Gillett.

41-10. "Death of Senator Gillett." *Amherst Graduates' Quarterly* 24 (August 1935): 384.

Notes Gillett's death from leukemia on July 31, 1935.

41-11. "Obituaries." *Harvard Alumni Bulletin*, 27 September 1935, p. 24.

41-12. *Representative Men of Massachusetts, 1890–1900*. Everett, Mass.: Massachusetts Publishing, 1898. 491 p.

41-13. RUSSELL, HENRY B. "Frederick H. Gillett: American Statesman." *Amherst Graduates' Quarterly* 21 (November 1931): 3–17.

A superficial outline of Gillett's career.

GILLETT AND MASSACHUSETTS HISTORY
AND POLITICS

41-14. ABRAMS, RICHARD M. *Conservatism in a Progressive Era: Massachusetts Politics, 1900–1912*. Cambridge, Mass.: Harvard University Press, 1964. 327 p.

41-15. HENNESSEY, MICHAEL E. *Four Decades of Massachusetts Politics, 1890–1935*. 1935. Reprint. Freeport, N.Y.: Books for Libraries Press, 1971. 562 p.

41-16. ———. *Twenty-five Years of Massachusetts Politics: From Russell to McCall, 1890–1915*. Boston: Practical Politics, 1917. 398 p.

41-17. HUTHMACHER, J. JOSEPH. *Massachusetts People and Politics, 1913–1933*. Cambridge, Mass.: Harvard University Press, 1959. 328 p.

41-18. JOHNSON, CLIFTON. *Hampden County, 1636–1936*. 3 vols. New York: American Historical Society, 1936.

41-19. LOCKWOOD, JOHN H., ET AL. *Western Massachusetts: A History, 1636–1925*. 4 vols. New York: Lewis Historical Publishing, 1926.

41-20. TOOMEY, DANIEL P., ED. *Massachusetts of Today*. Boston: Columbia Publishing, 1892. 619 p.

GILLETT'S POLITICAL ASSOCIATES

See also Cole (28-24), Griffin (35-92), Bullard (38-58), Longworth (38-72), Russell (38-82), and Timmons (43-18).

41-21. ASHBY, LEROY. *The Spearless Leader: Senator Borah and the Progressive Movement in the 1920s*. Urbana: University of Illinois Press, 1972. 325 p.

41-22. DOWNES, RANDOLPH C. *The Rise of Warren Gamaliel Harding, 1865–1920*. Columbus: Ohio State University Press, 1970. 734 p.

41-23. FUESS, CLAUDE M. *Calvin Coolidge: The Man from Vermont*. 1940. Reprint. Westport, Conn.: Greenwood Press, 1966. 522 p.

41-24. HOOVER, HERBERT C. *The Memoirs of Herbert Hoover: The Cabinet and the Presidency, 1920–1933*. 3 vols. New York: Macmillan, 1952.

41-25. McCOY, DONALD R. *Calvin Coolidge: The Quiet President*. New York: Macmillan, 1967. 472 p.

41-26. MURRAY, ROBERT K. *The Harding Era: Warren G. Harding and His Administration*. Minneapolis: University of Minnesota Press, 1969. 626 p.

41-27. NETHERS, JOHN L. *Simeon D. Fess: Educator and Politician.* Brooklyn: Pageant-Poseidon, 1973. 427 p.

41-28. WAYMAN, DOROTHY GODFREY. *David I. Walsh: Citizen-Patriot.* Milwaukee: Bruce Publishing, 1952. 366 p.

41-29. WHITE, WILLIAM ALLEN. *A Puritan in Babylon: The Story of Calvin Coolidge.* 1938. Reprint. Gloucester, Mass.: Peter Smith, 1973. 460 p.

GILLETT AND THE SPEAKERSHIP

41-30. [GILBERT, CLINTON W.]. *Behind the Mirrors: The Psychology of Disintegration at Washington.* New York: G. P. Putnam's Sons, 1922. 236 p.

41-31. KEYES, FRANCES PARKINSON. *Capital Kaleidoscope: The Story of a Washington Hostess.* New York: Harper and Brothers, 1937. 358 p.

41-32. MURRAY, ROBERT K. *The Politics of Normalcy: Governmental Theory and Practice in the Harding Coolidge Era.* New York: W.W. Norton, 1973. 162 p.

41-33. "The New Speaker." *Outlook,* 11 March 1925, p. 357.

41-34. PALMER, FREDERICK. "Congress Improves, Says Gillett." *Collier's,* 14 June 1924, p. 14.

41-35. "The Progress of the World: The New Congress at Work." *American Review of Reviews* 69 (January 1924): 15.

41-36. ZIEGER, ROBERT H. *Republicans and Labor, 1919–1929.* Lexington: University of Kentucky Press, 1969. 303 p.

GILLETT AND FOREIGN POLICY

41-37. FLEMING, DENNA FRANK. *The Treaty Veto of the American Senate.* 1930. Reprint. New York: Garland Publishing, 1971. 325 p.

41-38. ————. *The United States and the League of Nations, 1918–1920.* 1932. Reprint. New York: Russell and Russell, 1968. 593 p.

41-39. ————. *The United States and the World Court.* 1945. Reprint. New York: Russell and Russell, 1968. 593 p.

41-40. ————. *The United States and World Organization, 1920–1933.* 1938. Reprint. New York: AMS Press, 1966. 569 p.

41-41. HUDSON, MANLEY O. *The World Court, 1921–1931.* Boston: World Peace Foundation, 1931. 245 p.

41-42. JESSUP, PHILIP C. *The United States and the World Court.* 1929. Reprint. New York: Garland Publishing, 1972. 365 p.

41-43. MICKEY, DAVID HOPWOOD. "Senatorial Participation in Shaping Certain United States Foreign Relation Policies, 1921–1941." Ph.D. dissertation, University of Nebraska, 1954. 737 p. 08526.

41-44. WHEELER-BENNETT, J. W. *Information on the World Court, 1918–1928.* London: George Allen and Unwin, 1929. 208 p.

42. Nicholas Longworth
(1869–1931)
(Speaker, Sixty-ninth through Seventy-first Congresses)

Nicholas Longworth was born into one of the most prominent families of Cincinnati's business and social elite on November 5, 1869. He graduated from Harvard University in 1891 and received his law degree from the Law School of Cincinnati College in 1894. Although his family was wealthy, which made it unnecessary for Longworth to actively pursue a legal career, he soon attracted attention for his achievements as a lawyer and a politician.

Longworth, who devoted much of his energy to the Republican party, was elected to the Cincinnati board of education in 1898. There he attracted the interest of Cincinnati's Republican boss, George B. Cox. As Cox's protégé, he was elected to the state house of representatives in 1899 and the state senate in 1901. Longworth was groomed for success at each step on the political ladder. He was elected to the Fifty-eighth Congress in 1902, and with one exception he was reelected to every Congress until his death in 1931.

Polished, refined, and a musician of some distinction, Longworth was a consummate social and political being, equally at home in smoke-filled back rooms and in elegant ballrooms. His marriage at the White House in 1906 to the president's daughter, Alice Lee Roosevelt, was one of the most memorable social events in the history of Washington, D.C. But the private poker games with Speaker Cannon and other House leaders were even more important for Longworth's career. At these late-night sessions Longworth was initiated into the workings of the House as run by Uncle Joe Cannon, and he also became an important cog in the House Republican leadership.

When his father-in-law, Theodore Roosevelt, broke with the regular Republican party in 1912, Longworth remained loyal to the party. Although he lost his seat in Congress for one term, his loyalty was later repaid. From 1923 to 1925 he served as Republican floor leader under Speaker Gillett. When Gillett moved on to the Senate in 1925, Longworth became Speaker, a post he held through the end of the Seventy-first Congress in 1931.

Speaker Longworth restored the speakership to a position of political leadership. He flatly stated his intention to take the majority party leadership with him to the Speaker's chair and to rule according to the Republican platform. Like Cannon, Longworth used informal behind-the-scenes meetings to keep the legislative process functioning. The Speaker was able to learn the mood of the House and to develop his own strategies through an informal institution known as the Board of Education. The board was made up of bipartisan leaders who met for drinks and conversation in a first-floor hideaway on the House side of the Capitol.

Longworth, ever the civilized gentleman, insisted that members of the House observe proper congressional etiquette and not indulge in personal attacks when referring to members of the Senate. He died on April 9, 1931, while on a visit to Aiken, South Carolina.

MANUSCRIPT COLLECTIONS

Library of Congress, Manuscript Division, Washington, D.C.
  Longworth Papers, 1782–1936.
  Ca. 3,000 items.
  Restricted.
  MC 92.
  Most of Longworth's papers were destroyed by his widow after his death. The Library of Congress collection comprises chiefly scrapbooks and speeches from 1915 to 1930. A number of Longworth letters exist in scattered collections at the Cincinnati Historical Society, Cincinnati, Ohio, and in the Theodore Roosevelt Papers and the William Howard Taft Papers in the Library of Congress Manuscript Division.

BOOKS, ARTICLES, AND DISSERTATIONS

WORKS BY NICHOLAS LONGWORTH

The following works are listed chronologically by year of publication.

42-1. LONGWORTH, NICHOLAS. "Bettering Our Diplomatic and Consular Service." *Independent*, 5 July 1906, pp. 19–23.

Longworth advocated improving the consular service.

42-2. ———. "The Democratic Tariff." *Outlook,* 31 May 1913, pp. 248–51.

An attack upon the Underwood tariff.

42-3. ———. "American Tariff Policies Adapted to the Present Economic Situation in Relation to Foreign Trade." *Proceedings of the Academy of Political Science* 9 (February 1921): 82–88.

42-4. ———. "Why a Republican Congress." *Forum* 68 (November 1922): 977–82.

An article defending Harding's record and assailing the Democratic Congress.

42-5. ———. "A Close-up on Congress." *World Review,* 6 December 1926, p. 163.

An examination of the nature of the House of Representatives.

BIOGRAPHY, BIOGRAPHICAL SKETCHES, AND EULOGIES

42-6. CHAMBRUN, CLARA LONGWORTH DE. *The Making of Nicholas Longworth: Annals of an American Family.* 1933. Reprint. Freeport, N.Y.: Books for Libraries Press, 1971. 322 p.

Written by his sister, this is the only attempt at a full-length biography of Longworth.

42-7. "Death of Speaker Longworth." *Current History* 34 (May 1931): 274.

42-8. MENCKEN, H. L. "One Who Will Be Missed." *American Mercury* 24 (September 1931): 35–36.

Praises Longworth for possessing a realism seldom found in politics.

42-9. "Nicholas Longworth." *Nation,* 22 April 1931, p. 441.

42-10. "Obituaries." *Harvard Alumni Bulletin,* 23 April 1931, p. 892.

42-11. *Ohio's Progressive Sons.* Cincinnati: Queen City Publishing, 1905. 843 p.

Includes a very brief sketch of Longworth.

42-12. SHAW, ALBERT. "The Progress of the World: The Late Nicholas Longworth." *Review of Reviews* 83 (May 1931): 23–24.

42-13. STIMSON, GEORGE P. "The Speaker—and the Longworths." In *The Law in Southwestern Ohio,* pp. 154–64. Cincinnati: Cincinnati Bar Association, 1972.

42-14. U.S. CONGRESS. HOUSE. *Memorial Services Held in the House of Representatives of the United States, Together with Remarks Presented in Eulogy of Nicholas Longworth.* 72d Cong., 1st sess., 1931–32. Washington, D.C.: Government Printing Office, 1932. 103 p.

A collection of brief eulogies by Longworth's congressional colleagues.

LONGWORTH AND OHIO HISTORY AND POLITICS

42-15. ANDERSON, ELAINE S. "The Ohio Election of 1910: Harding and the Republicans." *Northwest Ohio Quarterly* 38 (Winter 1966): 15–35.

42-16. CHAMBRUN, CLARA LONGWORTH DE. *Cincinnati: Story of the Queen City.* New York: Charles Scribner's Sons, 1939. 342 p.

42-17. EVANS, NELSON W. *A History of Taxation in Ohio.* Cincinnati: Robert Clarke, 1906. 220 p.

42-18. FESS, SIMEON D. *Ohio: A Four Volume Reference Library.* 4 vols. Chicago: Lewis Publishing, 1937.

42-19. TURNER, GEORGE KIBBE. "The Thing above the Law: The Rise and Rule of George B. Cox, and His Overthrow by Young Hunt and the Fighting Idealists of Cincinnati." *McClure's* 38 (March 1912): 575–91.

LONGWORTH'S POLITICAL ASSOCIATES

See also Cole (28-24), Crissey (35-87), Roosevelt (35-110), Lowitt (38-73), Norris (38-77), Manners (38-139), Warren (39-8), Butt (40-70), Fisher (43-15), Timmons (43-18), and Martin (48-15).

42-20. ADAMS, SAMUEL HOPKINS. *Incredible Era: The Life and Times of Warren Gamaliel Harding.* 1939. Reprint. New York: Octagon Books, 1979. 456 p.

42-21. CASSINI, COUNTESS MARGUERITE. *Never a Dull Moment: The Memoirs of Countess Marguerite*

Cassini. New York: Harper and Brothers, 1956. 366 p.

42-22. FURMAN, BESS. *Washington By-Line: The Personal History of a Newspaperwoman.* New York: Alfred A. Knopf, 1949. 348 p.

42-23. GERSON, NOEL B. *T.R.* Garden City, N.Y.: Doubleday, 1970. 441 p.

LONGWORTH AND THE SPEAKERSHIP

See also King (39-3).

42-24. A.F.C. "Backstage in Washington." *Outlook and Independent,* 14 May 1930, p. 60.

42-25. ———. "Backstage in Washington." *Outlook and Independent,* 22 April 1931, pp. 555–56.

42-26. BERDAHL, CLARENCE A. "Some Notes on Party Membership in Congress, II." *American Political Science Review* 43 (June 1949): 492–508.

42-27. BLYTHE, SAMUEL G. "Two Years Is a Long Time." *Saturday Evening Post,* 8 January 1927, p. 14.

42-28. CALHOUN, LUCY MERIWETHER. "Introducing the New Speaker." *World Review,* 14 December 1925, p. 177.

42-29. The Gentleman at the Keyhole. "Nicked!" *Collier's,* 7 December 1929, p. 44.

42-30. ———. "A Stranger in His Own Home Town." *Collier's,* 8 October 1927, p. 30.

42-31. GILFOND, DUFF. "Mr. Speaker." *American Mercury* 11 (August 1927): 451–58.

42-32. HARD, WILLIAM. "Leadership in the House." *Review of Reviews* 74 (August 1926): 159–64.

42-33. ———. "Nicholas Longworth." *Nation,* 23 January 1924, pp. 88–89.

42-34. ———. "Nicholas Longworth." *Review of Reviews* 71 (April 1925): 370–73.

42-35. KENKEL, JOSEPH FREDERICK. "The Tariff Commission Movement: The Search for a Nonpartisan Solution of the Tariff Question." Ph.D. dissertation, University of Maryland, 1962. 137 p. 63-00778.

42-36. MCARTHUR, LUCILE. "Idle Moments of a Lady in Waiting." *Saturday Evening Post,* 19 September 1931, p. 3.
   An anecdotal account of life in the Speaker's office by his secretary.

42-37. "Nicholas Longworth: A Contradictory Floor Leader of Congress." *Current Opinion* 76 (April 1924): 414–16.

42-38. NOGGLE, BURL. *Teapot Dome: Oil and Politics in the 1920s.* 1962. Reprint. Westport, Conn.: Greenwood Press, 1980. 234 p.

42-39. PAGE, WILLIAM TYLER. "Mr. Speaker Longworth." *Scribner's* 83 (March 1928): 272–80.

42-40. "The Speaker of the House." *Review of Reviews* 77 (March 1928): 320–21.

42-41. WILLS, HENRY TARLETON. *Scientific Tariff Making: A History of the Movement to Create a Tariff Commission.* New York: Blanchard Press, 1913. 332 p.

42-42. "You Can't Help Liking Nick." *Literary Digest,* 21 November 1925, pp. 44–48.

THE LONGWORTHS AND WASHINGTON SOCIETY

See especially the reminiscences of Alice Roosevelt Longworth (38-72). *See also* Slayden (40-86) and Keyes (41-31).

42-43. ALLEN, ROBERT S., AND PEARSON, DREW. *Washington Merry-Go-Round.* New York: Horace Liveright, 1931. 366 p.

42-44. BARRYMORE, ETHEL. *Memories: An Autobiography.* New York: Harper and Brothers, 1955. 310 p.

42-45. DANIELS, JONATHAN. *Washington Quadrille: The Dance beside the Documents.* Garden City, N.Y.: Doubleday, 1968. 370 p.

42-46. HAGEDORN, HERMANN. *The Roosevelt Family of Sagamore Hill.* New York: Macmillan, 1954. 435 p.

42-47. HOWARD, ELEANOR VINCENT. "This Week's Wedding at the White House." *Harper's Weekly,* 17 February 1906, pp. 222–27.

42-48. HURD, CHARLES W. *Washington Cavalcade.* New York: E. P. Dutton, 1948. 320 p.

42-49. "The Progress of the World: A Wedding at the White House." *Review of Reviews* 33 (March 1906): 261.

42-50. ROOSEVELT, ELEANOR BUTLER. *Day before*

Yesterday: The Reminiscences of Mrs. Theodore Roosevelt, Jr. Garden City, N.Y.: Doubleday, 1959. 478 p.

42-51. TEICHMANN, HOWARD. *Alice: The Life and Times of Alice Roosevelt Longworth.* Englewood Cliffs, N.J.: Prentice-Hall, 1979. 286 p.

43. John Nance Garner
(1868–1967)
(Speaker, Seventy-second Congress)

John Nance Garner was the second Speaker to become vice-president of the United States. Born in Red River County, Texas, on November 22, 1868, he was the fourth member of the family line (which traced its heritage back to Virginia) to bear the name John Nance. Garner enrolled at Vanderbilt University in Nashville, Tennessee, at the age of eighteen but withdrew after one term because of poor health. He returned to Clarksville, Texas, to study law and gained admittance to the bar in 1890. In 1892 he moved to Uvalde with the hope that the climate would cure his tuberculosis.

Garner's legal practice in Uvalde flourished, enabling him to gain control of two local banks. From 1898 to 1902 he served two terms in the Texas assembly, where his bill to divide Texas into five states passed only to be vetoed by the governor. As chairman of the redistricting committee, he designed the district that sent him to Congress in 1903. The Fifteenth District, which Garner represented continuously until 1933, was larger than the states of New Hampshire, Vermont, Massachusetts, Rhode Island, and Delaware combined.

Although he was a Democrat, Garner won the confidence and respect of Republican Speaker Joseph Cannon. Garner, who reportedly won much of his personal fortune at the poker table, became one of Cannon's card-playing cronies. Yet when the House revolted

against Cannon's control, Garner actively supported the measures to strip the Speaker of much of his power. As a Democratic leader in the House, he introduced both the principle of a graduated income tax and the inheritance features of the income tax law. He also supported the Eighteenth Amendment, which prohibited the manufacture, sale, or transportation of intoxicating liquors.

Garner owed much of his popularity to his homespun personality and behind-the-scenes contacts. Garner and Speaker Longworth established a Board of Education. Meeting in a Capitol hideaway for drinks, or as Garner put it, "striking a blow for liberty," board members would discuss legislation and take the pulse of the House. Garner became minority leader of the House in 1928 and succeeded Longworth as Speaker when the Democrats won control of the Seventy-second Congress in 1931. Garner continued the Board of Education and imparted his political savvy to John McCormack, Fred Vinson, and, most especially, his fellow Texan Sam Rayburn.

During his only term as Speaker of the House, Garner unsuccessfully championed a national sales tax. In 1932 he received more than ninety votes on each of the first three ballots for the Democratic presidential nomination. Garner then released his supporters to Franklin Delano Roosevelt and was rewarded with the vice-presidential nomination. He served as vice-president during FDR's first two terms (1933–41) but became increasingly opposed to the president's actions, especially the court-packing scheme. Garner finally broke with Roosevelt in 1940 over the president's decision to seek a third term. His bid to block FDR's renomination by offering himself as a candidate failed, and Garner retired from public office.

In 1941 Garner returned to Uvalde, where he spent his last twenty-six years as an elder statesman of the Democratic party. Widely known as Cactus Jack, he had been a colorful figure in American politics for thirty-eight years. United Mine Workers president John L. Lewis had once called him "a whiskey-drinking, cigar-smoking, poker-playing, evil old man." Lewis was at least partially correct. Garner died on November 7, 1967, just fifteen days short of his ninety-ninth birthday.

MANUSCRIPT COLLECTIONS

University of Texas, Eugene Barker History Center, Austin, Tex.

John Nance Garner Biographical File.

Garner burned his private papers shortly before his death, saving only a collection of newspaper clippings and cartoons now held at the University of Texas. Researchers therefore will have to examine the manuscript collections of his colleagues for correspondence from Garner.

BOOKS, ARTICLES, AND DISSERTATIONS

WORKS BY JOHN N. GARNER

43-1. FENLEY, FLORENCE. *Old Timers: Their Own Stories*. Uvalde, Tex.: Hornby Press, 1939. 254 p.

Includes a brief "tribute" by Garner.

The following items are arranged chronologically by year of publication and alphabetically thereunder.

43-2. GARNER, JOHN NANCE. *Memoranda upon Amendments to Indian Depredations Act Relative to Citizenship*. Washington, D.C.: Government Printing Office, 1911. 5 p.

43-3. ———. "Should a Graduated Tax Be Applied to Corporations?" *Congressional Digest* 7 (January 1928): 22.

Garner argues for a graduated tax to assist small businesses.

43-4. ———. "Should Quota Law Be Applied to Mexico?" *Congressional Digest* 7 (May 1928): 155–58.

Garner argues against the quota system.

43-5. ———. " 'A Regular Pepper Pot' is Texas Jack Garner." *Literary Digest,* 12 December 1931, p. 28.

A reflection on the changes in dress and personal appearance during his twenty-eight years in Congress.

43-6. ———. "Garner Speaks." *Democratic Bulletin* 7 (November 1932): 33.

Excerpts from Garner's campaign speeches.

43-7. ———. "Letter of Acceptance, Aug. 23, 1932." *Congressional Digest* 11 (August/September 1932): 224.

Garner's letter of acceptance of the vice-presidential nomination.

43-8. ———. "Jack Garner Says—." *Democratic Bulletin* 8 (March 1933): 17.

A note on being elected vice-president and a brief political autobiography.

43-9. ———. "This Job of Mine." *American Magazine* 118 (July 1934): 23.

Garner describes the vice-presidency as "the spare tire on the national automobile."

43-10. ———. "Democratic Leaders Discuss the Campaign Issues." *Congressional Digest* 15 (August/September 1936): 209.

Extracts from Garner's renomination acceptance speech.

43-11. ———. "Advice from an Elder Statesman: 'Cut Down on Spending.' " *U.S. News and
World Report,* 8 March 1957, pp. 60–73.

An in-depth interview with Garner.

43-12. ———. "John Garner at 90 Tells an
Inside Story." *U.S. News and World Report,* 21
November 1958, pp. 98–105.

Garner speaks out on the court-packing scheme
and his split with FDR.

43-13. ———. "Garner: 'He Couldn't Be
Elected without Our Lyndon.' " *U.S. News and
World Report,* 16 January 1967, pp. 44–45.

Garner urged Lyndon Johnson to accept the
vice-presidential nomination on the Kennedy
ticket.

BIOGRAPHIES, BIOGRAPHICAL SKETCHES, AND EULOGIES

Biographies

43-14. BROWN, GEORGE ROTHWELL. *The Speaker of
the House: The Romantic Story of John N. Garner.*
New York: Brewer, Warren, and Putnam, 1932.
162 p.

An anecdotal biography written for the Garner
campaign for the 1932 presidential nomination.

43-15. FISHER, OVIE CLARK. *Cactus Jack.* Waco,
Tex.: Texian Press, 1978. 200 p.

An admiring biography based upon extensive
local sources.

43-16. JAMES, MARQUIS. *Mr. Garner of Texas.* Indianapolis: Bobbs-Merrill, 1939. 158 p.

A brief, informal biography.

43-17. ROMANO, MICHAEL JOHN. "The Emergence of John Nance Garner as a Figure in American National Politics, 1924–1941." Ph.D. dissertation, St. John's University, 1974. 370 p.
74–14661.

With particular focus on Garner's political
career, Romano characterizes him as an inef-
fective leader.

43-18. TIMMONS, BASCOM N. *Garner of Texas: A
Personal History.* New York: Harper and Brothers,
1948. 294 p.

An important and comprehensive biography
that lacks, however, an index and bibliography.

Biographical Sketches

See also Moley (39-20).

43-19. COOKE, ALISTAIR. *Talk about America.* New
York: Alfred A. Knopf, 1968. 310 p.

43-20. MICHIE, ALLAN A., AND RYLICK, FRANK.
Dixie Demagogues. New York: Vanguard Press,
1939. 298 p.

Includes a negative assessment of Garner.

43-21. TEXAS MEMORIAL MUSEUM, AUSTIN. *John
Nance Garner Cartoons: Commemorating the Ninetieth
Birthday of the Former Speaker of the House of Represen-
tatives and Vice-President of the United States.* Austin:
Texas Memorial Museum, 1958. 207 p.

Includes a brief biographical sketch by Bascom
Timmons.

43-22. U.S. CONGRESS. HOUSE. *Unveiling of the
Bust of the Honorable John Nance Garner.* 78th Cong.,
1st sess, 1943. Washington, D.C.: Government
Printing Office, 1943. 9 p.

Includes brief addresses by Sam Rayburn and
Tom Connally.

43-23. WELCH, JUNE R. *The Texas Senator.* Dallas,
Tex.: G.L.A. Press, 1978. 179 p.

Includes a short biographical profile, "John
Garner Became Vice-President."

Eulogies

43-24. "Chairman of the Board." *Time,* 17
November 1967, p. 32.

43-25. "One of the Last of the Frontier Politicians." *U.S. News and World Report,* 20 November
1967, p. 18.

GARNER AND TEXAS HISTORY AND POLITICS

43-26. ADAMS, FRANK CARTER. *Texas Democracy: A
Centennial History of Politics and Personalities of the
Democratic Party, 1836–1936.* 4 vols. Austin: Dem-
ocratic Historical Association, 1937.

43-27. BARR, ALWYN. *Reconstruction to Reform:
Texas Politics, 1876–1906.* Austin: University of
Texas Press, 1971. 315 p.

43-28. BOSWORTH, ALLAN R. *Ozona Country*. New York: Harper and Row, 1964. 238 p.

43-29. FEHRENBACH, T. R. *Lone Star: A History of Texas and the Texans*. New York: Macmillan, 1968. 751 p.

43-30. GOULD, LEWIS L. *Progressives and Prohibitionists: Texas Democrats in the Wilson Era*. Austin: University of Texas Press, 1973. 339 p.

43-31. GRANTHAM, DEWEY W., JR. "Texas Congressional Leaders and the New Freedom, 1913–1917." *Southwestern Historical Quarterly* 53 (July 1949): 35–48.

43-32. GREEN, GEORGE NORRIS. *The Establishment in Texas Politics: The Primitive Years, 1938–1957*. Westport, Conn.: Greenwood Press, 1979. 306 p.

43-33. MCKAY, SETH SHEPARD. *Seven Decades of the Texas Constitution of 1876*. Lubbock, Tex., 1942. 245 p.

43-34. ———. *Texas Politics, 1906–1944*. Lubbock: Texas Tech Press, 1952. 486 p.

43-35. MUNZ, CHARLES C. "This Is America: The Garner Country." *Nation*, 15 July 1939, pp. 66–69.

43-36. NIELSEN, IDA L., AND GRAY, LEONA STEWART. *From Barracks to Bricks*. Uvalde, Tex.: Southwest Texas Junior College, 1972. 127 p.

43-37. *A Proud Heritage: A History of Uvalde County, Texas, Written by the People of Uvalde County*. Uvalde, Tex.: El Progresso Club, 1975. 496 p.

43-38. SUTTON, WALTER A. "Texas Congressmen and the Mexican Revolution of 1910." *Journal of the West* 13 (October 1974): 90–107.

43-39. WINKLER, ERNEST W. *Platforms of Political Parties in Texas*. Austin: University of Texas Press, 1916. 700 p.

GARNER'S POLITICAL ASSOCIATES

See also Cole (28-24), Roper and Lovette (28-38), Jones (40-80), Mullen (40-84), Arnett (40-134), Furman (42-22), Teichmann (42-51), Waller (44-22 and 44-65), Heacock (46-10), Rayburn (47-11), Allen (47-23), Dorough (47-26), and Steinberg (47-28).

43-40. ADAMS, HENRY H. *Harry Hopkins*. New York: G. P. Putnam's Sons, 1977. 448 p.

43-41. ARNETT, ALEX M. "Garner versus Kitchin: A Study of Craft and Statecraft." In *The Walter Clinton Jackson Essays in the Social Sciences*, edited by Vera Largent, pp. 133–45. Chapel Hill: University of North Carolina Press, 1942.

43-42. BARKLEY, ALBEN W. *That Reminds Me*. Garden City, N.Y.: Doubleday, 1954. 288 p.

43-43. BERLE, ADOLF A. *Navigating the Rapids, 1918–1971: From the Papers of Adolf A. Berle*. Edited by Beatrice Bishop Berle and Travis Beal Jacobs. New York: Harcourt Brace Jovanovich, 1973. 859 p.

43-44. BLAKE, ISRAEL GEORGE. *Paul V. McNutt: Portrait* Central Publishing, 1966. 399 p.

43-45. BLUM, JOHN MORTON. *From the Morgenthau Diaries: Years of Crisis, 1928–1938*. Vol. 1. Boston: Houghton Mifflin, 1959. 583 p.

43-46. BOWERS, CLAUDE G. *My Life: The Memoirs of Claude Bowers*. New York: Simon and Schuster, 1962. 346 p.

43-47. BYRNES, JAMES F. *All in One Lifetime*. New York: Harper and Brothers, 1958. 432 p.

43-48. CARLISLE, RODNEY PARKER. "The Political Ideas and Influence of William Randolph Hearst, 1928–1936." Ph.D. dissertation, University of California, Berkeley, 1965. 208 p. 65-13459.

43-49. CATLEDGE, TURNER. *My Life and the Times*. New York: Harper and Row, 1971. 319 p.

43-50. CONNALLY, THOMAS T., AND STEINBERG, ALFRED. *My Name Is Tom Connally*. New York: Thomas Y. Crowell, 1954. 376 p.

43-51. COTNER, ROBERT C. *James Stephen Hogg: A Biography*. Austin: University of Texas Press, 1959. 617 p.

43-52. DAVIS, POLLY ANN. *Alben W. Barkley: Senate Majority Leader and Vice-President*. New York: Garland Publishing, 1979. 343 p.

43-53. DINNEEN, JOSEPH F. *The Purple Shamrock: The Hon. James Michael Curley of Boston*. New York: W. W. Norton, 1949. 331 p.

43-54. FARLEY, JAMES A. *Behind the Ballots: The Personal History of a Politician.* 1938. Reprint. New York: Da Capo Press, 1973. 392 p.

43-55. ———. *Jim Farley's Story: The Roosevelt Years.* New York: McGraw-Hill, 1948. 388 p.

43-56. HEARST, WILLIAM RANDOLPH. *William Randolph Hearst: A Portrait in His Own Words.* Edited by Edmund D. Coblentz. New York: Simon and Schuster, 1952. 309 p.

43-57. HELM, WILLIAM P. *Harry Truman: A Political Biography.* New York: Duell, Sloan, and Pearce, 1947. 241 p.

43-58. HENDERSON, RICHARD B. *Maury Maverick: A Political Biography.* Austin: University of Texas Press, 1970. 386 p.

43-59. HINTON, HAROLD B. *Cordell Hull: A Biography.* Garden City, N.Y.: Doubleday, Doran, 1942. 377 p.

43-60. HORNBY, HARRY P. *Going Around.* Uvalde, Tex.: Hornby Press, 1945. 158 p.

43-61. ICKES, HAROLD L. *The Secret Diary of Harold L. Ickes.* 3 vols. New York: Simon and Schuster, 1953–54.

43-62. KOSKOFF, DAVID E. *The Mellons: The Chronicle of America's Richest Family.* New York: Thomas Y. Crowell, 1978. 602 p.

43-63. KROCK, ARTHUR. *Memoirs: Sixty Years on the Firing Line.* New York: Funk and Wagnalls, 1968. 508 p.

43-64. LUNDBERG, FERDINAND. *Imperial Hearst: A Social Biography.* 1936. Reprint. New York: Arno Press, 1970. 406 p.

43-65. O'CONNOR, HARVEY. *Mellon's Millions: The Biography of a Fortune.* New York: John Day, 1933. 443 p.

43-66. ROGERS, WILL. *The Autobiography of Will Rogers.* Edited by Donald Day. Boston: Houghton Mifflin, 1949. 410 p.

43-67. SMYRL, FRANK H. "Tom Connally and the New Deal." Ph.D. dissertation, University of Oklahoma, 1968. 254 p. 68-17599.

43-68. STEINBERG, ALFRED. *The Man from Missouri: The Life and Times of Harry S. Truman.* New York: G. P. Putnam's Sons, 1962. 447 p.

43-69. STOKES, THOMAS L. *Chip Off My Shoulder.* Princeton: Princeton University Press, 1940. 561 p.

43-70. STORKE, THOMAS M. *California Editor.* Los Angeles: Westernlore Press, 1958. 489 p.

43-71. SWAIN, MARTHA H. *Pat Harrison: The New Deal Years.* Jackson: University Press of Mississippi, 1978. 316 p.

43-72. SWANBERG, W. A. *Citizen Hearst: A Biography of William Randolph Hearst.* New York: Charles Scribner's Sons, 1961. 555 p.

43-73. TIMMONS, BASCOM N. *Jesse H. Jones: The Man and the Statesman.* 1956. Reprint. Westport, Conn.: Greenwood Press, 1975. 414 p.

43-74. TOMPKINS, C. DAVID. *Senator Arthur H. Vandenberg: The Evolution of a Modern Republican, 1884–1945.* Lansing: Michigan State University Press, 1970. 312 p.

43-75. TRUMAN, MARGARET. *Harry S. Truman.* New York: William Morrow, 1973. 602 p.

43-76. WALLACE, HENRY A. *The Price of Vision: The Diary of Henry A. Wallace, 1942–1946.* Edited by John Morton Blum. Boston: Houghton Mifflin, 1973. 707 p.

43-77. WHALEN, RICHARD J. *The Founding Father: The Story of Joseph P. Kennedy.* New York: New American Library, 1964. 541 p.

43-78. WHEELER, BURTON K. *Yankee from the West.* 1962. Reprint. New York: Octagon Books, 1977. 436 p.

43-79. WILLIAMS, T. HARRY. *Huey Long.* 1969. Reprint. New York: Vintage Books, 1981. 884 p.

GARNER'S CONGRESSIONAL CAREER AND SPEAKERSHIP

General

See also King (39-3) and Allen and Pearson (42-43).

43-80. BURNER, DAVID. *The Politics of Provincialism: The Democratic Party in Transition, 1918-1932.* New York: Alfred A. Knopf, 1968. 293 p.

43-81. GARNER, MRS. JOHN N. [MARIETTA]. "30 Years of Dictation." *Good Housekeeping* 94 (May 1932): 28.

43-82. The Gentleman at the Keyhole. "Rough and Tumble." *Collier's,* 20 August 1927, p. 29.

43-83. HARD, WILLIAM. "Leadership in the House." *Review of Reviews* 74 (August 1926): 159-64.

43-84. TUCKER, RAY T. "Tiger from Texas." *Outlook and Independent,* 26 November 1930, p. 492.

Garner and Tax Legislation

43-85. "The Attempt to Tax the Rich." *Outlook,* 5 March 1924, pp. 375-76.

43-86. "Danger of a Tax Deadlock." *Literary Digest,* 19 January 1924, pp. 8-9.

43-87. "The Hullabaloo over the Democratic Tax Plan." *Literary Digest,* 21 January 1933, pp. 3-5.

43-88. LAWRENCE, DAVID. "Your Money." *Saturday Evening Post,* 8 March 1924, p. 6.

43-89. "An Opposition Tax Bill Too." *Review of Reviews* 69 (February 1924): 132.

43-90. PAUL, RANDOLPH E. *Taxation in the United States.* Boston: Little, Brown, 1954. 830 p.

43-91. RATNER, SIDNEY. *American Taxation: Its History as a Social Force in Democracy.* New York: W. W. Norton, 1942. 561 p.

43-92. SCHWARZ, JORDAN A. "John Nance Garner and the Sales Tax Rebellion of 1932." *Journal of Southern History* 30 (May 1964): 162-80.

43-93. "Will the Garner Bill Endure a Roll Call?" *Outlook,* 5 March 1924, p. 376.

Garner and the Speakership

43-94. BILLINGS, CHARLES ALBERT. "The Utopian of Uvalde." *North American Review* 234 (October 1932): 321-26.

43-95. The Gentleman at the Keyhole. "Jack's Place." *Collier's,* 20 June 1931, p. 48.

43-96. GILBERT, CLINTON W. "John N. Garner." *Forum* 87 (May 1932): 312-17.

43-97. HERRING, E. PENDLETON. "American Government and Politics: First Session of the Seventy-second Congress." *American Political Science Review* 26 (October 1932): 846-74.

43-98. ———. "American Government and Politics: First Session of the Seventy-third Congress." *American Political Science Review* 28 (February 1934): 65-83.

43-99. LIPPMANN, WALTER. *Interpretations, 1931-1932.* Edited by Allan Nevins. New York: Macmillan, 1932. 361 p.

43-100. PRINGLE, HENRY F. "Democracy Back in Power." *Outlook and Independent,* 23 December 1931, p. 523.

43-101. ROBINSON, N. T. N. "Steps Taken to Organize the 72nd Congress." *Congressional Digest* 11 (January 1932): 1-5.

43-102. SCHRIFTGIESSER, KARL. *This Was Normalcy: An Account of Party Politics during Twelve Republican Years, 1920-1930.* 1948. Reprint. New York: Oriole Editions, 1973. 325 p.

43-103. "The Seventy-second Congress Convenes in Final Session." *Congressional Digest* 11 (December 1932): 316-17.

43-104. STEINER, GILBERT Y. *The Congressional Conference Committee: Seventieth to Eightieth Congresses.* Urbana: University of Illinois Press, 1951. 185 p.

43-105. STROUT, RICHARD LEE [PSEUD. T.R.B.]. "Washington Notes." *New Republic,* 18 November 1931, pp. 17-18.

43-106. ———. "Washington Notes." *New Republic,* 13 January 1932, pp. 242-43.

43-107. WOOLF, S. J. "Garner Revives a Jacksonian Tradition." *New York Times Magazine,* 22 November 1931, p. 3.

Speaker Garner and the Hoover Administration

See also Warren (39-8), Schwarz (39-14), and Hoover (41-24).

43-108. BURNER, DAVID. *Herbert Hoover: A Public Life*. New York: Alfred A. Knopf, 1979. 433 p.

43-109. HINSHAW, DAVID. *Herbert Hoover: American Quaker*. New York: Farrar, Straus, 1950. 469 p.

43-110. JOSLIN, THEODORE G. *Hoover Off the Record*. Garden City, N.Y.: Doubleday, Doran, 1934. 367 p.

43-111. LEONARD, JONATHAN NORTON. *Three Years Down*. New York: Carrick and Evans, 1939. 320 p.

43-112. MYERS, WILLIAM S., AND NEWTON, WALTER H. *The Hoover Administration: A Documented Narrative*. 1936. Reprint. St. Clair Shores, Mich.: Scholarly Press, 1971. 553 p.

43-113. OLSON, JAMES STUART. *Herbert Hoover and the Reconstruction Finance Corporation, 1931–1933*. Ames: Iowa State University Press, 1977. 155 p.

43-114. SMITH, GENE. *The Shattered Dream: Herbert Hoover and the Great Depression*. New York: William Morrow, 1970. 278 p.

43-115. WILBUR, RAY LYMAN, AND HYDE, ARTHUR MASTICK. *The Hoover Policies*. 1937. Reprint. New York: Garland Publishing, 1979. 667 p.

43-116. WILSON, CAROL GREEN. *Herbert Hoover: A Challenge for Today*. New York: Evans Publishing, 1968. 338 p.

GARNER AND THE VICE-PRESIDENCY

See also Barzman (29-86), Curtis and Wells (29-87), Harwood (29-88), Manchester (39-4), Martin (39-5), Schlesinger (39-6), Patterson (39-12), Porter (39-13), Bloom (39-18), Moley (39-19), Mooney (47-27), and Shanks (47-114).

43-117. ALSOP, JOSEPH, AND KINTNER, ROBERT. *Men around the President*. New York: Doubleday, Doran, 1939. 212 p.

43-118. BABSON, ROGER W. *Washington and the Revolutionists: A Characterization of Recovery Policies and of the People Who Are Giving Them Effect*. 1934. Reprint. Freeport, N.Y.: Books for Libraries Press, 1970. 336 p.

43-119. BEARD, CHARLES A. *American Foreign Policy in the Making, 1932–1940: A Study in Responsibilities*. 1946. Reprint. Hamden, Conn.: Archon Books, 1968. 336 p.

43-120. BELL, JACK. *The Splendid Misery: The Story of the Presidency and Power Politics at Close Range*. Garden City, N.Y.: Doubleday, 1960. 474 p.

43-121. "A Blank Check for Roosevelt." *Newsweek*, 17 February 1933, p. 5.

43-122. BURNS, JAMES MACGREGOR. *Roosevelt: The Lion and the Fox*. New York: Harcourt, Brace, 1956. 553 p.

43-123. CARTER, JOHN FRANKLIN. *The New Dealers*. New York: Simon and Schuster, 1934. 414 p.

43-124. CREEL, GEORGE. "The Vanishing Brain Trust." *Collier's*, 13 April 1935, p. 12.

43-125. DISALLE, MICHAEL V., AND BLOCHMAN, LAWRENCE G. *Second Choice*. New York: Hawthorn Books, 1966. 253 p.

43-126. DIVINE, ROBERT A. *The Illusion of Neutrality*. Chicago: University of Chicago Press, 1962. 370 p.

43-127. ELLIS, EDWARD ROBB. *A Nation in Torment: The Great American Depression, 1929–1939*. New York: Coward-McCann, 1970. 576 p.

43-128. "Emperor Receives Garner." *Literary Digest*, 9 November 1935, p. 12.

43-129. FARR, FINIS. *FDR*. New Rochelle, N.Y.: Arlington House, 1972. 439 p.

43-130. FREIDEL, FRANK. *F.D.R. and the South*. Baton Rouge: Louisiana State University Press, 1965. 102 p.

43-131. ———. *Franklin D. Roosevelt*. 4 vols. Boston: Little, Brown, 1952–72.

43-132. "Garner: He'd Follow Roosevelt Even to a Political Hades." *Newsweek*, 29 December 1934, p. 16.

43-133. "The Garners in Washington." *Democratic Digest* 12 (May 1935): 5.

43-134. "Garner: Vice-President Once Cowboy, Is Astute Politician." *Newsweek,* 30 December 1933, pp. 14–15.

43-135. GILBERT, CLINTON W. "Contact Man." *Collier's,* 18 February 1933, p. 25.

43-136. GOSNELL, HAROLD F. *Champion Campaigner: Franklin D. Roosevelt.* New York: Macmillan, 1952. 235 p.

43-137. GUNTHER, JOHN. *Roosevelt in Retrospect: A Profile in History.* New York: Harper and Brothers, 1950. 410 p.

43-138. "He Can't Fish until Congress Adjourns: Capital Watches for Garner to Make Reservations for Home." *Literary Digest,* 3 August 1935, pp. 6–7.

43-139. HENRY, LAURIN L. *Presidential Transitions.* Washington, D.C.: Brookings Institution, 1960. 755 p.

43-140. HURD, CHARLES W. "As Vice-President, Garner Is Different." *New York Times Magazine,* 23 April 1933, p. 8.

43-141. IMLER, JOSEPH A. "The First One Hundred Days of the New Deal: The View from Capitol Hill." Ph.D. dissertation, Indiana University, 1975. 371 p. 76-11395.

43-142. JONES, JESSE H., AND ANGLY, EDWARD. *Fifty Billion Dollars: My Thirteen Years with the RFC, 1932–1945.* 1951. Reprint. New York: Da Capo Press, 1975. 631 p.

43-143. KENNEDY, SUSAN ESTABROOK. *The Banking Crisis of 1933.* Lexington: University Press of Kentucky, 1973. 270 p.

43-144. "Leadership in Congress." *Review of Reviews* 95 (January 1937): 47–50.

43-145. LEE, ANTHONY. "This Vice-President of Ours." *American Magazine* 118 (July 1934): 22.

43-146. LEUCHTENBERG, WILLIAM E. *Franklin D. Roosevelt and the New Deal, 1932–1940.* New York: Harper and Row, 1963. 393 p.

43-147. LIPPMANN, WALTER. *Interpretations, 1933–1935.* Edited by Allan Nevins. New York: Macmillan, 1936. 399 p.

43-148. MILBURN, GEORGE. "The Statesmanship of Mr. Garner." *Harper's Magazine* 165 (November 1932): 669–82.

43-149. MOLEY, RAYMOND. *After Seven Years.* 1939. Reprint. New York: Da Capo Press, 1972. 446 p.

43-150. RAUCH, BASIL. *Roosevelt from Munich to Pearl Harbor: A Study in the Creation of a Foreign Policy.* New York: Barnes and Noble, 1967. 527 p.

43-151. ROLLINS, ALFRED B., JR., ED. *Franklin D. Roosevelt and the Age of Action.* New York: Dell Publishing, 1960. 384 p.

43-152. ROOSEVELT, ELLIOT, AND ROOSEVELT, JAMES B. *An Untold Story: The Roosevelts of Hyde Park.* New York: G. P. Putnam's Sons, 1973. 318 p.

43-153. ROOSEVELT, FRANKLIN D. *Complete Presidential Press Conferences of Franklin D. Roosevelt.* 20 vols. New York: Da Capo Press, 1972.

43-154. ———. *F.D.R.: His Personal Letters.* Edited by Elliot Roosevelt. 4 vols. New York: Duell, Sloan, and Pearce, 1947–50.

43-155. ———. *The Public Papers and Addresses of Franklin D. Roosevelt.* Edited by Samuel I. Rosenman. 13 vols. New York: Random House, 1938–50.

43-156. ROOSEVELT, JAMES B. *My Parents: A Differing View.* Chicago: Playboy Press, 1976. 369 p.

43-157. ROSEN, ELLIOT A. *Hoover, Roosevelt, and the Brain Trust: From Depression to New Deal.* New York: Columbia University Press, 1977. 446 p.

43-158. SULLIVAN, LAWRENCE. *Prelude to Panic: The Story of the Bank Holiday.* Washington, D.C.: Statesman Press, 1936. 126 p.

43-159. "Texas Jack Back." *Time,* 7 October 1940, pp. 13–14.

43-160. TUGWELL, REXFORD G. *The Brain Trust.* New York: Viking Press, 1968. 538 p.

43-161. ———. *The Democratic Roosevelt: A Biography of Franklin D. Roosevelt.* Garden City, N.Y.: Doubleday, 1957. 712 p.

43-162. TULLY, GRACE. *F.D.R.: My Boss.* New York: Charles Scribner's Sons, 1949. 391 p.

43-163. YOUNG, DONALD. *American Roulette: The History and Dilemma of the Vice-Presidency.* New York: Holt, Rinehart, and Winston, 1972. 433 p.

The 1932 Democratic Convention and Presidential Campaign

See also Eaton (28-12).

43-164. ALLEN, ROBERT S. "Texas Jack." *New Republic,* 16 March 1932, pp. 119–21.

43-165. ANDERSON, PAUL Y. "Presidential Possibilities: Texas John Garner." *Nation,* 20 April 1932, pp. 465–67.

43-166. "Backstage in Washington." *Outlook* 160 (March 1932): 170.

43-167. " 'Cactus Jack' Garner's Boom." *Literary Digest,* 12 March 1932, p. 8.

43-168. CARLSON, EARLAND I. "Franklin D. Roosevelt's Fight for the Presidential Nomination, 1928–1932." Ph.D. dissertation, University of Illinois, 1955. 469 p. 00-15190.

43-169. DEMOCRATIC PARTY. NATIONAL COMMITTEE, 1932–36. *Campaign Book of the Democratic Party: Candidates and Issues, 1932.* New York: Democratic National Committee, 1932. 103 p.

43-170. DEMOCRATIC PARTY. NATIONAL CONVENTION. CHICAGO, 1932. *Official Report of the Proceedings of the Democratic National Convention Held at Chicago . . . 1932.* Washington, D.C., 1932. 637 p.

43-171. "Garner's Campaign Bomb." *Literary Digest,* 6 August 1932, p. 8.

43-172. The Gentleman at the Keyhole. "Capital Chatterbox." *Collier's,* 20 February 1932, p. 21.

43-173. ———. "Head of the House." *Collier's,* 9 January 1932, p. 19.

43-174. ———. "Plain Speaker." *Collier's,* 6 February 1932, p. 20.

43-175. GILBERT, CLINTON W. "The Roosevelt Convention." *Collier's,* 4 June 1932, p. 24.

43-176. "John Nance Garner: A Thumb Nail Sketch." *Democratic Bulletin* 7 (August 1932): 12–13.

43-177. MURPHY, WILLIAM C., JR. "The G.O.P. versus Garner." *Commonweal,* 14 September 1932, pp. 462–64.

43-178. OULAHAN, RICHARD. *The Man Who: The Story of the 1932 Democratic Convention.* New York: Dial Press, 1971. 147 p.

43-179. PATENAUDE, LIONEL V. "The Garner Vote Switch to Roosevelt: 1932 Democratic Convention." *Southwestern Historical Quarterly* 79 (October 1975): 189–204.

43-180. PEEL, ROY V., AND DONNELLY, THOMAS C. *The 1932 Campaign: An Analysis.* 1935. Reprint. New York: Da Capo Press, 1973. 242 p.

43-181. ROBINSON, LLOYD. *The Hopefuls: Ten Presidential Campaigns.* Garden City, N.Y.: Doubleday, 1966. 186 p.

43-182. ROLLINS, ALFRED B., JR. *Roosevelt and Howe.* New York: Alfred A. Knopf, 1962. 479 p.

43-183. ROSEBOOM, EUGENE H. *A History of Presidential Elections: From George Washington to Richard M. Nixon.* New York: Macmillan, 1970. 639 p.

43-184. STILES, LELA. *The Man behind Roosevelt: The Story of Louis McHenry Howe.* Cleveland: World Publishing, 1954. 311 p.

43-185. TAYLOR, LEAH MARCILE. "Democratic Presidential Politics, 1918–1932." Ph.D. dissertation, Louisiana State University, 1973. 881 p. 74-07266.

43-186. WHITE, OWEN P. "Cactus Jack." *Collier's,* 23 January 1932, p. 12.

43-187. ———. "Garner on Parade." *Collier's,* 28 May 1932, p. 12.

43-188. "Why Speaker Garner?" *Christian Century,* 2 March 1932, pp. 276–77.

Garner's Split with FDR

43-189. ALLEN, ROBERT S. "Roosevelt's Defeat: The Inside Story." *Nation,* 31 July 1937, pp. 123–24.

43-190. Altman, O. R. "American Government and Politics: First Session of the Seventy-fifth Congress, January 5, 1937, to August 21, 1937." *American Political Science Review* 31 (December 1937): 1071–93.

43-191. Baker, Leonard. *Back to Back: The Duel between FDR and the Supreme Court.* New York: Macmillan, 1967. 311 p.

43-192. Bell, Ulric. "Little Jack Garner." *American Mercury* 47 (May 1939): 1–8.

43-193. Hyde, Henry M. "White House No-Man." *Saturday Evening Post,* 25 June 1938, p. 23.

43-194. Patenaude, Lionel V. "Garner, Sumners, and Connally: The Defeat of the Roosevelt Court Bill in 1937." *Southwestern Historical Quarterly* 74 (July 1970): 36–51.

43-195. "Santa Clauses." *Literary Digest,* 5 June 1937, pp. 5–6.

43-196. Stokes, Thomas L. "Garner Turns on F.D.R." *Nation,* 26 June 1937, pp. 722–23.

43-197. "Undeclared War." *Time,* 20 March 1939, pp. 11–13.

43-198. "VP Garner." *Time,* 9 January 1939, pp. 14–15.

43-199. "Where Does New Deal Go from Here?" *Literary Digest,* 26 June 1937, pp. 3–4.

Garner's 1940 Presidential Bid

43-200. Broun, Heywood. "A Sock for Garner." *New Republic,* 24 May 1939, p. 72.

43-201. "Congress Begins Looking at the Presidential Prospects." *Congressional Digest* 18 (May 1939): 129–31.

43-202. "Congress Swan Song." *Newsweek,* 3 August 1939, pp. 16–17.

43-203. Crawford, Kenneth G. "The Real John Garner." *Nation,* 5 August 1939, pp. 139–40.

43-204. Democratic Party. National Convention. Chicago, 1940. *Official Report of the Proceedings of the Democratic National Convention Held at Chicago . . . 1940.* Washington, D.C., 1940. 390 p.

43-205. "Democrats Divided." *Current History* 50 (July 1939): 7.

43-206. Donahoe, Bernard F. "New Dealers, Conservatives, and the Democratic Nominees of 1940." Ph.D. dissertation, University of Notre Dame, 1965. 287 p. 65-06785.

43-207. ———. *Private Plans and Public Dangers: The Story of FDR's Third Nomination.* South Bend, Ind.: University of Notre Dame Press, 1965. 256 p.

43-208. "Garner Band Wagon." *Newsweek,* 27 November 1939, p. 12.

43-209. "Garner Finale." *Newsweek,* 13 May 1940, pp. 31–32.

43-210. "Garner for President." *Current History* 50 (July 1939): 7.

43-211. "Hats in the Ring: Caucus Jack." *New Republic,* 26 February 1940, pp. 266–69.

43-212. Ickes, Harold L. "My Twelve Years with F.D.R." *Saturday Evening Post,* 10 July 1948, p. 32.

43-213. James, Marquis. "Poker-Playing, Whisky-Drinking, Evil Old Man!" *Saturday Evening Post,* 9 September 1939, p. 25.

43-214. Michie, Allan A. "Men Who Would Be President: John Nance Garner." *Nation,* 2 March 1940, pp. 299–302.

43-215. Moscow, Warren. *Roosevelt and Willkie.* Englewod Cliffs, N.J.: Prentice-Hall, 1968. 210 p.

43-216. "Mr. Garner's Silence." *Newsweek,* 5 August 1940, p. 56.

43-217. "Out for Deer." *Time,* 19 December 1938, p. 14.

43-218. Owens, John W. "Lewis vs. Garner: A Sign of the Political Times." *Current History* 51 (September 1939): 36–37.

43-219. Parmet, Herbert S., and Hecht, Marie B. *Never Again: A President Runs for a Third Term.* New York: Macmillan, 1968. 306 p.

43-220. Ross, Hugh. "Roosevelt's Third-Term Nomination." *Mid-America* 44 (April 1962): 80–94.

43-221. Shannon, J. B. "Presidential Politics in the South, 1938." *Journal of Politics* 1 (May 1939): 146–70.

GARNER IN RETIREMENT

43-222. "Cronies at Garner's Ninetieth." *Life,* 8 December 1958, pp. 163–64.

43-223. "Garner Leaves." *Time,* 27 January 1941, p. 14.

43-224. "Gonna Live to 93." *Time,* 30 October 1944, p. 17.

43-225. Maverick, Maury, Jr. "A Visit with Cactus Jack Garner." *True West* 10 (September/October 1962): 15.

43-226. Presley, James. "Lone Star VP at 90." *New York Times Magazine,* 16 November 1958, pp. 39–41.

43-227. Tolbert, Frank X. "What Is Cactus Jack Up To Now?" *Saturday Evening Post,* 21 November 1963, pp. 28–29.

43-228. Woolf, S. J. "Then and Now: 'Jack' Garner Likes His Texas Privacy." *New York Times Magazine,* 5 December 1948, pp. 34–37.

44. Henry Thomas Rainey
(1860–1934)
(Speaker, Seventy-third Congress)

Henry T. Rainey, a liberal, progressive Democrat for his twenty-nine years in Congress, served as Speaker of the House during the momentous first hundred days of President Franklin Delano Roosevelt's New Deal. Rainey was born in Carrollton, Illinois, on August 20, 1860. He attended Amherst, where he earned a bachelor's degree in 1883 and a master's degree in 1886. In 1885 he received a law degree from Union College of Law (now Northwestern University Law School). He practiced law at Carrollton until 1902, when he was elected to Congress as a Democrat.

Rainey served in every Congress from 1902 until his death in 1934, with the exception of the Sixty-seventh (1921–23). He was a consistent progressive who advocated low tariffs and championed prolabor legislation. His rise to prominence in the House was slow but steady. He supported the insurgency against Speaker Cannon in 1911. As a member of the ways and

Means Committee, he was able to influence tariff and taxation legislation. Rainey was the ranking minority member during the years of the Republican ascendancy in the 1920s. He became majority leader when the Democrats regained control of the House and elected John Nance Garner to the speakership in 1931.

As majority leader of the Seventy-second Congress, Rainey initiated a plan for an international conference to reduce tariffs, but the measure was vetoed by President Hoover. He supported farm relief by helping to frame the McNary-Haugen farm bills. He also supported the movement to construct a deep waterway from the Great Lakes to the Gulf of Mexico. After Garner was nominated and elected to the vice-presidency, Rainey appeared to be in line to succeed to the Speaker's chair. The Democratic party was split, however, along sectional and ideological lines. Southern conservatives, including Garner, opposed the election of a

Midwestern liberal and opted instead to support Democratic whip John McDuffie of Alabama. Other Democratic candidates included Joseph W. Byrns, William B. Bankhead, and Sam Rayburn, all of whom later served as Speaker. President Roosevelt supported Rainey, as did the majority of newly elected Democratic congressmen. In the party caucus of March 2, 1933, Rainey received 166 votes, compared with McDuffie's 112. On March 9, Congress confirmed Rainey's election to the speakership.

With flowing white hair, the six-foot, two-hundred-seventy-five-pound Rainey was a commanding figure presiding over the House. He was completely in accord with the New Deal, which he facilitated by giving priority to such relief measures as the National Recovery Act. Rainey served only one term as Speaker. He died in St. Louis, Missouri, on August 19, 1934.

MANUSCRIPT COLLECTIONS

Library of Congress, Manuscript Division, Washington, D.C.

    Henry T. Rainey Papers, 1904–34.

    20 containers.

    Register.

    NUCMC 63-389.

    MC 124.

Additional Rainey correspondence can be found at the presidential libraries of Herbert Hoover and Franklin D. Roosevelt in West Branch, Iowa, and Hyde Park, N.Y., respectively.

BOOKS, ARTICLES, AND DISSERTATIONS

WORKS BY HENRY T. RAINEY

The following works are listed chronologically by year of publication and alphabetically thereunder.

44-1. RAINEY, HENRY T. *The Panama Canal in Its Relation to a Deep Waterway from the Great Lakes to the Gulf.* Washington, D.C., 1903.

    House speech of December 15, 1903, arguing for federally funded improvements to Mississippi River transportation.

44-2. ———. *An Argument against Ship Subsidies: Speech of Hon. Henry T. Rainey, of Illinois, in the House of Representatives.* Washington, D.C.: Government Printing Office, 1904.

    House speech of April 5, 1904, against restrictive maritime legislation.

*44-3. ———. *The Deep Waterway: Some Suggestions to the General Assembly of the State of Illinois.* N.p., 1907. 13 p.

44-4. ———. "The Legal Effect of the Maximum Provision of the Aldrich-Payne Tariff Law." *Central Law Journal* 69 (December 1909): 414–16.

    An examination and criticism of the Payne-Aldrich tariff.

*44-5. ———. *Corn: Speech in the House of Representatives.* Washington, D.C.: Government Printing Office, 1914. 8 p.

    House speech of June 6, 1914.

44-6. ———. "Is the Sales Tax a Sound Method of Raising Federal Revenue?" *Congressional Digest* 11 (May 1932): 144.

    Rainey argues in the affirmative.

44-7. ———. "Should Congress Pass New Tariff Measure?" *Congressional Digest* 11 (March 1932): 76.

    Argues for a new tariff measure.

44-8. ———. "Henry T. Rainey Says." *Demo-

cratic Bulletin 8 (April 1933): 9.

A summary of the work of the new Congress in March 1933.

44-9. ———. "Our Country's Economic Strength and How to Preserve It." *Consensus* 18 (January 1934): 5–16.

An argument for bimetallism.

44-10. ———. "Duties of Speaker." In *Congressional Procedure,* by Floyd M. Riddick, pp. 343–44. Boston: Chapman and Grimes, 1941.

A brief statement outlining the Speaker's duties as the presiding officer of the House.

BIOGRAPHY, BIOGRAPHICAL SKETCHES, AND EULOGIES

The only biography of Rainey, Waller (44-22), is scholarly and comprehensive. *See also* Drury (38-49).

44-11. BLOCK, MARVIN W. "Henry T. Rainey of Illinois." *Journal of the Illinois State Historical Society* 65 (Summer 1972): 142–57.

44-12. FIELD, WALTER T. "The Amherst Illustrious: Speaker Rainey." *Amherst Graduates' Quarterly* 24 (November 1934): 22–24.

44-13. FROST, THOMAS GOLD. *Tales from the Siwash Campus.* New York: Appellate Law Printers, 1938. 333 p.

44-14. MORRISON, HUGH ALEXANDER, ED. *Hon. Henry Thomas Rainey . . . Record of Services as a Member and Speaker of the House of Representatives . . . as Given in the Indexes of the Congressional Record.* N.p., 1934. 1 p.

44-15. PALMER, JOHN M., ED. *The Bench and Bar of Illinois: Historical and Reminiscent.* 2 vols. Chicago: Lewis Publishing, 1899.

44-16. "Rainey of Illinois." *Commoner,* 2 November 1906, p. 3.

44-17. "Speaker Rainey, Legislative Marshal of the New Deal, Dies." *Literary Digest,* 25 August 1934, p. 6.

44-18. "Transition: Died, Henry Thomas Rainey." *Newsweek,* 25 August 1934, pp. 29–30.

44-19. TREADWAY, ALLEN T. "The Amherst Illustrious: The Congressional Leaders—Rainey, '83, and Snell, '94." *Amherst Graduates' Quarterly* 22 (May 1933): 209–18.

44-20. UHLE, LEE. "Gadfly Rainey." *Illinois History* 22 (May 1969): 186–87.

44-21. U.S. CONGRESS. HOUSE. *Memorial Services Held in the House of Representatives of the United States, Together with Remarks Presented in Eulogy of Henry T. Rainey, Late a Representative from Illinois.* 74th Cong., 1st sess., 1935. Washington, D.C.: Government Printing Office, 1936. 94 p.

44-22. WALLER, ROBERT A. *Rainey of Illinois: A Political Biography, 1903–34.* Urbana: University of Illinois Press, 1977. 260 p.

RAINEY AND ILLINOIS HISTORY AND POLITICS

44-23. TOWNSHEND, WALTER A., AND BOESCHENSTEIN, CHARLES. *Illinois Democracy: A History of the Party and Its Representative Members Past and Present.* 4 vols. Springfield, Ill.: Democratic Historical Association, 1935.

44-24. WALLER, ROBERT A. "The Illinois Waterway from Conception to Completion, 1908–1933." *Journal of the Illinois State Historical Society* 65 (Summer 1972): 125–41.

RAINEY'S POLITICAL ASSOCIATES

See also Cole (28-24), Roper and Lovette (28-38), Tarr (38-84), Warren (39-8), Bloom (39-18), Coletta (40-72), Glad (40-75), Brown (43-14), Fisher (43-15), Timmons (43-18), Burns (43-122), Freidel (43-131), Jones and Angly (43-142), Leuchtenberg (43-146), Roosevelt (43-153, 43-154, and 43-155), Steinberg (47-28), and Mooney (47-32).

44-25. BLACKORBY, EDWARD C. *Prairie Rebel: The Public Life of William Lemke.* Lincoln: University of Nebraska Press, 1963. 339 p.

44-26. DUNNE, EDWARD F. *Dunne: Judge, Mayor, Governor.* Chicago: Windermere Press, 1916. 848 p.

44-27. FITE, GILBERT C. *George N. Peek and the Fight for Farm Parity.* Norman: University of Oklahoma Press, 1954. 314 p.

RAINEY'S CONGRESSIONAL CAREER

See also Blakey and Blakey (39-1), King (39-3), Schwarz (39-14), Allen and Pearson (42-43), and Schwarz (43-92).

44-28. "Backstage in Washington." *Outlook and Independent,* 25 November 1931, p. 394.

44-29. DANIELS, ROGER. *The Bonus March: An Episode of the Great Depression.* Westport, Conn.: Greenwood Press, 1971. 370 p.

44-30. DOBSON, JOHN M. *Two Centuries of Tariffs: The Background and Emergence of the U.S. International Trade Commission.* Washington, D.C.: U.S. International Trade Commission, 1976. 144 p.

44-31. FLYNN, JOHN T. "The Trap That Jack Built." *Collier's,* 21 May 1932, p. 12.

44-32. GRASSMUCK, GEORGE L. *Sectional Biases in Congress on Foreign Policy.* Baltimore: Johns Hopkins Press, 1951. 181 p.

44-33. HILL, EDWIN C. *The American Scene.* New York: Witmark Educational Publications, 1933. 454 p.

44-34. KERWIN, JEROME G. *Federal Water-Power Legislation.* 1926. Reprint. New York: AMS Press, 1968. 396 p.

44-35. LISIO, DONALD J. *The President and Protest: Hoover, Conspiracy, and the Bonus Riot.* Columbia: University of Missouri Press, 1974. 346 p.

44-36. LOWRY, EDWARD G. "The Tariff Revisers." *Harper's Weekly,* 4 February 1911, p. 8.

44-37. MCCARRON, JOHN F. . . . *Contested Election Case of Henry T. Rainey vs. Guy L. Shaw.* Washington, D.C.: Judd and Detweiler, 1921. 16 p.

44-38. MINER, DWIGHT CARROLL. *The Fight for the Panama Route: The Story of the Spooner Act and the Hay-Herran Treaty.* 1940. Reprint. New York: Octagon Books, 1966. 469 p.

44-39. "Mr. Rainey's Kindergarten for Standpatters." *Commoner,* 20 April 1906, p. 6.

44-40. MUMFORD, WILLIAM. . . . *Contested Election Case of Henry T. Rainey, vs. Guy L. Shaw.* N.p., 1921. 22 p.

44-41. ———. . . . *Contest of Election: Henry T. Rainey, Contestant, vs. Guy L. Shaw, Contestee.* N.p., 1921. 32 p.

44-42. MUSTO, DAVID F. *The American Disease: Origins of Narcotic Control.* New Haven: Yale University Press, 1973. 354 p.

44-43. PEEK, GEORGE N., AND CROWTHER, SAMUEL. *Why Quit Our Own?* New York: D. Van Nostrand, 1936. 353 p.

44-44. PEIRCE, CLYDE. *The Roosevelt Panama Libel Cases: A Factual Study of a Controversial Episode in the Career of Teddy Roosevelt, Father of the Panama Canal.* New York: Greenwich Book Publishers, 1959. 150 p.

44-45. RAINEY, MRS. HENRY T. [ELLA]. "The Woman's Congressional Club." *New England Magazine* 46 (May 1909): 265–71.

44-46. SHOVER, JOHN L. *Cornbelt Rebellion: The Farmers' Holiday Association.* Urbana: University of Illinois Press, 1965. 239 p.

44-47. SULLIVAN, MARK. "The Most Important Thing." *Collier's,* 4 January 1913, p. 15.

44-48. U.S. CONGRESS. HOUSE. *Contested Election Case of Henry T. Rainey vs. Guy L. Shaw.* 67th Cong., 1st sess. H. Doc. 84. Washington, D.C.: Government Prnting Office, 1921. 56 p.

44-49. U.S. CONGRESS. HOUSE. COMMITTEE ON ELECTIONS, NO. 2. *Contested Election Case of Rainey vs. Shaw.* Washington, D.C.: Government Printing Office, 1921. 2 p.

44-50. U.S. CONGRESS. HOUSE. COMMITTEE ON FOREIGN AFFAIRS. *The Story of Panama: Hearings on the Rainey Resolution.* Washington, D.C.: Government Printing Office, 1913. 736 p.

RAINEY AND THE SPEAKERSHIP

See also Schlesinger (39-6), Herring (43-98), Strout (43-106), Imler (43-141), and Moley (43-149).

44-51. BRATTER, HERBERT M. "The Silver Episode." *Journal of Political Economy* 46 (December 1938): 802–37.

44-52. BRENNAN, JOHN A. *Silver and the First New Deal*. Reno: University of Nevada Press, 1969. 187 p.

44-53. BROWDER, ROBERT PAUL. *The Origins of Soviet-American Diplomacy*. Princeton: Princeton University Press, 1953. 256 p.

44-54. DIOGENES [PSEUD.]. "Democratic Strategists Prepare to Make New Deal Issue in This Fall's Congressional Elections as Administration Sighs for Stronger Hold over Party Majority in Lower House." *Literary Digest,* 5 May 1934, p. 13.

44-55. HARD, WILLIAM. "The Nation's New Leaders." *Current History* 38 (May 1933): 146–51.

44-56. "The Hullabaloo over the Democratic Tax Plan." *Literary Digest,* 21 January 1933, pp. 3–5.

44-57. JOHNSON, G. GRIFFITH, JR. *The Treasury and Monetary Policy, 1933–1938*. 1939. Reprint. New York: Russell and Russell, 1967. 230 p.

44-58. LINDLEY, ERNEST K. *The Roosevelt Revolution: First Phase*. 1933. Reprint. New York: Da Capo Press, 1974. 328 p.

44-59. "The New President's Call to Battle." *Literary Digest,* 11 March 1933, pp. 5–7.

44-60. PARIS, JAMES DANIEL. *Monetary Policies of the United States, 1932–1938*. 1938. Reprint. New York: AMS Press, 1972. 198 p.

44-61. RIDDICK, FLOYD M. "The House of Representatives and the President." *South Atlantic Quarterly* 34 (January 1935): 79–90.

44-62. RUDWICK, ELLIOT M. "Oscar De Priest and the Jim Crow Restaurant in the U.S. House of Representatives." *Journal of Negro Education* 35 (Winter 1966): 77–82.

44-63. "Speaker: Tammany Helps Rainey to Speakership." *Newsweek,* 11 March 1933, p. 10.

44-64. WALLER, ROBERT A. "The Selection of Henry T. Rainey as Speaker of the House." *Capitol Studies* 2 (Spring 1973): 37–47.

45. Joseph Wellington Byrns
(1869–1936)
(Speaker, Seventy-fourth Congress)

Although he was a conservative Southern Democrat, Speaker Joseph W. Byrns was instrumental in the passage of liberal New Deal legislation. By placing party loyalty above ideology, he pushed FDR's legislative program through Congress with an expertise that surprised even the president. Indeed, party loyalty was the key to Byrns's political success. Devotion to the Democratic party enabled him to serve twenty-seven consecutive years in Congress. During that period he rose from a lowly member of the Committee on Indian Affairs to the highest office in the House.

Byrns was born on July 20, 1869, in Cedar Hill, Tennessee, the eldest of six children. After an elementary education in a one-room schoolhouse, he moved with his family to Nashville, where he attended high school. He graduated from Vanderbilt University in 1890 and began to practice law in Nashville in 1891. Byrns had taken little interest in politics, but he was persuaded to run for the state legislature. He served three terms in the state house of representatives (1895–1901) and was speaker in his final term. After a single term in the state senate, he was defeated in a race for district attorney general. But in 1908 he defeated the incumbent congressman, John Wesley Gaines, and won election to the Sixty-first Congress. A genial, uncomplicated, homespun politician, Byrns retained the support of his home district throughout his congressional career and ran unopposed in most reelection campaigns.

In the House, Byrns rose to the speakership through the normal seniority route. His congressional service was unspectacular but steady and conscientious. As a member of the Appropriations Committee, he developed a reputation as a financial watchdog. In 1930 he moved up to the chairmanship of the committee, where he successfully opposed Garner and Rainey's proposal for a national sales tax. As early as 1934 he also suggested, as an economy measure, that the War and Navy departments be consolidated into a department of national defense.

In 1932 Byrns first challenged for the speakership but lost to Henry T. Rainey. Although he was elected majority leader, Byrns resigned from the chairmanship of the Appropriations Committee after suffering two mild heart attacks. He remained majority leader, however, and recovered sufficiently to succeed to the speakership following Rainey's death in 1934. President Roosevelt and New Deal Democrats feared that Byrns lacked the will and the ability to control the House, but he proved to be remarkably adept at expediting legislation, using persuasion rather than coercion. He also established an effective information-gathering system by utilizing fifteen deputy party whips to ascertain how members would vote on particular issues. On June 3, 1936, he suffered a heart attack in his apartment in the Mayflower Hotel; he died of a cerebral hemorrhage the following morning. President Roosevelt led the nation in mourning the death of his loyal Democratic colleague.

MANUSCRIPT COLLECTIONS

Springfield Public Library, Springfield, Tenn.
 Joseph W. Byrns Collection.
 Most of Byrns's papers were destroyed by fire while in private possession. A limited collection of Byrns materials, which includes scrapbooks and portions of his library, is available at the Springfield Public Library. Some Byrns correspondence can be found in the presidential libraries of Herbert Hoover and Franklin D. Roosevelt, in West Branch, Iowa, and Hyde Park, N.Y., respectively.

BOOKS, ARTICLES, AND DISSERTATIONS

WORKS BY JOSEPH W. BYRNS

See also U.S. Congress, House (44-21). The following works are listed chronologically by year of publication and alphabetically thereunder.

*45-1. BYRNS, JOSEPH W. *What Industry Owes to Alcohol: Extension of Remarks in the House of Representatives*. Washington, D.C., 1927. 3 p.
 House speech of March 3, 1927.

45-2. ———. "Should a Republican House Be Reelected?" *Congressional Digest* 9 (October 1930): 249.
 A critique of the Hoover administration and the Republican Congress.

45-3. ———. "Political Estimates of the Record of the Seventy-first Congress." *Congressional Digest* 10 (April 1931): 123–25.
 Another criticism of the record of the Republican Congress.

*45-4. ———. *The Jews' Contribution to the United States: Address of Hon. Joseph W. Byrns . . . before the Fourteenth Quinquennial Convention of B'nai B'rith.* Washington, D.C.: Government Printing Office, 1935. 2 p.

Speech given May 6, 1935.

45-5. ———. "Plans for the New Congress." *Vital Speeches,* 28 January 1935, pp. 264–66.

An outline of the domestic and economic issues facing the next session of Congress.

45-6. ———. "Problems of Congress." *Vital Speeches,* 13 January 1936, pp. 228–31.

A preview of upcoming legislation awaiting the second session of the Seventy-fourth Congress.

45-7. ———. "Duties of Floor Leader . . . Duties of Democratic Congressional Committee." In *Congressional Procedure,* by Floyd M. Riddick, pp. 344–45. Boston: Chapman and Grimes, 1941.

BIOGRAPHICAL SKETCHES AND EULOGIES

There is no adequate biography of Byrns. Galloway's master's thesis and article (45-10 and 45-11) are the only scholarly treatments of his life and political career.

45-8. "Byrns: 'Good Fellow' Who Has Worked Up to the Speakership." *Newsweek,* 5 January 1935, p. 14.

45-9. "Congress: Reaper's Return." *Time,* 15 June 1936, pp. 13–14.

An account of Byrns's death and funeral.

*45-10. GALLOWAY, J. M. "The Public Life of Joseph W. Byrns." Master's thesis, University of Tennessee, 1962.

45-11. ———. "Speaker Joseph W. Byrns: Party Leader in the New Deal." *Tennessee Historical Quarterly* 25 (Spring 1966): 63–76.

45-12. "Speakers: Joe Byrns Dies and an Old Friend Gets His Job." *Newsweek,* 13 June 1936, p. 9.

45-13. U.S. CONGRESS. HOUSE. *Memorial Services Held in the House of Representatives of the United States, Together with Remarks Presented in Eulogy of Joseph Wellington Byrns, Late a Representative from Tennessee.*

75th Cong., 1st sess., 1937. Washington, D.C.: Government Printing Office, 1938. 183 p.

45-14. "Vanderbilt Loses Distinguished Alumnus in Death of Joe Byrns." *Vanderbilt Alumnus* 21 (June 1936): 13.

BYRNS AND TENNESSEE HISTORY AND POLITICS

See also Moore and Foster (15-37), Grant (45-27), and Coode (45-38).

45-15. ISAAC, PAUL E. *Prohibition and Politics: Turbulent Decades in Tennessee, 1885–1920.* Knoxville: University of Tennessee Press, 1965. 301 p.

45-16. McRAVEN, WILLIAM HENRY. *Nashville: Athens of the South.* Chapel Hill: Scheer and Jervis, 1949. 303 p.

45-17. MINTON, JOHN DEAN. *The New Deal in Tennessee, 1932–1938.* New York: Garland Publishing, 1979. 351 p.

45-18. WALLER, WILLIAM, ED. *Nashville, 1900 to 1910.* Nashville: Vanderbilt University Press, 1972. 390 p.

BYRNS'S POLITICAL ASSOCIATES

See also Hull (38-67), Wearin (39-21), Timmons (43-18), Connally and Steinberg (43-50), Ickes (43-61), Krock (43-63), Swain (43-71), Freidel (43-131), Roosevelt (43-153, 43-154, and 43-155), Waller (44-22), Heacock (46-10), Steinberg (47-28), and Mooney (47-32).

45-19. BROWNLOW, LOUIS. *The Autobiography of Louis Brownlow.* 2 vols. Chicago: University of Chicago Press, 1955–58.

45-20. HOOPER, BEN W. *The Unwanted Boy: The Autobiography of Governor Ben W. Hooper.* Knoxville: University of Tennessee Press, 1963. 258 p.

45-21. OURSLER, FULTON. *Behold This Dreamer! An Autobiography by Fulton Oursler.* Edited by Fulton Oursler, Jr. Boston: Little, Brown, 1964. 501 p.

45-22. SMITH, ALFRED E. *Up to Now: An Autobiography.* New York: Viking Press, 1929. 431 p.

45-23. STEINBERG, ALFRED. *The Bosses*. New York: Macmillan, 1972. 379 p.

45-24. TERRAL, RUFUS. *Newell Sanders: A Biography*. Kingsport, Tenn.: Kingsport Press, 1935. 310 p.

45-25. TOWNSEND, FRANCIS E. *New Horizons: An Autobiography*. Edited by Jesse George Murray. Chicago: J. L. Stewart, 1943. 246 p.

BYRNS'S CONGRESSIONAL CAREER

See also Blakey and Blakey (39-1), Warren (39-8), Schwarz (39-14), Moley (39-19), Hard (42-32), Herring (43-97 and 43-98), Imler (43-141), Daniels (44-29), Hard (44-55), Lindley (44-58), Riddick (44-61), and Waller (44-65).

45-26. DIOGENES [pseud.]. "Congressional Revolt against the President's Economy Measures Is One of Many Indications of the Approach of Midway Political Campaigns." *Literary Digest*, 7 April 1934, p. 13.

45-27. GRANT, PHILIP A., JR. "Tennesseans in the 63d Congress, 1913–1915." *Tennessee Historical Quarterly* 29 (Fall 1970): 278–86.

45-28. HUBBARD, PRESTON J. *Origins of the T.V.A.: The Muscle Shoals Controversy, 1920–1932*. Nashville: Vanderbilt University Press, 1961. 340 p.

45-29. "The Month in Congress: Appropriations." *Congressional Digest* 12 (January 1933): 28.

45-30. "Outlook Bright." *Democratic Bulletin* 4 (December 1929): 25–26.

45-31. PERKINS, VAN L. "The AAA and the Politics of Agriculture: Agricultural Policy Formulation in the Fall of 1933." *Agricultural History* 39 (October 1965): 220–29.

45-32. ———. *Crisis in Agriculture: The Agricultural Adjustment Administration and the New Deal, 1933*. Berkeley: University of California Press, 1969. 245 p.

45-33. POWELL, BOLLING R., JR. *Compilation and Analysis of Congressional Debates on the Right of the Federal Government to Operate Electric Power Projects and on Related Subjects*. St. Louis: St. Louis Law Printing, 1935. 975 p.

45-34. WILMERDING, LUCIUS, JR. *The Spending Power: A History of the Efforts of Congress to Control Expenditures*. 1943. Reprint. Hamden, Conn.: Archon Books, 1971. 317 p.

BYRNS AND THE SPEAKERSHIP

See also Patterson (39-12), Bloom (39-18), Steiner (43-104), and Shanks (47-114).

45-35. ALTMAN, O. R. "American Government and Politics: Second Session of the Seventy-fourth Congress, January 3, 1936, to June 20, 1936." *American Political Science Review* 30 (December 1936): 1086–1107.

45-36. "Byrns: Mae West and 6,000 Others Outrank the Speaker." *Newsweek*, 15 June 1935, p. 7.

45-37. "Congress: New Speaker of the House Another 'Uncle Joe'?" *Newsweek*, 22 December 1934, pp. 8–9.

45-38. COODE, THOMAS H. "Tennessee Congressmen and the New Deal, 1933–1938." *West Tennessee Historical Society Papers* 31 (1977): 132–58.

45-39. "Death and Taxes: The President Explodes a Bomb, Congress Must Soak the Rich and Do It before It Goes Home." *Newsweek*, 29 June 1935, pp. 5–6.

45-40. DIOGENES [pseud.]. "Capitol Hill Shows That It Still Insists upon Its Own Organization of Congress by Assuring the Election of Joseph W. Byrns of Tennessee as Speaker of the House." *Literary Digest*, 22 December 1934, p. 12.

45-41. "Four Head-Liners in Congress: Byrns and Robinson, Democrats, and Snell and McNary, Republicans, Match Strategy on Floors of Two Houses." *Literary Digest*, 11 January 1936, pp. 36–37.

45-42. HATCHER, JOE. "Joe Byrns Joins John Garner to Preside over Congress." *Vanderbilt Alumnus* 20 (January/February 1935): 10–11.

45-43. HERRING, E. PENDLETON. "American Government and Politics: First Session of the Seventy-fourth Congress, January 3, 1935, to August 26, 1935." *American Political Science Review* 29 (December 1935): 985–1005.

45-44. RIDDICK, FLOYD M. "Leadership in the House." *South Atlantic Quarterly* 36 (January 1937): 1–13.

45-45. "Social Security: House Members Miss Ball Game to Provide for 'More Abundant Life.' " *Newsweek,* 27 April 1935, p. 7.

45-46. "Tho' Joe Byrns Was Not the President's Choice for Speaker, Since His Election Mr. Roosevelt Has Rejoiced in the Suave, Speedy Way the Tennessean Gets Things Done." *Literary Digest,* 6 July 1935, p. 13.

45-47. "Townsend Cited: House Acts after Filibuster in Behalf of Pension Promoter." *Literary Digest,* 6 June 1936, pp. 6–7.

45-48. TUCKER, RAY T. "New Deal Shepherds on Capitol Hill." *New York Times Magazine,* 3 February 1935, p. 9.

46. William Brockman Bankhead
(1874–1940)
(Speaker, Seventy-fourth through Seventy-sixth Congresses)

The third Speaker of the House during Franklin Roosevelt's presidency, William Brockman Bankhead was just as loyal a legislative lieutenant as Rainey or Byrns. Bankhead, whose father and brother were both powerful Alabama politicians, forsook an interest in the theater to enter politics. As a politician he won acclaim for his skills as a parliamentarian and his powers of quiet persuasion.

Bankhead was born in Moscow, Alabama, on April 12, 1874. His father, John Hollis Bankhead, was a powerful Alabama Democrat who served in the House of Representatives from 1887 to 1907 and in the Senate from 1907 to 1920. William Brockman Bankhead's older brother, John Hollis Bankhead II, served in the Senate from 1931 to 1946. The Bankhead family's fame was not confined to politics: William Brockman Bankhead's daughter, Tallulah Bankhead, was a glamorous and well-known actress in her own right.

Bankhead was educated at the University of Alabama, where he played fullback on the university's first football team and received a bachelor's degree in 1893 and a master's degree in 1896. In between those degrees, he earned a law degree from Georgetown University in 1895. He briefly toyed with the idea of a theatrical career after law school but was dissuaded by his parents. After an apprenticeship in a New York law firm, he returned to Alabama as his brother's law partner. He served in the state legislature (1900–1901) and as solicitor of the Fourteenth Judicial Circuit (1900–1914). He was elected as a Democrat to the Sixty-fifth Congress and served from 1917 until his death in 1940.

Although he was a Southern Democrat, Bankhead took an active interest in social legislation, especially in the areas of labor and agriculture. In 1920, for example, he secured passage of a bill that granted federal aid for the rehabilitation of workers crippled in industrial accidents. He also endorsed the La Guardia anti-injunction bill; in return he was consistently supported by organized labor.

As chairman of the Rules Committee in 1934, Bankhead used his position to facilitate passage of New Deal legislation by keeping debate and amendments to a minimum. He was briefly considered as a possible successor after Speaker Rainey died in 1934, but he withdrew in favor of Byrns. He was selected majority leader, however, in spite of a severe heart attack which he suffered on January 1, 1935.

After he returned to full strength in 1936,

Bankhead served as floor leader for only six months before Byrns's death elevated him to the speakership. As Speaker, Bankhead presided with great dignity while exerting his personal influence behind the scenes to maintain party unity. He found Roosevelt's court-packing scheme a difficult measure to support, but he consistently supported the president's legislative program. Although he was mentioned as a possible vice-presidential candidate in 1940, Roosevelt insisted upon Henry Wallace. Bankhead accepted the president's choice with his usual grace. He was campaigning vigorously for the Roosevelt-Wallace ticket when he collapsed in Baltimore. He died five days later on September 15, 1940.

MANUSCRIPT COLLECTIONS

Alabama Department of Archives and History, Montgomery, Ala.
William Brockman Bankhead Papers, 1894–1940.
32 boxes.
NUCMC 60-1175.

In addition to the major collection at the Alabama Department of Archives and History, other Bankhead correspondence is held in the Franklin D. Roosevelt Library in Hyde Park, N.Y.

BOOKS, ARTICLES, AND DISSERTATIONS

WORKS BY WILLIAM B. BANKHEAD

See also U.S. Congress, House (42-14 and 45-14). The following Bankhead works are listed chronologically by year of publication and alphabetically thereunder.

46-1. BANKHEAD, WILLIAM B. "Republicans and Democrats Express Their Views on Candidates and Policies." *Congressional Digest* 11 (August/September 1932): 219.
An election-year defense of Democratic measures and an attack on Hoover's policies.

46-2. ———. "Achievements of the Administration of Franklin D. Roosevelt." In *The Campaign Book of the Democratic Party: Candidates and Issues, 1936,* pp. 11–19. New York: Democratic National Committee, 1937.
A speech by Bankhead praising and defending the Democratic record of FDR's first term.

46-3. ———. "The Nation Celebrates the 150th Anniversary of the United States Congress." *Congressional Digest* 18 (April 1939): 113–14.
Bankhead stresses the international importance of American democracy.

46-4. ———. "I'm Proud to Be a Politician." *True Story* 43 (September 1940): 22.
Speaker Bankhead recalls his decision to enter politics rather than pursue his interest in the theater: "I do not feel that I missed any of the drama of life by abandoning the world of make-believe for the realm of reality."

46-5. ———. "We Should Think Less of Political Differences." *Vital Speeches,* 1 August 1940, pp. 613–16.
The text of Bankhead's keynote address to the 1940 Democratic National Convention. *See also* (46-6).

46-6. DEMOCRATIC PARTY. NATIONAL CONVENTION. CHICAGO, 1940. *Official Report of the Proceedings of the Democratic National Convention Held at Chicago . . . 1940.* Washington, D.C., 1940. 390 p.
Contains the text of Bankhead's keynote address as well as information concerning his bid for the vice-presidential nomination.

BIOGRAPHY, BIOGRAPHICAL SKETCHES, AND EULOGIES

See also Michie and Rylick (43-20).

46-7. "Bankhead, William Brockman." In *Current Biography: 1940,* pp. 46–47. New York: H. W. Wilson, 1940.

46-8. "Death of a Speaker." *Life,* 30 December 1940, p. 22.

46-9. HEACOCK, WALTER JUDSON. "William B. Bankhead and the New Deal." *Journal of Southern History* 21 (August 1955): 347–59.

46-10. ———. "William Brockman Bankhead: A Biography." Ph.D. dissertation, University of Wisconsin, 1952. 247 p.

The only scholarly, full-length study of Bankhead's career.

46-11. MARKS, HENRY S. *Who Was Who in Alabama.* Huntsville, Ala.: Strode Publishing, 1972. 200 p.

46-12. U.S. CONGRESS. HOUSE. *Memorial Services Held in the House of Representatives of the United States Together with Remarks Presented in Eulogy of William Brockman Bankhead, Late a Representative from Alabama.* 77th Cong., 1st sess. Washington, D.C.: Government Printing Office, 1942. 143 p.

Contains over twenty eulogies presented by Bankhead's congressional colleagues.

46-13. "William B. Bankhead." *Newsweek,* 23 September 1940, p. 20.

BANKHEAD AND ALABAMA HISTORY AND POLITICS

46-14. ACEE, JOE G. *Lamar County History.* Vernon, Ala.: Lamar Democrat, 1976. 188 p.

46-15. OWEN, MARIE BANKHEAD. *The Story of Alabama: A History of the State.* Vol. 5. New York: Lewis Historical Publishing, 1949.

46-16. OWEN, THOMAS McADORY. *History of Alabama and Dictionary of Alabama Biography.* Vol. 3. 1921. Reprint. Spartanburg, S.C.: Reprint, 1978. 1,000 p.

BANKHEAD'S POLITICAL ASSOCIATES

See also Grantham (36-21), Hull (38-67), Bloom (39-18), Wearin (39-21), Jones (40-80), Fisher (43-15), Blake (43-44), Farley (43-55), Swain (43-71), Timmons (43-73), Roosevelt (43-153, 43-154, and 43-155), Waller (44-22), Rayburn (47-11), Allen (47-23), Dorough (47-

26), Mooney (47-27), Steinberg (47-28), and Martin (48-15).

46-17. DIES, MARTIN. *Martin Dies' Story.* New York: Bookmailer, 1963. 283 p.

46-18. DILLON, MARY EARHART. *Wendell Willkie, 1892–1944.* 1952. Reprint. New York: Da Capo Press, 1972. 378 p.

46-19. HAYS, BROOKS. *A Hotbed of Tranquility: My Life in Five Worlds.* New York: Macmillan, 1968. 238 p.

46-20. ROSENMAN, SAMUEL I. *Working with Roosevelt.* 1952. Reprint. New York: Da Capo Press, 1972. 560 p.

46-21. SCHAPSMEIER, EDWARD L., AND SCHAPSMEIER, FREDERICK H. *Henry A. Wallace of Iowa: The Agrarian Years, 1910–1940.* Ames: Iowa State University Press, 1968. 327 p.

46-22. ZUCKER, NORMAN L. *George W. Norris: Gentle Knight of American Democracy.* Urbana: University of Illinois Press, 1966. 186 p.

BANKHEAD'S CONGRESSIONAL CAREER

See also Herring (45-43) and Tucker (45-48).

46-23. CLAPPER, RAYMOND. "Hugo Black: Nemesis of Subsidy Spoilsmen." *Review of Reviews and World's Work* 89 (April 1934): 18–20.

46-24. COLE, WAYNE S. *Senator Gerald P. Nye and American Foreign Relations.* 1962. Reprint. Westport, Conn.: Greenwood Press, 1980. 293 p.

46-25. "Cotton: Senate Passes Control Bill as Conservatives Howl." *Newsweek,* 7 April 1934, pp. 30–31.

46-26. "Farmers: Cotton by Quota." *Time,* 9 April 1934, p. 16.

46-27. "Free-for-All Fight Starts for Speakership of House." *Literary Digest,* 1 September 1934, p. 6.

46-28. HERRING, E. PENDLETON. "American Government and Politics: Second Session of the Seventy-third Congress, January 3, 1934, to June 18, 1934." *American Political Science Review* 28 (October 1934): 852–66.

46-29. "Leadership." *Time,* 14 January 1935, pp. 12–13.

46-30. Newby, I. A. "States' Rights and Southern Congressmen during World War I." *Phylon* 24 (Spring 1963): 34–50.

46-31. "Playing Part in Congress." *Literary Digest,* 4 January 1936, p. 30.

46-32. "Well Leader." *Time,* 6 January 1936, p. 10.

BANKHEAD AND THE SPEAKERSHIP

See also Patterson (39-12), Porter (39-13), Divine (43-126), Leuchtenberg (43-146), Baker (43-191), Donahoe (43-206), Parmet and Hecht (43-219), "Congress" (45-9), "Speakers" (45-12), and Altman (45-35).

46-33. Alexander, Albert. "The President and the Investigator: Roosevelt and Dies." *Antioch Review* 15 (March 1955): 106–17.

46-34. Altman, O. R. "American Government and Politics: First Session of the Seventy-fifth Congress, January 5, 1937, to August 21, 1937." *American Political Science Review* 31 (December 1937): 1071–93.

46-35. ———. "American Government and Politics: Second and Third Sessions of the Seventy-fifth Congress, 1937–38." *American Political Science Review* 32 (December 1938): 1099–1123.

46-36. Appleby, Paul H. "Roosevelt's Third-Term Decision." *American Political Science Review* 46 (September 1952): 754–65.

46-37. "Bankhead Birthday." *Newsweek,* 24 April 1939, p. 16.

46-38. Bloom, Sol. *Our Heritage: George Washington and the Establishment of the American Union.* New York: G. P. Putnams's Sons, 1944. 662 p.

46-39. Caridi, Ronald J. *Twentieth-Century American Foreign Policy: Security and Self-Interest.* Englewood Cliffs, N.J.: Prentice-Hall, 1974. 388 p.

46-40. "The Congress: First Days." *Time,* 29 November 1937, pp. 10–11.

46-41. "The Congress: 'Mr. Will' Goes Home." *Time,* 30 September 1940, p. 15.

46-42. "Democrats Form Battle Lines for Defense-Crisis Campaign." *Newsweek,* 22 July 1940, pp. 15–16.

46-43. Jonas, Manfred. *Isolationism in America, 1935-1941.* Ithaca, N.Y.: Cornell University Press, 1966. 315 p.

46-44. "New Speaker: Bankhead Named as Byrns Dies, and Government Goes On." *Literary Digest,* 13 June 1936, pp. 5–6.

46-45. "Relief: Theatre Lobby." *Time,* 3 July 1939, pp. 8–9.

46-46. Riddick, Floyd M. "American Government and Politics: First Session of the Seventy-sixth Congress, January 3 to August 5, 1939." *American Political Science Review* 33 (December 1939): 1022–43.

46-47. ———. "American Government and Politics: Third Session of the Seventy-sixth Congress, January 3, 1940, to January 3, 1941." *American Political Science Review* 35 (April 1941): 284–303.

46-48. ———. "Party Government in a Session of the House of Representatives." *South Atlantic Quarterly* 36 (October 1937): 361–75.

46-49. Shepardson, Whitney H., and Scroggs, William O. *The United States in World Affairs: An Account of American Foreign Relations, 1939.* New York: Harper and Brothers, 1940. 420 p.

46-50. "The Speaker." *Time,* 23 September 1940, pp. 16–17.

46-51. Tucker, Ray T. "A Master for the House." *Collier's,* 5 January 1935, p. 22.

46-52. "Washington Correspondents Name Ablest Congressmen in *Life* Poll." *Life,* 20 March 1939, pp. 13–17.

BANKHEAD'S DOMESTIC LIFE

46-53. Bankhead, Tallulah. "My Life with Father." *Coronet* 31 (November 1951): 56–60.

46-54. ———. *Tallulah: My Autobiography*. New York: Harper and Brothers, 1952. 335 p.

46-55. BRIAN, DENIS. *Tallulah, Darling: A Biography of Tallulah Bankhead*. New York: Pyramid Books, 1972. 285 p.

46-56. GILL, BRENDAN. *Tallulah*. New York: Holt, Rinehart, and Winston, 1972. 287 p.

46-57. ISRAEL, LEE. *Miss Tallulah Bankhead*. New York: G. P. Putnam's Sons, 1972. 384 p.

46-58. RAWLS, EUGENIA. *Tallulah: A Memory*. Birmingham: University of Alabama Press, 1979. 97 p.

46-59. "Speaker Bankhead Meets His Famous Daughter Tallulah." *Life,* 22 February 1937, p. 17.

46-60. "The Speaker of the House Speaks to His Gardener." *Life,* 28 December 1936, pp. 9–11.

46-61. "The Theater: One-Woman Show." *Time,* 22 November 1948, pp. 76–85.

46-62. TUNNEY, KIERNAN. *Tallulah: Darling of the Gods*. New York: E. P. Dutton, 1973. 228 p.

47. Sam Rayburn
(1882–1961)
(Speaker, Seventy-sixth through Seventy-ninth, Eighty-first, Eighty-second, and Eighty-fourth through Eighty-seventh Congresses)

Sam Rayburn was Speaker of the House of Representatives for seventeen years and two months, more than twice as long as Henry Clay. Longevity was but one measure of the greatness of the man whose nickname, Mr. Sam, easily merged into that of Mr. Speaker. The man and the office were one and the same for nearly an entire generation. Congress and the speakership apparently were Rayburn's only passions in life, and in fulfilling them he defined the standards by which subsequent Speakers would be measured.

He was born in a log cabin near Kingston, Tennessee, on January 6, 1882. The name his parents gave him, Samuel Taliafero Rayburn, seemed too "high-falutin," so he later shortened it, and he was known throughout his career simply as Sam Rayburn. The family moved to Fannin County, Texas, when Sam was five years old. Later they settled in Bonham, Texas, which, along with Washington, D.C., was to be his home for the rest of his life. At eighteen, Rayburn entered Mayo Normal College, where he did odd jobs as the college handyman. He taught school after graduation. In 1906, at the age of twenty-four, he successfully ran for the state house of representatives.

A politically ambitious young man, Rayburn obtained a law degree from the University of Texas in 1908 while serving in the state legislature. In his third term he became speaker of the state house at the age of twenty-nine. His ambition was to run for Congress and ultimately to become Speaker of the House. He was elected to the Sixty-third Congress as a Democrat in 1912 and served until his death (1913–61).

Although it took Rayburn more than twenty-seven years to realize his ambitions to the Speaker's chair, he was a patient and tireless legislator. He had few if any interests outside politics. His marriage in 1927 lasted only three months, which left Rayburn free to devote all of his energies to Congress. Early in his career he won the friendship and guidance of older, more experienced leaders such as Cordell Hull, Champ Clark, and most important, fellow Texan John Nance Garner. With Garner's help, Rayburn was appointed to the Committee on Interstate and Foreign Commerce, the only committee on which he served during his forty-eight years in Congress. When Garner became Speaker in 1931, Rayburn became chairman of the committee.

Prior to 1932, Rayburn had demonstrated his skills as a legislator but had not been a major figure in the Democratic party leadership. As Garner's campaign manager in 1932, however, he was thrust into prominence in state and national party affairs. Rayburn was largely responsible for persuading Garner to throw his support to Roosevelt in return for the vice-presidential nomination. He then worked to enact New Deal legislation by using the chairmanship of the Interstate and Foreign Commerce Committee to facilitate passage of the Securities Act of 1933 and the Public Utility Holding Company Act. For his part, Rayburn took the greatest pride in the 1936 act that funded the Rural Electrification Administration.

With William B. Bankhead's elevation to the speakership in 1937, Rayburn became House majority leader. After Bankhead's death Rayburn became Speaker, on September 16, 1940. He occupied the Speaker's chair for seventeen of the following twenty-one years. Only during the Eightieth and Eighty-third Congresses (1947–49 and 1953–55), when the Republicans held a majority, was he replaced by his good friend Joseph Martin.

As Speaker, Rayburn served with presidents Roosevelt, Truman, Eisenhower, and Kennedy; he also tutored a Texas protégé in the Senate, Lyndon Baines Johnson. Rayburn's success and longevity as Speaker were based on his leadership style. He preferred to avoid confrontation by exerting informal powers of persuasion behind the scenes. A master of discerning the feel of the House through constant conversations with other members, he did not need elaborate polls to know how the House stood on any particular issue. He also continued the practice of the Board of Education begun by Longworth. Moreover, he maintained a steady sense of the dignity of the House and always fulfilled his commitments to its members.

During his last year as Speaker, Rayburn was forced to abandon his quiet leadership style in a showdown with Howard W. Smith, the conservative chairman of the House Rules Committee. To counter Smith, who was blocking action on Kennedy's New Frontier proposals, Rayburn reluctantly moved to enlarge the committee from twelve to fifteen and won a narrow victory. Before the session ended, illness forced him to return to Bonham. Shortly after the public learned that he had cancer, Rayburn died, on November 18, 1961. John F. Kennedy, Harry S. Truman, Dwight D. Eisenhower, and Lyndon Baines Johnson all paid a final tribute at his funeral.

MANUSCRIPT COLLECTIONS

Sam Rayburn Library, Bonham, Tex.
  Sam Rayburn Papers, 1913–61.
  73 microfilm reels.
  Addition, 1905–45.
  NUCMC 66-1344, 74-965.
  The Sam Rayburn Library in Bonham,

Texas, is an indispensable source for the study of Rayburn's career and speakership. The library holds a vast collection of Rayburn's personal correspondence and speeches and maintains a bibliography of secondary works.

BOOKS, ARTICLES, AND DISSERTATIONS

WORKS BY SAM RAYBURN

Speeches

The following speeches are listed chronologically by year of publication and alphabetically thereunder.

47-1. RAYBURN, SAM. "Is the Securities Act Sound?" *Today,* 30 December 1933, p. 7.

Rayburn defends the financial soundness of the Securities Act of 1933.

47-2. ———. "Should the Federal Securities Act of 1933 Be Modified?" *Congressional Digest* 13 (May 1934): 149.

Another defense of the Securities Act, which Rayburn helped enact.

47-3. ———. "Should Power Utility Holding Companies Be Abolished?" *Congressional Digest* 14 (May 1935): 142.

Rayburn attacks the mismanagement of utlity holding companies.

47-4. ———. "The Last Congress: Constructive or Destructive—Which?" *Vital Speeches,* 15 July 1938, pp. 592–95.

Rayburn defends the record of the Seventy-fifth Congress in a radio speech of June 20, 1938.

47-5. ———. "We Must Have Unity." *Vital Speeches,* 1 February 1944, pp. 229–30.

In a House speech, Rayburn warns of the dangers to the Allies of suspicion and disunity.

47-6. ———. " 'Leadership Has Been Offered Us': Extend a Helping Hand to Democracies." *Vital Speeches,* 15 May 1947, pp. 471–72.

Rayburn defends President Truman's foreign aid program.

47-7. ———. "Democratic Tax Proposals." *Current History* 27 (August 1954): 116–17.

In excerpts from a speech of March 16, 1954, Rayburn offers alternatives to the Eisenhower tax program.

47-8. ———. "Party Leaders in Congress Appraise the Record of Republican 83d Congress." *Congressional Digest* 33 (October 1954): 241.

A wide-ranging attack on both the Eisenhower administration and the Republican congressional leadership.

47-9. ———. "As Speaker Rayburn Sees the Labor Issue." *U.S. News and World Report,* 24 August 1959, pp. 90–91.

The text of Rayburn's radio speech of August 10, 1959, concerning labor union controversies.

47-10. ———. "Should the Source of REA's Loan Funds Be Broadened and Its Interest Rates Adjusted to the U.S. Treasury's Borrowing Costs?" *Congressional Digest* 38 (April 1959): 107.

Rayburn defends the record of the Rural Electrification Act, which he co-authored in 1936.

47-11. ———. *Speak, Mister Speaker.* Edited by H. G. Dulaney, Edward Hake Phillips, and MacPhelan Reese. Bonham, Tex.: Sam Rayburn Foundation, 1978. 489 p.

An account of Rayburn's life drawn from his own correspondence, speeches, and interviews.

Articles

The following articles are listed chronologically by year of publication.

47-12. RAYBURN, SAM. "The Case for the Democrats." *Saturday Evening Post,* 6 October 1956, p. 32.

An election-year appeal on behalf of Democratic party social-welfare principles.

47-13. ———. "A Teacher Who Seized Time by the Forelock." *National Education Association Journal* 49 (March 1960): 25.

A tribute to Rayburn's teacher, Professor William L. Mayo.

Interviews

The following interviews with Rayburn are listed chronologically by year of publication and alphabetically thereunder.

47-14. "What Influences Congress: An Interview with Sam Rayburn." *U.S. News and World Report,* 13 October 1950, pp. 28–31.

Rayburn discusses the evolution of the speakership.

47-15. "What's Ahead Now: Leaders Appraise the Election." *U.S. News and World Report,* 12 November 1954, pp. 68–71.

An interview with Rayburn on the new Congress and the administration's legislative program.

47-16. "Interview with Speaker Rayburn: Democrats Not to Be 'Labor Party.'" *U.S. News and World Report,* 19 December 1958, pp. 41–43.

A wide-ranging feature interview.

47-17. "What Happened in the Election." *U.S. News and World Report,* 14 November 1958, p. 44.

Rayburn interprets the election results as a protest against the Eisenhower administration.

47-18. "Sam Rayburn Tells about the New Congress." *U.S. News and World Report,* 28 November 1960, pp. 42–44.

An interview on the relations between Congress and the incoming Kennedy administration.

47-19. "Sam Rayburn Takes a Look at the World." *U.S. News and World Report,* 9 October 1961, pp. 58–61.

Rayburn defends high defense expenditures "until the world settles down."

47-20. "The Speaker Speaks of Presidents." *New York Times Magazine,* 4 June 1961, p. 32.

Rayburn reminisces about presidents he has known from Wilson to Kennedy.

The Rayburn Papers

The following works provide an introduction and guide to the Rayburn Papers in the Rayburn Library in Bonham, Texas.

47-21. BROWN, D. CLAYTON. "The Sam Rayburn Papers: A Preliminary Investigation." *American Archivist* 35 (July/October 1972): 331–36.

47-22. RAYBURN, SAM. *Guide to the Microfilm Edition of the Sam Rayburn Papers.* Bonham, Tex.: Sam Rayburn Library, 1972. 208 p.

BIOGRAPHIES, BIOGRAPHICAL SKETCHES, AND EULOGIES

Biographies

47-23. ALLEN, EDWARD. *Sam Rayburn: Leading the Lawmakers.* Chicago: Encyclopedia Britannica Press, 1963. 191 p.

47-24. CHAMPAGNE, ANTHONY. *Congressman Sam Rayburn.* New Brunswick, N.J.: Rutgers University Press, 1984. 228 p.

47-25. DANIEL, EDWARD ODA. "Sam Rayburn: Trials of a Party Man." Ph.D. dissertation, North Texas State University, 1979. 339 p. 79-19720.

47-26. DOROUGH, C. DWIGHT. *Mr. Sam.* New York: Random House, 1962. 597 p.

47-27. MOONEY, BOOTH. *Roosevelt and Rayburn: A Political Partnership.* Philadelphia: J. B. Lippincott, 1971. 228 p.

47-28. STEINBERG, ALFRED. *Sam Rayburn: A Biography.* New York: Hawthorn Books, 1975. 391 p.

Biographical Sketches

See also Mooney (1-12), Moley (39-19 and 39-20), and Welch (43-23).

47-29. HARDEMAN, D. B. "Unseen Side of the Man They Called Mr. Speaker." *Life,* 1 December 1961, p. 21.

47-30. HINGA, DON. "Sam Rayburn: Texas Squire." *Southwest Review* 29 (Summer 1944): 471–80.

47-31. KORNITZER, BELA. *American Fathers and Sons.* New York: Hermitage House, 1952. 316 p.

47-32. MOONEY, BOOTH. *The Politicians, 1945–1960.* Philadelphia: J. B. Lippincott, 1970. 368 p.

Eulogies

47-33. "Laid to Rest." *Time,* 24 November 1961, pp. 14–15.

47-34. MILLER, HOPE RIDINGS. "In Memoriam: Mr. Sam." *Diplomat* 12 (December 1961): 20–21.

47-35. "Mr. Sam." *Newsweek,* 27 November 1961, p. 17.

47-36. "Mr. Sam's Presidents Say Farewell." *Life,* 24 November 1961, pp. 42–43.

47-37. "An Old Friend Writes of Sam Rayburn." *U.S. News and World Report,* 23 October 1961, p. 68.

47-38. PENNIMAN, HOWARD. "Washington Front: Speaker Sam Rayburn, Just a Democrat?" *America,* 2 December 1961, p. 320.

47-39. "Rayburn's Legacy." *Reporter,* 7 December 1961, pp. 25–26.

47-40. "RIP, Sam Rayburn." *National Review,* 2 December 1961, pp. 370–71.

47-41. "Sam Rayburn's Frontier." *Life,* 20 October 1961, p. 4.

47-42. "Speaker Rayburn: Death Ends an Era." *U.S. News and World Report,* 27 November 1961, p. 14.

47-43. U.S. CONGRESS. *Memorial Services Held in the House of Representatives and Senate of the United States, Together with Remarks Presented in Eulogy of Sam Rayburn, Late a Representative of Texas.* 87th Cong., 2d sess., 1962. Washington, D.C.: Government Printing Office, 1962. 482 p.

47-44. ———. *Mr. Speaker: Excerpts from the Congressional Record . . . in Tribute to the Honorable Sam Rayburn, of Bonham, Texas.* Washington, D.C.: Government Printing Office, 1952. 94 p.

47-45. U.S. CONGRESS. HOUSE. *The Leadership of Sam Rayburn: Collected Tributes of His Congressional Colleagues.* 87th Cong., 1st sess., 1961. Washington, D.C.: Government Printing Office, 1961. 118 p.

47-46. ———. *Proceedings at the Dedication of the Sam Rayburn Statue . . . January 6, 1965.* 89th Cong., 1st sess. Washington, D.C.: Government Printing Office, 1965. 37 p.

RAYBURN AND TEXAS HISTORY AND POLITICS

See also Green (43-32).

47-47. BANKS, JIMMY. *Money, Marbles, and Chalk: The Wondrous World of Texas Politics.* Austin: Texas Publishing, 1971. 277 p.

47-48. BLEDSOE, JAMES MARCUS. *A History of Mayo and His College.* Commerce, Tex.: Nelson System, 1946. 574 p.

47-49. FUERMANN, GEORGE M. *Reluctant Empire.* Garden City, N.Y.: Doubleday, 1957. 284 p.

47-50. GANTT, FRED, JR. *The Chief Executive in Texas: A Study in Gubernatorial Leadership.* Austin: University of Texas Press, 1964. 396 p.

47-51. HARDEMAN, D. B. "Shivers of Texas: A Tragedy in Three Acts." *Harper's Magazine* 213 (November 1956): 50–56.

47-52. "Politician at Work." *Time,* 24 May 1943, p. 16.

47-53. "Sam Rayburn." *U.S. News and World Report,* 11 December 1953, p. 16.
A note on the Texas feud between Rayburn and Governor Shivers.

47-54. "Sam Rayburn, Texan." *Newsweek,* 14 January 1946, p. 28.

47-55. WEEKS, OLIVER DOUGLAS. *Texas in the 1960 Presidential Election.* Austin: Institute of Public Affairs, University of Texas, 1961. 80 p.

47-56. ———. *Texas One-Party Politics in 1956.* Austin: Institute of Public Affairs, University of Texas, 1957. 50 p.

47-57. ———. *Texas Presidential Politics in 1952.* Austin: Institute of Public Affairs, University of Texas, 1953. 116 p.

47-58. YOUNG, VALTON J. *The Speaker's Agent.* New York: Vantage Press, 1956. 83 p.

RAYBURN'S POLITICAL ASSOCIATES

See also Hull (38-67), Jones (40-80), Romano (43-17), Timmons (43-18), Berle (43-43), Blum (43-45), Byrnes (43-47), Connally (43-50), Davis (43-52), Henderson (43-58), Ickes (43-61), Wallace (43-76), Heacock (46-10), Dies (46-17), Hays (46-19), Martin (48-15), and Gordon (49-38).

47-59. ACHESON, DEAN. *Present at the Creation: My Years at the State Department.* New York: W. W. Norton, 1969. 798 p.

47-60. ALLEN, ROBERT S., AND SHANNON, WILLIAM V. *The Truman Merry-Go-Round.* New York: Vanguard Press, 1950. 502 p.

47-61. ANDERSON, CLINTON P. *Outsider in the Senate: Senator Clinton Anderson's Memoirs.* New York: World, 1970. 328 p.

47-62. BAKER, ROBERT GENE. *Wheeling and Dealing: Confessions of a Capitol Hill Operator.* New York: W. W. Norton, 1978. 296 p.

47-63. CRAWFORD, ANN F., AND KEEVER, JACK. *John B. Connally: Portrait in Power.* Austin: Jenkins Publishing, 1973. 460 p.

47-64. DANIELS, JONATHAN. *Frontier on the Potomac.* 1946. Reprint. New York: Da Capo Press, 1972. 262 p.

47-65. ———. *White House Witness, 1942–1945.* Garden City, N.Y.: Doubleday, 1975. 299 p.

47-66. DOUGLAS, PAUL H. *In the Fullness of Time: The Memoirs of Paul H. Douglas.* New York: Harcourt Brace Jovanovich, 1972. 642 p.

47-67. DOUGLAS, WILLIAM O. *Go East, Young Man: The Early Years.* New York: Random House, 1974. 493 p.

47-68. EGGLER, BRUCE. *The Life and Career of Hale Boggs.* New Orleans: States-Item, 1973. 16 p.

47-69. EISELE, ALBERT. *Almost to the Presidency: A Biography of Two American Politicians.* Blue Earth, Minn.: Piper, 1972. 460 p.
A dual biography of Hubert Humphrey and Eugene McCarthy.

47-70. FONTENAY, CHARLES L. *Estes Kefauver: A Biography.* Knoxville: University of Tennessee Press, 1980. 424 p.

47-71. GORMAN, JOSEPH BRUCE. *Kefauver: A Political Biography.* New York: Oxford University Press, 1971. 434 p.

47-72. HATCH, ALDEN. *The Wadsworths of the Genesee.* New York: Coward-McCann, 1959. 315 p.

47-73. HÉBERT, F. EDWARD. *Last of the Titans: The Life and Times of Congressman F. Edward Hébert of Louisiana.* Lafayette: University of Southwestern Louisiana Press, 1976. 478 p.

47-74. HUMPHREY, HUBERT H. *The Education of a Public Man: My Life and Politics.* Garden City, N.Y.: Doubleday, 1976. 513 p.

47-75. INOUYE, DANIEL K. *Journey to Washington.* Englewood Cliffs, N.J.: Prentice-Hall, 1967. 297 p.

47-76. KINCH, SAM, AND LONG, STUART. *Allan Shivers: The Pied Piper of Texas Politics.* Austin: Shoal Creek, 1973. 247 p.

47-77. LILIENTHAL, DAVID E. *The Journals of David E. Lilienthal.* Vol. 2. New York: Harper and Row, 1964–66. 666 p.

47-78. McPHERSON, HARRY. *A Political Education.* Boston: Little, Brown, 1972. 467 p.

47-79. MARTIN, JOHN BARTLOW. *Adlai Stevenson and the World: The Life of Adlai E. Stevenson.* Garden City, N.Y.: Doubleday, 1977. 946 p.

47-80. ———. *Adlai Stevenson of Illinois: The Life of Adlai E. Stevenson.* Garden City, N.Y.: Doubleday, 1976. 828 p.

47-81. MESTA, PERLE. *Perle: My Story.* New York: McGraw-Hill, 1960. 251 p.

47-82. MILLER, WILLIAM. *Fishbait: The Memoirs of the Congressional Doorkeeper.* Englewood Cliffs, N.J.: Prentice-Hall, 1977. 389 p.

47-83. PEARSON, DREW. *Diaries, 1949–1959.* Edited by Tyler Abell. New York: Holt, Rinehart, and Winston, 1974. 592 p.

47-84. SCHEELE, HENRY Z. *Charlie Halleck: A Political Biography.* New York: Exposition Press, 1966. 287 p.

47-85. SCHWARTZ, BERNARD. *The Professor and the Commissions.* 1959. Reprint. Westport, Conn.: Greenwood Press, 1978. 275 p.

47-86. STEVENSON, ADLAI E. *The Papers of Adlai E. Stevenson.* Edited by Walter Johnson. 8 vols. Boston: Little, Brown, 1972–79.

47-87. Swados, Harvey. *Standing Up for the People: The Life and Work of Estes Kefauver.* New York: E. P. Dutton, 1972. 189 p.

47-88. Udall, Morris K. *Education of a Congressman: The Newsletters of Morris K. Udall.* Edited by Robert L. Peabody. Indianapolis: Bobbs-Merrill, 1972. 384 p.

RAYBURN'S CONGRESSIONAL CAREER AND SPEAKERSHIP

General

See also Sundquist (39-7) and Champagne (47-24).

47-89. Brown, D. Clayton. "Sam Rayburn and the Development of Public Power in the Southwest." *Southwestern Historical Quarterly* 78 (October 1974): 140–54.

47-90. Engler, Robert. *The Politics of Oil.* New York: Macmillan, 1961. 565 p.

47-91. Holmans, A. E. *United States Fiscal Policy, 1945–1959: Its Contribution to Economic Stability.* London: Oxford University Press, 1961. 342 p.

47-92. McAdams, Alan K. *Power and Politics in Labor Legislation.* New York: Columbia University Press, 1964. 346 p.

47-93. Nash, Gerald D. *United States Oil Policy: Business and Government in Twentieth Century America.* 1968. Reprint. Westport, Conn.: Greenwood Press, 1976. 286 p.

47-94. Neustadt, Richard E. *Presidential Power: The Politics of Leadership from FDR to Carter.* New York: John Wiley and Sons, 1980. 286 p.

47-95. Robinson, James A. "The Role of the Rules Committee in Arranging the Program of the U.S. House of Representatives." *Western Political Quarterly* 12 (September 1959): 653–69.

47-96. Splawn, Walter. "Rayburn of Texas." *Bunker's Monthly* 2 (October 1928): 523–26.

47-97. Truman, David B. *The Congressional Party: A Case Study.* New York: John Wiley and Sons, 1959. 336 p.

47-98. Westerfield, H. Bradford. *Foreign Policy and Party Politics: Pearl Harbor to Korea.* 1955. Reprint. New York: Octagon Books, 1972. 448 p.

Rayburn and the Wilson Administration

See also Grantham (43-31).

47-99. Link, Arthur S. *Wilson.* Vols. 2 and 3. Princeton: Princeton University Press, 1956–60.

47-100. Shanks, Alexander Graham. "Sam Rayburn in the Wilson Administration." *East Texas Historical Journal* 6 (March 1968): 63–76.

Rayburn and FDR's Administrations

See also Patterson (39-12), Porter (39-13), Smyrl (43-67), Burns (43-122), Freidel (43-131), Roosevelt (43-153 and 43-154), and Baker (43-191).

47-101. Baker, Leonard. *Roosevelt and Pearl Harbor.* New York: Macmillan, 1970. 356 p.

47-102. Bishop, Jim. *FDR's Last Year, April 1944–April 1945.* New York: William Morrow, 1974. 690 p.

47-103. Divine, Robert A. *Since 1945: Politics and Diplomacy in Recent American History.* New York: John Wiley and Sons, 1975. 251 p.

47-104. Flynn, John T. "Other People's Money." *New Republic,* 31 May 1933, pp. 69–70.

47-105. Hawley, Ellis W. *The New Deal and the Problem of Monopoly: A Study in Economic Ambivalence.* Princeton: Princeton University Press, 1966. 525 p.

47-106. Kimball, Warren F. *The Most Unsordid Act: Lend-Lease, 1939–1941.* Baltimore: Johns Hopkins Press, 1969. 281 p.

47-107. Langer, William L., and Gleason, S. Everett. *The Undeclared War, 1940–1941.* 1953. Reprint. Gloucester, Mass.: Peter Smith, 1968. 963 p.

47-108. "Leader Apparent." *Time,* 14 December 1936, p. 15.

47-109. "New Bill of Rights." *Time,* 18 January 1943, pp. 19–21.

47-110. "Rayburn: Miss Lou's Mr. Sam, Good Neighbor and 'Party Man.' " *Newsweek,* 26 December 1936, p. 20.

47-111. SARGENT, JAMES EDWARD. "The Hundred Days: Franklin D. Roosevelt and the Early New Deal, 1933." Ph.D. dissertation, Michigan State University, 1972. 520 p. 72-22281.

47-112. "The 79th Sits." *Time,* 15 January 1945, p. 20.

47-113. SHANKS, ALEXANDER GRAHAM. "Sam Rayburn and the New Deal, 1933–1936." Ph.D. dissertation, University of North Carolina, 1965. 273 p. 65-14390.

47-114. ———. "Sam Rayburn: The Texas Politician as New Dealer." *East Texas Historical Journal* 5 (March 1967): 51–59.

47-115. YOUNG, ROLAND A. *Congressional Politics in the Second World War.* 1956. Reprint. New York: Da Capo Press, 1972. 281 p.

Rayburn and the Truman Administrations

See also Steinberg (43-68).

47-116. BERMAN, WILLIAM C. *The Politics of Civil Rights in the Truman Administration.* Columbus: Ohio State University Press, 1970. 361 p.

47-117. "The Capital: Love Feast." *Time,* 15 August 1949, p. 14.

47-118. "Congress at the Halfway Mark: Speaker Sam Rayburn Will Need All His Persuasive Power to Steer 'Fair Deal' toward Enactment." *U.S. News and World Report,* 7 April 1950, pp. 39–40.

47-119. "Congress: By a Hair." *Time,* 16 May 1949, p. 24.

47-120. "Congress: Closed Minds." *Time,* 1 August 1949, pp. 9–10.

47-121. "Congress: Oil and Water." *Time,* 13 August 1951, pp. 21–22.

47-122. DANIELS, JONATHAN. *The Man of Independence.* 1950. Reprint. Port Washington, N.Y.: Kennikat Press, 1971. 384 p.

47-123. "The Democrats in the Smoke-Filled Room." *New Republic,* 12 July 1948, pp. 16–17.

47-124. DONOVAN, ROBERT J. *Conflict and Crisis: The Presidency of Harry S. Truman, 1945–1948.* New York: W. W. Norton, 1977. 473 p.

47-125. GOSNELL, HAROLD F. *Truman's Crises.* Westport, Conn.: Greenwood Press, 1980. 656 p.

47-126. "Job for Soothing Talents of Sam Rayburn: To Unify Democrats and Guide through House the Program Promised by President." *U.S. News and World Report,* 7 January 1949, pp. 39–40.

47-127. LEE, R. ALTON. *Truman and Taft-Hartley: A Question of Mandate.* Lexington: University of Kentucky Press, 1966. 254 p.

47-128. McCOY, DONALD R., AND RUETTEN, RICHARD T. *Quest and Response: Minority Rights and the Truman Administration.* Lawrence: University Press of Kansas, 1973. 427 p.

47-129. McNAUGHTON, FRANK, AND HEHMEYER, WALTER. *Harry Truman: President.* New York: McGraw-Hill, 1948. 294 p.

47-130. PHILLIPS, CABELL B. *The Truman Presidency: The History of a Triumphant Succession.* New York: Macmillan, 1966. 463 p.

47-131. "Rayburn's Rosy View." *Newsweek,* 29 November 1948, p. 21.

47-132. "Rayburn to the Rear." *New Republic,* 23 May 1949, pp. 7–8.

47-133. THOMPSON, FRANCIS H. *The Frustration of Politics: Truman, Congress, and the Loyalty Issue, 1945–1953.* Rutherford, N.J.: Fairleigh Dickinson University Press, 1979. 246 p.

47-134. TRUMAN, HARRY S. *Memoirs of Harry S. Truman.* 2 vols. Garden City, N.Y.: Doubleday, 1955–56.

Rayburn and the Eisenhower Administrations

47-135. ADAMS, SHERMAN. *Firsthand Report: The Story of the Eisenhower Administration.* New York: Harper and Brothers, 1961. 481 p.

47-136. "The Battle over 'Civil Rights.' " *U.S. News and World Report,* 16 August 1957, p. 16.

47-137. BENSON, EZRA TAFT. *Cross Fire: The Eight Years with Eisenhower.* 1962. Reprint. Westport, Conn.: Greenwood Press, 1976. 627 p.

47-138. BRANYAN, ROBERT L., AND LARSEN, LAWRENCE H. *The Eisenhower Administration, 1953–1961: A Documentary History.* 2 vols. New York: Random House, 1971.

47-139. "Congress: Compromised Compromise." *Time,* 2 September 1957, pp. 13–14.

47-140. "Congress: 'I Love This House.' " *Time,* 2 February 1959, pp. 11–14.

47-141. "Congress: What Mr. Sam Wants." *Time,* 24 March 1958, p. 24.

47-142. COUGHLAN, ROBERT. "Proprietors of the House." *Life,* 14 February 1955, p. 72.

47-143. EISENHOWER, DWIGHT D. *The White House Years.* 2 vols. Garden City, N.Y.: Doubleday, 1963–65.

47-144. "41 Years of Experience to Help—or Hinder—Ike." *U.S. News and World Report,* 19 November 1954, p. 88.

47-145. FRIER, DAVID A. *Conflict of Interest in the Eisenhower Administration.* Ames: Iowa State University Press, 1969. 238 p.

47-146. "If Rayburn Says 'No.'" *U.S. News and World Report,* 3 May 1957, pp. 44–46.

47-147. "A Leader with Troubles: Division in the Ranks." *U.S. News and World Report,* 7 September 1959, pp. 48–49.

47-148. "A Look Ahead: What Leaders Expect Congress to Do." *U.S. News and World Report,* 11 January 1957, p. 28.

47-149. "Mister Sam's Skid." *Newsweek,* 7 September 1959, pp. 36–38.

47-150. " 'Mister Sam' Steps Up Again." *Life,* 17 January 1955, pp. 36–37.

47-151. "The Political Campaign Gets Up Steam." *U.S. News and World Report,* 3 September 1954, pp. 98–107.

47-152. "Rayburn's Strategy: Help Ike If It Helps Democrats." *U.S. News and World Report,* 8 January 1954, pp. 51–53.

47-153. "Republican vs. Democrat: What's This about a 'Do-Nothing Congress'?" *U.S. News and World Report,* 13 April 1956, pp. 122–24.

47-154. "Sam Rayburn." *U.S. News and World Report,* 23 April 1954, p. 12.

47-155. "Sam Rayburn." *U.S. News and World Report,* 17 December 1954, p. 14.

47-156. "Who Are the 'Spenders' on Capitol Hill?" *U.S. News and World Report,* 13 July 1959, p. 4.

Rayburn, the Kennedy Administration, and the Rules Committee Fight of 1961

47-157. "Congress: At the Brink." *Time,* 3 February 1961, pp. 16–17.

47-158. "Congress: Darkened Victory." *Time,* 10 February 1961, pp. 11–14.

47-159. "Congress: Mr. Sam's House Rules." *Time,* 12 January 1959, pp. 20–21.

47-160. "Congress: Turmoil in the House." *Time,* 13 January 1961, p. 14.

47-161. "Congress: Unblocking the Road." *Time,* 27 January 1961, pp. 14–15.

47-162. "Help for Mr. Sam." *Newsweek,* 6 February 1961, pp. 27–28.

47-163. "Inside Story of a Fight for Control in Congress." *U.S. News and World Report,* 6 March 1961, p. 75.

47-164. "It Is Still the House That 'Mr. Sam' the Speaker Runs." *Newsweek,* 13 February 1961, pp. 26–28.

47-165. LASKY, VICTOR. *J.F.K.: The Man and the Myth.* New York: Macmillan, 1963. 653 p.

47-166. LINCOLN, EVELYN. *Kennedy and Johnson.* New York: Holt, Rinehart, and Winston, 1968. 207 p.

47-167. LORD, DONALD C. *John F. Kennedy: The Politics of Confrontation and Conciliation*. Woodbury, N.Y.: Barron's, 1977. 458 p.

47-168. O'DONNELL, KENNETH, AND POWERS, DAVID F. *Johnny, We Hardly Knew Ye: Memories of John Fitzgerald Kennedy*. Boston: Little, Brown, 1972. 434 p.

47-169. OPOTOWSKY, STAN. *The Kennedy Government*. New York: E. P. Dutton, 1961. 208 p.

47-170. PARMET, HERBERT S. *Jack: The Struggles of John F. Kennedy*. New York: Dial Press, 1980. 586 p.

47-171. "Rayburn Clears Track for Kennedy's Program." *U.S. News and World Report,* 30 January 1961, p. 8.

47-172. SALINGER, PIERRE. *With Kennedy*. Garden City, N.Y.: Doubleday, 1966. 391 p.

47-173. "Sam Rayburn Sizes Up 8 Presidents He Has Known." *U.S. News and World Report,* 13 March 1961, p. 56.

47-174. SCHLESINGER, ARTHUR M., JR. *A Thousand Days: John F. Kennedy in the White House.* Boston: Houghton Mifflin, 1965. 1,087 p.

47-175. SIDEY, HUGH. *John F. Kennedy: President*. New York: Atheneum, 1963. 400 p.

47-176. SMALLWOOD, JAMES. "Sam Rayburn and the Rules Committee Change of 1961." *East Texas Historical Journal* 11 (Spring 1973): 51–54.

47-177. SORENSEN, THEODORE C. *Kennedy*. New York: Harper and Row, 1965. 783 p.

47-178. "When Two Old-Timers Clashed: 'Mr. Sam' Won, But. . . ." *U.S. News and World Report,* 13 February 1961, p. 20.

47-179. WICKER, TOM. *JFK and LBJ: The Influence of Personality upon Politics*. New York: William Morrow, 1968. 297 p.

Rayburn and Lyndon Johnson

47-180. BAKER, LEONARD. *The Johnson Eclipse: A President's Vice-Presidency*. New York: Macmillan, 1966. 280 p.

47-181. CORMIER, FRANK. *LBJ: The Way He Was.* Garden City, N.Y.: Doubleday, 1977. 276 p.

47-182. EVANS, ROWLAND, AND NOVAK, ROBERT. *Lyndon B. Johnson: The Exercise of Power*. New York: New American Library, 1966. 597 p.

47-183. JOHNSON, LYNDON BAINES. *The Vantage Point: Perspectives of the Presidency, 1963–1969*. New York: Holt, Rinehart, and Winston, 1971. 636 p.

47-184. JOHNSON, SAM HOUSTON. *My Brother Lyndon*. Edited by Enrique Hank Lopez. New York: Cowles Book, 1970. 278 p.

47-185. "Last Roundup in Congress: Two Texans in the Saddle." *U.S. News and World Report,* 22 August 1958, pp. 56–58.

47-186. LYNCH, DUDLEY M. *The President from Texas: Lyndon Baines Johnson*. New York: Thomas Y. Crowell, 1975. 169 p.

47-187. MOONEY, BOOTH. *LBJ: An Irreverent Chronicle*. New York: Thomas Y. Crowell, 1976. 290 p.

47-188. SHERRILL, ROBERT G. *Accidental President*. New York: Grossman, 1967. 282 p.

47-189. SIDEY, HUGH. *A Very Personal Presidency: Lyndon Johnson in the White House*. New York: Atheneum, 1968. 305 p.

47-190. SINGER, KURT, AND SHERROD, JANE. *Lyndon Baines Johnson: Man of Reason*. Minneapolis: T. S. Denison, 1964. 384 p.

47-191. STEINBERG, ALFRED. *Sam Johnson's Boy: A Close-Up of the President from Texas*. New York: Macmillan, 1968. 871 p.

47-192. "Two Texans." *U.S. News and World Report,* 12 November 1954, p. 14.

47-193. "Two Texans Who Call the Signals." *U.S. News and World Report,* 17 January 1958, pp. 48–50.

47-194. VALENTI, JACK. *A Very Human President*. New York: W. W. Norton, 1975. 402 p.

47-195. WHITE, WILLIAM S. *The Professional: Lyndon B. Johnson*. Boston: Houghton Mifflin, 1964. 273 p.

47-196. ZEIGER, HENRY. *Lyndon B. Johnson: Man and President*. New York: Popular Library, 1963. 143 p.

Evaluations of Rayburn as Speaker of the House

See also McNeil (1-24), Jones (1-34), Robinson (1-41), Bolling (1-47 and 1-48), Peabody (1-55), Manley (1-63), Horn (1-70), Oleszek (1-91), Goodwin (38-97), Gross (38-98), and Davidson, Kovenack, and O'Leary (39-10).

47-197. ALSOP, JOSEPH, AND KINTNER, ROBERT. "Never Leave Them Angry: Sam Rayburn Tackles His Biggest Job." *Saturday Evening Post,* 18 January 1941, p. 22.

47-198. ANDERSON, JACK. *Washington Exposé*. Washington, D.C.: Public Affairs Press, 1967. 487 p.

47-199. ANDERSON, JACK, AND BOYD, JAMES. *Confessions of a Muckraker: The Inside Story of Life in Washington during the Truman, Eisenhower, Kennedy, and Johnson Years*. New York: Random House, 1979. 354 p.

47-200. BAILEY, STEPHEN K. *Congress Makes a Law: The Story behind the Employment Act of 1946*. New York: Columbia University Press, 1950. 282 p.

47-201. BIBBY, JOHN F., AND DAVIDSON, ROGER H. *On Capitol Hill: Studies in the Legislative Process*. Hinsdale, Ill.: Dryden Press, 1972. 300 p.

47-202. BONE, HUGH A. *Party Committees and National Politics*. Seattle: University of Washington Press, 1958. 256 p.

47-203. BOYD, EDWARD. "Mr. Speaker: The Dynamo of Capitol Hill." *American Magazine* 159 (April 1955): 24.

47-204. CATER, DOUGLASS. *Power in Washington: A Critical Look at Today's Struggle to Govern in the Nation's Capital*. New York: Random House, 1964. 275 p.

47-205. ———. "Stalemate on Capitol Hill." *Reporter,* 15 September 1960, pp. 31–32.

47-206. CLARK, JOSEPH S. *Congress: The Sapless Branch*. New York: Harper and Row, 1964. 268 p.

47-207. COHN, DAVID L. "Mr. Speaker." *Atlantic Monthly* 170 (October 1942): 73–78.

47-208. DEXTER, LEWIS ANTHONY. *The Sociology and Politics of Congress*. Chicago: Rand McNally, 1969. 300 p.

47-209. EMSWILER, MARILYN. "Mr. Speaker: Sam Rayburn." *Texas Historian* 33 (March 1973): 20–25.

47-210. FENNO, RICHARD F., JR. "The Internal Distribution of Influence: The House." In *The Congress and America's Future,* edited by David B. Truman, pp. 52–76. Englewood Cliffs, N.J.: Prentice-Hall, 1973.

47-211. "The Four Leaders Who Run Congress." *U.S. News and World Report,* 11 January 1957, p. 74.

47-212. GOODWIN, GEORGE, JR. "The Seniority System in Congress." *American Political Science Review* 53 (June 1959): 412–36.

47-213. HAGGIN, B. H. "Speaker Rayburn and the FCC." *New Republic,* 24 July 1944, p. 104.

47-214. HEALY, PAUL F. "They're Just Crazy about Sam." *Saturday Evening Post,* 24 November 1951, p. 22.

47-215. HINCKLEY, BARBARA. "Congressional Leadership Selection and Support: A Comparative Analysis." *Journal of Politics* 32 (May 1970): 268–87.

47-216. ———. *The Seniority System in Congress*. Bloomington: Indiana University Press, 1971. 146 p.

47-217. ———. *Stability and Change in Congress*. New York: Harper and Row, 1971. 216 p.

47-218. IRISH, MARIAN D. "The Southern One-Party System and National Politics." *Journal of Politics* 4 (February 1942): 80–94.

47-219. LITTLE, DWAYNE LEE. "The Political Leadership of Speaker Sam Rayburn, 1940–1961." Ph.D. dissertation, University of Cincinnati, 1970. 469 p. 71-01528.

47-220. MAYHEW, DAVID R. *Party Loyalty among Congressmen: The Difference between Democrats and*

Republicans, 1947–1962. Cambridge, Mass.: Harvard University Press, 1966. 189 p.

47-221. "Mister Speaker." *Time,* 27 September 1943, pp. 19–22.

47-222. " 'Mr. Democrat' Sets a Record for Service." *U.S. News and World Report,* 16 March 1959, p. 26.

47-223. "Mr. Speaker Sam." *Newsweek,* 10 January 1955, pp. 18–20.

47-224. PEARSON, DREW, AND ANDERSON, JACK. *The Case against Congress: A Compelling Indictment of Corruption on Capitol Hill.* New York: Simon and Schuster, 1968. 473 p.

47-225. PHILLIPS, CABELL B. "Dozen Key Men in Congress." *New York Times Magazine,* 3 January 1960, pp. 6–7.

47-226. ———. "Twelve Key Members of the New Congress." *New York Times Magazine,* 2 January 1949, pp. 6–7.

47-227. PRICE, H. DOUGLAS. "The Congressional Career: Then and Now." In *Congressional Behavior,* edited by Nelson W. Polsby, pp. 14–27. New York: Random House, 1971.

47-228. "Rancher Rayburn." *Newsweek,* 16 November 1942, p. 64.

47-229. RAPOPORT, DANIEL. *Inside the House.* Chicago: Follett Publishing, 1975. 260 p.

47-230. "Rayburn Ropes a Steer." *Time,* 20 April 1942, p. 15.

47-231. "Realist." *Business Week,* 21 September 1940, p. 7.

47-232. SALTER, JOHN THOMAS, ED. *Public Men In and Out of Office.* 1946. Reprint. New York: Da Capo Press, 1972. 513 p.

47-233. "Sam Rayburn: Using 42 Years of Savvy to Help the Democrats." *Business Week,* 4 December 1954, pp. 166–70.

47-234. "Speaker Rayburn." *Newsweek,* 23 September 1940, p. 20.

47-235. "Speaker Sam Rayburn." *U.S. News,* 3 January 1947, p. 61.

47-236. VOORHIS, JERRY. "Rayburn of Texas." *New Republic,* 10 July 1944, pp. 44–46.

47-237. WHITE, WILLIAM S. *Home Place: The Story of the U.S. House of Representatives.* Boston: Houghton Mifflin, 1965. 175 p.

47-238. ———. *The Responsibles.* New York: Harper and Row, 1972. 275 p.

47-239. ———. "Sam Rayburn: The Untalkative Speaker." *New York Times Magazine,* 27 February 1949, p. 10.

47-240. ———. "The Ten Who Will Run Congress." *New York Times Magazine,* 2 January 1955, pp. 6–7.

47-241. ———. "Then Martin, Now Rayburn, and So On." *New York Times Magazine,* 6 February 1955, p. 17.

47-242. WRIGHT, JAMES C. *You and Your Congressman.* Rev. ed. New York: G. P. Putnam and Sons, 1976. 313 p.

RAYBURN AND DEMOCRATIC PARTY PRESIDENTIAL POLITICS

See also Martin (39-5), Farley (43-54 and 43-55), Bell (43-120), DiSalle and Blochman (43-125), Carlson (43-168), Democratic Party, National Committee (43-169), Oulahan (43-178), Patenaude (43-179), Democratic Party, National Convention (43-204), Donahoe (43-206 and 43-207), and Ross (43-220).

47-243. "At the Conventions: 'Mr. Speaker' and His Friend." *U.S. News and World Report,* 10 August 1956, p. 22.

47-244. COLLIER, EVERETT. "Rayburn for President? A Footnote to the 1952 Election." *Texas Quarterly* 9 (Winter 1966): 102–6.

47-245. COTTER, CORNELIUS P., AND HENNESSY, BERNARD C. *Politics without Power: The National Party Committees.* New York: Atherton Press, 1964. 246 p.

47-246. DAVID, PAUL T.; MOOS, MALCOLM; AND GOLDMAN, RALPH M., EDS. *Presidential Nominating Politics in 1952.* 5 vols. Baltimore: Johns Hopkins Press, 1954.

47-247. DEMOCRATIC PARTY. NATIONAL CONVEN-
TION. CHICAGO, 1944. *Official Report of the Proceedings.* Chicago, 1944. 399 p.

47-248. ———. PHILADELPHIA, 1948. *Democracy at
Work: The Official Report of the Democratic National
Convention.* Philadelphia: Local Democratic Politi-
cal Committee of Pennsylvania, 1949. 574 p.

47-249 ———. CHICAGO, 1952. *Official Report of the
Proceedings.* Washington, D.C.: Democratic
National Committee, 1955. 754 p.

47-250. ———. CHICAGO, 1956. *Official Report of
the Proceedings.* Washington, D.C.: Democratic
National Committee/Beacon Press, 1960. 901 p.

47-251. ———. LOS ANGELES, 1960. *Official Report
of the Proceedings.* Washington, D.C.: National
Document Publishers, 1964. 833 p.

47-252. " 'Mr. Sam,' the Delegate, No Gavel
Wielder This Time." *U.S. News and World Report,*
11 July 1960, p. 21.

47-253. "Old Hand." *U.S. News and World
Report,* 21 December 1956, p. 18.

47-254. SEVAREID, ARNOLD ERIC, ED. *Candidates,
1960: Behind the Headlines in the Presidential Race.*
New York: Basic Books, 1959. 369 p.

THE RAYBURN LIBRARY

47-255. " 'Mr. Sam' Dedicates His Own Memorial." *Life,* 21 October 1957, p. 38.

47-256. " 'Mr. Sam' Rayburn Has a Great
Day." *U.S. News and World Report,* 18 October
1957, p. 20.

47-257. NORDYKE, LEWIS. "A Tribute to 'Mr.
Sam.'" *New York Times Magazine,* 6 October 1957,
p. 60.

47-258. "Salute to 'Mr. Sam.'" *Newsweek,* 21
October 1957, p. 68.

RAYBURN'S FINAL ILLNESS AND DEATH

47-259. "Congress: The Grand Old Man."
Newsweek, 11 September 1961, pp. 30–31.

47-260. "Congress: Mister Sam." *Time,* 13 October 1961, pp. 26–27.

47-261. "Congress: Mr. Sam." *Newsweek,* 16
October 1961, pp. 16–17.

47-262. " 'Mr. Sam' Goes Home for a Rest."
U.S. News and World Report, 11 September 1961,
p. 23.

48. Joseph William Martin, Jr.
(1884–1968)
(Speaker, Eightieth and Eighty-third Congresses)

Joseph W. Martin, Jr., was born in North
Attleboro, Massachusetts, on November 3,
1884. His father was a blacksmith, and his
mother was a loyal Republican who exerted a
strong influence over her unmarried son. Martin learned politics from the ground up while
working from the age of six, as a newsboy, a
helper in his father's blacksmith shop, and a
night telephone operator. He also became well
known and popular for his proficiency as a
shortstop on high-school and semi-professional
baseball teams. After graduation from high
school in 1902, Martin became a reporter on
the *North Attleboro Leader* and shortly thereafter
on the *Attleboro Sun.* In 1908 he joined with nine
other investors to buy the *North Attleboro Evening
Chronicle* with the assurance that he would be
made editor. The paper prospered, and over

the years Martin was able to obtain full owner-ship. In 1914 he acquired an insurance agency in North Attleboro as an investment.

In 1911 Martin was elected as a Republican to the Massachusetts House of Representatives. Three years later he was elected to the Massachusetts Senate. Following his defeat in 1917, he returned to journalism, though he remained active in the state Republican party as a presidential elector in 1920 and executive secretary in 1922. He was elected to Congress in 1924 when the party's nominee died a week after the primary. Martin was subsequently reelected to every Congress until his defeat in 1966. During his tenure he served on the Foreign Affairs Committee (1925–39) and the House Rules Committee (1929–39). He became assistant Republican floor leader in 1937 and was Republican minority leader from 1939 to 1946, 1949 to 1953, and 1955 to 1959. He served as Speaker of the House in the Eightieth and Eighty-third Congresses (1947–49 and 1953–55).

During the 1930s and 1940s, Martin led House Republicans in opposition to the New Deal and Roosevelt's foreign policy. Although he was philosophically and politically opposed to the New Deal, he did support a revision of the Works Progress Administration and an improved revision of the social security system. He was active in the passage of the arms embargo and opposed Roosevelt's policies, which he felt were leading the nation into World War II. He endorsed the draft, however, and once war had been declared, Martin gave the president his full support.

Martin, who was prominent in national party politics for much of his career, was permanent chairman of the Republican National Conventions in 1940, 1944, 1948, 1952, 1956, and 1960. In 1940 Wendell Willkie selected Martin to serve as his campaign manager and as Republican National Chairman.

Martin's first term as Speaker was during Harry Truman's presidency. As Speaker, he aided passage of tax-reduction legislation, the Marshall Plan, Taft-Hartley labor legislation, the Twenty-Second Amendment—which limited the tenure of presidents to two terms—and legislation that altered the line of succession to the presidency by placing the Speaker of the House next in line after the vice-president. Though Martin and Truman respected one another, they clashed over the president's handling of both the Korean War and the recall of General Douglas MacArthur.

Martin's second term as Speaker was not a satisfying one. Even with a Republican in the White House and the party in control of the House, Martin was stymied by what he perceived to be President Eisenhower's moderate and politically naive course. After the party lost control of the House for the third successive time in 1958, House Republican members turned on Martin. Led by Charles Halleck, they voted Martin out of his position as minority leader in 1959. He lost the 1966 congressional election to Margaret Heckler and left Congress in 1967. Martin died in Florida of acute appendicitis on March 6, 1968.

MANUSCRIPT COLLECTIONS

Stonehill College, Cushing Martin Library, North Easton, Mass.

Joseph W. Martin, Jr., Papers, 1919–66. 90 ft. 10,500 items.

Included in the Martin Papers at Stonehill College are correspondence, speeches, press releases, diaries, appointment books, scrapbooks, newspaper clippings, and a few artifacts.

BOOKS, ARTICLES, AND DISSERTATIONS

WORKS BY JOSEPH W. MARTIN, JR.

See also U.S. Congress, House (44-21) and U.S. Congress (47-43 and 47-44).

48-1. BRIDGES, SEN. HENRY STYLES, AND MARTIN, REP. JOSEPH W., JR. *Republican Accomplishments in the Eighty-second Congress.* Washington, D.C.: Government Printing Office, 1952. 25 p.

A review of the Eighty-second Congress with criticism of the opposition.

The following works are listed chronologically by year of publication and alphabetically thereunder.

48-2. MARTIN, JOSEPH W., JR. "Would the Domestic Allotment Plan Help the American Farmer?" *Congressional Digest* 12 (February 1933): 40-56.

Includes extracts from Martin's remarks against the allotment plan.

48-3. ———. "Will the Administration's Soil Conservation Act Prove to Be Legal?" *Congressional Digest* 15 (March 1936): 87-96.

Martin speaks in opposition to the Roosevelt administrations's conservation policy.

48-4. ———. "The Heart and Spirit of America." *Vital Speeches,* 15 August 1939, pp. 653-55.

Martin lauds education and the American political system as the heart and spirit of America.

48-5. ———. "Let Us Now Go Forward." *Vital Speeches,* 1 June 1939, pp. 489-92.

Martin calls for a return to Americanism to put the unemployed back to work.

48-6. ———. "The Country Needs a Strong Opposition Party." *Vital Speeches,* 1 May 1941, pp. 436-37.

Martin states that a "virile" Republican party is needed to preserve the two-party system and a free America.

48-7. ———. "130,000,000 Free People Working in Unison." *Vital Speeches,* 1 February 1942, pp. 247-49.

Martin calls upon every American to put forth the effort and sacrifice needed to win the war.

48-8. ———. "Worldwide Abolition of Conscription." *Journal of the National Education Association* 34 (December 1945): 180-81.

Martin argues in support of his House resolution to promote worldwide abolition of conscription.

48-9. ———. "Republican Leader of the House." *U.S. News and World Report,* 14 November 1952, pp. 72-73.

An interview with Martin on the outcome of the 1952 election.

48-10. ———. "Liberty, Intelligence, Our Nation's Safety." *Vital Speeches,* 1 August 1954, pp. 613-15.

Martin warns against the Communist conspiracy.

48-11. ———. "A Reply to Churchill's Proposal for 'Coexistence' with the Reds: Speaker Martin of the House of Representatives Says Soviets Have Broken Every Treaty with Free Nations." *U.S. News and World Report,* 16 July 1954, pp. 82-84.

Text of a speech in which Martin denies the feasibility of coexistence with the Soviet Union.

48-12. ———. "The Case for the Republicans." *Saturday Evening Post,* 13 October 1956, p. 34.

Martin discusses Eisenhower's health, the administration's record, and Republican philosophy.

48-13. ———. "What Leaders Expect Congress to Do: Interview with Joseph W. Martin, Jr." *U.S. News and World Report,* 11 January 1957, pp. 29-30.

Martin briefly answers ten questions on the business of the new session of Congress.

48-14. ———. "The Greatest Convention Ever: I Remember Willkie." *Saturday Evening Post,* 9 July 1960, p. 21.

Includes selections from Martin's memoirs (48-15).

48-15. ———. *My First Fifty Years in Politics.* As told to Robert J. Donovan. 1960. Reprint. Westport, Conn.: Greenwood Press, 1975. 261 p.

Martin's anecdotal autobiography.

BIOGRAPHICAL SKETCHES AND EULOGIES

There is no full-length biography of Martin or even an adequate biographical sketch. The most complete biographical material is still to be found in his autobiography, Martin (48-15).

48-16. "Martin, Joseph W(illiam), Jr." In *Current Biography, 1948*, pp. 422–25. New York: H. W. Wilson, 1949.

48-17. "Mr. Republican." *Newsweek,* 18 March 1968, pp. 52–53.

48-18. U.S. CONGRESS. HOUSE. *Memorial Addresses and Other Tributes in the Congress of the United States on the Life and Public Services of Joseph William Martin, Jr.* 90th Cong., 2d sess., 1968. H. Doc. 376. Washington, D.C.: Government Printing Office, 1968. 113 p.

A collection of eulogies presented by Martin's congressional colleagues.

MARTIN'S POLITICAL ASSOCIATES

See also Fausold (38-62), Truman (43-75), Moscow (43-215), Dillon (46-18), Steinberg (47-28), Mooney (47-32), Acheson (47-59), Allen and Shannon (47-60), Mesta (47-81), Miller (47-82), Scheele (47-84), McNaughton and Hehmeyer (47-129), Truman (47-134), Adams (47-135), and Steinberg (47-191).

48-19. BARNARD, ELLSWORTH. *Wendell Willkie: Fighter for Freedom.* Marquette: Northern Michigan University Press, 1966. 611 p.

48-20. BARNES, JOSEPH. *Willkie: The Events He Was Part of, the Ideas He Fought For.* New York: Simon and Schuster, 1952. 405 p.

48-21. BARONE, LOUIS A. "Republican House Minority Leader Bertrand H. Snell and the Coming of the New Deal, 1931–1939." Ph.D. dissertation, State University of New York at Buffalo, 1969. 226 p. 70-17305.

48-22. BROWN, JOHN MASON. *Through These Men: Some Aspects of Our Passing History.* New York: Harper and Brothers, 1956. 302 p.

48-23. HOWARD, KATHERINE G. *With My Shoes Off.* New York: Vantage Press, 1977. 347 p.

48-24. JOHNSON, DONALD BRUCE. *The Republican Party and Wendell Willkie.* Urbana: University of Illinois Press, 1960. 354 p.

48-25. KILMAN, ED, AND WRIGHT, THEON. *Hugh Roy Cullen: A Story of American Opportunity.* New York: Prentice-Hall, 1954. 376 p.

48-26. MILLER, MERLE. *Plain Speaking: An Oral Biography of Harry S. Truman.* New York: Berkley Publishing, 1974. 448 p.

48-27. PARMET, HERBERT S. *Eisenhower and the American Crusades.* New York: Macmillan, 1972. 660 p.

48-28. VANDENBERG, ARTHUR H. *The Private Papers of Senator Vandenberg.* Edited by Arthur H. Vandenberg, Jr. Boston: Houghton Mifflin, 1952. 599 p.

MARTIN'S CONGRESSIONAL CAREER AND SPEAKERSHIP

General

See also Jones (1-34), Peabody (1-55 and 1-56), Manley (1-63), Patterson (39-12), Porter (39-13), Holmans (47-91), Westerfield (47-98), and Lee (47-127).

48-29. BENDINER, ROBERT. *Obstacle Course on Capitol Hill.* New York: McGraw-Hill, 1964. 231 p.

48-30. COFFIN, TRIS. "A Man of the Good Old Days." *New Republic,* 17 February 1947, pp. 18–20.

48-31. "The Gentleman from Martin, Mr. North Attleboro." *Time,* 15 March 1968, p. 20.

48-32. "Greatest Single Act of Statesmanship." *Commonweal,* 27 July 1945, pp. 348–49.

48-33. JONES, CHARLES O. *Party and Policy-Making: The House Republican Policy Committee.* New Brunswick, N.J.: Rutgers University Press, 1964. 174 p.

48-34. KAY, HUBERT. "Joe Martin and the People." *Life,* 1 January 1940, pp. 48–54.

48-35. "No Time for Sentiment." *Time,* 23 September 1966, p. 24.

48-36. "Old Joe's Revenge." *Time*, 19 September 1960, pp. 24–25.

48-37. "Review of the 76th Congress." *Newsweek*, 14 August 1939, pp. 11–13.

48-38. "Tax Soliloquy." *Time*, 22 March 1943, p. 12.

Martin and the Truman Administration

48-39. BAILEY, GILBERT. "Field Study in American Politics: A Tour with Speaker Joe Martin through His District Leads One to Ask: 'Do Issues Count'?" *New York Times Magazine*, 28 September 1947, p. 7.

48-40. "Bland, Silent Joe." *New Republic*, 6 October 1947, pp. 5–6.

48-41. "The Boys in the Smoke-Filled Room." *New Republic*, 21 June 1948, pp. 12–13.

48-42. DAVIES, RICHARD O. *Housing Reform during the Truman Administration*. Columbia: University of Missouri Press, 1966. 197 p.

48-43. GERVASI, FRANK. "The G.O.P.'s Off Stage Prompter." *Collier's*, 24 January 1948, p. 14.

48-44. "Joe Martin Day: Stronghold of Democratic Party Honors Its Favorite Republican." *Life*, 1 September 1947, p. 34.

48-45. "Joe Martin's Way." *Newsweek*, 19 April 1948, pp. 26–27.

48-46. "Keys to Joseph Martin's Power in Congress and Convention: Friendliness, Energy, Political Experience in Republican Ranks." *U.S. News and World Report*, 25 June 1948, pp. 37–39.

48-47. LINDLEY, ERNEST K. "Vandenberg, Martin, and Taft." *Newsweek*, 12 January 1948, p. 22.

48-48. "Martin Will Run House in Congress Which Will Cut Costs, Curb Power of President." *Life*, 18 November 1946, p. 36.

48-49. "Mr. Speaker." *Time*, 18 November 1946, pp. 23–25.

48-50. "Muffled Boom." *Time*, 1 September 1947, p. 12.

48-51. "Politics: Fall River Joe Martin Day." *Newsweek*, 1 September 1947, p. 18.

48-52. "Presidency: Man in Line." *Newsweek*, 21 July 1947, p. 18.

48-53. "Roles of Speaker Martin and the UMW's Lewis in Coal Settlement: Presidential Boom for One, Paying Off of Old Scores for Other." *U.S. News and World Report*, 23 April 1948, pp. 34–35.

48-54. "The Shape of Things." *Nation*, 17 April 1948, pp. 405–6, and 1 May 1948, p. 455.

48-55. SMITH, BEVERLY. "What Joe Martin Wants to Do." *Saturday Evening Post*, 18 January 1947, p. 12.

48-56. "Speaker-Apparent." *Newsweek*, 18 November 1946, pp. 36–37.

48-57. "Washington's Amendment." *Newsweek*, 6 January 1947, p. 17.

Martin and the Truman-MacArthur Controversy

48-58. CARIDI, RONALD J. *The Korean War and American Politics: The Republican Party as a Case Study*. Philadelphia: University of Pennsylvania Press, 1968. 319 p.

48-59. HIGGINS, TRUMBULL. *Korea and the Fall of MacArthur*. New York: Oxford University Press, 1960. 229 p.

48-60. MACARTHUR, DOUGLAS. *Reminiscences*. New York: McGraw-Hill, 1964. 438 p.

48-61. SCHLESINGER, ARTHUR M., JR., AND ROVERE, RICHARD H. *The MacArthur Controversy and American Foreign Policy*. 1951. Reprint. New York: Farrar, Straus, and Giroux, 1965. 366 p.

48-62. SPANIER, JOHN W. *The Truman-MacArthur Controversy and the Korean War*. Cambridge, Mass.: Harvard University Press, 1959. 311 p.

48-63. "Stars in His Eyes." *Newsweek*, 23 May 1955, p. 32.

48-64. WHITNEY, COURTNEY. *MacArthur: His Rendezvous with History*. New York: Alfred A. Knopf, 1956. 547 p.

48. JOSEPH WILLIAM MARTIN, JR.

Martin and the Eisenhower Administration

See also Benson (47-137), Branyan and Larsen (47-138), Coughlan (47-142), Eisenhower (47-143), and "The Four Leaders" (47-211).

48-65. "Battle for a Tax." *Time,* 6 July 1953, pp. 9–10.

48-66. "Joe Martin Sizes Up the 83rd." *Newsweek,* 24 November 1952, pp. 24–25.

48-67. "Joseph W. Martin, Jr." *U.S. News and World Report,* 4 December 1953, p. 16, and 25 December 1953, p. 12.

48-68. "Lord of the Citadel." *Time,* 9 August 1954, pp. 16–20.

48-69. "Martin and Taft and Ike over Who's Boss." *Newsweek,* 30 March 1953, pp. 24–25.

48-70. "Martin, MacArthur, and an Elephant (Rampant) Move In." *Life,* 12 January 1953, p. 17.

48-71. "Minority Leader Martin Wants U.S. Spending Cut." *U.S. News and World Report,* 28 November 1958, p. 19.

48-72. REICHARD, GARY W. *The Reaffirmation of Republicanism: Eisenhower and the Eighty-third Congress.* Knoxville: University of Tennessee Press, 1975. 303 p.

48-73. "Republicans: Smoothing and Stirring." *Time,* 27 September 1954, p. 17.

48-74. "Seer in Congress." *U.S. News and World Report,* 12 July 1957, p. 16.

48-75. "The Way to Get a Law Passed." *U.S. News and World Report,* 13 August 1954, p. 54.

Ouster of Martin from the Minority Leadership in 1959

48-76. "Republican Revolt." *Newsweek,* 19 January 1959, p. 20.

48-77. "Republicans: Old Joe Out." *Time,* 19 January 1959, pp. 16–17.

48-78. STEELE, JOHN L. "G.O.P. Tactics That Toppled a Veteran Leader." *Life,* 19 January 1959, p. 26.

48-79. "We'll Miss You, Joe Martin." *Life,* 19 January 1959, p. 37.

MARTIN AND REPUBLICAN PARTY PRESIDENTIAL POLITICS

See also Parmet and Hecht (43-219).

48-80. ABELS, JULES. *Out of the Jaws of Victory.* New York: Henry Holt, 1959. 336 p.

48-81. ALLEN, ROBERT S. "The Presidential Aspirants Speak Out: Joseph W. Martin, Jr." *Collier's,* 20 March 1948, p. 22.

48-82. "Chairman Martin." *Current History* 52 (September 1940): 14.

48-83. LURIE, LEONARD. *The King Makers.* New York: Coward, McCann, and Geoghegan, 1971. 271 p.

48-84. "Martin: An Old Hand on House Gavel." *U.S. News and World Report,* 14 November 1952, p. 56.

48-85. "Republicans: Mr. Willkie's Man Farley." *Time,* 9 September 1940, pp. 15–17.

48-86. "Republican Spokesman." *Life,* 6 October 1947, p. 49.

48-87. WILLIAMSON, S. T. "Leaders in the GOP Derby." *New York Times Magazine,* 22 February 1948, pp. 18–19.

49. John William McCormack
(1891–1980)
(Speaker, Eighty-seventh through Ninety-first Congresses)

John W. McCormack served in Congress for more than thirty-three years before he became Speaker of the House in 1962. For all but four of the previous twenty-two years he had been majority leader of the House under Sam Rayburn. As a Boston Irish-Catholic Democrat of the old school of politics, Speaker McCormack weathered criticisms of his age and his opposition to House reform for five terms (1962–71).

McCormack was born in South Boston on December 21, 1891, the eldest child of Joseph and Ellen O'Brien McCormack. He left school in the eighth grade after his father died. He held several odd jobs, including one as an office boy in a legal firm, where he studied law prior to his admittance to the Massachusetts bar in 1913. A successful legal practice in Boston was interrupted by military duty during World War I. After the armistice, he returned to Boston and embarked a political career.

Following two terms in the Massachusetts House of Representatives (1920–22), McCormack served two more terms in the state senate, where he became Democratic floor leader in 1925. Three years later he won a special election to fill a vacancy in the Seventieth Congress. McCormack served in the House from November 6, 1928, until his retirement on January 3, 1971, at the close of the Ninety-first Congress.

At the outset of his congressional career McCormack became a protégé of Speaker Garner and his lieutenant, Sam Rayburn. He was given a spot on the House Ways and Means Committee in his second term, an honor no second-term congressman had ever received. McCormack supported Rayburn's bid for the position of majority leader in 1936; when Rayburn became Speaker in 1940, he, in turn, chose McCormack as his successor.

As a New Deal Democrat, McCormack sup-

ported Franklin Roosevelt's domestic and foreign policies, but he stood out from many New Dealers in his ardent and vocal opposition to communism. In 1934 he chaired a special committee known as the McCormack-Dickstein Committee (the forerunner to the House Un-American Activities Committee) to investigate un-American activities. An amendment that he sponsored to the Smith Act made it a crime to belong to any party advocating the overthrow of the government.

Following Rayburn's illness and death in 1961, McCormack succeeded to the speakership. Although there were some who were apprehensive owing to his age (seventy) and the highly partisan role he had played as majority leader, he proved to be an effective Speaker, skillful at conciliation. Even though he had often differed with the Kennedy family in Massachusetts politics, he was able to work for President Kennedy's programs. Following Kennedy's assassination in 1963, Speaker McCormack was next in line to the presidency after Vice-President Lyndon Johnson, a situation that alarmed some members of his own party.

The real opposition to McCormack came from a group of young, liberal Democrats, led by Richard Bolling and Morris Udall, who thought that the Speaker was using his position to block House reform. They believed that the cumbersome committee structure and the seniority system were preventing the passage of needed civil rights and welfare legislation. Their efforts to unseat the Speaker, however, proved futile. McCormack finally retired in 1971 after the revelation that an aide had allowed the Speaker's office to be used, without McCormack's knowledge, for fraudulent transactions. McCormack died in retirement on November 22, 1980.

MANUSCRIPT COLLECTIONS

Boston University Library, Boston, Mass.
  John W. McCormack Papers, 1936–71.
  66 ft.
  NUCMC 77-846.

BOOKS, ARTICLES, AND DISSERTATIONS

WORKS BY JOHN W. McCORMACK

See also U.S. Congress, House (45-13), U.S. Congress (47-43 and 47-44), and U.S. Congress, House (47-45, 47-46, and 48-18).

49-1. *Face the Nation, 1954–1955: The Collected Transcripts from the CBS Radio and Television Broadcasts.* Vol. 1. New York: Holt Information Systems, 1972. 465 p.

Includes the transcript of a broadcast interview with McCormack of March 20, 1955.

The following works by McCormack are listed chronologically by year of publication and alphabetically thereunder.

49-2. McCORMACK, JOHN W. "Should Congress Enact a Federal Sedition Law?" *Congressional Digest* 14 (October 1935): 236–53.

McCormack warns of the need for a federal sedition law to regulate and prevent "communistic" subversion.

49-3. ———. "Communism—Its Method." *National Republic* 24 (June 1936): 1.

McCormack expresses his opposition to communism and discusses its relationship to the labor movement.

49-4. ———. "Personal Liberty." *Annals of the American Academy of Political and Social Science* 185 (May 1936): 154–61.

A warning that the rights of the individual must be zealously guarded.

49-5. ———. "America Is on the March." *Vital Speeches,* 1 February 1942, pp. 244–47.

McCormack interprets the war as a battle to preserve liberty, peace, and the right of self-government.

49-6. ———. "Did the 81st Congress Make a Satisfactory Record?" *Congressional Digest* 30 (January 1951): 30.

Majority Leader McCormack defends his party's record and attacks the opposition as "men of minute vision."

49-7. ———. "Party Leaders Appraise Record of the 84th Congress." *Congressional Digest* 35 (October 1956): 246.

A partisan interpretation of the Eighty-fourth Congress.

49-8. ———. "What to Look for in the New Session: Interview with John W. McCormack, Speaker of the House." *U.S. News and World Report,* 22 January 1962, pp. 38–41.

McCormack professes loyalty to President Kennedy and promises to support his program.

49-9. ———. "Eulogy to John F. Kennedy." *Vital Speeches,* 1 December 1963, pp. 98–99.

McCormack's eulogy to Kennedy, presented in the Capitol Rotunda. *See also* U.S. Congress (49-12).

49-10. ———. "America: Today and Yesterday, as Speaker McCormack Sees Things after 42 Years in Congress." *U.S. News and World Report,* 27 July 1970, pp. 58–62.

A lengthy interview in which McCormack warns against the tendency to appease communism and defends the welfare state.

49-11. ———. "Should Direct Popular Election of the President Be Adopted?" *Congressional Digest* 49 (January 1970): 10.

McCormack argues that direct election of the president is the only way that the democratic principle of one man, one vote, can be realized.

49-12. U.S Congress. *Memorial Addresses in the Congress of the United States and Tributes in Eulogy of John Fitzgerald Kennedy, Late a President of the United States*. 88th Cong., 2d sess. Washington, D.C.: Government Printing Office, 1964. 911 p.

Includes both McCormack's memorial address and the eulogy delivered in the Capitol Rotunda.

BIOGRAPHICAL SKETCHES AND EULOGIES

See also O'Neill (51-4).

49-13. *The American Catholic Who's Who, 1942–1943*. Vol. 5. Detroit, Mich.: Walter Romig, 1943. 496 p.

49-14. Lichtenstein, Nelson, and Schoene-baum, Eleanora W., eds. *Political Profiles: The Kennedy Years*. New York: Facts on File, 1976. 621 p.

49-15. Lichtenstein, Nelson; Schoenebaum, Eleanora W.; and Levine, Michael L., eds. *Political Profiles: The Johnson Years*. New York: Facts on File, 1976. 741 p.

49-16. Schoenebaum, Eleanora W., ed. *Political Profiles: The Nixon-Ford Years*. New York: Facts on File, 1979. 787 p.

49-17. U.S. Congress. *Memorial Addresses and Other Tributes in the Congress of the United States on the Life and Contributions of John W. McCormack*. 97th Cong., 1st sess. Washington, D.C.: Government Printing Office, 1981. 81 p.

MCCORMACK AND MASSACHUSETTS POLITICS

See Hennessey (41-15).

MCCORMACK'S POLITICAL ASSOCIATES

See also Barkley (43-42), Whalen (43-77), Dies (46-17), Rayburn (47-11), Dorough (47-26), Steinberg (47-28), Douglas (47-66), Miller (47-82), Scheele (47-84), Udall (47-88), Truman (47-134), Wright (47-242), and Clancy and Elder (51-6).

49-18. Curley, James Michael. *I'd Do It Again: A Record of My Uproarious Years*. Englewood Cliffs, N.J.: Prentice-Hall, 1957. 372 p.

49-19. Hays, Brooks. *A Southern Moderate Speaks*. Chapel Hill: University of North Carolina Press, 1959. 231 p.

49-20. Koskoff, David E. *Joseph P. Kennedy: A Life and Times*. Englewood Cliffs, N.J.: Prentice-Hall, 1974. 643 p.

49-21. McCarthy, Joe. *The Remarkable Kennedys*. New York: Dial Press, 1960. 190 p.

49-22. Marcantonio, Vito. *I Vote My Conscience: Debates, Speeches, and Writings of Vito Marcantonio, 1935–1950*. Selected and edited by Annette T. Robinson. New York: Vito Marcantonio Memorial, 1956. 494 p.

49-23. Miller, Clem. *Member of the House: Letters of a Congressman*. Edited by John W. Baker. New York: Charles Scribner's Sons, 1962. 195 p.

49-24. Shaffer, Samuel. *On and Off the Floor: Thirty Years as a Correspondent on Capitol Hill*. New York: Newsweek Books, 1980. 304 p.

MCCORMACK'S CONGRESSIONAL CAREER

General

See also Robinson (1-41), Manley (1-63), Paul (43-90), Allen and Shannon (47-60), Truman (47-97), Bailey (47-200), Irish (47-218), and Phillips (47-226).

49-25. Altmeyer, Arthur J. *The Formative Years of Social Security*. Madison: University of Wisconsin Press, 1966. 314 p.

49-26. Carroll, Holbert N. *The House of Representatives and Foreign Affairs*. Pittsburgh: University of Pittsburgh Press, 1958. 365 p.

49-27. Crosby, Donald F. *God, Church, and the Flag: Senator Joseph R. McCarthy and the Catholic Church, 1950–1957*. Chapel Hill: University of North Carolina Press, 1978. 307 p.

49-28. "John W. McCormack." *U.S. News and World Report*, 4 October 1940, p. 42.

49-29. "John W. McCormack." *U.S. News and World Report,* 4 March 1955, p. 14.

49-30. "John W. McCormack." *U.S. News and World Report,* 13 January 1956, p. 12.

49-31. "McElroy and Ike Say This about a 'First Blow.' " *U.S. News and World Report,* 16 March 1959, pp. 38–39.

49-32. MacRae, Duncan, Jr. *Dimensions of Congressional Voting: A Statistical Study of the House of Representatives in the Eighty-first Congress.* Berkeley: University of California Press, 1958. 390 p.

49-33. "New Floor Boss." *Newsweek,* 7 October 1940, p. 20.

49-34. "U.S. under Fire—Storm over Foreign Policy." *U.S. News and World Report,* 7 December 1956, pp. 53–56.

49-35. Westphal, Albert C. F. *The House Committee on Foreign Affairs.* New York: Columbia University Press, 1942. 268 p.

The New Deal and World War II

See also Porter (39-13), Wallace (43-76), Baker (43-191 and 47-101), Bishop (47-102), Kimball (47-106), and Langer and Gleason (47-107).

49-36. Beard, Charles A. *President Roosevelt and the Coming of the War, 1941: A Study in Appearances and Realities.* 1948. Reprint. Hamden, Conn.: Archon Books, 1968. 614 p.

49-37. Burns, James MacGregor. *Roosevelt: The Soldier of Freedom.* New York: Harcourt Brace Jovanovich, 1970. 722 p.

49-38. Gordon, Ira Lester. "John McCormack and the Roosevelt Era." Ph.D. dissertation, Boston University, 1976. 330 p. 76-21280.

The McCormack-Dickstein Committee

49-39. Buckley, William F., Jr. *The Committee and Its Critics.* Chicago: Henry Regnery, 1962. 352 p.

49-40. Diamond, Sander. *The Nazi Movement in the United States, 1924–41.* Ithaca, N.Y.: Cornell University Press, 1974. 380 p.

49-41. Goodman, Walter. *The Committee: The Extraordinary Career of the House Committee on Un-American Activities.* New York: Farrar, Straus, and Giroux, 1968. 564 p.

49-42. Latham, Earl. *The Communist Controversy in Washington from the New Deal to McCarthy.* Cambridge, Mass.: Harvard University Press, 1966. 446 p.

49-43. Ogden, August Raymond. *The Dies Committee: A Study of the Special House Committee for the Investigation of Un-American Activities, 1938–1944.* Washington, D.C.: Catholic University of America Press, 1945. 318 p.

MCCORMACK'S SPEAKERSHIP

General

See also Ripley (1-59 and 1-60), Shepsle (1-67), Sundquist (39-7), Evans and Novak (47-182), Lynch (47-186), Steinberg (47-191), Hinckley (47-217), Rapoport (47-229), and Bendiner (48-29).

49-44. Bell, Jack. *The Johnson Treatment: How Lyndon Johnson Took Over the Presidency and Made It His Own.* New York: Harper and Row, 1965. 305 p.

49-45. "Close, But No Cigar." *Newsweek,* 19 March 1962, pp. 32–33.

49-46. Curry, James E. "McCormack Trades a Dead Horse." *Christian Century,* 9 January 1957, pp. 45–47.

49-47. Goldman, Eric F. *The Tragedy of Lyndon Johnson.* New York: Alfred A. Knopf, 1969. 531 p.

49-48. Healy, Paul F. "Speaker of the House." *Columbia* 44 (March 1964): 9.

49-49. "Interviews with Winners and Losers." *U.S. News and World Report,* 18 November 1968, pp. 82–84.

49-50. "Is Congress Being Too 'Generous'?" *U.S. News and World Report,* 25 August 1969, pp. 70–71.

49-51. "A Look at Government's Top-Ranking Democrat." *U.S. News and World Report,* 8 September 1969, pp. 14–16.

49-52. "McCormack Seeks Tax Rebate for Church." *Christian Century,* 2 July 1952, p. 773.

49-53. "McCormack's Power—Next to Speaker Cannon's." *U.S. News and World Report,* 18 January 1965, p. 20.

49-54. MEANS, C. PAUL. "The Speaker Speaks Out on Defense." *Armed Forces Management* 8 (March 1962): 15–17.

49-55. "Men to Watch: McCormack, Mills, Kuchel." *Business Week,* 5 January 1962, p. 30.

49-56. "Protecting the Freshmen." *New Republic,* 4 September 1965, pp. 10–11.

49-57. "Republican Rumble." *Time,* 24 September 1965, pp. 26–27.

49-58. RIESELBACH, LEROY N. *Congressional Politics.* New York: McGraw-Hill, 1973. 426 p.

49-59. RIPLEY, RANDALL B. *Majority Party Leadership in Congress.* Boston: Little, Brown, 1969. 194 p.

49-60. "Uprising on a Minor Bill Hurts McCormack." *Business Week,* 17 March 1962, p. 42.

49-61. VIORST, MILTON. "The Speaker vs. the 'Hardliners.' " *Reporter,* 24 October 1963, pp. 43–44.

49-62. WEAVER, WARREN, JR. *Both Your Houses: The Truth about Congress.* New York: Praeger Publishers, 1972. 307 p.

McCormack's Election to the Speakership

See also "Congress" (47-259).

49-63. "Congressmen Kennedy Must Count On." *U.S. News and World Report,* 15 January 1962, pp. 37–38.

49-64. "Filling Mr. Sam's Shoes." *Newsweek,* 15 October 1962, pp. 30–31.

49-65. "Good Old John?" *Newsweek,* 16 October 1961, p. 27.

49-66. "McCormack for Speaker?" *U.S. News and World Report,* 23 October 1961, p. 57.

49-67. "Mister Sam's Successor." *Time,* 24 November 1961, pp. 14–15.

49-68. "Mr. Speaker." *Time,* 19 January 1962, pp. 16–21.

49-69. "The New 'Mr. Speaker'? McCormack Next in Line." *U.S. News and World Report,* 27 November 1961, p. 16.

49-70. "The New Speaker." *Newsweek,* 15 January 1962, pp. 15–19.

49-71. "Next in Line for House Speaker." *U.S. News and World Report,* 16 October 1961, p. 23.

49-72. "Rayburn's Illness May Touch Off Democratic Fight." *Business Week,* 7 October 1961, p. 46.

49-73. "Sam's Successor?" *Time,* 8 September 1961, p. 24.

49-74. "Speaker John." *Newsweek,* 27 November 1961, pp. 17–18.

49-75. " 'Speaker' McCormack? He Has Seniority, But. . . ." *U.S. News and World Report,* 18 September 1961, p. 23.

49-76. "The Successor." *Time,* 13 October 1961, p. 27.

49-77. "Wanted: A Man for Rayburn's Shoes." *Business Week,* 14 October 1961, pp. 28–29.

49-78. WHITE, WILLIAM S. "Farewell and Hail." *Harper's Magazine* 225 (July 1962): 84–85.

McCormack and the Kennedy Administration

See also Lasky (47-165), Lord (47-167), O'Donnell and Powers (47-168), Opotowsky (47-169), Parmet (47-170), and Wicker (47-179).

49-79. BLAIR, JOAN, AND BLAIR, CLAY, JR. *The Search for JFK.* New York: G. P. Putnam's Sons, 1976. 608 p.

49-80. "Campaigner McCormack: He'll Face Kennedys Again." *U.S. News and World Report,* 25 June 1962, p. 26.

49-81. COUGHLAN, ROBERT. "Old Rivalries on a Changed Battlefield." *Life,* 29 June 1962, pp. 63–72.

49-82. "Kennedy vs. McCormack: Family Ties Stir Row in Primary." *Business Week,* 16 June 1962, pp. 35–36.

49-83. "McCormack vs. Kennedy: A Feud That Never Was." *Newsweek,* 15 January 1962, pp. 16–17.

49-84. "Speakership Poses Problem for Kennedy." *Business Week,* 25 November 1961, p. 39.

McCormack and the Succession Crisis

See also Harwood (29-88).

49-85. "If Something Happened to the President." *U.S. News and World Report,* 16 December 1963, p. 37.

49-86. "McCormack and Hayden: No Plan to Quit." *U.S. News and World Report,* 23 December 1962, p. 12.

49-87. "The Men in Line for the Presidency Now." *U.S. News and World Report,* 2 December 1963, p. 14.

49-88. OBERDORFER, DON. "The Job John McCormack Dreads." *Saturday Evening Post,* 21 March 1964, pp. 66–68.

49-89. RESTON, JAMES. *Sketches in the Sand.* New York: Alfred A. Knopf, 1967. 479 p.

49-90. "Size-Up of New 'Vice President.' " *U.S. News and World Report,* 30 December 1963, pp. 26–27.

49-91. "The Succession: A Heartbeat Away." *Newsweek,* 16 December 1963, pp. 23–24.

49-92. "The Succession: Next in Line." *Time,* 27 December 1963, p. 16.

49-93. "What Sort of a President Would John McCormack Make?" *Esquire* 62 (July 1964): 90–93.

McCormack and House Reform

See also Bolling (1-47 and 1-48), Davidson, Kovenack, and O'Leary (39-10), and Bibby and Davidson (47-201).

49-94. "Bolling Is Right." *New Republic,* 11 November 1967, pp. 8–9.

49-95. "Gamble for the Gavel." *Newsweek,* 9 January 1969, pp. 24–25.

49-96. "House Democrats Plan Revolt against Speaker." *Business Week,* 6 April 1968, p. 41.

49-97. "House Speaker: Target of Rebels." *U.S. News and World Report,* 2 March 1970, p. 18.

49-98. "Kennedy Victory . . . Other New Leaders." *U.S. News and World Report,* 13 January 1969, pp. 16–18.

49-99. MATSUNAGA, SPARK, AND CHEN, PING. *Rulemakers of the House.* Urbana: University of Illinois Press, 1978. 208 p.

49-100. MURPHY, THOMAS P. *The New Politics Congress.* Lexington, Mass.: Lexington Books, 1974. 330 p.

49-101. "Old Jawn." *Newsweek,* 6 March 1967, p. 28.

49-102. SHERRILL, ROBERT G. "Insurgents in Caucus: Club Business on the Hill." *Nation,* 27 January 1969, pp. 102–4.

49-103. "Speaking Out on the Speaker." *Time,* 27 January 1969, p. 20.

49-104. STROUT, RICHARD LEE [PSEUD. T.R.B.]. "The Sapless Branch." *New Republic,* 24 January 1970, p. 4.

49-105. "Such Ingratitude." *Nation,* 23 February 1970, pp. 195–96.

McCormack and the Sweig-Voloshen Scandal

49-106. " 'Call Marty.' " *Newsweek,* 27 October 1969, p. 36.

49-107. "House Democrats Face Split over Scandal Charges." *Business Week,* 1 November 1969, pp. 45–46.

49-108. "Indictments for Two." *Time,* 26 January 1970, p. 16.

49-109. "Indictments in 'Influence' Case." *U.S. News and World Report,* 26 January 1970, p. 11.

49-110. Lambert, William. "The Murky Men from the Speaker's Office." *Life,* 31 October 1969, pp. 52–58.

49-111. "McCormack Faces *Life.*" *Newsweek,* 3 November 1969, p. 36.

49-112. "McCormack's Reapers?" *Newsweek,* 26 January 1970, p. 16.

49-113. "Scandals in Congress: The Record." *U.S. News and World Report,* 10 November 1969, pp. 25–27.

49-114. "The Speaker's Family." *Time,* 31 October 1969, pp. 18–20.

49-115. "The Voloshen Connection." *Time,* 24 October 1969, pp. 26–27.

49-116. Winter-Berger, Robert W. *The Washington Pay-Off: An Insider's View of Corruption in Government.* Secaucus, N.J.: Lyle Stuart, 1972. 341 p.

Retirement

49-117. "End of an Era in Congress." *U.S. News and World Report,* 1 June 1970, p. 35.

49-118. "McCormack: A Symbol Retires." *Time,* 1 June 1970, p. 14.

49-119. "Mr. Speaker Yields the Gavel." *Newsweek,* 1 June 1970, pp. 26–27.

MCCORMACK AND DEMOCRATIC PARTY PRESIDENTIAL POLITICS

See also Martin (39-5), Sorensen (47-177), David, Moos, and Goldman (47-246), and Sevareid (47-254).

49-120. Martin, John Frederick. *Civil Rights and the Crisis of Liberalism: The Democratic Party, 1945–1976.* Boulder, Colo.: Westview Press, 1979. 301 p.

49-121. Thomson, Charles A. H., and Shattuck, Frances M. *The 1956 Presidential Campaign.* Washington, D.C.: Brookings Institution, 1960. 382 p.

50. Carl Bert Albert
(1908–)
(Speaker, Ninety-second through Ninety-fourth Congresses)

Carl Albert, a scholar and a politician, was born in McAlester, Oklahoma, on May 10, 1908. His father was a poor cotton farmer and coal miner. Albert attended the University of Oklahoma, where he majored in political science and was president of the student council in his senior year. After he graduated Phi Beta Kappa in 1931, Albert earned two law degrees as a Rhodes Scholar at Oxford University (1933–34).

After his return to the United States, Albert was admitted to the Oklahoma bar in 1935 and worked for the Federal Housing Authority Administration in Oklahoma City. He joined the legal department of the Ohio Oil Company in 1940. During World War II he served in the Judge Advocate General's Department of the U.S. Army Air Forces and was awarded a Bronze Star for meritorious service in the Pacific theater. In 1946 Albert was elected to

Congress as a Democrat from Oklahoma's Third District.

During his tenure, in the Eightieth through Ninety-fourth Congresses (1947–77), Albert was a consistently liberal Democrat. Throughout his congressional career he supported the party leadership and carefully studied House procedures and members' voting records. Speaker Rayburn and Majority Leader McCormack, impressed by Albert's abilities, chose him majority whip in 1955. After Rayburn's death, Albert became majority leader in 1962, when he defeated a strong challenge from Congressman Richard Bolling. Following McCormack's retirement, Albert was selected Speaker of the House in 1971.

Although he preferred the behind-the-scenes persuasion techniques favored by Rayburn and McCormack, Albert sometimes resorted to the exercise of power. During the fight for President Johnson's anti-poverty program, for instance, Albert threatened to block proposed projects in the districts of opposition congressmen. As majority leader, he was the primary legislative advocate of the Great Society and of Johnson's foreign policy, including the military involvement in Vietnam. As chairman of the 1968 Democratic National Convention in Chicago, Albert ruled against motions by anti-war delegates supporting George McGovern and Eugene McCarthy. He remained a strong supporter of the Johnson and Nixon administrations' war policies until 1973, when he endorsed cutting off the funds for the bombing of Cambodia.

Albert's selection as Speaker in 1971 to succeed John McCormack was a confirmation of the continuing tradition whereby the majority leader assumes the speakership upon the death or retirement of his predecessor. Many within his own party thought that Albert was a weak Speaker, unable to maintain party unity or to develop Democratic alternatives to Nixon's policies. He did respond to calls for reform by giving more power to the majority party caucus, and he did gain control over the Rules Committee in 1973 by appointing new members who were loyal to him.

When confronted with the prospect of higher office, Albert displayed the reticence of a scholar. Twice he was second in line to the presidency—once after Vice-President Spiro Agnew resigned and again after Richard Nixon resigned—but on both occasions he showed little interest in becoming president. Albert had planned to retire in 1978, at the age of 70, but he decided not to seek reelection in 1976. The growing opposition within the party to his leadership and adverse publicity concerning his drinking problem may have contributed to his decision to retire early.

MANUSCRIPT COLLECTIONS

University of Oklahoma, Carl Albert Congressional Research and Studies Center, Norman, Okla.

Carl Albert Collection, 1946–77.
Ca. 1,100 ft.
The collection is closed to research use until 1985. A multivolume guide is in preparation.

BOOKS, ARTICLES, AND DISSERTATIONS

WORKS BY CARL ALBERT

Books

See also U.S. Congress 7-43 and 47-44), U.S. Congress, House (47-45), and U.S. Congress (49-12).

The following works by Albert are listed chronologically by year of publication and alphabetically thereunder.

50-1. ALBERT, CARL B. *Family Record of John Henry Ware*. Washington, D.C., 1972. 107 p.

A combined biography, genealogy, and local

history revolving around a cousin of Albert's great-grandfather's.

50-2. ———. *My Albert Line.* N.p., 1976. 321 p.
Albert's own compilation of facts about his family history, including a lengthy section on his parents and himself.

50-3. ———. *The Office and Duties of the Speaker of the House of Representatives.* Washington, D.C.: Government Printing Office, 1976. Unpaginated.
Speaker Albert details and analyzes the powers and functions of the speakership.

50-4. ALBERT, CARL B., ET AL., COMPS. *Abner Chaffin of Jackson County, Tennessee.* Provo, Utah, 1966. 190 p.
A genealogy of the family into which Albert's great-grandfather married.

Articles

The following works are listed chronologically by year of publication.

50-5. ALBERT, CARL B. "Commentary: Not Sold." *American Libraries* 4 (July/August 1973): 408.
Albert writes to oppose the Nixon administration's revenue-sharing proposal for education, arguing that it is a roundabout way of withdrawing federal support for education.

50-6. ———. "Recollections of My Early Life." *Chronicles of Oklahoma* 52 (Spring 1974): 30–37.
Contains the Speaker's reminiscences of his early childhood in southeastern Oklahoma.

Speeches

The following speeches are listed chronologically by year of publication and alphabetically thereunder.

50-7. ALBERT, CARL B. "A Comparison of Views by Congressional Leadership on the Record of the Eighty-seventh Congress." *Congressional Digest* 41 (December 1962): 296.
Albert defends the record of the Eighty-seventh Congress.

50-8. ———. "The Major Issues of the Eighty-seventh Congress as Viewed by House and Senate Leaders." *Congressional Digest* 41 (December 1962): 300.
Majority Leader Albert gives his views on a variety of issues, including civil rights, education, farm legislation, and foreign aid.

50-9. ———. "Should the Level of Federal Spending Proposed in the Fiscal 1964 Budget Be Substantially Reduced?" *Congressional Digest* 42 (May 1963): 151.
Albert argues that the Republicans' proposed $15 billion budget reduction would cut into the indispensable functions of government.

50-10. ———. "The Question of the Effectiveness of the Administration's Poverty Program." *Congressional Digest* 45 (March 1966): 84.
A speech in support of the federal poverty program as an effort to strengthen American family life.

50-11. ———. "Should Direct Popular Election of the President Be Adopted?" *Congressional Digest* 49 (January 1970): 14.
An argument in favor of abolition of the electoral college.

50-12. ———. "Should Congress Reject Pending Proposals to Grant 'Cease and Desist' Powers to the EEOC?" *Congressional Digest* 50 (November 1971): 271.
A speech in support of the Equal Employment Opportunities Commission.

50-13. ———. "Controversy over the Nixon Administration Proposal for a Federal Spending Ceiling." *Congressional Digest* 51 (December 1972): 305.
Albert voices his opposition to the administration's request to increase the national debt limit and impose a ceiling on federal expenditures.

Interviews

50-14. "A Democratic Appraisal of Nixon's Record So Far." *U.S. News and World Report,* 24 August 1970, pp. 58–61.

Albert criticizes the Nixon administration for not showing any initiative on legislation and defends Congress against charges of inaction.

50-15. *Face the Nation, 1958: The Collected Transcripts from the CBS Radio and Television Broadcasts.* Vol. 4. New York: Holt Information Systems, 1972. 409 p.

In an interview of December 14, 1958, Albert reveals his opposition to curbing the power of the House Rules Committee.

50-16. *Face the Nation, 1960–1961: The Collected Transcripts from the CBS Radio and Television Broadcasts.* Vol. 6. New York: Holt Information Systems, 1972. 499 p.

In a debate with Republicans Charles Halleck and Everett Dirksen, Albert and fellow Democrat Mike Mansfield defend the Kennedy administration's legislative program.

50-17. *Face the Nation, 1963–1964: The Collected Transcripts from the CBS Radio and Television Broadcasts.* Vol. 7. New York: Holt Information Systems, 1972. 425 p.

In a December 1, 1963, interview, Albert assesses the impact of Kennedy's assassination, claims that Johnson assigns top priority to the civil rights bill, and predicts a landslide victory for Johnson in 1964.

50-18. *Face the Nation, 1973: The Collected Transcripts from the CBS Radio and Television Broadcasts.* Vol. 16. Metuchen, N.J.: Scarecrow Press, 1975. 398 p.

In a January 28, 1973, interview, Albert wavers on the question of whether Congress need take any action to prevent future Vietnams and argues for a balance of power between Congress and the executive.

50-19. "What New Laws Congress Will Pass." *Nation's Business* 54 (January 1966): 63–68.

Majority Leader Albert voices his opinion that upcoming legislation would center on labor and civil rights issues.

50-20. "Winners and Losers: What They Say." *U.S. News and World Report,* 20 November 1972, pp. 58–59.

Speaker Albert interprets the election results as an indication of public satisfaction with the actions of the Democratic Congress.

BIOGRAPHICAL SKETCHES AND GENEALOGIES

See Lichtenstein and Schoenebaum (49-14), Lichtenstein, Schoenebaum, and Levine (49-15), Schoenebaum (49-16), and Albert (50-2 and 50-4).

ALBERT'S POLITICAL ASSOCIATES

See also Hébert (47-73), Miller (47-82), Scheele (47-84), Udall (47-88), Wright (47-242), and Clancy and Elder (51-6).

50-21. ABZUG, BELLA S. *Bella! Ms. Abzug Goes to Washington.* Edited by Mel Ziegler. New York: Saturday Review Press, 1972. 314 p.

50-22. FORD, GERALD R. *A Time to Heal: The Autobiography of Gerald R. Ford.* New York: Harper and Row, 1979. 454 p.

50-23. NIXON, RICHARD MILHOUS. *RN: The Memoirs of Richard Nixon.* New York: Grosset and Dunlap, 1978. 1,120 p.

ALBERT'S CONGRESSIONAL CAREER

See also Bolling (1-47 and 1-48), Peabody (1-55), Ripley (1-59), Davidson, Kovenack, and O'Leary (39-10), Wicker (47-179), Rieselbach (49-58), "Mister Sam's Successor" (49-67), and Murphy (49-100).

50-24. "An Adequate Number of Democrats." *Time,* 15 January 1965, pp. 16–20.

50-25. "The Boy from Bug Tussle." *Business Week,* 23 March 1963, pp. 30–31.

50-26. "Carl Albert: Nose Counter from Bug Tussle." *Time,* 12 January 1962, p. 13.

50-27. "House Majority Leader: Albert and Bolling Seek Job." *U.S. News and World Report,* 4 December 1961, p. 18.

50-28. "Little Giant from Bug Tussle." *Saturday Evening Post,* 24 March 1962, pp. 94–97.

50-29. "Majority Winner?" *Newsweek,* 4 December 1961, p. 17.

50-30. "The New Men Begin to Chafe." *Business Week,* 9 February 1963, pp. 23–24.

50-31. POLSBY, NELSON W. "Two Strategies of Influence: Choosing a Majority Leader, 1962." In *New Perspectives on the House of Representatives,* edited by Robert L. Peabody and Nelson W. Polsby, pp. 324–54. 3d ed. Chicago: Rand McNally, 1977.

ALBERT'S SPEAKERSHIP

General

See also Shepsle (1-67), Rapoport (47-229), Shaffer (49-24), Weaver (49-62), and Matsunaga and Chen (49-99).

50-32. BRADY, JAMES. "Class." *Esquire* 84 (August 1975): 123.

50-33. GREEN, MARK, WITH CALABRESE, MICHAEL. *Who Runs Congress?* 3d ed. New York: Bantam Books, 1979. 343 p.

50-34. "House Speaker Condemns Cuts in Aid for Library Services." *Library Journal,* 15 March 1973, p. 817.

50-35. MOORE, ROBIN; PERDUE, LEW; AND ROWE, NICK. *The Washington Connection.* New York: Condor, 1977. 333 p.

50-36. PEABODY, ROBERT L. "Committees from the Leadership Perspective." In *Changing Congress: The Committee System,* edited by Norman L. Ornstein, pp. 133–46. *Annals* 411 (January 1974).

50-37. THOMSON, SUZI PARK. *Suzi: The Korean Connection.* As told to Robin Moore and Gene Zack. New York: Condor, 1978. 441 p.

Albert's Election to the Speakership

See also "End of an Era" (49-117).

50-38. "Congress Gets Ready to Battle Nixon." *Business Week,* 9 January 1971, pp. 66–70.

50-39. FISCHER, JOHN. "The Coming Upheaval in Washington." *Harper's Magazine* 241 (October 1970): 21–40.

50-40. "Profile of the New Congress." *U.S. News and World Report,* 25 January 1971, pp. 42–43.

50-41. TEMPLIN, PHILLIP S. "The House: Changing of the Guard." *America,* 21 November 1970, p. 421.

Albert and House Reform

50-42. "Albert Has Dashed the Reformer's Hopes." *Business Week,* 11 December 1971, pp. 32–33.

50-43. DAVIDSON, ROGER H., AND OLESZEK, WALTER J. *Congress against Itself.* Bloomington: Indiana University Press, 1977. 306 p.

50-44. ORNSTEIN, NORMAN J., AND ROHDE, DAVID W. "Political Parties and Congressional Reform." In *Parties and Elections in an Anti-Party Age: American Politics and the Crisis of Confidence,* edited by Jeff Fishel, pp. 280–94. Bloomington: Indiana University Press, 1978.

50-45. SCHLESINGER, STEPHEN C. *The New Reformers: Forces for Change in American Politics.* Boston: Houghton Mifflin, 1975. 238 p.

The Presidential Succession and Watergate Crises

50-46. "Carl Albert's Plan for a Smooth Succession." *Time,* 12 November 1973, p. 37.

50-47. "The Coming Battle between President and Congress." *Time,* 1 February 1971, pp. 12–17.

50-48. "The Crack in the Constitution." *Time,* 15 January 1973, pp. 12–19.

50-49. DREW, ELIZABETH. *Washington Journal: The Events of 1973–1974.* New York: Random House, 1975. 428 p.

50-50. "Good Soldier." *Newsweek,* 2 December 1974, p. 40.

50-51. KOPKIND, ANDREW. "Carl Albert: Every Other Inch a President." *Ramparts,* January 1974, pp. 18–20.

50-52. "The Most Likely to Succeed." *Newsweek,* 1 June 1970, p. 27.

50-53. "The Reluctant Dragoon." *Time,* 5 November 1973, p. 31.

50-54. SHERRILL, ROBERT G. "Running from the Presidency." *New York Times Magazine,* 9 December 1973, p. 34.

50-55. "The Stand-in from Bug Tussle." *Newsweek,* 5 November 1973, p. 37.

50-56. WOODWARD, BOB, AND BERNSTEIN, CARL. *The Final Days.* New York: Simon and Schuster, 1976. 476 p.

ALBERT AND THE 1968 DEMOCRATIC NATIONAL CONVENTION

50-57. CHESTER, LEWIS; HODGSON, GODFREY; AND PAGE, BRUCE. *An American Melodrama.* New York: Viking Press, 1969. 814 p.

50-58. ENGLISH, DAVID, AND THE STAFF OF THE *Daily Express. Divided They Stand.* London: Michael Joseph, 1969. 428 p.

50-59. KNAPPMAN, EDWARD W. *Presidential Election 1968.* New York: Facts on File, 1968. 328 p.

50-60. MAILER, NORMAN. *Miami and the Seige of Chicago: An Informal History of the Republican and Democratic Conventions of 1968.* New York: World Publishing, 1968. 223 p.

50-61. *The Presidential Nominating Conventions, 1968.* Washington, D.C.: Congressional Quarterly Service, 1968. 291 p.

50-62. SHADEGG, STEPHEN C. *Winning's a Lot More Fun.* London: Macmillan, 1969. 278 p.

51. Thomas P. O'Neill, Jr.
(1912–)
(Speaker, Ninety-fifth Congress)

Thomas P. ("Tip") O'Neill, Jr., was born into a political environment in North Cambridge, Massachusetts, on December 9, 1912. His grandfather was an immigrant who fled the great Irish potato famine in 1845. His mother died nine months after he was born, and he was raised by a French-Canadian housekeeper, several nuns, and his father, who was the city's sewer commissioner. O'Neill's father, a significant figure in community politics, understood the importance of Democratic party loyalty. Politics was the mechanism by which Boston's Irish advanced in the face of an entrenched Brahmin establishment, a lesson that O'Neill's father imparted to his son. The political figures who frequented the O'Neill home and the colorful street-corner rallies that he witnessed all acclimated young O'Neill to the world of politics.

O'Neill attended St. John's High School and Boston College; he graduated in 1936, but he received his primary education in politics at the local hangout, Barry's Corner. His nickname was derived from another "Tip" O'Neill, a professional ballplayer who specialized in hitting foul tips. Together with his childhood cronies, he progressed from cards and baseball to political associations. In his senior year at Boston College, O'Neill placed fifth in a race for four seats on the Cambridge City Council.

In 1936 O'Neill was elected as a Democrat to the Massachusetts House of Representatives, which he entered in 1937 at the age of twenty-four. By ably using patronage and influence to benefit his constituents, O'Neill remained in the state legislature until 1952. He rose to the minority leadership in 1946 and became speaker in 1949. A successful insurance business, the support of loyal friends, and a stable home, which included his wife, Mildred Miller O'Neill, and five children, made his political career possible.

When John F. Kennedy decided to run for the Senate in 1952, O'Neill successfully campaigned to replace him in Congress. He entered the Eighty-third Congress in 1953 and followed a leadership course similar to the one that he had taken in the Massachusetts legislature. He forged a strong friendship with Majority Leader John McCormack, who occasionally invited him into the inner circle of the House leadership, Speaker Rayburn's Board of Education. In 1955 he was rewarded for his party loyalty with an appointment to the powerful Rules Committee.

O'Neill broke with the party leadership only on rare occasions. One such occasion concerned the war in Vietnam. Convinced that the war was unwinnable and that continued Amer-

ican involvement would only bring futher discord and division at home, he came out in opposition to the war and to President Johnson's policies in 1967. Four years later he became majority whip under Speaker Albert and Majority Leader Hale Boggs. In 1973 O'Neill was elected majority leader after Boggs died in a plane crash. As whip and later as majority leader, he managed the flow of information and legislation in a tightly organized manner.

One of the issues that O'Neill managed was the attempt to impeach President Nixon for his involvement in the Watergate scandal. He also championed passage of anti-impoundment legislation and the War Powers Act of 1973. Meanwhile, two other scandals had removed his key Democratic rivals, Wayne Hays and Wilbur Mills. After Speaker Albert retired in 1976, O'Neill ran unopposed for the Democratic nomination and was easily elected Speaker of the Ninety-fifth Congress. As Speaker since 1977, he has restored much of the leadership, initiative, and prestige to the speakership.

MANUSCRIPT COLLECTIONS

John F. Kennedy Library, Waltham, Mass.
   Thomas P. O'Neill Papers, 1969–71.
   25 ft.
   NUCMC 78-355.

BOOKS, ARTICLES, AND DISSERTATIONS

WORKS BY THOMAS P. O'NEILL, JR.

See also U.S. Congress, House (47-45), U.S. Congress (49-12), and "Winners and Losers" (50-20).

51-1. *Face the Nation, 1975: The Collected Transcripts from the CBS Radio and Television Broadcasts*. Vol. 18. Metuchen, N.J.: Scarecrow Press, 1976. 382 p.
   In an interview of July 27, 1975, O'Neill voiced opposition to the Ford administration's energy program and Turkish arms deal.

51-2. MERYMAN, RICHARD. "Thomas P. O'Neill, Jr.: The Man from Barry's Corner." *Yankee* 42 (July 1978): 64.
   An interview concerning O'Neill's early years in North Cambridge, Massachusetts, and his entry into politics.

51-3. O'NEILL, THOMAS P., JR. "Should Congress Repeal the 'Right to Work' Provisions of the Taft-Hartley Act?" *Congressional Digest* 44 (August/September 1965): 200.

O'Neill argues that a closed shop is a democratic measure.

51-4. ———. "Unforgettable John McCormack." Edited by Mary McSherry. *Reader's Digest* 118 (May 1981): 123–27.

A compassionate remembrance of O'Neill's colleague and predecessor.

51-5. "When People Complain That Congress Is Loafing. . . ." *U.S. News and World Report*, 27 May 1974, pp. 27–29.

O'Neill, in an interview, denies that Congress is dragging its feet on impeachment.

BIOGRAPHY AND BIOGRAPHICAL SKETCH

See also Meryman (51-2).

51-6. CLANCY, PAUL, AND ELDER, SHIRLEY. *Tip: A Biography of Thomas P. O'Neill, Speaker of the House.* New York: Macmillan, 1980. 246 p.

A well-written journalistic account of O'Neill's rise from the world of Boston politics to the speakership.

O'NEILL'S POLITICAL ASSOCIATES

See also Hébert (47-73), Miller (47-82), Udall (47-88), Lasky (47-165), Parmet (47-170), Steinberg (47-191), Ford (50-22), and Nixon (50-23).

51-7. GLAD, BETTY. *Jimmy Carter: In Search of the Great White House.* New York: W. W. Norton, 1980. 546 p.

51-8. LASKY, VICTOR. *Jimmy Carter: The Man and the Myth.* New York: Richard Marek, 1979. 419 p.

51-9. PRICE, RAYMOND, JR. *With Nixon.* New York: Viking Press, 1977. 398 p.

O'NEILL'S CONGRESSIONAL CAREER

See also Matsunaga and Chen (49-99), Peabody (50-36), Thomson (50-37), Davidson and Oleszek (50-43), Ornstein and Rohde (50-44), and Schlesinger (50-45).

51-10. "An Apple That Fell Near the Tree." *Time,* 4 February 1974, pp. 16–17.

51-11. BRESLIN, JIMMY. *How the Good Guys Finally Won.* New York: Viking Press, 1975. 192 p.

51-12. FIORINA, MORRIS P. *Congress: Keystone of the Washington Establishment.* New Haven: Yale University Press, 1977. 105 p.

51-13. "Is Stalemate Hurting U.S.?" *U.S. News and World Report,* 21 July 1975, pp. 33–34.

51-14. "Judging Nixon: The Impeachment Session." *Time,* 4 February 1974, pp. 14–22.

51-15. "Key Changes in Congress." *U.S. News and World Report,* 15 January 1973, p. 25.

O'NEILL'S SPEAKERSHIP, 1977–1980

See also Green and Calabrese (50-33).

51-16. "Awful Timing." *Time,* 8 May 1978, p. 12.

51-17. "The Budget: Who's In Charge Here?" *Newsweek,* 23 June 1980, p. 29.

51-18. "Congress Gives Carter Mixed Grades on First Report Card." *U.S. News and World Report,* 28 March 1977, p. 22.

51-19. GOLDMAN, PETER, WITH LINDSAY, JOHN J., AND HUBBARD, HENRY W. "The New Kings of the Hill." *Newsweek,* 17 January 1977, pp. 17–18.

51-20. HENRY, WILLIAM A., III. "The Unlikely Cult Figure." *New Republic,* 11 February 1978, pp. 18–21.

51-21. "How House Leader Views Election, Carter, Congress." *U.S. News and World Report,* 11 August 1980, pp. 23–24.

51-22. JONES, ROCHELLE, AND WOLL, PETER. *The Private World of Congress.* New York: Free Press, 1979. 264 p.

51-23. KEEFE, WILLIAM J. *Congress and the American People.* Englewood Cliffs, N.J.: Prentice-Hall, 1980. 177 p.

51-24. MATHEWS, TOM, AND HUBBARD, HENRY W. "The Man of the House." *Newsweek,* 17 January 1977, pp. 18–20.

51-25. Mathews, Tom; Hubbard, Henry W.; and Clift, Eleanor. "Tiffing with Tip." *Newsweek,* 14 August 1978, pp. 19–20.

51-26. O'Hara, Joseph A. "Of Many Things." *America,* 18 December 1976.

51-27. "O'Neill and Wright: They'll Push White House Plans—But No Blank Checks." *U.S. News and World Report,* 20 December 1976, p. 26.

51-28. Peabody, Robert L. "House Party Leadership in the 1970s." In *Congress Reconsidered,* edited by Lawrence C. Dodd and Bruce I. Oppenheimer, pp. 137–55. Washington, D.C.: Congressional Quarterly Press, 1981.

51-29. Roberts, Steven V. "The Politics of Loyalty." *New Leader,* 29 January 1979, pp. 5–7.

51-30. Ross, Irwin. " 'Tip' O'Neill: Speaker of the House." *Reader's Digest* 111 (November 1977): 137–41.

51-31. Safire, William L. *Safire's Washington.* New York· Times Books, 1980. 534 p.

51-32. Seligman, Daniel. "Keeping Up: The Bostonians." *Fortune,* 8 September 1980, p. 33.

51-33. Shogan, Robert. *Promises to Keep: Carter's First Hundred Days.* New York: Thomas Y. Crowell, 1977. 300 p.

51-34. "Soothing the Speaker." *Time,* 14 August 1978, p. 12.

51-35. "The Speaker and Oversight." *Government Executive* 11 (January 1979): 20–21.

51-36. "A Speaker's Life." *Economist,* 28 May 1977, p. 34.

51-37. "A Surprise in the House." *Newsweek,* 20 December 1976, pp. 25–26.

51-38. Thimmesch, Nick. "Portrait of the Speaker as a Party Man." *New York,* 20 February 1978, p. 10.

51-39. ———. "Tip O'Neill: Warts and All." *Saturday Evening Post* 251 (March 1979): 14–19.

51-40. "Tip at the Top." *Newsweek,* 15 January 1973, pp. 15–16.

51-41. "Tip: 'Give 'Em Enough Rope.' " *Newsweek,* 24 November 1980, p. 47.

51-42. Tolchin, Martin. "An Old Pol Takes on the New President." *New York Times Magazine,* 24 July 1977, p. 6.

51-43. "Tougher Leaders for Congress." *U.S. News and World Report,* 21 June 1976, p. 16.

51-44. "Two Who Will Run the House." *Time,* 20 December 1976, p. 23.

51-45. Uslaner, Eric M. "Policy Entrepreneurs and Amateur Democrats in the House of Representatives: Toward a More Party-Oriented Congress?" In *Legislative Reform: The Policy Impact,* edited by Leroy N. Rieselbach, pp. 105–16. Lexington, Mass.: Lexington Books, 1978.

51-46. "What It's Like to Be Speaker of the House." *U.S. News and World Report,* 6 June 1977, pp. 70–71.

51-47. "Who Runs America?" *U.S. News and World Report,* 17 April 1978, pp. 30–39.

O'NEILL'S SPEAKERSHIP, 1981–1984

51-48. Adler, Jerry. "The 'Extra Mile' to Nowhere." *Newsweek,* 10 May 1982, pp. 38–42.

51-49. Ajemian, Robert. "Tip O'Neill on the Ropes." *Time,* 18 May 1981, p. 17.

51-50. Alpern, David M. "Tip: Happy at Last." *Newsweek,* 15 November 1982, p. 45.

51-51. Alter, J. "With Friends Like These. . . ." *Washington Monthly* 14 (January 1983): 12–14.

51-52. Beatty, J. "The Life of the Party." *New Republic,* 24 January 1983, pp. 16–20.

51-53. "Beyond Tip's Cap." *New Republic,* 4 July 1983, pp. 5–7.

51-54. Cato [pseud.]. "Letter from Washington." *National Review,* 13 November 1981, p. 1315.

51-55. ———. "Letter from Washington." *National Review,* 28 May 1982, p. 602.

51-56. GOLDMAN, PETER; BORGER, GLORIA; AND CLIFT, ELEANOR. "The Honeymoon Is Over." *Newsweek*, 29 June 1981, pp. 36–37.

51-57. HITCHENS, CHRISTOPHER. "Minority Report." *Nation*, 10 March 1984, p. 278.

51-58. "Immigration Reform Again." *America*, 22 October 1983, pp. 221–22.

51-59. JACKSON, STUART. "Reagan and O'Neill Butt Heads." *Businessweek*, 4 April 1983, p. 111.

51-60. LAMBRO, DONALD. "Kemp-Roth Meets the O'Neill Gang." *National Review*, 29 May 1981, pp. 605–10.

51-61. McGRATH, PETER; HUBBARD, HENRY W.; AND BORGER, GLORIA. "Tip and His Fleeced Flock." *Newsweek*, 10 August 1981, pp. 22–23.

51-62. MAGNUSON, ED. "The Summit That Failed." *Time*, 10 May 1982, pp. 10–12.

51-63. "O'Neill's Tunnel Could Jam Everyone's Highways." *Businessweek*, 5 March 1984, pp. 18–19.

51-64. "A Question of Humbler Than Thou." *Time*, 29 June 1981, p. 18.

51-65. "Reagan, Democrats Now Playing for Keeps." *U.S. News and World Report*, 29 June 1981, p. 9.

51-66. SHAPIRO, WALTER. "Immigration: Failure of Will." *Newsweek*, 17 October 1983, p. 32.

51-67. "The Speaker Gets a Lecture on Taiwan." *Newsweek*, 11 April 1983, p. 53.

51-68. "Speaker O'Neill's Season of Discontent." *U.S. News and World Report*, 21 November 1983, p. 13.

51-69. STANLEY, ALESSANDRA. "Tip Topped!" *Time*, 28 May 1984, p. 36.

51-70. STARR, MARK, AND BORGER, GLORIA. "Not Ready for Prime Time." *Newsweek*, 28 May 1984, p. 24.

51-71. STONE, MARVIN. "Snookered by Tip O'Neill." *U.S. News and World Report*, 17 October 1983, p. 100.

51-72. THOMAS, EVAN. "Playing Politics with Immigration." *Time*, 17 October 1983, p. 19.

51-73. "Tip O'Neill Maneuvers to Keep the F-18 Intact." *Businessweek*, 28 March 1983, p. 40.

51-74. "Tip O'Neill Plays His Own China Card." *U.S. News and World Report*, 11 April 1983, p. 13.

51-75. TOLCHIN, MARTIN. "Troubles of Tip O'Neill." *New York Times Magazine*, 16 August 1981, pp. 30–31.

Author Index

AUTHOR INDEX

Billings, Charles A., 43-94
Billington, Monroe L., 40-67, 40-136
Billington, Ray A., 16-125
Binkley, Robert W., 9-185
Binkley, Wilfred E., 1-69, 9-225
Binkley, William C., 16-166
Birdsall, Richard D., 6-2, 6-9
Bishop, Farnham, 16-185
Bishop, Jim, 47-102
Bishop, William W., 41-5
Bitner, Harry, 1-93
Blackman, Emily C., 27-30
Blackorby, Edward C., 44-25
Blaine, Harriet B., 30-220
Blaine, James G., 30-1–30-16
Blaine, John E., 30-49
Blair, Clay, Jr., 49-79
Blair, Joan, 49-79
Blake, Israel G., 43-44
Blakeley, George T., 9-113
Blakey, Gladys C., 39-1
Blakey, Roy G., 39-1
Blanding, William F., 35-55
Bledsoe, James M., 47-48
Blennerhassett, Harman, 5-53
Bliss, George, 6-46
Blochman, Lawrence G., 43-125
Block, Marvin W., 44-11
Bloom, Sol, 46-38
Bloom, Vera, 39-18
Bluff, Harry, 14-31
Blum, John M., 38-131, 40-68, 43-45, 43-76
Blythe, Samuel G., 42-27
Boeschenstein, Charles, 44-23
Bohner, Charles H., 21-93
Bolles, Blair, 38-33
Bolling, Richard, 1-47, 1-48
Bolton, Ethel S., 21-57
Bond, Beverly W., Jr., 5-58, 5-59
Bone, Hugh A., 47-202
Boney, F. N., 17-41
Bonner, James C., 36-14
Borden, Morton, 6-15, 16-229
Borger, Gloria, 51-56, 51-61, 51-70
Borome, Joseph A., 9-63, 21-16
Bosworth, Allan R., 43-28
Boucher, Chauncey S., 17-2, 25-39
Bourne, Edward G., 16-126, 16-186, 16-187, 23-4
Boutell, Henry S., 38-153, 38-154
Boutwell, George S., 30-74
Bowden, Robert D., 38-249
Bowers, Claude G., 3-37, 6-36, 16-225, 38-56, 43-46
Bowles, Samuel, 29-95, 29-96

Bowling, Kenneth R., 3-38
Boyd, Anne M., 1-94
Boyd, Edward, 47-203
Boyd, George A., 5-26
Boyd, James, 47-199
Boyd, James P., 30-22, 34-13
Boyd, Linn, 23-1–23-3
Boyd, Thomas B., 30-144
Boykin, Edward C., 10-13
Boykin, Samuel, 22-16
Braden, Waldo W., 38-250
Bradford, Gamaliel, 30-34, 30-35, 30-222
Bradley, Erwin S., 16-72, 27-31
Brady, David W., 28-49, 35-119, 39-9
Brady, James, 50-32
Braeman, John, 38-57
Bragg, Jefferson D., 24-67
Brant, Irving, 5-27
Branyan, Robert L., 47-138
Bratter, Herbert M., 44-51
Brauer, Kinley J., 21-78
Breese, Donald H., 25-40
Brennan, J. Fletcher, 33-30
Brennan, John A., 44-52
Brent, Robert A., 16-205
Breslin, Jimmy, 51-11
Brian, Denis, 46-55
Brichford, Maynard J., 27-38
Bridges, Henry S., 48-1
Brigance, William N., 9-263, 22-57, 30-44
Briggs, John E., 37-28
Brigham, Johnson, 30-36
Brisbin, James S., 29-74
Broadus, John A., 25-29
Brock, William R., 9-218, 29-58
Brockunier, S. Hugh, 4-32
Brockett, Linus P., 27-27
Broesamle, John J., 40-115
Brooks, Addie L., 15-85
Brooks, N. C., 16-188
Brooks, Noah, 29-97, 30-37
Brooks, Philip C., 9-145
Brooks, Robert P., 17-2, 22-1, 22-53
Brooks, Sydney, 28-50
Brooks, U. R., 25-54
Broun, Heywood, 43-200
Broussard, James H., 11-19
Browder, Robert P., 44-53
Brown, D. Clayton, 47-21, 47-89
Brown, Everett S., 5-28, 5-39, 7-65, 9-230
Brown, George R., 1-49, 43-14
Brown, George W., 24-40
Brown, Harry J., 30-87, 30-112
Brown, James, 9-251

AUTHOR INDEX

AUTHOR INDEX

Polakoff, Keith I., 30-137
Polk, James K., 16-1–16-3, 16-10, 16-11,
    16-17–16-24
Polk, Sarah C., 16-238
Pollard, James E., 16-40
Polsby, Nelson W., 1-56–1-58, 47-227, 50-31
Poore, Benjamin P., 10-49
Porter, David L., 39-13
Porter, James M., 16-52
Porter, Robert P., 35-59
Potter, David, 10-26, 10-40, 10-41
Powell, Bolling R., Jr., 45-33
Powers, David F., 47-168
Powers, G. C., 30-79
Powers, Samuel L., 28-35
Pratt, Julius W., 16-146, 40-89
Prentice, George D., 9-97
Prescott, William H., 21-14
Presley, James, 43-226
Price, Glenn W., 16-178
Price, H. Douglas, 47-227
Price, Miles O., 1-93
Price, Raymond, Jr., 51-9
Prichard, Walter, 24-100
Prince, Benjamin F., 33-17, 33-38
Prince, Carl E., 5-23
Pringle, Henry F., 35-109, 38-146, 43-100
Prucha, Francis P., 15-83
Pukl, Joseph M., Jr., 16-65–16-67
Pulliam, David L., 19-11
Purcell, Richard J., 4-32

-Q-
Quaife, Milo M., 16-2
Quint, Alonzo H., 24-57

-R-
Rainey, Henry T., 44-1–44-10
Rainey, Mrs. Henry T. (Ella), 44-45
Rakove, Jack N., 4-20
Ramage, C. J., 22-23
Ramsdell, H. J., 30-156
Rand, Clayton, 22-24
Randall, Emilius O., 33-39
Randall, Henry S., 6-45
Randall, James G., 15-70, 24-112, 28-7
Randall, Samuel J., 32-1–32-4
Randel, William P., 25-63
Rapoport, Daniel, 47-229
Ratner, Sidney, 43-91
Ratzlaff, Robert K., 11-22
Rauch, Basil, 16-160, 43-150
Rawley, James A., 10-42
Rawls, Eugenia, 46-58

Ray, Joseph M., 40-80
Ray, P. O., 23-14
Rayback, Joseph G., 16-113, 16-221
Rayburn, Sam, 47-1–47-13, 47-22
Redlich, Fritz, 11-38
Reed, Emily H., 24-79
Reed, George I., 31-29, 33-39
Reed, Thomas B., 9-10, 35-1–35-46
Reese, MacPhelan, 47-11
Reeves, Jesse S., 14-37, 16-217
Reeves, Thomas C., 30-120
Regier, Cornelius C., 38-257
Reichard, Gary W., 48-72
Reid, Virginia H., 24-124
Reid, Whitelaw, 16-161, 33-44
Reid, William G., 17-80
Remick, Henry C., 1-38
Remini, Robert V., 7-55, 9-234, 12-11, 12-12, 14-29
Republican Party National Conventions, 29-37,
    29-38, (1876) 30-138, (1920) 41-8
Resh, Richard W., 16-169
Reston, James, 49-89
Reynolds, John S., 25-64
Rhett, Robert B., 17-63
Rhodes, James F., 10-4, 28-8, 35-123
Rice, Jessie P., 21-108
Rich, Robert, 21-87, 21-88
Richards, Henry M. M., 3-7, 3-19, 3-31
Richards, Julian W., 37-19, 37-40
Richardson, Albert D., 29-84, 29-101
Richardson, Charles F., 15-103
Richardson, James D., 16-25, 17-74
Richardson, Leon B., 30-121
Riddick, Floyd M., 1-39, 44-10, 44-61, 45-7, 45-44,
    46-46–46-48
Riddle, Albert G., 28-36
Riddle, Donald W., 21-109
Riddleberger, Patrick W., 29-47
Ridgway, Erman J., 40-129
Ridpath, John C., 30-29
Rieselbach, Leroy N., 49-58, 51-45
Riker, Dorothy, 20-13
Riley, Stephen T., 6-27
Ripley, Randall B., 1-40, 1-50, 1-59, 1-60, 49-59
Ripley, Roswell S., 16-194
Rippy, J. Fred, 16-162
Rips, Rae E., 1-94
Risjord, Norman K., 7-56, 9-141, 9-142
Rives, George L. 9-173
Rives, William C., 6-19, 12-29
Robbins, D. P., 31-33
Robbins, Roy M., 9-196, 27-51
Roberson, Jere W., 15-87
Roberts, A. Sellew, 24-101

Scott, James B., 34-30
Scott, Nancy N., 15-71
Scott, W. W., 13-11
Scroggs, William O., 46-49
Seager, Robert, II, 9-11, 16-99
Sealsfield, Charles, 9-258
Sears, Louis M., 16-218
Sebba, Gregor, 22-53
Sedgwick, H. D., 6-6
Sedgwick, Sarah C., 6-12
Sedgwick, Theodore, 6-1
Seidensticker, Oswald, 3-8
Seilhamer, George O., 1-83
Seitz, Don C., 29-92, 30-45
Selbey, John, 16-179
Seligman, Daniel, 51-32
Sellers, Charles G., Jr., 16-35, 16-41, 16-42
Setser, Vernon G., 9-198
Sevareid, Arnold E., 47-254
Seward, Frederick W., 15-72, 16-100
Seward, William H., 16-100
Sewell, Richard H., 24-33
Shackford, James A., 16-101
Shackford, John B., 16-101
Shadegg, Stephen C., 50-62
Shaffer, Samuel, 49-24
Shaler, Nathaniel S., 9-124
Shanks, Alexander G., 47-100, 47-113, 47-114
Shanks, Henry T., 17-70
Shannon, Fred A., 32-38
Shannon, J. B., 43-221
Shannon, William V., 47-60
Shapiro, Samuel, 24-36
Shapiro, Walter, 51-66
Sharkey, Robert P., 30-70
Sharp, Walter R., 29-25
Shattuck, Frances M., 49-121
Shaw, Albert, 42-12
Shaw, William H., 26-21
Shenk, Hiram H., 32-12
Shenton, James P., 16-102
Shepard, Edward M., 16-114
Shepard, Rebecca A., 31-23
Shepard, William R., 9-177
Shepardson, Whitney H., 46-49
Shepsle, Kenneth A., 1-67
Sherburne, John H., 5-47
Sherman, John, 28-40
Sherman, Thomas H., 30-31
Sherman, William T., 24-58, 24-59, 30-11
Sherrill, Robert, 47-188, 49-102, 50-54
Sherrod, Jane, 47-190
Shields, Johanna N., 17-37
Shimmell, L. S., 32-13

Shippee, Lester B., 16-148
Shipton, Clifford K., 4-9, 6-7
Shoemaker, Floyd C., 40-49, 40-63
Shogan, Robert, 51-33
Shover, John L., 44-46
Shryock, Richard H., 22-39
Sidey, Hugh, 47-175, 47-189
Sievers, Harry J., 29-48, 30-124
Silbey, Joel H., 10-16, 17-38
Simkins, Francis B., 25-65
Simms, Henry H., 10-27, 10-44, 17-10, 17-27, 27-43
Simms, William G., 11-16
Simon, John Y., 24-47
Simpson, Albert F., 12-26
Simpson, Craig M., 17-57
Simpson, John E., 22-25, 22-56, 22-65
Sinclair, Barbara, 39-15
Singer, Kurt, 47-190
Singletary, Otis A., 16-195
Sioussat, St. George L., 14-2, 15-17, 15-56, 15-57, 16-12, 16-13, 16-68
Sitterson, Joseph C., 7-44
Sizer, Theodore, 4-10
Slayden, Ellen M., 40-86
Smalley, George W., 35-61
Smallwood, James, 47-176
Smith, Alfred E., 45-22
Smith, Arthur D. H., 16-103
Smith, Beverly, 48-55
Smith, Charles P., 26-23
Smith, Charles W., Jr., 13-43
Smith, Elbert B., 7-32, 16-222, 22-60
Smith, Gene, 43-114
Smith, George W., 24-60
Smith, Henry H., 28-53
Smith, James M., 5-40
Smith, Joe P., 24-125
Smith, Joseph, 30-207
Smith, Justin H., 9-150, 16-180, 16-196
Smith, Margaret (Bayard), 9-259
Smith, Oliver H., 20-18
Smith, Samuel L. G., 9-108
Smith, T. Berry, 40-104
Smith, Theodore C., 9-143, 24-126, 30-92, 30-174
Smith, Walter B., 11-40
Smith, Willard H., 29-15, 29-26, 29-27, 29-54, 29-71
Smith, William E., 26-24
Smith, William H., 1-14, 31-34
Smith, William L., 16-104
Smith, Zachariah F., 9-101
Smyrl, Frank H., 43-67
Snowden, Yates, 25-66

AUTHOR INDEX

Woodward, C. Vann, 32-48, 32-49, 35-118
Woodward, Walter C., 20-39
Woody, Robert H., 25-65
Woolf, S. J., 43-107, 43-228
Woollen, William W., 20-7
Wortham, Thomas, 16-199
Wrage, Ernest J., 9-263
Wright, David M., 11-41, 11-42
Wright, James C., 47-242
Wright, Theon, 48-25
Wright, William C., 15-118
Wynkoop, Henry, 3-63

-X-

X.M.C., 35-154

-Y-

Yates, Richard, 38-87
Yearns, Wilfred B., 17-82, 22-91
Young, Bob, 16-198

Young, Donald, 43-163
Young, George B., 30-165
Young, James S., 2-13
Young, Jan, 16-198
Young, Klyde H., 29-90
Young, Roland A., 47-115
Young, Valton J., 47-58
Younger, Edward, 17-77, 30-130

-Z-

Zack, Gene, 50-37
Zahler, Helene S., 9-205
Zeiger, Henry, 47-196
Zieger, Robert H., 41-36
Ziegler, Mel, 50-21
Zilversmit, Arthur, 6-24
Zimmerman, Charles, 29-34
Zinn, Charles, 1-92
Zucker, Norman L., 46-22
Zwelling, Shomer S., 16-134

Subject Index

Entries relating to the text and not the bibliography are in *italic type*.

-A-

Abbot, Abiel, 11-6
Abzug, Bella S., 50-21
Acheson, Dean, 47-59
Adams, Charles Francis, 21-92, 21-98
Adams, Charles Francis, Jr., 26-26
Adams, Henry, 35-83
Adams, John, 3-49, 5-47, 6-37
Adams, John Quincy, 7-22, 7-26, 9-152, 9-162, 12-8, 14-22, 14-27, 16-78
Adams-Onís Treaty, 9-145
Agricultural Adjustment Administration, 45-31–45-32
Alabama: history and politics of, 13-30, 46-11, 46-15–46-16
Alaman, Lucas, 16-173
Alaska, purchase of, 24-122–24-124
Albemarle Co., Va., 14-19, 14-21
Albert, Carl Bert: *biographical sketch of, pp. 272–73; manuscript collections, p. 273;* biographical sketches and genealogies, 49-14–49-16, 50-2, 50-4; congressional career, 1-47–1-48, 1-55, 1-59, 39-10, 47-179, 49-58, 49-67, 49-100, 50-24–50-31; and 1968 Democratic National Convention, 50-57–50-62; political associates, 47-73, 47-82, 47-84, 47-88, 47-242, 50-21–50-23, 51-6; Speakership: 1-67, 47-229, 49-24, 49-62, 49-99, 50-32–50-37, election, 49-117, 50-38–50-41, and House reform, 50-42–50-45, presidential succession and Watergate crisis, 50-46–50-56; works by: articles, 50-5–50-6, books, 47-43–47-45, 49-12, 50-1–50-4, interviews, 50-14–50-20, speeches, 50-7–50-13
Aldrich, Nelson W., 35-112
Alien and Sedition Laws, 5-40
Allison, William B., 30-123
American Colonization Society, 9-212, 9-216, 12-24
American System, 9-185–9-186, 9-193
Americus, Ga., 36-20
Ames, Fisher, 6-14
Anderson, Clinton P., 47-61
Andrew, John A., 21-35, 21-107, 24-34

Anti-imperialism, 34-53, 35-161, 35-165, 35-170–35-171
Arkansas, slavery in, 12-25
Arthur, Chester A., 30-108, 30-120
Atchison, David R., 17-53
Athens, Ga., 22-32, 22-37, 22-80
Atkinson, Edward, 34-33

-B-

Bacon, Robert, 34-30
Bailey, Joe, 40-65
Baker, Newton D., 40-73
Baker, Robert G., 47-62
Ballston Spa, N.Y., 12-5
Baltimore, Md., 24-40
Bancroft, George, 16-7, 16-87, 16-95
Bankhead, Tallulah, 46-53–46-59, 46-61–46-62
Bankhead, William Brockman: *biographical sketch of, pp. 244–45; manuscript collections, p. 245;* and Alabama history and politics, 46-14–46-16; biographical sketches, 43-20, 46-7–46-9, 46-11, 46-13; biography, 46-10; congressional career, 45-43, 45-48, 46-23–46-32; domestic life, 46-53–46-62; eulogies, 46-12; political associates, 36-21, 38-67, 39-18, 39-21, 40-80, 43-15, 43-44, 43-55, 43-71, 43-73, 43-153–43-155, 44-22, 46-17–46-22, 47-11, 47-23, 47-26–47-28, 48-15; and the Speakership, 39-12–39-13, 43-126, 43-146, 43-191, 43-206, 43-219, 45-9, 45-12, 45-35, 46-33–46-52; works by, 42-14, 45-13, 46-1–46-6
Bank of the United States, 9-200, 9-202, 11-29, 11-36, 11-39–11-41
Banks, Nathaniel Prentice: *biographical sketch of, pp. 122–23; manuscript collections, p. 123;* and anti-slavery politics and the Republican party, 15-106, 24-24–24-34; biography and biographical sketches, 21-70, 24-13–24-16; and Civil War: Department of the Gulf, 24-67–24-86, freedmen and the Louisiana labor system, 24-87–24-99, and Louisiana cotton and sugar industries, 24-100–24-103, military operations, 22-87, 24-39–24-66, and Reconstruction, 24-104–24-115; congressional career and Speakership, 24-17–24-23; and Fenian

ABOUT THE AUTHOR

Donald R. Kennon is associate historian at the U.S. Capitol Historical Society. He is co-author of *Washington Past and Present: A Guide to the Nation's Capital.*

THE JOHNS HOPKINS UNIVERSITY PRESS

**The Speakers of the U.S. House
of Representatives**

This book was composed in Baskerville by
BG Composition, Inc.

It was printed on 60 lb. Lakewood text paper
and bound by Bookcrafters.